KU-792-263

FRANK WOOD'S

BOOK-KEEPING AND ACCOUNTS

Seventh Edition

Frank Wood BSc(Econ), FCA

and

Sheila Robinson BA(Hons), Cert Ed, FMAAT

BLACKBURN COLLEGE LIBRARY

 Prentice Hall
FINANCIAL TIMES

An imprint of **Pearson Education**
Harlow, England • London • New York • Boston • San Francisco • Toronto • Sydney • Singapore • Hong Kong
Tokyo • Seoul • Taipei • New Delhi • Cape Town • Madrid • Mexico City • Amsterdam • Munich • Paris • Milan

Pearson Education Limited

Edinburgh Gate
Harlow
Essex CM20 2JE
England

and Associated Companies throughout the world

Visit us on the World Wide Web at:
www.pearsoned.co.uk

BLACKBURN COLLEGE
UCL

BB32202

Browns Books	29/09/09
657.2WOO	33.65

First published 1981
Second edition published 1986
Third edition published 1992
Fourth edition published 1997
Fifth edition published 2001
Sixth edition published 2004
Seventh edition published 2009

© Longman Group Limited 1981
© Longman Group UK Limited 1986, 1992
© Financial Times Professional Limited 1997
© Pearson Education Limited 2001, 2004, 2009

The rights of Frank Wood and Sheila Robinson to be identified as authors
of this work have been asserted by them in accordance with the Copyright,
Designs and Patents Act 1988.

All rights reserved. No part of this publication may be reproduced, stored
in a retrieval system, or transmitted in any form or by any means, electronic,
mechanical, photocopying, recording or otherwise, without either the prior
written permission of the publisher or a licence permitting restricted copying
in the United Kingdom issued by the Copyright Licensing Agency Ltd,
Saffron House, 6–10 Kirby Street, London EC1 8TS.

ISBN: 978-0-273-71805-5

British Library Cataloguing-in-Publication Data
A catalogue record for this book is available from the British library

Library of Congress Cataloging-in-Publication Data
Wood, Frank, 1926–2000.
    Frank Wood's book-keeping and accounts / Frank Wood and Sheila
Robinson. – 7th ed.
        p. cm.
    Includes bibliographical references and index.
    ISBN 978-0-273-71805-5
    1. Bookkeeping.   2. Accounting.   I. Robinson, Sheila I.   II. Title.
III. Title: Book-keeping and accounts.
    HF5636.W86 2009
    657—dc22

                                    2008039450

10 9 8 7 6 5 4 3 2 1
11   10   09

Typeset in 10.5/12.5pt Garamond Book by 35
Printed and bound by Rotolito Lombarda, Italy

The publisher's policy is to use paper manufactured from sustainable forests.

Contents

Part 4 Adjustments to financial statements

Part 5 Financial statements of other organisations

Part 6 Associated accounting topics

Preface to the seventh edition

The highly successful *Book-keeping and Accounts* has become an essential textbook for students undertaking studies of book-keeping and accounting for the first time. It is a well-recognised text used by lecturers teaching students undertaking the Association of Accounting Technicians (AAT) Foundation and Intermediate Examinations, the AAT's Diploma Pathway, International Association of Book-keepers (IAB), A Level Examinations, and the Oxford Cambridge and Royal Society of Arts (OCR) examinations, and as a general text for personnel employed in the accountancy profession. In this new fully updated seventh edition I have introduced four new chapters:

The Accounting System – an overview of the process of recording source documents through to the preparation of the financial statements.

Business Documentation – explains the documents used within a business's trading activity.

Computers and Accounting Systems – provides an overview of the uses of computer technology in processing accounting data.

Professional Ethics – an introduction to ethical behaviour in the workplace.

I have thoroughly reviewed and updated the book to reflect the recent changes in financial and technological developments and legislation. Particular reference is made to the chapters shown below:

Chapter 18 Value added tax (VAT) – now includes reference to VAT requirements when businesses trade with EC member states.

Chapter 20 Business banking – developments in the way money is transferred.

Chapter 37 Limited company accounts – has been rewritten to cover the changes brought about by the Companies Act 2006.

Both the 'Learning Objectives' and the 'Chapter Summary' have been revised to reflect the changes in the financial environment and any changes in the accountancy examining bodies' syllabuses. The glossary has been enlarged to cover new and revised aspects of the text.

I have acknowledged comments from lecturers who have made constructive suggestions about the previous edition and have incorporated these where appropriate. The text comprehensively covers the financial aspects of various accountancy examining bodies at foundation and intermediate level. It is important that students and tutors are fully conversant with the syllabus of the bodies whose examinations they intend to take.

Sheila Robinson 2008

Acknowledgements

The author would like to thank the following people for their help and assistance in producing the seventh edition of this book:

Rosemary Evans, a Chief Examiner for the AAT, for her review of certain chapters.

Professor David Hunt, President of the Institute of Financial Accountants, for his suggestions and help with the chapter on 'Ethics'.

Malcolm Robinson, Chartered Engineer, for his support, encouragement and help throughout the production of this text and for diligently checking the manuscript proofs.

Adrian Veale, Account Manager and former council member of the AAT, for his advice and review of the chapter on 'Limited company accounts'.

Karen Woodburn, Partner in an accountancy practice. for reviewing the 'VAT Chapter'.

I am grateful to the following examining bodies for their kind permission to use past assessment papers and sample questions from examination papers:

Association of Accounting Technicians (AAT)
Assessment and Qualifications Alliance (AQA) and the various GCSE examining bodies
City and Guilds Pitman Qualifications
Oxford, Cambridge and RSA Examinations (OCR)

Acknowledgements

We are grateful to the following for permission to reproduce copyright material:

Exercise 9.7x from Northern Examinations and Assessments, Paper 1, Level H, Paper ref 1407, Question 3., AQA(AEB)/AQA/NEAB/AQA examination materials are reproduced by permission of the Assessment and Qualifications Alliance; Exercise 19.3 from OCR Bk-k, Stage 1, Paper ref JUN 107, June 1998, Question 2, OCR (Oxford, Cambridge and RSA Examinations); Exercise 19.4x from OCR Bk-k, Stage 1, Paper ref NOV 107, Nov 1998, Question 1, OCR (Oxford, Cambridge and RSA Examinations); Exercises 20.6x, 23.6x, 25.4x, 26.8x, 30.7x, 32.4, 32.5x, 35.8x from *Administration and Assessment Manual*, AAT (2002); Exercise 20.7 from *Administration and Assessment Manual*, AAT (2000); Exercise 22.3X from Southern Examining Group, Paper 2, Level F, Paper ref 3260/2, Question 1 (part), AQA(AEB)/AQA/NEAB/AQA examination materials are reproduced by permission of the Assessment and Qualifications Alliance; Exercise 23.8x from Northern Examinations and Assessments, Paper 2, Level F, Paper ref 1403, Question 3, AQA(AEB)/AQA/NEAB/AQA examination materials are reproduced by permission of the Assessment and Qualifications Alliance; Exercise 24.4x from OCR Bk-k, Stage 1, Paper ref MAR 107, Mar 1999, Question 1, OCR (Oxford, Cambridge and RSA Examinations); Exercise 25.6 from Bk-k & A/c, Level 2, Paper ref NU-BKA 12/70032, Question 3, City & Guilds; Exercise 27.5x from Southern Examining Group, Paper 3, Level H, Paper ref 3260/3, Question 2, AQA(AEB)/AQA/NEAB/AQA examination materials are reproduced by permission of the Assessment and Qualifications Alliance; Exercise 27.6x from Northern Examinations and Assessments, Paper 2, Level H, Paper ref 1408, Question 5, AQA(AEB)/AQA/NEAB/AQA examination materials are reproduced by permission of the Assessment and Qualifications Alliance; Exercise 28.4 from Southern Examining Group, Paper 3, Level H, Paper ref 3260/3, Question 3, AQA(AEB)/AQA/NEAB/AQA examination materials are reproduced by permission of the Assessment and Qualifications Alliance; Exercise 28.5x from Northern Examinations and Assessments, Paper 1, Level H, Paper ref 1407, Question 4, AQA(AEB)/AQA/NEAB/AQA examination materials are reproduced by permission of the Assessment and Qualifications Alliance; Exercise 29.8 from Bk-k & A/c, Level 2, Paper ref NU-BKA 12/01058, Question 5, City & Guilds; Exercise 29.9x from Southern Examining Group, Paper 2 Level F, Paper ref 3260/2, Question 2, AQA(AEB)/AQA/NEAB/AQA examination materials are reproduced by permission of the Assessment and Qualifications Alliance; Exercise 30.6 from *Administration and Assessment Manual*, AAT (1999); Exercises 31.6, 31.7x, 35.8x from *Administration and Assessment Manual*, AAT (1998); Exercises 32.3, 35.5 from *Administration and Assessment Manual*, AAT (2001); Exercise 32.6x from Assessment and Qualifications Alliance, Paper 2, Level F, Paper ref 3122/F, Question 1 (part), AQA(AEB)/AQA/NEAB/AQA examination materials are reproduced by permission of the Assessment and Qualifications Alliance; Exercise 33.2 from Bk-k & A/c, Level 2, Paper ref NU-BKA 12/90093, Question 2, City & Guilds; Exercise 33.3x from Bk-k & A/c, Level 2, Paper ref NU-BKA 12/01054, Question 2, City & Guilds; Exercise 33.8x from Northern Examinations and Assessments, Paper 3, Level H, Paper ref 1408, Question 4, AQA(AEB)/AQA/NEAB/AQA examination materials are reproduced by permission of the Assessment and Qualifications Alliance; Exercise 34.10 from Southern Examining Group, Paper 3, Level H, Paper ref 3260/3, Question 5, AQA(AEB)/AQA/NEAB/AQA examination materials are reproduced by permission of the Assessment and Qualifications Alliance; Exercise 34.11x from OCR, Stage 1, Paper ref JUN 201, June 1999, Question 1, OCR (Oxford, Cambridge and RSA Examinations); Exercise 34.12x from Southern Examining Group, Paper 1, Level F, Paper ref 3260/1, Question 8, AQA(AEB)/AQA/NEAB/AQA examination materials are reproduced by permission of the Assessment and Qualifications Alliance; Exercise 35.9x from A/c, Level 3, Paper ref NU-ACC 13/70111, Question 3, City & Guilds; Exercise 36.6 from A/c, Level 3, Paper ref NU-ACC 13/70111, Question 1, City & Guilds; Exercise 36.7x from Assessment and Qualifications Alliance, Paper 2, Level F, Paper ref 3122/F, Question 4, AQA(AEB)/AQA/NEAB/AQA examination materials are reproduced by permission of the Assessment and Qualifications Alliance; Exercise 37.6 from A/c, Level 3, Paper ref NU-ACC 13/70111, Question 2, City & Guilds; Exercise 37.7x from Northern Examinations and Assessments, Paper 2, Level H, Paper ref 1408, Question 3, AQA(AEB)/AQA/NEAB/AQA examination materials are reproduced by permission of the Assessment and Qualifications Alliance; Exercise 37.8x from Southern Examining Group, Paper 3, Level H, Paper ref 3260/3, Question 6, AQA(AEB)/AQA/NEAB/AQA examination materials are reproduced by permission of the Assessment and Qualifications Alliance; Exercise 38.3 from Southern Examining Group, Paper 3, Level H, Paper ref 3260/3, Question 4, AQA(AEB)/AQA/NEAB/AQA examination materials are reproduced by permission of the Assessment and Qualifications Alliance; Exercise 38.5x from A/c, Level 3, Paper ref NU-ACC 13/70107, Question 4, City & Guilds; Exercise 38.6x from Southern Examining Group, Paper 2, Level F, Paper ref 3260/2, Question 3, AQA(AEB)/AQA/NEAB/AQA examination materials are reproduced by permission of the Assessment and Qualifications Alliance; Exercise 39.2x from A/c, Level 3, Paper ref NU-ACC 13/70111, Question 5, City & Guilds; Exercise 39.3x from Northern Examinations and Assessments, Paper 1, Level H, Paper ref 1407, Question 5, AQA(AEB)/AQA/NEAB/AQA examination materials are reproduced by permission of the Assessment and Qualifications Alliance.

PART 1

Introduction to principles of accounting

This part of the book is concerned with the basic principles of the double entry system of book-keeping. It also includes capital and revenue expenditure.

CHAPTER 1

Introduction to accounting principles

Learning objectives

After you have studied this chapter you should be able to:

- understand the need for accounting and its importance in business and management
- appreciate the difference between book-keeping and accounting
- understand that the accounting sequence is the basis for preparing financial statements
- understand the concept of financial control
- know that the two most important financial statements are:
  1 the trading and profit and loss account
  2 the balance sheet
- identify the main users of accounting information
- distinguish between the different types of business organisations.

1.1 Aims of a business

A vital aspect of any business is proper financial management. The owners of the business would have invested money in what they considered to be a viable enterprise based on a particular expertise. They may also have borrowed money to help to finance the business. This investment needs to be used carefully so that the business can flourish and generate a profit. Most businesses start with a sound idea and great enthusiasm by the owners who commit much time and effort to establishing a customer base. To ensure that the effort and financial commitment are not wasted it is essential that proper financial control is used as part of good management practice. Too many businesses fail in the early stages due to lack of sound financial control. Well-established and successful businesses will undoubtedly have good accounting procedures and financial management which not only keep the owners aware of the financial status of the business but generate information for external parties such as Her Majesty Revenue and Customs (HMRC).

1.2   Definitions of book-keeping and accounts

Book-keeping is the process of recording, in the book accounts or on computer, the financial effect of business transactions and managing such records. The process of recording the financial information is the initial stage in the preparation of financial statements.

Accounting is the skill or practice of maintaining accounts and preparing reports to aid the financial control and management of a business.

1.3   The accounting sequence

In order that the business can satisfy all interested parties it must follow certain accounting procedures and practices in a formal sequence. Essentially this sequence can be stated as shown in Exhibit 1.1. Each part of the sequence can be explained briefly, as set out below.

Exhibit 1.1 The accounting sequence

Recording accounting data

Each business must install a system to collect and record all the financial transactions that are carried out. This includes cash received and paid out, goods bought and sold, items bought for use in the business, and so on.

Classifying data

Once the data has been recorded, it has to be classified so that it can be of use to the business. For instance, if a leisure business sells both sports equipment and camping gear, it would be of value to the proprietor to know the sales figures for the separate parts of the business.

Summarising data

Summarising the data of the various financial transactions provides the managers of the business with information in a concise form.

Communicating information

When the information from the above three procedures has been prepared, it then needs to be presented in a formal way as the business's accounts and business reports.

1.4 Basic concept of financial control

All businesses whether small, i.e. sole traders, through to very large ones such as multinational corporations use the same concept of financial control (see Exhibit 1.2). This can best be illustrated using a straightforward example such as a market trader who buys and sells goods. Such a person would operate his or her business as shown in Exhibit 1.3.

Exhibit 1.2 **The basis of a business**

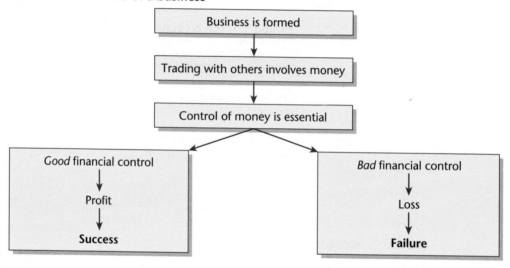

Exhibit 1.3

Financial control	
Trader invests in goods using his own money	Buys goods for £10,000
Being a good salesperson he is able to sell goods at more than he paid for them	Sells all the goods for £15,000
The difference between the cost of goods and selling price is profit	£ Selling price 15,000 *Less* Cost price 10,000 Profit 5,000
However, he has incurred expenses in actually selling the goods, i.e. market rents, transport, which must be deducted from this profit	*Less* Expenses 3,000 **Profit now** £2,000

Financial control is a major function of a business but there are other aspects that are needed to provide success:

● a competitive product and/or service
● a good strategy
● a competent workforce.

None of these would be of any use unless there is a market (people or businesses willing to buy the product and/or service).

It is, however, a fact that businesses, which practice good recording of financial data, will have the information to make sound management decisions with a far better chance of success.

1.5 Importance and need for accounting

As stated earlier, businesses must operate profitably otherwise they will cease to exist. The **financial statements** produced by a business's accounting department aim to show clearly the profit or loss that has been made and the financial position of the business.

The two most important statements are:

1 the trading and profit and loss account
2 the balance sheet.

Both these statements have to be checked and verified by a firm of auditors as part of the legal requirements for correct financial reporting. It is essential that accurate financial information is available to the auditors to enable them to fulfil their functions properly.

There are, however, other groups who are keenly interested in the activities of the business. The main interested parties are shown in Exhibit 1.4.

Exhibit 1.4

Interested party	Reason
HMRC	Legally required to collect tax such as employees' tax, national insurance contributions, business tax, VAT, etc.
Investors	Could be private individuals, companies, banks, etc. who will want to monitor the performance of the business to ensure it is profitable.
Suppliers	They will need to be assured of the viability of the business before accepting orders.
Customers	Before placing orders with a business they will need to know that it is financially stable.
Employees	They need to know of a business's financial status usually via unions or professional bodies.

1.6   Planning and decision making

Financial statements provide management with the means to measure the financial performance of the business. They will have the information to enable them to make rational decisions and to formulate revised plans as necessary. For example, the statements might show an unexpected rise in the cost of purchased goods, which is likely to affect the profits and cash flows of the business, and action would be needed to deal with this situation. Financial plans are usually known as **budgets**.

1.7   Types of organisations

Organisations are classified according to their structure and financial make-up and are mainly classified as follows. The classification will determine an organisation's legal status and what financial reporting is required of it:

- A **sole trader** is an individual trading alone in his or her own name, or under a recognised trading name. He or she is solely liable for all business debts, but when the business is successful can take all the profits.
- A **partnership** is a group of a minimum of two people up to a maximum of 20, who together carry on a particular business with a view to making a profit. This topic will be covered in Chapter 36.
- **Limited companies**, both private and public:
  - A **private limited company** is a legal entity with at least two shareholders. The liability of the shareholders is limited to the amount that they have agreed to invest.
  - A **public limited company** is also a legal entity with limited shareholder liability, but unlike a private company it can ask the public to subscribe for shares in its business. See Chapter 37.
- **Non-trading organisations** include clubs, associations and other non-profit-making organisations which are normally run for the benefit of their members to engage in a particular activity rather than to make a profit. Their financial statements will take the form of income and expenditure accounts, to be covered in Chapter 35.

Chapter summary

- The basis of business is trading with others and good financial control is essential if the organisation is to succeed.
- Book-keeping is the recording of business financial transactions.
- Accounting is the practice of maintaining accounts and preparing financial statements.
- The accounting sequence is as follows:
  - recording accounting data
  - classifying data
  - summarising data
  - communicating information.

- Financial control means ensuring that the sales of a business are greater than the cost incurred by the business, thus providing a profit.
- The two most important financial statements are:
  - the trading and profit and loss account
  - the balance sheet.
- A number of groups or agencies have a keen interest in the financial performance of a business:
  - HMRC
  - investors
  - suppliers
  - customers
  - employees.
- Organisations can include:
  - sole traders
  - partnerships
  - private limited companies
  - public limited companies
  - non-trading organisations.

Reminder: A glossary of accounting terms can be found in Appendix A at the end of the book.

EXERCISES

1.1 State briefly the importance of good financial control to the owners of a business.

1.2 There are a number of bodies or individuals, other than the owners, who will have an interest in the financial performance statements of a business. List these interested parties and explain briefly the reasons for their interest.

1.3 List the main types of business organisation and explain each one's basic structure.

CHAPTER 2

The accounting system

Learning objectives

After you have studied this chapter you should be able to:

- describe and explain the accounting system
- understand the source documents used within an organisation
- understand the need for books of original entry and what each one is used for
- appreciate how the books of original entry are used alongside the ledgers employing the double entry system of book-keeping
- distinguish between personal and impersonal ledgers
- distinguish between the different types of ledgers
- appreciate that at the end of the financial year the accounts are balanced off and a trial balance prepared
- understand that from the final trial balance the financial statements are prepared consisting of the trading and profit and loss account and the balance sheet.

2.1 Introduction

This chapter gives an overview of the **accounting system** starting with the source documents that are used initially to enter a transaction in the books of account. It explains the books of original entry and provides an introduction to the double entry system of book-keeping and the ledgers. The difference between personal and impersonal accounts is discussed together with the meaning of real and nominal accounts.

Finally, a summary is given of the procedures followed by organisations at the end of the accounting year to 'balance off' the accounts and prepare the trial balance. From the final trial balance the financial statements are prepared which show the results of the year's trading, be it a profit or loss, together with the **balance sheet** that indicates the financial position of the organisation at a specific point in time.

All the topics covered in this overview chapter are dealt with thoroughly in later chapters.

2.2 The accounting system

Traditionally businesses operate on a 12-month cycle, which may be the same as the calendar year January to December or perhaps the same as the tax year which runs from 6 April of one year to 5 April of the following year. Alternatively, some businesses operate from the date the business first began, for example 1 September of one year to 31 August of the following year.

During the 12-month period the business receives many documents of a financial nature that have to be entered in the books of account using either a manual or a computerised system. At the end of each month the books are usually 'balanced off' and a trial balance drawn up from which the financial statements may be prepared. Also, at the end of each month, outstanding accounts are usually settled, wages and salaries paid and monies received during the month are all recorded.

If the organisation uses a computerised system of accounting then, at the end of each month, a great deal of useful information can also be obtained such as the amount of money outstanding each month and the length of time the debt has been owing, and the amount of money that the organisation owes. Other financial information is also available that enables management to carry out an appraisal of the business, to budget and to forward plan. While this information is also available using a manual system of book-keeping it is not as readily available or as easily reformatted and processed as the information from a computerised system.

It is usual for the financial statements of a business to be prepared on an annual basis since they are required for taxation purposes and for the use by the owners of the business.

This chapter shows how source documents are recorded in the accounting records of an organisation and the various stages that are followed in preparing the financial statements (*see* Exhibit 2.1).

2.3 Source documents

Source documents are documents where original information is found, for example, sales and purchase invoices and credit notes. All businesses and organisations which are involved in either trading activities or providing a service use these important documents.

Invoice An invoice is a document prepared by the seller when they sell goods or provide services on credit. The invoice, usually numbered for easy identification and for filing in a suitable storage system, contains the following information:

- seller's name and address
- purchaser's name and address
- purchaser's order number and date
- date of delivery
- description of goods and services supplied including part number and catalogue reference
- quantity and price per item

Exhibit 2.1 The accounting system for a profit-making organisation

Collect financial information from business documentation

From the original documentation enter the data
in the books of original entry

Use the double entry system to post entries from the books
of original entry to the ledgers

Balance off the ledger accounts and prepare the trial balance to
check that balances from the ledgers are correct

Draw up the trading and profit and loss account to determine
the gross profit and net profit

Prepare the balance sheet to show assets, liabilities and capital
at the end of the accounting period

- total amount due
- terms and conditions of sale.

From a book-keeper's point of view the invoice is one of the most important documents since details of the transaction need to be entered in the books of account of both the seller and the buyer. In the seller's records the invoice is a sales invoice and in the purchaser's records it is a purchase invoice.

Credit note This document is raised by the supplier when goods have been returned by the purchaser due to their being damaged, faulty or supplied to the wrong specification, or when an overcharge has been made on an invoice. The amount owed by the customer will be reduced by the amount of the credit note. Credit notes are sometimes printed in red to distinguish them from invoices. Again, credit notes are important documents that need entering in the books of both the supplier and purchaser.

Debit note If the supplier agrees, goods bought previously may be returned. When this happens a debit note is raised by the purchaser and sent to the supplier giving details of the goods returned and the reason for their return. The debit note shows that the purchaser expects the seller to bear the charge.

Paying-in slips These are forms used for paying money into a bank account. The recipient of the money must record on the counterfoil of the bank paying-in slip details of the amount paid and by whom so that these may be recorded in the organisation's cash book.

Cheque counterfoil When a cheque is made out it is important to complete the counterfoil, entering details of the amount paid and to whom together with any other relevant information. The payment will also be recorded in the cash book.

Receipt This document acknowledges the receipt of money from a customer and is often issued when a customer purchases goods for cash rather than on credit. Again counterfoils are completed and used to enter the details of the receipt of cash in the cash book.

Bankers' Automated Clearing Service (BACS) receipt BACS enables the transfer of money between banks and other financial organisations. The supplier's bank can receive payment direct from the customer's bank. The customer usually sends an advice to the supplier giving details of the amount of the payment, which is then used to record the receipt in the books of account and later checked against the bank statement. This topic will be covered fully in Chapter 20.

Petty cash voucher A form used by anyone requesting payment for a small item of expenditure incurred on behalf of the business. The form gives details of the expense and should be signed and duly authorised. The petty cash voucher expenditure is recorded in the organisation's petty cash book.

Occasionally correspondence from a customer may be used as a source document to record a financial transaction that may be out of the ordinary. This may occur when a customer is unable to pay an outstanding amount and offers to settle the debt by giving the supplier an asset. Such a transaction would be entered in the journal (see Chapter 24). Internal documents such as a memorandum from a senior member of the organisation may be used in the same way.

It is important to note that all information of a financial nature must be supported by a source document and it is from this document that the details are entered in the business's book-keeping system. Source documents may also be referred to as **prime documents**.

2.4 Books of original entry

These are books in which the transaction is first entered. There are separate books for different types of transaction, as follows:

- **The journal** – this is used to record items that are much less common and sometimes complicated and are not recorded in any other book of original entry.
- **Sales day book** (also called **sales journal**) – a book used for listing sales invoices. It gives details of the date of the sale, to whom and the amount of the sale. Sales day books may also contain analysis columns to analyse sales between different goods, departments and so on.
- **Purchases day book** (also called **purchases journal**) – this is similar to the sales day book, but contains lists of purchase invoices received from suppliers of goods or services. The purchases day book may also contain analysis columns depending upon the accounting system.
- **Purchases returns day book** (also called **returns outwards day book** or journal) – this is used to record goods returned to suppliers.

- **Sales returns day book** (also called **returns inwards day book** or journal) – this is used to list any returns made by customers. This will lead to a credit note being issued to them.
- **Cash book** – this is another book of original entry used to enter cash and bank receipts and payments. The cash book provides a record of the business's bank account and also provides details of the amount of cash in hand. It is both a book of original entry and part of the double entry system as it contains the balances of both cash in hand and cash at bank.
- **Petty cash book** – a cash book used for making small (petty) payments, details of which are entered from petty cash vouchers supported if possible by a receipt.

2.5 An introduction to the double entry book-keeping system

The system of **double entry book-keeping** is a method of recording transactions in the books of account of a business. In the section above, source documents, which provide all the relevant information, were discussed followed by the books of original entry. The next important stage is to understand the double entry system of book-keeping.

Business transactions deal with money or money's worth and each transaction always affects two things. For example, if a firm buys goods valued at £500 and pays for them by cheque, two things will have occurred:

1 The stock of goods is increased by £500.
2 The money in the firm's bank account will have decreased by £500.

If the firm then pays cash for a piece of equipment, then:

1 The money in the cash account will be reduced.
2 The firm will have acquired equipment.

The dual aspect of treating each transaction is then recorded in an account. An account shows us the 'history' of a particular business transaction, for example, the bank account or equipment account. If manual accounting records are kept, then each account is usually shown on a separate page. If a computerised system is used, then each account is given a separate code number. The following shows an example of an account.

							Reference no.
Dr					Name of account		Cr
Date	Details	Folio	£	Date	Details	Folio	£
	Debit side				Credit side		

Double entry book-keeping is shown using a step-by-step approach in Chapters 4, 5 and 6.

2.6   The ledgers

In a double entry system the accounts, as mentioned above, are kept in a ledger. If the business is very small then only one ledger may be used, but once the business expands it is better to have more than one ledger to allow different members of staff to be able to record transactions at the same time.

Once details from the source documents are entered in the books of original entry then the next stage of the book-keeping procedure is to show the effect of the transactions by putting them into double entry accounts. The different types of ledgers used are as follows (their alternative names are shown in brackets).

Types of ledger		
Sales ledger (Debtors' ledger)	**Purchase ledger** (Creditors' ledger)	**General ledger** (Nominal ledger)
Shows records of customer's personal accounts.	Shows records of suppliers' personal accounts.	Contains the remaining double entry accounts, such as assets, capital, expenses and income.

2.7   Classification of accounts

Accounts are divided into **personal accounts** and **impersonal accounts**. Personal accounts are accounts that deal with people and businesses – in other words, the debtors and creditors – **debtors** being people who owe money to the business and **creditors** being people or businesses to whom money is owed. The debtors' accounts are maintained in the sales ledger, which may also be referred to as the debtors' ledger, the creditors' accounts are kept in the purchases ledger also referred to as the creditors' ledger.

Impersonal accounts are divided into real and nominal accounts:

● **Real accounts** are those which deal with possessions of the business, for example, buildings, machinery, computer equipment, fixtures and fittings, stock, etc.
● **Nominal accounts** are those in which expenses and income are recorded, for example, sales, purchases, wages, electricity, commissions received, etc.

Private ledger

In order to ensure privacy for the proprietor(s), the capital, drawings and other similar accounts are sometimes kept in a **private ledger**. This prevents office staff from seeing items of a confidential nature.

Exhibit 2.2 illustrates the classification of accounts.

Exhibit 2.2 Classification of accounts

2.8 Balancing off accounts and the trial balance

Businesses usually balance off their accounts at the end of each month and prepare what is called a **trial balance**. The trial balance is prepared for several reasons: first of all it is important to check periodically that the transactions have been entered correctly in the books of account; second it is useful to know how much money is outstanding and how much the business owes. Also, with the use of accounting software, the business can easily prepare draft financial statements showing the profit or loss to date and the financial position of the firm at a specific date. Both the trial balance and the financial statements are dealt with in later chapters of this book.

2.9 Financial statements

At the end of the financial year a trial balance is drawn up and from that and other information and adjustments the financial statements are prepared by an organisation. The financial statements include:

- the **trading and profit and loss account** which shows the gross and net profits or losses made during the period, and
- the balance sheet, which indicates the financial position of the business at a particular point in time.

As the name implies, the final accounts are the end product of the recording of all the business transactions throughout the financial year. Once prepared, they are used by the owner(s) of the business for information, interpretation and planning purposes.

2.10 Summary of the accounting system

This chapter has shown how the accounting procedures of a business are recorded and the information that is derived from those records. It may be useful to list them once again at this point. Source documents are received as follows:

Documents	Entered into book of original entry
Sales invoices	Sales day book (also called sales journal)
Credit notes (sent to customers)	Sales returns day book (also called returns inwards day book)
Purchase invoices	Purchases day book (also called purchases journal)
Credit notes (received from suppliers)	Purchases returns day book (also called returns outwards day book)
Cash and cheques received	Cash book (also a ledger account)
Cheques paid out	Cash book (also a ledger account)
Small cash payments	Petty cash book (also a ledger account for cash in hand)
Miscellaneous correspondence	The journal

Once the details of the transaction have been entered into the books of original entry, the information is then entered into the ledgers by means of the double entry system. This procedure is often referred to as **posting**. Sales transactions are posted to the sales ledger, purchases transactions are posted to the purchase ledger and items involving the real and nominal accounts are posted to the general ledger.

At the end of each month the books are balanced off and a trial balance prepared to check the arithmetical accuracy of the book-keeping entries. At the end of the accounting period the final trial balance is used to prepare the year-end accounts, i.e. the trading and profit and loss account and the balance sheet. The accounts are then presented to the owner(s) of the business for their information, interpretation and action in the form of planning and budgeting for the next accounting period, and for forward planning.

Chapter summary

- The accounting system is the sequence in which financial data is recorded and processed prior to the preparation of the financial statements at the end of the trading period.
- All information that is entered into the book-keeping records comes from a source document such as an invoice, credit note, debit note, cheque book counterfoil, paying-in book, petty cash voucher, etc.
- The books of original entry are used as a basis for posting the transactions to the double entry accounts in the various ledgers.
- At the end of the accounting period the accounts are balanced off and a trial balance prepared.
- The final trial balance is used to prepare the year-end accounts. These are the trading and profit and loss account, which shows the profit or loss made for the period, and the balance sheet, which shows the financial position of the business at a specific date.

- A summary of the accounting system is shown together with a recap of the various stages of the accounting procedures.

Reminder: There is a glossary of accounting terms in Appendix A at the end of the book.

EXERCISES

*Note: Questions with the suffix 'X' shown after the question number do **not** have answers shown at the back of the book. Answers to the other questions are shown in Appendix E.*

2.1 Source documents are very important.

(*a*) Describe the contents of both an invoice and a credit note.
(*b*) State when each of these would be used.

2.2 Describe the service offered by BACS and in what circumstances might a business use this facility.

2.3X The books of original entry are used to record initial accounting information and separate books are used for different types of transactions. List the various books used and give a brief explanation as to how each is used.

2.4 For what purpose would you use the following ledgers:

(*a*) General or nominal ledger
(*b*) Sales ledger
(*c*) Purchases ledger?

2.5X Distinguish between personal and impersonal accounts giving examples of what each might contain.

CHAPTER 3

The balance sheet and the accounting equation

Learning objectives

After you have studied this chapter you should be able to:

- understand the accounting equation
- understand what is meant by assets, liabilities and capital
- draw up balance sheets after different transactions have occurred
- explain the meaning of the terms assets, capital, liabilities, debtors and creditors.

3.1 Introduction

This chapter looks at one of the financial statements used in businesses called the **balance sheet**. The balance sheet is just one of the statements prepared at the end of the financial year, the other statements are the trading and profit and loss accounts. Although these are separate accounts they are usually shown as one financial statement, and will be discussed in later chapters.

The balance sheet is a financial statement that is usually prepared at the end of an organisation's financial year. Quite simply the statement details everything that the organisation *owns* and what it *owes* as at a specific date. The items an organisation owns are known as **assets** and what it owes are called **liabilities**. Also included in the balance sheet is the **capital**, which is the amount of money supplied by the owner(s) of the business.

3.2 The accounting equation

Accounting is based upon a concept known as the **accounting equation**, which is simply that at any point in time the total amount of resources supplied by the owner equals the resources in the business. Assuming that the owner of the new business supplies all the resources then this can be shown as follows:

> Resources supplied by the owner = Resources in the business

In accounting the various terms have special meanings. The amount of resources supplied by the owner is called **capital**. As mentioned above the actual resources that are in the business are called **assets**. If the owner of the business has supplied all of the resources, the accounting equation can be shown as:

Capital = Assets

In many cases other people besides the owner of the business will have supplied some of the assets. The amounts owing to these people for these assets is called **liabilities**, as stated above. When this is the case the accounting equation changes to:

Capital = Assets – Liabilities

This is the most common way in which the accounting equation is presented since the two sides of the equation will have the same totals because we are dealing with the same thing but from two different points of view. First, the value of the owners' investment in the business and secondly the value of what is owned by the business, which is ultimately owned by the owners.

Unfortunately, with this form of the accounting equation, it is no longer possible to see at a glance what value is represented by the resources in the business. This can be seen more clearly if you change assets and capital around to give an alternative form of the accounting equation:

Assets = Capital + Liabilities

This can then be replaced with words describing the resources of the business:

Resources: what they are = Resources: who supplied them
(Assets)   (Capital + Liabilities)

It is a fact that no matter how you present the accounting equation, the totals of both sides will *always* equal each other, and this will *always* be true irrespective of the number of transactions. The actual assets, capital and liabilities may change, but the total of the assets will always equal the total of capital + liabilities. Or, reverting to the more common form of the accounting equation, the capital will always equal the assets of the business minus the liabilities.

Assets consist of property of all kinds, such as buildings, machinery, equipment, stocks of goods and motor vehicles. Other assets include debts owed by customers and the amount of money in the bank account.

Liabilities include amounts owed by the business for goods and services supplied to the business, and expenses incurred by the business but still outstanding. Funds borrowed by the business are also included.

Capital is often called the owner's **equity** or **net worth**. This is comprised of the funds invested in the business by the owner plus any **profits** retained for use in the business less any share of the profits paid out to the owner by the business.

3.3 The balance sheet and the effects of business transactions

As mentioned above the balance sheet shows the financial position of an organisation at a point in time. In other words, it presents a snapshot of the organisation at the date when the balance sheet was prepared. It is in the balance sheet that the accounting equation is expressed.

The balance sheet is not the first accounting record to be made, nor the first record that you will learn to enter, but it is a convenient place to start considering accounting.

In the following activities you will see how a series of transactions affect the balance sheet.

1 The introduction of capital

On 1 January 2009, K Astley started in business and put £50,000 into a bank account for the business. The balance would appear:

K Astley
Balance Sheet as at 1 January 2009

	£
Assets: Cash at bank	50,000
Capital	50,000

Note how the top section of the balance sheet contains the assets and the bottom section contains the capital. The information is always presented in the balance sheet in this way.

2 The purchase of an asset by cheque

On 3 January 2009, Astley buys a small shop for £30,000. The effect of this transaction on the balance sheet is that the money in the bank is decreased and the new asset, shop, is added:

K Astley
Balance Sheet as at 3 January 2009

	£
Assets: Shop	30,000
Cash at bank	20,000
	50,000
Capital	50,000

Note how the two parts of the balance sheet 'balance': the total of the assets equals the total of the liabilities.

3 The purchase of an asset and the incurring of a liability

On 5 January 2009, Astley buys some goods for £5,000 from D Moore and agrees to pay for them some time within the following two weeks. The effect of this is that a new asset, **stock** of goods, is acquired, and a liability for the goods is created. A person to whom money is owed for goods is known in accounting language as a **creditor**. The balance sheet becomes:

K Astley
Balance Sheet as at 5 January 2009

		£
Assets:	Shop	30,000
	Stock of goods	5,000
	Cash at bank	20,000
		55,000
Less:	Creditor	5,000
		50,000
Capital		50,000

Note how the liability (the creditor) is shown as a deduction from the assets. This is exactly the same calculation as is presented in the most common form of the accounting equation.

4 Sale of an asset on credit

On 10 January 2009, goods which cost £1,000 were sold to P Hall for the same amount, the money to be paid at a later date. The effect is a reduction in the stock of goods and the creation of a new asset. A person who owes the business money is known in accounting terms as a **debtor**. The balance sheet now appears as:

K Astley
Balance Sheet as at 10 January 2009

		£
Assets:	Shop	30,000
	Stock of goods	4,000
	Debtor	1,000
	Cash at bank	20,000
		55,000
Less:	Creditor	5,000
		50,000
Capital		50,000

5 Sale of an asset for immediate payment

On 15 January 2009, goods which cost £2,000 were sold to M Clark for the same amount. Clark paid for them immediately by cheque. Here one asset, stock of goods, is reduced, while another asset, bank, is increased. The balance sheet after these transactions is now shown:

K Astley
Balance Sheet as at 15 January 2009

	£
Assets: Shop	30,000
Stock of goods	2,000
Debtor	1,000
Cash at bank	22,000
	55,000
Less: Creditor	5,000
	50,000
Capital	50,000

6 The payment of a liability

On 17 January 2009, Astley pays a cheque for £3,000 to D Moore in part payment of the amount owing. The asset of bank is therefore reduced, and the liability to the creditor is also reduced. The balance sheet now appears as shown below:

K Astley
Balance Sheet as at 17 January 2009

	£
Assets: Shop	30,000
Stock of goods	2,000
Debtor	1,000
Cash at bank	19,000
	52,000
Less: Creditor	2,000
	50,000
Capital	50,000

Note how the total of each part of the balance sheet has not changed. The business is still worth £50,000 to the owner K Astley.

7 Collection of an asset

P Hall, who owed Astley £1,000, makes a part payment of £750 by cheque on 31 January 2009. The effect is to reduce one asset, debtor, and to increase another asset, bank. The balance sheet after these transactions is now shown:

K Astley
Balance Sheet as at 31 January 2009

	£
Assets: Shop	30,000
Stock of goods	2,000
Debtor	250
Cash at bank	19,750
	52,000
Less: Creditor	2,000
	50,000
Capital	50,000

3.4 Equality of the accounting equation

It can be seen that every transaction has affected two items. Sometimes it has changed two assets by reducing one and increasing the other. In other cases, the effect has been different. You will notice, however, that in all cases apart from the very first (when the owner started the business by putting in cash of £50,000) no change has been made to the total of either section of the balance sheet and the equality between their two totals has remained the same. The accounting equation has held true throughout the example and, in fact, always will.

The effect of each of the seven accounting transactions, shown above, upon the two sections of the balance sheet is now illustrated in Exhibit 3.1.

Exhibit 3.1

Type of transaction	Effect			
1 Owner pays capital into the bank	↑	Increase asset (Bank)	↑	Increase capital
2 Purchase shop premises by cheque	↓	Decrease asset (Bank)	↑	Increase asset (Shop premises)
3 Buy goods on credit	↑	Increase asset (Stock of goods)	↑	Increase liability (Creditors)
4 Sale of goods on credit	↓	Decrease asset (Stock of goods)	↑	Increase asset (Debtors)
5 Sale of goods for cash or cheque	↑	Increase asset (Cash or bank)	↓	Decrease asset (Stock of goods)
6 Pay creditor	↓	Decrease asset (Bank)	↓	Decrease liability (Creditor)
7 Debtor pays money owing by cheque	↑	Increase asset (Bank)	↓	Decrease asset (Debtors)

Each transaction has, therefore, maintained the same total for assets as for capital + liabilities. This can be shown:

Number of transactions as above	Assets	Capital and Liabilities	Effect on balance sheet totals
1	+	+	Each side added to equally
2	− +		A minus and a plus both on the assets side thus cancelling out each other
3	+	+	Each side added to equally
4	− +		A minus and a plus on the assets side
5	+ −		A plus and a minus both on the assets side cancelling out each other
6	−	−	Each side reduced equally
7	+ −		A plus and a minus on the assets side

3.5 More detailed presentation of the balance sheet

The balance sheets shown in this chapter are presented in what is referred to as the 'vertical presentation'. This method will be used throughout the book since it is the most common method of presentation used today.

A more detailed balance sheet of K Astley is now shown in line with how you will learn to present the information in later stages of your studies:

K Astley
Balance Sheet as at 31 January 2009

		£
Fixed assets		
Shop		30,000
Current assets		
Stock of goods	2,000	
Debtor	250	
Cash at bank	19,750	
	22,000	
Less: Current Liabilities		
Creditor	2,000	20,000
		50,000
Capital		50,000

The terms **fixed assets**, **current assets** and **current liabilities** shown in the above balance sheet are explained below. The terms are dealt with more fully in Chapter 11.

● **Fixed assets** are assets which have an expected useful life of at least a year and beyond, for example, buildings, machinery, fixtures, motor vehicles. They are used in the business to enable it to carry on the purpose of earning income and are not intended for resale.

- **Current assets** are assets which change from day to day, for example, the value of stock in hand goes up and down as it is bought and sold. Similarly, the amount of money owing to us by debtors will change quickly, as we sell more to them on credit and they pay their debts. The amount of money in the bank will also change as we receive and pay out money.
- **Current liabilities** are those liabilities which have to be paid within the near future, for example, creditors for goods bought.

Chapter summary

- The balance sheet is a financial statement prepared at a particular point in time. It contains assets, capital and liabilities.
- The whole of accounting is based on the accounting equation namely that resources supplied by the owner (the capital) will always equal the resources in the business (the assets).
- Other people may also supply some of the assets to the business. The name given to any amounts that are owed by the business to other people are called liabilities.
- When assets are supplied by other people as well as the owner of the business the accounting equation becomes Capital = Assets − Liabilities.
- The two sides of the accounting equation are represented by the two sections of the balance sheet.
- The totals of each part of the balance sheet should always agree, i.e. balance.
- Every transaction affects two items in the accounting equation. Sometimes that may involve the same item being affected twice, once positively (going up) and once negatively (going down).
- Every transaction affects two items in the balance sheet.

Reminder: There is a glossary of accounting terms in Appendix A at the end of the book.

EXERCISES

*Note: Questions with the suffix 'X' shown after the question number do **not** have answers shown at the back of the book. Answers to the other questions are shown in Appendix E.*

3.1 Examine the following table and complete the gaps:

	Assets £	Liabilities £	Capital £
(a)	34,282	7,909	?
(b)	276,303	?	213,817
(c)	?	6,181	70,919
(d)	?	109,625	877,138
(e)	88,489	?	78,224
(f)	456,066	51,163	?

3.2X Examine the following table and complete the gaps:

	Assets £	Liabilities £	Capital £
(a)	?	59,997	604,337
(b)	346,512	?	293,555
(c)	47,707	?	42,438
(d)	108,129	11,151	?
(e)	515,164	77,352	?
(f)	?	19,928	179,352

3.3 Determine which are assets and which are liabilities from the following list:

(a) Computer equipment
(b) Stock of goods
(c) Loan from H Barlow
(d) Motor vehicles
(e) What we owe for advertising materials
(f) Bank balance.

3.4X Which of the following are assets and which are liabilities?

(a) Premises
(b) Debtors
(c) Cash in hand
(d) Creditors
(e) Loan from finance company
(f) Owing to bank
(g) Machinery
(h) Motor vehicles.

3.5 State which of the following are shown under the wrong headings for S Murphy's business:

Assets	Liabilities
Cash in hand	Money owing to bank
Creditors	Debtors
Premises	Stock of goods
Motor vehicles	
Loan from C Shaw	
Machinery	

3.6X Which of the following are shown under the wrong headings?:

Assets	Liabilities
Cash at bank	Machinery
Computer equipment	Motor vehicles
Creditors	Loan from W Barlow
Capital	
Debtors	
Stock of goods	

3.7 Ann Wood decides to open a retail shop selling greetings cards and gifts. Her uncle lends her £30,000 to help her with financing the venture. Ann buys shop premises costing £50,000, a motor vehicle for £10,000 and stock of goods for £5,000. Ann did not pay for her stock of goods in full and still owes £2,100 to her suppliers in respect of them. After the events described above and before she starts trading, Ann has £100 cash in hand and £7,000 cash at the bank.

You are required to calculate the amount of capital that Ann invested in her business.

3.8X Suman Patel decides to start his own retail business and his father agrees to lend him £3,000. Before starting trading he decides to buy some shop fittings costing £4,000 and a secondhand motor van costing £6,100.

Suman also buys a stock of goods for £5,720 paying £3,000 when he placed the order, the balance being due in two months. After paying for the above items Suman has £4,200 in the bank and £120 in cash.

You are required to calculate Suman's capital.

3.9 Draw up T Lymer's balance sheet, using the vertical presentation method, from the following information as at 31 December 2010.

	£
Capital	34,823
Delivery van	12,000
Debtors	10,892
Office furniture	8,640
Stock of goods	4,220
Cash at bank	11,722
Creditors	12,651

3.10X Draw up A Pennington's balance sheet as at 31 March 2010 from the following information:

	£
Premises	50,000
Plant and machinery	26,500
Debtors	28,790
Creditors	32,320
Bank overdraft	3,625
Stock	21,000
Cash in hand	35
Capital	90,380

3.11 Complete the columns to show the effects of the following transactions:

	Effects upon		
	Assets	Capital	Liabilities

(a) Bought goods on credit £400.
(b) F Drew lends the firm £500 by cheque.
(c) We return goods £50 to a supplier whose account was still outstanding.
(d) We pay a creditor £330 by cheque.
(e) The owner of the business introduces £5,000 into the firm by cheque.
(f) Bought computer £880 for office use paying by cheque.
(g) Sold goods for cash £45.
(h) A debtor pays us in cash £77.

For each item shown above, you are required to state how it changes assets, capital or liabilities.

For example the answer to (*a*) will be:

(*a*) *Assets*	*Capital*	*Liabilities*
+ £400	–	+ £400

The double entry system for assets, liabilities and capital

Learning objectives

After you have studied this chapter you should be able to:

- understand what is meant by the double entry system
- explain how the double entry system follows the rules of the accounting equation
- understand the rules for double entry book-keeping
- be able to draw up 'T accounts' and understand the terms 'debit' and 'credit'
- be able to record transactions affecting assets, liabilities and capital in the T accounts.

4.1 Nature of a transaction

In Chapter 3 we saw how various events changed two items in the balance sheet. Events which result in such changes are known as **transactions**. This means that if the proprietor of a business asks the price of some goods but does not buy them, then there is no transaction. If he or she later asks the price of some goods and then buys them, in this second case there is a transaction, since it would mean that two balance sheet items, i.e. stock of goods and cash at bank, will have changed.

4.2 The double entry system

The system of double entry book-keeping is a method of recording transactions in the books of account of a business. In the previous chapter we saw how every transaction affected two items. We now need to show these effects when the transaction is first recorded in the books of account. The information for every item that is entered into the books of account is obtained from a source document, i.e. an invoice, credit note, cheque book stub, paying in book, etc. (see Chapter 14). The next important stage is to understand the double entry system of book-keeping.

Business transactions deal with money or money's worth and each transaction always affects two things. For example, if a business buys goods valued at £500 and pays for them by cheque, two things have occurred:

1 the money in the business's bank account will have decreased by £500
2 the stock of goods is increased.

Here is another example: if a business buys a motor van costing £10,000 and pays for it by cheque then again two things have been affected:

1 the money in the business's bank account will have decreased by £10,000
2 the motor van will have been acquired for the business and that asset account will have increased.

This is the book-keeping stage of accounting and the process used is called **double entry**; sometimes this may also be referred to as **double entry book-keeping**, either term is correct.

In the previous chapter a new balance sheet was drawn up after each transaction. This can be done quite easily if there are only a few transactions per day. However, if there are hundreds of transactions per day then it will become impossible to draw up numerous balance sheets. There simply would not be enough time to carry out such a task.

Therefore, instead of constantly drawing up amended balance sheets after each transaction what we have instead is the double entry system. The basis of this system is that the transactions that have occurred are entered in the books of account, as mentioned above. An **account** shows us the 'history of' a particular business trans-action. It is the place in the records where all the information referring to a particular asset, liability or capital is entered, for example, the bank account or motor van account. If manual records are kept, then each account is usually shown on a separate page; if a computerised system is used, then each account is given a separate code number and the information is stored on the accounting package and back-up systems.

4.3 The accounts for double entry

Each account should be shown on a separate page. The double entry system divides each page into two halves. The left-hand side of each page is called the **debit** side, while the the right-hand side is called the **credit** side. The title of each account is written across the top of the account at the centre – see Exhibit 4.1. Note that the word 'Debit' is often shown in a short form as *Dr*, while 'Credit' is often shown as *Cr*.

Exhibit 4.1

Title of account written here					
Date	Details	£	Date	Details	£

Left-hand side of the page.
This is the 'debit' side.

Right-hand side of the page.
This is the 'credit' side.

The words 'debit' and 'credit' in book-keeping terms do not mean the same as in normal language and should be viewed differently from the start to avoid confusion. Students new to studying double entry may find it useful to think of 'IN' when looking at the entry of a debit item, and to think of 'OUT' when looking at the entry of a credit item. We will consider this later in Section 4.5.

4.4 Rules for double entry

Double entry is relatively easy to learn and understand if the following four rules are learnt and understood:

1 Double entry means that every transaction affects two things and should, therefore, be entered twice: once on the *Debit* side and once on the *Credit* side. Later on in your studies you may have more than two accounts to record a transaction, for example, when an item is purchased and part of it is paid for in cash and part paid by cheque.
2 The order in which the items are entered does not matter – although students may find it easier to deal with any cash or bank transaction first using the 'IN' and 'OUT' principle.
3 A **debit** entry is always an asset or an expense. A **credit** entry is a liability, capital or income.
4 To increase or decrease assets, liabilities or capital, as seen in Chapter 3, the double entry rules are as shown in Exhibit 4.2.

Exhibit 4.2

Accounts	To record	Entry in the account
Assets	↑ an increase	Debit
	↓ a decrease	Credit
Liabilities	↑ an increase	Credit
	↓ a decrease	Debit
Capital	↑ an increase	Credit
	↓ a decrease	Debit

Let's look once again at the accounting equation:

	Capital	=	Assets	–	Liabilities
To increase each item	Credit		Debit		Credit
To decrease each item	Debit		Credit		Debit

The double entry rules for liabilities and capital are the same, but they are the opposite of those for assets. Looking at the accounts the rules will appear as:

Capital account		Any asset account		Any liability account	
Decreases	Increases	Increases	Decreases	Decreases	Increases
–	+	+	–	–	+

In a real business, at least one full page would be taken for each account in the accounting books. However, as we have not enough space in this book to put each account on a separate page, we will list the accounts under each other.

4.5 The 'IN' and 'OUT' approach

To help students having difficulty in deciding on which side of each account the items should be entered, a useful hint is for them to think of the debit side being 'IN' to the account, and the credit side being 'OUT' of the account.

To give two examples of this approach, we will use the following:

Example 1: Paid cash £2,000 to buy machinery.

The double entry for this transaction would be as follows:

Effect	Action
(a) Machinery comes 'IN' (b) Cash goes 'OUT'	A *debit* entry in the Machinery account A *credit* entry in the Cash account

Example 2: Took £500 out of the cash in hand of the business and paid it into the bank account of the business.

The double entry for this transaction would be as follows:

Effect	Action
(a) Money comes 'IN' to the bank (b) Cash goes 'OUT' of the cash till	A *debit* entry in the Bank account A *credit* entry in the Cash account

4.6 T accounts

The type of accounts that are going to be demonstrated are known as **T accounts**. This is because the accounts are in the shape of a T, as illustrated in Exhibit 4.3.

Exhibit 4.3

Account title here: the top stroke of the T

Debit side   Credit side

The line divides the two sides and is the downstroke of the T.

4.7 Worked examples

The entry of a few transactions can now be attempted:

Example 3: The proprietor starts the business with £30,000 in cash on 1 August 2009.

Effect	Action
(a) Increases the *asset* of cash (b) Increases the *capital*	Debit the cash account – cash goes 'IN' Credit the capital account – cash comes 'OUT' of the owner's money

These are entered as follows:

Dr		Cash Account			Cr
	'IN'			'OUT'	
2009			£		
Aug 1			30,000		

Dr		Capital Account			Cr
	'IN'			'OUT'	
			2009		£
			Aug 1		30,000

The date of the transaction has already been entered. Now there remains the description which is to be entered alongside the amount. The double entry to the item in the cash account is completed by an entry in the capital account, and therefore the word 'Capital' will appear in the cash account. Similarly, the double entry to the item in the capital account is completed by an entry in the cash account, and therefore the word 'Cash' will appear in the capital account.

The finally completed accounts are therefore:

Dr		Cash Account			Cr
	'IN'			'OUT'	
2009			£		
Aug 1 Capital			30,000		

Dr		Capital Account			Cr
	'IN'			'OUT'	
			2009		£
			Aug 1 Cash		30,000

This method of entering transactions therefore fulfils the requirements of the double entry rules as shown in Section 4.4. Now let us look at the entry of some more transactions.

***Example* 4**: A motor van is bought for £17,500 cash on 2 August 2009.

Effect	Action
(a) Decreases the *asset* of cash (b) Increases the *asset* of motor van	Credit the cash account – Cash goes 'OUT' Debit the motor van account – Motor van comes 'IN'

Dr		Cash Account		Cr
	'IN'		'OUT'	
			2009	£
			Aug 2 Motor van	17,500

Dr		Motor Van Account		Cr
	'IN'		'OUT'	
2009		£		
Aug 2 Cash		17,500		

Example 5: Fixtures bought on credit from Shop Fitters for £1,500 on 3 August 2009.

Effect	Action
(*a*) Increases the *asset* of Fixtures	Debit the Fixtures account – Fixtures go 'IN'
(*b*) Increases the *liability* to Shop Fitters	Credit the Shop Fitters' account – Fixtures come 'OUT' of the supplier's account

Dr		Fixtures Account		Cr
	'IN'		'OUT'	
2009		£		
Aug 3 Shop Fitters		1,500		

Dr		Shop Fitters' Account		Cr
	'IN'		'OUT'	
			2009	£
			Aug 3 Fixtures	1,500

Example 6: Paid the amount owing in cash to Shop Fitters on 17 August 2009.

Effect	Action
(*a*) Decreases the *asset* of cash	Credit the cash account – Cash goes 'OUT'
(*b*) Decreases the *liability* to Shop Fitters	Debit the Shop Fitters' account – Cash goes 'IN' to the supplier's account

Dr		Cash Account		Cr
	'IN'		'OUT'	
			2009	£
			Aug 17 Shop Fitters	1,500

Dr		Shop Fitters' Account		Cr
	'IN'		'OUT'	
2009		£		
Aug 17 Cash		1,500		

Example 7: Transactions to date.

Taking the transactions numbered 3 to 6 above, the records will now appear thus:

Dr		Cash Account		Cr
	'IN'		'OUT'	
2009		£	2009	£
Aug 1 Capital		30,000	Aug 2 Motor Van	17,500
			Aug 17 Shop Fitters	1,500

Dr		Capital Account		Cr
	'IN'		'OUT'	
			2009	£
			Aug 1 Cash	30,000

Dr		Motor Van Account		Cr
	'IN'		'OUT'	
2009		£		
Aug 2 Cash		17,500		

Dr		Shop Fitter's Account		Cr
	'IN'		'OUT'	
2009		£	2009	£
Aug 17 Cash		1,500	Aug 3 Fixtures	1,500

Dr		Fixtures Account		Cr
	'IN'		'OUT'	
2009		£		
Aug 3 Shop Fitters		1,500		

Before you read further, you are required to work through Exercises 4.1 and 4.2 at the end of the chapter.

Example 8: Now you have actually made some entries in accounts, you are to go carefully through the example shown in Exhibit 4.4. Make certain you can understand every entry.

Exhibit 4.4

Transactions	Effect	Action	IN/OUT
2009 May 1 Started an engineering business putting £10,000 into a business bank (A) account.	Increases *asset* of bank. Increases *capital* of owner.	Debit bank account. Credit capital account.	IN OUT
May 3 Bought works machinery on credit from Unique Machines £2,750. (B)	Increases *asset* of machinery. Increases *liability* to Unique Machines.	Debit machinery account. Credit Unique Machines account.	IN OUT
May 4 Withdrew £2,000 cash from the bank and placed it in the cash box. (C)	Decreases *asset* of bank. Increases *asset* of cash.	Credit bank account. Debit cash account.	OUT IN
May 7 Bought a secondhand motor van paying in cash £1,800. (D)	Decreases *asset* of cash. Increases *asset* of motor van.	Credit cash account. Debit motor van account.	OUT IN
May 10 Sold some of the machinery for £150 on credit to B Barnes. (E)	Decreases *asset* of machinery. Increases *asset* of money owing from B Barnes.	Credit machinery account. Debit B Barnes account.	OUT IN
May 21 Returned some of the machinery, value £270 to Unique Machines. (F)	Decreases *asset* of machinery. Decreases *liability* to Unique Machines.	Credit machinery account. Debit Unique Machines account.	OUT IN
May 28 B Barnes pays the business the amount owing, £150, by cheque. (G)	Increases *asset* of bank. Decreases *asset* of money owing by B Barnes.	Debit bank account. Credit B Barnes account.	IN OUT
May 30 Bought another secondhand motor van for £4,200, paying by cheque. (H)	Decreases *asset* of bank. Increases *asset* of motor vans.	Credit bank account. Debit motor van account.	OUT IN
May 31 Paid the amount of £2,480 to Unique Machines by cheque. (I)	Decreases *asset* of bank. Decreases *liability* to Unique Machines.	Credit bank account. Debit Unique Machines account.	OUT IN

In account form this is shown thus:

Dr			Bank Account			Cr
	'IN'			'OUT'		
2009		£	2009			£
May 1 Capital	(A)	10,000	May 4 Cash	(C)		2,000
May 28 B Barnes	(G)	150	May 30 Motor van	(H)		4,200
			May 30 Unique			
			Machines	(I)		2,480

Dr			Cash Account			Cr
	'IN'			'OUT'		
2009		£	2009			£
May 4 Bank	(C)	2,000	May 7 Motor van	(D)		1,800

Dr			Capital Account			Cr
	'IN'			'OUT'		
			2009			£
			May 1 Bank	(A)		10,000

Dr			Machinery Account			Cr
	'IN'			'OUT'		
2009		£	2009			£
May 3 Unique			May 10 B Barnes	(E)		150
Machines	(B)	2,750	May 21 Unique			
			Machines	(F)		270

Dr			Motor Van Account			Cr
	'IN'			'OUT'		
2009		£				
May 7 Cash	(D)	1,800				
May 30 Bank	(H)	4,200				

Dr			Unique Machines Account			Cr
	'IN'			'OUT'		
2009		£	2009			£
May 21 Machinery	(F)	270	May 3 Machinery	(B)		2,750
May 31 Bank	(I)	2,480				

Dr			B Barnes Account			Cr
	'IN'			'OUT'		
2009		£	2009			£
May 10 Machinery	(E)	150	May 28 Bank	(G)		150

4.8 Abbreviation of 'Limited'

The abbreviation 'Ltd' will be seen in examples and exercises throughout the book and this refers to limited companies. When you see the name of a business, for example, Skinners Ltd, the suffix indicates a limited company. In our books, the transaction with Skinners Ltd will be entered in the same way as for any other customer or supplier.

4.9 Value Added Tax (VAT)

Students studying accountancy will be aware that in the UK many goods and services are subject to Value Added Tax (VAT). You will have noticed that in this chapter VAT has been ignored. This has been done deliberately to avoid confusion to the student since it was felt by the authors that it is best to concentrate on the principles of double entry book-keeping initially before including VAT. VAT will be introduced later in this book (see Chapters 18 and 19).

Chapter summary

- The chapter covers the concept of double entry book-keeping whereby every transaction affects two things. Each item has to be entered twice in the book-keeping records, once on the debit side of an account and once on the credit side of an account.
- Double entry follows the rules of the accounting equation.
- Transactions are entered into the accounts rather than directly into numerous balance sheets.
- The use of 'T accounts' to record information is discussed.
- The chapter contains a fully worked example illustrating how transactions cause increases and decreases in asset, liability and capital accounts.

EXERCISES

4.1 Complete the following table showing which accounts are to be credited and which are to be debited:

	Account to be debited	Account to be credited
(a) Bought motor van for cash		
(b) Bought office machinery on credit from J Grant & Son		
(c) Introduced capital in cash		
(d) A debtor, J Beach, pays us by cheque		
(e) Paid a creditor, A Barrett, in cash.		

4.2X Complete the following table showing which accounts are to be debited and which accounts are to be credited:

	Account to be debited	Account to be credited
(a) Bought computer equipment for office paying by cheque		
(b) A debtor, Bush Ltd, pays us by cheque		
(c) Owner of the business puts further money into the business by cheque		
(d) Paid a creditor, Ash & Co, by cheque		
(e) Bought office chair paying by cash		
(f) Bought a motor car paying by cheque		
(g) Mike Meredith lent the business £5,000 paying by cheque		
(h) Sold old motor van, received cash, £600		
(i) Paid a creditor, Skinners Ltd, by cash		
(j) Bought desk for computer paying by cheque.		

4.3 Write up the asset and liability and capital accounts to record the following transactions in the records of G Powell.

2009
July 1 Started business with £25,000 in the bank
July 2 Bought office furniture by cheque, £1,500
July 3 Bought machinery £7,500 on credit from Planers Ltd
July 5 Bought a secondhand van paying by cheque, £6,000
July 8 Sold some of the office furniture – not suitable for the firm – for £600 on credit to J Walker & Sons
July 15 Paid the amount owing to Planers Ltd, £7,500, by cheque
July 23 Received the amount due from J Walker, £600, in cash
July 31 Bought more machinery by cheque, £2,800.

4.4X You are required to open the asset, liability and capital accounts and record the following transactions for May 2009 in the records of John Morgan & Co.

2009
May 1 Started in business with £12,000 in cash
May 2 Paid £11,750 of the opening cash into a bank account for the business
May 4 Bought office furniture on credit from Office Supplies Ltd for £770
May 11 Bought computer equipment £2,000 paying by cheque
May 17 Bought benches for workroom on credit from Baxter's Ltd, £1,500
May 22 Returned one of the work benches, costing £500, which was broken to Baxter's Ltd. They agreed to credit our account.
May 24 Paid amount owing to Office Supplies Ltd by cheque
May 28 Bought secondhand motor van paying by cheque, £3,000
May 30 Bought secondhand work bench paying by cash, £100
May 31 Paid the amount outstanding to Baxter's Ltd by cheque.

4.5 Write up the asset, capital and liability accounts in the books of A Burton to record the following transactions:

2009
July 1 Started in business with £15,000 in the bank
July 3 Bought secondhand motor car and paid by cheque, £6,500

July 9 Bought office furniture from Cheetham & Co £1,150 paid by cheque
July 12 Bought computer on credit from Computext Ltd, £2,400
July 17 Took £200 out of the bank and put it in the cash till
July 19 Bought office chair and paid by cash, £42
July 25 Paid Computext Ltd £1,000 on account
July 27 Bought secondhand motor van, £2,450 paid by cheque
July 29 Bought desk for reception area and paid cash, £100
July 31 Paid the outstanding account to Computext Ltd by cheque.

4.6X Write up the various accounts needed in the books of S Russell to record the following transactions:

2009
April 1 Opened business with £10,000 in the bank
April 3 Bought office equipment for £700 on credit from J Saunders Ltd
April 6 Bought secondhand motor van, paying by cheque, £3,000
April 8 Borrowed £1,000 from H Thompson – he gave us the money by cheque
April 11 Russell put further capital into the firm in the form of cash, £500
April 12 Paid £350 of the cash in hand into the bank account
April 15 Returned some of the office equipment costing £200 – it was faulty – to J Saunders Ltd
April 17 Bought more office equipment, paying by cash, £50
April 19 Sold the motor van, as it had proved unsuitable, to R Jones for £3,000. R Jones will settle for this by three payments later this month
April 21 Received a loan in cash from J Hawkins, £400
April 22 R Jones paid us a cheque for £1,000
April 23 Bought a suitable secondhand motor van £3,600 on credit from Phillips Garages Ltd
April 26 R Jones paid us a cheque for £1,800
April 28 Paid £2,000 by cheque to Phillips Garages Ltd
April 30 R Jones paid us cash, £200.

CHAPTER 5

The double entry system for the asset of stock

Learning objectives

After you have studied this chapter you should be able to:

- understand the terms cost price and selling price, the monetary difference between the two being the profit which is one of the main aims of a business
- understand the need to use various accounts in recording the movement of stock, i.e. sales, purchases, sales returns (returns inwards) and purchases returns (returns outwards) accounts
- record the purchase and sale of goods both by credit and cash using the double entry system
- record the return of goods in the sales returns account using the double entry system when customers return goods to the firm
- record the return of goods in the purchases returns account using the double entry system when the firm returns goods to their supplier
- explain the meanings of the terms 'purchases' and 'sales' as used in accounting
- understand the differences in recording sales for cash compared with sales made on credit.

5.1 Introduction

As stated in Chapter 1 it is the aim of all commercial organisations to make a profit and to remain in business. Exhibit 1.3 demonstrated the need to sell goods for more than was paid for them and it is important to record the cost of goods purchased and the sale of goods at selling price. The accounts needed to record these transactions are now considered.

5.2 Stock movements

A business, on any particular date, will normally have goods which have been bought previously and have not yet been sold. These unsold goods are known as the business's 'stock' of goods. The stock of goods in a business is therefore constantly changing because some of it is bought, some of it is sold, some is returned to the suppliers and some is returned by the firm's customers.

To keep a check on the movement of stock, various accounts are opened as shown in the table below:

Account	Reason
Purchases Account	For the purchase of goods
Sales Account	For the sale of goods
Sales Returns Account	For goods returned to the firm by its customers
Purchases Returns Account	For goods returned by the firm to its suppliers

As stock is an asset, and these four accounts are all connected with this asset, the double entry rules are those used for assets.

We shall now look at some specific entries in the following sections.

5.3 Purchase of stock on credit

On 1 August 2009, goods costing £1,650 are bought on credit from D Henry.

First, the twofold effect of the transaction must be considered so that the book-keeping entries can be worked out. We have the following:

(a) *The asset of stock is increased.* An increase in an asset needs a debit entry in an account. Here, the account is a stock account showing the particular movement of stock; in this case it is the 'purchases' movement, so the account must be the purchases account.

(b) *There is an increase in a liability.* This is the liability of the firm to D Henry because the goods supplied have not yet been paid for. An increase in a liability needs a credit entry, and so in order to enter this part of the transaction a credit entry is made in D Henry's account.

Here again, we can use the idea of the debit side being 'IN' to the account, and the credit side being 'OUT' of the account. In this example, purchases have come 'IN', thus creating a debit in the Purchase Account; and the goods have come 'OUT' of D Henry, needing a credit in the account of D Henry. Thus:

Dr		Purchases Account		Cr
	'IN'		'OUT'	
2009		£		
Aug 1 D Henry		1,650		

Dr		D Henry Account		Cr
	'IN'		'OUT'	
		2009		£
		Aug 1 Purchases		1,650

5.4 Purchases of stock for cash

On 2 August 2009, goods costing £2,200 were bought, cash being paid for them immediately. As a result:

(*a*) *The asset of stock is increased.* Thus, a debit entry will be needed. The movement of stock is that of a purchase, so it is the Purchases Account which needs debiting. (Purchases have come 'IN' – debit the Purchases Account.)

(*b*) *The asset of cash is decreased.* To reduce an asset a credit entry is called for, and the asset is that of cash so the Cash Account needs crediting. (Cash has gone 'OUT' – credit the Cash Account.)

Dr	Purchases Account			Cr
	'IN'		'OUT'	
2009		£		
Aug 2 Cash		2,200		

Dr	Cash Account			Cr
	'IN'		'OUT'	
		2009		£
		Aug 2 Purchases		2,200

5.5 Sales of stock on credit

On 3 August 2009, a business sold goods on credit for £2,500 to K Leach. Then:

(*a*) *An asset account is increased.* This is the account showing that K Leach is a debtor for the goods. The increase in the asset of debtors requires a debit and the debtor is K Leach, so the account concerned is that of K Leach. (Goods have gone 'IN' to K Leach – debit K Leach's account.)

(*b*) *The asset of stock is decreased.* For this, a credit entry to reduce an asset is needed. The movement of stock is that of 'Sales' and so the account credited is the Sales Account. (Sales have gone 'OUT' – credit the Sales Account.)

Thus:

Dr	K Leach Account			Cr
	'IN'		'OUT'	
2009		£		
Aug 3 Sales		2,500		

Dr	Sales Account			Cr
	'IN'		'OUT'	
		2009		£
		Aug 3 K Leach		2,500

5.6 Sales of stock for cash

On 4 August 2009, goods are sold for £55, the cash for them being paid immediately. Then:

(a) *The asset of cash is increased.* A debit in the cash account is needed to show this. (Cash has come 'IN' – debit the Cash Account.)

(b) *The asset of stock is reduced.* The reduction of an asset requires a credit and the movement of stock is represented by 'Sales'. So the entry needed is a credit in the Sales Account. (Sales have gone 'OUT' – credit the Sales Account.)

Dr		Cash Account		Cr
	'IN'		'OUT'	
2009		£		
Aug 4 Sales		55		

Dr		Sales Account		Cr
	'IN'		'OUT'	
			2009	£
			Aug 4 Cash	55

5.7 Sales returns

Sales returns represent goods sold which have subsequently been returned by a customer. This could be for various reasons, such as:

- the goods sent to the customer are of the incorrect size, colour or model
- the goods have been damaged in transit
- the goods are of poor quality.

As the original sale was entered in the double entry system, so the return of those goods must also be entered.

On 5 August 2009, goods which had previously been sold to F Lowe for £290 have been returned by him. As a result:

(a) *The asset of stock was increased by the goods returned.* A debit representing an increase of an asset is needed, and this time the movement of stock is that of 'Sales Returns'. The entry required therefore is a debit in the Sales Returns Account. (The goods have come 'IN' – debit the Sales Returns Account.)

(b) *An asset is decreased.* The debt of F Lowe to the firm is now reduced, and to record this a credit is required in F Lowe's account. (The goods have come 'OUT' of F Lowe – credit the F Lowe Account.)

The movements are shown thus:

Dr		Sales Returns Account		Cr
	'IN'		'OUT'	
2009		£		
Aug 5 F Lowe		290		

Dr		F Lowe Account			Cr
'IN'			'OUT'		
			2009		£
			Aug 5 Sales returns		290

An alternative name for a sales returns account is a returns inwards account.

5.8 Purchases returns

Purchases returns represent goods which were purchased, and are now being returned to the supplier. As the original purchase was entered in the double entry system, so also is the return to the supplier of those goods.

On 6 August 2009, goods previously bought for £960 are returned by the firm to K Howe. Thus:

(*a*) *The liability of the firm to K Howe is decreased by the value of the goods returned to him*. The decrease in a liability needs a debit, this time in the K Howe Account. (The goods have gone 'IN' to K Howe – debit the K Howe Account.)

(*b*) *The asset of stock is decreased by the goods sent out*. A credit representing a reduction in an asset is needed, and the movement of stock is that of 'Purchases Returns', so the entry will be a credit in the purchases returns account. (The returns have gone 'OUT' – credit the Purchases Returns Account.)

Dr		K Howe Account			Cr
'IN'			'OUT'		
2009		£			
Aug 6 Purchase returns		960			

Dr		Purchases Returns Account			Cr
'IN'			'OUT'		
			2009		£
			Aug 6 K Howe		960

An alternative name for a purchases returns account is a returns outwards account.

5.9 A worked example

Enter the following transactions in suitable double entry accounts:

2009
May 1 Bought goods on credit £680 from D Small
May 2 Bought goods on credit £770 from A Lyon & Son
May 5 Sold goods on credit to D Hughes for £600
May 6 Sold goods on credit to M Spencer for £450

May 10 Returned goods £150 to D Small
May 12 Goods bought for cash, £1,000
May 19 M Spencer returned £160 goods to us
May 21 Goods sold for cash, £1,500
May 22 Paid cash to D Small, £530, on account
May 30 D Hughes paid the amount owing by him £600 in cash
May 31 Bought goods on credit £640 from A Lyon & Son.

The double entry accounts can now be shown as:

Dr		Purchases Account		Cr
	'IN'		'OUT'	
2009		£		
May 1 D Small		680		
May 2 A Lyon & Son		770		
May 12 Cash		1,000		
May 31 A Lyon & Son		640		

Dr		Sales Account		Cr
	'IN'		'OUT'	
			2009	£
			May 5 D Hughes	600
			May 6 M Spencer	450
			May 21 Cash	1,500

Dr		Purchases Returns Account		Cr
	'IN'		'OUT'	
			2009	£
			May 10 D Small	150

Dr		Sales Returns Account		Cr
	'IN'		'OUT'	
2009		£		
May 19 M Spencer		160		

Dr		D Small Account		Cr
	'IN'		'OUT'	
2009		£	2009	£
May 10 Purchases returns		150	May 1 Purchases	680
May 22 Cash		530		

Dr		A Lyon & Son Account		Cr
	'IN'		'OUT'	
			2009	£
			May 2 Purchases	770
			May 31 Purchases	640

Dr		D Hughes Account		Cr
	'IN'		'OUT'	
2009	£	2009		£
May 5 Sales	600	May 30 Cash		600

Dr		M Spencer Account		Cr
	'IN'		'OUT'	
2009	£	2009		£
May 6 Sales	450	May 19 Sales returns		160

Dr		Cash Account		Cr
	'IN'		'OUT'	
2009	£	2009		£
May 21 Sales	1,500	May 12 Purchases		1,000
May 30 D Hughes	600	May 22 D Small		530

5.10 Special meaning of 'sales' and 'purchases'

It must be emphasised that 'sales' and 'purchases' have a special meaning in accounting language.

Purchases in accounting means *the purchase of those goods which the firm buys with the prime intention of selling*. Sometimes the goods may be altered, added to or used in the manufacture of something else, but it is the element of *resale* that is important. To a firm that trades in computers, for instance, computers are purchases. If something else is bought, such as a motor van, such an item cannot be called purchases, even though in ordinary language it may be said that a motor van has been purchased. The prime intention of buying the motor van is for use by the company and not for resale.

Similarly, **sales** means the *sale of those goods in which the firm normally deals and that were bought with the prime intention of resale*. The description 'sales' must never be given to the disposal of other items.

If we did not keep to these meanings, it would result in the different kinds of stock accounts containing something other than goods sold or for resale.

5.11 Comparison of cash and credit transactions for purchases and sales

The difference between the records needed for cash and credit transactions can now be seen.

The complete set of entries for purchases of goods where they are paid for immediately by cash would be:

(*a*) **debit the purchases account**
(*b*) **credit the cash account**.

On the other hand, the complete set of entries for the purchase of goods on credit can be broken down into two stages. First, the purchase of the goods and second, the payment for them. The first part is:

(*a*) **debit the purchases account**
(*b*) **credit the supplier's account**.

The second part is:

(*c*) **debit the supplier's account**
(*d*) **credit the cash account**.

The difference can now be seen. With the cash purchase, no record is kept of the supplier's account. This is because cash passes immediately and therefore there is no need to keep a check of indebtedness (money owing) to a supplier. On the other hand, in the credit purchase the records should show to whom money is owed until payment is made. A study of cash sales and credit sales will reveal a similar difference.

Cash Sales	Credit Sales
Complete entry: ● debit cash account ● credit sales account	First part: ● debit customer's account ● credit sales account Second part: ● debit cash account ● credit customer's account

Chapter summary

- Goods must be sold at a higher price than the cost price to make a profit. If sold at a lower price than the cost price a loss would occur.
- Various accounts are used to record the movement of stock because stock is normally sold at a higher price than its cost.
- The accounts used to record the movement of stock are:
  - **purchases account** to record the purchases of stock as debit entries in the account since the goods come 'IN' to the firm
  - **sales account** for the sale of the goods as credit entries in the account because the goods go 'OUT' of the firm
  - **sales returns account** to record goods that a customer returns to the firm as debit entries since the goods are returned 'IN' to the firm
  - **purchases returns account** to record goods that the firm returns to its suppliers as the goods go 'OUT' of the firm.
- The special meaning in accounting terms of 'purchases' and 'sales', namely that purchases refer to goods bought for resale. Purchases of assets such as a motor van to be used in the business, are recorded separately in the asset account, motor van. Sales refers to goods sold in the normal course of business. The disposal of an asset

such as equipment should never be recorded in the sales account but recorded separately in a disposal account to be discussed later.

● Purchases for cash are *never* entered in the supplier's account while purchases on credit are *always* entered in the supplier's (creditor's) account.

● Sales for cash are *never* entered in the customer's account while sales on credit are *always* entered in the customer's (debtor's) account.

EXERCISES

5.1 Complete the following table showing which accounts are to be credited and which are to be debited:

	Account to be debited	Account to be credited
(a) Goods bought on credit from P Hart		
(b) Goods sold for cash		
(c) Bought motor car from Morgan Motors on credit		
(d) Bought goods on credit from Cohens Ltd		
(e) Returned some of the goods, which were faulty, to P Hart		
(f) Sold goods on credit to H Perkins		
(g) Goods sold, a cheque being received on the sale		
(h) Sold some of the office furniture for cash		
(i) H Perkins returned some of the goods to us		
(j) Goods brought on credit from P Griffith.		

5.2X Complete the following table:

	Account to be debited	Account to be credited
(a) Bought goods on credit from J Needham		
(b) Bought goods paying by cheque		
(c) Sold goods for cash		
(d) We returned goods to J Needham		
(e) Bought computer for the office on credit from Smith Computers Ltd		
(f) Sold goods on credit to H Broad		
(g) Goods returned to us by H Broad		
(h) Bought goods for cash		
(i) We paid a creditor, W Simms, by cheque		
(j) Bought motor car on credit from Smithy Garage.		

5.3 Paul Garner decided to start his own business and asks you to assist him by entering the following transactions in the books of account for March 2009:

2009
March 1 Started business with £4,000 in cash
March 2 Bought goods £1,230 on credit from Flynn Bros
March 4 Bought goods for cash, £345
March 7 Sold goods for cash, £120

March 10 Opened a bank account and took £3,500 out of the cash and put it in the bank

March 14 Bought a computer to use in the office paid by cheque, £1,000

March 16 Sold goods on credit to D Knott, £600

March 20 Bought goods £450 on credit from Flynn Bros

March 23 Sold goods on credit to Bateson's Ltd, £570

March 25 We returned goods to Flynn Bros, £75

March 27 Paid the amount due to Flynn Bros by cheque

March 30 Bateson's Ltd returned some faulty goods to us value, £109.

5.4 The following are the business transactions of Grace Andrews, a retailer of ladies wear, for the month of September 2010:

2010

Sept   1 Started in business with £10,000 in the bank and £100 of cash

Sept   3 Bought shop fittings £1,900 on credit from Duffy & Son

Sept   5 Bought goods on credit from Barrett's Fashions, £2,378

Sept   9 Bought computer for use within the business, £1,020 paid by cheque

Sept 10 Bought desk for office, £65 and paid cash

Sept 12 Sales of goods £800 paid into bank

Sept 15 Returned faulty goods to Barrett's Fashions, £180

Sept 22 Paid Duffy & Son by cheque, £1,900

Sept 25 Sales of goods £600 paid into bank

Sept 28 Bought goods on credit from Barrett's Fashions, £1,434

Sept 30 Sold goods for cash, £280

Sept 30 Bought secondhand motor car, £4,750.

As accounts assistant you have been asked to record the above transactions in the books of account for September 2010.

5.5X Ahmed's Ltd has just started his own business selling computer equipment and software. The following transactions took place during his first month of trading, June 2009. You are required to enter them into the books of account:

2009

June   1 Started in business with £20,000 in the bank

June   3 Bought stock of computers for resale £8,000 on credit from Computers Wholesale Ltd

June   4 Bought shop fittings paying by cheque, £1,690

June   8 Bought stock of software for resale, £1,000 paid by cheque

June   9 Bought motor car paying by cheque, £7,000

June 12 Sold goods, £1,700 by cheque

June 16 Returned faulty goods to Computers Wholesale Ltd, £900

June 20 Sold goods for cash, £340

June 26 Bought desk and chair for office, £300 paying by cheque

June 28 Sold goods on credit to Law & Co, £1,600

June 29 Paid Computers Wholesale Ltd £5,000 on account by cheque

June 30 Bought goods from Computers Wholesale Ltd on credit, £850

June 30 Law & Co return goods to us, £220

June 30 Sold goods, £2,300 by cheque.

5.6X You are to enter the following in the accounts needed:

2009

June   1 Started business with £1,000 cash

June   2 Paid £800 of the opening cash into a bank account for the firm

June 3 Bought goods on credit from H Grant, £330
June 4 Bought goods on credit from D Clark, £140
June 6 Sold goods on credit to B Miller, £90
June 8 Bought office furniture on credit from Barrett's Ltd, £400
June 10 Sold goods for cash, £120
June 13 Bought goods on credit from H Grant, £200
June 14 Bought goods for cash, £60
June 15 Sold goods on credit to H Sharples, £180
June 16 We returned goods worth £50 to H Grant
June 17 We returned some of the office furniture, cost £30, to Barrett's Ltd
June 18 Sold goods on credit to B Miller, £400
June 21 Paid H Grant's account by cheque, £480
June 23 B Miller paid us the amount owing in cash, £490
June 24 Sharples returned to us £50 of goods
June 25 Goods sold for cash, £150
June 28 Bought goods for cash, £370
June 30 Bought computer on credit from J Kelly, £600.

CHAPTER 6

The double entry system for expenses and revenues

Learning objectives

After you have studied this chapter you should be able to:

● understand the concept of profit and loss by comparing revenue with expenses
● see the effects of profits and losses on capital and the relationship to the accounting equation
● understand why separate accounts are used for each type of expense and revenue
● be able to record expenses and revenues using the double entry system
● understand the term 'drawings', be able to record them and recognise the effects of drawings on capital.

6.1 The nature of profit or loss

To an accountant, **profit** means the amount by which **revenues** are greater than **expenses** for a set of transactions. The term 'revenues' means the sales value of goods and services that have been supplied to customers. The term **expenses** means the value of all the assets that have been used up to obtain those revenues.

If, therefore, we had supplied goods and services valued for sale at £100,000 to customers, and the expenses incurred by us to be able to supply those goods and services amounted to £70,000, then the result would be a profit calculated as follows:

		£
Revenues	Goods and services supplied to customers for the sum of	100,000
Less Expenses	Value of all the assets used up to enable us to supply the above goods and services	70,000
Profit		30,000

On the other hand, it is possible for expenses to exceed revenues for a set of transactions. In this case the result is a loss. For example a **loss** would be incurred given the following.

		£
Revenues	What we have charged to our customers in respect of all the goods and services supplied to them	60,000
Less Expenses	Value of all the assets used up to supply these goods and services to our customers	(80,000)
Loss is therefore		(20,000)

6.2 The effect of profit and loss on capital

Businesses exist to make profits and so increase their capital. Let's look at the relationship between profits and capital in an example.

On 1 January the assets and liabilities of a firm are:

- Assets: Fixtures £10,000, Stock £7,000, Cash at the bank £3,000.
- Liabilities: Creditors £2,000.

The capital is found from the accounting equation:

> **Capital = Assets – Liabilities**

In this case capital works out at Assets £10,000 + £7,000 + £3,000 – Liabilities £2,000 = £18,000.

During January the whole of the £7,000 stock is sold for £11,000 cash. On 31 January the assets and liabilities have become:

- Assets: Fixtures £10,000, Stock nil, Cash at the bank £14,000.
- Liabilities: Creditors £2,000.

The capital can be calculated:

> Assets £10,000 + £14,000 – Liabilities £2,000 = £22,000

It can be seen that capital has increased from £18,000 to £22,000 = £4,000 increase because the £7,000 stock was sold for £11,000, a profit of £4,000. Profit, therefore, increases capital.

> **Old Capital + Profit = New Capital**
> **£18,000 + £4,000 = £22,000**

On the other hand, a loss would *reduce* the capital so:

> **Old Capital – Loss = New Capital**

6.3 Profit or loss and sales

Profit will be made when goods are sold at more than cost price, while the opposite will mean a **loss**.

6.4   Profit or loss and expenses

In Section 6.1 it was shown that profit was made when the goods were sold for more than the cost price. As well as the cost of the goods, a firm incurs other **expenses** such as rent, salaries, wages, telephone costs, motor expenses, and so on. Every £1 of expenses will mean £1 less profit.

All expenses could be charged to one Expense Account, but it would then be difficult to identify specific areas of the firm's expenditure, such as the amount spent on motor running costs or rent. To facilitate the need to know different types of expenses, a separate account is opened for each type of expense, for instance:

- Rent Account
- Telephone Account
- Stationery Account
- Salaries Account
- Advertising Account
- Motor Expenses Account
- Wages Account
- Insurance Account
- Postages Account

In the same way that separate accounts are opened for each type of expense, separate accounts are also opened for any additional *revenue* that the business may receive, such as rent received or bank interest received. Again, separate revenue accounts can be opened as follows:

- Rent Receivable Account
- Commission Received Account
- Bank Interest Received Account

It is purely a matter of choice in a business as to the name of each expense or revenue account. For example, an account for postage stamps could be called 'Postage Stamp Account', 'Postage Account' or even 'Communication Expenses Account'. Also some businesses amalgamate expenses, for example, 'Printing, Stationery and Advertising Account'. Infrequent or small items of expense are usually put into a 'Sundry Expenses Account' or 'General Expenses Account'.

6.5   Debit or credit?

We have to decide whether expense accounts are to be debited or credited with the amounts involved. Assets involve expenditure by the firm and are shown as debit entries. Expenses also involve expenditure by the firm and therefore should also be debit entries. Why? Because assets and expenses must ultimately be paid for. This payment involves a credit to the bank account (or to the cash account) so the original entry in the asset account or in the expense account must be a debit.

An alternative explanation may also be used for expenses. Every expense results in a decrease in an asset or an increase in a liability, and because of the accounting equation this means that the capital is reduced by each expense. The decreases in capital needs a debit entry and therefore expense accounts contain debit entries for expenses.

Revenue is the opposite of expenses and, therefore, appears on the opposite side to expenses – that is, revenue accounts appear on the credit side of the books. Pending the periodical calculation of profit, therefore, revenue is collected together in appropriately named accounts, and until it is transferred to the profit calculations it will need to be shown as a credit.

Consider, too, that expenditure of money pays for expenses, which are used up in the short term, or assets, which are used up in the long term – both for the purpose of winning revenue. Both of these are shown on the debit side of the accounts, while the revenue which has been won is shown on the credit side of the accounts.

6.6 Effect of transactions

A few illustrations will demonstrate the double entry required.

Example 1: Rent of £200 is paid in cash. Here the twofold effect is:

(a) *The total of the expenses of rent is increased* – a benefit goes 'IN'. As expense entries are shown as debits, and the expense is rent, so the action required is the debiting of the Rent Account.
(b) *The asset of cash is decreased* – money goes 'OUT'. This means crediting the Cash Account to show the decrease of the asset.

Summary: ● debit the rent account with £200 – 'IN'
         ● credit the cash account with £200 – 'OUT'.

Example 2: Motor expenses are paid with a cheque for £230. The twofold effect is:

(a) *The total of the motor expenses paid is increased* – a benefit is received 'IN'. To increase an expenses account needs a debit, and so the action required is to debit the Motor Expenses Account.
(b) *The asset of money in the bank is decreased* – money goes 'OUT'. This means crediting the Bank Account to show the decrease of the asset.

Summary: ● debit the motor expenses account with £230 – 'IN'
         ● credit the bank account with £230 – 'OUT'.

Example 3: £60 cash is paid for telephone expenses.

(a) *The total of telephone expenses is increased* – a benefit received goes 'IN'. Expenses are shown by a debit entry, and therefore to increase the expense account in question the action required is to debit the Telephone Expenses Account.
(b) *The asset of cash is decreased* – money goes 'OUT'. This needs a credit in the Cash Account to decrease the asset.

Summary: ● debit telephone expenses account with £60 – 'IN'
         ● credit the cash account with £60 – 'OUT'.

It is now possible to study the effects of some more transactions showing the results in the form of a table. See Exhibit 6.1.

Exhibit 6.1

	Increase	Action	Decrease	Action
June 1 Paid for postage stamps by cash £20	Expense of postages	Debit postage account (IN)	Asset of cash	Credit cash account (OUT)
2 Paid for advertising by cheque £290	Expense of advertising	Debit advertising account (IN)	Asset of bank	Credit bank account (OUT)
3 Paid wages by cash £900	Expense of wages	Debit wages account (IN)	Asset of cash	Credit cash account (OUT)
4 Paid insurance by cheque £420	Expense of insurance	Debit insurance account (IN)	Asset of bank	Credit bank account (OUT)

The above four examples can now be shown in account form:

Dr   **Cash Account**   Cr
'IN'		'OUT'	
			£
		June 1 Postages	20
		June 3 Wages	900

Dr   **Bank Account**   Cr
'IN'		'OUT'	
			£
		June 2 Advertising	290
		June 4 Insurance	420

Dr   **Advertising Account**   Cr
'IN'		'OUT'	
	£		
June 2 Bank	290		

Dr   **Insurance Account**   Cr
'IN'		'OUT'	
	£		
June 4 Bank	420		

Dr   **Postage Account**   Cr
'IN'		'OUT'	
	£		
June 1 Cash	20		

Dr   **Wages Account**   Cr
'IN'		'OUT'	
	£		
June 3 Cash	900		

6.7 Drawings

The owner may want to take cash out of the business for his or her private use. This is known as **drawings**. Money taken out as drawings will reduce capital.

Each amount taken as drawings will be debited to a drawings account and at the end of the year this is transferred to the capital account and will be explained later.

Example 4: On 25 August a proprietor takes £50 cash out of her business for her own use.

Effect	Action
1 Capital is decreased by £50 2 Cash is decreased by £50	Debit the drawings account £50 Credit the cash account £50

Dr		Cash Account		Cr
	'IN'		'OUT'	
				£
			Aug 25 Drawings	50

Dr		Drawings Account		Cr
	'IN'		'OUT'	
		£		
Aug 25 Cash		50		

Sometimes *goods* (rather than money) are taken for private use. These are also known as drawings. Entries for such transactions will be described later in the book.

6.8 Revenues and double entry

We have just looked at instances of expenses being recorded. There will also be the need to record revenues. We will now look at an example.

Example 5: On 5 June it is decided that part of a firm's premises are not needed at the moment. The firm agrees to sublet the surplus space to another firm and receives rent of £140 by cheque. Here, the twofold effect is:

(*a*) *The asset of the bank is increased* – money comes 'IN'. This means debiting the bank account to show the increase of the asset.

(*b*) *The total of the revenue of rent received is increased* – the benefit comes 'OUT' of rent received, so the action required is the crediting of the rent received account.

Summary: • debit the bank account with £140 – 'IN'
            • credit the rent received account with £140 – 'OUT'.

This will therefore appear as:

Dr		Bank Account		Cr
	'IN'		'OUT'	
		£		
June 5 Rent received		140		

Dr		Rent Received Account		Cr
	'IN'		'OUT'	
				£
		June 5 Bank		140

Chapter summary

- The calculation of profit is achieved by comparing revenues with expenses incurred in running the business.
- A loss occurs when the expenses incurred are more than the revenue earned.
- If a business makes a profit, that profit belongs to the owner of the business and consequently their capital is increased by that amount.
- When a loss is incurred then the owner must bear the losses and such a loss will reduce their capital account.
- It is important to record expenses in separate expense accounts to enable the business to identify various areas of expense such as motor expenses, stationery, etc.
- Different types of revenue should also be recorded in separate accounts to provide information of the income received.
- The procedure for recording expenses and revenue in the various accounts uses the double entry system.
- 'Drawings' are recorded in a separate account. They are then deducted from the owner's capital account and are never an expense of the business.

EXERCISES

6.1 Complete the following table:

	Account to be debited	Account to be credited
(a) Paid rent by cash		
(b) Paid for goods by cash		
(c) Received by cheque a refund of rates already paid		
(d) Paid general expenses by cheque		
(e) Received commissions in cash		
(f) Goods returned by us to T Jones		
(g) Goods sold for cash		
(h) Bought office fixtures by cheque		
(i) Paid wages in cash		
(j) Took cash out of business for private use.		

6.2X Complete the following table

	Account to be debited	Account to be credited
(a) Sold surplus stationery, receiving proceeds in cash		
(b) Paid salaries by cheque		
(c) Rent received for premises sublet, by cheque		
(d) Goods returned to us by Royal Products		
(e) Commission received by us previously in error, now refunded by cheque		
(f) Bought machinery by cheque		
(g) Paid lighting expenses in cash		
(h) Insurance rebate received by cheque		
(i) Buildings bought by cheque		
(j) Building repairs paid in cash.		

6.3 You are required to enter the following transactions in the double entry accounts of B Cartwright:

2010
Jan 1 Started business with £20,000 capital, which was deposited in the bank
Jan 3 Paid rent for premises by cheque, £1,000
Jan 4 Bought goods on credit from M Parkin for £580 and J Kane for £2,400
Jan 4 Purchased motor van for £5,000, paying by cheque
Jan 5 Cash sales of £1,005
Jan 10 Paid motor expenses in cash, £75
Jan 12 Paid wages in cash, £120
Jan 17 Bought goods on credit from M Parkin, £670
Jan 19 Paid insurance by cheque, £220
Jan 25 Sold goods for £800, payment being received as a cheque, which was banked immediately
Jan 31 Paid wages in cash, £135, and electricity by cheque, £78.

6.4X The following are the transactions of G Dunn for the month of May 2010. You are required to enter the transactions in the appropriate accounts using the double entry system.

2010
May 1 Started in business with £12,000 in the bank
May 2 Purchased goods £1,750 on credit from M Mills
May 3 Bought fixtures and fittings for £1,500, paying by cheque
May 5 Sold goods for cash, £1,300
May 6 Bought goods on credit for £1,140 from S Waite
May 10 Paid rent by cash, £250
May 12 Bought stationery, £87, paying by cash
May 18 Goods returned by us to M Mills, £230
May 21 Let off part of the premises receiving rent by cheque, £100
May 23 Sold goods on credit to M Street for £770
May 24 Bought a motor van, paying by cheque £3,000
May 30 Paid wages for the month, £648, by cash
May 31 The proprietor, G Dunn, took cash for himself amounting to £200.

6.5 You are required to enter the following transactions, completing the double entry in the records of K Walsh for the month of July 2009.

2009

July 1 Started in business with £8,000 in the bank

July 2 Paid for rent of premises by cheque, £375

July 3 Bought shop fittings for £800 paid by cheque

July 5 Bought goods on credit from A Jackson, £450; D Hill, £675; and E Frudd, £1,490

July 6 Paid insurance by cheque, £130

July 7 Bought motor van for £5,000 on credit from High Lane Motors

July 11 Cash sales of £1,500

July 13 Paid for printing and stationery by cheque, £120

July 15 Paid wages in cash, £200

July 18 Bought goods from A Jackson, £890, on credit

July 21 Cash sales, £780

July 25 Paid motor expenses, £89, by cash

July 30 Paid High Lane Motors, £5,000 by cheque

July 31 Paid wages in cash, £300, and stationery, £45, in cash.

6.6X Write up the following transactions in the books of J Blake for March 2009:

2009

March 1 Started business with £15,000 capital in cash

March 2 Paid £14,000 of the cash into a bank account for the business

March 2 Bought goods on credit from J Paul for £592

March 4 Paid for rent of premises by cash, £250, and bought a secondhand motor van for £3,000, paying by cheque

March 5 Bought goods, paying by cheque for £2,100

March 9 Sold goods to E Ford for £323 and received a cheque

March 11 Paid for printing of stationery, £45, by cash

March 14 Cash sales of £490

March 18 Goods returned by us to J Paul, £67

March 19 Bought goods from J Paul on credit, £720

March 21 Paid for advertising, £60, by cheque

March 24 Sold goods for cash, £500

March 25 Paid the following expenses by cheque: wages, £540; motor expenses, £110; stationery, £82

March 28 Paid J Paul £1,245 by cheque

March 31 Sold goods for cash, £526.

6.7X Enter the following transactions using double entry for S Littleton for the month of April 2009:

2009

April 1 Started in business with capital of £7,500 in the bank account and £1,000 in cash

April 3 Bought a motor car, £4,000, paying by cheque

April 5 Paid for rent of office, £275 in cash

April 7 Paid for motor expenses, £50 in cash

April 9 Paid for telephone charges, £95 by cheque

April 14 Bought stock of goods on credit from K Woodburn, £2,300, and A Veale, £2,600

April 16 Sold goods, £1,900, receiving the money by cheque

April 19 Paid for motor expenses, £60 in cash

April 20 Returned faulty goods to A Veale, £240

April 25 Cash sales of £875, paid for insurance, £180 in cash

April 28 Paid salaries, £1,210 by cheque

April 29 Paid K Woodburn £1,500 on account by cheque

April 30 Bought further goods from K Woodburn on credit, £770.

CHAPTER 7

Balancing off accounts

Learning objectives

After you have studied this chapter you should be able to:

- understand what is meant by 'balancing off' accounts
- balance off accounts at the end of a period and bring down the opening balance to the next period
- distinguish between a debit balance and a credit balance
- prepare accounts in a three-column format, as used in computerised accounts.

7.1 Introduction

In the preceding chapter the entries into the various accounts have been shown. However, at the end of a period, usually monthly, each account will require 'balancing off'. Balancing off simply means finding the difference between the total of the debit entries and the total of the credit entries in a particular account. The 'difference' between the two sides is known as the 'balance' and this figure is inserted on the side of the account that shows the least amount of money. If both sides of the account are then totalled up, they should agree, having inserted the 'balance'; if they do not add up correctly, then an error may have been made in the calculation of the balance or perhaps in adding up the account. The calculation will then need to be rechecked.

Sometimes an account simply requires closing off; this is when both the debit and credit sides total up to exactly the same amount and thus there is no balance.

In the following examples we will consider balancing off accounts at the end of a period and bringing down the balances to the next accounting period.

7.2 Accounts for debtors

Where debtors have paid their accounts

So far we have considered how to record transactions in the accounting books by means of debit and credit entries. At the end of each accounting period the figures in each account are examined to see what they reveal. One of the most obvious reasons for this is to find out how much money our customers owe us for goods we have sold to them. As mentioned above this procedure is usually carried out monthly.

We will now look at the account of one of our customers, K Tandy, for transactions in August 2009.

Dr		K Tandy Account		Cr
2009	£	2009		£
Aug 1 Sales	144	Aug 22 Bank		144
Aug 19 Sales	300	Aug 28 Bank		300

This shows that during the month of August we sold a total of £444 in goods to Tandy, and have been paid a total of £444 by him. At the close of business at the end of August he therefore owes us nothing; his account can be closed off on 31 August 2009 by inserting the totals on each side, as follows:

Dr		K Tandy Account		Cr
2009	£	2009		£
Aug 1 Sales	144	Aug 22 Bank		144
Aug 19 Sales	300	Aug 28 Bank		300
	444			444

Notice that totals in accounting are shown with a single line above them, and a double line underneath. Totals on accounts at the end of a period are always shown on a level with one another, as shown in the following completed account for C Lee:

Dr		C Lee Account		Cr
2009	£	2009		£
Aug 11 Sales	177	Aug 30 Bank		480
Aug 19 Sales	203			
Aug 22 Sales	100			
	480			480

In this account, C Lee also owed us nothing at the end of August 2009, as she had paid us for all sales to her.

If an account contains only one entry on each side and they are equal, you don't need to include totals. For example:

Dr		K Wood Account		Cr
2009	£	2009		£
Aug 6 Sales	214	Aug 12 Bank		214

Where debtors still owe for goods

Not all customers will have paid their accounts by the end of the month and will have amounts outstanding on their account. In these cases, the totals of each side would not equal each other. Let us look at the account of D Knight for August 2009:

Dr		D Knight Account		Cr
2009	£	2009		£
Aug 1 Sales	158	Aug 28 Bank		158
Aug 15 Sales	206			
Aug 30 Sales	118			

You will see that the debit side adds up to £482 and the credit side adds up to £158. The difference of £324 (i.e. £482 − £158) represents sales of £206 and £118 not paid for and is, therefore, still owing to us on 31 August 2009.

In double entry, we only enter figures as totals if the totals on both sides of the account agree. We do, however, want to close off the account for August, but showing that Knight owes us £324. If he owes £324 at close of business on 31 August 2009, then he will still owe us that same figure when the business opens on 1 September 2009. We show this by **balancing the account**, which is done in five stages:

1 Add up both sides to find out their totals. Do not write anything permanent in the account at this stage, but you could write the figures lightly in pencil.
2 Deduct the smaller total from the larger total to find the balance.
3 Now enter the balance on the side with the smallest total. This now means the totals will be equal.
4 Enter totals on a level with each other.
5 Now enter the balance on the line below the totals. The balance below the totals should be on the opposite side to the balance shown above the totals.

Against the balance above the totals, complete the date column by showing the last day of that period. Below the totals show the first day of the next period against the balance. The balance above the totals is described as balance *carried down*. The balance below the total is described as balance *brought down*.

Knight's account when 'balanced off' will appear as shown in Exhibit 7.1.

Exhibit 7.1

Dr		D Knight Account		Cr
2009	£	2009		£
Aug 1 Sales	158	Aug 28 Bank		158
Aug 15 Sales	206	Aug 31 Balance		
Aug 30 Sales	118		carried down	324
	482			482
Sept 1 Balance brought down	324			

Stage 5: enter balance to start off entries for following month.

Stage 4: enter totals level with each other.

Stage 3: enter balance here so that totals will be equal.

We can now look at another account prior to balancing:

Dr		H Henry Account		Cr
2009	£	2009		£
Aug 5 Sales	300	Aug 24 Sales returns		50
Aug 28 Sales	540	Aug 29 Bank		250

We will abbreviate 'carried down' to 'c/d' and 'brought down' to 'b/d' from now on.

Dr		H Henry Account		Cr
2009	£	2009		£
Aug 5 Sales	300	Aug 24 Sales returns		50
Aug 28 Sales	540	Aug 29 Bank		250
		Aug 31 Balance c/d		540
	840			840
Sept 1 Balance b/d	540			

Notes:
- The date given for the balance c/d is the last day of the period which is finishing and that for the balance b/d is given as the opening date of the next period.
- As the total of the debit side originally exceeded the total of the credit side, *the balance is said to be a debit balance*. This being a personal account (i.e. for a person), the person concerned is said to be a debtor – the accounting term for anyone who owes money to the firm.

If accounts contain only one entry, it is unnecessary to enter the total. A double line ruled under the entry will mean that the entry is its own total. For example:

Dr		B Walters Account		Cr
2009	£	2009		£
Aug 18 Sales	51	Aug 31 Balance c/d		51
Sept 1 Balance b/d	51			

7.3 Accounts for creditors

Exactly the same principles apply when the balances are carried down to the credit side. *This balance is known as a 'credit balance'*. We can look at two accounts of our suppliers which are to be balanced off.

Dr		E Williams Account		Cr
2009	£	2009		£
Aug 21 Bank	100	Aug 2 Purchases		248
		Aug 18 Purchases		116

Dr   **K Patterson Account**   Cr

2009	£	2009	£
Aug 14 Purchases returns	20	Aug 8 Purchases	620
Aug 28 Bank	600	Aug 15 Purchases	200

We now add up the totals and find the balance, i.e. stages 1 and 2. When balanced off, these will appear as:

Dr   **E Williams Account**   Cr

2009	£	2009	£
Aug 21 Bank	100	Aug 2 Purchases	248
Aug 31 Balance c/d	264	Aug 18 Purchases	116
	364		364
		Sept 1 Balance b/d	264

Stage 3: enter balance here so that totals will be equal.	**Stage 4:** enter totals level with each other.

Stage 5: enter balance to start off entries for following month.

Dr   **K Patterson Account**   Cr

2009	£	2009	£
Aug 14 Purchases returns	20	Aug 8 Purchases	620
Aug 28 Bank	600	Aug 15 Purchases	200
Aug 31 Balance c/d	200		
	820		820
		Sept 1 Balance b/d	200

The accounts of E. Williams and K. Patterson have credit balances. They are **creditors** – the accounting term for anyone to whom money is owed.

The type of accounts which have been demonstrated so far are often known as 'T accounts' (see Section 4.6) since the accounts are in the shape of a letter T. The following accounts show the three-column method, which is used in computerised accounting systems.

Before you read further, attempt Exercises 7.1 and 7.2 at the end of this chapter.

7.4 Three-column accounts

Through the main part of this book, the type of account used shows the left-hand side of the account as the debit side and the right-hand side as the credit side. However, when most computers are used, the style of the ledger account is different. It appears as three columns of figures, there being one column for debit entries, another column for credit entries, and the last column for the balance. If you have a current account at a bank, your bank statements will normally be shown using this method.

The accounts used in this chapter will now be redrafted to show the ledger accounts drawn up in this way.

K Tandy Account

	Debit	Credit	Balance (and whether debit or credit)
2009	£	£	£
Aug 1 Sales	144		144 Dr
Aug 19 Sales	300		444 Dr
Aug 22 Bank		144	300 Dr
Aug 28 Bank		300	0

C Lee Account

	Debit	Credit	Balance
2009	£	£	£
Aug 11 Sales	177		177 Dr
Aug 19 Sales	203		380 Dr
Aug 22 Sales	100		480 Dr
Aug 30 Bank		480	0

K Wood Account

	Debit	Credit	Balance
2009	£	£	£
Aug 6 Sales	214		214 Dr
Aug 12 Bank		214	0

D Knight Account

	Debit	Credit	Balance
2009	£	£	£
Aug 1 Sales	158		158 Dr
Aug 15 Sales	206		364 Dr
Aug 28 Cash		158	206 Dr
Aug 31 Sales	118		324 Dr

H Henry Account

	Debit	Credit	Balance
2009	£	£	£
Aug 5 Sales	300		300 Dr
Aug 24 Sales returns		50	250 Dr
Aug 28 Sales	540		790 Dr
Aug 29 Bank		250	540 Dr

B Walters Account

	Debit	Credit	Balance
2009	£	£	£
Aug 18 Sales	51		51 Dr

E Williams Account

	Debit £	Credit £	Balance £
2009			
Aug 2 Purchases		248	248 Cr
Aug 18 Purchases		116	364 Cr
Aug 21 Bank	100		264 Cr

K Patterson Account

	Debit £	Credit £	Balance £
2009			
Aug 8 Purchases		620	620 Cr
Aug 14 Purchases returns	20		600 Cr
Aug 15 Purchases		200	800 Cr
Aug 28 Bank	600		200 Cr

You will notice in the above accounts that the balance is calculated after every entry. This can be done quite simply when using a computer accounting package since the software can automatically calculate the new balance after each entry.

However, when manual methods are being used, it is often too much work to have to calculate a new balance after each entry. Also, the greater the number of calculations, the greater the possibility of errors. For these reasons, it is usual for students to use two-sided accounts. However, it is important to note that there is no difference in principle; the final balances are the same using either method.

Chapter summary

- This chapter describes what is meant by 'balancing off' accounts at the end of a period.
- Balance off appropriate accounts at the end of a period and bring down the opening balance to the beginning of the next period.
- Opening balances brought down on the debit side are referred to as debit balances whereas those brought down on the credit side are known as credit balances.
- 'Debtors' are people or organisations who owe money to the business. Their accounts in your accounting records show a greater value on the debit side, hence they are your debtors.
- 'Creditors' are people or organisations that the business owes money to. Their accounts in your accounting records show a greater value on the credit side, hence they are your creditors.
- 'T accounts' are used generally for recording transactions where there is a manual system of accounting.
- Computerised accounting packages use three-column accounts. Illustrations of preparing three-column accounts are shown.
- Both the 'T accounts' and the three-column accounts show the same information and the balances will be identical whichever method is used.

EXERCISES

7.1 Enter the following items in the appropriate debtors' accounts (i.e. your customers' accounts) only; do *not* write up other accounts. Then balance off each of these personal accounts at the end of the month. (Keep your answer – it will be used as a basis for question 7.3.)

2010
May 1 Sales on credit to D Binns £1,035, C Cade £450, H Teate £630
May 3 Sales on credit to J Watts £627, M Lowe £99
May 9 Sales returns from D Binns £60, H Teate £30
May 12 C Cade paid us by cheque, £450
May 16 H Teate paid us by cheque, £600
May 25 D Binns paid us £450 on account in cash
May 31 Sales on credit to J Watts, £135.

7.2 Enter the following in the appropriate creditors' accounts (i.e. your suppliers' accounts) only. Do *not* write up the other accounts. Then balance off each of these personal accounts at the end of the month. (Keep your answer – it will be used as the basis for question 7.4X.)

2009
July 2 Purchases on credit from G Birks £687, A Weale £180, T Potts £1,012
July 5 Purchases on credit from K Lee £150, B Dixon £1,320
July 11 We returned goods to T Potts £33, G Birks £87
July 17 Purchases on credit from G Birks, £120
July 21 We paid B Dixon by cheque, £1,320
July 27 We paid G Birks £300 on account by cash
July 31 We returned goods to A Weale, £42.

7.3 Redraft each of the accounts given in your answer to 7.1 as three-column ledger-style accounts.

7.4X Redraft each of the accounts given in your answer to 7.2 as three-column ledger-style accounts.

7.5 Enter the following in the personal accounts (i.e. the creditor and debtor accounts) only; do *not* write up the other accounts. Balance off each personal account at the end of the month. After completing this, state which of the balances represent debtors and which represent creditors.

2009
Oct 1 Sales on credit to T Tickle £690, S Ames £330,
Oct 3 Purchases on credit D Stott £116, D Owen £347, J Rhodes £98
Oct 9 Sales on credit to S Ames £645, T Johnson £376
Oct 11 Purchases on credit from D Owen £135, J Ahmed £367
Oct 14 Sales returns from S Ames £45, T Tickle £46
Oct 19 We returned goods to D Owen £36, D Stott £19
Oct 23 We paid D Stott by cheque, £97
Oct 25 T Tickle paid us by cheque, £674
Oct 29 We paid J Ahmed by cash, £367
Oct 30 S Ames paid us £500 on account by cheque
Oct 31 T Johnson paid us by cheque, £376.

7.6X Enter the following in the necessary personal accounts; do *not* write up the other accounts. Balance each personal account at the end of the month. (Keep your answer – it will be used as the basis of question 7.8X.)

2009
Aug 1 Sales on credit to L Sterling £445, L Lindo £480, R Spencer £221
Aug 4 Goods returned to us by L Sterling £15, R Spencer £33
Aug 8 Sales on credit to L Lindo £66, R Spencer £129, L Banks £465
Aug 9 We received a cheque for £430 from L Sterling
Aug 12 Sales on credit to R Spencer £235, L Banks £777
Aug 19 Goods returned to us by L Banks £21, R Spencer £25
Aug 22 We received cheques as follows: R Spencer £300, L Lindo £414
Aug 31 Sales on credit to L Lindo £887, L Banks £442.

7.7X Enter the following, which are personal accounts only. Bring down balances at end of the month. After completing this, state which of the outstanding balances represent debtors and which represent creditors.

2009
May 1 Credit sale B Flynn £241, R Kelly £29, J Long £887, T Fryer £124
May 2 Credit purchases from S Wood £148, T DuQuesnay £27, R Johnson £77, G Henriques £108
May 8 Credit sales to R Kelly £74, J Long £132
May 9 Credit purchases from T DuQuesnay £142, G Henriques £44
May 10 Goods returned to us by J Long £17, T Fryer £44
May 12 Cash paid to us by T Fryer, £80
May 15 We returned goods to S Wood £8, G Henriques £18
May 19 We received cheques from J Long £500, B Flynn £241
May 21 We sold goods on credit to B Flynn £44, R Kelly £280
May 28 We paid by cheque the following: S Wood £140; G Henriques £50; R Johnson £60
May 31 We returned goods to G Henriques, £4.

7.8X Redraft each of the accounts given in your answer to 7.6X as three-column accounts.

CHAPTER 8

The trial balance

Learning objectives

After you have studied this chapter you should be able to:

- understand the purpose of a trial balance
- understand why the trial balance totals should equal one another
- draw up a trial balance from a given set of figures
- appreciate that some kinds of errors can be made but the trial balance totals will still equal one another
- understand what steps to take if the trial balance doesn't balance.

8.1 Introduction

A trial balance is an essential stage in ensuring the accuracy of the book-keeping entries prior to the preparation of the financial statements. It is a list of account titles and their balances in the ledger on a specific date. The trial balance lists the name of each account together with the balance shown in either the debit or credit columns. Since every entry in double entry book-keeping should have a corresponding credit entry then, provided no errors have occurred, the two columns should agree when totalled.

It is important to note that the trial balance is not part of the double entry system, it is merely a list of balances drawn up to check the arithmetical accuracy of the book-keeping entries. It does, however, serve two purposes:

1 It checks the accuracy of the double entry transactions.
2 It facilities the preparation of the financial statements of the business (this is a topic covered in Part 2).

8.2 | Total debit entries = total credit entries

Using the double entry system of book-keeping it has been shown that:

- for each debit entry there is a credit entry
- for each credit entry there is a debit entry.

All the items recorded in all the accounts on the debit side should equal *in total* all the items recorded on the credit side of the accounts. We need to check that for each debit entry there is also a credit entry. In order to do so, we prepare a trial balance which may be drawn up at the end of a period.

Each account needs to be balanced off, as shown in the previous chapter, and the balances entered in the trial balance. If the outstanding balance is a debit balance it would be entered in the debit column of the trial balance; if a credit balance it would be entered in the credit column. The trial balance would then be totalled and if both sides agree this is proof that certain types of errors have not been made. However, some errors may have occurred which the trial balance does not detect. This is discussed in Section 8.5 and later in Chapters 32 and 33.

Using the worked exercise from Section 5.9, the trial balance would be as follows:

Trial Balance as at 31 May 2009		
	£	£
Purchases	3,090	
Sales		2,550
Purchases returns		150
Sales returns	160	
A Lyon & Son		1,410
M Spencer	290	
Cash	570	
	4,110	4,110

Here the two sides 'balance', in other words both the debit column and the credit column add up to the same amount: £4,110.

This form of trial balance is the easiest to extract when there are more than a few transactions during the period and it is the one accountants use. As mentioned in the introduction to this chapter, the main purposes of preparing a trial balance is to ensure that no errors have been made and to facilitate the preparation of the financial statements. The financial statements consist of a 'profit and loss account' which shows how much profit the business has earned in a period. The 'balance sheet' shows what the assets and liabilities of a business are at the end of a period. Both these financial statements are dealt with in Part 2.

8.3 | A worked example

The following accounts, for K Potter, have been entered up for May 2009 and balanced off. Note the entries used to 'balance off' the accounts have been highlighted.

K Potter's Books:

Dr		£		Cr	£
			Bank Account		

Dr		£	Cr		£
2009			2009		
May 1	Capital	9,000	May 21	Machinery	550
May 30	T Monk	300	May 29	T Wood	860
			May 31	Balance c/d	7,890
		9,300			9,300
June 1	Balance b/d	7,890			

Dr		£	Cr		£
			Cash Account		
2009			2009		
May 5	Sales	180	May 30	K Young	170
May 12	Sales	210	May 31	Balance c/d	220
		390			390
June 1	Balance b/d	220			

Dr		£	Cr		£
			T Wood Account		
2009			2009		
May 6	Purchases returns	40	May 2	Purchases	900
May 29	Bank	860			
		900			900

Dr		£	Cr		£
			K Young Account		
2009			2009		
May 28	Purchases returns	80	May 3	Purchases	250
May 30	Cash	170	May 18	Purchases	190
May 31	Balance c/d	190			
		440			440
			June 1	Balance b/d	190

Dr		£	Cr		£
			T Monk Account		
2009			2009		
May 10	Sales	590	May 23	Sales returns	140
			May 30	Bank	300
			May 31	Balance c/d	150
		590			590
June 1	Balance b/d	150			

Dr		£	Cr		£
			C Howe Account		
2009			2009		
May 22	Sales	220	May 25	Sales returns	10
			May 31	Balance c/d	210
		220			220
June 1	Balance b/d	210			

Dr		AB Ltd Account		Cr
		2009		£
		May 31 Machinery		2,700

Dr		Capital Account		Cr
		2009		£
		May 1 Bank		9,000

Dr		Purchases Account		Cr
2009	£	2009		£
May 2 T Wood	900	May 31 Balance c/d		1,340
May 3 K Young	250			
May 18 K Young	190			
	1,340			1,340
June 1 Balance b/d	1,340			

Dr		Sales Account		Cr
2009	£	2009		£
May 31 Balance c/d	1,200	May 5 Cash		180
		May 10 T Monk		590
		May 12 Cash		210
		May 22 C Howe		220
	1,200			1,200
		June 1 Balance b/d		1,200

Dr		Sales Returns Account		Cr
2009	£	2009		£
May 23 T Monk	140	May 31 Balance c/d		150
May 25 C Howe	10			
	150			150
June 1 Balance b/d	150			

Dr		Purchases Returns Account		Cr
2009	£	2009		£
May 31 Balance c/d	120	May 6 T Wood		40
		May 28 K Young		80
	120			120
		June 1 Balance b/d		120

Dr		Machinery Account		Cr
2009	£	2009		£
May 21 Bank	550	May 31 Balance c/d		3,250
May 31 AB Ltd	2,700			
	3,250			3,250
June 1 Balance b/d	3,250			

After each account has been balanced off, a trial balance can then be prepared as follows:

K Potter Trial Balance as at 31 May 2009		
	Dr £	Cr £
Bank	7,890	
Cash	220	
K Young		190
T Monk	150	
C Howe	210	
AB Ltd		2,700
Capital		9,000
Purchases	1,340	
Sales		1,200
Sales returns	150	
Purchases returns		120
Machinery	3,250	
	13,210	13,210

8.4 The uses of the trial balance

Trial balances may be used:

- to check that the books 'balance', i.e. that every debit entry has been accompanied by a credit entry
- to ascertain the net amount of the error(s), should an error(s) have been made
- as a basis from which the financial statements are prepared, i.e. the trading account, the profit and loss account and the balance sheet (these will be explained in Part 2).

8.5 Trial balance and errors

Students new to accounting often assume that when a trial balance 'balances', the entries in the accounts must be correct. *This, however, may not be true.* It means that certain types of error have not been made, but there are several types of error that will not affect the balancing of a trial balance, such as omitting a transaction altogether. Another example might be a credit sale of £87 to a customer that is inadvertently debited to the sales account instead of being credited; the customer's account then being credited instead of being debited. Since both the debit and the credit entries are of the same amount then this will not affect the agreement of the trial balance.

Examples of the errors which would be revealed, provided there are no compensating errors which cancel them out, are addition errors, using one figure for the debit entry and another figure for the credit entry, entering only one aspect of a transaction, and so on. These will be considered in greater detail in later chapters.

8.6 Steps to take if the trial balance does not balance

If the trial balance does not balance, i.e. the two totals are different, then this is evidence that one or more errors have been made in either the double entry book-keeping or in the preparation of the trial balance itself. In this case, the following eight steps should be taken to locate the error(s):

1 If the trial balance is badly written and contains many alterations, then rewrite it.
2 Again add each side of the trial balance. If you added the numbers 'upwards' the first time, then start at the top and work 'downwards' the second time, and vice versa.
3 Find the amount of the discrepancy and then check in the accounts for a trans-action of this amount and, if located, ensure that the double entry has been carried out correctly.
4 Halve the amount of the discrepancy. Check to see whether there is a transaction for this amount and, if located, ensure the double entry has been carried out correctly. This type of error may have occurred if an item had been entered on the wrong side of the trial balance.
5 If the amount of the discrepancy is divisible by nine, this indicates that when the figure was originally entered it may have had digits transposed, for example £63 entered in error as £36, or £27 entered as £72.
6 Check that the balance on each account has been correctly calculated and entered onto the trial balance in the right column using the correct amount.
7 Ensure that every outstanding balance from all the ledgers and the cash book have been included in the trial balance and tick each balance after ensuring it is entered correctly.
8 If the error has still not been identified, then the error must be sought in the accounts themselves. It may be necessary to check all the entries from the date of the last trial balance.

8.7 Multiple-choice self-test questions

A growing practice of examining boards is to set multiple-choice questions in Accounting. This type of question certainly gives an examiner the opportunity to cover large parts of the syllabus briefly but in detail. Students who omit to study areas of the syllabus will be caught out by an examiner's use of multiple-choice questions. No longer will it be possible to say that it is highly probable that a certain topic will not be tested – the examiner can easily cover it with a multiple-choice question.

We have deliberately set blocks of multiple-choice questions at given places in this book, rather than a few at the end of each chapter. Such questions are relatively easy to answer a few minutes after reading the chapter, and so by asking the questions later your powers of recall and understanding are far better tested. It also gives you practice at answering a few questions in one block, as in an examination.

Each multiple-choice question has: a 'stem', namely that part which poses the problem; a 'key', which is the one correct answer; and a number of 'distractors', i.e.

incorrect answers. The key plus the distractors are known as the 'options'. If you do not know the answer you should guess. You may be right by chance, or you may remember something subconsciously. In any event, unless the examiner warns otherwise, he will expect you to guess if you don't know the answer.

You should now attempt Set 1 in Appendix C, which contains 20 multiple-choice questions.

Chapter summary

- A trial balance is a list of account titles and their balances in the ledger at a specific date which is prepared to check the arithmetical accuracy of the book-keeping entries.
- A trial balance also assists in the preparation of the financial statements.
- A worked example of a trial balance is shown.
- The balancing of a trial balance does not always indicate that no errors have been made since certain errors can be made and the trial balance will still agree.
- What steps to take if a trial balance does not balance.

EXERCISES

8.1 You are required to enter the following transactions for the month of May 2009, for a small electrical retailer. Balance the accounts off and extract a trial balance as at 31 May 2009.

2009
May 1 Started in business with capital of £2,500, which was paid into the bank
May 2 Bought goods on credit from the following: D Ellis £540; C Mendez £87; K Gibson £76
May 4 Sold goods on credit to: C Bailey £430; B Hughes £62; H Spencer £176
May 6 Sold goods for cash, £500
May 8 Paid rent by cash, £120
May 9 C Bailey paid us £250 by cheque on account
May 10 H Spencer paid us £150 on account by cheque
May 12 We paid the following by cheque: K Gibson £76; D Ellis £370 on account
May 15 Bought stationery for cash, £60
May 18 Bought goods on credit from: D Ellis £145; C Mendez £234
May 19 Paid rent by cash, £120
May 25 Sold goods on credit to: C Bailey £90; B Hughes £110; H Spencer £128
May 31 Paid C Mendez £87 by cheque.

8.2 Enter up the books from the following details of a Do-it-yourself Shop for the month of March, and extract a trial balance as at 31 March 2009.

2009
March 1 Started business with £8,000 in the bank
March 2 Bought goods on credit from the following persons: K Henriques £76;
            M Hyatt £27; T Braham £560
March 5 Cash sales, £870
March 6 Paid wages in cash, £140
March 7 Sold goods on credit to: H Elliott £35; L Lane £42; J Carlton £72

March 9 Bought goods for cash, £46
March 10 Bought goods on credit from: M Hyatt £57; T Braham £98
March 12 Paid wages in cash, £140
March 13 Sold goods on credit to: L Lane £32; J Carlton £23
March 15 Bought shop fixtures on credit from Betta Ltd, £500
March 17 Paid M Hyatt by cheque, £84
March 18 We returned goods to T Braham, £20
March 21 Paid Betta Ltd a cheque for £500
March 24 J Carlton paid us his account by cheque, £95
March 27 We returned goods to K Henriques, £24
March 30 J King lent us £600 by cash
March 31 Bought a motor van paying by cheque, £4,000.

8.3X Record the following transactions in the books of C Hilton. Balance off the accounts and extract a trial balance as at 30 June 2009.

2009
June   1 C Hilton started in business with £9,000 in cash
June   2 Paid £8,000 of the cash into a bank account
June   4 Paid rent for shop £300 by cheque
June   6 Bought goods on credit from Moorlands & Co. £675; J Swain £312; B Merton £225
June 12 Sold goods for cash, £450
June 13 Bought fixtures, paying by cheque, £230
June 15 Sold goods on credit T Green £180; K Wood £367; P Brown £256
June 18 Sold goods for cash, £220
June 20 Paid Moorlands & Co by cheque £675 and B Merton £225
June 21 Returned goods to J Swain £112 and paid the outstanding balance on their account by cheque
June 24 Bought goods on credit from Moorlands & Co £220 and J Swain £92
June 26 Paid wages in cash, £366
June 27 Cash drawings, £200
June 29 Bought motor van, paying by cheque, £4,000
June 30 Sold goods on credit to T Green £300; K Wood £50; P Brown £60
June 30 Received cheques from the following: T Green £180 and K Wood £367

8.4X You are required to enter the following transactions in the necessary accounts for April 2010 of a home furnishing business. At the end of the month balance off the accounts and prepare a trial balance.

2010
April   1 Started in business with £15,000 in the bank
April   3 Bought goods on credit from: Bowman Furnishers £320; Howe Homes £460; W Hunt £1,800; J Bond £620
April   7 Cash sales, £480
April   9 Paid rent by cheque, £500
April 11 Paid rates by cheque, £190
April 12 Sold goods on credit to: L Clark £480; K Allen £96; R Gee £1,170
April 14 Paid wages in cash, £400
April 17 We returned faulty goods to: Bowman Furnishers £28; J Bond £60
April 20 Bought goods on credit from: J Bond £220; W Hunt £270; Bowman Furnishers £240
April 23 Goods were returned to us from: K Allen £20; L Clark £40
April 25 Bought motor car on credit from Bates Motors, £5,000
April 26 Cash sales, £175

April 27 We paid the following by cheque: Bowman Furnishers £532; Howe Homes £460; W Hunt £2,070

April 28 Bought secondhand motor van, £3,000 paid by cheque

April 29 Bought stationery and paid in cash, £56

April 30 Received cheques from: L Clark £440; K Allen £76

April 30 Paid Bates Motors by cheque, £5,000.

8.5 Correct and balance the following trial balance.

Trial balance of P Brown as at 31 May 2009		
	Dr £	Cr £
Capital		20,000
Drawings	7,000	
General expenses		500
Sales	38,500	
Purchases		29,000
Debtors		6,800
Creditors	9,000	
Bank balance (Dr)	15,100	
Cash		200
Plant and equipment		5,000
Heating and lighting		1,500
Rent	2,400	

8.6 Reconstruct the trial balance after making the necessary corrections.

Trial balance of S Higton as at 30 June 2009		
	Dr £	Cr £
Capital	19,956	
Sales		119,439
Stationery	1,200	
General expenses	2,745	
Motor expenses		4,476
Cash at bank	1,950	
Stock 1 July 2008	7,668	
Wages and salaries		9,492
Rent and rates	10,500	
Office equipment	6,000	
Purchases	81,753	
Heating and lighting		2,208
Rent received	2,139	
Debtors	10,353	
Drawings		4,200
Creditors		10,230
Motor vehicle	7,500	
Interest received	1,725	
Insurance		3,444
	153,489	153,489

8.7X From the following list of balances, prepare a trial balance as at 31 December 2010 for Ms Anita Hall:

	£
Plant and machinery	21,450
Motor vehicles	26,000
Premises	80,000
Wages	42,840
Purchases	119,856
Sales	179,744
Rent received	3,360
Telephone, printing and stationery	3,600
Creditors	27,200
Debtors	30,440
Bank overdraft	2,216
Capital	131,250
Drawings	10,680
General expenses	3,584
Lighting and heating	2,960
Motor expenses	2,360

CHAPTER 9

Capital and revenue expenditures

Learning objectives

After you have studied this chapter you should be able to:

- distinguish between expenditure that is capital in nature and that which is revenue
- understand that some expenditure is part capital expenditure and part revenue expenditure
- understand that if revenue expenditure is incorrectly treated as capital expenditure, or vice versa, then both the financial statements and the profit therein will be affected.

9.1 Introduction

This chapter will deal with the distinction between capital and revenue expenditure and show the importance of careful classification, which can ultimately affect the recorded profits and the balance sheet valuations of a business.

9.2 Capital expenditure

Capital expenditure is incurred when a business spends money to either:

- buy fixed assets, or
- add to the value of an existing fixed asset.

Included in such amounts should be the costs of:

- acquiring fixed assets
- bringing them into the business
- legal costs of buying buildings
- carriage inwards on machinery bought
- any other cost needed to get the fixed asset ready for use.

9.3 Revenue expenditure

Revenue expenditure is expenditure that does not increase the value of fixed assets but is incurred in the day-to-day running expenses of the business.

The difference from capital expenditure can be seen when considering the cost of running a motor vehicle for a business. The expenditure incurred in acquiring the motor vehicle is classed as capital expenditure, while the cost of the petrol used to run the vehicle is revenue expenditure. This is because the revenue expenditure is used up in a few days and does not add to the value of the fixed asset.

9.4 Difference between capital and revenue expenditure

The difference between capital and revenue expenditure can be seen more generally in the following table (Exhibit 9.1). Revenue expenditure is the day-to-day running expense of the business and, as such, is chargeable to the trading and profit and loss account. Capital expenditure, in contrast, results in an increase in the fixed assets shown in the balance sheet.

Exhibit 9.1

Capital	Revenue
Premises purchased	Rent of premises
Legal charges for conveyancing	Legal charges for debt collection
New machinery	Repairs to machinery
Installations of machinery	Electricity costs of using machinery
Additions to assets	Maintenance of assets
Motor vehicles	Current Road Fund Tax
Delivery charges on new assets	Carriage on purchases and sales
Extension costs of new offices	Redecorating existing offices
Cost of adding air-conditioning to room	Interest on loan to purchase air-conditioning

9.5 Joint expenditure

In certain cases, an item of expenditure will need dividing between capital and revenue expenditure. Suppose a builder was engaged to carry out some work on your premises, the total bill being £60,000. If one-third of this was for repair work and two-thirds for improvements, then £20,000 should be charged to the profit and loss account as revenue expenditure, and £40,000 should be identified as capital expenditure and added to the value of the firm's premises and shown as such in the balance sheet. See Exhibit 9.2.

Exhibit 9.2 Joint expenditure

Builder's cost for repairs and improvements to premises £60,000

9.6 Incorrect treatment of expenditure

If one of the following occurs:

- capital expenditure is incorrectly treated as revenue expenditure, or
- revenue expenditure is incorrectly treated as capital expenditure,

then both the balance sheet figures and trading and profit and loss account figures will be incorrect. This means that the net profit figure will also be incorrect.

If capital expenditure is incorrectly posted to revenue expenditure – for example, if the purchase of a photocopier is posted in error to the stationery account instead of the office equipment account – then:

> **Net profit** would be understated, *and*
> **Balance sheet** values would not include the value of the asset.

If revenue expenditure is incorrectly posted to capital expenditure – for example if stationery is posted to office equipment instead of the stationery account – then:

> **Net profit** would be overstated, *and*
> **Balance sheet** values would be overvalued.

If the expenditure affects items in the trading account, then the **gross profit** figure will also be incorrect.

9.7 Treatment of loan interest

If money is borrowed to finance the purchase of a fixed asset, then interest will have to be paid on the loan. The **loan interest**, however, is *not* a cost of acquiring the asset but is simply a cost of financing its acquisition. This means that loan interest is revenue expenditure and *not* capital expenditure, and should be charged to the profit and loss account.

9.8 Capital and revenue receipts

When an item of capital expenditure is sold, the receipt is called a capital receipt. Suppose a motor van is bought for £10,000, and sold five years later for £2,000. The £10,000 was treated as capital expenditure; the £2,000 received is treated as a capital receipt.

Revenue receipts are sales or other revenue items, such as rent receivable or commissions receivable.

Chapter summary

- It is important to distinguish between expenditure that is classified as 'capital' and that which is 'revenue' since this can ultimately affect the recording of profits and balance sheet valuations.
- Expenditure can be either:

Capital expenditure	*or*	Revenue expenditure
(a) Buying fixed assets		(a) For daily running expenses of the business
(b) Adding value to fixed assets		(b) Not adding value to fixed asset

- Some items are both capital and revenue expenditure and the costs involved need to be apportioned carefully.
- If capital expenditure or revenue expenditure is mistaken one for the other, then either gross or net profit (or both) will be incorrectly stated. The value of the assets in the balance sheet will also be affected.
- It is also important to classify capital receipts, i.e. the sale of a fixed asset, from revenue receipts which are accounted for from sales or other revenue items.

EXERCISES

9.1 Newton Data Systems specialises in providing computer services to small commercial businesses.

You are required to state whether the following transactions should be classified as capital or revenue expenditure, giving reasons for your choice:

(*a*) Salaries of the computer operators.
(*b*) Purchase of new computer for use in the office.
(*c*) Purchase of computer printout paper.
(*d*) Insurance of all the company's computer hardware.
(*e*) Cost of adding additional storage capacity to a mainframe computer to be used by the company.
(*f*) Cost of providing additional security to the company's offices.

9.2 Cairns Engineering Company extracted the following information from their financial records:

	£
(*a*) New stationery and brochures	411
(*b*) Purchase of new pickup truck	18,000
(*c*) Purchase of new lathe	5,200
(*d*) Delivery cost of new lathe	200
(*e*) Electricty (including new wiring £1,800, part of premises improvement)	3,900
(*f*) Wages (including wages of two of Cairn's employees for improvement work on Cairns premises, amount involved £20,000)	65,000

You are required to:
- State whether each of the items listed above are capital or revenue expenditure and state how much the company has spent on each category for the year.
- Briefly explain the difference between capital and revenue expenditure.

9.3X (*a*) Star Fashions Ltd, which manufactures children's clothing, is planning to purchase a new cutting machine costing £20,000. Would the following items of expenditure be classed as capital or revenue expenditure?

    (i) The purchase price of the cutting machine.

    (ii) The cost of installing the machine.

    (iii) The significant cost of initial training for the staff to operate the new machine.

    (iv) The cost of future repairs and maintenance of the machine.

(*b*) If capital expenditure is treated as revenue expenditure, then:

    (i) How would the total expenses and the net profit for the period be affected?

    (ii) What effect would the error have on the value of the fixed assets in the balance sheet?

9.4 T Taylor has drawn up his financial statements for the year ended 31 December 2009. On examining them, you find that:

(*a*) Taylor has debited the cost of office equipment £311 to the purchases account.

(*b*) Taylor has debited the cost of repairing office equipment £290 to the motor repairs account.

(*c*) Sale of a building for £10,000 has been credited to the sales account.

(*d*) Repayment of a loan £500 has been debited to the loan interest account.

From his figures he had calculated gross profit as £95,620 and net profit as £28,910.

Ignoring any adjustments for depreciation, calculate revised figures of gross and net profits after taking (*a*) to (*d*) into account.

9.5X S Simpson has calculated her gross profit for the year to 30 June 2009 as £129,450 and her net profit as £77,270. You find that Simpson's books show:

(*a*) Sale of a motor vehicle for £4,100 has been credited to the sales account.

(*b*) Fixtures, bought for £750, have been debited to the repairs account.

(*c*) Receipt of a loan for £6,000 has been credited to the sales account.

(*d*) Repairs to motor vehicles £379 have been debited to the general expenses account.

Ignoring any adjustments for depreciation, calculate the revised figures of gross and net profits.

9.6X A business has incorrectly charged some of its expenditure in its final accounts. The incorrect figures shown were as follows:

(*a*) Gross profit £216,290

(*b*) Net profit £110,160

(*c*) Fixed assets £190,000

(*d*) Current assets £77,600.

Required:

You are to show, for each of the following, the effects on the calculations of (*a*) gross profit, (*b*) net profit, (*c*) fixed assets in the balance sheet and (*d*) current assets in the balance sheet. (Ignore depreciation.)

    (i)   Motor van costing £5,500 debited to motor expenses account.

    (ii)   Carriage outwards £77 debited to fixtures account.

    (iii) Rent £2,000 debited to buildings account.

    (iv) Machinery £6,000 debited to fixtures account.

    (v)   Office equipment £790 debited to purchases account.

    (vi) Discounts allowed £2,380 debited to machinery account.

9.7X (*a*) For each of the following transactions place *one* tick (✓) in the appropriate column to indicate whether the item is an example of capital expenditure, revenue expenditure, revenue receipt or capital receipt.

Transaction (i) is done as an example for you.

Transaction	Capital expenditure	Capital receipt	Revenue expenditure	Revenue receipt
(i) Purchase of goods for resale			✓	
(ii) Rent received for office sublet				
(iii) Purchase of stationery for office use				
(iv) Sale of old equipment no longer required				
(v) Cost of building an extension to premises				
(vi) Sale of stock				
(vii) Repairs to existing premises				

(*b*) How should items of capital expenditure be treated when preparing final accounts?

NEAB (GCSE)

PART 2

The financial statements of sole traders

This part of the book is concerned with preparing the financial statements of sole traders from the double entry records. A chapter on accounting concepts, standards and policies is also included.

CHAPTER 10

Trading and profit and loss account: an introduction

Learning objectives

After you have studied this chapter you should be able to:

- understand why profit is calculated
- explain the purpose of the trading account and profit and loss account
- calculate the cost of goods sold, gross profit and net profit
- understand the difference between gross profit and net profit
- understand that an adjustment needs to be made for the stock of unsold goods at the end of the trading period
- close off sales, purchases and relevant expense accounts at the end of the trading period by double entry; and transfer the balances to the trading account and profit and loss account
- prepare a trading account and profit and loss account from a trial balance
- transfer the net profit and drawings to the capital account at the end of the period
- appreciate that after preparing the trading account and profit and loss account all remaining balances in the books of account are required for preparation of the balance sheet.

10.1 | Purpose of the trading and profit and loss account

The trading and profit and loss account is one of the most important financial statements and, as stated in Chapter 1, it is a requirement for correct financial reporting. Its purpose is to show how much profit or loss has been made over a period of time. It is prepared at least once a year but could easily be made available for a shorter period if required, especially with the use of accounting software.

The main purpose of a trading and profit and loss account is for the owners to be able to see how profitably the business is being run. Chapter 1 details other groups who will be interested in the financial results of a business, such as banks, if the business requires a loan, and the tax authorities.

10.2 Uses of the trading and profit and loss account

One of the most important uses of the trading and profit and loss account is that of comparing the results obtained with the results expected. In a trading organisation, much attention is paid to how much profit is made, before deducting expenses. This is the **gross profit** and it appears in the first section of the trading and profit and loss account. The amount of gross profit is of major interest. In the next section of the account the **net profit** is shown and again this is equally important to the owners and other groups.

Gross profit: (calculated in the Trading Account)	This is the excess of sales over the **cost of goods sold** in the period.
Net profit: (calculated in the Profit and Loss Account)	This is what is left of the gross profit after all other expenses have been deducted.

It would be possible to have one account called a **trading account**, and another called a **profit and loss account**. Normally they are combined together to form one account called the **trading and profit and loss account**.

10.3 Horizontal and vertical format for the trading and profit and loss account

In Section 10.4, we will look at the trading and profit and loss account drawn up using the horizontal style. The left-hand side is the debit side, while the right-hand side is the credit side of the accounts. These accounts can therefore be seen as part of the double entry system, and students should be able to understand why each item is shown as a debit or a credit in them.

In Section 10.8, we will see how the trading and profit and loss account can be shown using a vertical style.

10.4 Preparation of a trading and profit and loss account

A trial balance needs to be drawn up before a trading and profit and loss account can be prepared. This contains nearly all the information needed. (Later on in this book you will see that certain adjustments have to be made, but we will ignore these at this stage.) Set out in Exhibit 10.1 is the trial balance of K Wade made up to the end of his first year's trading. This information is needed to prepare his trading and profit and loss account for the year ended 31 December 2009. For now, we will assume that K Wade has no closing stock at 31 December 2009.

To calculate gross profit

Remember that:

Sales – Cost of Goods Sold = Gross Profit

Exhibit 10.1

K Wade		
Trial Balance as at 31 December 2009		
	Dr £	Cr £
Sales		39,650
Purchases	27,150	
General expenses	2,550	
Fixtures and fittings	6,840	
Debtors	2,460	
Creditors		2,180
Capital		8,800
Drawings	7,750	
Bank	3,820	
Cash	60	
	50,630	50,630

We could in fact calculate this by simply using arithmetic. However, we must remember that we are using double entry methods. The answer will be the same whether normal arithmetic or proper double entry methods are used. To enable you to see fully how the calculations are performed using double entry, we will show the balances for sales and purchases, as in Exhibit 10.1, and how the entries are made to transfer these items into the calculations within the trading account.

The following steps should be carried out:

Step 1 Transfer the credit balance of the sales account to the credit of the trading account portion of the trading and profit and loss account.

Debit: sales account
Credit: trading account.

Step 2 Transfer the debit balance of the purchases account to the debit of the trading account.

Debit: trading account
Credit: purchases account.

Remember that, in this case, there is no stock of unsold goods. This means that purchases = **cost of goods sold**.

Step 3 If sales are greater than the cost of goods sold, the difference is gross profit. (If not, the answer would be a **gross loss**.) We will carry this gross profit figure from the trading account part down to the profit and loss part.
The double entry for gross profit is:

Debit: trading account
Credit: profit and loss account.

The double entry for the above transfers are shown in Exhibit 10.2.

Exhibit 10.2

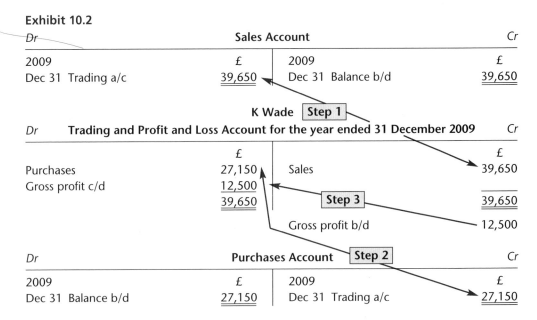

Notice that, after the trading account has been completed, there are no balances remaining in the sales and purchases accounts. They are now said to be 'closed'.

To calculate net profit and record it

Remember that:

> **Gross Profit – Expenses = Net Profit**

Remember also (from Chapter 6) that:

> **Old Capital + Net Profit = New Capital**

The double entry needed to carry out these calculations is:

Step 1 Transfer the debit balances on expenses accounts to the debit of the profit and loss account.

> Debit: profit and loss account
> Credit: expenses accounts.

Step 2 Transfer the net profit, when found, to the capital account to show the increase in capital.

> Debit: profit and loss account
> Credit: capital account.

The results are shown in Exhibit 10.3.

Exhibit 10.3

K Wade

Dr	Trading and Profit and Loss Account for the Year ended 31 December 2009			Cr
		£		£
Purchases		27,150	Sales	39,650
Gross profit c/d		12,500		
		39,650		39,650
General expenses		2,550	Gross profit b/d	12,500
Net profit		9,950		
		12,500		12,500

Step 1

Dr	General Expenses Account			Cr
2009		£	2009	£
Dec 31 Balance b/d		2,550	Dec 31 Profit and loss a/c	2,550

Dr	Capital Account		Step 2	Cr
			2009	£
			Dec 31 Balance b/d	8,800
			Dec 31 Net profit	9,950
				18,750

Note: See Section 10.5 for completion of this account.

10.5 Completion of capital account

You have seen that we credit the capital account with the amount of net profit. We have, therefore, recorded the increase in capital.

In the trial balance, Exhibit 10.1, we can see that there are drawings of £7,750. **Drawings** are withdrawals of capital.

After entering the net profit in the capital account we can now complete the account. To do this we transfer the drawings to the capital account. Thus:

Debit: capital account
Credit: drawings account.

The completed capital and drawings accounts are as follows:

Dr	Drawings Account			Cr
2009		£	2009	£
Dec 31 Balance b/d		7,750	Dec 31 Capital	7,750

Dr		Capital Account		Cr
2009	£	2009		£
Dec 31 Drawings	7,750	Dec 31 Balance b/d		8,800
Dec 31 Balance c/d	11,000	Dec 31 Net profit		9,950
	18,750			18,750
		2010		
		Jan 1 Balance b/d		11,000

10.6 Stock of unsold goods at end of period

Usually some of the goods bought (purchases) have not been sold by the end of the accounting period.

We have already seen that gross profit is calculated as follows:

> **Sales – Cost of Goods Sold = Gross Profit**

However, purchases only equals cost of goods sold if there is no stock at the end of a period. We can calculate cost of goods sold as follows:

What we bought in this period:	Purchases
Less Goods bought but not sold in this period:	Closing Stock
	= Cost of Goods Sold

Remember, we are concerned here with the trading and profit and loss account of a business where there is no opening stock. In Section 12.5 we will look at the later years of a business.

Now let us look at the preparation of a trading and profit and loss account for B Swift. His trial balance is shown as Exhibit 10.4 and was drawn up after his first year of trading:

Exhibit 10.4

B Swift Trial Balance as at 31 December 2009		
	Dr £	Cr £
Sales		38,500
Purchases	29,000	
Rent	2,400	
Electricity	1,500	
General expenses	600	
Fixtures and fittings	5,000	
Debtors	6,800	
Creditors		9,100
Bank	15,100	
Cash	200	
Drawings	7,000	
Capital		20,000
	67,600	67,600

Note: On 31 December 2009, at the close of trading, B Swift had goods costing £3,000 that were unsold.

The cost of goods sold figure will be:

	£
Purchases	29,000
Less Closing stock	3,000
Cost of goods sold	26,000

The gross profit will be:

	£
Sales	38,500
Less Cost of goods sold	26,000
Gross profit	12,500

The net profit will be:

	£	£
Gross profit		12,500
Less Expenses		
Rent	2,400	
Electricity	1,500	
General expenses	600	
		4,500
Net profit		8,000

The double entry for the above transactions is now shown in Exhibit 10.5.

Exhibit 10.5

Dr		**Sales Account**		Cr
2009	£	2009		£
Dec 31 Trading a/c	38,500	Dec 31 Balance b/d		38,500

Dr		**Purchases Account**		Cr
2009	£	2009		£
Dec 31 Balance b/d	29,000	Dec 31 Trading a/c		29,000

Dr		**Rent Account**		Cr
2009	£	2009		£
Dec 31 Balance b/d	2,400	Dec 31 Profit and loss a/c		2,400

Dr		Electricity Account		Cr
2009	£	2009		£
Dec 31 Balance b/d	1,500	Dec 31 Profit and loss a/c		1,500

Dr		General Expenses Account		Cr
2009	£	2009		£
Dec 31 Balance b/d	600	Dec 31 Profit and loss a/c		600

To record the stock we need to:

> Debit: stock account
> Credit: trading account

as shown below:

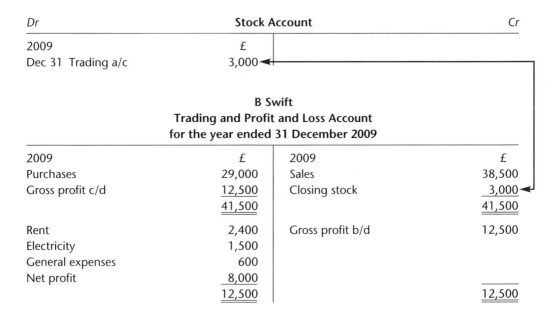

Dr		Stock Account		Cr
2009	£			
Dec 31 Trading a/c	3,000			

B Swift
Trading and Profit and Loss Account
for the year ended 31 December 2009

2009	£	2009	£
Purchases	29,000	Sales	38,500
Gross profit c/d	12,500	Closing stock	3,000
	41,500		41,500
Rent	2,400	Gross profit b/d	12,500
Electricity	1,500		
General expenses	600		
Net profit	8,000		
	12,500		12,500

The figures shown in Exhibit 10.5 show that there is now a balance on the stock account. We had to record it there because at 31 December 2009 we had an asset, namely £3,000 of stock, but there was no record of that fact in our books. We have now brought our records up to date by showing the stock in our accounts. Without the stock account at 31 December 2009, our records would have been incomplete.

10.7 The capital account

The capital account for B Swift can now be completed, thus:

Dr		Capital Account		Cr
2009	£	2009		£
Dec 31 Drawings	7,000	Jan 1 Cash		20,000
Dec 31 Balance c/d	21,000	Dec 31 Net profit from profit		
		and loss a/c		8,000
	28,000			28,000
		2010		
		Jan 1 Balance b/d		21,000

Dr		Drawings Account		Cr
2009	£	2009		£
Dec 31 Balance b/d	7,000	Dec 31 Capital		7,000

10.8 The vertical style for trading and profit and loss accounts

The trading and profit and loss account shown above is written in the *horizontal* format to demonstrate how the double entry system works. However, the trading and profit and loss account is more often shown in the *vertical* format, and it is this format that we will use in future in this book. You may wish to carry on preparing the horizontal format trading and profit and loss account before drawing up the vertical format, until you are sure you understand how to double enter directly into the vertical format.

The trading and profit and loss account of B Swift, in the vertical format, is shown below:

B Swift
Trading and Profit and Loss Account for the year ended 31 December 2009

	£	£
Sales		38,500
Less Cost of goods sold		
Purchases	29,000	
Less Closing stock	3,000	
		26,000
Gross profit		12,500
Less Expenses		
Rent	2,400	
Electricity	1,500	
General expenses	600	
		4,500
Net profit		8,000

You can see that the figures used are exactly the same using either the horizontal or vertical methods of display. The vertical method is a more modern presentation method. It is intended to make accounts easier to understand for those without an in-depth understanding of accounting and the double entry system.

10.9 The balances remaining in the books of account

Taking Exhibit 10.5, including the adjustment of closing stock valued at £3,000, we can now ascertain the balances still remaining in the books of account after the preparation of the trading and profit and loss accounts. The following accounts have been closed in this process:

Sales Purchases	} transferred to trading account
Rent Electricity General expenses	} transferred to profit and loss account
Drawings	} transferred to capital account

With the remaining balances we can draw up a trial balance which is now shown in Exhibit 10.6.

Exhibit 10.6

<table>
<tr><td colspan="3" align="center">B Swift
Trial Balance as at 31 December 2009
(after Trading and Profit and Loss
Accounts completed)</td></tr>
<tr><td></td><td align="center">Dr
£</td><td align="center">Cr
£</td></tr>
<tr><td>Fixtures and fittings</td><td>5,000</td><td></td></tr>
<tr><td>Debtors</td><td>6,800</td><td></td></tr>
<tr><td>Creditors</td><td></td><td>9,100</td></tr>
<tr><td>Stock</td><td>3,000</td><td></td></tr>
<tr><td>Bank</td><td>15,100</td><td></td></tr>
<tr><td>Cash</td><td>200</td><td></td></tr>
<tr><td>Capital</td><td></td><td>21,000</td></tr>
<tr><td></td><td>30,100</td><td>30,100</td></tr>
</table>

The one account that was not in the original trial balance was the stock account. It was not brought into our books until the trading account was prepared. These balances will be used when we look at the balance sheets in the next chapter. They are also carried forward to the next accounting period.

Chapter summary

- The trading and profit and loss account is prepared to determine the profit/losses made in the period.
- One of the main uses of the trading and profit and loss account is to provide information on the profit/losses made in the period and compare these figures with previous year's results.
- How to calculate the cost of goods sold, gross profit and net profit.
- How to close off the sales, purchases and relevant expense accounts at the end of a period and post the entries to the trading and profit and loss account.
- How to transfer the net profit and drawings to the capital account at the end of a period.
- How to treat stock of unsold goods at the end of a period.
- The preparation of the trading and profit and loss account from a trial balance using both the horizontal and vertical methods of presentation.
- Any balances still remaining in the books of account after preparation of the trading and profit and loss account represent assets, liabilities and capital. These balances are entered into the Balance Sheet (see the next chapter) and then carried forward to the next accounting period.

EXERCISES

Note: All answers should show the vertical layout of the trading and profit and loss accounts.

10.1 From the following details of I Simpson, draw up her trading and profit and loss account using the vertical style for the year ended 31 December 2009, this being her first year of trading:

Year to 31 December 2009	£
Purchases	24,190
Sales	38,220
Rent	4,170
Wages and salaries	5,390
Postage and stationery	840
Electricity expenses	710
General expenses	370

Note: At 31 December 2009, the stock was valued (at cost) at £4,310.

10.2X From the following details of C Newman, draw up his trading and profit and loss account using the vertical style for his first year of trading for the year ended 31 December 2009.

Year to 31 December 2009	£
Rent	4,990
Motor expenses	2,370
Sundry expenses	410
Travel expenses	600
Office expenses	720
Sales	57,090
Purchases	42,910

Note: Stock at 31 December 2009 amounted in value to £8,220.

10.3 From the following trial balance of G Singh, extracted after one year's trading, prepare the trading and profit and loss account for the year ended 31 December 2009. A balance sheet is not required.

G Singh
Trial Balance as at 31 December 2009

	Dr £	Cr £
Sales		73,848
Purchases	58,516	
Wages	8,600	
Motor expenses	2,080	
Rates	2,680	
Insurance	444	
General expenses	420	
Premises	20,000	
Motor vehicle	12,000	
Debtors	7,800	
Creditors		6,418
Cash at bank	6,616	
Cash in hand	160	
Drawings	8,950	
Capital		48,000
	128,266	128,266

Stock at 31 December 2009 was valued at £10,192.

(Retain your answer – it will be used later in Exercise 11.1.)

10.4X From the following trial balance of R Cairns after his first year's trading, you are required to draw up a trading and profit and loss account for the year ended 30 June 2009.

R Cairns
Trial Balance as at 30 June 2009

	Dr £	Cr £
Sales		99,082
Purchases	71,409	
Rates	2,000	
Printing and stationery	562	
Electricity	1,266	
Wages	9,492	
Insurance	605	
Premises	145,000	
Computer equipment	8,000	
Debtors	9,498	
Sundry expenses	1,518	
Creditors		3,618
Cash at bank	6,541	
Drawings	12,200	
Motor vehicle	16,500	
Motor expenses	3,109	
Capital		185,000
	287,700	287,700

Stock at 30 June 2009 was valued at £11,498.

(Retain your answer – it will be used later in Exercise 11.2X.)

10.5 Mrs P Stewart commenced trading as a card and gift shop with a capital of £6,855 on 1 April 2009. At the end of her first year's trading on 31 March 2010, she was able to identify from her accounting records that she had received £24,765 sales in the year. These sales had cost her £13,545 to purchase, and she had £2,345 cards and gifts, at cost, in stock on 31 March 2010. In the year she had also spent £2,100 on staff wages, and drawn personal cash of £5,500. Other overhead costs incurred were:

	£
Rent and rates	1,580
Electricity	565
Motor expenses	845
Insurance	345
General expenses	245

On 31 March 2010, Mrs P Stewart had cash in hand of £135, a bank balance of £2,675, and owed £3,285 to creditors. Mrs Stewart's business owned a car, which had a value of £5,875 at 31 March 2010. She had also bought shelving and fixtures and fittings in the year to the value of £1,495.

You are required to draw up the trading and profit and loss account for the first year's trading.

(*Exam hint*: Before you attempt to draw up the trading and profit and loss account, it would be a good idea to extract the trial balance at 31 March 2010 from the information given.) The closing stock figure should be shown as a note at the foot of the trial balance.

(Keep your answer – it will be used later in Exercise 11.3.)

10.6X Miss R Burgess has just completed her first year of trading for the year ended 30 April 2009, as a manufacturer of model railway accessories. Her initial capital was £9,025. At 30 April 2009, she was owed £5,600 by customers, and owed £4,825 to suppliers. She calculated that she had stock in hand, at cost, at the year end of £7,670, and her bank account was overdrawn by £2,560. The petty cash float held £25 at 30 April 2009.

From her records, she calculated her income and expenditure for the year ended 30 April 2009 as:

	£
Sales	56,540
Purchases	34,315
Rent of factory	6,000
Drawings	10,000
Motor expenses	1,735
Insurance	345
General expenses	780
Salaries	7,550

Miss R Burgess had plant and equipment to the value of £3,750 and a van worth £2,850 at 30 April 2009.

You are required to draw up the trading and profit and loss account for the first year's trading.

(Keep your answer – it will be used later in Exercise 11.5X.)

10.7X A business has been trading for one year. Extract a trading and profit and loss account for the year ended 30 June 2009 for M Kent. The trial balance as at 30 June 2009 is as follows:

M Kent Trial Balance as at 30 June 2009		
	Dr £	Cr £
Rent and rates	1,560	
Insurance	305	
Lighting expenses	516	
Motor expenses	1,960	
Salaries and wages	4,850	
Sales		35,600
Purchases	30,970	
Trade expense	806	
Motor van	3,500	
Creditors		3,250
Debtors	6,810	
Shop fixtures	3,960	
Shop buildings	28,000	
Cash at bank	1,134	
Drawings	6,278	
Capital		51,799
	90,649	90,649

Stock at 30 June 2009 was £9,960.
(Keep your answer – it will be used later in Exercise 11.6X.)

CHAPTER 11

The balance sheet

Learning objectives

After you have studied this chapter you should be able to:

- define a balance sheet
- understand that a balance sheet is prepared from the remaining balances in the trial balance after preparation of the trading and profit and loss accounts
- explain why a balance sheet is not part of the double entry system
- explain the meaning of the terms fixed assets, current assets, current liability and long-term liability
- prepare a balance sheet using the vertical method of presentation
- understand the importance of the term net current assets/working capital
- know which items appear in the owner's capital account.

11.1 Definition and content of a balance sheet

A **balance sheet** is a financial statement setting out the book values of assets, liabilities and capital 'as at' a particular point in time. In simple terms a balance sheet shows what a business '*owns*' and what it '*owes*' at a specific date.

Details of the assets, liabilities and capital have to be found in the records of the business and then written out as a balance sheet. These details are readily available since they consist of all the balances remaining in the records once the trading and profit and loss account for the period have been completed. All balances remaining have to be assets, liabilities or capital since the other balances should have been closed off when the trading and profit and loss account was completed.

11.2 Preparing a balance sheet

Let us look at Exhibit 11.1, the trial balance of B Swift (from Exhibit 10.6) as on 31 December 2009 after the trading and profit and loss account had been prepared.

Exhibit 11.1

B Swift Trial Balance as at 31 December 2009 (after Trading and Profit and Loss Accounts completed)		
	Dr £	Cr £
Fixtures and fittings	5,000	
Debtors	6,800	
Creditors		9,100
Stock	3,000	
Bank	15,100	
Cash	200	
Capital		21,000
	30,100	30,100

We can now draw up a balance sheet as at 31 December 2009, and this is shown in Exhibit 11.2. The layout is discussed further in Section 11.4.

Exhibit 11.2

B Swift
Balance Sheet as at 31 December 2009

	£	£
Fixed assets		
Fixtures and fittings		5,000
Current assets		
Stock	3,000	
Debtors	6,800	
Cash at bank	15,100	
Cash in hand	200	
	25,100	
Less Current liabilities		
Creditors	9,100	
Net current assets		16,000
Long-term liabilities		
Long-term loan		–
Net assets		21,000
Financed by:		
Capital account		
Cash introduced		20,000
Add net profit for the year		8,000
		28,000
Less Drawings		7,000
		21,000

11.3 No double entry in balance sheets

It may seem strange to you to learn that balance sheets are *not* part of the double entry system.

If accounts are drawn such as the cash account, rent account, sales account, trading and profit and loss account, and so on, we are writing up part of the double entry system. We make entries on the debit and credit sides of these accounts.

In preparing a balance sheet, we do not enter anything in the various accounts. We do not actually transfer the fixtures balance or the stock balance, or any of the others, to the balance sheet. All that we do is to list the balances for assets, capital and liabilities to form a balance sheet. This means that none of these accounts have been closed off. *Nothing is entered in the accounts.*

When the next accounting period starts, these accounts are still open containing balances. As a result of business transactions, entries are then made in these accounts to add to, or deduct from, the amounts shown in the accounts using normal double entry.

If you see the word 'account' you will know that it is part of the double entry system, and it will include debit and credit entries. If the word 'account' cannot be used, it is not part of double entry. For instance:

Trial balance: A list of balances to see whether the records are correct.

Balance sheet: A list of balances arranged according to whether they are assets, capital or liabilities.

11.4 Balance sheet layout

The balance sheet is one of the most important financial statements and as such it is important that the reader of this statement finds it easy to follow and understand. Over the years various ways of presenting the financial information have evolved. The present format of the balance sheet is shown in Exhibit 11.2 above.

You will see that the balance sheet starts by listing all the assets which the business 'owns' as at the date of the balance sheet. The assets are split into two categories, fixed and current assets, and this is followed by details of the funds acquired to finance the business.

In Appendix B there is a model layout of the financial statements of a sole trader, namely the Trading and Profit and Loss Account and Balance Sheet. You may find it useful to take a copy of these layouts and use them when undertaking exercises on the preparation of the financial statements.

Assets

Assets are shown under two headings, namely fixed assets and current assets.

Fixed assets

Fixed assets are assets that:

- are expected to be of use to the business for a long time
- are to be used in the business, and
- were not bought only for the purposes of resale.

Examples are buildings, machinery, motor vehicles, fixtures and fittings.

Fixed assets are listed first in the balance sheet starting with those that the business will keep the longest, down to assets with the shortest life expectancy. For instance:

Fixed assets
1 Land and buildings
2 Fixtures and fittings
3 Machinery
4 Motor vehicles

Current assets

Current assets are assets that are likely to change in the near future and usually within 12 months of the balance sheet date. They include stock of goods for resale at a profit, amounts owed by debtors, cash at bank and any cash in hand. These are listed starting with the asset that is least likely to be turned into cash, finishing with cash itself. The accepted order is listed as:

Current assets
1 Stock
2 Debtors
3 Cash at bank
4 Cash in hand

Liabilities

There are two categories of liabilities, **current liabilities** and **long-term liabilities**.

Current liabilities

Current liabilities are liabilities due for repayment in the short term, usually within one year. Examples are bank overdrafts, amounts due to creditors for the supply of goods for resale.

Current liabilities are deducted from the current assets, as shown in Exhibit 11.2, to give the **net current assets** or **working capital**. This figure is very important in accounting since it shows the amount of resources the business has in the form of readily available cash to meet everyday running expenses.

Long-term liabilities

Long-term liabilities are liabilities not due for repayment in the near future. Examples are bank loans, loans from others such as friends or relatives, and mortgages. Long-term liabilities are deducted from the total figure of assets plus the net current assets as illustrated in Exhibit 11.2.

Capital account

This is the proprietor's or partners' account with the business. It will start with the balance brought forward from the previous accounting period, to which is added any personal cash introduced into the business and the net profit made by the business in this accounting period. Deducted from the capital account will be amounts drawn from the business and any loss made by the business. The final balance on the capital account should equal the net assets or net liabilities figure – and hence the balance sheet balances. Exhibit 11.3 gives the standard format.

Exhibit 11.3

Capital Account		
	£	£
Balance b/d		X
Add Cash introduced		X
Net profit for the period		X
		X
Less Drawings	X	
Net loss for the period	X	
		X
		X

It is important to note that the balance sheet shows the position of the business at one point in time: the balance sheet date, i.e. 'as at 31 December 2009'. It is like taking a snapshot of the business at one moment in time. On the other hand the trading and profit and loss account shows the profit/loss of that business for a period of time (normally a year), i.e. 'for the year ended 31 December 2009'.

Chapter summary

- A balance sheet is a financial statement which lists the book values of assets, liabilities and capital 'as at' a specific date. It shows what a business 'owns' and 'owes' at a particular point in time.
- The balance sheet is prepared from the remaining balances in the trial balance after the trading and profit and loss account has been completed.
- The balance sheet is *not* part of the double entry system.
- Most balance sheets are set out using the vertical method of presentation which shows the assets divided into two categories namely fixed assets and current assets followed by current liabilities, long-term liabilities and capital.
- The term 'fixed assets' means assets of a more permanent nature such as land and building, equipment and cars that are owned by the business. These are listed in the balance sheet in descending order with the most permanent asset shown first.
- The term 'current assets' refers to assets that are likely to change within one year, for example, stock, debtors, cash at bank and cash in hand. These are listed in order of liquidity with the least liquid of the assets shown first, i.e. stock and the most liquid asset shown at the bottom, i.e. cash in hand.

- The term net current assets or working capital is an important figure in accounting since it represents the amount of readily available resources available for paying everyday running expenses.
- The capital account contains money invested by the owner of the business plus the net profit for the period less amounts taken out by the owner in the form of 'drawings'. If there is no net profit then a net loss will have been incurred.

EXERCISES

11.1 Complete exercise 10.3 by drawing up a balance sheet as at 31 December 2009 for G Singh.

11.2X Complete exercise 10.4X by drawing up a balance sheet as at 30 June 2009 for R Cairns.

11.3 Complete exercise 10.5 by drawing up a balance sheet as at 31 March 2010 for Mrs P Stewart.

11.4 Miss V Holland had been trading for a number of years as a cheese retailer, making up accounts each year to 30 June. As at 30 June 2009 she was able to extract the following information from her accounting records and has asked you as her accountant to draw up the balance sheet at that date:

(a) She owed amounts to businesses that had supplied her with cheese, totalling £4,565
(b) She was owed £2,375 by a customer who bought goods on credit
(c) She had cash in hand of £150
(d) Her bank account was overdrawn by £1,785
(e) She had stock of cheese unsold totalling £1,465
(f) She had a van that was used for deliveries and that was valued at £3,400 on 30 June 2009
(g) She had equipment valued at £2,885 at the year end
(h) She had introduced £2,000 of her own money in the year, when she was nearing her over-draft limit
(i) The business made a net profit of £2,525 in the year to 30 June 2009
(j) Miss V Holland drew £50 each week, for the whole year, and had no other drawings from the business
(k) The business had a loan from V Holland's mother for £2,000. This was not due to be repaid until the year 2012.

11.5X Complete exercise 10.6X by drawing up a balance sheet as at 30 April 2009 for Miss R Burgess.

11.6X Complete exercise 10.7X by drawing up a balance sheet as at 30 June 2009 for M Kent.

CHAPTER 12

Financial statements: further considerations

Learning objectives

After you have studied this chapter you should be able to:

- record sales returns and purchases returns in the trading and profit and loss account
- understand that carriage inwards on goods purchased is treated as part of the cost of goods sold
- realise that carriage outwards is an expense to be entered in the profit and loss account
- adjust financial statements properly for both the opening and closing stocks of the period
- explain why the cost of putting goods into a saleable condition should be charged to the trading account
- prepare a trading and profit and loss account if either a gross loss or net loss occurs.

12.1 Sales returns and purchases returns

When firms deal with the purchase and sale of goods it is inevitable that there are occasions when goods have to be returned by the purchaser to the supplier because they are damaged, faulty or perhaps not to the specification ordered. The goods will be returned to the supplier accompanied by a returns note which gives details of the goods being returned and the reason together with details of the order number, date, etc.

Purchases returns (also called returns outwards)

When a business returns goods to a supplier for one of the above-mentioned reasons they are known as **purchases returns** or **returns outwards**. The book-keeping entries are as follows:

> Debit: supplier's account (i.e. the creditor)
> Credit: the purchases returns (or returns outwards) account.

The purchases returns account is kept separate from the purchases account to enable a check to be made on the amount of goods being returned.

Sales returns (also called returns inwards)

If goods are returned by a customer (debtor) then they are referred to as **sales returns** or **returns inwards**. The book-keeping entries would be as shown below:

> Debit: sales returns (or returns inwards) account
> Credit: customer's (debtors') account.

The sales returns are again kept separate from the sales account to enable a check to be made on the amount of goods being returned to the firm.

12.2 Dealing with returns in the trading account

In Chapter 10 the sales returns and purchases returns accounts were deliberately omitted so that the first sight of the trading and profit and loss accounts would not be too difficult. Since a large number of firms will return goods to their suppliers (purchases returns), and have goods returned to them (sales returns), then these returns must be taken into consideration when calculating the gross profit.

In the trading account the sales returns and purchases returns are dealt with as follows:

- sales returns should be deducted from **sales**
- purchases returns should be deducted from **purchases**.

Suppose that in Exhibit 10.1 the trial balance of K Wade, rather than simply containing a sales account balance of £39,650 and a purchases account balance of £27,150 the balances showing stock movement had been:

K Wade
Trial Balance as at 31 December 2009 (extract)

	Dr £	Cr £
Sales		40,000
Purchases	27,350	
Sales returns	350	
Purchases returns		200

If we compare the two trial balances, i.e. the one shown in Exhibit 10.1 and the one shown above, the gross profit amount will be exactly the same. Sales in the original example were £39,650, while in the above example the sales returns is deducted from sales as follows:

	£
Sales	40,000
Less Sales returns	350
Net sales	39,650

Purchases were originally shown as £27,150 but in the above example purchases returns will need to be deducted from purchases to ascertain the amount of goods retained by the firm as shown below:

		£
Purchases		27,350
Less Purchases returns		200
Net purchases		27,150

The trading account using the figures from the above example will now appear as in Exhibit 12.1.

Exhibit 12.1

K Wade
Trading and Profit and Loss Account for the year ended 31 December 2009

	£	£
Sales		40,000
Less Sales returns		350
		39,650
Less Cost of goods sold		
Purchases	27,350	
Less Purchases returns	200	27,150
Gross profit		12,500

The gross profit in the above example is £12,500 which is exactly the same amount as shown in Exhibit 10.3. You will notice that the trading and profit and loss account prepared in Exhibit 10.3 was prepared using the horizontal method. The trading and profit and loss account shown above in Exhibit 12.1 has been presented using the vertical method of presentation which will be used on all further examples in this book.

Student hint:
Many students have difficulty deciding whether sales returns should be deducted from sales or purchases figures and vice versa. The same applies to the purchases returns figure. The following illustration shows that the returns are always deducted from the figure on the opposite side so forming an 'X' on the trial balance:

K Wade
Trial Balance as at 31 December 2009 (extract)

	Dr £	Cr £
Sales		40,000
Purchases	27,350	
Sales returns	350	
Purchases returns		200

12.3 Carriage

When a firm buys goods from a supplier the cost of delivering or transporting the goods also has to be paid. In accountancy terms this cost of transport is often referred to as 'carriage'. Carriage charges for transporting goods purchased into a firm is known as **carriage inwards**, whereas, carriage charges for the delivery of goods to a firm's customers is known as **carriage outwards**.

Carriage inwards

When goods are purchased, the cost of carriage inwards may be included as part of the price, or, alternatively, the firm may have to pay for it separately. Suppose the firm was buying exactly the same goods from different suppliers. One supplier might sell them for £100 and not charge anything for carriage. Another supplier might sell the goods for £95, but you would have to pay £5 to a courier for carriage inwards, i.e. a total of £100. In both cases the goods cost £100. Therefore, to keep the cost of buying goods on the same basis carriage inwards is *always* added to the cost of purchases in the trading account.

Carriage outwards

Carriage outwards is the cost of delivering the goods to the firm's customers. It is an expense and not part of the selling price of the goods. Carriage outwards is always charged as an expense in the profit and loss account.

12.4 Dealing with carriage in the trading and profit and loss account

Suppose that in the illustration shown earlier of K Wade the goods had been bought for the same total figure of £27,350 but, in fact, £27,200 was the figure for purchases and £150 for carriage inwards. Let us also assume that part of the general expenses figure of £2,550, in Exhibit 10.1 was, in fact, carriage outward amounting to £400.

The trial balance would appear as in Exhibit 12.2.

Exhibit 12.2

K Wade		
Trial Balance as at 31 December 2009 (extract)		
	Dr	Cr
	£	£
Sales		40,000
Purchases	27,200	
Sales returns	350	
Purchases returns		200
Carriage inwards	150	
Carriage outwards	400	
General expenses	2,150	

The trading and profit and loss account would then be shown in Exhibit 12.3.

Exhibit 12.3

K Wade Trading and Profit and Loss Account for the year ended 31 December 2009	£	£
Sales		40,000
Less Sales returns		350
		39,650
Less Cost of goods sold		
Purchases	27,200	
Less Purchases returns	200	
	27,000	
Add Carriage inwards	150	27,150
Gross profit		12,500
Less Expenses:		
General expenses	2,150	
Carriage outwards	400	2,550
Net profit		9,950

It can be seen that the three versions of K Wade's trial balance have all been concerned with the same overall amount of goods bought and sold by the business, at the same overall prices. Therefore, in each case, the same gross profit of £12,500 is shown. The net profit of £9,950 also remains the same.

Before you proceed further you are advised to attempt Exercises 12.1 and 12.2X.

12.5 The second year of a business

Following on from Exhibit 11.2 in the previous chapter, we assume that B Swift carries on his business for another year. He then extracts a trial balance as on 31 December 2010 as shown as Exhibit 12.4. Closing stock as at that date was valued at £5,500.

Exhibit 12.4

B Swift Trial Balance as at 31 December 2010	Dr £	Cr £
Sales		67,000
Purchases	42,600	
Electricity	1,900	
Rent	2,400	
Wages: store assistant	5,200	
General expenses	700	
Carriage outwards	1,100	
Buildings	20,000	
Fixtures and fittings	7,500	
Debtors	12,000	
Creditors		9,000
Bank	1,200	
Cash	400	
Loan from J Marsh		10,000
Drawings	9,000	
Capital		21,000
Stock (at 31 December 2009)	3,000	
	107,000	107,000

Adjustments needed for stock

So far we have prepared the accounts for new businesses only. When a business starts it has no stock brought forward. B Swift started his new business on 1 January 2009 so his first year of trading ended on 31 December 2009 when he had a closing stock of £3,000. Therefore, when preparing his trading and profit and loss account for that year we are only concerned with the closing stock figure of £3,000. When we prepare the trading and profit and loss account for the second year we can see the difference.

In the trading and profit and loss account for the first year of trading, i.e. the year ended 31 December 2009, only one stock figure appears; that is the closing stock of £3,000. This figure of closing stock for the year ended 31 December 2009 becomes the opening stock for the second year of trading and will be entered into the trading account in Swift's second year of trading. Therefore, both opening and closing stock figures are shown in the trading and profit and loss account for the year ended 31 December 2010.

The stock figure shown in the trial balance given in Exhibit 12.4 is that brought forward from the previous year on 31 December 2009; it is, therefore, the opening stock. The closing stock at 31 December 2010 can only be found by stocktaking, assume that it amounts to £5,500.

The opening and closing stock account figures for Swift for the two years can now be summarised as follows:

Trading Account for period ⟶	Year to 31 December 2009	Year to 31 December 2010
Opening stock 1.1.2009	None	
Closing stock 31.12.2009	£3,000	
Opening stock 1.1.2010		£3,000
Closing stock 31.12.2010		£5,500

Double entry for stock

To enable you to understand the double entry aspect of stock, both the stock account and the trading account for B Swift for the year ended 31 December 2010 are shown below:

Dr		Stock Account		Cr
2009	£	2009		£
Dec 31 Trading a/c	3,000	Dec 31 Balance c/d		3,000
2010		2010		
Jan 1 Balance b/d	3,000	Dec 31 Trading a/c (Opening stock)		3,000
Dec 31 Trading a/c (Closing stock)	5,500	Dec 31 Balance c/d		5,500
	8,500			8,500

B Swift
Trading and Profit and Loss Account for the year ended 31 December 2010

	£		£
Opening stock	3,000	Sales	67,000
Purchases	42,600	Closing stock	5,500
Gross profit c/d	26,900		
	72,500		72,500

The stock at 31 December 2010 is £5,500 and had not been entered into the accounts previously. The entries above show how this has been recorded using double entry:

Debit: stock account £5,500
Credit: trading account £5,500.

Calculation of cost of goods sold

Let us now calculate the cost of goods sold for B Swift for the year ended 31 December 2010:

	£
Stock of goods at start of the year	3,000
Add Purchases	42,600
Total goods available for sale	45,600
Less What remains at the end of the year:	
(i.e. Closing stock)	5,500
Therefore the cost of goods that have been sold	40,100

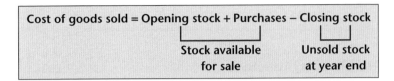

Cost of goods sold = Opening stock + Purchases – Closing stock

Stock available for sale

Unsold stock at year end

The gross profit can now be found by taking into consideration the effect the closing stock has on the gross profit. Remember that sales less cost of goods sold equals gross profit therefore:

	£
Sales	67,000
Less Cost of goods sold (see above)	40,100
Gross profit	26,900

Now the trading and profit and loss account and balance sheet can be drawn up as shown in Exhibits 12.5 and 12.6.

Exhibit 12.5

B Swift Trading and Profit and Loss Account for the year ended 31 December 2010		
	£	£
Sales		67,000
Less Cost of goods sold		
Opening stock	3,000	
Add Purchases	42,600	
	45,600	
Less Closing stock	5,500	
		40,100
Gross profit		26,900
Less Expenses		
Wages	5,200	
Carriage outwards	1,100	
Electricity	1,900	
Rent	2,400	
General expenses	700	
		11,300
Net profit		15,600

Exhibit 12.6

B Swift Balance Sheet as at 31 December 2010	£	£
Fixed assets		
Buildings		20,000
Fixtures and fittings		7,500
		27,500
Current assets		
Stock	5,500	
Debtors	12,000	
Cash at bank	1,200	
Cash in hand	400	
	19,100	
Less Current liabilities		
Creditors	9,000	
Net current assets		10,100
		37,600
Long-term liabilities		
Loan from J Marsh		10,000
Net assets		27,600
Financed by		
Capital account		
Balance at 1 January 2009		21,000
Add Net profit for the year		15,600
		36,600
Less Drawings		9,000
		27,600

12.6 Financial statements

The term **financial statements** is often used to mean collectively the trading and profit and loss account and the balance sheet which are produced at the end of a trading period. They used to be referred to as **final accounts** but this term can be quite misleading since none of the financial statements are really 'accounts' in the book-keeping sense. Many people do, however, still refer to them as the 'final accounts' or just simply 'the accounts' of a business.

12.7 Other expenses in the trading account

The costs of putting goods into a saleable condition should be charged in the trading account. In the case of a trader these are relatively few. An example might be a trader who sells clocks packed in boxes. If he bought the clocks from one source and the boxes from another source, both of these items would be charged in the trading account as purchases. In addition, if a person is paid wages to pack the clocks, then such wages would be charged in the trading account. The wages of shop assistants who sold the clocks would be charged in the profit and loss account. The wages of the person packing the clocks would be the only wages in this instance concerned with 'putting the goods into a saleable condition'.

For goods imported from abroad it is usual to find that the costs of import duty, marine insurance and freight charges are also treated as part of the cost of goods sold and are, therefore, debited to the trading account.

12.8 Losses incurred by a business

So far, we have looked at the situation in which both a gross profit and a net profit have been made by a business. This will not always be the case in every business. For all kinds of reasons, such as poor trading conditions, bad management, or unexpected increases in expenses, the business may trade at a loss for a given period.

We will look at two cases, A Barnes, who made a gross profit but a **net loss** for the year, and K Jackson, who made both a gross loss and a net loss. The details for the trading and profit and loss accounts for the year ended 31 December 2009 for Barnes and Jackson are as follows:

	A Barnes	K Jackson
	£	£
Opening stock 1 January 2009	3,500	9,200
Sales	21,000	33,000
Purchases	15,000	29,800
Closing stock 31 December 2009	2,200	4,800
Other expenses	6,300	3,900

The trading and profit and loss accounts for each business can now be prepared, see Exhibits 12.7 and 12.8.

Exhibit 12.7

A Barnes
Trading and Profit and Loss Account
for the year ended 31 December 2009

	£	£
Sales		21,000
Less Cost of goods sold		
Opening stock	3,500	
Add Purchases	15,000	
	18,500	
Less Closing stock	2,200	16,300
Gross profit		4,700
Less Other expenses		6,300
Net loss		1,600

In the above example of A Barnes a gross profit of £4,700 was made but since expenses of £6,300 were greater than that the final result is a net loss of £1,600.

Exhibit 12.8

K Jackson
Trading and Profit and Loss Account
for the year ended 31 December 2009

	£	£
Sales		33,000
Less Cost of goods sold		
Opening stock	9,200	
Add Purchases	29,800	
	39,000	
Less Closing stock	4,800	34,200
Gross loss		1,200
Add Other expenses		3,900
Net loss		5,100

In the above example of K Jackson a gross loss of £1,200 occurred since the cost of goods sold amounted to £34,200 while sales were only £33,000. Added to this gross loss of £1,200 were the expenses of £3,900 for the period and a resultant net loss of £5,100.

Recording losses in the capital account

If a net loss occurs then it will be recorded in the owner's capital account as follows:

Debit: capital account
Credit: profit and loss account.

12.9 Step-by-step guide to preparing financial statements (preliminary level)

Many students have difficulty in the preparation of the financial statements and in remembering the layout. The following step-by-step guide should help you in their preparation:

Preparing the financial statements

1 Before starting the exercise, rule lines connecting each item. This avoids selecting a wrong figure that is easily done under the stress of an examination.
2 Decide which section of the financial statement each item should be entered *before* you start, i.e. trading account, profit and loss account section or the balance sheet. On the left-hand side of the trial balance use the following abbreviations to identify where each item should be entered:
   ● T for trading account
   ● P/L for profit and loss account
   ● BS for the balance sheet.

3 An *almost* inviolable rule:
- Each item displayed in the trial balance must only be entered *once* in the final accounts.
- Any item below a trial balance exercise should be dealt with *twice* (i.e. in the exercises following notice the closing stock figure is shown under the totals of the trial balance).

Dealing with adjustments in financial statements

1 **Sales returns** and **purchases returns:**
   (a) sales returns – deduct from sales in the trading account
   (b) purchases returns – deduct from purchases in the trading account.
2 **Carriage inwards** and **carriage outwards:**
   (a) carriage inwards – add to purchases in the trading account
   (b) carriage outwards – charge as an expense in the profit and loss account.

Note: In Appendix B you will find a model layout of the trading and profit and loss account and balance sheet of a sole trader. Further step-by-step instructions in the preparation of the financial statements are also shown in Chapter 29.

Chapter summary

- The sales returns should always be deducted from the sales and the purchases returns deducted from the purchases; both are shown in the trading account.
- The name 'carriage' means the cost of transport.
- Carriage inwards is the cost of transporting the goods purchased 'into' the firm and, as such, is always *added* to the cost of purchases in the trading account.
- Carriage outwards is the cost of delivering the goods sold to the customers and is shown as an expense in the profit and loss account.
- When a new business first starts it has no opening stock; however, at the end of the first year of trading stocktaking is carried out to ascertain the amount of stock unsold, the closing stock.
- The closing stock of one year becomes the opening stock of the next year.
- A stock account is updated to record the closing stock figure and to carry forward the balance from one period to the next.
- When preparing a trading account for the first year of business only the closing stock figure is shown since there is no opening stock.
- In the second year of business both the opening and closing stock figures are shown in the trading account.
- The calculation of the figure for *cost of goods sold* is shown which appears under this heading in the trading account.
- The preparation of the trading and profit and loss account is shown including adjustments for sales returns, purchases returns, carriage inwards, and both opening and closing stocks in the trading account. Carriage outwards is shown as an expense in the profit and loss account.

- A balance sheet is shown indicating the entry of the closing stock figure under the 'current asset' section.
- Any expenses incurred with getting the goods into a saleable condition are charged in the trading account.
- How to prepare a trading and profit and loss account if either a gross loss or net loss occurs.

EXERCISES

12.1 From the following details, prepare the trading account for the year ended 31 December 2009 for T Clarke.

		£
Carriage inwards		670
Sales		38,742
Purchases		26,409
Stocks of goods:	1 January 2009	6,924
	31 December 2009	7,489

12.2X The following details for the year ended 31 March 2008 are available. Prepare the trading account for that year for M Parkin.

		£
Stocks:	31 March 2007	16,492
	31 March 2008	18,504
Purchases		36,905
Carriage inwards		1,122
Sales		54,600

12.3 Prepare the trading and profit and loss account for the year ended 31 December 2009, in respect of T Mann, from the following details:

		£
Sales returns		490
Purchases returns		560
Purchases		31,000
Sales		52,790
Stocks of goods:	1 January 2009	5,690
	31 December 2009	4,230
Carriage inwards		1,700
Salaries and wages		5,010
Rent		1,460
Motor expenses		3,120
General expenses		420
Carriage outwards		790

12.4X A trading and profit and loss account for the year ended 31 December 2009 is to be prepared for K Lake from the following:

		£
Carriage outwards		490
Carriage inwards		210
Sales returns		1,500
Purchases returns		1,580
Salaries and wages		6,250
Rent		1,750
Sundry expenses		360
Sales		99,500
Purchases		64,570
Stocks of goods:	1 January 2009	18,280
	31 December 2009	17,360

12.5 From the following trial balance of Suzanne Curtis, draw up a trading and profit and loss account for the year ended 30 June 2009, and balance sheet as at that date.

	Dr	Cr
	£	£
Stock 1 July 2008	14,208	
Carriage outwards	1,200	
Carriage inwards	1,860	
Sales returns	1,230	
Purchases returns		1,932
Purchases	71,244	
Sales		111,600
Salaries and wages	23,172	
Rent and rates	1,824	
Insurance	468	
Motor expenses	2,656	
Telephone and internet	2,624	
Electricity	996	
General expenses	1,884	
Buildings	50,000	
Motor vehicles	10,800	
Fixtures and fittings	2,100	
Debtors	23,376	
Creditors		20,386
Cash at bank	2,892	
Drawings	7,200	
Capital		85,816
	219,734	219,734

Stock at 30 June 2009 was £17,700.

12.6X The trial balance shown below was extracted from the books of J Collins on 31 March 2009. Prepare the trading and profit and loss account for the year ended 31 March 2009 and a balance sheet as at that date using the trial balance and the note regarding stock.

J Collins
Trial Balance as at 31 March 2009

	Dr £	Cr £
Sales		74,400
Purchases	46,224	
Stock 1 April 2008	15,104	
Carriage outwards	1,304	
Carriage inwards	936	
Salaries and wages	11,788	
Printing and stationery	810	
Telephone	756	
Travel expenses	490	
Rent	1,824	
Rates	1,080	
Sundry expenses	2,808	
Computer equipment	9,600	
Fixtures and fittings	2,400	
Debtors	18,308	
Creditors		12,180
Cash at bank	15,504	
Cash in hand	480	
Drawings	8,540	
Capital		51,376
	137,956	137,956

Stock at 31 March 2009 was £19,992.

12.7X G Bowyer manufactures sportswear, and for the year ended 31 October 2009 his sales were £76,540. He also paid carriage outwards of £4,275 to transport the sportswear to customers.

The materials purchased in the year amounted to £33,325, with an additional amount paid for carriage inwards of £2,715. Bowyer had stock of £8,255 on 1 November 2008, and of £7,985 on 31 October 2009. He was owed £6,285 by customers, and owed £4,825 to suppliers on 31 October 2009. His bank balance was overdrawn by £3,335, and he had equipment valued at £11,125 and a van valued at £2,225 on that date.

His overheads for the year ended 31 October 2009 were:

	£
Rent and rates	6,000
Motor expenses	3,110
Salaries	7,450
Telephone	495
Insurance	500
General expenses	750

He drew £3,675 in the year to 31 October 2009 and had a balance brought forward on his capital account on 1 November 2008 of £5,485.

You are required to draw up, in the vertical format, the trading and profit and loss account for the year ended 31 October 2009, and a balance sheet for G Bowyer at that date.

12.8 The following is the trial balance of J Smailes as at 31 March 2009. Draw up a set of final accounts for the year ended 31 March 2009 in vertical format.

	Dr	Cr
	£	£
Stock 1 April 2008	18,160	
Sales		92,340
Purchases	69,185	
Carriage inwards	420	
Carriage outwards	1,570	
Purchases returns		640
Wages and salaries	10,240	
Rent and rates	3,015	
Communication expenses	624	
Commissions payable	216	
Insurance	405	
Sundry expenses	318	
Buildings	20,000	
Debtors	14,320	
Creditors		8,160
Fixtures	2,850	
Cash at bank	2,970	
Cash in hand	115	
Loan from K Ball		10,000
Drawings	7,620	
Capital		40,888
	152,028	152,028

Stock at 31 March 2009 was £22,390.

12.9X L Stokes drew up the following trial balance as at 30 September 2009. You are required to draft trading and profit and loss accounts for the year to 30 September 2009 and a balance sheet as at that date in vertical format.

	Dr	Cr
	£	£
Loan from P Owens		5,000
Capital		25,955
Drawings	8,420	
Cash at bank	3,115	
Cash in hand	295	
Debtors	12,300	
Creditors		9,370
Stock 30 September 2008	23,910	
Motor van	4,100	
Office equipment	6,250	
Sales		130,900
Purchases	92,100	
Sales returns	550	
Carriage inwards	215	
Purchases returns		307
Carriage outwards	309	
Motor expenses	1,630	
Rent	2,970	
Telephone charges	405	
Wages and salaries	12,810	
Insurance	492	
Office expenses	1,377	
Sundry expenses	284	
	171,532	171,532

Stock at 30 September 2009 was £27,475.

CHAPTER 13

Accounting concepts, standards and policies

Learning objectives

After you have studied this chapter you should be able to:

- understand how the regulatory framework of accounting operates and provides 'rules' which are used in the preparation and presentation of financial statements
- understand why financial statements can be used for several different purposes
- define an accounting concept
- appreciate the fundamental and basic concepts of accounting
- distinguish between 'objectivity' and 'subjectivity'
- appreciate the development of accounting standards SSAPs and FRSs
- understand the Statement of Principles of Financial Reporting which sets out the principles required for the preparation and presentation of financial statements
- understand the importance of confidentiality.

13.1 Introduction

So far in this book we have dealt with recording transactions and Part 2 dealt with the preparation of the financial statements (final accounts) of a sole trader from a trial balance. There are, however, other issues to consider with the preparation of the financial statements which are known as accounting concepts or 'rules' of accounting.

These concepts or rules have evolved over the years for practical as much as theoretical reasons. As a consequence this has made the preparation of the financial statements more standardised enabling the information to be more easily understood and reliable, and to enable clearer comparisons between different businesses.

13.2 Definition of an accounting concept

A concept may be defined as an idea. Thus, an **accounting concept** is an assumption that underlies the preparation of the financial statements of the organisation. These are accounting procedures that have developed over the years to form the 'basic rules of accounting'.

13.3 Fundamental accounting concepts

The four important accounting concepts which are used in preparing periodic financial statements of a business are shown in Exhibit 13.1.

Exhibit 13.1

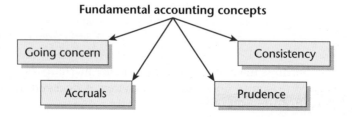

Going concern concept

The **going concern concept** implies that the business will continue to operate for the foreseeable future. In other words, it is assumed that the business will continue to trade for a long period of time and there are no plans to cease trading and/or liquidate the business.

Accruals concept (or matching concept)

The **accruals concept** says that net profit is the difference between revenues and expenses rather than the difference between cash received and cash paid.

$$\text{Revenues} - \text{Expenses} = \text{Net Profit}$$

Sales are **revenues** when the goods or services are sold and *not* when the money is received, which can be later in the accounting period. Purchases are **expenses** when goods are bought, *not* when they are paid for. As we shall see in Chapter 29, items such as rent, insurance and motor expenses are treated as expenses when they are incurred, not when they are paid for. Adjustments are made when preparing financial statements for expenses owing and those paid in advance (prepayments). Other adjustments that have to be made include adjusting for depreciation of fixed assets and for probable bad debts, both of which will be discussed later.

Identifying the expenses used up to obtain the revenues is referred to as *matching* expenses against revenues, which is why this concept is also called the **matching concept**.

By showing the actual expenses *incurred* in a period matched against revenues *earned* in the same period, a correct figure of net profit will be shown in the profit and loss account.

Consistency concept

The **consistency concept** requires that the same treatment be applied when dealing with similar items not only in one period but in all subsequent periods. The concept states that when a business had adopted a method for the accounting treatment of an item it should treat all similar items that follow in the same way when preparing the financial statements. Examples of when the consistency concept is used include:

- methods of depreciation (see Chapter 26)
- stock valuation (see later in this chapter and Chapter 31).

This concept is important since it assists in analysis of financial information and decision making, and it is vital that the organisation uses the same accounting principles each year. If the organisation was constantly changing its methods then this would result in misleading profits being calculated and inaccurate analyses, hence the reason why the convention of consistency is used. However, this does not mean that the business must always use a particular method; it may make changes provided it has good reason to do so and each change is declared in the notes to the financial statements.

Prudence concept

When preparing financial statements accountants often have to use their judgement in determining the valuation of a particular asset or perhaps deciding whether an outstanding debt will ever be paid. It is the accountant's duty and responsibility to ensure that the financial statements are prepared as accurately as possible in disclosing the appropriate facts about a business. Therefore, the accountant should ensure that assets are not overvalued and similarly all liabilities should be identified. In other words, the accountant should display a certain amount of caution when forecasting a business's net profit or when valuing assets for balance sheet purposes.

The **prudence concept** means that accountants will take the figure that will understate rather than overstate the profit. They must also ensure that all losses are recorded in the books but equally so ensure that profits are not anticipated by recording them before they have been gained.

The term '**conservatism**' was widely used to describe this concept until it was generally replaced by 'prudence'. (Refer also to Section 13.9 FRS 18.)

13.4   Other accounting concepts

In addition to the fundamental accounting concepts there are several other concepts and conventions which are followed when preparing the financial statements of a business.

Business entity concept

The **business entity concept** implies that the affairs of a business are to be treated as being quite separate from the personal activities of the owner(s) of the business. In other words, only the activities of the business are recorded and reported in the firm's financial statements. Any transactions involving the owner(s) are kept separate and are excluded.

The only time that the personal resources of the owner(s) affect the business's accounting records is when they introduce new capital into the business or take drawings.

Realisation concept

This accounting concept considers that profit should only be included in the profit and loss account when it is reasonably certain that it has been earned. Profit is normally said to be earned when:

- goods or services are provided to the buyer, and
- the buyer incurs liability for them.

This concept of profit is known as the **realisation concept**. Note that it is *not*:

- when the order is received, or
- when the customer pays for the goods.

Historical cost concept

The assets of the business are recorded in the accounting records at cost price, i.e. the actual price paid for them, and this is known as the **historical cost concept**. For example, if a building cost £100,000 it will appear in the balance sheet at that value.

The advantage of using the cost method of valuation is that the assets can be easily verified since there will be a source document (invoice) which can be used to check the amount entered in the books of account.

Money measurement concept

This concept states that only transactions and activities that can be measured in terms of money and whose monetary value can be assessed with reasonable objectivity will be entered into the accounting records.

Materiality concept

This concept applies when the value of an item is relatively insignificant and as such does not warrant separate recording, for example, the purchase of a box of paper clips, calculator or small clock for the office. Such small expenditures are regarded as 'not material' and their purchase would not be recorded in separate expense accounts but grouped together in a sundry or general expense account.

Dual aspect concept

The concept whereby all transactions affect two aspects and as such affect two double entry accounts, one on the debit side and one on the credit side. The two aspects are always equal to each other. In other words:

$$\text{Assets} = \text{Capital} + \text{Liabilities}$$

As mentioned above double entry is the name given to the method of recording the transactions under the **dual aspect concept**.

13.5 Objectivity and subjectivity

It is especially important in accounting that the procedures or methods used are agreed by everyone, this approach is said to be *objective*. If, however, the owner(s) wish to use their own method or procedure that other people may not agree to, then this approach would be *subjective*.

Financial accounting seeks **objectivity** (rather than **subjectivity**) and must have rules which lay down the way in which the activities of the business are recorded. As we have already seen from the above these rules are known as **accounting concepts**.

13.6 Accounting policies

These constitute the specific accounting bases which have been used consistently by a business and were appropriate in the preparation of the financial statements. An example would be the method of depreciation used, such as the straight line method, to depreciate a fixed asset (see later chapters on depreciation). If this method of depreciation was used for many years then this would become the business's accounting policy for depreciation.

13.7 Accounting standards

At one time there were quite wide differences in the ways that accountants calculated profits, but in the late 1960s a number of high profile cases in the UK led to a widespread outcry against the lack of uniformity in financial reporting. Therefore, the past 40 years or so have seen many changes and developments in the financial reporting system.

Initially the Accounting Standards Committee (ASC) was formed by the UK accounting bodies in 1971 and this committee was responsible for issuing many Statements of Standard Accounting Practice (SSAPs) which accountants and auditors were expected to comply with. This body was replaced with the Accounting Standards Board (ASB) in 1990 and while this body took over the practices still in use at the time (SSAPs) they developed further standards known as Financial Reporting Standards (FRSs). More recently we have seen the introduction of Statement of Principles for Financial Reporting (SOP) which aims to set out the principles to be followed when preparing the financial statements.

13.8 Statement of Principles for Financial Reporting

The Statement of Principles for Financial Reporting was developed by the ASB in 1999 and recently updated in 2007. The Statement's objectives are used to form the basis on which financial statements are prepared and presented. It aims to provide a logical and consistent form of reference to be used by the ASB in the development of financial reporting standards. The Statement of Principles is not, however, an accounting standard, instead it is to be used as an aid to the standard setting process.

The eight key areas identified in the Statement of Principles of Financial Reporting are as follows:

1 The objective of financial statements
2 The reporting entity
3 The qualitative characteristics of financial information
4 The elements of financial statements
5 Recognition in financial statements
6 Measurement in financial statements
7 Presentation of financial information
8 Accounting for interests in other entities.

Each of the above areas is dealt with fully in the Statement of Principles document published by the ASB, however, at this stage in your studies it is only necessary to note its contents. You will cover the Statement of Principles in greater detail later on in your studies.

13.9 Examples of accounting standards

As mentioned in Section 13.7 the ASC and ASB were responsible for the introduction of:

● Statements of Standard Accounting Practice (SSAPs)
● Financial Reporting Standards (FRSs)
● The Statement of Principles for Financial Reporting (SOP).

All accountants are expected to adhere to the contents of SSAPs, FRSs and SOP when preparing financial statements: they are in effect the 'rules' by which accountants must conform. We will now look at some of the accounting standards you will be required to be familiar with at this stage of your studies.

SSAP 5 Accounting for Value Added Tax

This accounting standard was first issued in 1974 prior to the introduction of Value Added Tax, usually abbreviated to VAT. VAT is a tax charged on the supply of most goods and services in the UK. It is collected by traders and borne by the final consumer. Once the tax is collected it is paid, at regular intervals, to HM Revenue & Customs which is responsible for the administration of VAT.

When a business has a turnover (sales) over a certain threshold then it must register for VAT. However, not all business have to be registered since some may be exempt from registration, such as small businesses whose turnover is below the threshold for VAT registration. Some goods and services are not taxable, for example postal services. All businesses who are registered for VAT must keep proper accounting records of all their business transactions. (This topic is covered in greater depth in Chapter 18.)

SSAP 9 Stocks and long-term contracts

Since there are many different types of businesses and conditions within them there simply cannot be one system of valuation for stocks and work-in-progress. This accounting standard sets out broad guidelines to be followed when placing a valuation on stock. The standard states: *'that stock should be valued at the lower of cost or net realisable value'*.

It also states that *'profit should not'*, except in the case of long-term contracts such as a large construction project, be recognised in advance, but immediate account should be made of anticipated losses.

In the Balance Sheet stock should be classified into the different types of stocks held. For example in manufacturing accounts (to be covered later in Chapter 38) there are usually three types of stock as follows:

- stock of raw materials
- stock of work-in-progress
- stock of finished goods.

Net realisable value consists of the expected selling price *less* any expenses necessary to sell the product. This may be below cost because of stock deterioration, obsolescence and similar factors.

SSAP 9 defines *'cost'* as being:

That expenditure which has been incurred in the normal course of the business in bringing the product or service to its present location and condition. This expenditure should include, in addition to the costs of purchase, such costs of conversion as are appropriate to that location and condition.

Cost of purchase comprises the purchase price including import duties, transport and handling costs and any other directly attributable costs, less trade discounts, rebates and subsidies.

Cost of conversion comprises:

- costs which are specifically attributable to units of production, i.e. direct labour, direct expenses and subcontracted work
- production overheads based on the normal level of activity, taking one year with another, including fixed production overheads. (Selling and distribution costs should not, however, be included in these costs.)
- other overheads, if any, attributable in the particular circumstances of the business to bring the product or service to its present location and condition.

(Stock valuation is covered more fully in Chapter 31.)

FRS 15: Tangible fixed assets

This accounting standard states that all fixed assets that have a useful and economic life should be depreciated with one exception, freehold land. Freehold land is not normally depreciated since land lasts for ever unless it is subject to depletion or loss of value for reasons which may be applicable in certain circumstances, such as land erosion, extraction of minerals, dumping of toxic wastes, etc.

'FRS 15: Tangible fixed assets' replaced 'SSAP 12: Accounting for depreciation' in 1999 and prior to that freehold land and buildings were not subject to depreciation since it was argued that property values tended to rise rather than fall. With the introduction of SSAP 12 and subsequently FRS 15 it became necessary to charge depreciation on the useful life of property/buildings but not, as stated above, freehold land. The standard also stated that the cost of freehold land and buildings be separated to allow the building element to be depreciated.

Depreciation should be applied to all fixed assets that have a useful economic life. It should be provided by allocating the cost of the use of the fixed asset as an expense and charged to the profit and loss account during the particular accounting period. There are various methods of depreciation which can be applied but the method selected should be that which produces the most appropriate allocation of depreciation in relation to the benefit received in the accounting period. Depreciation is usually calculated on the value of the assets as shown in the balance sheet.

(This topic is covered more fully in Chapters 26 and 27.)

FRS 18 Accounting policies

'SSAP 2: Disclosure of accounting policies' was the first UK accounting standard that recognised that users of financial statements who wished to analyse and evaluate final accounts could not do this effectively unless they knew which method(s) and techniques had been used in their preparation. SSAP 2 was issued to help to bring about an improvement in the quality of financial reporting and it dealt with four of the fundamental accounting concepts, namely:

● going concern
● accruals
● consistency
● prudence.

These fundamental accounting concepts were discussed in Section 13.3 above.

In 2000, 'SSAP 2: Disclosure of accounting policies' was replaced by 'FRS 18: Accounting policies'. FRS 18 concentrates upon accounting policies and looks at the various methods and techniques used in the preparation of financial statements. The accounting policies set out the method in which the various accounting transactions are recorded and subsequently reflected in the financial statements of the business. The objective of the financial statement is always 'to give a true and fair view' and be consistent with accounting standards which should be reviewed regularly to ensure that those applied are still appropriate.

When a business selects an accounting policy it should ensure that it fits within the framework of the four 'objectives':

1 Relevance – the financial statements should provide those analysing and evaluating them sufficient information to enable them to make business decisions.
2 Reliability – such information must be reliable, accurate and neutral.
3 Comparability – users must be able to compare one year's statements with previous years' financial statements.
4 Understandability – financial statements must be able to be understood by users with accounting and business knowledge.

Examples of accounting policies

- Which method of depreciation to use, i.e. straight line or reducing balance method (see Chapters 26 and 27).
- The basis for valuing the closing stock of a business, i.e. LIFO (last in first out), FIFO (first in first out) or AVCO (average cost) – refer to Chapter 31.

13.10 Confidentiality

Although confidentiality is not a concept of accounting, employees who work within financial departments of an organisation and have access to its financial information should recognise that this information is confidential. They should not disclose sensitive information to anyone within the organisation except to those authorised to receive it.

Such information should only be disclosed 'outside' the organisation to bodies such as HM Revenue and Customs as this is required by legislation.

The organisation's auditors/accountants will also require access to the financial records to enable the preparation of the business's financial statements.

Chapter summary

- Financial statements are prepared for the use of the owner(s) of the business and other stakeholders.
- An 'accounting concept' is an accounting procedure developed over the years to form the 'basic rules of accounting'.
- Appreciate that the need for general agreement on accounting issues has led to the development of concepts and conventions.
- The fundamental accounting concepts are: going concern, accruals, consistency and prudence. In addition there are many other concepts pertinent to organisations when preparing their financial statements.
- Objectivity is using a method that everyone can agree to whereas subjectivity is using a method that other people may not agree to, possibly derived from one's own personal preferences.
- Accounting policies are specific accounting bases selected and consistently used by an organisation.
- The development of accounting standards SSAPs and FRSs.
- Statement of Principles for Financial Reporting sets out the principles required in the preparation and presentation of financial statements.
- 'SSAP 5 Accounting for VAT' outlines the procedures for the collection and payment of value added tax.
- 'SSAP 9 Stocks and long-term contracts' states that stock must be valued at the lower of cost or net realisable value.
- 'FRS 15 Tangible fixed assets' deals with the depreciation charged on fixed assets. One exception to this rule is that of freehold land which does not depreciate except in certain circumstances such as in mining.

- 'FRS 18 Accounting policies' outlines the underlying procedures for the preparation and presentation of the financial statements of an organisation.
- Appreciate the importance of confidentiality.

EXERCISES

13.1 Which accounting concept is used in each of the following accounting treatments? Explain.

(*a*) The cost of a tape dispenser has been charged to an expense account, although in fact it could still be in use in ten years' time.

(*b*) A sole proprietor has sold his private house, but has not recorded anything about it in the business records.

(*c*) A debt has been written off as a bad debt even though there is still a chance that the debtor eventually may be able to pay it.

(*d*) A machine has been bought for an exceedingly low figure, and it has been entered in the asset account at that figure even though it is worth more.

(*e*) An expert says that the value of the management team to the company is worth well over a million pounds, yet nothing is entered for it in the books.

(*f*) A motor van broke down in December 2008. The repair bill for it was not paid until 2008 yet it has been treated as a 2008 expense.

(*g*) A customer saw a carpet in 2008 and said he might well buy it. He phoned in 2008 and asked for the carpet to be delivered. The item was not treated as a sale in 2007 but was treated as a sale in 2009.

(*b*) The final day of the financial year saw the passing of a law that would render trading in our sort of goods illegal, and the business will have to close. The accountant says that our stock figure cannot be shown at cost in the balance sheet.

(*i*) We have been told that we cannot show our asset of motor cars at cost in one year and at cost plus the price increase the next year when the manufacturer increases prices of all cars, which also includes our unsold stock.

(*j*) We have shown all items of machinery costing less than £100 as machinery operating expenses.

13.2X When preparing the final accounts of your company, name the accounting concepts you should follow to deal with each of the following:

(*a*) Electricity consumed during the accounting period is still unpaid at the year end.

(*b*) The owner of the company has invested her private assets in the company.

(*c*) A debtor who owes the company a large amount has been declared bankrupt, and the outstanding amount due to the company is now considered to be irrecoverable.

(*d*) The company has suffered substantial losses in the past few years, and it is extremely uncertain whether the company can continue to operate next year.

13.3X Accounting concepts and conventions are used in preparing financial statements of a business.

(*a*) Briefly explain any three of the following concepts:
   (i)   Going concern
   (ii) Accruals
   (iii) Consistency
   (iv) Prudence.

(*b*) Objectivity is important in analysing and preparing accounting information. Explain the term 'objectivity', giving an example as to how it might be applied.

13.4 Explain briefly what you understand by the 'historical cost concept'. Give an advantage in using the cost method of valuation.

13.5 As an accounts clerk you have been checking the aged debtor list and have noticed that an account due from the Priory Paper Co for £187.00 has been outstanding for over six months. No response is gained from enquiries by telephone or letter and a visit is made to Priory's last known address by one of your sales representatives. She discovers that the premises are now occupied by a printing company whose owner tells her that the owner of Priory Paper Co is rumoured to have gone abroad.

Which accounting concept would you follow and what action would you recommend your company to take in dealing with this matter?

13.6X Describe how stock should be valued using the accounting standard 'SSAP 9 Stocks and long-term contracts'.

13.7 'FRS 18 Accounting policies' is concerned with the preparation and presentation of financial statements. Name the four 'objectives' which the accounting standard recommends organisations should consider when selecting accounting policies.

13.8 James works in the payroll department of a printing company. While having lunch a colleague asks him if he could let him know how much one of the managers earns. James is uncertain how to respond to his colleague's request and asks you as, Payroll Manager, what he should do. Draft an email to James advising him what to do in these circumstances.

PART 3

Books of original entry

This part is concerned with the books and journals into which transactions are first entered, together with chapters on business banking and VAT.

CHAPTER 14

Business documentation

Learning objectives

After you have studied this chapter you should be able to:

- understand the various documentation used in the buying and selling process
- follow the purchasing process from the quotation to the purchase order and subsequently the advice note, delivery note and invoice
- appreciate the documents used when goods or services are not satisfactory, i.e. the returns notes and credit notes
- understand the need for the supplier to send a statement of account to the purchaser at the end of the month
- appreciate the use of a remittance advice which is usually provided by the purchaser of the goods or services.

14.1 Introduction

All businesses and organisations are involved in trading, i.e. the buying and selling of goods and/or services in order to make a profit. The financial transaction of buying and selling involves some very important documents which are used by both the buyer and the seller. The documents have been in general use for many years and are part of an established procedure. Their proper use enables trading to proceed smoothly and in the event of a dispute between a buyer and a seller, the matter can normally be settled quickly. Since both parties use the same documents they will be dealt with in the sequence normally found in the trading activity.

A diagram of the flow of documents is shown in Exhibit 14.1.

Exhibit 14.1 The trading activity

Action by seller (supplier)	THE FLOW OF DOCUMENTS	
	Sequence	Action by buyer (purchaser)
Sends	QUOTATION →	Receives
Receives	← PURCHASE ORDER	Sends
Sends	ADVICE NOTE →	Receives
Sends	DELIVERY NOTE → (with goods)	Receives and raises goods received note
Sends	INVOICE →	Receives
Receives and raises goods received note	← RETURNS NOTE* (if goods are faulty, etc.)	Sends
Sends after approval to give credit	CREDIT NOTE* →	Receives
Sends	STATEMENT OF ACCOUNT →	Receives
Receives	← REMITTANCE ADVICE (payment)	Sends

* Both the returns note and the credit note would only be used if there was some problem with the goods supplied.

14.2 Quotation

At the request of a prospective purchaser a company will issue a **quotation** (an offer to supply goods or services). The quotation will normally be in the form of a formal document detailing what is to be supplied, when, where and the price. It will also state the terms, usually known as the conditions of sale, under which the company is prepared to supply the goods or services. Some suppliers may have a standard range of products to offer and choose to issue a catalogue as the quotation from which purchasers may order goods.

The quotation is a very important document since it could well be the starting point for a contract between the supplier and the purchaser. On receiving the quotation the purchaser should check it to ensure it meets the full requirements. Only then should the purchaser consider raising a purchase order.

An example of a quotation is shown in Exhibit 14.2.

Exhibit 14.2 Quotation

Morridge Products Ltd
Moor Top Lane
Leek

Telephone: 01538 703101
Fax: 01538 703203
VAT Reg No: 761 9849 16

QUOTATION

Stoke Engineering Co Ltd   Date: 4 March 2009
Blythe End Works   Our Ref: 2432
Stoke-on-Trent

Thank you for your enquiry of 24 Feb 2009. We are pleased to quote for the supply of the following:

Quantity	Description	Part No	Price each
120	Suspension arm	B402	£38.50
60	Axle shaft	B424	£27.65
120	Backplate	B432	£43.20

Delivery: 6 weeks from receipt of your order.
Terms: Strictly net with payment within 30 days from date of invoice.
VAT: Prices quoted are exclusive of VAT.
Prices: Include delivery to your works in one consignment.

Signed   *P T Thompson*
         Sales Manager

14.3 Purchase order

When a business or organisation decides to buy goods or engage the services of another company it usually issues a **purchase order**.

This document contains the following information:

- name and address of supplier
- purchase order number
- date of order
- details of the goods or services ordered including part numbers or catalogue references
- quantity required
- delivery date
- authorised signature of a senior member of the company such as the buyer.

It is normally raised by the customer's purchasing office and then sent to the supplier. Once it has been accepted by the supplier a formal contract will exist between the two parties.

An example of a purchase order is shown in Exhibit 14.3.

Exhibit 14.3 **Purchase order**

PURCHASE ORDER		

Stoke Engineering Co Ltd
Blythe End Works
Stoke-on-Trent

Telephone: 01782 923116   Order No: ST 6032
Fax: 01782 923431   Date: 12 March 2009
VAT Reg No: 964 7688 21

Morridge Products Ltd
Moor Top Lane
Leek

Please supply the following:

120 off	Suspension arm	Part No B402	£38.50 each
60 off	Axle shaft	Part No B424	£27.65 each
120 off	Backplate	Part No B432	£43.20 each

Delivery required: by end of May 2009 to our works.

If there are any queries regarding this order please contact the undersigned immediately.

Signed   *A Barton*
              Buyer

14.4 Advice note

An **advice note** is sent to the customer before the goods are despatched. This means that the customer will know that the goods are on the way and when they should arrive. If the goods do not arrive within a reasonable time then the customer will notify the supplier so that enquiries may be made with the carrier to establish what has happened to the goods.

The advice note is usually raised as part of a pack of documents including the delivery note and the invoice since the information on each document is essentially the same. Only the invoice will have the price details and total amount due. The delivery note is explained in Section 14.5 and the invoice in Section 14.6.

An advice note is shown in Exhibit 14.4.

Exhibit 14.4 Advice note

Morridge Products Ltd
Moor Top Lane
Leek

Telephone: 01538 703101
Fax: 01538 703203
VAT Reg No: 761 9849 16

Stoke Engineering Co Ltd   Date: 2 May 2009
Blythe End Works   Our Ref: 2432
Stoke-on-Trent

Your Order No: ST 6032

ADVICE NOTE

We have today despatched the items shown below by *Coopers Transport*

Quantity	Description	Part No
120	Suspension arm	B402
60	Axle shaft	B424
120	Backplate	B432

Please advise us if the goods have not been received within *3 days*.

14.5 Delivery note

When the company supplying the goods is ready to despatch them to the purchaser they prepare a **delivery note** (sometimes called a despatch note). As mentioned in Section 14.4 this document is normally prepared at the same time as the invoice, usually by using a suitable accounting software package. The document contains the following information:

- name and address of purchaser
- date and number of customer's purchase order
- details of goods despatched including their description and part number or catalogue reference
- quantity being supplied
- delivery address and any relevant instructions, i.e. must be delivered between 8 a.m. and 6 p.m.

Price details are not shown on this document. When a supplier uses its own transport or the services of a carrier a copy of the delivery note will be signed by the receiving company and this note will be returned to the supplier. This copy will be safely filed as it may be needed as 'proof of delivery' of the goods should a dispute arise as to their safe receipt.

Exhibit 14.5 shows a delivery note.

Exhibit 14.5 Delivery note

Morridge Products Ltd
Moor Top Lane
Leek

Telephone: 01538 703101
Fax: 01538 703203
VAT Reg No: 761 9849 16

Stoke Engineering Co Ltd   Date: 2 May 2009
Blythe End Works   Our Ref: 2432
Stoke-on-Trent

Your Order No: ST 6032

DELIVERY NOTE

Please receive the following:

Quantity	Description	Part No
120	Suspension arm	B402
60	Axle shaft	B424
120	Backplate	B432

Would you please acknowledge receipt of the goods by signing this note and pass accompanying copy to the driver making the delivery.

Received by: *M Jordan*   Date: *4 May 2009*

14.6 Invoice

An invoice is a document prepared by the seller whenever it sells goods or provides services on credit. The invoice is usually numbered for easy identification and for filing in a suitable storage system. It contains the following information:

- seller's name and address
- seller's VAT registration number
- purchaser's name and address
- purchaser's order number and date
- date of delivery
- description of goods and services supplied including part number and catalogue reference
- quantity
- price per item
- VAT payable
- total amount due
- terms and conditions of sale.

From a book-keeper's point of view the invoice is one of the most important documents since details of the transaction need to be entered in the books of account of both the seller and the buyer. The following Chapters 15 and 16 deal with the entry of invoices.

Exhibit 14.6 shows an invoice.

Exhibit 14.6 Invoice

INVOICE
Morridge Products Ltd **Moor Top Lane** **Leek**
Telephone: 01538 703101 Fax: 01538 703203 VAT Reg No: 761 9849 16

Invoice to

Stoke Engineering Co Ltd   Invoice No: 5/232
Blythe End Works   Advice Note: 2432
Stoke-on-Trent

Your Order No: ST 6032   Date/Tax point: 2 May 2009

Quantity	Description	Part No	Price each £	Amount £
120	Suspension arm	B402	38.50	4,620.00
60	Axle shaft	B424	27.65	1,659.00
120	Backplate	B432	43.20	5,184.00
		Total		11,463.00
		VAT at $17\frac{1}{2}$%		2,006.03
		Amount due		13,469.03

Terms: Strictly net within 1 month
E&OE

14.7 Pro-forma invoice

In certain circumstances a **pro-forma invoice** is raised and sent to the purchaser who will then make payment before any goods or services are supplied. A supplier might take this action if a purchaser is unknown to the supplier, has not yet established creditworthiness or is known to the supplier as a late or inconsistent payer.

14.8 Returns note

In certain circumstances a purchaser needs to return goods to the supplier because they are damaged, faulty or perhaps not to the specification ordered. The goods will be returned to the supplier accompanied by a **returns note** or **sales returns** note which gives details of the goods being returned and the reason together with the details of the order number, date, etc. On receiving the returns note and goods the supplier will raise a goods received note which tells the departments concerned of the return of these goods. A senior member of staff will then have to decide whether or not it is appropriate to give credit for the returned goods.

Exhibit 14.7 shows a returns note.

Exhibit 14.7 Returns note

RETURNS NOTE	
Stoke Engineering Co Ltd	**Return Note No: 1186**
Blythe End Works	
Stoke-on-Trent	
Telephone: 01782 923116	
Fax: 01782 923431	
VAT Reg No: 964 7688 21	**Date:** 13 May 2009

Morridge Products Ltd
Moor Top Lane
Leek

We have today returned the following goods:

23 off Axle shaft, Part No B424

Returned as agreed between our Mr J Barton and your Mr A Lowe due to 50 mm diameter being oversize.

J Barton   Inspection Department

14.9 Credit note

Once the supplier has decided to give credit then a **credit note** will be raised for the value of the returned goods including the applicable amount of VAT. The note will then be sent to the customer.

A credit note is usually printed in red to distinguish it from an invoice and while it contains similar information to that found in an invoice some details will differ. For instance, the customer may only have returned a part of a consignment and this will need to be clearly identified on the credit note.

Again credit notes are important documents which need to be entered in the books of account as the amount owed by the buyer will be reduced by the amount of the credit note. Chapter 17 deals with the entry of credit notes.

Exhibit 14.8 illustrates a credit note which, as mentioned above, is usually printed in red.

Exhibit 14.8 Credit note

CREDIT NOTE				
Morridge Products Ltd				
Moor Top Lane				
Leek				
Telephone: 01538 703101				
Fax: 01538 703203				
VAT Reg No: 761 9849 16				

Stoke Engineering Co Ltd		Credit Note No: 532/00	
Blythe End Works		Our Invoice No: 5/232	
Stoke-on-Trent		Your Reference: 1186	
Your Order No: ST 6032		Date/Tax point: 20 May 2009	

Quantity	Description	Part No	Price each	Amount
23	Axle shaft	B424	£27.65	£635.95

Goods returned as faulty.

Total	£635.95
VAT at $17\frac{1}{2}$%	£111.29
Amount credited	£747.24

14.10 Statement of account

At the end of each month businesses send out a document known as a **statement of account**. This statement contains details of all the customer's transactions during the previous month, starting off with the opening balance outstanding from the previous month plus the amounts owing from the current month's invoices. Any amounts that are paid are deducted together with any credit note allowances. This gives the total amount outstanding which is then due for payment at the end of the month.

On receipt of the statement of account the customer should check the details with their own records to ensure that they agree with the statement. Provided the invoices listed on the statement have been approved for payment then arrangements will be made to pay the account. Chapter 17 covers the preparation of statements of account.

Exhibit 14.9 shows a statement of account.

Exhibit 14.9 Statement of account

STATEMENT OF ACCOUNT

Morridge Products Ltd
Moor Top Lane
Leek

Telephone: 01538 703101
Fax: 01538 703203
VAT Reg No: 761 9849 16

Stoke Engineering Co Ltd
Blythe End Works
Stoke-on-Trent

Statement date: 31 May 2009
Account number: 2432
Page number: 1

Date	Reference	Debit	Credit	Balance
		£	£	£
30/4/09	Balance from previous statement			931.28
2/5/09	Invoice No 5/232	13,469.03		14,400.31
7/5/09	Payment received		931.28	13,469.03
20/5/09	Credit note No 532/00		747.24	12,721.79
	Total outstanding			12,721.79

Terms: Strictly net 30 days from date of invoice
Payment due 30/6/09
E&OE

14.11 Remittance advice

When payment is made from one business to another it is important that the recipient of the money has details of the payment so that the money may be correctly allocated. Therefore, the business making the payment usually includes a **remittance advice**. This document is rather like a statement, and may in fact be prepared at the same time, in that it shows details of the business's most recent transactions and final balance outstanding which is represented by the accompanying cheque or advice if the payment is made by BACS (see Chapter 20).

If any invoice has not been paid for any reason it will be left outstanding and can then be queried. A remittance advice is shown in Exhibit 14.10.

Exhibit 14.10 Remittance advice

	REMITTANCE ADVICE			
Stoke Engineering Co Ltd **Blythe End Works** **Stoke-on-Trent**		Remittance advice: 6/962		
Telephone: 01782 923116 Fax: 01782 923431 VAT Reg No: 964 7688 21		Date: 28 June 2009		
Morridge Products Ltd Moor Top Lane Leek		Account No: 2432		
Date	*Invoice or credit note No*	*Invoice*	*Credit note*	*Payment*
2/5/2009 20/5/2009	5/232 532/00	13,469.03	747.24	13,469.03 (747.24)
			TOTAL PAYMENT	12,721.79

14.12 Goods received note (GRN)

When goods are received the purchaser will raise a **goods received note** (GRN) which details exactly what goods have been received. This note is raised as part of the purchaser's internal procedure and is used to advise various departments of their arrival. These departments will include:

- buying office – so that the progress of orders can be monitored
- materials office – so stock records can be updated
- accounts department – the invoice from the supplier will be checked with the GRN as proof of delivery before payment is authorised.

It is important to both the supplier and the purchaser that details on the purchase order, invoice and GRN are correct so as to avoid possible disputes which could result in delayed payment and the loss of goodwill.

If the supplier receives faulty goods back from the purchaser then they will also raise a GRN to inform all the departments concerned of the return of the goods.

A goods received note is shown as Exhibit 14.11.

Exhibit 14.11 Goods received note

Stoke Engineering Co Ltd				GRN No _____
Goods Received Note		Copies	Accounts Dept ———— White	
			Purchasing Dept ———— Pink	
O/No _____			Material control ———— Green	
			Inspection ————— Blue	
Supplier Ref _____			With Goods ————— Yellow	
Description	Part No	Quantity		Remarks
Received by (signature) _____			Date _____	
Carrier _____				

14.13 Abbreviations

Business documents frequently contain abbreviations and terms of trade the most common of which are as follows:

Carriage paid   Another word for carriage is transport costs. Thus carriage paid indicates that the cost of transport has been included in the cost of the goods.

COD   This abbreviation stands for 'cash on delivery' and means that the goods must be paid for on delivery.

E&OE   On some invoices and other documents you will see the initials 'E & OE' printed at the bottom of the invoice. This abbreviation stands for 'errors and omissions excepted'. Basically, this is a warning that there may possibly be errors or omissions which could mean that the figures shown could be incorrect, and that the recipient should check the figures carefully before taking any action concerning them.

Ex works   This means that the price of the goods does not include delivery costs.

Net monthly   This phrase frequently appears at the foot of an invoice and means that the full amount of the invoice is due for payment within one month of the date of the invoice.

Chapter summary

- Organisations use many documents within their trading activity (see Exhibit 14.1).
- A 'quotation' is a formal document, containing details of the goods or services required, issued by the seller following a prospective buyer's enquiry.
- Once the buyer has decided to purchase the goods or services it issues a 'purchase order' to the supplier. This document details the goods or services required by the purchaser.
- Upon receipt of the purchase order the supplier issues an 'advice note' informing the buyer of the date of despatch of the goods or services.
- Accompanying the goods will be a delivery note (sometimes called a despatch note). This document contains details of the goods being delivered, but without the price details. The recipient will then sign for the receipt on delivery.
- An 'invoice' is then sent by the supplier to the buyer detailing the goods or services supplied and the amount outstanding. The payment details are also included on the invoice.
- A pro-forma invoice is a type of invoice that is occasionally raised when the seller wishes to secure payment prior to the goods or services being supplied.
- When goods are faulty or unsatisfactory they are often returned to the supplier by the buyer who issues a returns note to accompany the goods. The supplier, upon receipt, will then issue the purchaser with a credit note which will give details of the amount to be deducted from the original invoice.
- Usually, at the end of the month, the purchaser receives a statement of account from the supplier detailing the invoices and credit notes issued during the particular period and the total amount outstanding and due for payment. Any payment made should be accompanied by a remittance advice detailing the invoices included in the payment.
- A goods received note is a document raised by the purchaser when the goods or services are received and shows the exact details of goods received.

EXERCISES

14.1 Describe the functions of the following documents:

(a) remittance advice
(b) goods received note (GRN)
(c) credit note
(d) invoice.

14.2X (a) What is the purpose of a pro-forma invoice?
(b) What does it mean if goods are sold COD?
(c) What does 'terms net' on an invoice mean?
(d) What does the term 'ex works' mean?
(e) What does E&OE on an invoice mean?

14.3 You are asked to complete the following sentences:

(*a*) Clover Designs Ltd sends a .... to a supplier to order goods.

(*b*) An .... is sent to the buyer before the goods are delivered to let it know that the goods will be despatched shortly.

(*c*) An .... is sent by the seller to the buyer of goods or services to advise it of how much is owed for the goods or services supplied.

(*d*) Clover Designs Ltd sends a .... with a payment to a supplier to indicate which invoices are being paid.

14.4X You are employed as an accounts clerk for a printing company. At the end of each month one of your tasks is to prepare statements of account to be sent to customers. Below are details from the account of one of your customers John Ashley Ltd.

Invoices sent during the month:

May 2	Invoice No. 7821	£43.75
May 8	Invoice No. 7955	£35.00
May 17	Credit Note No. 304	£10.20
May 23	Invoice No. 8204	£74.50
May 28	Received cheque	£51.50

The amount outstanding on May 1 amounted to £101.50

You are required to draft a statement of account showing details of how much John Ashley Ltd has outstanding at the end of May.

CHAPTER 15

Division of the ledger: sales day book and sales ledger

Learning objectives

After you have studied this chapter you should be able to:

- appreciate how the books of original entry are used alongside the ledgers
- distinguish between a cash sale and a credit sale and the way each are recorded in the books of account
- prepare a sales invoice and appreciate the need for copy invoices
- enter invoices into the sales day book and post transactions to the appropriate accounts in the sales ledger and general ledger
- explain the difference between trade discount and cash discount
- appreciate the documentation used in the sale of goods
- understand the importance of internal control
- appreciate the need for credit control over debtors
- understand why 'factoring' is used by organisations.

15.1 Introduction

In Chapter 2 we discussed the accounting cycle within which a business operates during its financial year. This included recording all the trading activities from the source document in the day books, posting to the various ledgers and the preparation of the financial statements at the end of the accounting period.

As a business expands additional accounting record books are required to enable the system of recording transactions to be made easier and more efficient. A **book of original entry** is where a transaction is first recorded. All transactions that are entered into the book-keeping system originate from a **source document** such as an invoice, credit note, cheque book stub, paying-in slip, and so on. In the next two chapters we will be looking at invoices and credit notes that are raised when goods or services are sold to customers and perhaps returned if a problem arises with the goods, when a credit would be issued. Chapters 20 and 21 cover the banking system and cash books, which illustrate how cash and cheques are recorded in the accounting records.

15.2 The books commonly used

The various books used in accounting are shown linked in Exhibit 15.1.

Exhibit 15.1

15.3 Cash sales

When goods are purchased by a customer who pays for them immediately by cash, then there is no necessity to enter the sale of these goods into the sales day book or the sales ledger since the customer is not in debt to the business. Keeping details of these customers' names and addresses is, therefore, not needed.

15.4 Credit sales

In many businesses most of the sales will be made on credit rather than for cash. In fact, the sales of some businesses or organisations will consist entirely of credit sales.

For each credit sale the supplier will send a document to the buyer showing details and prices of the goods sold. This document is known as a sales invoice to the supplier and a purchase invoice to the buyer. An example of an invoice was shown in Exhibit 14.6; a further example is now shown in Exhibit 15.2.

Exhibit 15.2

Your Purchase Order 10/A/980		J Blake 7 Over Warehouse Leicester LE1 2AP

Invoice No: 16554
To: D Poole & Co
     Deansgate Restaurant
     45 Charles Street
     Manchester M1 5ZN
	INVOICE	1 September 2009

Quantity and description	Per unit	Total
	£	£
21 cases Cape Glory Pears	20	420
5 cartons Kay's Flour	4	20
6 cases Joy's Sauce	20	120
		560
Terms: 1¼% cash discount if paid within one month		

Most businesses have individually designed invoices but inevitably they follow a generally accepted accounting format. All invoices will be numbered and contain the names and addresses of both the supplier and the customer. In Exhibit 15.2 the supplier is J Blake and the customer is D Poole & Co.

15.5 Copies of sales invoices

Once the goods have been despatched to the buyer a **sales invoice** is made out by the supplier. The top copy of the sales invoice is sent to the buyer, further copies are retained by the supplier for use within the organisation. For example, one copy is usually sent to the accounts department to enable the sale of goods on credit to be recorded in the sales day book and sales ledger, another copy may be passed to the sales department, and so on.

15.6 Entering credit sales into the sales day book

As mentioned above, a copy of the sales invoice is passed to the accounts department where the supplier enters this into the sales day book. This book is merely a list, showing the following:

- date of sale
- name of customer to whom the goods have been sold
- invoice number
- final amount of invoice.

There is no need to show details of the goods sold in the sales day book. This can be found by looking at copy invoices.

Exhibit 15.3 shows a **sales day book**, which illustrates how the invoices are entered starting with the entry of the invoice shown in Exhibit 15.2. (Assume that the entries are on page 26 of the day book.)

Exhibit 15.3

		Invoice No	Folio	Amount £
2009				
Sept	1 D Poole & Co	16554		560
	8 T Cockburn	16555		1,640
	28 C Carter	16556		220
	30 D Stevens & Co	16557		1,100
				3,520

Sales Day Book *(page 26)*

15.7 Posting credit sales to the sales ledger

Instead of having one ledger for all accounts, a sales ledger is used for recording credit sale transactions.

1 The credit sales are now posted, one by one, to the **debit** side of each customer's account in the sales ledger.
2 At the end of each period, the total of the credit sales is posted to the **credit** of the sales account in the general ledger.

It may be easier to use 'IN' and 'OUT', as shown in Chapter 4, to post these transactions; i.e. the goods sold go 'into' each individual customer's account and they come 'out' of the sales account. This is now illustrated in Exhibit 15.4.

Exhibit 15.4 Posting credit sales

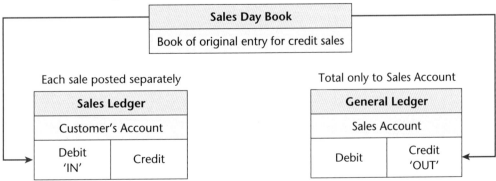

15.8 An example of posting credit sales

The sales day book in Exhibit 15.3 is now shown again. This time posting is made to the sales ledger and the general ledger. Notice the completion of the folio columns with the ledger reference, as stated above, and the page number of the ledger (see Exhibit 15.5).

Exhibit 15.5

Sales Day Book			(page 26)
	Invoice No	Folio	Amount
2009			£
Sept 1 D Poole & Co	16554	SL 12	560
8 T Cockburn	16555	SL 39	1,640
28 C Carter	16556	SL 125	220
30 D Stevens & Co	16557	SL 249	1,100
Transferred to Sales Account		GL 44	3,520

	Sales Ledger			*(page 12)*
Dr	*D Poole & Co Account*			*Cr*

2009	Folio	£
Sept 1 Sales	SB 26	560

				(page 39)
Dr	*T Cockburn Account*			*Cr*

2009	Folio	£
Sept 8 Sales	SB 26	1,640

				(page 125)
Dr	*C Carter Account*			*Cr*

2009	Folio	£
Sept 28 Sales	SB 26	220

				(page 249)
Dr	*D Stevens & Co Account*			*Cr*

2009	Folio	£
Sept 30 Sales	SB 26	1,100

	General Ledger			*(page 44)*
Dr	*Sales Account*			*Cr*

		2009	Folio	£
		Sept 30 Credit sales for the month	SB 26	3,520

Alternative names for the sales day book are the 'sales book' and the 'sales journal'. Before you continue, you should now attempt Exercise 15.3.

15.9 Trade discounts

Suppose you are a supplier of goods to three different categories of customers:

1 traders who buy many goods from you
2 traders who buy only a few items from you
3 direct to the general public.

The traders themselves have to sell the goods to the general public in their own areas. They have to make a profit to help finance their business, so they will want to pay you less than the retail price.

The traders who buy in large quantities will not want to pay as much as traders who buy in small quantities. You want to attract large customers, and so you are prepared to sell to such traders at a lower price.

This means that your selling prices are at three levels:

1 to traders buying large quantities
2 to traders buying small quantities
3 to the general public.

As a supplier you will provide the same retail price list to each category of customer. However, a reduction (discount), called a **trade discount** is given to traders 1 and 2. An example illustrating this is shown in Exhibit 15.6.

Exhibit 15.6

You are selling a particular make of food mixing machine. The retail price is £200. Traders **(1)** are given 25% trade discount, traders **(2)**, 20% and the general public who pay the full retail price. The prices paid by each type of customer would be:

		Trader (1) £		Trader (2) £	General public (3) £
Retail price		200		200	200
Less Trade discount	(25%)	50	(20%)	40	nil
Price to be paid by customer		150		160	200

15.10 Sales invoice with trade discount

Exhibit 15.7 is an invoice for goods supplied by R Grant (Catering Supplies) to D Poole & Co. The items supplied by R Grant (Catering Supplies) are the same as supplied by J Blake – see Exhibit 15.2; however, you will notice that R Grant (Catering Supplies) uses **trade discounts** to encourage customers to buy from him.

By comparing Exhibits 15.2 and 15.7 you can see that the prices paid by D Poole & Co were the same. It is simply the method of calculating the price that is different.

Exhibit 15.7

INVOICE

R GRANT (CATERING SUPPLIES)
Higher Side Preston PR1 2NL

Telephone: (01703) 33122
Fax: (01703) 22331

D Poole & Co
Deansgate Restaurant
45 Charles Street
Manchester M1 5ZN

Invoice No: 30756
Account No: P/4298
Date: 1 September 2009

Your Purchase Order 11/A/G80

Quantity	Per unit	Total
	£	£
21 cases Cape Glory Pears	25	525
5 cartons Kay's Flour	5	25
6 cases Joy's Sauce	25	150
		700
Less 20% Trade Discount		140
		560

15.11 Trade discounts and cash discounts compared

As trade discount is simply a way of calculating sales prices, no entry for trade discount should be made in the double entry records or in the sales day book.

The recording of Exhibit 15.7 in R Grant's (Catering Supplies) sales day book and D Poole's personal account will appear thus:

Sales Day Book			(page 87)
	Invoice No	Folio	Amount
2009			£
Sept 2 D Poole & Co	30756	SL 32	560

Sales Ledger (page 32)

Dr			D Poole & Co Account	Cr

2009	Folio	£	
Sept 2 Sales	SB 87	560	

To compare with cash discounts:

● trade discounts are not shown in double entry accounts
● cash discounts *are* shown in double entry accounts.

15.12 Other documentation

As already stated in Chapter 14, trading activities involve the use of various documents. Each business will have its own system of making out documents. All but the very smallest organisations will have their documents prepared via accounting software.

The sales invoice is the document from which the book-keeping records are prepared. There will usually be several other documents prepared at the same time, so that the business may properly organise the despatch of the goods to ensure that they are safely received. These are listed below for R Grant (Catering Supplies).

Advice note

Advice notes are sent to customers before goods are despatched to advise them of the delivery date. (Refer to Section 14.4.) The advice note for R Grant (Catering Supplies) is shown in Exhibit 15.8.

Exhibit 15.8

ADVICE NOTE	R GRANT (CATERING SUPPLIES) Higher Side Preston	No 178554
30 August 2009	PR1 2NL	Tel: (01703) 33122 Fax: (01703) 22331

J. Jones, Head Buyer
D Poole & Co
Deansgate Restaurant
45 Charles Street
Manchester M1 5ZN

Your order No 11/A/G80
Despatch details: 27 cases and 5 cartons

Quantity	Cat No	Description	Price
21 cases	M566	Cape Glory Pears	£25 each
5 cartons	K776	Kay's Flour	£5 each
6 cases	J865	Joy's Sauce	£25 each
			All less 20%

Delivery to:
  D Poole & Co, Warehouse 2,
  Longmills Trading Estate, Manchester M14 2TT

Delivery note

When goods are sent out, they usually have a **delivery note** to accompany them (see Section 14.5). The delivery note for R Grant (Catering Supplies) is shown in Exhibit 15.9.

Exhibit 15.9

DELIVERY NOTE	R GRANT (CATERING SUPPLIES)	No 194431
	Higher Side	
	Preston	Tel: (01703) 33122
11 September 2009	PR1 2NL	Fax: (01703) 22331

J. Jones, Head Buyer
D Poole & Co
Deansgate Restaurant
45 Charles Street
Manchester M1 5ZN

Order No 11/A/G80
Despatch details: 27 cases, 5 cartons by road

Quantity	Cat No	Details
21 cases	M566	Cape Glory Pears
5 cartons	K776	Kay's Flour
6 cases	J865	Joy's Sauce

Delivery to: Warehouse 2, Longmills Trading Estate,
Manchester M14 2TT

Received 27 cases and 5 cartons

Signed   ....

On behalf of ....

Other documents

Each business may vary in the type and number of documents used; these were discussed in Chapter 14.

15.13 Manufacturer's recommended retail price

Looking at an item displayed in a shop window, you will frequently see something like the following:

Digital LCD TV: Manufacturer's Recommended Retail Price	£500
Less discount of 20%	£100
You pay only	£400

Very often the manufacturer's recommended retail price is a figure above what the manufacturer would expect the public to pay for its product. Probably, in the case shown, the manufacturer would have expected the public to pay around £400 for its product.

The inflated figure used for the 'manufacturer's recommended retail price' is simply a sales gimmick. Most people like to feel they are getting a bargain. The salesmen know that someone would usually prefer to get '20% off' and pay £400, rather than for the price simply be shown as £400 with no mention of a discount.

15.14 Credit control

Credit control is a crucial function in any organisation that sells goods and/or provides services on credit. It should follow a strict procedure to monitor that debtors pay in full and on time. A business that does not receive payment when it is due may reach the stage when it can no longer pay its creditors. In these circumstances, it is very likely to fail.

The following procedures will help the business to maintain a positive cash flow situation:

1 Set a credit limit for each debtor which should not be exceeded. The limit should take account of the debtor's payment record and its importance to the business as a customer.
2 As soon as the payment date has been reached, check to see whether payment has been made or not. Failure to pay on time may mean you refuse to supply any more goods unless payment is made quickly.
3 Where payment is not forthcoming, after investigation it may be necessary to take legal action to sue the customer for the debt. This will depend on the circumstances.
4 It is important that customers are made aware of what will happen if they do not pay their account by the due date.

15.15 Internal checks

Sales invoices

When sales invoices are prepared they should be checked very carefully. It is important to ensure that the correct quantity of goods supplied is invoiced at the correct price. This also applies to services; they too, need to be invoiced at the correct amount. To avoid the possibility of errors being made or indeed fraud occurring it is prudent to have different members of staff involved at the various stages of invoice preparation. One member of staff may prepare the invoice, which is then passed to another senior member for checking and approving, before the invoice is sent to the customer.

Purchase invoices

For purchase invoices it is equally important for these to be checked. The purchaser needs to ensure that the goods or services to which the purchase invoice refers have been received and are as per the order and specification. It then needs to check that the goods or services are charged at the correct amount and calculations on the invoice are correct. This is discussed further in Chapter 16, in particular Section 16.6.

15.16 Factoring

One of the problems that face many businesses is the time taken by debtors to pay their accounts. Few businesses have so much cash available to them that they do not mind how long the debtor takes to pay. It is a fact that many businesses that become bankrupt do so, not because the business is not making profits, but because the business has run out of cash funds. Once that happens, the confidence factor in business evaporates, and the business then finds that very few people will supply it with goods, and it also cannot pay its employees. Closure of the firm then generally happens fairly quickly.

In the case of debtors, the cash problem may be alleviated by using the services of a financial intermediary called a 'factor'. **Factoring** is a financial service designed to improve the cash flow of healthy, growing companies, enabling them to make better use of management time and the money tied up in trade credit to customers. In essence, factors provide their clients with three closely integrated services, covering sales accounting and collection, credit management (which can include protection against bad debts), and the availability of finance against sales invoices.

15.17 Slip system

Some organisations avoid using day books by using the **slip system**. This involves putting information such as lists of invoices in 'slip' form, which can then be entered directly into the ledger accounts. The entry into the appropriate day book is thus eliminated.

For instance, banks use the slip system, whereby a customer makes out a paying-in slip to pay money into his or her account, and the slip is then used to enter the details of the transaction and become the documentary evidence.

Nowadays, with most organisations using computerised accounting systems, invoices tend to be collated into batches prior to entry. The invoices are then entered directly onto the system and the total checked, with the slip, prior to processing the invoices by computer.

The advantages of the slip system are that:

- it is easy to operate
- it is quicker than using day books
- it minimises the risk of error, i.e. batch totals should be verified before processing when using a computerised system of accounting.

The disadvantages are:

- if invoices are lost, this can cause problems
- the risk of fraud is increased
- it is not easy to analyse items, for example, sales of different kinds of goods.

Chapter summary

- As the business expands so does the requirement of additional books to record the accounting transactions.
- Books of original entry are where a transaction is entered first from the source document, i.e. invoice, credit note, etc.
- There are various books of original entry, sales and purchases day books, sales returns and purchases returns day books, the journal, petty cash book and cash book.

- When goods or services are sold for cash it is not necessary to enter the details into the sales day book and sales ledger since the customer is not in debt to the business.
- When goods or services are sold on credit then an invoice will need to be prepared and sent to the buyer. This document is known as a 'sales invoice' to the supplier and a 'purchase invoice' to the buyer. Several copies of the invoice are usually made to enable the accounts staff to record the sale in the books of account, other copies may be required for internal use.
- Sales invoices are a 'source document' and are entered into the sales day book which is a book of original entry. They are then posted to each individual customer's account in the sales ledger. At the end of the period total sales will be posted to the sales account in the general ledger.
- Trade discount is a discount or reduction given to a customer when calculating the price of goods. No entry is made of trade discount in the accounting records.
- Other documentation involved in the trading activity include an advice note, delivery note, etc.
- Credit control within an organisation is important for the business to maintain a healthy cash flow.
- Other areas that are important include the checking of invoices prior to entry in the books of account and before payment is made.
- Factoring is offered to businesses to help improve their cash flow. This involves 'selling' its debtors to a factoring company who then become responsible for collecting debts as they become due. The factoring company retains a percentage of the amount collected for its services.

EXERCISES

15.1 For each of the following types of transactions, state the book of original entry, and the ledger and type of account, in which you would enter the transaction:

(*a*) Sales invoice
(*b*) Bank receipt
(*c*) Purchase invoice
(*d*) Bank payment
(*e*) Sales credit note
(*f*) Sales returns
(*g*) Purchases credit note
(*h*) Closing stock.

15.2X (*a*) State which document(s) would be entered into the following books of original entry:
    (i)   Purchases day book
    (ii) Sales returns day book
    (iii) Cash book
    (iv) Sales day book
    (v) Purchases returns day book.
(*b*) Distinguish between personal and impersonal accounts.

15.3 You are to enter up the sales day book from the following details. Post the items to the relevant accounts in the sales ledger and then show the transfer to the sales account in the general ledger.

```
2009
Mar   1  Credit sales to J Gordon        £187
Mar   3  Credit sales to G Abrahams      £166
Mar   6  Credit sales to V White          £12
Mar  10  Credit sales to J Gordon         £55
Mar  17  Credit sales to F Williams      £289
Mar  19  Credit sales to C Richards       £66
Mar  27  Credit sales to V Wood           £28
Mar  31  Credit sales to L Simes          £78
```

15.4X   Enter up the sales day book from the following, then post the items to the relevant accounts in the sales ledger. Show the transfer to the sales account in the general ledger.

```
2009
May   1  Credit sales to J Johnson        £305
May   3  Credit sales to T Royes          £164
May   5  Credit sales to B Howe            £45
May   7  Credit sales to M Lee            £100
May  16  Credit sales to J Jakes          £308
May  23  Credit sales to A Vinden         £212
May  30  Credit sales to J Samuels      £1,296
```

15.5   During April 2009 the following credit sales were made by Dabell's Stationery Supplies Ltd:

Date	Debtor	Invoice no.	Amount £
1 April	Fisher & Co	6265	1,459
3 April	Elder (Office Supplies)	6266	73
5 April	Haigh (Mfr) Ltd	6267	56
11 April	Ardern & Co (Solicitors)	6268	1,598
15 April	I Rafiq	6269	540
20 April	Royle's Business Systems	6270	2,456
22 April	Fisher & Co	6271	23
22 April	Ardern & Co (Solicitors)	6272	345
25 April	Elder (Office Supplies)	6273	71
27 April	Haigh (Mfr) Ltd	6274	176

Required:

(a) Draw up a sales day book and enter the above invoices into the day book for the month of April 2009. The next sales day book page no. is 26.

(b) The sales ledger showed the following balances at 1 April 2009.

Customer	Amount outstanding £	Sales ledger ref.
Ardern & Co (Solicitors)	472	SL1
Elder (Office Supplies)	75	SL2
Fisher & Co	231	SL3
Haigh (Mfr) Ltd	1,267	SL4
I Rafiq	330	SL5
Royle's Business Systems	750	SL6

Open an account for each of the firm's customers in the sales ledger and enter the balances outstanding on 1 April 2009.

(c) Post the sales invoices for the month of April to the appropriate ledger account in the sales ledger.

(d) During April the firm received cheques from Fisher & Co for £231, I Rafiq for £330 and £1,000 on account from Haigh (Mfr) Ltd. Post the cheques to the customer's accounts in the sales ledger.

(e) Balance each account off at the end of April and draw up a list of outstanding debtors.

15.6X Morton's Garage is situated on the outskirts of Macclesfield and sells petrol and accessories in addition to carrying out repairs and maintenance on vehicles. At 1 January 2009 Morton's sales ledger showed the following balances on their customers' accounts:

	£	
C Crawford	1,078	Dr
S Brocklehurst	563	Dr
L Price & Partners	321	Dr
D Woolham & Co	146	Dr

During January 2009 the garage issued the following invoices in respect of credit sales of petrol, accessories and repairs.

2009	Invoice no.	Name	Amount £
2 Jan	37542	D Woolham & Co	230
6 Jan	37543	C Crawford	345
7 Jan	37544	S Brocklehurst	1,980
9 Jan	37545	L Price & Partners	523
13 Jan	37546	D Woolham & Co	56
18 Jan	37547	L Price & Partners	200
21 Jan	37548	C Crawford	340
24 Jan	37549	C Crawford	45
29 Jan	37550	S Brocklehurst	845
31 Jan	37551	L Price & Partners	721

On 31 January 2009 the garage proprietor, Mr Morton, received cheques from the following customers, who settled their account for the previous month:

Customer	Amount of cheque £
C Crawford	1,078
L Price & Partners	321
D Woolham & Co	146

Required:
Carry out the following tasks using your own reference numbers:

(a) Draw up a sales day book and enter the above invoices into the day book and total it for the month of January 2009.

(b) Open an account for each customer and enter the balances as at 1 January 2009. Post the sales from the day book to each account and the amounts received.

(c) Balance the customers' accounts at 31 January 2009 and bring down the balances.

(d) Post the total sales to the sales account in the general ledger.

15.7 Why is it important to ensure that sales invoices are thoroughly checked before being sent out to customers?

15.8 What is meant by the term 'factoring'?

Purchases day book and purchases ledger

Learning objectives

After you have studied this chapter you should be able to:

- appreciate the documentation used when purchasing goods or services
- enter purchase invoices into the purchases day book
- post the purchases day book to the purchase ledger
- authorise and code invoices for payment.

16.1 Purchase orders

An organisation uses a document called a **purchase order** when ordering goods or services from a supplier (see Section 14.3).

16.2 Purchase invoices

When organisations purchase goods or services from suppliers on credit they are sent a purchase invoice detailing the goods or services and their price.

In the previous chapter, Exhibit 15.2 showed an invoice raised by J Blake, the supplier, and sent to D Poole & Co, the buyer. The invoice is common to both parties since it details the goods supplied and the amount outstanding.

1 In the books of D Poole & Co it is a **purchase invoice**.
2 In the books of J Blake it is a **sales invoice**.

16.3 Entering invoices into the purchases day book

Upon receipt of the purchase invoice for goods and services supplied on credit, the purchaser enters the details in its **purchases day book**. This book is merely a list showing the following:

- date of purchase
- name of supplier from whom the goods were purchased
- reference number of the invoice
- final amount of invoice.

There is no need to show details of the goods bought in the purchases day book; this can be found by looking at the invoices themselves. Exhibit 16.1 is an example of a purchases day book.

Exhibit 16.1

Purchases Day Book			(page 49)
	Invoice No	Folio	Amount
2009			£
Sept 2 R Simpson	9/101		670
8 B Hamilton	9/102		1,380
19 C Brown	9/103		120
30 K Gabriel	9/104		510
			2,680

In the same way that sales invoices are used for entering up the sales day book, the purchase invoices are used as the source for entering up the purchases day book. These are known as **source documents**.

The purchases day book is also known as the 'purchases book' or the 'purchases journal'.

16.4 Posting credit purchases to the purchases ledger

We now have a separate purchases ledger. The double entry is as follows:

- The credit purchases are posted one by one, to the **credit** of each supplier's account in the purchases ledger.
- At the end of each period, the total of the credit purchases is posted to the **debit** of the purchases account in the general ledger.

Again, you may find it easier to use 'IN' and 'OUT', as discussed in Chapters 4 and 15; i.e. the goods purchased come from each supplier and therefore their accounts are entered on the 'OUT' side. The total purchases for the period are then entered on the 'IN' side of the purchases account since the goods are coming 'IN' to us. This is illustrated in Exhibit 16.2.

Exhibit 16.2 Posting credit purchases

16.5   A worked example of posting credit purchases

The purchases day book in Exhibit 16.1 is shown again below. This time, posting is made to the purchases ledger and the general ledger. Note the completion of the folio columns. This time the individual invoices are posted from the purchases day book (abbreviated PDB) to the individual creditors' accounts in the purchases ledger (abbreviated PL) and to the general ledger (abbreviated GL). The reference details, i.e. the abbreviated initials of the specific ledger or day book, are recorded followed by the page reference number.

Purchases Day Book			*(page 49)*
	Invoice No	*Folio*	*Amount*
2009			£
Sept 2 R Simpson	9/101	PL 16	670
8 B Hamilton	9/102	PL 29	1,380
19 C Brown	9/103	PL 55	120
30 K Gabriel	9/104	PL 89	510
Transferred to purchases account		GL 63	2,680

Purchases Ledger   *(page 16)*

Dr   *R Simpson Account*   Cr

			Folio	£
	2009			
	Sept 2	Purchases	PB 49	670

(page 29)

Dr   *B Hamilton Account*   Cr

			Folio	£
	2009			
	Sept 8	Purchases	PB 49	1,380

(page 55)

Dr		C Brown Account			Cr
		2009		Folio	£
		Sept 19 Purchases		PB 49	120

(page 89)

Dr		K Gabriel Account			Cr
		2009		Folio	£
		Sept 30 Purchases		PB 49	510

General Ledger *(page 63)*

Dr	Purchases Account			Cr
2009	Folio	£		
Sept 30 Credit purchases for the month	PB 49	2,680		

16.6   Authorisation and coding of invoices

Authorisation of purchase invoices

When purchase invoices are received from various suppliers of goods or services, it is important to check the invoices for accuracy in the calculations and to ensure that the goods invoiced have been received and agree with the relevant purchase order and specifications.

On receipt, each purchase invoice should be numbered, recorded and stamped with an appropriate rubber stamp (see Exhibit 16.3), to enable the invoice to be checked and coded.

Exhibit 16.3

Invoice no	
Purchase order no	
Goods received	
Extensions	
Passed for payment	
Code	

Coding of invoices

After stamping, it is necessary to perform the **coding of invoices**. Each invoice should be sent to the department responsible for ordering the goods, the invoice should be checked and, if everything is satisfactory, it is coded, passed for payment by a department head and returned to the accounts department for entry into the books of account and, ultimately, payment.

Organisations using computer accounting software need to give unique numbers to all their various accounts so that the software can recognise them instantly:

● *Purchases Ledger*   Suppliers are given account numbers – for example:

	Account number
Blackshaws	0207
Harvey Construction Ltd	0243
Morridge Products	0275
Travis and Humphreys	0284

● *Sales Ledger*   Customers' account numbers may be thus:

	Account number
Heath Manufacturing Ltd	1084
Office Supplies Ltd	1095
Seddon & Sons	1098
Yeoman's Supplies	1099

● *General Ledger*   Examples of account codes are as follows:

	Account number
Capital account	4003
Motor expenses account	4022
Printing and stationery account	4074
Sales account	4000
Purchases account	5000

A register of code numbers allocated to specific accounts must be maintained and updated as necessary. This register may be a manual one or held on the computer system.

Chapter summary

- An organisation uses a document called a purchase order when ordering goods or services from a supplier.
- When organisations purchase goods or services from suppliers they are sent a purchase invoice detailing the goods or services and their price. The invoice is used by both buyer and seller, to the buyer it is a purchase invoice and to the seller a sales invoice.
- Only invoices relating to goods bought on credit are entered into the purchases day book which is merely a list showing details of each credit purchase, i.e. the date of purchase, name of supplier, reference number and amount due.
- Each purchase invoice is then posted to the individual customer's account in the purchases ledger.
- At the end of the period, usually a month, the total purchases are posted to the purchases account in the general ledger.
- Many organisations have a system of coding the invoices prior to entry into the books of account. Part of this process involves authorising the invoice for payment.

EXERCISES

16.1 B Mann has the following purchases for the month of May 2009:

2009
May   1   From K King: 4 radios at £30 each, 3 music centres at £160 each.
          Less 25% trade discount.
May   3   From A Bell: 2 washing machines at £200 each, 5 vacuum cleaners at £60 each, 2 dish
          dryers at £150 each. Less 20% trade discount.
May 15   From J Kelly: 1 music centre at £300 each, 2 washing machines at £250 each. Less
          25% trade discount.
May 20   From B Powell: 6 radios at £70 each, less 33$\frac{1}{3}$% trade discount.
May 30   From B Lewis: 4 dish dryers at £200 each, less 20% trade discount.

Required:
(a) Enter up the purchases day book for the month.
(b) Post the transactions to the suppliers' accounts, use your own folio references.
(c) Transfer the total to the purchases account in the general ledger.

16.2X A Rowland has the following purchases for the month of June 2009:

2009
June   2   From C Lee: 2 sets golf clubs at £250 each, 5 footballs at £20 each.
           Less 25% trade discount.
June 11   From M Elliott: 6 cricket bats at £20 each, 6 ice skates at £30 each, 4 rugby balls at
           £25 each. Less 25% trade discount.
June 18   From B Wood: 6 sets golf trophies at £100 each, 4 sets golf clubs at £300 each. Less
           33$\frac{1}{3}$% trade discount.
June 25   From B Parkinson: 5 cricket bats at £40 each. Less 25% trade discount.
June 30   From N Francis: 8 goal posts at £70 each. Less 25% trade discount.

Required:
(a) Enter up the purchases day book for the month.
(b) Post the items to the suppliers' accounts, use your own folio references.
(c) Transfer the total to the purchases account in the general ledger.

16.3 You are employed as accounts assistant for a catering company, Surprise Desserts, that specialises in making desserts for sale to local restaurants, hotels and shops. During July 2009 the following purchases invoices are received.

2009		£	Invoice no.
July 1	Barton Foods Ltd	78.50	201
July 3	Henmore Eggs	56.26	202
July 8	Barton Foods Ltd	101.30	203
July 10	Fernley & Co	98.00	204
July 12	Henmore Eggs	48.20	205
July 14	Bridge Catering Co	142.00	206
July 19	Ruffoni Creams	132.82	207
July 23	Fernley & Co	43.20	208
July 25	Ace Packaging Co	217.75	209
July 31	Henmore Eggs	62.60	210

Required:

(a) Draw up a purchases day book, enter the invoices and total it up at the end of the month.

(b) Open accounts for each of the suppliers, use your own folio numbers and post the invoices to the suppliers' accounts in the purchase ledger.

(c) Post the totals to the purchases account in the general ledger.

16.4X (a) As accounts assistant for a builders' merchants you are responsible for approving invoices prior to payment at the end of each month. List the steps you would take in authorising an invoice for payment.

(b) The company has recently purchased four concrete mixers which are shown in the catalogue at £260 less 25% trade discount and a further 2.5% cash discount if the invoice is settled within 7 days. Assuming the invoice is paid within 7 days what is the total amount the firm would have to pay for the concrete mixers? Ignore VAT.

16.5X You are employed as a sales assistant for a small company, Wilshaws Ltd, who sell farm supplies. As the company employs the minimum administrative staff, one of your duties is to look after the purchases ledger. This task involves entering the invoices received from suppliers into the day book and posting to the relevant creditors' accounts in the ledger.

Wilshaw's purchase invoices received for November 2009 are as follows:

Date	Supplier	Our Inv No	Total
2009			£
Nov 1	Bould & Co	SR2103	104.26
Nov 3	Hambleton's	SR2104	140.57
Nov 7	Farm Supplies Co	SR2105	448.12
Nov 10	Worthington's Ltd	SR2106	169.91
Nov 12	Sigley Bros	SR2107	47.00
Nov 15	Hambleton's	SR2108	259.09
Nov 20	Harlow's Mfr	SR2109	84.96
Nov 20	Bould & Co	SR2110	29.14
Nov 25	Clark & Robinson	SR2111	61.63
Nov 30	T Adams Ltd	SR2112	233.83

Required:

(a) Draw up a purchases day book, enter the invoices, and total up at the end of the month.

(b) Open accounts for each of the suppliers, using your own folio numbers, and post the invoices to the suppliers' accounts in the purchases ledger.

(c) Post the totals to the purchases account in the general ledger.

CHAPTER 17

Sales returns day book and purchases returns day book

Learning objectives

After you have studied this chapter you should be able to:

- appreciate the need for sales returns and purchases returns to be made when goods or services are unsatisfactory
- enter credit notes in the Sales Returns Day Book and post to the appropriate individual customer's account in the Sales Ledger
- at the end of the period post the total of the Sales Returns Day Book into the Sales Returns Account in the General Ledger
- enter debit notes in the Purchases Returns Day Book and post to the appropriate individual customer's account in the Purchases Ledger
- at the end of the period post the total of the Purchases Returns Day Book to the Purchases Returns Account in the General Ledger
- appreciate the need for keeping separate returns accounts
- reconcile ledger accounts with suppliers' statements
- make appropriate book-keeping entries for sales made via credit card.

17.1 Sales returns (returns inwards) and purchases returns (returns outwards)

When goods are bought and sold it is inevitable that occasionally they are unsuitable for various reasons, such as when the goods are:

- faulty or damaged
- not suitable for the particular requirement, for example, wrong type, size, colour
- part of an incomplete consignment
- subject to an overcharge on the invoice.

When this happens the supplier will need to make an allowance to the customer to correct the situation.

Note: there are alternative names which are used for sales and purchases returns. Sales returns are often referred to as **returns inwards** while purchases returns are known as **returns outwards**.

17.2 Sales returns (returns inwards) and credit notes

As mentioned above, if the goods supplied are unsuitable then the supplier will need to rectify the situation. Since the customer (debtor) will have already been sent an invoice at the time the goods were delivered they will be in debt to the supplier (creditor) for the value of the goods. Therefore, when the supplier makes an allowance for goods that have been returned, or a reduction in price has been agreed, the supplier will issue a **credit note** to the customer (debtor) showing the amount of the agreed reduction.

Exhibit 17.1 shows an example of a credit note. (Note that credit notes are usually printed in red to distinguish them from invoices.)

Exhibit 17.1

CREDIT NOTE		
R GRANT (CATERING SUPPLIES)		
Higher Side Preston PR1 2NL		
	Telephone:	(01703) 33122
	Fax:	(01703) 22331
D Poole & Co		
Deansgate Restaurant	Credit Note No:	0/37
45 Charles Street	Account No:	P/4298
Manchester M1 5ZN	Date:	8 September 2009

Quantity	Per unit	Total
	£	£
2 cases Cape Glory Pears	25	50
Less 20% Trade Discount		10
		40

17.3 Book-keeping entries for credit notes

Credit notes are source documents and are listed in a separate day book called the **sales returns day book** (or alternatively, returns inwards day book). The book-keeping entries are:

Sales ledger   Credit the individual customer accounts (debtor's) with the amount of each credit note.

General ledger   Debit the Sales Returns Account with the total of the sales returns day book at the end of the period.

Again, you may find it easier to use 'IN' and 'OUT' as discussed previously; i.e. goods returned to us are entered on the 'IN' side of the sales returns account since the goods are coming 'IN' to us, and on the 'OUT' side of the individual customers' accounts.

17.4 Example of a sales returns day book

An example of a sales returns day book (returns inwards day book) showing the items posted from the sales returns day book (abbreviated SRDB) to the sales ledger (SL) and the general ledger (GL) is shown in Exhibit 17.2.

Exhibit 17.2

Sales Returns Day Book			(page 10)
	Note No	Folio	Amount
2009			£
Sept 8 D Poole & Co	9/37	SL 12	40
17 A Brewster	9/38	SL 58	120
19 C Vickers	9/39	SL 99	290
29 M Nelson	9/40	SL 112	160
Transferred to sales returns account		GL 114	610

Sales Ledger (page 12)

Dr　　　　　　　　　D Poole & Co Account　　　　　　　　　Cr

			2009	Folio	£
			Sept 8 Sales returns	SRDB 10	40

(page 58)

Dr　　　　　　　　　A Brewster Account　　　　　　　　　Cr

			2009	Folio	£
			Sept 17 Sales returns	SRDB 10	120

(page 99)

Dr　　　　　　　　　C Vickers Account　　　　　　　　　Cr

			2009	Folio	£
			Sept 19 Sales returns	SRDB 10	290

(page 112)

Dr　　　　　　　　　M Nelson Account　　　　　　　　　Cr

			2009	Folio	£
			Sept 29 Sales returns	SRDB 10	160

General Ledger (page 114)

Dr　　　　　　　　　Sales Returns Account　　　　　　　　　Cr

2009	Folio	£	
Sept 30 Returns for the month	SRDB 10	610	

17.5 Purchases returns (returns outwards) and debit notes

When a business buys goods for resale but then has to return some of the goods for any of the reasons already discussed they are known as 'purchases returns' or 'returns outwards'. When this occurs a document known as a **debit note** is sent by the business to the supplier giving details of a claim for an allowance in respect of goods returned.

Exhibit 17.3 shows an example of a debit note.

Exhibit 17.3

DEBIT NOTE		
R GRANT (CATERING SUPPLIES)		
Higher Side Preston PR1 2NL		
	Telephone: (01703) 33122	
	Fax: (01703) 22331	
B Hamilton Food Supplies		
20 Fourth Street	Debit Note No: 9/34	
Kidderminster	Account No: H/3752	
KD2 4PP	Date: 11 September 2009	

Quantity	Per unit	Total
	£	£
4 cases Canadian Salmon	60	240
Less 25% Trade Discount		60
		180
Returned damaged in transit		

17.6 Book-keeping entries for debit notes

Debit notes are source documents and are listed in a purchases returns day book (or alternatively, the returns outwards book). This is then used for posting the items as follows:

Purchases ledger Debit the individual suppliers' (creditor's) accounts with the amount of each debit note.

General ledger Credit the Purchases Returns Account with the total of the purchases returns day book at the end of the period.

Using 'IN' and 'OUT', the entries would be as follows: the goods returned by us to the supplier go 'IN' to the suppliers' accounts and come 'OUT' of the purchases returns account.

17.7 A worked example of a purchases returns day book

An example of a purchases returns day book (returns outwards day book), showing the items posted from the purchases returns day book (PRDB) to the purchases ledger (PL) and the general ledger (GL), is shown in Exhibit 17.4.

Exhibit 17.4

Purchases Returns Day Book			(page 7)
	Note No	Folio	Amount £
2009			
Sept 11 B Hamilton	9/34	PL 29	180
16 B Rose	9/35	PL 46	100
28 C Blake	9/36	PL 55	30
30 S Saunders	9/37	PL 87	360
Transferred to purchases returns account		GL 116	670

Purchases Ledger (page 29)

Dr — B Hamilton Account — Cr

2009	Folio	£	
Sept 11 Purchases returns	PRDB 7	180	

(page 46)

Dr — B Rose Account — Cr

2009	Folio	£	
Sept 16 Purchases returns	PRDB 7	100	

(page 55)

Dr — C Blake Account — Cr

2009	Folio	£	
Sept 28 Purchases returns	PRDB 7	30	

(page 87)

Dr — S Saunders Account — Cr

2009	Folio	£	
Sept 30 Purchases returns	PRDB 7	360	

General Ledger (page 116)

Dr — Purchases Returns Account — Cr

			2009	Folio	£
			Sept 30 Returns for the month	PRDB 7	670

17.8 Double entry and returns

Exhibit 17.5 shows how double entry is made for both sales returns (returns inwards) and purchases returns (returns outwards).

Exhibit 17.5 Posting sales returns and purchases returns

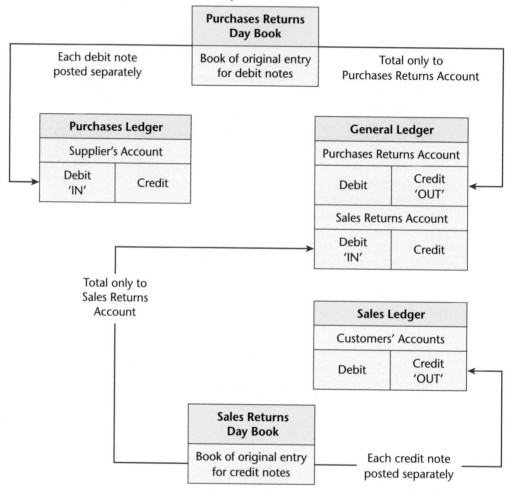

Note that full coverage of the treatment of sales returns and purchases returns in the final accounts has already been shown in Sections 12.1 and 12.2.

17.9 Reasons for keeping separate returns accounts

It might be thought that the sales returns could have been debited to the sales account rather than to a separate sales returns account. This would result in only the net figure of sales appearing in the trading account.

It is important for the owners of a business to check the amount of sales being returned. This may show that too many faulty goods are being sold, involving the business in unnecessary costs, such as carriage outwards, packing expenses, and so on. Showing the figures separately will highlight an excessive amount of returns.

Similar considerations will apply with purchases returns, and therefore a separate purchases returns account is kept.

17.10 Statements

At the end of each month a **statement of account** should be sent to each debtor that owes money on the last day of that month. It is really a copy of the debtor's account in the seller's books. It should show:

● the amount owing at start of the month
● the amount of each sales invoice sent to the debtor during the month
● any credit notes sent to the debtor during the month
● cash and cheques received from the debtor during the month
● the amount due from the debtor at the end of the month.

Debtors will use these statements to see whether the accounts in their own accounting records agrees with their account in our records. If in our books a debtor is shown as owing £798 then, depending on items in transit between us, the debtors books should show us as a creditor for £798.

The statements also act as a reminder to debtors that money is owed, and will show the date by which payment should be made.

An example of a statement is shown in Exhibit 17.6.

Exhibit 17.6

STATEMENT

R GRANT (CATERING SUPPLIES)
Higher Side Preston PR1 2NL

Telephone: (01703) 33122
Fax: (01703) 22331

Accounts Department
D Poole & Co
Deansgate Restaurant
45 Charles Street
Manchester M1 5ZN

Date: 30 September 2009

Date	Details	Debit	Credit	Balance
2009		£	£	£
Sept 1	Balance b/f			880
Sept 2	Invoice 30956	560		1,440
Sept 3	Returns 9/37		40	1,400
Sept 25	Bank		880	520
Sept 30	Balance owing c/f			520

All accounts due and payable within one month

17.11 Reconciliation of our ledger accounts with suppliers' statements

A supplier's statement of account should be checked against its ledger account in the business's own books and the balance reconciled before making a payment. Sometimes, because of the differences in timing, the balance on a supplier's statement on a certain date can differ from the balance on that supplier's account in the business's purchases ledger. This is similar to a bank statement where the balance may differ from that in the cash book and require the preparation of a **bank reconciliation statement** to reconcile the two balances. This is dealt with in Chapters 20 and 23.

If the balance on the statement of account does differ from the supplier's account in the purchases ledger, then it will be necessary to check the statement against the ledger account and reconcile the difference by preparing a supplier's reconciliation statement.

The reasons for the differences in balances may be due to:

- goods returned by the customer but not recorded by the supplier until after the statement of account has been issued
- a supplier sending goods to a customer, together with an invoice, but neither being received by the customer until a later date: the customer is, therefore, unable to enter the invoice in their books of the account until receipt
- payments in transit
- other errors which may be made by either the supplier or buyer when entering data, i.e. transposing figures, or an error in the calculation of a balance where manual accounts are maintained.

Exhibit 17.7 shows the account of C Young Ltd in the purchases ledger of A. Hall Ltd and the statement of account received from the supplier, C Young Ltd, together with the reconciliation.

Exhibit 17.7

(a) Purchases ledger   A Hall Ltd Books

Dr		C Young Ltd Account		Cr
2009	£	2009		£
Jan 10 Bank	1,550	Jan 1 Balance b/d		1,550
Jan 29 Returns (i)	116	Jan 6 Purchases		885
Jan 31 Balance c/d	1,679	Jan 18 Purchases		910
	3,345			3,345
		Feb 1 Balance b/d		1,679

(b) Supplier's statement

C Young Ltd
Market Place, Leeds

STATEMENT

Account Name: A Hall Ltd
Account Number: H93   Date: 31 January 2009

	Debit	Credit	Balance
	£	£	£
2009			
Jan 1 Balance			1,550 Dr
Jan 4 Invoice No 3250	885		2,435 Dr
Jan 13 Payment received		1,550	885 Dr
Jan 18 Invoice No 3731	910		1,795 Dr
Jan 31 Invoice No 3894	425		2,220 Dr

Comparing the purchases ledger account with the supplier's statement, two differences can be seen:

1 A Hall Ltd returned goods value £116 to C Young Ltd, but it had not received them and recorded them in its books by the end of January.
2 C Young Ltd sent goods to A Hall Ltd, but the latter had not received them and therefore had not entered the £425 in its books by the end of January.

A reconciliation statement can be drawn up by A Hall Ltd as on 31 January 2009.

Reconciliation of Supplier's Statement
C Young Ltd as on 31 January 2009

		£	£
Balance per our purchases ledger			1,679
Add Purchases not received by us	(ii)	425	
Returns not received by supplier	(i)	116	
			541
Balance per supplier's statement			2,220

17.12 Sales and purchases via credit cards

Nowadays, consumers are increasingly using credit cards to purchase goods and services. In effect, the sales are 'cash sales', as far as the purchasers are concerned: they have seen and received goods or obtained services and in their eyes they have paid for them by using their credit card. Such sales are very rarely sales to anyone other than the general public, as compared with sales to professionals in a specific trade.

Once a customer has received the goods or services from the seller, he or she does not need to be entered in the sales ledger as a debtor. All the selling company is then interested in, from a recording point of view, is collecting the money from the credit card company.

The book-keeping entries are as follows:

Sales of items via credit cards:	**Debit:**	Credit card company
	Credit:	Cash sales
Receipt of money from credit card company:	**Debit:**	Bank
	Credit:	Credit card company
Commission charged by credit card company:	**Debit:**	Selling expenses
	Credit:	Credit card company

Credit cards are discussed in more detail in Chapter 20.

Chapter summary

- A credit note is a document issued by a supplier and sent to a purchaser showing details of an allowance made in respect of unsatisfactory goods or services.
- Credit notes are entered into a sales returns day book. The total returns for the month are posted to the debit side of the sales returns account in the general ledger. Each transaction is also posted to the credit side of the individual customers' accounts in the sales ledger.
- A useful hint: goods returned to us are entered on the 'IN' side of the sales returns account and on the 'OUT' side of the individual customers' accounts.
- A debit note is a document sent to a supplier claiming an agreed allowance for unsatisfactory goods or services.
- Debit notes are entered into a purchases returns day book. Each transaction is then posted to the debit side of the individual suppliers' accounts in the purchases ledger. The total returns for the month are posted to the credit side of the purchases returns account in the general ledger.
- A useful hint: the goods returned by us to the supplier go 'IN' to the suppliers' accounts and come 'OUT' of the purchases returns account.
- To keep a note of the number of returns being made it is important to have separate accounts for sales returns and purchases returns.
- Statements are issued by suppliers and sent to their customers, i.e. their debtors, requesting payment of amounts due. The debtor uses the statement to check the suppliers' records against their own and if correct will make payment against the statement.
- Statements are also used to reconcile the records of the supplier to those of the customer. Differences are identified and if errors or discrepancies have arisen then amendments can be made.
- Credit card sales are treated as cash sales. Commission charged by the credit card company is treated as a selling expense.

EXERCISES

17.1   You are to enter up the purchases day book and the purchases returns day book from the following details, then post the items to the relevant accounts in the purchases ledger, and then show the transfers to the general ledger at the end of the month.

2009

May   1 Credit purchase from H Lloyd, £119

May   4 Credit purchases from the following: D Scott £98; A Simpson £114; A Williams £25; S Wood £56

May   7 Goods returned by us to the following: H Lloyd £16; D Scott £14

May 10 Credit purchase from A Simpson, £59

May 18 Credit purchases from the following: M White £89; J Wong £67; H Miller £196; H Lewis £119

May 25 Goods returned by us to the following: J Wong £5; A Simpson £11

May 31 Credit purchases from: A Williams £56; C Cooper £98.

17.2X Enter up the sales day book and the sales returns day book from the following details. Then post to the customers' accounts and show the transfers to the general ledger.

2009

June   1 Credit sales to: A Simes £188; P Tulloch £60; J Flynn £77; B Lopez £88

June   6 Credit sales to: M Howells £114; S Thompson £118; J Flynn £66

June 10 Goods returned to us by: A Simes £12; B Lopez £17

June 20 Credit sales to M Barrow, £970

June 24 Goods returned to us by S Thompson, £5

June 30 Credit sales to M Parkin, £91.

17.3 Framework Ltd is a small company which specialises in framing pictures, photographs, certificates, etc. At the beginning of the new financial year 1 January 2009 the following balances appeared in the ledgers:

Sales Ledger

	£
J Forbes (Fancy Gifts)	745 Dr
J Goodwin & Co	276 Dr
L & P Moss	390 Dr

Purchases Ledger

	£
M & P Fitzsimons	800 Cr
L Horne	450 Cr
M Ward & Sons	245 Cr

During January 2009 the following transactions took place:

Jan   2 Purchased goods from L Horne, £650

Jan   3 Purchased goods from M Ward & Sons, £334

Jan 11 Sold goods to J Goodwin & Co, £328

Jan 12 Received credit note from L Horne, £42, in respect of goods returned as unsuitable

Jan 22 Purchased goods from M & P Fitzsimons, £756

Jan 23 Sold goods to J Forbes (Fancy Gifts), £1,234

Jan 27 Sold goods to L & P Moss, £2,500

Jan 28 Received credit note from M & P Fitzsimons, £200

On 31 January the company received a cheque from J Forbes (Fancy Gifts) for £745 and a cheque for £200 on account from L & P Moss.

On the same date the company paid cheques to M & P Fitzsimons £500 on account and M Ward & Sons £245.

Required:

(*a*) Open personal accounts for the debtors and creditors and enter the outstanding balances at 1 January 2009.

(*b*) Post the above transactions to the accounts in the sales and purchases ledgers.

(*c*) Balance off the accounts at 31 January and bring the balances down.

Note: Day books and postings to the general ledger are not required.

17.4X You are employed as an accounts clerk for Elder's Printing Co, 36 High Street, Shrewsbury SH4 8JK. One of your tasks is to prepare statements of account which are sent out to customers at the end of each month. Two of the customers' accounts are shown below.

Sales Ledger

Dr		D Hammond Ltd Account			Cr
2009	£		2009		£
Jan 1 Balance b/d	1,403		Jan 7 Bank		1,380
Jan 3 Sales	177		Jan 12 Credit note		23
Jan 10 Sales	527				
Jan 25 Sales	200				

Dr		Alex Richards Ltd Account			Cr
2009	£		2009		£
Jan 1 Balance b/d	346		Jan 7 Bank		292
Jan 7 Sales	27		Jan 7 Discount		8
Jan 9 Sales	521		Jan 12 Credit note		46
Jan 27 Sales	400				
Jan 31 Sales	53				

The addresses of the above customers are as follows:

D Hammond Ltd	Alex Richards Ltd
Bay House	Unit 12
Heath Road	Greenways Industrial Estate
Shrewsbury	Chester
SH7 3KL	CE21 9HU

Required:

(*a*) Balance each of the above accounts off, and state the amount owing by each of the customers.

(b) Draft a statement of account to be sent to each customer.

17.5X As accounts clerk for Perris Design Company one of your tasks is to reconcile the company's suppliers' accounts statements with the purchases ledger accounts prior to payment. Shown below are two statements which have been received from two of your suppliers; Bennetts Ltd and Kirkhams Products Ltd.

   Prepare reconciliation statements reconciling the statements with the ledger accounts.

STATEMENT

BENNETTS LTD
The Green, Brentwood, Essex.

Tel: 0277 371832
Date: 31st July 2009

Customer:
  Perris Design Co
  Deansgate
  Ipswich.

Account No: 47310

Date 2009	Description/reference	Debit £ p	Credit £ p	Balance £ p
30 June	Balance b/f			252.41
2 July	002361 Inv.	84.96		
9 July	003123 Inv.	42.50		379.87
16 July	Cash		252.41	127.46
23 July	003972 Inv.	696.32		823.78
30 July	003989 Inv.	121.50		945.28

AMOUNT NOW DUE

Interest will be charged on overdue accounts

STATEMENT

KIRKHAMS PRODUCTS LTD
Riverside Works, Romford.

Tel: 0708 649685
Date: 31st July 2009

Customer:
  Perris Design Co
  Deansgate
  Ipswich.

Account No: PX/32971

Date	Description/reference	Debit £ p	Credit £ p	Balance £ p
July 1	Balance b/f			1,829.00
July 15	Invoice No. 49606	531.75		
July 13	Invoice No. 822663	54.62		
July 21	Invoice No. 84133	459.23		
July 24	Invoice No. 82624	68.42		2,943.02
July 30	Cash		1,432.30	1,510.72

AMOUNT NOW DUE   N.B. Our Inv. No. 821503 for £396.70 is overdue

Interest will be charged on overdue accounts

PURCHASES LEDGER

Dr   Bennetts Ltd a/c   Cr

2009				2009			
July 10	Bank	252.41		July 1	Balance b/d	252.41	
27	Returns	63.50		2	Purchases	84.96	
31	Balance c/d	760.28		9	Purchases	42.50	
				23	Purchases	696.32	
		1,076.19				1,076.19	
				Aug 1	Balance b/d	760.28	

Dr   Kirkhams Products Ltd   Cr

2009				2009			
July 30	Bank	1,432.30		July 1	Balance b/d	1,829.00	
30	Purchases Returns	54.62		15	Purchases	531.75	
31	Balance c/d	1,387.68		13	Purchases	54.62	
				21	Purchases	459.23	
		2,874.60				2,874.60	
				Aug 1	Balance b/d	1,387.68	

Value added tax (VAT)

Learning outcomes

After you have studied this chapter you should be able to:

- understand how the value added tax system operates in the UK
- understand how VAT is collected and paid to HM Revenue and Customs (HMRC)
- distinguish between the various rates of VAT
- appreciate exempt businesses
- prepare sales invoices including charges for VAT
- record VAT transactions in the book-keeping system
- complete a VAT Return form.

18.1 Introduction to VAT

VAT is a tax charged on the supply of most goods and services supplied by businesses within the UK. In the UK, businesses with a certain amount of turnover (sales) must be registered for VAT. The turnover threshold usually increases each year as part of the Chancellor of the Exchequer's budget. VAT is administered in the UK by HMRC that has a very useful website at www.hmrc.gov.uk where all aspects of VAT can be found.

Once a business has been registered for VAT it is issued with a VAT Registration Number which must be quoted on all businesses documentation, for example, order forms, invoices, etc. When the business makes a sale of its goods or supplies a service to a customer VAT is added to the purchase price of the goods, this is known as **output VAT**. Any purchases or services bought by the supplier are also subject to VAT; from the purchaser's point of view this is known as **input VAT**.

There are exceptions to the goods and services supplied to which VAT is charged and this will be discussed later on in this chapter.

VAT is collected by businesses and paid to HMRC, usually on a quarterly basis. However, some businesses may decide to opt for the payment of VAT on an annual basis. There is also a scheme known as the **flat rate scheme** whereby businesses calculate VAT as a percentage of annual sales thereby avoiding the necessity to calculate input and output VAT on individual transactions. This scheme was designed to help small businesses and to eliminate the work involved in accounting for VAT.

18.2 Payment of VAT

Once a business has been registered for VAT it is required to complete a VAT Return (see Exhibit 18.5 later) each quarter (or each year if it is using the annual basis of return) in which details of the business's purchases and sales and the VAT elements are listed. The VAT due for payment to HMRC is calculated as follows:

● the amount of VAT charged on sales, i.e. output VAT

  less

● the amount of VAT paid on purchases, i.e. input VAT.

In most cases businesses have to pay the difference between output VAT and input VAT to HMRC. However, some businesses have more input VAT than output VAT and in these circumstances the business will receive a refund of VAT from HMRC.

18.3 VAT rates

There are three rates of VAT in operation at the time of writing:

● standard rate, currently 17.5%
● reduced rate, currently 5%
● zero rate.

18.4 Goods and services applicable to VAT

Standard rate VAT

Most goods and services are subject to VAT at the standard rate of 17.5%.

Reduced rate VAT

This reduced rate of 5% applies to certain goods and services such as:

● domestic fuel or power
● installation of energy saving materials
● grant funded installation of heating equipment
● security goods or connection of gas supplies
● renovation and alteration of dwellings and residential conversions
● women's sanitary products
● child car seats.

Zero-rated goods and services

Some goods and services are zero-rated which means that VAT on these products is charged at 0%. Some examples are:

● food for human consumption (there are some exceptions such as chocolate biscuits, some confectionery, etc.)

- books and periodicals
- clothing and footwear for young children.

Exempt goods and services

There are also goods and services which are exempt from accounting for VAT. Such businesses neither add VAT onto the selling price of their goods or services nor do they obtain a refund of VAT on the amount they pay on the products they purchase. Examples of **exempt supplies** are:

- financial services
- postal services
- certain types of education.

18.5 Zero-rated businesses

In the section above, the concept of **zero-rated supplies** was introduced where the rate of VAT charged was 0%. Since supplies in these businesses are sold a rate of VAT (albeit 0%), any input VAT incurred, relating to the business, may be reclaimed.

Example 1: A book dealer sells £100,000 worth of books in a year and, during that year, purchases book shelving for £10,000 plus VAT.
   The VAT reclaimable is therefore:

	Net (£)	VAT (£) @ 17.5%
Sales	100,000	Nil
Purchases	10,000	1,750
VAT reclaimable		1,750

A further example that would fall into this category would be a shop selling young children's shoes. The business would apply the 0% rate of VAT to the selling price of the children's shoes and would be able to reclaim any input VAT it paid out on the purchase of goods or services incurred in running the shop.

18.6 Exempted businesses

There are businesses that deal in goods and services that are exempt from VAT, as shown in Section 18.4. The important thing to note here is that unlike zero-rated businesses, businesses selling exempt products do not charge VAT on their product sales and are *not* able to reclaim input VAT they pay on their goods and services purchased. The type of businesses falling into this category are as follows:

- Those dealing with financial matters, such as banks and credit card companies.
- Small businesses that are not registered for VAT since their turnover is below the VAT registration threshold. These small businesses do not have to register for VAT unless they want to, in which case they would need to keep full accounting VAT records and charge VAT on the sale of their goods and services.

- Businesses that are registered for VAT can deregister if their turnover falls below a certain level.

The important thing to note is that input VAT directly attributable to exempt supplies or to non-VAT registered businesses cannot be reclaimed from HMRC.

Example 2: An insurance company sells £100,000 worth of insurance, and purchases furniture for its office for £10,000 plus VAT.

This business cannot reclaim the £1,750 input VAT on the furniture as it does not have any vatable supplies. The total amount paid for the furniture, £11,750, will be the cost to the business. Contrast this situation with the zero-rated supplier in Example 1 above, which was able to reclaim £1,750.

18.7 Partly exempt business

Some VAT registered traders will sell some goods that are exempt from VAT and others that are either standard-rated or zero-rated. These businesses may reclaim part of the input VAT paid by them, but not all of it. The rules are complicated, but in essence the input VAT reclaimable will be proportionate to the standard- and zero-rated percentage of the business's total annual turnover.

18.8 How the VAT system works

In Exhibit 18.1 it can be seen that VAT is payable to HMRC whenever a sale is made. This progressive method of tax collection ensures a steady flow of funds for the government.

A toymaker manufactures toys from scraps of material and sells them to a wholesaler for £200 plus VAT. The wholesaler sells these to a retailer for £300 plus VAT, who in turn retails the toys to a number of private customers who are not VAT registered.

Exhibit 18.1 Calculation of VAT at 17.5% payable to HMRC

	Net (£)	Vat (£)	Type of VAT	VAT due to HMRC
Toymaker				
Sale of toys	200.00	35.00	Output	
less cost of materials	–	–		
VAT		35.00		£35
Wholesaler				
Sale of toys	300.00	52.50	Output	
less cost of toys	200.00	35.00	Input	
VAT		17.50		£17.50
Retailer				
Sale of toys	400.00	70.00	Output	
less cost of toys	300.00	52.50	Input	
VAT		17.50		£17.50
				£70.00

Exhibit 18.1 shows the total tax of £70 has been paid to HMRC at various stages in the distribution of the toys. It also shows that the retailer has charged its customers a total output VAT of £70. These customers are not VAT registered and have no input VAT to offset against the £70 paid by them.

18.9 Different methods of accounting for VAT

How VAT appears in the ledger accounts and in the financial statements depends on which of the following categories businesses fall into:

- **Businesses that can recover VAT paid** - all businesses except exempted firms do not incur VAT as an expense. They either:
  - obtain a refund of the VAT they have paid in the case of a zero-rated business, or
  - collect VAT from their customers, deduct the VAT paid on goods and services bought by them and simply remit the balance owing to HMRC as in **standard-rated businesses**.
- **Businesses that cannot recover VAT paid** - this applies to all businesses that are treated as exempted businesses and are unable to obtain refunds for any tax paid (refer to Section 18.6).

The following section outlines the double entry requirements for recording VAT in the above categories.

18.10 Book-keeping entries for businesses that can recover VAT paid

Standard-rated businesses

Value added tax and sales invoices

These businesses will have to add VAT to the value of the sales invoice. It must be pointed out that this is based on the amount of the invoice *after* any trade discount has been deducted. Exhibit 18.2 is an invoice drawn up from the following details. On 2 March 2009, W Frank & Co, Hayburn Road, Stockport, sold the following goods to R Bainbridge Ltd, 267 Star Road, Colchester. Bainbridge's Order Number was A/4/559, for the following items:

> 200 Rolls T56 Black Tape at £6 per 10 rolls
> 600 Sheets R64 Polythene at £10 per 100 sheets
> 7,000 Blank Perspex B49 Markers at £20 per 1,000.

All of these goods are subject to VAT at the rate of 17.5%. A trade discount of 25% is given by Frank & Co. The sales invoice is numbered 8851.

Exhibit 18.2

W Frank & Co **Hayburn Road** **Stockport SK2 5DB**	

INVOICE No 8851

Date/tax point: 2 March 2009

To: R Bainbridge
267 Star Road
Colchester CO1 1BT

Your order no: A/4/559
Account no: F/1896

	£
200 Rolls T56 Black Tape @ £6 per 10 rolls	120
600 Sheets R64 Polythene @ £10 per 100 sheets	60
7,000 Blank Perspex B49 Markers @ £20 per 1,000	140
	320
Less Trade Discount 25%	80
	240
Add VAT 17.5%	42
	282
VAT Registration No: 469 2154 42	

The sales day book will normally have an extra column for the VAT contents of the sales invoice (see Chapter 19). This is needed to make it easier to account for VAT. The entry of several sales invoices in the sales day book and in the ledger accounts can now be examined for our sample case.

W Frank & Co sold the following goods during the month of March 2009:

	Total of invoice, after trade discount deducted but before VAT added	VAT 17.5%
2009	£	£
March 2 R Bainbridge Ltd (*see* Exhibit 18.2)	240	42
March 10 S Lange & Son	200	35
March 17 K Bishop	160	28
March 31 R Andrews & Associates	80	14

Sales Day Book					Page 58
2009	Invoice No	Folio	Total £	VAT £	Net £
March 2 R Bainbridge Ltd	8851	SL 77	282	42	240
March 10 S Lange & Son	8852	SL 119	235	35	200
March 17 K Bishop	8853	SL 185	188	28	160
March 31 R Andrews & Associates	8854	SL 221	94	14	80
Transferred to General Ledger			799	119	680
				GL 90	GL 76

Now that the sales day book has been written up, the next task is to enter the amounts of the invoices in the individual customers' accounts in the sales ledger. These are simply charged with the full amounts of the invoices, including VAT.

As an instance of this, K Bishop will be shown as owing £188. When she pays her account she will pay £188. It will then be the responsibility of W Frank & Co to ensure that the figure of £28 VAT in respect of this item is included in the total cheque payable to HMRC.

Sales Ledger Page 77

Dr			R Bainbridge Ltd				Cr
2009		Folio	£				
March 2 Sales		SB 58	282				

Page 119

Dr			S Lange & Son				Cr
2009		Folio	£				
March 10 Sales		SB 58	235				

Page 185

Dr			K Bishop				Cr
2009		Folio	£				
March 17 Sales		SB 58	188				

Page 221

Dr			R Andrews & Associates				Cr
2009		Folio	£				
March 31 Sales		SB 58	94				

In total, therefore, the personal accounts have been debited with £799, this being the total of the amounts that the customers will have to pay. The actual sales of the firm are not £799; the amount that is actually sales is £680, the other £119 being simply the VAT that W Frank & Co are collecting on behalf of the government.

The double entry is made in the general ledger thus:

● credit the sales account with the sales content only, i.e. £680
● credit the VAT account with the VAT content only, i.e. £119.

These are shown as:

General Ledger Page 76

Dr			Sales				Cr
			2009		Folio	£	
			March 31 Credit sales		SB 58	680	
			for the month				

Dr		Value Added Tax		Cr
	2009		Folio	£
	March 31	Sales Book: VAT	SB 58	119

Value added tax and purchases

In the case of a taxable business, it will have to add VAT to its sales invoices, but it will *also* be able to get a refund of the VAT it pays on its purchases.

Instead of paying VAT to HMRC and then claiming a refund of the VAT on purchases, the business can offset the amount paid as VAT on purchases against the amount payable as VAT on sales. This means that only the difference has to be paid to HMRC. It is shown as:

	£
(a) Output VAT collected on sales invoices	xxx
(b) Less Input VAT already paid on purchases	xxx
(c) Net amount to be paid to HMRC	xxx

In certain fairly rare circumstances *(a)* may be less than *(b)*. If that were to be the case, then it would be HMRC that would refund the difference *(c)* to the firm. Such a settlement between the firm and HMRC will take place at least every three months.

The recording of purchases in the purchases day book and purchases ledger follows a similar method to that of sales, but with the personal accounts being credited instead of debited. We can now look at the records of purchases for W Frank & Co, whose sales have been dealt with in Exhibit 18.2. The firm made the following purchases for March 2009:

	Total invoice, after trade discount deducted but before VAT added	VAT 17.5%
2009	£	£
March 1 E Lyal Ltd (*see* Exhibit 18.3)	200	35
March 11 P Portsmouth & Co	280	49
March 24 J Davidson	40	7
March 29 B Cofie & Son Ltd	80	14

Before looking at the recording of these in the purchases records, compare the first entry for E Lyal Ltd with Exhibit 18.3 to ensure that the correct amounts have been shown.

Exhibit 18.3

E Lyal Ltd
College Avenue
St Albans
Hertfordshire ST2 4JA

INVOICE No K 453/A

Date/tax point: 1/3/2009
Your order no BB/667

To: W Frank & Co   Terms: Strictly net 30 days
     Hayburn Road   VAT Reg. No: 236 4054 56
     Stockport

	£
50 metres of BYC plastic 1 metre wide x £3.60 per metre	180
1,200 metal tags 500mm x 10p each	120
	300
Less Trade Discount at 33⅓%	100
	200
Add VAT 17.5%	35
	235

The purchases day book can now be entered up.

Purchases Day Book				Page 38
	Folio	Total	VAT	Net
2009		£	£	£
March 1 E Lyal Ltd	PL 15	235	35	200
March 11 P Portsmouth & Co	PL 70	329	49	280
March 24 J Davidson	PL 114	47	7	40
March 29 B Cofie & Son Ltd	PL 166	94	14	80
Transferred to General Ledger		705	GL 90 105	GL 54 600

These transactions are entered in the purchases ledger. Once again, there is no need for the VAT to be shown as separate amounts in the accounts of the suppliers.

Purchases Ledger   *Page 15*

Dr   *E Lyal Ltd*   Cr

	2009	Folio	£
	March 1 Purchases	PB 38	235

Page 70

Dr   *P Portsmouth & Co*   Cr

	2009	Folio	£
	March 11 Purchases	PB 38	329

Page 114

Dr			J Davidson				Cr
			2009		Folio	£	
			March 24 Purchases		PB 38	47	

Page 166

Dr			B Cofie & Son Ltd				Cr
			2009		Folio	£	
			March 29 Purchases		PB 38	94	

The personal accounts have been credited with a total of £705, this being the total of the amounts which W Frank & Co will have to pay to them. The actual cost of purchases is not, however, £705. You can see that the correct amount is £600. The other £105 is the VAT that the various firms are collecting for HMRC. This amount is also the figure for VAT that is reclaimable from HMRC by W Frank & Co.

The debit entry in the purchases account is, therefore, £600, as this is the actual cost of the goods to the firm. The other £105 is entered on the debit side of the VAT account. Notice that there is already a credit of £119 in the VAT account in respect of the VAT added to sales.

General Ledger

Page 54

Dr			Purchases				Cr
2009		Folio	£				
March 31 Credit purchases							
for the month		PB 38	600				

Page 90

Dr			Value Added Tax				Cr
2009		Folio	£	2006		Folio	£
March 31 Purchases Day				March 31 Sales Day			
Book: VAT		PB 38	105	Book: VAT		SB 38	119
March 31 Balance c/d			14				
			119				119
				April 1 Balance b/d			14

In the final accounts of W Frank & Co, the following entries would be made:

(*a*) trading account for the month ended 31 March 2009:
  ● debited with £600 as a transfer from the purchases account
  ● credited with £680 as a transfer from the sales account
(*b*) balance sheet as at 31 March 2009:
  ● balance of £14 (credit) on the VAT account would be shown as a current liability, as it represents the amount owing to HMRC for VAT
(*c*) Note that in the trial balance at 31 March 2009
  ● balance of £14 would be shown as:
      VAT owing to HMRC (credit) £14.

Zero-rated businesses

These businesses:

(*a*) Do not have to add VAT onto their sales invoices, as their rate of VAT is zero or nil.
(*b*) They can, however, reclaim from HMRC any VAT paid on goods or services bought.

Accordingly, because of (*a*) no VAT is entered in the sales day book; VAT on sales does not exist. Because of (*b*) the purchases day book and purchases ledger will appear exactly in the same manner as for taxable firms, as already shown in the case of W Frank & Co. The VAT account will only have debits in it, being the VAT on purchases. Any balance on this account will be shown in the balance sheet as a debtor.

18.11 VAT and cash discounts

Where a cash discount is offered for prompt payment, VAT is calculated on an amount represented by the value of the invoice less such a discount. Even if the cash discount is lost because of late payment, the VAT will not change.

Exhibit 18.4 shows an example of such a sales invoice, assuming a cash discount offered of 2.5% and a VAT rate at 17.5%.

Exhibit 18.4

ATC Ltd
18 High Street
London WC2E 9AN

INVOICE No ZT 48910

VAT Reg No: 313 5924 71
Date/tax point: 11 May 2009
Your order no: TS/778

To: R Noble
     Belsize Road
     Edgeley
     Stockport

	£
500 paper dispensers @ £20 each	10,000
Less Trade Discount @ 20%	2,000
	8,000
Add VAT 17.5%	1,365*
Terms – 2.5% cash discount is paid within one month.	9,365

*The VAT has been calculated on the net price of £8,000 *less* the cash discount 2.5%, i.e. £7,800. Then the VAT at 17.5% on £7,800 is calculated as £1,365.

18.12 Book-keeping entries for businesses that cannot get refunds of VAT paid

Since these businesses do not add VAT onto the value of their sales invoices, there is obviously no entry for VAT in the sales day book or the sales ledger. They do not get a refund of VAT on purchases. This means that there will not be a VAT account; all that will happen is that VAT paid is included as part of the cost of the goods bought.

Assume that the only purchase made in a month was of goods for £120 + VAT £21 from D Oswald. The entries relating to it will appear as:

Purchases Day Book			Page 11
2009		Folio	£
May 16 D Oswald Ltd		PL 14	141
			141
			GL 17

	Purchases Ledger		Page 14
Dr	D Oswald Ltd		Cr
	2009	Folio	£
	May 16 D Oswald Ltd	PB 11	141

	General Ledger			Page 17
Dr		Purchases		Cr
2009	Folio	£	2009	£
May 31 Credit purchases			May 31 Transfer to	
for the month	PB 11	141	Trading Account	141

Trading Account for the month ended 31 May 2009 (extract)

	£	£
Sales		XXX
Less **Cost of goods sold**		
Purchases		141

18.13 VAT included in gross amount

Often only the gross amount of an item is known. This figure will, in fact, be made up of the net amount plus VAT. To find the amount of VAT that has been added to the net amount, a formula capable of being used with any rate of VAT is:

$$\frac{\% \text{ rate of VAT}}{100 + \% \text{ rate of VAT}} \times \text{Gross Amount} = \text{VAT in } \pounds$$

Suppose that the gross amount of sales was £940 and the rate of VAT was 17.5%. To find the amount of VAT and the net amount before VAT was added, you insert this information into the formula:

$$\text{VAT} = \frac{17.5}{(100 + 17.5)} \times £940 = \frac{17.5}{117.5} \times £940 = 140.$$

Therefore, the net amount was £800, which, with VAT £140 added, becomes £940 gross.

18.14 VAT on items other than sales and purchases

VAT is not just paid on purchases of raw materials and goods for resale. It is also payable on many items of expense and on the purchase of fixed assets.

Businesses that *can* get refunds of VAT paid will not include VAT as part of the cost of the expense or fixed asset. Businesses that *cannot* get refunds of VAT paid will include the VAT cost as part of the expense or fixed asset. For example, two businesses buying similar items would treat the following items as shown:

	Business that can reclaim VAT		Business that cannot reclaim VAT	
Buys Machinery £200 + VAT £35	Debit Machinery	£200	Debit Machinery	£235
	Debit VAT Account	£35		
Buys Stationery £160 + VAT £28	Debit Stationery	£160	Debit Stationery	£188
	Debit VAT Account	£28		

18.15 VAT owing

VAT owing by or to the business can be included with debtors or creditors, as the case may be. There is no need to show the amount(s) owing as separate items.

18.16 Relief from VAT on bad debts

It is possible to claim relief on any debt that is more than six months old and has been written off in the accounts. Should the debt later be paid, the VAT refunded will then have to be paid back to HMRC.

18.17 Purchase of cars

Normally, the VAT paid on a car bought for a business is not reclaimable.

Exhibit 18.5

	Value Added Tax Return	For Official Use	
HM Customs and Excise	For the period 01.04.10 to 30.06.10	SPECIMEN	

Bayley (Supplies) Ltd
Park Lane
Congleton
CW12 7EJ

Registration Number	Period
531 8210 44	06.10

You could be liable to a financial penalty if your completed return and all the VAT payable are not received by the due date.

Due date: 31.07.10

For Official Use

Before you fill in this form please read the notes on the back and the VAT leaflets *"Filling in your VAT return"* and *"Flat rate scheme for small businesses"*, if you use that scheme. Fill in all boxes clearly in ink, and write 'none' where necessary. Don't put a dash or leave any box blank. If there are no pence write "00" in the pence column. **Do not** enter more than one amount in any box.

For official use			£	p
	VAT due in this period on **sales** and other outputs	**1**	15,050	00
	VAT due in this period on **acquisitions** from other EC Member States	**2**	NONE	
	Total VAT due (**the sum of boxes 1 and 2**)	**3**	15,050	00
	VAT reclaimed in this period on **purchases** and other inputs (including acquisitions from the EC)	**4**	9,975	00
	Net VAT to be paid to Customs or reclaimed by you (Difference between boxes 3 and 4)	**5**	5,075	00
	Total value of **sales** and all other outputs excluding any VAT. **Include your box 8 figure**	**6**	86,000	00
	Total value of **purchases** and all other inputs excluding any VAT. **Include your box 9 figure**	**7**	57,000	00
	Total value of all **supplies** of goods and related costs, excluding any VAT, to other EC Member States	**8**	NONE	00
	Total value of all **acquisitions** of goods and related costs, excluding any VAT, from other EC Member States	**9**	NONE	00

If you are enclosing a payment please tick this box. ✓

DECLARATION: You, or someone on your behalf, must sign below.

I, ... CHARLES BAYLEY .... declare that the
(Full name of signatory in BLOCK LETTERS)
information given above is true and complete.

Signature ...... C. Bayley ...... Date 14 July 2010

A false declaration can result in prosecution

F

VAT 100

18. 21   Sales and purchases to EC Member States

In the above example, Bayley (Supplies) Ltd, it was assumed that the company had not made any sales to or purchased goods from EC Member States. However, in the past few years more and more UK businesses are dealing with European firms; in these cases it will be necessary to complete boxes 8 and 9. This is now illustrated with the following example:

Example 2: Let us assume that in the example above, Bayley (Supplies) Ltd sold £20,000 of goods and also purchased £10,000 of goods from EC Member States in the quarter ended 30 June 2010. These transactions would need to be included in the VAT return as follows:

- Box 8 – enter the £20,000 of goods sold to EC Member States, this figure is then added to the total in Box 6 (i.e. £86,000 + £20,000 = £106,000).
  Note: Sales to EC Member States do not have VAT charged on them provided the company has obtained the VAT registration number from the overseas business.
- The company's acquisitions of £10,000 is dealt with as shown below:
  1 In Box 9 enter the value of the acquisition, i.e. £10,000.
  2 Calculate the VAT on the acquisition, i.e. 17.5% of £10,000 = £1,750.
  3 In Box 2 enter the figure of VAT £1,750.
  4 Add Box 1 and 2 together to give £15,050 + £1,750 = £16,800 and enter this figure into box 3.
  5 In Box 4 add the figure of VAT to the VAT reclaimed figure, i.e. £1,750 + £9,975 = £11,725.
  6 In Box 5 the amount of VAT due to be paid remains the same as in our first example, i.e. £5,075.
  7 In Box 7 add the value of the acquisitions, i.e. £10,000, to the total purchases figure of £57,000 to give a figure of £67,000.

The VAT Return is now completed and is shown in Exhibit 18.6.

Exhibit 18.6

	Value Added Tax Return	For Official Use
HM Customs and Excise	For the period 01.04.10 to 30.06.10	SPECIMEN

Bayley (Supplies) Ltd.
Park Lane
Congleton
CW12 YEJ

Registration Number	Period
531 8210 44	06.10

You could be liable to a financial penalty if your completed return and all the VAT payable are not received by the due date.

Due date: 31.07.10

For Official Use

Before you fill in this form please read the notes on the back and the VAT leaflets *"Filling in your VAT return"* and *"Flat rate scheme for small businesses"*, if you use that scheme. Fill in all boxes clearly in ink, and write 'none' where necessary. Don't put a dash or leave any box blank. If there are no pence write "00" in the pence column. **Do not enter more than one amount in any box.**

For official use			£	p
	VAT due in this period on **sales** and other outputs	**1**	15,050	00
	VAT due in this period on **acquisitions** from other EC Member States	**2**	1,750	00
	Total VAT due (**the sum of boxes 1 and 2**)	**3**	16,800	00
	VAT reclaimed in this period on **purchases** and other inputs (including acquisitions from the EC)	**4**	11,725	00
	Net VAT to be paid to Customs or reclaimed by you (**Difference between boxes 3 and 4**)	**5**	5,075	00
	Total value of **sales** and all other outputs excluding any VAT. Include your box 8 figure	**6**	106,000	00
	Total value of **purchases** and all other inputs excluding any VAT. Include your box 9 figure	**7**	67,000	00
	Total value of all **supplies** of goods and related costs, excluding any VAT, to other EC Member States	**8**	20,000	00
	Total value of all **acquisitions** of goods and related costs, excluding any VAT, from other EC Member States	**9**	10,000	00

If you are enclosing a payment please tick this box. ☑

DECLARATION: You, or someone on your behalf, must sign below.

I, ... CHARLES BAYLEY ...... declare that the
(Full name of signatory in BLOCK LETTERS)

information given above is true and complete.

Signature ...... C. Bayley. ...... Date 14 JULY 2010

A false declaration can result in prosecution

F

VAT 100

Note: All firms registered for VAT that make sales to firms registered for VAT in EC Member States will also be required to complete an 'EC Sales List'. The form lists details of the firm's EC supplies and is supplied with the VAT Form 100 from HMRC.

18.22 VAT on goods taken for private use

If a trader takes some goods out of his own business stock for his own private use, the trader should be charged with any VAT due on these goods.

For instance, suppose that Smith, a furniture dealer, takes a table and chairs out of stock for permanent use in his own home. The cost to the business has been (cost price + value added tax). Therefore the proprietor's drawing should be charged with both the cost price of goods plus the VAT.

The double entry needed, assuming goods taken of £1,000 + VAT at 17.5%, would, therefore, be:

	£	£
Dr Drawings	1,175	
Cr Purchases		1,000
Cr VAT		175

There can be complicating circumstances, outside the scope of this book, that might influence the amount of VAT to be charged on such drawings.

Chapter summary

- Value added tax (VAT) is a tax levied on sales by the UK government. It is described as an 'indirect tax' and ultimately the tax is paid by the final consumer of the goods or services.
- VAT is administered in the UK by HM Revenue and Customs.
- There are currently three rates of VAT, namely: standard rate, currently 17.5%; reduced rate, currently 5%; and zero rate.
- The way in which the VAT system operates is explained whereby VAT is paid at various stages in the distribution chain.
- Businesses may be classified as standard-rated, zero-rated, exempt or partially exempt.
- The book-keeping entries for the recording of VAT in the books of account is shown for the various types of business.
- When preparing sales invoices the trade discount is deducted before VAT is added.
- If a business allows cash discount for prompt payment the VAT is calculated on the sales value less any cash discount offered. If the cash discount is lost because of late payment the VAT will not change.
- VAT may also be charged on items of expense and the purchase of fixed assets. The book-keeping entries vary depending upon whether the firm is able to reclaim the VAT paid or not.
- At the end of a particular period, either quarterly or annually, a VAT return form is completed and sent to HMRC together with any payment due. Alternatively, there may be a refund due.

EXERCISES

18.1 On 1 May 2009, D Wilson Ltd, 1 Hawk Green Road, Stockport, sold the following goods on credit to G Christie & Son, The Golf Shop, Hole-in-One Lane, Marple, Cheshire:

Order No A/496
3 sets of 'Boy Michael' golf clubs at £240 per set.
150 Watson golf balls at £8 per 10 balls.
4 Faldo golf bags at £30 per bag.
Trade discount is given at the rate of $33^1/_3$%.
All goods are subject to VAT at 17.5%.

Required:
(*a*) Prepare the sales invoice to be sent to G Christie & Son. The invoice number will be 10586.
(*b*) Show the entries in the personal ledgers of D Wilson Ltd and G Christie & Son.

18.2 The following sales have been made by S Thompson Ltd during the month of June 2009. All the figures are shown 'net' after deducting trade discount, but before adding VAT at the rate of 17.5%.

2009
August	1	to M Sinclair & Co	£160
"	8	to M Brown & Associates	£240
"	19	to A Axton Ltd	£80
"	31	to T Christie	£40

You are required to enter up the sales day book, sales ledger and general ledger in respect of the above items for the month.

18.3 The following sales and purchases were made by R Colman Ltd during the month of May 2009:

	Net	VAT added
2009	£	£
May 1 Sold goods on credit to B Davies & Co	160	28
" 4 Sold goods on credit to C Grant Ltd	200	35
" 10 Bought goods on credit from:		
– G Cooper & Son	400	70
– J Wayne Ltd	240	42
" 14 Bought goods on credit from B Lugosi	40	7
" 16 Sold goods on credit to C Grant Ltd	120	21
" 23 Bought goods on credit from S Hayward	40	7
" 31 Sold goods on credit to B Karloff	80	14

Enter up the sales and purchases day books, sales and purchases ledgers, and the general ledger for the month of May 2009. Carry the balance down on the VAT account.

18.4X On 1 March 2009, C Black, Curzon Road, Stockport, sold the following goods on credit to J Booth, 89 Andrew Lane, Stockport, under Order No 1697:

20,000 coils sealing tape   @ £4.70 per 1,000 coils
40,000 sheets A5 paper   @ £4.50 per 1,000 sheets
30,000 sheets A4 paper   @ £4.20 per 1,000 sheets
All goods are subject to VAT at 17.5%.

Required:
(*a*) Prepare the sales invoice to be sent to J Booth.
(*b*) Show the entries in the personal ledgers of J Booth and C Black.

18.5   At the quarter ending 30 June 2009 the following details of purchases, sales and VAT were extracted from the books of Ivy & Co.

	Purchases		Sales	
2009	*Net*	*VAT*	*Net*	*VAT*
	£	£	£	£
April	50,000	8,750	52,600	9,205
May	42,000	7,350	48,000	8,400
June	55,000	9,625	60,000	10,500

Required:
(*a*) Write up and balance the VAT account in the books of Ivy & Co for the quarter ended 30 June 2009.
(*b*) Explain the significance of the outstanding balance and how it will be cleared.

18.6X   The following information was extracted from the books of Mason Motors Ltd for the quarter ended 31 December 2009.

	Purchases		Sales	
2009	*Net*	*VAT*	*Net*	*VAT*
	£	£	£	£
October	37,600	6,580	75,000	13,125
November	39,400	6,895	62,000	10,850
December	52,000	9,100	68,000	11,900

Required:
(*a*) From the above details write up the VAT account for the quarter ended 31 December 2009.
(*b*) For what period of time must VAT records be kept?
(*c*) What book-keeping records would be required to record a cash refund of £120 (including VAT) to a customer?

18.7   You have been asked to prepare the sales invoice amount for photographic equipment recently delivered to your customer, Lawton Photography. The total amount of equipment supplied amounted to £2,320. The customer is entitled to the following discounts:

● trade discount 12.5%
● cash discount 2.5% (for payment within 7 days).

Required:
Calculate the amount of the sales invoice showing all your workings.

18.8X   (*a*) Photoprint Ltd recently purchased 22 reams of special printing paper for Job No. 67 at a cost of £3.75 per ream each plus VAT. When the job was complete Photoprint Ltd charged the customer £235.00 inclusive of VAT. How much VAT is owed to HMRC in respect of Job No. 67?

(b) The following amounts include VAT at a rate of 17.5%:

£47.00

£2.35

£62.60

£3.76

For each item calculate both the net and VAT amounts.

CHAPTER 19

VAT entries from sales and purchases day books

Learning objectives

After you have studied this chapter you should be able to:

- enter invoices into analytical sales and purchases day books
- post transactions from analytical sales and purchases day books to the personal accounts in the sales and purchases ledgers
- post totals from the analytical day books to the general ledger
- complete a VAT account from the day books.

19.1 Introduction

In Chapters 15 and 16, the sales and purchases day books were shown using only one total column for the value of the goods sold or purchased. Often goods are subject to VAT, as discussed in the previous chapter. In that chapter you will have noticed that additional columns were used to take account of the VAT, as shown in the Sales Day Book in Exhibit 18.2 and the Purchases Day Book in Exhibit 18.3.

In addition to accounting for VAT, many businesses find it useful to analyse their sales and purchases between different types of goods bought and sold, or perhaps between different departments. For example, a coffee shop may sell refreshments and gifts and wish to ascertain the profit on the two different sales areas. In this example it would be advantageous to analyse both sales and purchases to reflect the goods/services bought or sold in each area. The purchases day book could be ruled as follows:

Purchases Day Book						
Date	Details	Folio	Total	VAT	Gifts	Food
			£	£	£	£

19.2 Entering sales invoices into an analytical sales day book

When a business requires additional information from its records, the books can easily be adapted to meet particular needs.

Let us consider a retail computer shop that sells hardware and software to the public, local businesses and schools. The proprietor, Mr Harlow, wishes to monitor the sales of each of these lines separately. Exhibit 19.1 shows an example of Mr Harlow's **analytical sales day book**.

Exhibit 19.1

	Sales Day Book					(page 7)
Date	Details	Folio	Total	VAT	Software	Hardware
			£	£	£	£
April 1	Mount Hey School	SL 1	705	105		600
3	Ashby Marketing	SL 2	564	84	480	
15	Davenport Manufacturing	SL 3	4,700	700		4,000
20	St James College	SL 4	23,500	3,500		20,000
			29,469	4,389	480	24,600
				GL 3	GL 1	GL 2

19.3 Posting credit sales

Each sale now has to be posted to the individual debtors accounts in the sales ledger, as follows:

(i) The total of each sales invoice (i.e. the net price of the goods plus VAT) is posted to each individual debtors account on the debit side, since the goods are going 'into' their account.

(ii) At the end of the period, the sales day book is added up and the totals posted on the credit, or 'OUT', side of the following accounts:
- sales of software account
- sales of hardware account
- VAT account.

The results are shown below:

	Sales Ledger			SL 1
Dr	Mount Hey School			Cr
		Folio	£	
April 1 Sales		SB 7	705	

			SL 2
Dr	Ashby Marketing Co		Cr

	Folio	£	
April 3 Sales	SB 7	564	

			SL 3
Dr	Davenport Manufacturing Co		Cr

	Folio	£	
April 15 Sales	SB 7	4,700	

			SL 4
Dr	St James College		Cr

	Folio	£	
April 20 Sales	SB 7	23,500	

General Ledger

			GL 1
Dr	Sale of Software		Cr

		Folio	£
	April 30 Credit sales for April	SB 7	480

			GL 2
Dr	Sale of Hardware		Cr

		Folio	£
	April 30 Credit sales for April	SB 7	24,600

			GL 3
Dr	VAT		Cr

		Folio	£
	April 30 VAT on credit sales for April	SB 7	4,389

19.4 Entering purchase invoices into an analytical purchases day book

Another business might wish to monitor its purchases that might include goods for resale and business expenses such as electricity, motor expenses, etc. The example shown in Exhibit 19.2 illustrates how a business could analyse its purchase invoices using an **analytical purchases day book**.

Exhibit 19.2

			Purchases Day Book				(page 3)
Date	Details	Folio	Total	VAT	Goods	Motor Exp	Stationery
			£	£	£	£	£
Nov 1	Bould & Co	PL 1	4,230	630	3,600		
10	Sigley's (Stat)	PL 2	47	7			40
17	T Adams Ltd	PL 3	940	140	800		
30	Robinson's Garage	PL 4	188	28		160	
			5,405	805	4,400	160	40
				GL 3	GL 1	GL 2	GL 3

19.5 Posting credit purchases

Each purchase now has to be posted to the individual creditors' accounts in the purchase ledger, as follows:

(i) The *total* of each purchase invoice (i.e. the net price of the goods, plus VAT) is posted to each individual creditor's account on the *credit* side, since the goods are coming 'OUT' of their accounts.

(ii) At the end of the period, the purchases day book is added up and the totals are posted on the *debit*, or 'IN', side of the following accounts:
- purchases account
- motor expenses account
- stationery account
- VAT account.

	Purchases Ledger			PL 1
Dr	Bould & Co			Cr
			Folio	£
	Nov 1 Purchases		PB 3	4,230

				PL 2
Dr	Sigley's Stationers			Cr
			Folio	£
	Nov 10 Purchases		PB 3	47

				PL 3
Dr	T Adams Ltd			Cr
			Folio	£
	Nov 17 Purchases		PB 3	940

				PL 4
Dr	Robinson's Garage			Cr
			Folio	£
	Nov 30 Purchases		PB 3	188

General Ledger   GL 1

Dr			Purchases			Cr
		Folio	£			
Nov 30 Credit purchases for November		PB 3	4,400			

GL 2

Dr			Motor Expenses			Cr
		Folio	£			
Nov 30 Purchases day book		PB 3	160			

GL 3

Dr			Stationery			Cr
		Folio	£			
Nov 30 Purchases day book		PB 3	40			

GL 4

Dr			VAT			Cr
		Folio	£			
Nov 30 Purchases day book		PB 3	805			

19.6 Further example of the VAT account

In the above sections it has been shown that VAT is recorded in a separate column in both the sales and purchases day book. You have also seen that the total of the VAT columns have been transferred into the VAT account at the end of each month. In the same way that VAT is recorded in the sales and purchases day books there are also separate VAT columns in both the sales returns and purchases returns day books. Taking these into account the VAT account is as follows:

Dr	**VAT Account**	Cr
(Input tax)		*(Output tax)*
VAT on purchases		VAT on sales and/or services
VAT on sales returns		VAT on purchase returns
VAT on expenses		VAT on other income
VAT on purchases of fixed assets (except cars)*		VAT on sale of fixed assets*

*The purchase and sale of fixed assets is discussed later on in this book in Chapters 26 and 27.

The following example shows the VAT account including sales, purchases, sales returns and purchases returns.

Example: The following financial information has been extracted from the books of Morridge Products Ltd for the period 1 January to 31 March 2009. Prepare the VAT account for the quarter ended 31 March 2009 and state the amount of VAT to be paid to HMRC.

	Purchases		Purchases Returns	
2009	Net (£)	VAT (£)	Net (£)	VAT (£)
January	20,000	3,500	1,000	175
February	15,000	2,625	400	70
March	18,000	3,150	–	–
	53,000	9,275	1,400	245

	Sales		Sales Returns	
2009	Net (£)	VAT (£)	Net (£)	VAT (£)
January	40,000	7,000	1,200	210
February	28,000	4,900	–	–
March	35,000	6,125	800	140
	103,000	18,025	2,000	350

The account is shown below:

Dr		VAT Account		Cr
2009		2009		
Jan 31 Purchases Day Book	3,500	Jan 31 Sales Day Book		7,000
Jan 31 Sales Returns Day Book	210	Jan 31 Purchases Returns Day Book		175
Feb 28 Purchases Day Book	2,625	Feb 28 Sales Day Book		4,900
Mar 31 Purchases Day Book	3,150	Feb 28 Purchases Returns Day Book		70
Mar 31 Sales Returns Day Book	140	Mar 31 Sales Day Book		6,125
Mar 31 Balances c/d	8,645			
	18,270			18,270
		Apr 1 Balance b/d		8,645

The amount of VAT due to be paid to HMRC for the quarter ended 31 March 2009 is £8,645. Until this payment is made it is a liability and would appear in the trial balance on the credit side as follows:

Trial balance as at 31 March 2009

	Dr £	Cr £
VAT owing to HMRC		8,645

In some cases where the VAT on **inputs** exceeds the output VAT then a refund would be due to the company from HMRC. For example if input VAT for the quarter ended 30 June 2009 amounted to £1,000 and the output VAT was £750 then a refund of £250 would be due to the company. This would appear on the trial balance as a debit entry, see below:

Trial balance as at 30 June 2009

	Dr £	Cr £
VAT due from HMRC	250	

19.7   Advantages of analysis books

The advantages of analysis books are that businesses can be provided with exactly the information that they need, at the time when they want it. Different firms have different needs, and they therefore analyse their books in different ways.

Analysis books enable businesses to do such things as:

● calculate the profit or loss made by each part of a business
● draw up control accounts for the sales and purchases ledgers (see Chapter 25)
● keep a check on the sales of each type of goods
● keep a check on goods sold in different locations, departments or sections
● identify purchasers of each type of good offered for sale.

Chapter summary

● Many organisations use analytical day books for entering sales and purchases invoices, they are books of original entry.
● Analytical day books are especially useful for the recording of VAT since the day book contains several analysis columns allowing the VAT content of an invoice to be recorded. The additional columns enable further analysis to be made, for example, recording sales for different sections of the business or different types of expenditure in the purchases day book.
● Invoices are entered and analysed according to the type of sale or expense at the time the transaction is recorded.
● The total amount of the invoice (i.e. the amount of the goods plus the VAT) is posted to the individual debtors' or creditors' account.
● At the end of the month the total of the VAT column and other columns, appropriately analysed, will be posted to the accounts in the general ledger.
● At the end of the period the VAT account is prepared from the sales, purchases, sales returns and purchases returns accounts.
● There are many advantages of using analytical day books.

EXERCISES

19.1   The Curtain Design Company sells both ready-made and custom-made curtains to local hotels, nursing homes and the public. It operates an analytical sales day book, where it analyses the sales into sales of ready-made curtains and custom-made curtains.

The following invoices were sent during November 2009. All goods are subject to VAT at 17.5%.

Date	Customer	Ready-made £	Custom-made £
Nov 1	Jarvis Arms Hotel		2,300
Nov 8	Springs Nursing Home	1,000	
Nov 15	J P Morten	220	
Nov 17	Queen's Hotel		1,500
Nov 30	W Blackshaw	90	

You are required to:

(*a*) record the above transactions in an analytical sales day book

(*b*) post the invoices to the personal accounts in the sales ledger

(*c*) post the totals to the appropriate accounts in the general ledger.

19.2 The Hall Engineering Company manufactures small engineering components for the motor-car industry. It operates an analytical purchases day book, in which the purchases invoices are recorded.

During May 2009, the following invoices were received. All goods are subject to VAT at 17.5%.

			£
May 1	Black's Engineering Co	Engineering goods	520
May 3	Ace Printing Co	Printing catalogues	145
May 24	Morgan's Garage	Petrol Account	120
May 26	Martin's Foundry	Engineering parts	700
May 28	Office Supplies	Stationery	126
May 29	Black's Engineering Co	Engineering parts	220

Required:

(*a*) Enter the purchase invoices in an analytical purchases day book using the following analysis columns:
  ● Engineering parts
  ● Printing and stationery
  ● Motor expenses
  ● VAT.

(*b*) Post the transactions to the personal accounts in the purchases ledger.

(*c*) Post the totals to the appropriate accounts in the general ledger.

19.3 Smart Campers supplies an extensive range of camping equipment and accessories. It has three branches, situated at Horsforth, Moortown and Otley. Sales day books are kept at Head Office and are compiled from information received from branches.

During the month of May 2009, credit sales were as follows. All sales are subject to VAT at 10%.

2 May
 Outdoor Centre
 Moortown branch
 12 Flair cool boxes at £15.90 each
 6 Camping stoves at £29.95 each
 All less trade discount 20%

8 May
 Premier Leisure
 Horsforth branch
 10 Explorer rucksacks at £34.99 each
 Less trade discount 20%
 12 Trekker ridge tents at £59.95 each
 Less trade discount 15%

16 May
 Airedale Sport
 Otley branch
 8 Palma cool bags at £7.85 each
 12 Flair cool boxes at £15.90 each
 All less trade discount 20%

28 May	Empire Products
	Moortown branch
	14 Dome tents at £47.90 each
	8 Trekker ridge tents at £59.95 each
	All less trade discount 15%

You are required to draw up a sales day book with analysis columns as follows: Total, Horsforth, Moortown, Otley and VAT. Once that has been done, enter the above transactions for May 2009.

OCR

19.4X Adel Garden Centre divides its purchases of stock into two main departments: Outdoor Furniture and Garden Tools. Credit purchases during the month of October 2009 were as set out below, with VAT at 10% to be included on all transactions.

2 October	Oakland Supplies
	6 steel spades at £18.75 each
	8 garden forks at £10.50 each
	Less trade discount 20%
14 October	Airedale Products
	4 patio furniture sets at £49.60 each
	Less trade discount 15%
22 October	Oakland Supplies
	6 garden tool sets at £34.90 each
	4 garden forks at £10.50 each
	Less trade discount 20%
	8 sun loungers at £39.95 each
	Less trade discount 25%
20 October	Airedale Products
	1 patio furniture set invoiced on 14 October was returned because it was damaged. A credit note was issued.
28 October	Oakland Supplies
	2 garden tool sets were returned because they were faulty. A credit note was issued.

You are required to do the following:
(*a*) Draw up a purchases day book and purchases returns day book with analysis columns for Total, Outdoor Furniture, Garden Tools and VAT. Enter the date, name of supplier and the amounts of money into the appropriate columns. (Details of invoices are NOT required in the day books.)
(*b*) Total the day books.
(*c*) Write up the purchases ledger accounts from the day books, and balance the accounts at the end of the month.

OCR

Business banking

Learning objectives

After you have studied this chapter you should be able to:

● appreciate the legal relationship with the bank and the customer
● differentiate between current, deposit and loan accounts
● understand the various methods of transferring money by the banking system
● appreciate the services offered by a bank
● understand the clearing system
● be aware of the security measures necessary when using electronic methods of banking
● appreciate the use of the bank statement.

20.1 Introduction

The trading activity, in which all businesses are engaged, involves the transfer of money as goods and/or services are bought and sold. In order to facilitate money transfer all businesses will require a bank account. Banks can offer their business customers three main types of accounts:

1 *Current accounts* are used for regular payments into and out of a bank account. A cheque book will be given by the bank to the holder of the account, who will use it to make payments to people to whom they owe money. Payment may also be made by standing order or direct debit. The holder will be given a paying-in book to enable money to be paid into their current account. An overdraft facility can often be made available by the bank but prior arrangements need to be made. Current accounts do not normally earn interest but more recently some banks have been offering interest on these accounts to attract customers.

2 *Deposit accounts* are for holding money that is not required for making payments in the foreseeable future, i.e. savings. Interest is given by the bank on money kept in such accounts.

3 *Loan accounts* provide funds to an individual or business usually to finance the purchase of a capital item such as a motor vehicle, plant and equipment. Loans are usually for a fixed period, for example, three years, and interest is charged to the customer.

The opening of such accounts will involve a contract between the ban_ customer clearly stating the relationship between the two parties and the relating to the operation of the account/s.

The banking system has changed dramatically over the past few years and there _ now a number of different ways in which money can be transferred between bus nesses and their customers.

20.2 Transferring money

This can be received or paid by a business or organisation by various methods, including the following:

- cash
- **cheques**
- debit cards
- **credit cards**
- bank giro credit transfer
- BACS – this is the **Bankers' Automated Clearing Service**
- **standing order**
- **direct debits**
- paying-in slips.

20.3 Cash

Receiving cash

Cash is still used extensively in the retail business by customers purchasing goods. Security is a major problem in a number of ways for the business receiving the cash as shown below:

- it must be counted and checked to ensure that it corresponds with any documentation showing the amount to be received
- it must be stored safely and taken to the bank as soon as possible
- counterfeit money can be in circulation and detection equipment could be needed to prevent this type of fraud
- there should be regular internal checks to ensure that the persons handling cash are honest and funds do not go astray.

Most cash sales are made where electronic cash tills are in operation and these issue receipts automatically. The receipts should be kept by customers, not only as proof of payment, but, as evidence of the purchase should the goods have to be returned if faulty or unsuitable.

The electronic operation of the system ensures that the amount of cash received over a particular period is recorded automatically. The amounts received can easily be checked against the till records enabling cash deposits to the bank to be readily made.

A till receipt is shown in Exhibit 20.1.

Exhibit 20.1 Receipt for a cash sale

	MILO'S SUPERSTORE MANCHESTER
Name of store _____	VAT No. 212 5212 78
VAT registration number _____	RECEIPT
	Superjet travel game 17.50
Goods bought _____ {	Bulendo magic tricks 11.25
	Junior chess set 9.12
Total price due _____	3 items: TOTAL 37.87
Cash given _____	CASH 40.00
Change to be given _____	CHANGE 2.13
	Please keep receipt for refunds or queries
Location of cash till _____	Cash till No. 5
Date/time/reference number of transaction __	14/12/2009 11.58 1216 44/16

Cash that needs to be banked will be detailed on a paying-in slip – this is described in Section 20.14.

Paying by cash

When payments are made by a business it is safer and easier to use a non-cash method such as cheques or the BACS system (this is described in Section 20.9). Many firms who employ weekly paid staff still pay wages in cash and this method involves all the security problems which have been discussed previously. However, small value purchases can be made using the petty cash system. This is described in Chapter 22.

20.4 Cheques

Receiving cheques

Most customers who have received goods and/or services pay for them by cheque. These customers will have established a credit account with the business after credit worthiness checks have been carried out.

Cheques received from these well-established credit account customers should be carefully examined for the following:

- that the cheque is drawn payable to the receiver
- that the correct amount is stated both in words and in figures
- that the cheque is dated and is not out of date or postdated
- that the cheque has been properly signed.

If any of these factors are not in order the cheque will have to be returned to the drawer for amendment or for a new cheque to be issued. Cheques sent by post will not be accompanied by bank guarantee cards. It is not a legal requirement to issue a receipt for payment by cheque since the cheque is evidence of such payment. In spite of this many businesses do issue receipts.

When casual customers purchase goods and pay for them by cheque the business will only accept such payment when the cheque is supported by a **bank guarantee/ debit card**. The card company that has issued the card will guarantee to pay the cheque amount due. These cards usually have a cheque guarantee limit of £100. Cheques received by the business should be paid into the bank as soon as possible using paying-in slips.

Paying by cheque

When a business pays by cheque for goods or services it must be signed by an authorised signatory. The person signing the cheque for the business must have the approval of the company. The bank will also have previously been notified of the name of this person and will have carried out checks to verify this person's identity. They are legally bound to carry out this procedure to prevent fraud and to counter money-laundering activities. Larger businesses will usually insist on at least two authorised signatories to ensure proper payments are made.

It is vital that the business's account has sufficient money in it to cover the amounts paid otherwise the bank will not process the cheque.

The person writing the cheque and using it for payment is known as the **drawer**. The person to whom the cheque is paid is known as the **payee** and the **drawee** is the bank. A completed cheque is shown in Exhibit 20.2.

Exhibit 20.2

The completed cheque shows that J Woodstock, the drawer, is paying K Marsh, the sum of £72.85 on 22 May 2009. The counterfoil, at the left-hand side of the cheque, is also completed and retained by J Woodstock as a record of the transaction. It will be used to enter the details in the cash book which is covered in a later chapter.

Security of cheques

All cheques used by businesses will be crossed with two diagonal lines pre-printed on the face of the cheque as shown in Exhibit 20.2. This ensures that it must be paid into a bank account, building society account or saving account. The bank will ensure that it is paid into the payee's account if the words 'A/c Payee Only' are written between the diagonal lines.

Cheque clearing

It is important to understand that when a cheque is sent from one business to another it takes time to clear or process it. The business receiving the cheque will pass this to its bank who will in turn seek approval from the drawer's bank to transfer the amount shown on the cheque. The process involves an exchange centre where each bank collects the cheques drawn on accounts held with the centre. Typically the process takes three to five working days. It is important that cheques received by a business are banked on the same day to ensure that the funds are received as early as possible.

At the time of writing, the Office of Fair Trading (OFT) is in negotiation with the banking industry to clarify the cheque clearing cycle.

20.5 Credit cards

Receiving money by credit card

Credit cards are a method for customers to purchase goods without needing to pay by cash or make out a cheque. They can also be used when the customer wishes to make a purchase by telephone, fax or via the internet. Credit cards are issued by organisations such as Visa and Mastercard who operate the system. A recent development has been the 'chip and pin' system which involves the bank issuing a card with a unique four-digit number to each customer.

The business will have an electronic card acceptance point into which the customer places the card. When the system has recognised the card the customer is requested to enter his or her unique number and upon validation the purchase value will be accepted. The business bank account will be credited with the purchase sum automatically. This new system has resulted in a substantial reduction in fraudulent transactions. It has eliminated the need for the business to check the card details and the customer's signature which saves time. However, extreme care should be taken when entering the PIN number so that it cannot be seen by other customers or employees.

When customers are remote from the business they will have to provide the following information:

● card number – 16-digit and on some occasions the last 3 digits of the security number on the reverse side of the card
● expiry date of the card
● name printed on the card.

Again the purchase sum is transferred automatically to the business and the customer's account with the company is charged.

Paying by credit card

Some organisations provide business credit cards to their staff usually to pay for such things as hotel accommodation, travel expenses, etc. When these are used the charge will be made to the business, not to the person who has used the card. The business will set limits of expenditure on the card and will require copy vouchers and any other form of receipt to be handed in regularly. These will then be compared with the monthly account received from the credit card company.

20.6 Debit cards

Debit cards are issued by a number of banks in conjunction with Visa, Mastercard, etc., and are used in a very similar way to credit cards. Customers operate the same 'chip and pin' system, the crucial difference is that at the time of making payment by debit card, funds are electronically transferred from the purchaser's bank to the supplier's bank account.

Most banks now provide their customers with debit cards having more than one function. In addition to being able to make payments without making out a cheque, debit cards can act as a cheque guarantee card, usually up to £100 maximum, and also for making withdrawals from cash machines both in the UK and abroad. This is a popular way for customers to purchase all types of goods and services since it is quick and efficient, cash free and from the point of view of the supplier payment is guaranteed once the purchase has been validated by the system.

The most important aspect of using debit cards is to ensure that the customer has adequate funds in his or her account before attempting to use these facilities.

20.7 Electronic funds transfer at point of sale (EFTPOS)

The **EFTPOS** system is used when credit card and debit card transactions are made as described in Sections 20.5 and 20.6. In the case of credit cards the supplier usually receives payment within two days whereas the use of debit cards means the purchaser's bank account is debited at the point of sale and the supplier's bank account is credited with the customer's purchase amount.

20.8 Bank giro credit transfer

This is a safe and convenient way of receiving and paying money. Money paid by this method will be received directly into the business's bank account and the sums received will be shown on its bank statement.

Paying by this method requires the business to prepare the payments in the usual way but in addition prepares a list and bank giro credit slips detailing each payee's banking details and the amount due. The list and slips are then sent to the bank with one cheque to cover all the payments. These will be automatically sent to the various bank accounts through a centralised system.

This form of money transfer is still in use but larger organisations have adopted the BACS system.

20.9 BACS (Bankers' Automated Clearing Service)

The service enables the business to receive money due to it and to make payments. BACS is a company owned by the Bank of England, the high street banks and some building societies, which offers a computerised payment transfer system that organisations may use to pay not only wages and salaries but also creditors, dividends, grants, pensions, etc.

Processing the transfers is a three-day cycle. Information is stored by the BACS system to enable payments to be made on pre-set days, such as salary payments.

It is important to note that a remittance advice should be sent to the supplier when using BACS. Failing this the supplier will not know that the payment has been made until they receive their bank statement. They may also have difficulty in tracing the identity of the business paying the amount.

When the business receives payment from their customers they will also need a remittance advice from the customer for exactly the same reason as explained above and to know which invoices have been covered by the payment.

20.10 Standing order

A person may make a regular payment from their bank account, or receive a regular amount into their account by standing order. This is a straightforward method of making regular fixed payments over which the payer has full control. The steps necessary to make payments by a standing order are as follows:

- **payer** instructs the bank in writing to pay a certain amount, on a particular day to a specific organisation
- bank makes payment via the computer banking system.

The payer can instruct the bank to cease or amend the payment at any time by giving written notification.

20.11 Direct debit

This has become a common method of paying both fixed and variable amounts of money. Many businesses offer discounts on payment since they are so anxious for their customers to use this method. The system of operation is as follows:

- the proposed receiver (**payee**) of the money sends a mandate to the payer
- **payer** completes the mandate and returns it to the payee
- payee sends the mandate to the payer's bank who will arrange to send the money to the payee's bank via the computer banking system.

The amounts that the payer has authorised to be withdrawn from their own account can vary as the payee makes changes. Typical examples of variations are usually increases in insurance premiums, business rates and loan repayments. It is normal for the payee to advise the payer of such increases.

Payees prefer this method of regular payment since they have control over them and should the payer wish to cancel a direct debit they have to do so through the bank/payee. While this method of payment is convenient for both parties, the payer should exercise great care in giving permission for the setting up of direct debits.

The process of setting up a direct debit mandate as described above is quite laborious and time-consuming. However, it is now possible to set up a direct debit by telephone or online using the **Automated Direct Debit Instruction Service (AUDDIS)**. This is a fast way of arranging for a business to make repayments almost immediately for, say, the purchase of computer equipment and to pay by instalments. The safeguards of the Direct Debit Guarantee apply to both a paper-based mandate and paperless mandate.

20.12 Large transfers of money

Bank drafts

When a business wants to make a large purchase from a supplier with whom they have no credit account it could mean it having to use a **bank draft**. A bank draft is raised by the business's bank from funds held by the business and is passed to the supplier for whom it is a secure and guaranteed method of payment.

Clearing House Automated Payments System (CHAPS)

The **CHAPS** computerised system has been developed to facilitate the same-day transfer of large amounts of money. It is particularly useful for the sale and purchase of residential and commercial property.

20.13 Internet business transactions

Most businesses nowadays have websites where the goods or services on offer can be viewed and purchases made online. Since the purchaser and supplier are remote from each other transactions are made using a credit card or a debit card. The use of these cards is covered in Sections 20.5 and 20.6.

The online facilities provided by businesses for selling their goods/services are being used increasingly. Consumers can quickly search a number of like suppliers for the keenest prices and best delivery, without leaving home. The supplier will then despatch the goods to them.

Security of online buying is still of concern and businesses must ensure they have systems installed to guard against attempted fraud. Fraudulent transactions can come from a number of sources including:

- computer hackers accessing consumers' and businesses' files
- cloning of credit and debit cards which are then used to access legitimate consumers' bank accounts

- identity fraud where the criminal can apply to a bank for credit/debit cards based on the victim's details.

The encoding of data ('encryption') needs to be constantly reviewed and updated to prevent this type of crime.

20.14 Paying-in slips

A paying-in slip is prepared when the business wants to pay money into its current account. Details of cash and cheques, that are to be paid into the bank, are entered on the slip. The completed slip, cash and cheques are then taken to the bank. Normally a business deals with one particular branch of its bank but the bank giro credit shown in Exhibit 20.3 can be used to pay money into its account at any branch of any bank.

Exhibit 20.3

(a) Face of paying-in slip

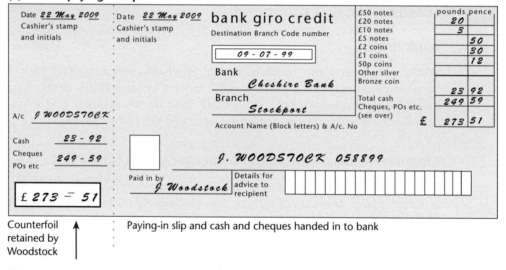

Counterfoil retained by Woodstock

Paying-in slip and cash and cheques handed in to bank

(b) Reverse side of paying-in slip

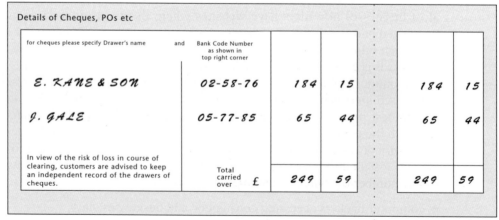

20.15 Bank statements

All the monies received and paid out of a business's current account are recorded in its cash book. The bank will also have a record of the transactions in its account for the business and will issue a statement of account on a regular basis, usually monthly.

It is important for the business to check the bank statement against the bank column in its own cash book to ensure that there are no errors (see Section 21.2). A bank reconciliation statement is usually prepared to reconcile the bank's balance with those in the business's cash book. This topic is covered in Chapter 23.

Chapter summary

- The trading activity is emphasised as meaning the sale of goods and/or services between organisations.
- Fundamental to the trading activity is the receipt and payment of money.
- There are three main bank accounts, namely the current, deposit and loan accounts.
- Transferring money in the business can be carried out in various ways: cash, cheque, credit cards, debit cards, EFTPOS, bank giro credit transfer, BACS, standing order and direct debits.
- Larger sums of money can be transferred via bank draft or by using the clearing house automated payments system (CHAPS).
- Internet business transactions are becoming more and more popular for the online sale and purchase of goods and services. It is important to ensure good security measures are in place to avoid fraudulent transactions taking place.
- Each of the above methods is discussed and reasons given as to why a business might use a particular method(s).
- Paying-in slips are described since they can be used to deposit both cash and cheques into a bank account.
- The use of the bank statement enables the business to check bank transactions against its cash book records.

EXERCISES

20.1   Businesses in the retail sector are highly likely to receive cash from their customers in payment for goods/services. State what steps a business should take in the handling, storage and transfer of cash to a bank.

20.2   State briefly what other non-cash methods are available to businesses in both receiving and paying out money.

20.3   BACS is an organisation formed to handle the transfer of money between businesses. State the full name of BACS and briefly describe how the organisation carries out this function.

20.4 Morridge Products Ltd receives a cheque which has the normal crossing but, in addition, the words 'A/c payee only' have been written between the lines. Explain how a bank would process this cheque.

20.5X Direct debits are a convenient method of making payments. Explain how the system operates and say what the advantages are for the payer and payee.

20.6X The cheque below has been received today.

      Northern Bank   **46-30-28**
      1 Main Street
      Dudley DY7 3AV

                                           Date   *31 June 2009*

      PAY *Senator Safes*   £   *552.00*

      Five hundred and twenty-five

      pounds only   BBP Limited

      ⑈100744⑈ 46⑈3028⑆ 33357800⑈

(*a*) Give *three* reasons why the cheque will not be honoured by the bank.
(*b*) What is the branch sort code number on the cheque?
(*c*) What document would you expect to be sent with a cheque in payment of an account?

AAT

20.7 Howard Photographics banks with The Central Bank and has recently sent a cheque to a supplier, Ben Brown Ltd. Give the name of the drawer, the drawee and the payee.

AAT

CHAPTER 21

Cash books

Learning objectives

After you have studied this chapter you should be able to:

● enter data into two and three column cash books

● balance off the cash book at the end of a period

● use folio columns for cross-referencing purposes

● enter 'contra' items in the cash book

● understand and complete entries for discounts allowed and discounts received both in the cash book, and at the end of a period, in the discount accounts in the general ledger.

21.1 Introduction

The cash book consists of the cash account and the bank account put together in one book. Initially, we showed these two accounts on different pages of the ledger; now it is easier to put the two sets of account columns together. This means that we can record all money received and paid out on a particular date on the same page.

In the cash book, the debit column for cash is put next to the debit column for bank. The credit column for cash is put next to the credit column for bank.

21.2 Drawing up a cash book

In Exhibit 21.1 the cash account and bank account are shown as separate accounts whereas in Exhibit 21.2 the cash and bank accounts are shown together in a cash book. The bank columns contain details of the payments made by cheque and direct transfer from the bank account and the money received and paid into the bank account. The bank will also keep a copy of the customer's account in its own records.

Periodically, or on request, the bank sends a copy of the account in its books to the business. This document is known as a **bank statement**. Upon receipt of the bank statement the business will check the transactions against the bank columns in its own cash book to ensure that there are no errors.

Exhibit 21.1

Dr		Cash Account		Cr
2009	£	2009		£
Aug 2 T Moore	33	Aug 8 Postage		20
Aug 5 K Charles	25	Aug 12 C Potts		19
Aug 15 F Hughes	37	Aug 28 Stationery		25
Aug 30 H Howe	18	Aug 31 Balance c/d		49
	113			113
Sept 1 Balance b/d	49			

Dr		Bank Account		Cr
2009	£	2009		£
Aug 1 Capital	1,000	Aug 7 Rates		105
Aug 3 W P Ltd	244	Aug 12 F Small Ltd		95
Aug 16 K Noone	408	Aug 26 K French		268
Aug 30 H Sanders	20	Aug 31 Balance c/d		1,204
	1,672			1,672
Sept 1 Balance b/d	1,204			

Exhibit 21.2

Dr			Cash Book			Cr
	Cash	Bank			Cash	Bank
2009	£	£	2009		£	£
Aug 1 Capital		1,000	Aug 7 Rates			105
" 2 T Moore	33		" 8 Postage		20	
" 3 W P Ltd		244	" 12 C Potts		19	
" 5 K Charles	25		" 12 F Small Ltd			95
" 15 F Hughes	37		" 26 K French			268
" 16 K Noone		408	" 28 Stationery		25	
" 30 H Sanders		20	" 31 Balance c/d		49	1,204
" 30 H Howe	18					
	113	1,672			113	1,672
Sept 1 Balances b/d	49	1,204				

'Money in' 'Money out'

21.3 Cash paid into the bank

In Exhibit 21.2 the payments into the bank were cheques received by the business, which were banked on receipt. We must now consider cash being paid into the bank.

1 Let us look at the position when a customer pays his account in cash, and later, a part of this cash is paid into the bank. The receipt of the cash is debited to the cash column on the date received, the credit entry being in the customer's personal account. The cash banked has the following effect, needing action as shown:

Effect	Action
(a) Asset of cash is decreased	Credit the asset account, i.e. the cash account that is represented by the cash column in the cash book.
(b) Asset of bank is increased	Debit the asset account, i.e. the bank account that is represented by the bank column in the cash book.

Now let us look at an example:

Example 1: A cash receipt of £100 from M Davies on 1 August 2009, later followed by the banking on 3 August of £80 of this amount, would appear in the cash book as follows:

Dr			Cash Book			Cr
	Cash £	Bank £			Cash £	Bank £
2009	100		2009		80	
Aug 1 M Davies			Aug 3 Bank			
Aug 3 Cash		80				

The details column shows entries against each item stating the name of the account in which the completion of double entry has taken place. Against the cash payment of £80 appears the word 'bank', meaning that the debit £80 is to be found in the bank column, and the opposite applies.

2 Where the whole of the cash received is banked immediately, the receipt can be treated in exactly the same manner as a cheque received, i.e. it can be entered directly in the bank column.

3 If the business requires cash it can present one of its own cheques to the bank that would exchange it for cash.

The twofold effect and the action required is:

Effect	Action
(a) Asset of bank is decreased	Credit the asset account, i.e. the bank column in the cash book.
(b) Asset of cash is increased	Debit the asset account, i.e. the cash column in the cash book.

This can be shown in the following example:

Example 2: A withdrawal of £75 cash on 1 June 2009 from the bank would appear in the cash book as:

Dr			Cash Book		Cr
	Cash £	Bank £		Cash £	Bank £
2009 June 1 Bank	75		2009 June 1 Cash		75

Both the debit and credit entries for this item are in the same book. When this happens it is known as a **contra** item.

21.4 The use of folio columns

As already illustrated the 'details column' in an account contains the name of the account in which the other part of the double entry has been entered. Anyone looking through the books should, therefore, be able to find the other half of the double entry in the ledgers. However, when many books are being used, just to mention the name of the other account may not be enough information to find the other account quickly. More information is needed, and this is given by using **folio columns**.

In each account and in each book being used, a folio column is added, always shown on the left of the money columns. In this column, the name of the other book and the number of the page in the other book where the other part of the double entry was made is stated against each and every entry. The double entry must always be completed before the folio columns are filled in.

An entry for receipt of cash from C Kelly whose account was on page 45 of the sales ledger, and the cash recorded on page 37 of the cash book, would have the following folio column entries:

- in the cash book, the folio column entry would be SL 45
- in the sales ledger, the folio column entry would be CB 37.

Note how each of the titles of the books is abbreviated so that it can fit into the space available in the folio column. Each of any contra items (transfers between bank and cash) being shown on the same page of the cash book and would use the letter 'C' (for 'contra') in the folio column. There is no need to also include a page number in this case. The act of using one book as a means of entering transactions into the accounts, in order to complete the double entry, is known as **posting** the items.

21.5 Advantages of folio columns

The advantages of using folio columns are as follows:

- Folio references are essential to help locate where entries have been posted to (see Section 21.4).
- Entering references in the folio columns confirms the transaction has been posted. Therefore, any item without a reference can easily be identified and subsequently posted.

21.6 Example of a cash book with folio columns

The following transactions are written up in the form of a cash book. The folio columns are filled in as though double entry had been completed to other accounts.

2009		£
Sept 1	Proprietor puts capital into a bank account for the business	10,940
Sept 2	Received cheque from M Boon	115
Sept 4	Cash sales	1,102
Sept 6	Bought stationery and paid by cash	35
Sept 7	Banked £400 of the cash held by the business	400
Sept 15	Cash sales paid direct into the bank	40
Sept 23	Paid cheque to S Wills	277
Sept 29	Withdrew cash from bank for business use	120
Sept 30	Paid wages in cash	518

Dr					Cash Book				Cr
		Folio	*Cash* £	*Bank* £			*Folio*	*Cash* £	*Bank* £
2009					2009				
Sept 1	Capital	GL 1		10,940	Sept 6	Stationery	GL 65	35	
" 2	M Boon	SL 98		115	" 7	Bank	C	400	
" 4	Sales	GL 87	1,102		" 23	S Wills	PL 23		277
" 7	Cash	C		400	" 29	Cash	C		120
" 15	Sales	GL 87		40	" 30	Wages	GL 39	518	
" 29	Bank	C	120		" 30	Balances	c/d	269	11,098
			1,222	11,495				1,222	11,495
Oct 1	Balances	b/d	269	11,098					

'Money in' 'Money out'

The abbreviations used in the folio column are as follows: GL = General Ledger; SL = Sales Ledger; C = Contra; PL = Purchases Ledger.

21.7 Cash discounts

Businesses prefer it if customers pay their accounts quickly. A firm may accept a smaller sum in full settlement if payment is made within a certain period of time. The amount of the reduction of the sum to be paid is known as a **cash discount**. The term 'cash discount' thus refers to the allowance given for quick payment. It is still called a cash discount even if the account is paid by cheque or by direct transfer into the bank account.

The rate of cash discount is usually stated as a percentage. Full details of the percentage allowed, and the period within which payment is to be made, are quoted on all sales documents by the selling company. A typical period during which a discount may be allowed is one month from the date of the original transaction.

21.8 Discounts allowed and discounts received

A firm may have two types of cash discounts in its books. These are:

- **Discounts allowed** – cash discounts allowed by a business to its customers when they pay their accounts quickly.
- **Discounts received** – cash discounts received by a business from its suppliers when it pays their accounts quickly.

We can now see the effect of discounts by looking at two examples.

Example 1: W Clarke owed us £100. He pays on 2 September 2009 by cash within the time limit laid down and the business allows him 5% cash discount. So he will pay £100 − £5 cash discount = £95 in full settlement of his account.

Effect	Action
1 Of cash: Cash is increased by £95. Asset of debtors is decreased by £95.	Debit: Cash Account, i.e. enter £95 in debit column of cash book. Credit: W Clarke £95.
2 Of discounts: Asset of debtors is decreased by £5. (After the cash was paid there remained a balance of £5. As the account has been paid this asset must now be cancelled.) Expenses of discounts allowed increased by £5.	Credit: W Clarke £5. Debit: Discounts allowed account £5.

This means that W Clarke's debt of £100 has now been shown as fully settled, and exactly how the settlement took place has also been shown.

Example 2: The business owed S Small £400 and pays him on 3 September 2009 by cheque. Since it pays within the specified 30 days it can claim $2\frac{1}{2}$% cash discount. The business will pay S Small £400 less £10 cash discount = £390 in full settlement of the account.

Effect	Action
1 Of cheque: Asset of bank is reduced by £390. Liability of creditors is reduced by £390.	Credit: Bank, i.e. enter in credit bank column, £390. Debit: S Small's account £390.
2 Of discounts: Liability of creditors is reduced by £10. (After the cheque was paid, the balance of £10 remained. As the account has been paid, the liability must now be cancelled.) Revenue of discounts received increased by £10.	Debit: S Small's account £10. Credit: Discounts received account £10.

The accounts in the business's books for both W Clarke and S Small would be as follows:

Cash Book (*page 32*)

	Folio	Cash	Bank		Folio	Cash	Bank
		£	£			£	£
2009				2009			
Sept 2 W Clarke	SL 12	95		Sept 3 S Small	PL 75		390

Dr , *Cr*

General Ledger (*page 18*)
Discounts Received Account

	Folio	£		Folio	£
			2009		
			Sept 2 S Small	PL 75	10

Dr , *Cr*

(*page 17*)
Discounts Allowed Account

	Folio	£		Folio	£
2009					
Sept 2 W Clarke	SL 12	5			

Dr , *Cr*

Sales Ledger (*page 12*)
W Clarke Account

	Folio	£		Folio	£
2009			2009		
Sept 1 Balance	b/d	100	Sept 2 Cash	CB 32	95
			Sept 2 Discount	GL 17	5
		100			100

Dr (left), *Cr* (right)

Purchases Ledger (*page 75*)
S Small Account

	Folio	£		Folio	£
2009			2009		
Sept 3 Bank	CB 32	390	Sept 1 Balance	b/d	400
Sept 3 Discounts	GL 18	10			
		400			400

Dr (left), *Cr* (right)

It is accounting custom to enter the word 'Discount' in the personal accounts, not stating whether it is a discount received or a discount allowed.

21.9 Discount columns in the cash book

The discounts allowed account and the discounts received account are in the general ledger, along with all the other revenue and expense accounts. It has already been stated that every effort should be made to avoid too much reference to the general ledger.

In the case of discounts, this is done by adding an extra column on each side of the cash book in which the amounts of discounts are entered. Discounts received are entered in the discounts column on the credit side of the cash book, and discounts allowed in the discounts column on the debit side of the cash book.

The cash book, if completed for the two examples so far dealt with, would appear thus:

		Folio	Discount £	Cash £	Bank £			Folio	Discount £	Cash £	Bank £
Cash Book											*(page 32)*
2009						2009					
Sept 2	W Clarke	SL 12	5	95		Sept 3	S Small	PL 75	10		390

There is no alteration to the method of showing discounts in the personal accounts.

To make entries in the discount accounts in the General Ledger

Total of discounts column on receipts side of cash book } Enter on debit side of Discounts Allowed Account

Total of discounts column on payments side of cash book } Enter on credit side of Discounts Received Account

21.10 A worked example

The following is an example of a three-column cash book for the whole of a month, showing the ultimate transfer of the totals of the discounts columns to the discount accounts in the General Ledger.

2009		£
May 1	Balances brought down from April:	
	Cash Balance	29
	Bank Balance	654
	Debtors accounts:	
	B King	120
	N Campbell	280
	D Shand	40
	Creditors accounts:	
	U Barrow	60
	A Allen	440
	R Long	100
May 2	B King pays us by cheque, having deducted $2^{1}/_{2}$% cash discount £3	117
May 8	We pay R Long his account by cheque, deducting 5% cash discount £5	95
May 11	We withdrew £100 cash from the bank for business use	100
May 16	N Campbell pays us his account by cheque, deducting $2^{1}/_{2}$% discount £7	273
May 25	We paid expenses in cash	92
May 28	D Shand pays us in cash after having deducted $2^{1}/_{2}$% cash discount	38
May 29	We pay U Barrow by cheque less 5% cash discount £3	57
May 30	We pay A Allen by cheque less $2^{1}/_{2}$% cash discount £11	429

(page 64)

Dr					**Cash Book**				Cr
	Folio	Discount	Cash	Bank		Folio	Discount	Cash	Bank
2009		£	£	£	2009		£	£	£
May 1 Balances	b/d		29	654	May 8 R Long	PL 58	5		95
May 2 B King	SL 13	3		117	May 11 Cash	C			100
May 11 Bank	C		100		May 25 Expenses	GL 77		92	
May 16 N Campbell	SL 84	7		273	May 29 U Barrow	PL 15	3		57
May 28 D Shand	SL 91	2	38		May 30 A Allen	PL 98	11		429
					May 31 Balances	c/d		75	363
		12	167	1,044			19	167	1,044
Jun 1 Balances	b/d		75	363					

Sales Ledger — *Page 13*

Dr			*B King Account*			Cr
2009	Folio	£	2009	Folio	£	
May 1 Balance	b/d	120	May 2 Bank	CB 64	117	
			May 2 Discount	CB 64	3	
		120			120	

Page 84

Dr			*N Campbell Account*			Cr
2009	Folio	£	2009	Folio	£	
May 1 Balance	b/d	280	May 16 Bank	CB 64	273	
			May 16 Discount	CB 64	7	
		280			280	

Page 91

Dr			*D Shand Account*			Cr
2009	Folio	£	2009	Folio	£	
May 1 Balance	b/d	40	May 28 Cash	CB 64	38	
			May 28 Discount	CB 64	2	
		40			40	

Purchases Ledger — *Page 15*

Dr			*U Barrow Account*			Cr
2009	Folio	£	2009	Folio	£	
May 29 Bank	CB 64	57	May 1 Balance	b/d	60	
May 29 Discount	CB 64	3				
		60			60	

Page 58

Dr			R Long Account			Cr
2009	Folio	£	2009	Folio	£
May 8 Bank	CB 64	95	May 1 Balance	b/d	100
May 8 Discount	CB 64	5			
		100			100

Page 98

Dr			A Allen Account			Cr
2009	Folio	£	2009	Folio	£
May 30 Bank	CB 64	429	May 1 Balance	b/d	440
May 30 Discount	CB 64	11			
		440			440

General Ledger

Page 77

Dr			Expenses Account			Cr
2006	Folio	£		Folio	£
May 25 Cash	CB 64	92			

Page 88

Dr			Discounts Received Account			Cr
	Folio	£	2009	Folio	£
			May 31 Cash book	CB 64	19

Page 90

Dr			Discounts Allowed Account			Cr
2009	Folio	£		Folio	£
May 31 Cash book	CB 64	12			

Is the above method of entering discounts correct? You can easily check. See the following:

Discounts in Ledger Accounts	Debits		Credits	
		£		£
Discounts received	U Barrow	3	Discounts	
	R Long	5	Received	
	A Allen	11	Account	£19
		19		
				£
Discounts allowed	Discounts		B King	3
	Allowed		N Campbell	7
	Account	£12	D Shand	2
				12

You can see that proper double entry has been carried out. Equal amounts, in total, have been entered on each side of the accounts.

21.11 Bank overdrafts and the cash book

A business may borrow money from a bank by means of a **bank overdraft**. This means that the business is allowed to pay more out of the bank account, by paying out cheques, than the total amount available in the account.

Up to this point the bank balances have all been money at the bank, and so they have all been assets, i.e. debit balances. When the account is overdrawn, the business owes money to the bank and so the account is a liability and the balance a credit one.

Taking the cash book shown, suppose that the amount payable to A Allen was £1,429 instead of £429. Thus the amount in the bank account, £1,044, is exceeded by the amount withdrawn. The cash book would appear as follows:

Dr				Cash Book			Cr
	Discount	Cash	Bank		Discount	Cash	Bank
2009	£	£	£	2009	£	£	£
May 1 Balances b/d		29	654	May 8 R Long	5		95
" 2 B King	3		117	" 11 Cash			100
" 11 Bank		100		" 25 Expenses		92	
" 16 N Campbell	7		273	" 29 U Barrow	3		57
" 28 D Shand	2	38		" 30 A Allen	11		1,429
" 31 Balance c/d			637	" 31 Balance c/d		75	
	12	167	1,681		19	167	1,681
Jun 1 Balance b/d		75		Jun 1 Balance b/d			637

On a balance sheet, a bank overdraft will be shown as an item included under the heading Current Liabilities.

Full coverage of the treatment of discounts allowed and discounts received in the financial statements is shown in Chapter 29.

Chapter summary

- A cash book is made up of a cash account and a bank account put together into one book.
- Entries made on the debit side of the cash book are in respect of monies received via cash, cheque or bank transfer. The money comes 'into' the business and is therefore entered on the debit 'in' side of the cash book.
- Entries made on the credit side of the cash book are in respect of monies paid out via cash, cheque or bank transfer. Money is paid 'out' of the business so entries are made on the 'out' side of the account.

- Folio columns are used in the cash book so that items may easily be traced to other accounts in the ledgers and to provide assurance that the double entries have been completed.
- Cash discounts are given to encourage prompt payment of outstanding accounts. The discount is referred to as cash discount irrespective of whether the account is settled by cash, cheque or bank transfer.
- Discount allowed is the amount of discount allowed by a business to its customers when their accounts are settled promptly and within the time limit.
- Discount received is when the business's suppliers allow them to deduct discount if they pay the account within the stated terms of trade.
- Discounts allowed and received are entered into the appropriate column in the cash book, totalled at the end of the period, and the amount transferred to the discount accounts in the general ledger.
- Should the balance at the bank go into an overdraft position then the balance brought down will appear on the credit side of the cash book.

EXERCISES

21.1 A two-column cash book is to be written up from the following, carrying the balances down to the following month:

2009
Jan 1 Started business with £4,000 in the bank
Jan 2 Paid for fixtures by cheque, £660
Jan 4 Cash sales £225: Paid rent by cash, £140
Jan 6 T Thomas paid us by cheque, £188
Jan 8 Cash sales paid direct into the bank, £308
Jan 10 J King paid us in cash, £300
Jan 12 Paid wages in cash, £275
Jan 14 J Walters lent us £500 paying by cheque
Jan 15 Withdrew £200 from the bank for business use
Jan 20 Bought stationery paying by cash, £60
Jan 22 We paid J French by cheque, £166
Jan 28 Cash drawings £100
Jan 30 J Scott paid us by cheque, £277
Jan 31 Cash sales £66.

21.2 You work for Stott & Co, a medium-sized clothes manufacturer, whose offices and works are situated in Derby. As book-keeper to the firm, one of your main duties is to enter up the cash book on a regular basis.

Required:
From the information given below, enter up the transactions for May 2009, balance off at the end of the month, and bring the balances down.

	£
May 1 Balances b/d	
Cash in hand	14.72
Bank (overdrawn)	820.54

May	2	Bought stationery by cash	10.00
May	3	Banked cheques received from:	
		P Wrench	432.36
		R Whitworth	634.34
		J Summers	341.00
May	6	South West Rail Ltd, cheque for travel expenses of company secretary to London	37.50
May	9	Paid the following accounts by cheque:	
		Fabulous Fabrics Ltd	450.80
		Mellors Manufacturing Co	348.32
May	12	Received from cash sale	76.00
May	14	Paid employees PAYE and NI to the HMRC, by cheque	221.30
May	17	Received cheque from Trentam Traders	32.81
May	20	Foreign currency drawn from bank for director's visit to Italy	250.00
		Bank charges re currency	3.20
May	24	Received cash from sale of goods	350.00
May	26	Cash to bank	300.00
May	27	Salaries by cheque	5,720.00
May	31	Received cheques from the following:	
		J Summers	1,231.00
		Bradnop Manufacturing Co	725.00
		Taylors	2,330.50

(NVQ Level 2)

21.3X As a trainee accounts clerk at Jepsons & Co you have as one of your tasks the job of entering up the business's cash book at the end of each month.

Required:
From the details listed below, enter up the cash book for February 2009, balance off at the end of the month, and bring the balances down.

2009			£
Feb	1	Balances brought down from January:	
		Cash in hand	76.32
		Cash at bank	2,376.50
Feb	2	Paid electricity bill by cheque	156.00
Feb	4	Paid motor expenses by cash	15.00
Feb	6	Received cheques from the following debtors:	
		D Hill	300.00
		A Jackson	275.00
		H Wardle	93.20
Feb	7	Paid for stationery by cash	3.70
Feb	10	Sold goods for cash	57.10
Feb	12	Paid for purchases from Palmer & Sons by cheque	723.50
Feb	14	Received loan by cheque from D Whitman	500.00
Feb	16	Paid Wright Brothers by cheque for repairs to office machinery	86.20
Feb	17	The proprietor, Stan Jepson, took cash for his own use.	50.00
		He asks you to pay his personal telephone bill by cheque to the post office	140.60
Feb	22	J Smith paid his account by cheque	217.00
Feb	23	Petrol bill paid by cash	21.00
Feb	26	Received cheque for sale of goods	53.00

	£
Feb 27 Bought new photocopier from Bronsons of Manchester and paid by cheque	899.00
Feb 28 Paid monthly salaries by cheque	2,400.00

21.4 Enter up a three-column cash book from the following details. Balance off at the end of the month, and show the relevant discount accounts as they would appear in the general ledger.

2009

May 1 Started business with £6,000 in the bank

May 1 Bought fixtures paying by cheque, £950

May 2 Bought goods paying by cheque, £1,240

May 3 Cash sales £407

May 4 Paid rent in cash, £200

May 5 N Morgan paid us his account of £220 by a cheque for £210, we allowed him £10 discount

May 7 Paid S Thompson & Co £80 owing to them by means of a cheque £76, they allowed us £4 discount

May 9 We received a cheque for £380 from S Cooper, discount having been allowed £20

May 12 Paid rates by cheque, £410

May 14 L Curtis pays us a cheque for £115

May 16 Paid M Monroe his account of £120 by cash £114, having deducted £6 cash discount

May 20 P Exeter pays us a cheque for £78, having deducted £2 cash discount

May 31 Cash sales paid direct into the bank, £88.

21.5 From the following details, write up a three-column cash book, balance off at the end of the month, and show the relevant discount accounts as they would appear in the general ledger.

2009

Mar 1 Balances brought forward:

   Cash in hand £211

   Cash at bank £3,984

Mar 2 We paid each of the following accounts by cheque, in each case we deducted a 5% discount: T Adams £80; C Bibby £260; D Clarke £440

Mar 4 C Potts pays us a cheque for £98

Mar 6 Cash sales paid direct into the bank, £49

Mar 7 Bought stationery £65 and paid by cash

Mar 9 The following persons pay us their accounts by cheque, in each case they deducted a discount of $2\frac{1}{2}$%: R Smiley £160; J Turner £640; R Pimlott £520

Mar 12 Paid motor expenses by cash, £100

Mar 18 Cash sales, £98

Mar 21 Paid for insurance by cheque, £120

Mar 23 Paid expenses by cash, £60

Mar 28 Received a cheque for £500 being a loan from R Godfrey

Mar 31 Paid for stationery by cheque, £27.

21.6X You are to write up a three-column cash book for M Pinero from the details that follow. Then balance off at the end of the month and show the discount accounts in the general ledger.

2009

May 1 Balances brought forward:

   Cash in hand £58

   Bank overdraft £1,470

May 2 M Pinero pays further capital into the bank, £1,000

May 3 Bought office fixtures by cheque, £780

May 4 Cash sales, £220

May 5 Banked cash, £200

May 6 We paid the following by cheque, in each case deducting $2\frac{1}{2}$% cash discount:
B Barnes £80; T Horton £240; T Jacklin £400

May 8 Cash sales, £500

May 12 Paid motor expenses in cash, £77

May 15 Cash withdrawn from the bank, £400

May 16 Cash drawings, £120

May 18 The following firms paid us their accounts by cheque, in each case deducting a 5%
discount: L Graham £80; B Crenshaw £140; H Green £220

May 20 Wages paid in cash, £210

May 22 T Weiskopf paid us his account in cash, £204

May 26 Paid insurance by cheque, £150

May 28 We banked all the cash in our possession except for £20 in the cash till

May 31 Bought motor van, paying by cheque, £4,920.

CHAPTER 22

Petty cash and the imprest system

Learning objectives

After you have studied this chapter you should be able to:

- understand why organisations use a petty cash book
- recognise the need for a petty cash voucher
- understand the imprest system
- make entries in a petty cash book
- post the appropriate amounts from the petty cash book to the various accounts in the general ledger at the end of the period.

22.1 Introduction to petty cash

All types of organisations from very small ones to large businesses usually incur small items of expenditure. The type of expenditure incurred would be such items as the purchase of postage stamps or perhaps the posting of a parcel to a customer, travel expenses, cleaning materials and stationery. The items purchased are usually paid for in cash by a member of staff, on behalf of the organisation, who then seeks reimbursement of the amount spent. A petty cash book is used to record these transactions. Larger amounts of expenditure will be paid for by cheque and recorded in the cash book as discussed in the previous chapter.

The petty cash book is a book of original entry since items are entered here first and it also acts as a ledger account for the cash in hand at any point of time.

22.2 Petty cash voucher

When a person incurs expenditure on behalf of the organisation they need to complete a **petty cash voucher** in order to reclaim the amount of money spent.

This will show details of the expense incurred together with a receipt (if possible), the amount spent including VAT and signed by the person making the claim. The petty cash voucher will then need to be authorised for payment. Often the petty cashier is able to authorise payments up to a specific limit, for example £25.00, with any amount above that usually being authorised by a manager or accountant.

When the petty cash voucher is entered into the petty cash book it will be numbered for future reference purposes and then filed. An example of a petty cash voucher is shown in Exhibit 22.1.

Exhibit 22.1

Petty Cash Voucher	No. _1_
	Date _2 May 2009_

Description	Amount		
		£	p
Stationery		14	10
(including VAT £2.10)			

Signature _Ken Boardman_
Authorised _Sandra Ashford_

22.3 The imprest system

The **imprest system** is where the cashier gives the petty cashier enough cash to meet the needs of the following period. At the end of the period, the cashier finds out the amounts spent by the petty cashier, and tops up the petty cashier's cash by an amount equal to that spent. The petty cash in hand should then be equal to the original amount with which the period was started. Exhibit 22.2 shows an example of this method.

Exhibit 22.2

		£
Period 1	The cashier gives the petty cashier	100
	The petty cashier pays out in the period	78
	Petty cash now in hand	22
	The cashier now gives the petty cashier the amount spent	78
	Petty cash in hand at the end of period 1	100
Period 2	The petty cashier pays out in the period	84
	Petty cash now in hand	16
	The cashier now gives the petty cashier the amount spent	84
	Petty cash in hand end of period 2	100

It may be necessary to increase the fixed sum, often called the **cash float**, to be held at the start of each period. In the above case, if we had wanted to increase the float at the end of the second period to £120, then the cashier would have given the petty cashier an extra £20, i.e. £84 + £20 = £104.

Advantages of using the petty cash imprest system

- A junior member of the accounts department, usually called the petty cashier, can be given the task of operating the system thus allowing the cashier to concentrate on other areas of work.
- Small items of expenditure incurred by the organisation are entered into the petty cash book and only the totals at the end of the period are posted to the appropriate accounts in the general ledger. Thus eliminating the main cash book and ledger accounts of numerous transactions.
- The imprest system enables the cash to be checked at any time since the amount paid out, represented by the petty cash vouchers, and the cash in hand should equal the float at the beginning of the period.

22.4 Worked example of an analytical petty cash book

A small company offering secretarial services to local businesses incurs the following items of expenditure during May 2009. The items shown in Exhibit 22.3 will initially require entering in the petty cash book.

Exhibit 22.3

2009

May 1 The petty cashier received a cash float of £200.00 from the cashier
May 2 Stationery £14.10 including VAT £2.10 (see petty cash voucher no. 1)
May 4 Postage stamps, £22.00
May 6 Tea and coffee for office visitors, £8.00
May 9 Travel expenses, £16.00
May 10 Computer disks, £12.80 including VAT £1.91
May 12 Postage on parcel, £3.60
May 15 Office cleaner, £25.00
May 22 Milk for office, £4.20
May 25 Received £6.00 from Anita Kerr, office manager, for personal photocopying*
May 27 Office cleaner, £25.00
May 27 Cleaning materials, £4.40 plus VAT 77p, total spent £5.17
May 31 Travel expenses, £23.00
May 31 The cashier reimbursed the petty cashier with the amount spent during the month.

Each of the above items will have had a petty cash voucher completed by the person who had incurred the expenditure on behalf of the business. For illustration purposes just one petty voucher is shown, petty cash voucher no. 1, see previous Exhibit 22.2.

*Receipts

Occasionally, a member of staff may wish to purchase stamps from the petty cashier or perhaps have some photocopying done for their own personal use. In these cases the petty cashier will issue a receipt to the staff member for the amount received. For example, see Exhibit 22.4.

Exhibit 22.4

RECEIPT			
Received from: Anita Kerr		**Date:** 25 May 2009	
The sum of: Six pounds only		**No.** 26	
		£	p
Cheque		–	–
Cash		6	00
		6	00
Re: Photocopying			
		Kim Patel	
		WITH THANKS	

The above items of expenditure and the receipt are entered in the petty cash book as illustrated in Exhibit 22.5.

Exhibit 22.5

Petty Cash Book   *(page 31)*

Receipts £ p	Date	Details	Voucher Number	Total £ p	VAT £ p	Postage £ p	Cleaning £ p	Travel Expenses £ p	Stationery £ p	Sundry Expenses £ p
	2009									
200.00	May 1	Cash	CB 19							
	May 2	Stationery	1	14.10	2.10				12.00	
	May 4	Postage stamps	2	22.00		22.00				
	May 6	Tea, coffee	3	8.00						8.00
	May 9	Travel expenses	4	16.00				16.00		
	May 10	Computer disks	5	12.80	1.91				10.89	
	May 12	Postage on parcel	6	3.60		3.60				
	May 15	Office cleaner	7	25.00			25.00			
	May 22	Milk	8	4.20						4.20
6.00	May 25	Anita Kerr								
		Photo-copying	26							
	May 27	Office cleaner	9	25.00			25.00			
	May 27	Cleaning materials	10	5.17	0.77		4.40			
	May 31	Travel expenses	11	23.00				23.00		
				158.87	4.78	25.60	54.40	39.00	22.89	12.20
	May 31	Balance	c/d	47.13	GL 17	GL 19	GL 29	GL 44	GL 56	GL 60
206.00				206.00						
47.13	June 1	Balance	b/d							
152.87	June 1	Cash	CB 22							

Reimbursement equals the total amount spent in May 2009 (£158.87 – £6.00 Receipt ∴ £152.87 reimbursed)

Total amount spent in May 2009

Entering the petty cash book

On 1 May the petty cashier received £200.00 cash from the main cashier. This is the amount of the float for the period of May.

The cashier would enter this item on the credit side of the cash book, the money comes 'OUT' of the bank. The debit entry is now shown on the 'Receipts' side of the petty cash book, the money comes 'INTO' the petty cash. Note the folio reference 'CB 19' (Cash Book page 19) is also entered to cross-reference the entry.

Each petty cash voucher is then entered in date order as follows:

- Enter the date.
- Enter the details of each payment.
- A voucher number is then given to each petty cash voucher and entered on the voucher itself and in the 'voucher number' column.
- The total amount of the expenditure incurred is then entered in the 'total' column.
- The expenditure is then analysed into an appropriate expense column.
- If VAT has been incurred then the VAT amount is entered in the 'VAT' column and the remaining expense in the appropriate column. For example, the petty cash voucher shown in Exhibit 22.1 is for stationery amounting to £14.10. In the total column £14.10 is entered, £2.10 is then entered in the VAT column and the cost of the stationery £12.00 is then entered in the stationery column.

Any money received from the sale of sundry items to a member of staff, as in the case of Anita Kerr who had some personal photocopying, then the receipt of the cash is entered into the 'receipts' column, in this example £6.00. The date, details and receipt number are also entered in the appropriate columns.

The petty cash book now requires balancing off at the end of the month as follows:

- Add up the 'total' column.
- Add up each of the expense columns. The total of all the expense columns added together should now equal the amount shown in the 'total' column.
  In Exhibit 22.5 this would be:

	£ p
VAT	4.78
Postage	25.60
Cleaning	54.40
Travel expenses	39.00
Stationery	22.89
Sundry expenses	12.20
Total	158.87

- The petty cashier now needs to calculate the amount of money needed to restore the imprest to £200.00 for the beginning of the next period. This is as follows:

	£ p
Amount of float at beginning of May	200.00
Money received during month	
Anita Kerr – Photocopying	6.00
	206.00
Less Amount spent (see above)	158.87
Cash in hand at 31 May 2009	47.13
Amount of float	200.00
Less Cash in hand at 31 May 2009	47.13
Cash required to restore the imprest	152.87

- The balance of cash in hand at 31 May 2009, £47.13, is now entered into the petty cash book and shown as '*balance c/d*', £47.13 (see Exhibit 22.5).
- The '*receipts*' and '*total*' columns are now added up and should equal each other, i.e. £206.00. These totals should be shown on the same line and both double underlined.
- The '*Balance b/d*' on 1 June, £47.13, is now entered in the *receipts* column and underneath that entry the amount received from the cashier to restore the imprest £152.87 is also entered.

The double entry for each of the expense columns is now carried out:

- The total of each expense column is debited to the expense account in the general ledger.
- The folio number of each general ledger account is entered under each of the expense columns in the petty cash book. This enables cross-referencing and also means that the double entry to the ledger account had been completed.

The double entry for all the items in Exhibit 22.5 appears as Exhibit 22.6.

Exhibit 22.6

Cash Book (Bank column only)   *Page 19*

Dr						Cr
		2009		Folio	£	
		May 1 Petty Cash		PCB 31	200.00	
		June 1 Petty Cash		PCB 31	152.87	

General Ledger   *Page 17*

VAT Account

Dr					Cr
2009		Folio	£		
May 31 Petty Cash		PCB 31	4.78		

                                                                      Page 19

Postages Account

Dr					Cr
2009		Folio	£		
May 31 Petty Cash		PCB 31	25.60		

Page 29

Dr   Cleaning Account   Cr

2009		Folio	£	
May 31 Petty Cash		PCB 31	54.40	

Page 44

Dr   Travel Expenses Account   Cr

2009		Folio	£	
May 31 Petty Cash		PCB 31	39.00	

Page 56

Dr   Stationery Account   Cr

2009		Folio	£	
May 31 Petty Cash		PCB 31	22.89	

Page 60

Dr   Sundry Expenses Account   Cr

2009		Folio	£	
May 31 Petty Cash		PCB 31	12.20	

Paying creditors from petty cash

Occasionally a creditor may be paid their account out of the petty cash. If this arises then the book-keeping entries would be to record the payment in the petty cash book, using a column headed 'ledger accounts', then post the item to the debit side of the creditor's account in the purchase ledger. This transaction is very rare and would only occur where the item to be paid was small, or if a refund was made out of petty cash to a customer who may have overpaid their account.

22.5 Bank cash book

In a business with both a cash book and a petty cash book, the cash book is often known as a **bank cash book**. This means that *all* cash payments are entered in the petty cash book, and the bank cash book will contain *only* bank columns and discount columns. When this arrangement is in operation, any cash sales will be paid directly into the bank.

Chapter summary

- The petty cash book is used to record transactions involving small items of expenditure incurred by a member of staff on behalf of the organisation.
- Claims for reimbursement of monies paid out are usually made on a petty cash voucher. The voucher should be completed with all the relevant details together with receipt (if possible), duly signed and authorised.

- The imprest system is used by many organisations to operate the petty cash system. Here an amount of money called a 'float' is given to the petty cashier at the start of a period. At the end of the period the amount spent by the petty cashier is reimbursed by the cashier to restore the imprest to its original amount.
- The advantages of using a petty cash system is that it enables a junior member of staff to be appointed petty cashier so allowing the cashier or accountant to concentrate on other areas of work.
- Using the petty cash book saves both the cash book and the ledger account from containing many small items of expenditure.
- The imprest system enables the cash to be checked at any time.
- Entries made into the petty cash book include not only petty cash vouchers for expenses incurred on behalf of the business but also receipts of money that may have been received in respect of sundry sales to staff members.
- The petty cash book is totalled, balanced off and the double entry completed with postings to the ledger accounts in the general ledger.
- The name of the cash book is sometimes called a bank cash book when it only contains bank columns. Cash sales having been banked direct and the petty cash book used for small sundry cash items.

EXERCISES

22.1 You are employed as accounts clerk for Kitchen Designs who operate their petty cash using the imprest system. At the beginning of the month there was £18.52 left in the petty cash box from the previous month and the cashier has just given you £131.48 to restore the imprest to £150.

The following are details of the petty cash vouchers that have been authorised for payment by the cashier for June 2009, together with a receipt for cash received.

2009		£
June	1 Window cleaner	10.00
June	3 Postage stamps	7.60
June	4 Petrol (including VAT of £5.60)	37.60
June	6 Stationery (including VAT of £1.45)	9.75
June	10 Sold stamps to Jean Ford £2.00 (receipt no. 8)	
June	14 Office cleaner	20.00
June	16 Parcel postage	1.35
June	19 Magazine for reception (no VAT)	3.00
June	21 Computer disks (including VAT £1.05)	7.95
June	23 Petrol (including VAT £2.10)	14.10
June	27 Refreshments for clients (no VAT)	4.20
June	29 Office cleaner	20.00

Required:

(a) Enter the balance brought down and the cash received to restore the imprest in the petty cash book on 1 June 2009. The petty cash book page number to use is 47.

(b) Enter the above transactions into the petty cash book using the following analysis columns, VAT, postage, cleaning, motor expenses, stationery and sundry expenses. The next petty cash voucher number is 32.

(c) Total and balance the petty cash book on 30 June and bring down the balance on 1 July. Show the amount of cash received from the cashier to restore the imprest to £150.

22.2X Singh's Estate Agents operates their petty cash system on a fortnightly basis using the imprest system with a float of £100. On 15 October 2009 there was an opening balance of £23.40 in the petty cash box. The following transactions took place during the period commencing 15 October 2009.

2009	£
Oct 15 Received amount from cashier to restore the imprest	
Oct 16 Envelopes and files (including VAT of £1.66)	11.66
Oct 17 Tea, coffee and milk (for clients no VAT)	7.40
Oct 18 Special delivery postage charges	8.60
Oct 20 Office cleaner	20.00
Oct 20 Cleaning materials (including VAT 63p)	4.23
Oct 23 Received £3.50 from M Lloyd for sale of stationery (receipt no. 78)	
Oct 23 Postage stamps	7.00
Oct 25 Travel expenses	16.42
Oct 27 Flowers for reception (including VAT 74p)	4.99
Oct 28 Photocopying paper (including VAT £1.40)	9.40
Oct 31 Received cash to restore imprest	

Required:

(a) Enter the balance brought down and the cash received to restore the imprest on 15 October 2009 in the petty cash book page 33.

(b) Enter the above transactions into the petty cash book using the following analysis columns, VAT, postage, cleaning, travel expenses, stationery and sundry expenses. The next petty cash voucher number is 80.

(c) Total and balance the petty cash book on 31 October and bring down the balance on 1 November. Show the amount of cash received from the cashier to restore the imprest to £100.

22.3X Jane Porter has recently introduced a petty cash book using the imprest system. The monthly imprest is £100. On 1 March 2009 the balance of petty cash in hand was £15.20 and on this day the imprest was restored when cash for the appropriate amount was given to the petty cash clerk.

During March the following petty cash vouchers were prepared:

Voucher Number	Date	Details
187	March 5	Travel expenses £8.90
188	March 8	Postage £4.75
189	March 11	Visitor's train fare £14.50
190	March 17	Stationery £14.40 *plus* VAT at 17.5%
191	March 23	Registration fee on parcel £8.84
192	March 27	Stationery items totalling £21.15 *including* VAT at 17.5%

Tasks:

(a) Enter the above petty cash vouchers into a petty cash book using the following analysis columns, travel expenses, postage, stationery and VAT. Total the analysis columns on 31 March. Balance the petty cash book on 31 March and bring down the balance.

(b) List the main items of information that should be found on a petty cash voucher.

(c) Explain why it is important for the petty cash clerk to keep all petty cash vouchers.

Southern Examining Group AQA

Please note that this question is NOT from the live examinations for the current specification.

22.4 You work for S Dickinson (Estate Agents) as a receptionist, although some of your duties include administration tasks and dealing with the firm's petty cash, which is operated using the imprest system. A float of £120 is used by the firm for petty cash and this is given to you on 1 March.

Required:

(*a*) From the following petty cash vouchers (Exhibit 22.7), you are required to enter them in the petty cash book using analysis columns as you think appropriate. Balance off at the end of the month and obtain cash to restore the imprest from Ms Dickinson.

(*b*) Post the petty cash expense columns to the accounts in the general ledger and enter the cash obtained to restore the imprest in the cash book.

(*c*) What are the advantages to using the imprest system? Draft a short memo outlining these to Ms Dickinson.

(NVQ Level 2)

Exhibit 22.7

	No	1
Petty Cash Voucher		
	Date	2/3/2009

For what required	Amount	
	£	p
Postage Stamps	6	50
	6	50
Signature	A. Bond	
Passed by	SMD	

	No	2
Petty Cash Voucher		
	Date	3rd March 2009

For what required	Amount	
	£	p
Second-class rail fare to Stourbridge	23	—
	23	—
Signature	G. Jones	
Passed by	SMD	

	No	3
Petty Cash Voucher		
	Date	7th March 2009

For what required	Amount	
	£	p
Parcel Post to London	4	—
	4	—
Signature	A. Bond	
Passed by	SMD	

	No	4
Petty Cash Voucher		
	Date	9th March 2009

For what required	Amount	
	£	p
Window cleaning	8	—
	8	—
Signature	C. Cotton	
Passed by	SMD	

Exhibit 22.7 (*continued*)

	No	5
Petty Cash Voucher		
Date	12th March 2009	

For what required	Amount	
	£	p
Envelopes	2	64
VAT		46
	3	10
Signature	A. Bond	
Passed by	SMD	

	No	6
Petty Cash Voucher		
Date	14th March 2009	

For what required	Amount	
	£	p
Tea etc (Hospitality)	6	40
	6	40
Signature	A. Bond	
Passed by	SMD	

	No	7
Petty Cash Voucher		
Date	16th March 2009	

For what required	Amount	
	£	p
Petrol	10	—
(including VAT)		
	10	—
Signature	G. Jones	
Passed by	SMD	

	No	8
Petty Cash Voucher		
Date	19th March 2009	

For what required	Amount	
	£	p
Computer Discs	11	06
VAT @ 17.5%	1	94
	13	—
Signature	S. Dickinson	
Passed by	SMD	

	No	9
Petty Cash Voucher		
Date	20 March 2009	

For what required	Amount	
	£	p
Dusters & Polish	1	47
17.5% VAT		26
	1	73
Signature	J. Pratt	
Passed by	SMD	

	No	10
Petty Cash Voucher		
Date	23 March 2009	

For what required	Amount	
	£	p
Postage Stamps	2	40
	2	40
Signature	A. Bond	
Passed by	SMD	

Exhibit 22.7 *(continued)*

No	11

Petty Cash Voucher

Date *27th March 2009*

For what required	Amount	
	£	p
Payment of creditors:–		
J. Cheetham (A/c No C44)	7	30
	7	30

Signature   *S. Dickinson*

Passed by   *SMD*

No	12

Petty Cash Voucher

Date *31st March 2009*

For what required	Amount	
	£	p
Magazines, Newspapers	6	40
etc. (for reception)		
	6	40

Signature   *A. Bond*

Passed by   *SMD*

22.5X You are employed as junior accountant's assistant of Morridge Products Ltd and one of your main tasks is that of petty cashier. The company uses an analytical petty cash book with columns for travelling expenses, postage, stationery, cleaning, sundry expenses and VAT, and they operate the imprest system.

Required:

(*a*) On 1 January 2009 the company's accountant, Mr Brammer, restores the petty cash float to £100 and gives you the petty cash vouchers shown in Exhibit 22.8. You are required to enter them in the petty cash book, balance off the book at the end of January, and obtain reimbursement from Mr Brammer to restore the imprest.

(*b*) Mr Brammer is anxious for you to become involved with all the financial aspects of the business and would like you to complete the book-keeping entries by posting the totals of the 'petty cash analysis columns' to the relevant accounts in the general ledger.

(*c*) Unfortunately, you have to go in hospital for a few days and will probably be absent from work for a couple of weeks. Mr Brammer asks you to write out a set of instructions in note form on the operation of the petty cash book as Jenny Cadwaller, his secretary, will be taking over in your absence. Ensure the instructions are clear, concise and easy to follow.

(NVQ Level 2)

Exhibit 22.8

No	1

Petty Cash Voucher

Date _1st Jan 2009_

For what required	Amount	
	£	p
Travelling Expenses to Crewe	5	36
	5	36

Signature _Jim Steadman_

Passed by _G Brammer_

No	2

Petty Cash Voucher

Date _5 Jan 2009_

For what required	Amount	
	£	p
Office Cleaning	10	—
	10	—

Signature _A. Duffy_

Passed by _G. Brammer_

No	3

Petty Cash Voucher

Date _9 Jan 2009_

For what required	Amount	
	£	p
Parcel to Northampton	1	98
	1	98

Signature _Tom Finikin_

Passed by _G Brammer_

No	4

Petty Cash Voucher

Date _10 Jan 2009_

For what required	Amount	
	£	p
Milk & Coffee for Office	6	50
	6	50

Signature _J. Cadwaller_

Passed by _G. Brammer_

No	5

Petty Cash Voucher

Date _12 Jan 2009_

For what required	Amount	
	£	p
Air-mail Stationery	7	15
VAT	1	25
	8	40

Signature _J. Cadwaller_

Passed by _G. Brammer_

No	6

Petty Cash Voucher

Date _15 Jan 2009_

For what required	Amount	
	£	p
Light Bulbs & 3 plugs.	3	64
VAT		64
	4	28

Signature _Tom Finikin_

Passed by _G Brammer_

Exhibit 22.8 (*continued*)

No	7

Petty Cash Voucher

Date _21 Jan 2009_

For what required	Amount	
	£	p
Office cleaning	20	—
	20	—

Signature _A. Duffy_

Passed by _G Brammer_

No	8

Petty Cash Voucher

Date _22 Jan 2009_

For what required	Amount	
	£	p
1 Ream Copier Paper	4	30
+ VAT		75
	5	05

Signature _J. Cadwaller_

Passed by _G. Brammer_

No	9

Petty Cash Voucher

Date _24 Jan 2009_

For what required	Amount	
	£	p
Car Allowance: Manchester – Visiting Customer	15	—
	15	—

Signature _J. Steadman_

Passed by _G. Brammer_

No	10

Petty Cash Voucher

Date _24 Jan 2009_

For what required	Amount	
	£	p
Financial Times & Economist for Reception	2	10
	2	10

Signature _J. Cadwaller_

Passed by _G Brammer_

No	11

Petty Cash Voucher

Date _30 Jan 2009_

For what required	Amount	
	£	p
Milk	1	50
	1	50

Signature _P. Fisher_

Passed by _G. Brammer_

No	12

Petty Cash Voucher

Date _31 Jan 2009_

For what required	Amount	
	£	p
First Class Stamps	4	80
	4	80

Signature _J. Cadwaller_

Passed by _G. Brammer_

Bank reconciliation statements

Learning objectives

After you have studied this chapter you should be able to:

● understand the reason for preparing bank reconciliation statements
● reconcile cash book balances with bank statement balances
● understand how bank overdrafts affect the reconciliation process
● make necessary entries in the account for dishonoured cheques.

23.1 Completing entries in the cash book

In Chapter 21 we saw how businesses record monies coming into and out of the business in their cash book. Cash items being entered in the 'cash columns' and cheques and other bank items being entered in the 'bank columns'.

In the business bank account the bank will also be recording monies paid into and out of the account in the bank's own records. If all the items entered in the cash book were the same as those entered in the business's account with the bank, then obviously the bank balance per the business's books and the bank balance per the bank's books would equal each other. However, this is not usually the case. There may be items paid into or out of the business bank account which have not been recorded in the cash book. There may also be items entered in the cash book which have not yet been entered in the bank's records of the business's account. To see if any differences have occurred the business will need to obtain a bank statement from the bank and use this to compare its records with those of the bank. Banks usually issue bank statements to their customers on a regular basis but one can easily be obtained from the bank on request.

An example of a cash book and a bank statement is shown in Exhibit 23.1. The items that are the same in both sets of records are ticked off.

Exhibit 23.1

Dr	Cash Book (bank columns only)						Cr
2009			£	2009			£
June 1 Balance b/f			80	June 27 I Gordon	✓		35
June 28 D Jones	✓		100	June 29 B Tyrell			40
				June 30 Balance c/d			105
			180				180
July 1 Balance b/d			105				

Bank Statement	Dr	Cr	Balance	
2009	£	£	£	
June 26 Balance b/f ✓			80	Cr
June 28 Banking ✓		100	180	Cr
June 30 I Gordon ✓	35		145	Cr

By comparing the cash book and the bank statement, it can be seen that the only item that was not in both of these was the cheque payment to B Tyrell for £40 in the cash book. The reason why this was entered in the cash book but does not appear on the bank statement is simply one of timing. The cheque had been posted to B Tyrell on 29 June, but there had not been time for it to be banked by Tyrell and passed through the banking system. Such a cheque is called an **unpresented cheque** because it has not yet been presented at the drawer's bank.

To prove that the balances are not different because of errors, even though they show different figures, a bank reconciliation statement is drawn up. This is shown in Exhibit 23.2.

Exhibit 23.2

Bank Reconciliation Statement as at 30 June 2009

	£
Balance in hand as per cash book	105
Add unpresented cheque: Tyrell	40
Balance in hand as per bank statement	145

It would have been possible for the bank reconciliation statement to have started with the bank statement balance:

Bank Reconciliation Statement as at 30 June 2009

	£
Balance in hand as per bank statement	145
Less unpresented cheque: Tyrell	40
Balance in hand as per cash book	105

You should notice that the bank account is shown as a debit balance in the business's cash book because, to the business, it is an asset. In the bank's books the bank account is shown as a credit balance because this is a liability of the bank to the business.

23.2 Some reasons for differences in balances

We can now look at a more complicated example in Exhibit 23.3. Similar items in both cash book and bank statement are shown ticked.

Exhibit 23.3

Dr			Cash Book		Cr
2009		£	2009		£
Dec 27 Total b/f		2,000	Dec 27 Total b/f		1,600
Dec 29 J Potter	✓	60	Dec 28 J Jacobs	✓	105
Dec 31 M Johnson (B)		220	Dec 30 M Chatwood (A)		15
			Dec 31 Balance c/d		560
		2,280			2,280
2010					
Jan 1 Balance b/d		560			

Bank Statement

2009		Dr £	Cr £	Balance £
Dec 27 Balance b/f				400 Cr
Dec 29 Cheque	✓		60	460 Cr
Dec 30 J Jacobs	✓	105		355 Cr
Dec 30 BGC*: L Shaw (C)			70	425 Cr
Dec 30 Bank charges (D)		20		405 Cr

*BGC = bank giro credit.

The balance brought forward in the bank statement £400 is the same figure as that in the cash book, i.e. totals b/f £2,000 − £1,600 = £400. However, items (A) and (B) are in the cash book only, and (C) and (D) are on the bank statement only. We can now examine these in detail:

(A) This is a cheque recently sent by us to Mr Chatwood. It has not yet passed through the banking system nor been presented to our bank, and it is therefore an **unpresented cheque**.

(B) This is a cheque banked by us on our visit to the bank when we collected the copy of our bank statement. As we handed this banking item over the counter at the same time as the bank clerk gave us our bank statement, naturally it has not yet been entered on the statement.

(C) A customer, L Shaw, has paid his account by instructing his bank to pay us direct through the banking system, instead of paying by cheque. Such a transaction is usually called a **bank giro credit (BCG)**.

(D) The bank has charged us £20 for keeping our bank account and all the work connected with it. Instead of sending us an invoice they have simply taken the money out of our bank account.

Having taken into account the above differences the bank reconciliation statement can now be prepared. As mentioned earlier there are two ways in which a bank reconciliation statement can be prepared. You can start with the balance as shown in the cash book (see first example shown below) or, alternatively, you can start with the balance as shown on the bank statement in the second example. Examining bodies may ask for either method of presentation so ensure you know exactly which method is required before attempting the question.

Bank Reconciliation Statement as at 31 December 2009

	£	£
Balance in hand as per cash book		560
Add Unpresented cheque – M Chatwood	15	
Bank giro credits	70	
		85
		645
Less Bank charges	20	
Bank lodgement not yet entered on bank statement	220	
		240
Balance in hand as per bank statement		405

A bank reconciliation statement starting with the bank statement balance appears thus:

Bank Reconciliation Statement as at 31 December 2009

	£	£
Balance in hand as per bank statement		405
Add Bank charges	20	
Bank lodgement not yet entered on bank statement	220	
		240
		645
Less Unpresented cheque – M Chatwood	15	
Bank giro credits	70	
		85
Balance in hand as per bank statement		560

23.3 Writing up the cash book before attempting a reconciliation

The easiest way to do a reconciliation is to complete the cash book first. All items on the bank statement will then be in the cash book. This means that the only differences will be items in the cash book but not on the bank statement. At the same time, any errors found in the cash book by such a check can be corrected.

Although this would be the normal way to proceed before actually drawing up a bank reconciliation statement, it is possible that an examiner will ask you not to do it this way. If, in Exhibit 23.3 the cash book had been written up before the bank reconciliation statement was drawn up, then the cash book and the reconciliation statement would have appeared as follows in Exhibit 23.4.

Exhibit 23.4

Dr		Cash Book		Cr
2009	£	2009		£
Dec 27 Total b/fwd	2,000	Dec 27 Total b/fwd		1,600
Dec 29 J Potter	60	Dec 28 J Jacobs		105
Dec 31 M Johnson	220	Dec 30 M Chatwood		15
Dec 31 BGC:		Dec 31 Bank charges*		20
L Shaw*	70	Dec 31 Balance c/d		610
	2,350			2,350
2010				
Jan 1 Balance b/d	610			

*Adding items that appear in the bank statement but not in the cashbook.

Bank Reconciliation Statement as on 31 December 2009

	£
Balance in hand as per cash book	610
Add Unpresented cheque – M Chatwood	15
	625
Less Bank lodgement not yet entered on bank statement	220
Balance in hand as per bank statement	405

23.4 Bank overdrafts

When there is a bank overdraft (shown by a credit balance in the cash book), the adjustments needed for reconciliation work are opposite to those needed for a debit balance.

Exhibit 23.5 shows a cash book, and a bank statement showing an overdraft. Only the cheque for G Cumberbatch (A) £106 and the cheque paid to J Kelly (B) £63 need adjusting. Work through the reconciliation statement in Exhibit 23.5 and then compare the reconciliation statements in Exhibits 23.4 and 23.5.

Exhibit 23.5

Dr		Cash Book (bank columns only)		Cr
2009	£	2009		£
Dec 5 I Howe	308	Dec 1 Balance b/f		709
Dec 24 L Mason	120	Dec 9 P Davies		140
Dec 29 K King	124	Dec 27 J Kelly (B)		63
Dec 31 G Cumberbatch (A)	106	Dec 29 United Trust		77
Dec 31 Balance c/f	380	Dec 31 Bank charges		49
	1,038			1,038
		2010		
		Jan 1 Balance b/f		380

Bank Statement

2009	Dr £	Cr £	Balance £
Dec 1 Balance b/f			709 O/D
Dec 5 Cheque		308	401 O/D
Dec 14 P Davies	140		541 O/D
Dec 24 Cheque		120	421 O/D
Dec 29 K King: BGC		124	297 O/D
Dec 29 United Trust: Standing order	77		374 O/D
Dec 31 Bank charges	49		423 O/D

Note: On a bank statement an overdraft is often shown with the letters O/D following the amount; or else it is shown as a debit balance, indicated by the letters DR after the amount.

Bank Reconciliation Statement as at 31 December 2009

	£
Overdraft as per cash book	380
Add Bank lodgements not on bank statement	106
	486
Less Unpresented cheque	63
Overdraft per bank statement	423

Now compare the reconciliation statements in Exhibits 23.4 and 23.5. This comparison reveals the following:

	Exhibit 23.4 Balances	Exhibit 23.5 Overdrafts
Balance/Overdraft per cash book	XXXX	XXXX
Adjustments		
Unpresented cheque	PLUS	LESS
Banking not entered	LESS	PLUS
Balance/Overdraft per bank statement	XXXX	XXXX

Adjustments are, therefore, made in the opposite way when there is an overdraft.

23.5 Dishonoured cheques

When a cheque is received from a customer and paid into the bank, it is recorded on the debit side of the cash book. It is also shown on the bank statement as a deposit to the bank. However, at a later date, it may be found that the customer's bank will not pay us the amount due on the cheque. The cheque is therefore worthless. It is known as a **dishonoured cheque**.

There are several possible reasons for this. As an example, let us suppose that K King gave us a cheque for £5,000 on 20 May 2009. We banked it, but on 25 May 2009 our bank returned the cheque to us. Typical reasons are:

● King had put £5,000 in figures on the cheque, but had written it in words as five thousand five hundred pounds. You will have to give the cheque back to King for amendment or reissue.

- King had put the year 2008 on the cheque instead of 2009. Normally, cheques are considered 'stale' six months after the date on the cheque; in other words, the banks will not pay cheques over six months' old.
- King simply did not have sufficient funds in his bank account. Suppose he had previously only got a £2,000 balance and yet he has given us a cheque for £5,000. His bank has not allowed him to have an overdraft. In such a case the cheque would be dishonoured. The bank would write on the cheque 'refer to drawer', and we would have to get in touch with King to see what he was going to do to settle his account.

In all of these cases the bank would show the original banking as being cancelled, by showing the cheque paid out of our bank account. As soon as this happens, they will notify us. We will then also show the cheque being cancelled by a credit in the cash book. We will then debit that amount to this account.

When King originally paid his account, our records would appear as:

Dr		K King Account			Cr
2009		£	2009		£
May 1 Balance b/d		5,000	May 20 Bank		5,000

Dr		Bank Account			Cr
2009		£			
May 20 K King		5,000			

After our recording the dishonoured cheque, the records will appear as:

Dr		K King Account			Cr
2009		£	2009		£
May 1 Balance b/d		5,000	May 20 Bank		5,000
May 25 Bank: cheque dishonoured		5,000			

Dr		Bank Account			Cr
2009		£	2009		£
May 20 K King		5,000	May 25 K King: cheque dishonoured		5,000

In other words, King is once again shown as owing us £5,000.

23.6 Some other reasons for differences in balances

As you will recall from Chapter 20, both standing orders and direct debits can be set up to move money regularly out of one bank account and into another. As far as bank reconciliation statements are concerned, both of these types of payments will have passed through the bank account but will not have been entered in the cash book.

23.7 Terms used in banking

There are many terms used in the banking system with which a student of accountancy needs to be familiar. In Chapter 20 many of these were discussed in detail. As a recap some of these are listed below together with additional terms:

- Bank charges and interest – charges made by the bank for providing the services of a bank account while interest charged is for making funds available to a business when it is overdrawn.
- Bank giro credits (also referred to as credit transfers) – a method used by businesses to pay creditors, wages and salaries.
- Bank lodgement – money deposited by a business into its account at the bank.
- Bank overdraft – an overdraft is a facility provided by the bank where it will continue to make payments from a current account even though there are insufficient funds to cover the payment. This is a short-term loan, on which the bank charges interest on a day-to-day basis.
- Bank reconciliation statement – a calculation comparing the cash book balance with the bank statement balance.
- Bankers' Automated Clearing Service (BACS) – a computerised payment transfer system that is a very popular way of paying creditors, wages and salaries.
- Direct debits – where the business gives permission for an organisation to collect amounts owing direct from its bank account. This method is often used to pay mortgages, insurance premiums, etc.
- Dishonoured cheques – when a bank dishonours a cheque it will not process the cheque because there are insufficient funds in the drawer's (the person making the payment) account.
- Out-of-date cheques – a cheque becomes 'stale' six months after the date on the cheque. Banks will not generally pay cheques over six months old.
- Standing order – instructions given by a business to a bank to pay specified amounts at given dates.
- Unpresented cheques – cheques that have been sent but have not yet gone through the recipient's bank account.

Chapter summary

- The purpose of preparing a bank reconciliation statement is to find the reasons for the differences in the balance as shown in the cash book with that shown on the bank statement.
- By preparing a bank reconciliation statement errors may be identified in either the cash book or the bank statement and be corrected.
- The differences in balances may be caused by quite valid reasons and are usually due to the varying dates that the business and the bank record monies paid into and out of their particular account.
- It is easier to write up the cash book first before preparing a bank reconciliation statement since the only differences will be items in the cash book but not on the bank statement.

● If the account is showing a bank overdraft then preparing a bank reconciliation statement is the opposite to when there is a balance in the account.
● If a business receives a cheque from a customer which ultimately 'bounces', i.e. there are insufficient funds in the account for the cheque to be paid, then it is known as a 'dishonoured cheque'.
● How to make the appropriate entries in the account to record a dishonoured cheque.
● Typical terms used in banking are summarised.

EXERCISES

23.1 The following are extracts from the cash book and the bank statement of J Roche. You are required to:

(*a*) write the cash book up to date, and state the new balance as on 31 December 2009
(*b*) draw up a bank reconciliation statement as on 31 December 2009.

Dr		Cash Book		Cr
2009	£	2009		£
Dec 1 Balance b/f	1,740	Dec 8 A Dailey		349
Dec 7 T J Masters	88	Dec 15 R Mason		33
Dec 22 J Ellis	73	Dec 28 G Small		115
Dec 31 K Wood	249	Dec 31 Balance c/d		1,831
Dec 31 M Barrett	178			
	2,328			2,328

Bank Statement

2009	Dr £	Cr £	Balance £
Dec 1 Balance b/f			1,740
Dec 7 Cheque		88	1,828
Dec 11 A Dailey	349		1,479
Dec 20 R Mason	33		1,446
Dec 22 Cheque		73	1,519
Dec 31 BGC: J Walters		54	1,573
Dec 31 Bank charges	22		1,551

23.2X The following are extracts from the cash book and bank statement of Preston & Co:

Dr		Cash Book		Cr
2009	£	2009		£
Dec 1 Balance b/d	8,700	Dec 6 S Little		1,745
Dec 7 T J Blake	440	Dec 14 L Jones		165
Dec 20 P Dyson	365	Dec 21 E Fraser		575
Dec 30 A Veale	945	Dec 31 Balance c/d		9,155
Dec 31 K Woodburn	300			
Dec 31 N May	890			
	11,640			11,640

Bank Statement

2009	Dr £	Cr £	Balance £
Dec 1 Balance b/d			8,700
Dec 9 Cheque		440	9,140
Dec 10 S Little	1,745		7,395
Dec 19 L Jones	165		7,230
Dec 20 Cheque		365	7,595
Dec 26 BGC: P Todd		270	7,865
Dec 31 Bank charges	110		7,755

You are required to:

(a) write up the cash book and state the new balance on 31 December 2009

(b) prepare a bank reconciliation statement as on 31 December 2009.

23.3 The bank statement for James Baxter for the month of March 2009 is as follows:

Bank Statement

2009	Dr £	Cr £	Balance £
Mar 1 Balance b/d			2,598 O/D
8 L Young	61		2,659 O/D
16 Cheque		122	2,537 O/D
20 A Duffy	104		2,641 O/D
21 Cheque		167	2,474 O/D
31 BGC: A May		929	1,545 O/D
31 Standing Order: Oak plc	100		1,645 O/D
31 Bank charges	28		1,673 O/D

The cash book for March 2009 is shown below:

Dr		Cash Book		Cr
2009	£	2009		£
Mar 16 N Morris	122	Mar 1 Balance b/d		2,598
" 21 P Fraser	167	" 6 L Young		61
" 31 Southern Elect. Co	160	" 30 A Duffy		104
" 31 Balance c/d	2,804	" 30 C Clark		490
	3,253			3,253

You are required to:

(a) write the cash book up to date

(b) draw up a bank reconciliation statement as at 31 March 2009.

23.4X   Following is the cash book (bank columns) of E Flynn for December 2009:

Dr		Cash Book		Cr
2009	£	2009		£
Dec 6 J Hall	155	Dec 1 Balance b/d		3,872
Dec 20 C Walters	189	Dec 10 P Wood		206
Dec 31 P Miller	211	Dec 19 M Roberts		315
Dec 31 Balance c/d	3,922	Dec 29 P Phillips		84
	4,477			4,477

The bank statement for the month is:

2009	Dr £	Cr £	Balance £
Dec 1 Balance			3,872 O/D
Dec 6 Cheque		155	3,717 O/D
Dec 13 P Wood	206		3,923 O/D
Dec 20 Cheque		189	3,734 O/D
Dec 22 M Roberts	315		4,049 O/D
Dec 30 Mercantile: Standing order	200		4,249 O/D
Dec 31 K Saunders: BGC		180	4,069 O/D
Dec 31 Bank charges	65		4,134 O/D

You are required to:
(a) write the cash book up to date to take the necessary items into account
(b) draw up a bank reconciliation statement as on 31 December 2009.

23.5   On 31 December 2009 the bank columns of K Talbot's cash book showed a balance of £4,500. The bank statement as at 31 December 2009 showed a credit balance of £8,850 on the account. You checked the bank statement with the cash book and found that the following had not been entered in the cash book:

(i)   A standing order to RB Insurance for £600 had been paid by the bank.
(ii) Bank interest receivable of £720 had not been entered into the account.
(iii) Bank charges of £90 had been made.
(iv) A credit transfer of £780 from KB Ltd had been paid direct into the account.
(v)   Talbot's deposit account balance of £4,200 had been transferred into her bank current account.
(vi) A returned cheque of £210, dishonoured by C Hill, had been entered on the bank statement.

You also found that two cheques, payable to L Young £750 and K Clark £870, had been entered in the cash book but had not been presented for payment. In addition, a cheque for £2,070 had been paid into the bank on 31 December 2009 but had not been credited on the bank statement until 2 January 2010.

Required:
(a) Starting with the cash book debit balance of £4,500, write the cash book up to date.
(b) Draw up a bank reconciliation statement as on 31 December 2009.

23.6X On 28 June Senator Safes received the following bank statement as at 24 June 2009.

	SOUTH BANK plc			
	High Street, Webley, W36 OKW			
To: Senator Safes	Account No: 721982716			24 June 2009
	STATEMENT OF ACCOUNT			
Date	Details	Paid out	Paid in	Balance
2009		£	£	£
3 June	Balance b/f			7,000C
5 June	Cheque No 326705	300		6,700C
5 June	Cheque No 326710	6,900		200D
5 June	Cheque No 326711	300		500D
10 June	Bank Giro Credit			
	C Maguire		9,100	8,600C
11 June	Cheque No 326713	76		8,524C
14 June	Direct Debit			
	Bamber Limited	1,300		7,224C
20 June	Direct Debit			
	Webley MBC	100		7,124C
24 June	Bank charges	52		7,072C
D = Debit	C = Credit			

The cash book as at 28 June 2009 is shown below.

Cash Book

Date 2009	Details	Bank £	Date 2009	Cheque No	Details	Bank £
1 June	Balance b/f	6,700	1 June	326710	B Groom Limited	6,900
26 June	P Kramer	3,100	1 June	326711	KKD Limited	300
26 June	L Jones	82	6 June	326712	F Bolton	250
			7 June	326713	Leigh & Company	76

(a) check the items on the bank statement against the items in the cash book
(b) write out the cash book and update as needed
(c) total the cash book and clearly show the balance carried down
(d) prepare a bank reconciliation statement as at 28 June 2009.

AAT

23.7X Cunningham & Co is an old-established firm of accountants in Huddersfield. You have been employed as book-keeper to the company to assist the senior partner, Mr Cunningham, with the accounting records and day-to-day routine duties. The company's policies when dealing with both payments and receipts is extremely strict. All cash and cheques received are to be banked immediately. Any payments over £10 must be made by cheque. Small cash payments are all paid by the petty cash system.

One of your tasks is to enter the company's cash book and reconcile this with the bank statement. This task must be carried out on a weekly basis.

Required:

(*a*) Having obtained the company's cheque book and paying-in book (Exhibits 23.6 and 23.7), enter up the cash book (bank columns only) for the week commencing 3 November 2009. Unfortunately, on that date the company was overdrawn by £2,356.00.

(*b*) Balance up the cash book at the end of the week and bring the balance down.

(*c*) From the bank statement (Exhibit 23.8) you are required to prepare:

   (i) The corrected cash book balance as at 10 November 2009.

   (ii) A bank reconciliation statement as at 10 November 2009.

(NVQ Level 2)

Exhibit 23.6 Details of cheque book stubs – Cunningham & Co

Date _3 Nov 2009_ Payee _Post Office_ _____ _Stamps_ _____ **Amount £ 146.50** 001763	Date _3 Nov 2009_ Payee _The Law_ _____ _Society_ _____ **Amount £ 121.80** 001764	Date _4 Nov 2009_ Payee _Bayleys_ _____ _Office Supplies_ _____ **Amount £ 94.10** 001765
Date _5 Nov 2009_ Payee _Lower Bents_ _____ _Garage_ _(Petrol A/c – Sept)_ **Amount £ 450.15** 001766	Date _6 Nov 2009_ Payee _Wages_ _____ _____ **Amount £ 489.20** 001767	Date _10 Nov 2009_ Payee _Petty Cashier_ _____ _(Restoring_ _Imprest)_ **Amount £ 46.00** 001768

Exhibit 23.7 Details from paying-in book – Cunningham & Co

Date _3 Nov 2009_	Date _5 Nov 2009_	Date _6 Nov 2009_
A/c _Cunningham & Co_	A/c _Cunningham & Co_	A/c _Cunningham & Co_
Cash	Cash _Bent Garage £221.00_ _P Ralphs £53.00_	Cash _Mr Prince £130.50_
Cheques _Mrs Stoddard £540.00_	Cheques _Gardeners £1500.00_	Cheques _Stephens & Smith £523.10_
£ 540.00	£ 1774.00	£ 653.60

Date _7 Nov 2009_	Date _7 Nov 2009_
A/c _Cunningham & Co_	A/c _Cunningham & Co_
Cash	Cash _Brindle Bros £165.50_
Cheques _Rileys (Printers) & Co £759.00_	Cheques _Robert Andrews Ltd £325.00_
£ 759.00	£ 490.50

Exhibit 23.8 Bank statement – Cunningham & Co

TUDOR BANK			CONFIDENTIAL		
High Street **Huddersfield**			**Account:** Cunningham & Co Chestergate Huddersfield		
Account No: 0012770123			Sheet No: 67 Date: 8 November 2009		

2009		Dr	Cr	Balance	
Nov 3 Balance b/d				2,356.00	O/D
3 Cheque	001763	146.50		2,502.50	O/D
3 Deposit			540.00	1,962.50	O/D
5 Deposit			1,774.00	188.50	O/D
6 S/O Noble Insurance		62.00		250.50	O/D
6 Cheque	001767	489.20		739.70	O/D
6 Deposit			653.60	86.10	O/D
7 Deposit			759.00	672.90	
7 Bank charges		22.45		650.45	
7 Cheque	001765	94.10		556.35	

23.8X The following are extracts from the cash book and bank statement of Noshin Choudhary for the month of February 2009.

Dr	Cash Book (Bank columns only) – N Choudhary				Cr
2009		£	2009		£
Feb 1	Balance b/d	2200	Feb 10	J Fairhurst	157
8	P Burlace	98	16	B Shaw	243
18	P Burlace	140	28	T Rungren	130
28	J Garcia	124	28	Balance c/d	2,032
		2,562			2,562

N Choudhary Bank Statement as at 28 February 2009

2009	Debit £	Credit £	Balance £
Feb 1 Balance b/d			2,200
8 Cheque		98	2,298
13 J Fairhurst	157		2,141
18 Cheque		140	2,281
20 B Shaw	243		2,038
26 Standing order	42		1,996
28 Bank charges	26		1,970
28 Credit transfer		91	2,061

Using the above information:

(*a*) bring the cash book up to date to show a corrected bank balance

(*b*) prepare a statement reconciling the *corrected* cash book balance with the bank statement.

NEAB (GCSE)

CHAPTER 24

The journal

Learning objectives

After you have studied this chapter you should be able to:

● identify the journal as an original book of entry
● use the journal for entering a range of different transactions
● post items from the journal to the ledgers
● appreciate the advantages of using a journal.

24.1 Introduction

In earlier chapters we have seen that transactions are initially entered into a book of original entry. For example, all items involving receipts and payments are recorded in the cash book while purchase and sales invoices are entered in the respective day books. Occasionally it is necessary to record a much less common transaction like writing off a bad debt or perhaps when a debtor is unable to pay an outstanding invoice and offers a fixed asset in full settlement of the debt. It is just as important to record these transactions as it is to record the purchase of goods for resale. Such a transaction is therefore recorded in another book of original entry – the **journal**.

The journal is like a diary in which details of less common transactions are recorded prior to them being posted to the ledger accounts. For each transaction the following details are recorded:

● the date
● the name of the accounts to be debited and credited and the amount
● a description and explanation of the transaction, which is known as the **narrative**
● a reference number for the source document as proof of the transaction.

24.2 Typical uses of the journal

Some of the main uses of the journal are listed below. It must not be thought that this list is a fully detailed one:

- the purchase and sale of fixed assets on credit
- writing off bad debts
- opening entries – the entries needed to open a new set of books
- other items: adjustments to any of the entries in the ledgers
- the correction of errors.

The layout of the journal can be shown as follows:

The Journal

Date		Folio	Dr	Cr
	The name of the account to be debited. The name of the account to be credited. The narrative.			

It can be seen that on the first line the name of the account to be *debited* is entered while the second line gives the account to be *credited*. The name of the account to be credited is indented slightly and not shown directly under the name of the account to be debited, because this makes it easier to distinguish between the debit and credit items.

It should be remembered that the journal is not a double entry account; it is a form of diary, and entering an item in the journal is not the same as recording an item in an account. Once the journal entry has been made, the entry into the double entry accounts can be made.

Examples of the uses of the journal are given more fully in Section 24.4.

24.3   Journal entries and examination questions

One of the areas that examiners of book-keeping and accounting often highlight when preparing the Examiner's Report is the student's ability in answering questions involving journal entries. This is not because questions involving journal entries are more difficult but many students seem to suffer some sort of mental block when answering them. The problem in tackling journal questions occurs because students do not view the journal as a form of diary. In fact, diary entries contain specific instructions about particular transactions which need to be recorded in the ledger. In other words, the student initially needs to think double entry, i.e. which account needs to be debited and then which account should be credited. These instructions then need to be noted in the journal in three stages:

1 the account to be debited
2 the account to be credited
3 a description of the transaction.

To help you when dealing with journal entries we will first show what the entries are in the double entry accounts and then how to write up the journal for each of the entries. We will now look at a few examples, including the folio references.

24.4 Examples of journal entries

1 Purchase and sale of fixed assets

Example 1: A drilling machine was bought on credit from Toolmakers Ltd for £5,500 on 1 July 2009 (ignore VAT). This transaction involves the acquisition of a new drilling machine, which is an asset, but the business also incurs a liability since it has purchased the machine on credit from Toolmakers Ltd. From what you have learnt in earlier chapters you will know that the acquisition of an asset is a debit entry in the Machinery Account and the liability to Toolmakers Ltd is a credit entry in its account.

General Ledger

Dr			Machinery Account		(Folio GL 1) Cr
2009		*Folio*	£		
Jul 1 Toolmakers		PL 55	5,500		

Purchase Ledger

Dr	Toolmakers Ltd Account			(Folio PL 55) Cr
	2009		*Folio*	£
	Jul 1 Machinery		GL 1	5,500

Now we have to record these entries in the journal. Remember, the journal is simply a kind of diary, not in account form but in ordinary written form. It says which account has to be debited, which account has to be credited, then gives a narrative that simply describes the nature of the transaction.

For the transaction above, the journal entry will appear as follows:

The Journal

Date	Details	Folio	Dr	Cr
2009			£	£
Jul 1	Machinery	GL 1	5,500	
	Toolmakers	PL 55		5,500
	Purchase of milling machine on credit,			
	purchases invoice no. 7/159			

Example 2: A business purchases a laptop for use by one of the managers at a cost of £600 plus VAT at 17.5% on credit from Newdata Systems Ltd on 12 May 2009.

This example includes VAT so initially it is necessary to calculate the VAT payable, i.e. 17.5% of £600 = £105 making the total amount owing to Newdata Systems Ltd £705. Assuming that the business is registered for VAT and can claim a refund of the VAT paid (see Section 18.14) the double entry required to enter this transaction would be:

General Ledger

Dr			Computer Equipment Account	(Folio GL 16) Cr

2009	Folio	£
May 12 Newdata Systems Ltd	PL 37	600

Dr			VAT Account	(Folio GL 73) Cr

2009	Folio	£
May 12 Newdata Systems Ltd	PL 37	105

Purchase Ledger

Dr		Newdata Systems Ltd Account	(Folio PL 37) Cr

	2009	Folio	£
	May 12 Journal	GL 16	705

Note that the cost of purchasing the laptop is £600 since the business will be able to reclaim £105 VAT. If, however, the business had not been registered for VAT then the cost would be £705.

The journal entries to record the above transaction are as follows:

The Journal

Date	Details	Folio	Dr	Cr
2009			£	£
May 12	Computer equipment	GL 16	600	
May 12	VAT	GL 73	105	
May 12	Newdata Systems Ltd	PL 37		705
	Purchase of laptop on credit,			
	Purchase invoice no. 7890			

Example 3: Some office furniture which is no longer required is sold for £300 on credit to K King on 2 July 2009. Here again, it is not difficult to work out what entries are needed in the double entry accounts. They are as follows:

Sales Ledger

Dr			K King Account	(Folio SL 79) Cr

2009	Folio	£
Jul 2 Office furniture	GL 51	300

General Ledger

Dr		Office Furniture Account	(Folio GL 51) Cr

	2009	Folio	£
	Jul 2 K King	SL 79	300

These are shown in journal form as follows:

The Journal

Date	Details	Folio	Dr	Cr
			£	£
2009				
Jul 2	K King	SL 79	300	
	Office furniture	GL 51		300
	Sale of some office furniture no longer required –			
	see letter ref: CT 568			

2 Writing off bad debts

Example 4: A debt of £78 owing to us from H Mander is written off as a bad debt on 31 August 2009. As the debt is now of no value, we have to stop showing it as an asset. This means that we will need to credit H Mander's account to cancel the amount out of his account. A bad debt is an expense so we will debit the amount to the bad debts account.

In double entry form this is shown as:

General Ledger

Dr			Bad debts Account	(Folio GL 16) Cr
2009	Folio	£		
Aug 31 H Mander	SL 99	78		

Sales Ledger

Dr			H Mander Account			(Folio SL 99) Cr
2009	Folio	£	2009	Folio	£
Aug 1 Balance	b/d	78	Aug 31 Bad debts	GL 16	78

The journal entry showing the same transaction would be as follows:

The Journal

Date	Details	Folio	Dr	Cr
			£	£
2009				
Aug 31	Bad debts	GL 16	78	
	H Mander	SL 99		78
	Debt written off as bad. See letter in file 9/8906			

3 Opening entries

Example 5: J Brew, after being in business for some years without keeping proper records, now decides to keep a double entry set of books. On 1 July 2009, he establishes that his assets and liabilities are as follows:

- *Assets*: Motor van £4,840, Fixtures £700, Stock £390,
  Debtors – B Young £95, D Blake £45,
  Bank £5,080, Cash £20.
- *Liabilities*: Creditors – M Quinn £129, C Walters £41.

The assets therefore total (£4,840 + £700 + £390 + £95 + £45 + £5,080 + £20) = £11,170; and the liabilities total (£129 + £41) = £170. The capital in the business consists of assets minus liabilities, which in Brew's case is £11,170 − £170 = £11,000.

We must start the writing up of the books on 1 July 2009. To do this:

1 Open asset accounts, one for each asset. Each opening asset is shown as a debit balance.
2 Open liability accounts, one for each liability. Each opening liability is shown as a credit balance.
3 Open an account for the capital. Show it as a credit balance.

Record the details of the above transactions in the journal.
    Exhibit 24.1 shows:

● the journal
● the opening entries in the double entry accounts.

Exhibit 24.1

The Journal

Page 5

Date	Details	Folio	Dr	Cr
2009			£	£
July 1	Motor van	GL 1	4,840	
	Fixtures	GL 2	700	
	Stock	GL 3	390	
	Debtors – B Young	SL 1	95	
	D Blake	SL 2	45	
	Bank	CB 1	5,080	
	Cash	CB 1	20	
	Creditors – M Quinn	PL 1		129
	C Walters	PL 2		41
	Capital	GL 4		11,000
	Assets and liabilities at the date entered			
	to open the books		11,170	11,170

General Ledger

Page 1

Dr   *Motor Van Account*   Cr

2009		Folio	£		
July 1	Balance	J 5	4,840		

Page 2

Dr   *Fixtures Account*   Cr

2009		Folio	£		
July 1	Balance	J 5	700		

Page 3

Dr   *Stock Account*   Cr

2009		Folio	£		
July 1	Balance	J 5	390		

Dr				Capital Account			Page 4 Cr
				2009	Folio	£	
				July 1 Balance	J 5	11,000	

Sales Ledger   Page 1

Dr				B Young Account			Cr
2009	Folio	£					
July 1 Balance	J 5	95					

Page 2

Dr				D Blake Account			Cr
2009	Folio	£					
July 1 Balance	J 5	45					

Purchases Ledger   Page 1

Dr				M Quinn Account			Cr
				2009	Folio	£	
				July 1 Balance	J 5	129	

Page 2

Dr				C Walters Account			Cr
				2009	Folio	£	
				July 1 Balance	J 5	41	

Cash Book   Page 1

Dr		Cash	Bank		Cr
2009	Folio	£	£		
July 1 Balances	J 5	20	5,080		

Once the opening balances have been recorded in the books, the day-to-day transactions are entered in the normal way. Opening entries are needed only *once* in the life of the business.

4 Other items

These can be of many kinds and it is impossible to write out a complete list. Several examples are as follows:

Example 6: K Young, a debtor, owes £2,000 on 1 July 2009. He was unable to pay his account in cash, but offers a motor car in full settlement of the debt. The offer is accepted on 5 July 2009.

The personal account is now no longer owed and therefore needs to be credited. On the other hand, the firm now has an extra asset, a motor car, and therefore the motor car account needs to be debited.

The double entry records are therefore:

Sales Ledger

Dr				K Young Account		(SL 333) Cr
2009	Folio	£		2009	Folio	£
July 1 Balance	b/d	2,000		July 5 Motor car	GL 171	2,000

General Ledger

Dr			Motor Car Account	(GL 171) Cr
2009	Folio	£		
July 5 K Young	SL 333	2,000		

This is shown in the journal as follows:

The Journal

		Folio	Dr	Cr
2009			£	£
July 5	Motor car	GL 171	2,000	
	K Young	SL 333		2,000
	Accepted motor car in full settlement of debt			
	per letter dated 5/7/2009			

***Example* 7**: T Jones is a creditor. On 10 July 2009 his business is taken over by A Lee, to whom the debt of £150 is to be paid. Here, one creditor is being exchanged for another. The action needed is to cancel the amount owing to T Jones by debiting his account, and to show it owing to A Lee by opening an account for A Lee and crediting it.

The double entry records are therefore thus:

Dr				T Jones Account		(SL 92) Cr
2009	Folio	£		2009	Folio	£
July 10 A Lee	SL 44	150		July 1 Balance	b/d	150

Dr			A Lee Account		(SL 44) Cr
			2009	Folio	£
			July 10 T Jones	SL 92	150

The journal entries are thus:

The Journal

		Folio	Dr	Cr
2009			£	£
July 10	T Jones	SL 92	150	
	A Lee	SL 44		150
	Transfer of indebtedness as per letter ref G/1335			

Example 8: An office photocopier bought on credit from RS Ltd for £1,310 was found to be faulty and returned to the supplier on 12 July 2009. The supplier agreed to make an allowance of the full amount outstanding, £1,310, which the business accepted.

The double entry records are therefore thus:

Purchase Ledger

Dr			RS Ltd Account			(PL 124) Cr
2009	Folio	£	2009	Folio	£	
July 12 Office machinery	GL 288	1,310	July 1 Balance	b/d	1,310	

General Ledger

Dr			Office machinery Account			(GL 288) Cr
2009	Folio	£	2009	Folio	£	
July 1 Balance	b/d	1,310	July 12 RS Ltd	PL 124	1,310	

The journal entries are thus:

The Journal

		Folio	Dr	Cr
2009			£	£
July 12	RS Ltd	PL 124	1,310	
	Office machinery	GL 288		1,310
	Faulty photocopier returned to supplier.			
	Full allowance given. See letter 10/7/2009			

5 Correction of errors

Journal entries for these will be found in Chapters 32 and 33.

6 Recap on journal entries

Remember that when entering an unusual transaction that needs to go via the journal you need to think double entry, i.e. which account needs to be debited and which account should be credited. In the above examples we have shown the double entry accounts first followed by the journal entry. This is to help the student to overcome the problem in recording journal entries. However, in practical circumstances the journal entry is always done first followed by posting the transaction from the journal to the double entry accounts, see Exhibit 24.2.

Exhibit 24.2

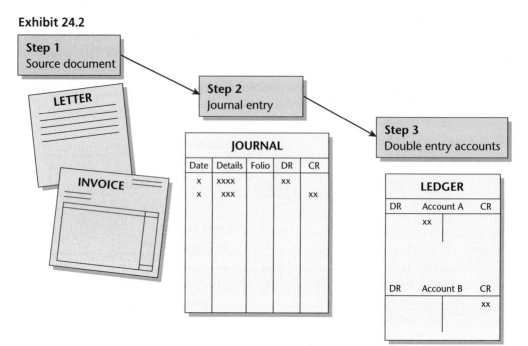

24.5 Advantages of using the journal

Recording transactions in the journal has the following advantages:

● There is less chance of further errors occurring by ensuring that the item is recorded properly and posted in the appropriate double entry accounts.
● Without such a record in the journal fraudulent transactions could occur more easily.
● There is a permanent record of the transaction with reference to the prime source document.
● If a record of the transaction is kept it saves relying on a member of staff to remember all the details. Also, if the member of staff leaves then it becomes almost impossible at a later date to understand why a particular book-keeping entry was made in the accounting books.

Despite these advantages many businesses do not use a journal.

24.6 Examination guidance

Later on in your studies, you may find that some of the journal entries become rather more complicated than those you have seen so far. The best plan for nearly all students would be to follow this advice during examinations:

● On your examination answer paper, write a heading entitled 'Workings'. Then under that show the double entry accounts.
● Now put a heading entitled 'Answer', and show the answer in the form of the journal, as shown in this chapter.

See Exhibit 24.3.

Exhibit 24.3

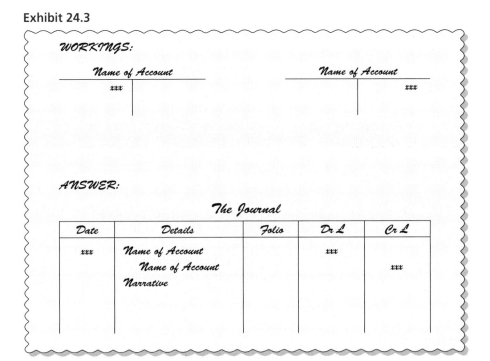

WORKINGS:

Name of Account	Name of Account
xxx	xxx

ANSWER:

The Journal

Date	Details	Folio	Dr £	Cr £
xxx	Name of Account		xxx	
	Name of Account			xxx
	Narrative			

If you are already confident about dealing with these questions and you feel that you can manage them without showing your workings, then you may wish to leave out your workings from your answer.

If the question asks for 'journal entries' you must *not* fall into the trap of just showing the double entry accounts, as you could get no marks at all even though your double entry records are correct. The examiner wants to see the *journal* entries, and you must show them as your answer.

Chapter summary

- The journal is an original book of entry and is used to record rare or exceptional transactions that do not appear in the other books of original entry.
- Typical uses of the journal include the purchase and sale of fixed assets, writing off bad debts, correction of errors and opening entries.
- When preparing a journal entry the date is entered first followed by the name of the account to be debited and amount, this is followed by entering the name of the account to be credited, slightly indented, and the amount. Finally, a narrative, giving a brief description of the transaction is written.
- Since many students have problems answering examination questions involving journal entries it is recommended that they prepare 'a working section' to show

the double entry aspect prior to preparing the journal entry which usually forms the 'Answer' to the question.

● The advantages of using the journal include:

(*a*) a reduced possibility of an error occurring

(*b*) a permanent record of the transaction

(*c*) less risk of fraudulent transactions.

EXERCISES

24.1   Show the journal entries to record the following:

2009

Jan 1 Bought computer on credit from Data Systems for £4,000

Jan 5 Goods taken from the business for own use, £120. The goods were not paid for by the proprietor

Jan 8 A debt of £220 owing to us by J Oddy is written off as a bad debt

Jan 15 Bought a motor vehicle from Smithy Garage paying by cheque, £15,500

Jan 29 J Street owes us £250. She is unable to pay her debt and we agree to take some filing cabinets valued at £250 from her to cancel the debt.

Narratives are not required.

24.2X   Show the journal entries for April 2009 necessary to record the following items:

(*a*) Apr 1 Bought fixtures on credit from J Harper, £1,809

(*b*) Apr 4 We take £500 goods out of the business stock without paying for them

(*c*) Apr 9 £28 worth of the goods taken by us on 4 April are returned back into stock by us. We do not take any money for the return of the goods

(*d*) Apr 12 K Lamb owes us £500. He is unable to pay his debt. We agree to take some office equipment from him at the value and so cancel the debt

(*e*) Apr 18 Some of the fixtures bought from J Harper, £65 worth, are found to be unsuitable and are returned to him for full allowance

(*f*) Apr 24 A debt owing to us by J Brown of £68 is written off as a bad debt

(*g*) Apr 30 Office equipment bought on credit from Super Offices for £2,190.

24.3   (*a*) J Green's financial position at 1 May 2009 is as follows:

		£
Bank		2,910
Cash		160
Equipment		5,900
Premises		25,000
Creditors:	R Smith	890
	T Thomas	610
Debtors:	J Carnegie	540
Loan from:	J Higgins	4,000

You are required to show the opening entries needed to open a double entry set of books for Green as at 1 May 2009. Then open up the necessary accounts in J Green's ledger to record the above, as well as the succeeding transactions.

(*b*) During May 2009, Green's transactions were as follows:

2009

May   2 Bought goods from T Thomas on credit, £2,100

May   5 Paid R Smith on account by cheque, £500

May 12 Repaid J Higgins by cheque, £1,000

May 24 Sold goods to J Carnegie on credit, £2,220

May 31 Total cash sales for the month £8,560, of which £8,000 banked on 31 May

May 31 J Carnegie returned goods to us, £400

May 31 Paid loan interest to Higgins by cheque, £200.

You are required to post all accounts and to extract a trial balance as at 31 May 2009, but only the cash book needs balancing down. Note that the sales, purchases and returns day books are *not* needed.

24.4X   M Maxwell is in business as a trader. During February 2009, the following transactions took place:

February

  3 Purchased a motor vehicle from J Saunders costing £5,000 paying 50% of the total cost by cheque with the remainder due in 6 months.

  8 Purchased fixtures and fittings on credit from J McNulty. List price £200 less trade discount of 15%.

  9 M Maxwell put a further £10,000 into the business, 25% went into cash and the remainder into the firm's bank account.

10 A Robinson, a debtor owing £250 was declared bankrupt. M Maxwell received 10% of the amount outstanding by cheque. The remainder to be written off to bad debts.

16 It was found that the £5,000 paid for the motor vehicle purchased on 3 February included Road Fund Licence valued at £150.

22 An account of £50 for petrol for M Maxwell's private car had been posted to the firm's Motor Expenses Account.

24 Rent received of £125 had been posted to the Commissions Received Account.

24 Purchased a piece of machinery on credit from C Mattey. The list price was £6,000 but a trade discount of 20% was allowed.

26 The machine, purchased on 24 February, had chipped paintwork. Maxwell kept it but Mattey agreed to a credit of £100.

You are required to enter these transactions (including cash) into the journal, giving suitable brief narratives.

OCR

Control accounts

Learning objectives

After you have studied this chapter you should be able to:
- understand the need for control accounts
- prepare a sales ledger control account
- prepare a purchase ledger control account
- know the sources of information for control accounts
- understand the double entry aspect of control accounts
- appreciate the advantages of control accounts
- understand the meaning and use of memorandum accounts.

25.1 Need for control accounts

Where a business is small all the accounts may be contained in one ledger and at the end of the accounting period a trial balance could easily be drawn up as a test of the arithmetical accuracy of the accounts. However, it must be remembered that certain errors may not be revealed by the trial balance (refer to Chapter 8). If the trial balance totals disagree, the books could easily and quickly be checked to find the errors.

However, as the business grows the accounting requirements also expand and the work has to be divided up into various separate ledgers and, consequently, errors are not as easily identifiable. The error or errors could be very difficult to find and it may be necessary to check every item in every ledger. Therefore, what is required is a type of trial balance for each ledger, and this requirement is met by the **control account**. Thus it is only the ledgers where the control accounts do not balance that need detailed checking to locate any errors.

25.2 The principle of control accounts

The principle on which control accounts is based is simple. In Exhibit 25.1 you will see that the individual ledger accounts feed into the respective control accounts. Therefore, if the total of the opening balances for each individual ledger account is

Exhibit 25.1 The principle of control accounts

known, together with information of the total additions and total deductions made into these accounts during a particular period, then the total amount outstanding at the end of that period can be calculated.

The total amount outstanding in the control account can then be checked against a list of the individual balances of the ledger accounts. Provided that no errors have occurred then the two total figures should agree. As mentioned in Section 25.1 control accounts act like mini trial balances and if an error has occurred it can be identified more easily if control accounts are maintained since a control account failing to balance would mean the error lies within that particular ledger.

Let us now look at the following sales ledger. Suppose there were only four accounts in the sales ledger for the month of May 2009 as shown below:

Sales Ledger

Dr   T Allen Account   Cr

2009		£	2009		£
May	1 Balance b/d	850	May	7 Bank	820
"	4 Sales	900	"	7 Discounts allowed	30
"	30 Sales	350	"	31 Balance c/d	1,250
		2,100			2,100
Jun	1 Balance b/d	1,250			

Dr   P May Account   Cr

2009		£	2009		£
May	1 Balance b/d	1,500	May	9 Sales returns	200
"	28 Sales	400	"	14 Bank	900
			"	14 Discounts allowed	20
			"	31 Balance c/d	780
		1,900			1,900
Jun	1 Balance b/d	780			

Dr   K White Account   Cr

2009		£	2009		£
May	1 Balance b/d	750	May	20 Sales returns	110
"	15 Sales	600	"	31 Balance c/d	1,240
		1,350			1,350
Jun	1 Balance b/d	1,240			

Dr		C Young Account		Cr
2009	£	2009		£
May 1 Balance b/d	450	May 28 Bad debts		450

A **control account**, in this case a *sales ledger* **control account**, would consist only of the totals of each of the items in the sales ledger. Let us therefore first list the totals for each type of item.

May 1 Balances b/d: £850 + £1,500 + £750 + £450 = £3,550
Sales in May: £900 + £350 + £400 + £600 = £2,250
Cheques received in May: £820 + £900 = £1,720
Discounts allowed in May: £30 + £20 = £50
Sales returns in May: £200 + £110 = £310
Bad debts written off in May: £450

Now, looking at the totals only, it is possible to draw up a sales ledger control account. Debits are shown as usual on the left-hand side, and credits on the right-hand side. Thus:

Dr		Sales Ledger Control Account		Cr
2009	£	2009		£
May 1 Balance b/d	3,550	May 31 Bank		1,720
" 31 Sales for the month	2,250	" 31 Discounts allowed		50
		" 31 Sales returns		310
		" 31 Bad debts		450
		" 31 Balances c/d (A)		?
	5,800			5,800
Jun 1 Balances b/d (B)	?			

From your studies so far of double entry, you should be able to see that the Balance c/d (A) is the figure needed to balance the account, i.e. the difference between the two sides, i.e. £5,800 − £2,530 = £3,270.

We can now look at the ledger and see if that is correct. The balances are £1,250 + £780 + £1,240 = £3,270. As this has now proved to be correct, the figure of £3,270 can be shown in the sales ledger control account as the balances carried down (A) and the balances brought down (B).

In the above straightforward example, there were only four ledger accounts. Suppose instead that there were 400 – or 4,000 or 40,000 – ledger accounts. In these cases, the information concerning the totals of each type of item cannot be obtained so easily.

Remember that the main purpose of a control account is to act as a check on the accuracy of the entries in the ledgers. The total of a list of all the balances extracted from the ledger should equal the balance on the control account. If not, a mistake, or even many mistakes, may have been made and will have to be found.

25.3　Information for control accounts

The following tables show where information is obtained from in order to draw up control accounts.

Sales Ledger Control	Source
A Opening debtors	List of debtors' balances drawn up at the end of the previous period.
B Credit sales	Total from sales day book.
C Sales returns	Total of sales returns day book.
D Cheques received	Cash book: Bank column on received side. List extracted or total of a special column for cheques which have been included in the cash book.
E Cash received	Cash book: Cash column on received side. List extracted or total of a special column which have been included in the cash book.
F Discounts allowed	Total of discounts allowed column in the cash book.
G Closing debtors	List of debtors' balances drawn up at the end of the period.

Refer to Exhibit 25.2.

Purchases Ledger Control	Source
A Opening creditors	List of creditors' balances drawn up at the end of the previous period.
B Credit purchases	Total from purchases day book.
C Purchases returns	Total of purchases returns day book.
D Cheques paid	Cash book: Bank column on payments side. List extracted or total of a special column which have been included in the cash book.
E Cash paid	Cash book: Cash column on payments side. List extracted or total of a special column which have been included in the cash book.
F Discounts received	Total of discounts received column in the cash book.
G Closing creditors	List of creditors' balances drawn up at the end of the period.

Refer to Exhibit 25.3.

25.4　Form of control accounts

Control accounts are normally prepared in the same form as an account, with the totals of the debit entries in the ledger on the left-hand side of the control accounts, and the totals of the various credit entries in the ledger on the right-hand side.

　Exhibit 25.2 shows how information is used to construct a sales ledger control account for the month of May 2009. The letters A, B, C, etc. from the above tables, relate to the items in the diagram.

Exhibit 25.2 Sales ledger control account – source of data

Sales Day Book B		Sales Returns Day Book C

Total of credit sales
for May 2009

Total of sales returns
for May 2009

Sales Ledger Control Account

2009		£	2009		£
May 1	Balances b/d	A	May 31	Sales returns	C
31	Sales	B	31	Bank	D
			31	Discounts allowed	F
			31	Cash	E
			31	Balances c/d	G
		H*			H*

Cash Book (Receipts side)	E	Total of cash received from debtors in May 2009
	D	Total of cheques received from debtors in May 2009
	F	Total discounts allowed to debtors in May 2009

	Sales Ledger	
Total of all balances on 1 May 2009	A	
	G	Total of all balances on 31 May 2009

* H: If the two totals labelled H are not equal to each other, then there is an error somewhere in the books.

Exhibit 25.3 now shows the construction of a **purchases ledger control account** for May 2009.

Exhibit 25.3 Purchases ledger control account – source of data

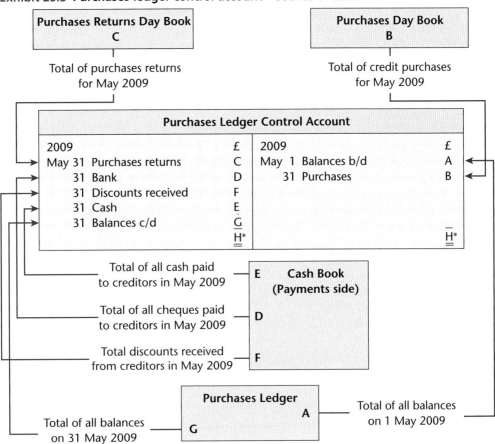

* H: If the two totals labelled H are not equal to each other, then there is an error somewhere in the books.

Exhibit 25.4 shows an example of a sales ledger control account for a sales ledger in which all the entries are arithmetically correct.

Exhibit 25.4

Sales ledger	£
Debit balances on 1 January 2009	1,894
Total credit sales for the month	10,290
Cheques received from customers in the month	7,284
Cash received from customers in the month	1,236
Sales returns from customers during the month	296
Debit balances on 31 January as extracted from the sales ledger	3,368

Dr			Sales Ledger Control Account		Cr
2009		£	2009		£
Jan 1 Balances b/d		1,894	Jan 31 Bank		7,284
31 Sales		10,290	31 Cash		1,236
			31 Sales returns		296
			31 Balances c/d		3,368
		12,184			12,184

We have proved the ledger to be arithmetically correct because the totals of the control account equal each other. If the totals were not equal, then this would prove that there is an error somewhere.

Exhibit 25.5 shows an example where an error is found to exist in a purchases ledger. The ledger will have to be checked in detail, the error found, and the control account then corrected.

Exhibit 25.5

Purchases ledger	£
Credit balances on 1 January 2009	3,890
Cheques paid to suppliers during the month	3,620
Purchases returns to suppliers in the month	95
Bought from suppliers in the month	4,936
Credit balances on 31 January as extracted from the purchases ledger	5,151

Dr		Purchases Ledger Control Account		Cr
2009	£	2009		£
Jan 31 Bank	3,620	Jan 1 Balances b/d		3,890
31 Purchases returns	95	31 Purchases		4,936
31 Balances c/d	5,151			
	8,866*			8,826*

*As can be seen from the totals at the bottom of the control account, there is a £40 (£8,866 – £8,826) error in the purchases ledger. We will have to check that ledger in detail to find the error.

Notice that a double line does not appear under the totals figures. We will not finalise the account (and double rule it) until the error is traced and corrected.

25.5 Other transfers

Transfers to bad debt accounts will have to be recorded in the sales ledger control account because they involve entries in the sales ledgers.

Similarly, a contra account, whereby the same business is both a supplier and a customer and inter-indebtedness is set off, will also need entering in the control accounts. An example of this follows:

(i)   The business has sold A Hughes £600 goods on 1 May
(ii)   Hughes has supplied the business with £880 goods on 12 May
(iii) The £600 owing by Hughes is set off against £880 owing to him on 30 May
(iv) This leaves £280 owing to Hughes on 31 May

	Sales Ledger		
Dr	A Hughes Account		Cr
	£		
May 1 Sales	(i) 600		

Purchases Ledger

Dr			A Hughes Account			Cr
			May 12 Purchases	(ii)	£	880

The set-off now takes place:

Sales Ledger

Dr			A Hughes Account			Cr
		£				£
May 1 Sales	(i)	600	May 30 Set-off: Purchases			
		____	ledger	(iii)	600
		====				

Purchases Ledger

Dr			A Hughes Account			Cr
		£				£
May 30 Set-off: Sales ledger	(iii)	600	May 12 Purchases	(ii)	880
May 31 Balance c/d	(iv)	280			____
		880			880
		====			====
			Jun 1 Balance b/d	(iv)	280

The transfer of the £600 will appear on the credit side of the sales ledger control account and on the debit side of the purchases ledger control account.

Students often find it difficult to work out which side of each control account contra items (set-offs) are shown. Think of it as cash received and cash paid, the entries go on the same sides of the control accounts as these items. Thus a contra item will appear on the credit side of the sales ledger control account (the same side as cash received from debtors) and will appear on the debit side of the purchases ledger control account (the same side as cash paid to creditors would appear). Remember this and you won't get it wrong.

25.6   A more complicated example

Exhibit 25.6 shows a worked example of a more complicated control account. You will see that there are sometimes credit balances in the sales ledger as well as debit balances. Suppose, for instance, that we sold £500 goods to W Young, she then paid in full for them, and then afterwards she returned £40 goods to us. This would leave a credit balance of £40 on the account, whereas usually the balances in the sales ledger are debit balances.

There may also be reason to write off a debt as bad where a business finds it impossible to collect the debt. If this happens, the double entry would be as follows:

> Debit: bad debts account
> Credit: individual debtors' accounts.

Ultimately, the bad debts account would be credited and the profit and loss account would be debited (see Chapter 28). The sales ledger control account would also be credited, as shown in Exhibit 25.6.

Exhibit 25.6

2009		£
Aug 1	Sales ledger – debit balances	3,816
Aug 1	Sales ledger – credit balances	22
Aug 31	Transactions for the month:	
	Cash received	104
	Cheques received	6,239
	Sales	7,090
	Bad debts written off	306
	Discounts allowed	298
	Sales returns	664
	Cash refunded to a customer who had overpaid his account	37
	Dishonoured cheques	29
	Interest charged by us on overdue debt	50
	At the end of the month:	
	Sales ledger – debit balances	3,429
	Sales ledger – credit balances	40

Dr			Sales Ledger Control Account			Cr
2009		£	2009			£
Aug 1	Balances b/d	3,816	Aug 1	Balances b/d		22
Aug 31	Sales	7,090	Aug 31	Cash		104
	Cash refunded	37		Bank		6,239
	Bank: dishonoured			Bad debts		306
	cheques	29		Discounts allowed		298
	Interest on debt	50		Sales returns		664
	Balances c/d	40		Balances c/d		3,429
		11,062				11,062

25.7 Control accounts and double entry

When a business operates control accounts, it has to decide where the control accounts should be kept within the book-keeping system. There are two options:

1 keep the control accounts within the double entry system
2 keep control accounts as memorandum accounts.

These two options are discussed next.

Control accounts within the double entry system

In order to maintain the control accounts within the general ledger, the control account becomes part of the double entry system and the individual debtors and creditors accounts become memorandum accounts (see Exhibit 25.7).

Exhibit 25.7 Control account as part of a double entry system

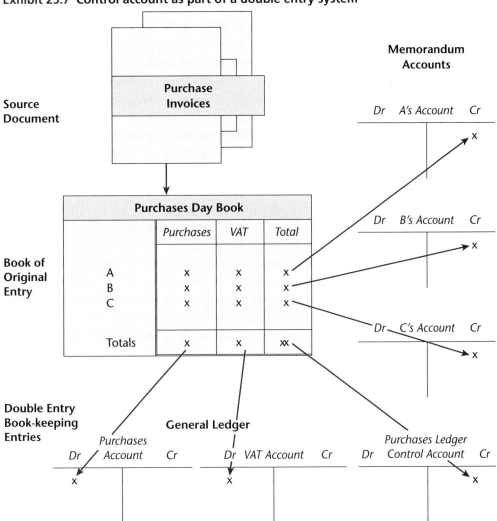

In Exhibit 25.7, the balance of outstanding creditors is taken from the control account and included in the trial balance at the end of the month or year end, as required. In this case, the personal accounts of the creditors (i.e. A Account, B Account, C Account, etc.) are not part of the double entry and are referred to as **memorandum accounts**. It is, however, important to balance the memorandum accounts periodically with the purchases ledger control accounts so that errors can be located and corrected. The same procedure would apply to the sales.

Control accounts as memorandum accounts

In order to maintain the control accounts in the sales and purchases ledgers, the control accounts become memorandum accounts. Using this method, the debtors' and creditors' personal accounts are included in the double entry system via the sales and purchases ledgers, while the control account becomes the memorandum account.

Exhibit 25.8 illustrates this procedure with the purchase ledger. The sales would be similar.

If a transaction involving either a debtor or creditor is made via the journal, for example, writing off a bad debt, it is necessary to record the entry in both the individual debtor or creditor ledger account and also in the respective control account.

Exhibit 25.8 Control account as a memorandum account

25.8 Control accounts and computerised accounting systems

Control accounts are used by many organisations especially those using manual accounting systems. For organisations using computerised accounting systems the control accounts are an integral part of the accounting package and are prepared automatically. This is because computerised systems ensure that all double entry transactions are completed upon entry thereby ensuring that the ledgers all balance. However, even these businesses with computerised accounting packages often prepare their own manual control accounts to ensure that the ledgers balance and to detect any errors.

25.9 Advantages of control accounts

There are several advantages an organisation can benefit from by using control accounts as shown below:

- *Location of error* – By preparing control accounts any arithmetical errors that may have occurred are identified. Also, if a clerk has inadvertently omitted entering an invoice or payment in the personal accounts these too would be identified since the control account acts as a mini trial balance. However, it must be pointed out that there are other errors that may still be contained in the ledgers such as mispostings or compensating errors.
- *Prevention of fraud* – Normally the control accounts are under the supervision of a senior member of the accounting team or accounts manager. This makes fraud more difficult since any transaction entered into a ledger account must also be included in the control account. Since a different member of staff would be responsible for maintaining the ledgers, from the member supervising the control account, it would be more difficult to carry out fraudulent transactions. Therefore the supervisor or manager provides an internal check on the procedures.
- *Information for management* – For management purposes the balances on the control accounts can always be taken to equal debtors and creditors without waiting for an extraction of individual balances. Management control is thereby aided because the speed at which information is obtained is one of the prerequisites of efficient control.

25.10 Other sources of information for control accounts

With a large organisation there may well be more than one sales ledger or purchase ledger. The accounts in the sales ledger may be divided up in ways such as:

- *Alphabetically* – thus we may have three sales ledgers, split: A–F, G–O and P–Z.
- *Geographically* – this could be split: Europe, Far East, Africa, Australasia, North and South America.

For each ledger we must therefore have a separate control account.

Note that many students become confused when making postings to control accounts. You might find it useful to remember that when posting entries to control accounts the entry goes on the same side as it would in the personal account. Another useful hint can also be applied when entering 'contra' or 'set-off' items:

here, think of the contra or set-off as *cash* and enter the item where you would normally enter cash on the respective control account (as mentioned previously in Section 25.5).

25.11 Multiple-choice questions

Now attempt set No. 2 of the multiple-choice questions in Appendix C. This set contains 35 questions.

Chapter summary

- As a business expands it becomes increasingly difficult to trace any error(s) that may have occurred. Tracing an error may involve checking every item in every ledger which is very time consuming. Therefore, what is needed is a type of trial balance for each ledger and this requirement is met by the control account.
- Control accounts are prepared usually at the end of each month or period. The account contains the total of the various individual personal account balances which are held in subsidiary ledgers such as the 'sales ledger' or 'purchase ledger'. By comparing the balance on the control account with the total outstanding balances in a subsidiary ledger the arithmetical accuracy can be checked. Errors can more easily be located and rectified.
- Control accounts contain information gathered from the various accounting books including, sales and purchase day books, sales returns and purchases returns day books and cash book. These items are entered into the control accounts in 'total', i.e. total credit sales for the month, total monies received from the debtors for the month, and so on.
- Transfers from one ledger to another may be called 'contra entries' or sometimes 'set-offs'. Remember to enter these on the same side in the control account as you would normally enter cash either received or paid.
- If the sales ledger control account and the purchase ledger control account are maintained in the general ledger, then they are part of the double entry system and the sales ledger accounts and purchases ledger accounts (i.e. the personal accounts) are classed as 'memorandum accounts'.
- If, however, the sales ledger and purchases ledger are part of the double entry system, then the control accounts are classed as 'memorandum accounts'.
- The advantages of using control accounts include helping to locate errors and the prevention of fraud. They also provide information to management on the totals of outstanding debtors and creditors at any point in time. Such information is easily and speedily obtained from the control account.
- Finally, remember that when making entries into the control accounts the entry goes on exactly the same side as it would in the personal accounts. Think of 'contra items' or 'set-offs' as cash and enter them on the same side you would normally enter cash on the respective control account.

EXERCISES

25.1   You are required to prepare a sales ledger control account from the following:

2009		£
May 1	Sales ledger balances	4,560
	Total of entries for May:	
	Sales day book	10,870
	Sales returns day book	460
	Cheques and cash received from customers	9,615
	Discounts allowed	305
May 31	Sales ledger balances	5,050

25.2   You are to prepare a sales ledger control account from the following. Deduce the closing figure for the sales ledger balance as at 31 March 2009.

2009		£
Mar 1	Sales ledger balances	6,708
	Totals for March:	
	Discounts allowed	300
	Cash and cheques received from debtors	8,970
	Sales day book	11,500
	Bad debts written off	115
	Sales returns day book	210
Mar 31	Sales ledger balances	?

25.3X   Draw up a purchases ledger control account from the following:

2009		£
June 1	Purchases ledger balances	3,890
	Totals for June:	
	Purchases day book	5,640
	Purchases returns day book	315
	Cash and cheques paid to creditors	5,230
	Discounts received	110
June 30	Purchases ledger balances	?

25.4X   The following is a summary of sales activities during the month of November.

	£
Balance of debtors at 1 November 2009	220,617
Goods sold on credit	99,300
Money received from credit customers	109,262
Sales returns from credit customers	2,000
Journal credit to correct an error	550

(*a*) Prepare a debtors control account from the above details. Show clearly the balance carried down at 30 November 2009, and brought down at 1 December 2009.
The following closing balances were in the Subsidiary (Sales) Ledger on 30 November.

Robertson Mechanics	£15,016	Dr
Parkes and Company	£52,109	Dr
JJP Limited	£13,200	Dr
Components Limited	£42,982	Dr
OKK Parts	£44,798	Dr
Stevens Limited	£550	Dr
Mechanics Supplies	£40,000	Dr

(b) Reconcile the balances shown above with the debtors control account balance you have calculated in part (a).

	£
Debtors control account balance as at 30 November 2009	
Total of Subsidiary (Sales) Ledger accounts as at 30 November 2009	_____
Difference	======

(c) What may have caused the difference you calculated in part (b) above?

Association of Accounting Technicians

25.5X Draw up a sales ledger control account from the following.

2009		£
Apr 1	Debit balances	4,960
	Credit balances	120
	Totals for April:	
	Sales day book	8,470
	Cash and cheques received from debtors	7,695
	Discounts allowed	245
	Debit balances in the sales ledger set off against credit balances in the purchases ledger	77
Apr 30	Debit balances	?
	Credit balances	46

25.6 On 1 January 2009, the balances on Shery Tatupu's sales ledger were as follows:

	£	
L Barker	62	Cr
D Blackhurst	1,466	Dr
H Brackenbridge	58	Cr

During the three months ended 31 March 2009, the following transactions took place:

	Credit sales	Cash sales	Sales returns	Payments received on account by cheque	Discount allowed by cheque
	£	£	£	£	£
L Barker	18,642	946	–	15,023	142
D Blackhurst	16,428	–	88	16,009	–
H Brackenbridge	19,886	887	–	17,332	227

You are required to:

(*a*) write up the sales ledger accounts for the quarter ended 31 March 2009

(*b*) prepare the sales ledger control account for the quarter ended 31 March 2009

(*c*) reconcile the control account balance with the ledger account balances.

City & Guilds Pitman qualifications

25.7X Carl Barber runs a small business selling electrical components to wholesalers. Since he has numerous debtors and creditors he keeps sales and purchase ledgers and maintains both sales and purchases control accounts.

The following information is available from Carl's books for the year ended 31 December 2009.

	£
Balances as at 1 January 2009:	
Purchase ledger debit balance	131
Purchase ledger credit balance	7,794
Sales ledger debit balance	10,030
Sales ledger credit balance	71
Totals for the year:	
Cash received in respect of debit balance in purchase ledger	131
Purchases day book	50,099
Purchases returns day book	669
Sales day book	79,660
Discounts allowed	2,910
Discounts received	1,843
Cheques paid to suppliers	46,634
Cheques received from customers	69,015
Sales returns day book	1,578
Bad debts written off	408
Amount due from debtor offset against amount due to the same firm in our	
creditors' ledger (offset via contra)	543

Note: The credit balance of £71 in the Sales Ledger brought forward on 1 January 2009 is to be carried forward as at 31 December 2009.

Required:

(*a*) Prepare Carl's sales ledger control account as at 31 December 2009.

(*b*) Prepare Carl's purchases ledger control account as at 31 December 2009.

(*c*) Why is it important to maintain control accounts? Discuss the advantages.

PART 4

Adjustments for financial statements

This part is concerned with the adjustments that are needed and the use of the extended trial balance in preparing the financial statements.

CHAPTER 26

Depreciation of fixed assets

Learning objectives

After you have studied this chapter you should be able to:

- define depreciation
- explain why depreciation is charged
- calculate depreciation using both the straight line method and the reducing balance method.

26.1 Introduction

In Chapter 9 we considered the distinction between capital and revenue expenditure. Capital expenditure involves the purchase of fixed assets. This chapter covers the need for charging depreciation on these assets and the causes of depreciation.

The methods of calculating depreciation usually involve either the straight line or reducing balance method.

The double entry aspect of recording transactions showing the purchase of fixed assets, charges for depreciation and the disposal of assets will be shown in Chapter 27.

26.2 Depreciation of fixed assets

Fixed assets are those assets of material value that are:

- of long life, and
- to be used in the business, and
- not bought with the intention of being resold.

However, fixed assets such as machinery, motor vehicles, fixtures and even buildings do not last for ever. If the amount received (if any) on disposal is deducted from the cost of buying them, the difference is called **depreciation**.

The only time that depreciation can be calculated accurately is when the fixed asset is finally disposed of, and the difference between the cost to its owner and the amount received on disposal is then calculated. If a motor vehicle were to be bought for £10,000 and sold five years later for £2,000, then the amount of depreciation is £10,000 − £2,000 = £8,000.

26.3 Depreciation as an expense

Depreciation is part of the original cost of a fixed asset consumed during its period of use by the business. It is an expense for services consumed, in the same way as expenses for items such as wages, rent or electricity. Since depreciation is an expense, it will have to be charged to the profit and loss account and will, therefore, reduce net profit.

You can see that the only real difference between the cost of depreciation for a motor vehicle and the cost of petrol for the motor vehicle is that the petrol cost is used up in a day or two, whereas the cost of depreciation for the motor vehicle is spread over several years. Both are costs to the business.

26.4 Causes of depreciation

The principal causes of depreciation are:

- physical deterioration
- economic factors
- the time factor
- depletion.

These are described in greater detail below.

Physical depreciation

Physical depreciation can come in two basic forms:

- *Wear and tear* When a motor vehicle, or machinery, or fixtures and fittings are used, they eventually wear out. Some last many years, but others last only a few. This is even true of buildings, although some may last for a very long time.
- *Erosion, rust, rot and decay* Land may be eroded or wasted away by the action of wind, rain, sun or the other elements of nature. Similarly, the metals in motor vehicles or machinery will rust away. Wood will rot eventually. Decay is a process, which will be present due to the elements of nature and a lack of proper attention.

Economic factors

Economic factors may be said to be the reasons for an asset being put out of use even though it is in good physical condition. The two main factors are usually **obsolescence** and **inadequacy**, described further thus:

- *Obsolescence* This is the process of becoming out of date. For instance, over the years there has been great progress in the development of synthesisers and electronic devices used by leading commercial musicians. The old equipment will therefore have become obsolete, and much of it will have been taken out of use by such musicians. This does not mean that the equipment is worn out. Other people may well buy the old equipment and use it, possibly because they cannot afford to buy new up-to-date equipment.

● *Inadequacy* This arises when an asset is no longer used because of the growth and change in the size of the business. For instance, a small ferryboat that is operated by a business at a coastal resort will become entirely inadequate when the resort becomes more popular. When this occurs it would be more efficient and economical to operate a larger ferryboat, and so the smaller boat will be taken out of use by the business. In this case, it does not mean that the ferryboat is no longer in good working order; it may be sold to a business at a smaller resort.

Both obsolescence and inadequacy do not necessarily mean that the asset is destroyed. It is merely put out of use by the business, and another business will often buy it. For example, many of the aeroplanes no longer used by the large airlines are bought by smaller airlines.

The time factor

Obviously time is needed for wear and tear, erosion, and for obsolescence and inadequacy to take place. However, there are fixed assets to which the time factor is connected in a different way. These are assets that have a legal life fixed in terms of years.

For instance, you may agree to rent some buildings for ten years. Such an agreement is normally called a **lease**. When a lease expires, it is worth nothing to you as it has finished; whatever you paid for the lease is now of no value.

A similar asset is where you buy a patent with complete rights, so that only you are able to produce something using that patent. When the patent's time has expired, it then has no value. The usual length of life of a patent is 16 years.

Instead of using the term depreciation, the term **amortisation** is often used for these assets.

Depletion

Other assets are of a 'wasting' character, perhaps due to the extraction of raw materials from them. The materials are then either used by the business to make something else, or are sold in their raw state to other businesses. Natural resources such as mines, quarries and oil wells come under this heading.

To provide for the consumption of an asset of a wasting character is called provision for **depletion**.

26.5 Land and buildings

Prior to the accounting regulation known as SSAP 12 'Accounting for depreciation' which applied after 1977, freehold and long leasehold properties were very rarely subject to a charge for depreciation. It was contended that, as property values tended to rise instead of fall, it was inappropriate to charge depreciation.

However, SSAP 12 requires that depreciation be charged over the property's useful life, with the exception that freehold land will not normally require a provision for depreciation. This is because land does not normally depreciate. Buildings do, however, eventually fall into disrepair or become obsolete and must be subject to a charge for depreciation each year. When a revaluation of property takes place, the depreciation charge must be on the revalued figure.

As discussed in Chapter 13 many of the accounting standards have recently been replaced with Financial Reporting Standards (FRSs).

FRS 15 'Tangible fixed assets' replaced SSAP 12 in 1999 and repeated the requirements of the original standard and also dealt with the problem of the distinction between the cost of freehold land and the cost of the buildings upon it, by insisting that each cost should be separated (see Section 13.9).

26.6 Appreciation

At this stage, readers may well begin to ask themselves about the assets that increase (appreciate) in value. The answer to this is that normal accounting procedure would be to ignore any such **appreciation**, as to bring appreciation into account would be to contravene both the historical cost concept and the prudence concept (as discussed in Chapter 13). However, one of the problems when SSAP 12 was introduced was that the UK was in the middle of a property boom when businesses could see the market value of their properties rising. At the same time, they were being instructed by the accounting standard to charge their profit and loss account with depreciation that represented a fall in the value of the property over the period. Not surprisingly, this didn't make sense. Therefore, SSAP 12 allowed fixed assets to be revalued and for depreciation to then be calculated on the basis of the revalued amount. FRS 15 also permits this to be done.

26.7 Provision for depreciation as an allocation of cost

Depreciation in total over the life of an asset can be calculated quite simply as cost less amount receivable when the asset is put out of use by the business. If the item is bought and sold within one accounting period, then the depreciation for that period is charged as a revenue expense in arriving at that period's net profit. The difficulties start when the asset is used for more than one accounting period, and an attempt has to be made to charge each period with the depreciation for that period.

Even though depreciation provisions are now regarded as allocating cost to each accounting period (except for accounting for inflation), it does not follow that there is any 'true' method of performing even this task. All that can be said is that the cost should be allocated over the life of the asset in such a way as to charge it as equitably as possible to the periods in which the asset is used.

The difficulties involved are considerable, and some of them are now listed.

● Apart from a few assets, such as a lease, how accurately can a business assess an asset's useful life? Even a lease may be put out of use if the premises leased have become inadequate.
● How does one measure 'use'? A car owned by a business for two years may have been driven one year by a very careful driver and another year by a reckless driver. The standard of driving will affect the motor car and also the amount of cash

receivable on its disposal. How should such a business apportion the car's depreciation costs?

● There are other expenses beside depreciation, such as repairs and maintenance of the fixed asset. As both of these affect the rate and amount of depreciation, should they not also affect the depreciation provision calculations?

● How can a business possibly know the amount receivable in a number of years' time when the asset is put out of use?

These are only some of the difficulties. Therefore, the methods of calculating provisions for depreciation are mainly accounting customs.

26.8 Methods of calculating depreciation charges

The two main methods in use for calculating depreciation charges are the **straight line method** and the **reducing balance method**. Most accountants think that, although other methods may be needed in certain cases, the straight line method is the one that is generally most suitable. Both methods are now described.

Straight line method

This method involves the cost price of an asset, the estimated years of its use and the expected disposal value. The depreciation charge each year can be calculated thus:

$$\text{Depreciation charge per year} = \frac{\text{Cost price} - \text{Disposal value}}{\text{Number of years of use}}$$

For example, if a car was purchased for £22,000 and the business decided to keep it for four years and then sell it for £2,000, the depreciation to be charged would be:

$$\frac{\text{Cost price} - \text{Disposal value}}{\text{Number of years of use}} = \frac{£22,000 - £2,000}{4} = £5,000 \text{ depreciation per year}$$

The depreciation charge of £5,000 would then be charged for four years.

If, after four years, the car had no disposal value, the charge for depreciation would have been:

$$\frac{\text{Cost price}}{\text{Number of years of use}} = \frac{£22,000}{4} = £5,500 \text{ depreciation each year for 4 years}$$

This method may sometimes be referred to as the 'fixed instalment method'.

Reducing balance method

Depreciation to be charged involves deciding on a percentage amount to be used each year. This percentage is then deducted from the cost price for the first year and in subsequent years from the reducing balances. This is illustrated in the following example:

Example: if a machine is bought for £10,000 and depreciation is to be charged at 20%, the calculations for the first three years would be as follows:

	£
Cost	10,000
First year: depreciation (20% of £10,000)	2,000
	8,000
Second year: depreciation (20% of £8,000)	1,600
	6,400
Third year: depreciation (20% of £6,400)	1,280
Net book value at the end of the third year	5,120

Note that **net book value** means the cost of a fixed asset with depreciation deducted. It is sometimes simply known as 'book value'. This method is sometimes referred to as the 'diminishing balance method'.

Using this method means that much larger amounts are charged in the earlier years of use as compared with the latter years of use. It is often said that repairs and upkeep in the early years will not cost as much as when the asset becomes old. This means that:

In the early years		In the later years
A higher charge for depreciation	will tend	A lower charge for depreciation
+	to be	+
A lower charge for repairs	fairly	A higher charge for repairs
and upkeep	equal to	and upkeep

The worked example in Section 26.9 gives a comparison of the calculations using the two methods, when the same cost applies to both methods.

26.9 A worked example

A business has just bought a machine for £8,000. It will be kept in use for four years, and then it will be disposed of for an estimated amount of £500. The business's management asks for a comparison of the amounts charged as depreciation using both methods.

For the straight line method the depreciation is calculated as follows:

$$\frac{\text{Cost price} - \text{Disposal value}}{\text{Number of years of use}} = \text{Depreciation per year}$$

$$\frac{£8,000 - £500}{4} = \frac{£7,500}{4}$$

$$= £1,875 \text{ depreciation per year}$$

For the reducing balance method a percentage figure of 50% will be used.

	Method 1 Straight Line		Method 2 Reducing Balance
	£		£
Cost	8,000		8,000
Depreciation: year 1	1,875	(50% of £8,000)	4,000
	6,125		4,000
Depreciation: year 2	1,875	(50% of £4,000)	2,000
	4,250		2,000
Depreciation: year 3	1,875	(50% of £2,000)	1,000
	2,375		1,000
Depreciation: year 4	1,875	(50% of £1,000)	500
Disposal value	500		500

Exhibit 26.1 illustrates the fact that using the reducing balance method there is a much higher charge for depreciation in the early years, and lower charges in the later years: whereas for the straight line method the charge remains the same each year.

Exhibit 26.1 A comparison of depreciation methods

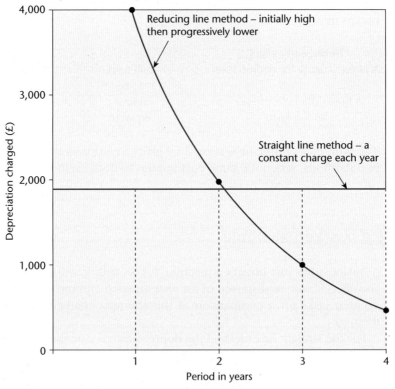

Other methods

There are many more methods of calculating depreciation but they are outside the scope of this book. Special methods are often used in particular industries, where there are circumstances which are specific to that industry.

26.10 Depreciation provisions and assets bought or sold

There are two main methods of calculating depreciation provisions for assets bought or sold during an accounting period.

1 Ignore the dates during the year that the assets were bought or sold and merely calculate a full period's depreciation on the assets in use at the end of the period. Thus, assets sold during the accounting period will have no provision made for depreciation for that last period irrespective of how many months they were in use. Conversely, assets bought during the period will have a full period of depreciation provision charged even though they may not have been owned throughout the whole period.

2 Provide for depreciation made on the basis of one month's ownership equals one month's depreciation. Fractions of months are usually ignored. This is obviously a more precise method than method 1.

The first method is the one normally used in practice. However, for examination purposes, where the dates on which the assets are bought and sold are shown, you should use method 2. If no such dates are given then, obviously, method 1 is the one to use. Often the question will indicate which method to use so it is important to read the instructions carefully before attempting your answer.

Chapter summary

● Depreciation is charged on fixed assets in use during an accounting period.
● Fixed assets are defined as those assets of material value that are intended to be used in the business over a period of time and have not been bought with the intention of resale.
● Depreciation is an expense of the business and as such is charged to the profit and loss account.
● The main causes of depreciation are physical deterioration, economic factors, the time factor and depletion.
● The increase in value over the cost of an asset, usually land and buildings, is called appreciation.
● The straight line method is where an equal amount of depreciation is charged each year.
● The reducing balance method is where a fixed percentage for depreciation is taken from the cost of the asset in the first year. In the second and later years the same percentage is taken from the reduced balance (i.e. cost *less* depreciation already charged).

EXERCISES

26.1 K Richardson runs a small manufacturing business and purchases a new machine for £40,000. It has an estimated life of five years and a scrap value of £5,000. Richardson is not sure whether to use the straight line or reducing method of depreciation for the purpose of calculating depreciation on the machine.

You are required to calculate the depreciation on the machine using both methods, showing clearly the balance remaining in the machine account at the end of the five years for each method. Assume that 40% per annum is to be used for the reducing balance method.

26.2 A printing press cost £37,500 and will be kept for four years when it will be traded in at an estimated value of £15,360. Show the calculations of the figures for depreciation (to the nearest £) for each of the four years using:

(a) the straight line method, and
(b) the reducing balance method, using a depreciation rate of 20%.

26.3X A motor vehicle costs £19,200 and will be kept for four years, and then sold for an estimated value of £1,200. Calculate the depreciation for each year using:

(a) the reducing balance method, using a depreciation rate of 50%, and
(b) the straight line method.

26.4X A photocopier costs £5,120. It will be kept for five years, and then sold at an estimated figure of £1,215. Show the calculations of the figures for depreciation for each year using:

(a) the straight line method, and
(b) the reducing balance method, using a depreciation rate of 25%.

26.5X A tractor cost £72,900 and has an estimated life of five years after which it will be traded in at an estimated value of £9,600. Show your calculations of the amount of depreciation each year using:

(a) the reducing balance method at a rate of $33\frac{1}{3}$%, and
(b) the straight line method.

26.6 A dumper is bought for £6,000. It will last for three years and will then be sold back to the supplier for £3,072. Show the depreciation calculations for each year using:

(a) the reducing balance method with a rate of 20%, and
(b) the straight line method.

26.7X From the following information, which shows the depreciation for the first two years of use for two assets, you are required to answer the questions set out below.

	Machinery	Fixtures
	£	£
Cost Year 1	8,000	3,600
Year 1 Depreciation	1,600	900
	6,400	2,700
Year 2 Depreciation	1,600	675
	4,800	2,025

(a) Which type of depreciation method is used for each asset?
(b) What will be the book value of each of the assets after four years of use?
(c) If, instead of the method used, the machinery had been depreciated by the alternative method but using the same percentage rate, what would have been the book value after four years? (Calculate your answer to the nearest £.)

26.8X   Harry Green is the owner of HG Computers, a business that buys and sells computer equipment whose financial year end is 31 October 2009. As book-keeper to the company you have just prepared the trial balance which you pass to Harry Green. Harry looks at the figures in the trial balance and tells you that he:

- sees that there is an account called 'Computer equipment at cost';
- understands that he has several computers that he uses to run the business;
- hopes to keep these computers for about three years;
- thought that all his computers were treated as stock.

Task:

Write a memo to Harry Green explaining why computers used by the business would not be classified as stock.

AAT

CHAPTER 27

Double entry records for depreciation and the disposal of assets

Learning objectives

After you have studied this chapter you should be able to:

● incorporate depreciation calculations into the accounting records
● record the disposal of fixed assets and the adjustments needed to the provision for depreciation accounts.

27.1 Recording depreciation

The fixed asset accounts show the assets at cost price while the depreciation is shown separately accumulating in a **provision for depreciation account**. The following example illustrates the accounting records.

Example: A business purchases machinery for use in the business's workshop for £2,000 on 1 January 2009. The company uses the reducing balance method of depreciation using a rate of 20% per annum and their financial year end is 31 December. The accounting records for the first three years are illustrated in Exhibit 27.1.

1 The machinery is purchased on 1 January 2009 and paid for by cheque:
   ● **Debit** the machinery account £2,000
   ● **Credit** the bank account £2,000 (not shown in our example).
2 At the end of the financial year the asset is depreciated at 20% per annum using the reducing balance method. First of all we need to calculate the amount of depreciation to be charged each year:

	£
Cost of machinery	2,000
First year: depreciation (20% of £2,000)	400
Reduced balance year 1	1,600
Second year: depreciation (20% of £1,600)	320
Reduced balance year 2	1,280
Third year: depreciation (20% of £1,280)	256
Net book value at end of third year	1,024

Note: Net book value = Cost price – Depreciation
= 2,000 – 976 = £1,024

3 To record the depreciation:
- **Debit** the 'profit and loss account' with the amount of depreciation each year.
- **Credit** the 'provision for depreciation – machinery account' with the amount of the depreciation charged each year.

4 In the balance sheet the asset and total depreciation would be shown under the fixed asset section as follows:
- The asset, i.e. 'machinery', is always shown at **cost price**, i.e. £2,000.
- The total depreciation to date, i.e. £400 + £320 + £256 = £976, is shown as a deduction from the cost price of the machinery to arrive at the **net book value**, £2,000 – £976 = £1,024.

Exhibit 27.1

Dr		Machinery Account			Cr
2009		£	2009		£
Jan 1	Cash	2,000	Dec 31 Balance c/d		2,000
2010			2010		
Jan 1	Balance b/d	2,000	Dec 31 Balance c/d		2,000
2011			2011		
Jan 1	Balance b/d	2,000	Dec 31 Balance c/d		2,000
2012					
Jan 1	Balance b/d	2,000			

Dr		Provision for Depreciation – Machinery Account		Cr
2009		£	2009	£
Dec 31 Balance c/d		400	Dec 31 Profit and loss a/c	400
2010			2010	
Dec 31 Balance c/d		720	Jan 1 Balance b/d	400
			Dec 31 Profit and loss a/c	320
		720		720
2011			2011	
Dec 31 Balance c/d		976	Jan 1 Balance b/d	720
			Dec 31 Profit and loss a/c	256
		976		976
			2012	
			Jan 1 Balance b/d	976

Profit and Loss Account (extracts) for the year ended 31 December

		£
2009	Depreciation	400
2010	Depreciation	320
2011	Depreciation	256

Now, the balance on the Machinery Account is shown on the balance sheet at the end of each year, less the balance on the Provision for Depreciation Account.

Balance Sheet (extracts) as at 31 December

	Cost	Total depreciation	Net book value
	£	£	£
2009			
Machinery	2,000	400	1,600
2010			
Machinery	2,000	720	1,280
2011			
Machinery	2,000	976	1,024

Another example can now be given in Exhibit 27.2. This is of a business with financial years ending 30 June. A motor car is bought on 1 July 2009 for £8,000. Another car is bought on 1 July 2010 for £11,000. Each car is expected to be in use for five years, and the disposal value of the first car is expected to be £500 and of the second car £1,000. The method of depreciation to be used is the straight line method. The first two years' accounts are shown in the Exhibit.

Depreciation per year – straight line method:

Motor Car No. 1 bought on 1 July 2009 at a cost price of £8,000.

$$\text{Depreciation charge per year} = \frac{\text{Cost price} - \text{Disposal value}}{\text{Number of years of use}}$$

$$= \frac{8,000 - 500}{5}$$

$$= £1,500 \text{ depreciation charge per year}$$

Motor Car No. 2 bought on 1 July 2010 at a cost price of £11,000.

$$\text{Depreciation charge per year} = \frac{\text{Cost price} - \text{Disposal value}}{\text{Number of years of use}}$$

$$= \frac{11,000 - 1,000}{5}$$

$$= £2,000 \text{ depreciation charge per year}$$

Note: The entries in the cash book have not been shown in this example.

Exhibit 27.2

Dr		Motor Cars Account			Cr
2009		£	**2010**		£
Jul 1	Bank	8,000	Jun 30 Balance c/d		8,000
2010			**2011**		
Jul 1	Balance b/d	8,000	Jun 30 Balance c/d		19,000
Jul 1	Bank	11,000			
		19,000			19,000
2011					
Jul 1	Balance b/d	19,000			

Dr		Provision for Depreciation – Motor Cars Account		Cr
2010	£	2010		£
Jun 30 Balance c/d	1,500	Jun 30 Profit and loss a/c		1,500
		Jul 1 Balance b/d		1,500
2011		2011		
Jun 30 Balance c/d	5,000	Jun 30 Profit and loss a/c		3,500
	5,000			5,000
		Jul 1 Balance b/d		5,000

Profit and Loss Account (extracts) for the year ended 30 June

	£
2010 Depreciation	1,500
2011 Depreciation	3,500

Balance Sheet (extract) as at 30 June 2010

	Cost	Total depreciation	Net book value
	£	£	£
Motor car	8,000	1,500	6,500

Balance Sheet (extract) as at 30 June 2011

	Cost	Total depreciation	Net book value
	£	£	£
Motor cars	19,000	5,000	14,000

27.2 The disposal of a fixed asset

Reason for accounting entries

When an asset is sold it will need deleting from the accounts. This means that the cost of that asset needs to be taken out of the asset account. In addition, the depreciation of the asset that has been sold will have to be taken out of the depreciation provision. Finally, the profit or loss on sale, if any, will have to be calculated.

When we charge depreciation on a fixed asset, we are having to make estimates. We cannot be absolutely certain how long we will keep an asset in use, nor can we be certain at the date of purchase how much the asset will be sold for on disposal. Nor will we always estimate correctly. This means that when the asset is disposed of, the cash received for it is usually different from our original estimate.

Accounting entries needed

On the sale of a fixed asset, i.e. machinery, the following entries are needed.

A Transfer the cost price of the asset sold to an assets disposal account (in this case a machinery disposals account):

- **debit** machinery disposals account
- **credit** machinery account.

B Transfer the depreciation already charged to the assets disposal account:
  - **debit** provision for depreciation – machinery account
  - **credit** machinery disposals account.

C For the amount received on disposal:
  - **debit** cash book
  - **credit** machinery disposal account.

D Transfer the difference (i.e. the amount to balance the machinery disposal account) to the profit and loss account.
  - (a) If the machinery disposals account shows a difference on the debit side of the account, it is a profit on sale:
    - **debit** machinery disposals account
    - **credit** profit and loss account.
  - (b) If the machinery disposals account shows a difference on the credit side of the account, it is a loss on sale:
    - **debit** profit and loss account
    - **credit** machinery disposals account.

These entries can be illustrated by looking at those needed if the machinery already shown in Exhibit 27.1 was sold. The records to 31 December 2011 show that the cost of the machine was £2,000 and a total of £976 has been written off as depreciation, leaving a net book value of (£2,000 − £976) = £1,024. If, therefore, the machine is sold on 2 January 2012 for *more than* £1,024, a profit on sale will be made; if, on the other hand, the machine is sold for *less than* £1,024, then a loss on disposal will be incurred.

Exhibit 27.3 shows the entries needed when the machine has been sold for £1,070 and a small profit on sale has been made. Exhibit 27.4 shows the entries where the machine has been sold for £950, thus incurring a loss on the sale. In both cases the sale is on 2 January 2012 and no depreciation is charged for the two days' ownership in 2012. The letters (A) to (D) in Exhibits 27.3 and 27.4 are references to the sequence of instructions shown above. Note: Cash book entries are not shown.

Exhibit 27.3

Dr				Machinery Account				Cr
2009			£	2012				£
Jan 1	Cash		2,000	Jan 2	Machinery disposals	(A)		2,000

Dr				Provision for Depreciation: Machinery Account				Cr
2012			£	2012				£
Jan 2	Machinery disposals	(B)	976	Jan 1	Balance b/d			976

Dr					Machinery Disposals Account				Cr
2012				£	2012				£
Jan	2	Machinery	(A)	2,000	Jan 2	Cash	(C)		1,070
Dec 31		Profit and			2	Provision for			
		loss a/c	(D)	46		depreciation	(B)		976
				2,046					2,046

Profit and Loss Account for the year ended 31 December 2012

		£
Gross Profit		xxx
Add Profit on sale of machinery	(D)	46

Exhibit 27.4

Dr		Machinery Account				Cr
2009		£	2012			£
Jan 1	Cash	2,000	Jan 2	Machinery disposals	(A)	2,000

Dr			Provision for Depreciation: Machinery Account			Cr
2012			£	2012		£
Jan 2	Machinery disposals	(B)	976	Jan 1 Balance b/d		976

Dr			Machinery Disposals Account			Cr
2012			£	2012		£
Jan 2	Machinery	(A)	2,000	Jan 2 Cash	(C)	950
				2 Provision for depreciation	(B)	976
				Dec 31 Profit and loss	(D)	74
			2,000			2,000

Profit and Loss Account for the year ended 31 December 2012

		£
Gross Profit		xxx
Less Loss on sale of machinery	(D)	74

In this chapter, all unnecessary difficulties have been avoided. For instance, all assets have been bought, or sold, on the first day of a financial year. Exactly what happens when assets are sold or bought part way through the year is dealt with in *Business Accounting 1* by Frank Wood and Alan Sangster.

27.3 Depreciation provisions and the replacement of assets

Making a provision for depreciation does not mean that money is invested somewhere to finance the replacement of the asset when it is put out of use. It is simply a book-keeping entry, and the end result is that lower net profits are shown because the provisions have been charged to the profit and loss account.

It is not surprising to find that people who have not studied accounting misunderstand the situation. They often think that a provision is the same as money kept somewhere with which to replace the asset eventually.

On the other hand, lower net profits may also mean lower drawings by the owner(s) of the business. If this is the case, then there will be more money in the bank with which to replace the asset. However, there is no guarantee that lower profits mean lower drawings.

Note: A step-by-step guide dealing with depreciation in final accounts is shown in Section 29.14.

Chapter summary

- Fixed assets are shown at cost price in the appropriate asset account, any depreciation charge is shown separately and accumulating in a 'Provision for depreciation account'.
- The depreciation charge for the period is then debited to the Profit and Loss Account.
- In the balance sheet the asset is shown at cost price, less the accumulated depreciation so giving the 'Net book value' of the asset.
- On disposal of a fixed asset the book-keeping entries will involve a new account, i.e. 'asset disposal account'. It is then necessary to transfer the cost price of the asset, the accumulated depreciation and the cash received to this account when the asset is sold. The balancing figure in the asset disposal account may be either a profit or loss on disposal.
- If there is a profit on disposal this will then be added to the gross profit in the profit and loss account.
- If there is a loss on disposal this will be charged as an expense in the profit and loss account.
- Providing for depreciation does not mean that funds are invested elsewhere for financing the replacement of the asset.

EXERCISES

27.1 A White, an exporter, bought a new car for his business on 1 January 2009 for £12,500. He decided to write off depreciation at the rate of 20%, using the reducing balance method.
Show the following for each of the financial years ended 31 December 2009, 2010 and 2011.

(*a*) motor cars account
(*b*) provision for depreciation account
(*c*) extracts from the profit and loss accounts
(*d*) extracts from the balance sheets.

27.2X H Slater, a jewellery manufacturer, purchased a new machine for £18,000 on 1 November 2009. Her business year end is 31 October, but she cannot decide which method of depreciation she should use in respect of the machine – the straight line method or the reducing balance method.

Required:
In order to assist her in making a decision, draw up the machinery account and the provision for depreciation account for the three years from 1 November 2009 using:

(*a*) the straight line method
(*b*) the reducing balance method.

Each account must indicate which method is being used, and each account should be balanced at the end of each of the three years. In both cases the rate of depreciation is to be 10%, and calculations should be made to the nearest £.

(c) Also show the extracts from the profit and loss accounts and balance sheets for each of the three years.

27.3 On 1 January 2009, which was the first day of a financial year, T Young bought networked computer hardware for £9,500. It is to be depreciated by the straight line method at the rate of 20%, ignoring salvage value. On 1 January 2012 the system was sold for £4,250.

Show the following for the complete period of ownership.

(a) The computer account.
(b) The provision for depreciation.
(c) The computer disposal account.
(d) The extracts from profit and loss accounts for four years.
(e) The extracts from three years' balance sheets – 2009, 2010 and 2011.

27.4 Show the relevant disposal account for each of the following cases, including the transfers to the profit and loss account.

(a) Motor vehicle: cost £12,000; depreciated £9,700 to date of sale; sold for £1,850.
(b) Machinery: cost £27,900; depreciated £19,400 to date of sale; sold for £11,270.
(c) Fixtures: cost £8,420; depreciated £7,135 to date of sale; sold for £50.
(d) Buildings: cost £200,000; depreciated straight line 5% on cost for 11 years to date of sale; sold for £149,000.

27.5X Wai Lan Chung owns a Chinese restaurant. The business's fixed assets include some kitchen equipment which cost £38,000 when it was purchased on 1 January 2008.

It was decided that kitchen equipment should be depreciated using the straight line method. It was estimated that the equipment has a useful life of five years and a likely scrap value of £2,000. Depreciation is recorded in the accounts on 31 December each year.

On 28 March 2010 some of the kitchen equipment was sold for cash £520. The equipment had cost £4,400 on 1 January 2008; at date of sale the equipment had a net book value of £2,000.

Tasks:
(a) Give *one* cause of depreciation.
(b) Explain why it is important for businesses to make an annual charge for depreciation of fixed assets.
(c) Prepare the disposal account recording the profit or loss on the sale of the kitchen equipment.

Southern Examining Group AQA

Please note that this question is NOT from the live examinations for the current specification.

27.6X (a) What is meant by the term depreciation?
(b) Which accounting concept is being ignored if a business changes the method of charging depreciation each year?
(c) Name *two* methods of charging depreciation provision.
(d) The accountant for a business recommends that, because of the size of the organisation, all items of machinery less than £500 should be treated as revenue expenditure. What accounting concept or convention is being applied in this example?

(*e*) A business whose financial year ends on 31 December each year purchased a delivery van by cheque for £20,000 on 1 January 2009. Depreciation is to be charged on delivery vans at 20% p.a. on cost. The delivery van was sold on 30 June 2011 for a cheque of £13,000. Depreciation is not charged in the year of disposal. Show the *relevant entries* in *each* of the following accounts for the years ended 31 December 2009, 2010 and 2011:

(i) delivery van account

(ii) provision for depreciation account

(iii) delivery van disposal account

(iv) profit and loss account.

NEAB (GCSE)

CHAPTER 28

Bad debts and provisions for doubtful debts

Learning objectives

After you have studied this chapter you should be able to:

- understand how bad debts are written off
- understand why provisions for doubtful debts are made
- make the accounting entries necessary for recording a provision for doubtful debts
- make the accounting entries for increasing or reducing the provision for doubtful debts
- make all the entries in respect of the provision for doubtful debts in the profit and loss account and balance sheet
- make accounting entries in respect of bad debts recovered.

28.1 Bad debts

If a business finds that it is impossible to collect a debt, then that debt should be written off as a **bad debt**. This could happen if the debtor is suffering a loss in the business, or may even have gone bankrupt and is thus unable to pay the debt. A bad debt is, therefore, an expense on the business that is owed the money.

An example of debts being written off as bad is shown next.

Example 1: We sold £50 goods to K Leeming on 5 January 2009, but that business became bankrupt. On 16 February 2009 we sold £240 goods to T Young. Young managed to pay £200 on 17 May 2009, but it became obvious that he would never be able to pay the final £40.

When drawing up our final accounts to 31 December 2009, we decided to write these off as bad debts. The accounting entries are shown in the table below.

Accounting entries	Explanation
Debit: Bad debts account	To transfer the amount of unpaid debt to the bad debts account
Credit: Debtor's account	To reduce the liability of the debtor who is unable to settle the debt
Debit: Profit and loss account	To record the amount of bad debts of the period concerned
Credit: Bad debts account	To transfer the amount of bad debts to profit and loss account

The accounts would appear as follows:

Dr		K Leeming Account			Cr
2009		£	2009		£
Jan 5	Sales	50	Dec 31	Bad debts	50

Dr		T Young Account			Cr
2009		£	2009		£
Feb 16	Sales	240	May 17	Cash	200
			Dec 31	Bad debts	40
		240			240

Dr		Bad Debts Account			Cr
2009		£	2009		£
Dec 31	K Leeming	50	Dec 31	Profit and loss a/c	90
Dec 31	T Young	40			
		90			90

Profit and Loss Account for the year ended 31 December 2009 (extract)

	£	
Gross profit		xxx
Less Expenses:		
Bad debts	90	90

28.2 Provisions for doubtful debts

Let us look, as an example, at the accounts of K Clark, who started in business on 1 January 2009 and has just completed his first year of trading on 31 December 2009.

He has sold goods for £50,000 and they cost him £36,000, so his gross profit was (£50,000 − £36,000) = £14,000. However, included in the £50,000 sales was a credit sale to C Yates for £250. C Yates has died, leaving no money, and he had not paid his account. The £250 debt is therefore a bad debt and should be charged in the profit and loss account as an expense.

Beside that debt, a credit sale of £550 on 1 December 2009 to L Hall is unlikely to get paid. Although Clark is not certain of this he has been informed that Hall has not paid debts owing to other businesses. As Clark had given three months' credit to Hall, the debt is not repayable until 28 February 2010.

However, he has been requested by his bank to provide it with his financial statements for the year 2009. Unfortunately, Clark cannot wait until after 28 February 2010 to see whether the debt of £550 owing by Hall will be paid or not.

If it is not paid then it will become a bad debt but in the meantime it is a **doubtful debt**.

What, therefore, can Clark do? When he presents his financial statements to the bank he wants to achieve the following objectives:

(*a*) to charge as expenses in the profit and loss account for the year 2009 an amount representing sales of that year for which he will never be paid
(*b*) to show in the balance sheet as correct a figure as possible for the true value of debtors at the balance sheet date.

He can carry out (*a*) above by writing off Yates' debt of £250 and then charging it as an expense in his profit and loss account.

For (*b*) he cannot yet write off Hall's debt of £550 as a bad debt because he is not certain about it being a bad debt. If he does nothing about it, then the debtors shown on the balance sheet will include a debt that is probably of no value. The debtors on 31 December 2009, after deducting Yates' £250 bad debt, amount to £10,000.

The answer to this is as shown in Exhibit 28.1.

Exhibit 28.1

K Clark
Trading and Profit and Loss Account
for the year ended 31 December 2009

	£	£
Sales		50,000
Less Cost of goods sold:		36,000
Gross profit		14,000
Less Expenses:		
Other expenses	5,000	
Bad debts	250	
Provision for doubtful debts	550	
		5,800
Net profit		8,200

K Clark
Balance Sheet as at 31 December 2009 (extracts)

	£	£
Debtors	10,000	
Less Provision for doubtful debts	550	
		9,450

Exactly how we will do the double entry for this is explained in Section 28.4 following. What we have achieved so far is to show bad debts and **provision for doubtful debts** as an expense in the year when the sales were made. The debtors are also shown at probably what is their true value.

28.3 Provisions for doubtful debts: estimating provisions

The estimates of provisions for doubtful debts can be made thus:

● by looking into each debt, and estimating which ones will be bad debts
● by estimating, on the basis of experience, what percentage of the debts will result in bad debts.

It is well known that the longer a debt is owing, the more likely it will become a bad debt. Some businesses draw up an **ageing debtors schedule**, showing how long debts have been owing. Older debtors need higher percentage estimates of bad debts than newer debtors. Exhibit 28.2 gives an example of such an ageing schedule.

Exhibit 28.2 Ageing schedule for doubtful debts

Period debt owing	Amount	Estimated percentage doubtful	Provision for doubtful debts
	£		£
Less than 1 month	5,000	1	50
1 month to 2 months	3,000	3	90
2 months to 3 months	800	4	32
3 months to 1 year	200	5	10
Over 1 year	160	20	32
	9,160		214

In the above example the calculation of the provision for doubtful debts has been specifically detailed. Many businesses do not go to this level of detail; instead they apply a percentage based upon the experience that has been established within the business over a number of years. For example, they may decide to use 5% of the debtors figure as a provision for doubtful debts.

28.4 Accounting entries for provisions for doubtful debts

When a decision has been taken as to the amount of provision to be made, then the accounting entries needed for the provision relate to the year in which provision is *first* made, as follows:

● **Debit**: profit and loss account with the amount of provision
● **Credit**: provision for doubtful debts account.

Let us look at an example that shows the entries needed for a provision for doubtful debts.

Example 2: As at 31 December 2009, the debtors' figure for a business amounted to £10,000 after writing off £422 of definite bad debts. It is estimated that 2% of debts (i.e. £10,000 × 2% = £200) will eventually prove to be bad debts, and it is decided to make a provision for these. The accounts would appear as follows:

Profit and Loss Account for the year ended 31 December 2009 (extracts)

	£	£
Gross profit		xxx
Less Expenses:		
Bad debts	422	
Provision for doubtful debts	200	622

Dr	Provision for Doubtful Debts Account			Cr
2009		£	2009	£
Dec 31 Balance c/d		200	Dec 31 Profit and loss a/c	200
			2010	
			Jan 1 Balance b/d	200

In the balance sheet, the balance on the provision for doubtful debts will be deducted from the total of debtors, thus:

Balance Sheet (extracts) 31 December 2009

	£	£
Current assets		
Debtors	10,000	
Less Provision for doubtful debts	200	9,800

28.5 Increasing the provision

Taking the same example as shown in Example 2 above, let us suppose that at the end of the following year, on 31 December 2010, the doubtful debts provision needed to be increased. This was because the provision was kept at 2% but the debtors had risen to £12,000. Not included in the figure of £12,000 debtors is £884 in respect of debts that had already been written off as bad debts during the year. A provision of £200 had been brought forward from the *previous* year, but we now want a total provision of £240 (i.e. 2% of £12,000). All that is needed is a provision for an extra £40.

The double entry will be:

● **Debit**: profit and loss account
● **Credit**: provision for doubtful debts account,

and the relevant accounts will look as set out below.

Profit and Loss Account (extracts) for the year ended 31 December 2010

	£	£
Gross profit		xxx
Less Expenses:		
Bad debts	884	
Provision for doubtful debts	40	

Dr		Provision for Doubtful Debts Account		Cr
2010	£	2010		£
Dec 31 Balance c/d	240	Jan 1 Balance b/d		200
		Dec 31 Profit and loss a/c		40
	240			240
		2011		
		Jan 1 Balance b/d		240

Balance Sheet as at 31 December 2010 (extracts)

Current assets	£	£
Debtors	12,000	
Less Provision for doubtful debts	240	11,760

28.6 Reducing the provision

Outstanding debtors can reduce as well as increase and if a business finds that the amount outstanding has decreased it may decide to reduce the provision for doubtful debts. Reducing a provision is the opposite of increasing a provision.

In the provision for doubtful debts account a credit balance is shown, therefore, to reduce it we would need a debit entry in the provision account. The credit would be in the profit and loss account. Again, using Example 2 above, let us assume that on 31 December 2011 the debtors figure had fallen to £10,500 but the provision remained at 2%, i.e. £210 (2% of £10,500). As the provision had previously been £240, it now needs a reduction of £30. Bad debts of £616 had already been written off during the year and are not included in the debtors figure of £10,500.

The double entry is:

- **Debit**: provision for doubtful debts account
- **Credit**: profit and loss account,

and the relevant accounts look thus:

Profit and Loss Account (extracts) for the year ended 31 December 2011

	£	£
Gross profit		xxx
Add Reduction in provision for doubtful debts		30
		xxx
Less Expenses:		
Bad debts	616	616

Dr		Provision for Doubtful Debts Account		Cr
2011	£	2011		£
Dec 31 Profit and loss a/c	30	Jan 1 Balance b/d		240
Dec 31 Balance c/d	210			
	240			240
		2012		
		Jan 1 Balance b/d		210

Balance Sheet as at 31 December 2011 (extracts)

Current assets	£	£
Debtors	10,500	
Less Provision for doubtful debts	210	10,290

The main points that you have to remember about provisions for doubtful debts are:

Year 1 - provision first made:
(*a*) debit profit and loss account with full provision
(*b*) show in balance sheet as a deduction from debtors.

Later years:
(*a*) only the increase, or decrease, in the provision is shown in the profit and loss account, as follows:
   - *to increase*: debit the profit and loss account, and credit the provision for doubtful debts account.
   - *to decrease*: credit the profit and loss account, and debit the provision for doubtful debts account.
(*b*) the balance sheet will show the amended figure of the provision as a deduction from debtors.

28.7 A worked example

Let us now look at a comprehensive example.

Example 3: A business started on 1 January 2009 and its financial year end is 31 December. A table of debtors, the bad debts written off and the estimated doubtful debts at the rate of 2% of debtors at the end of each year, as well as the double entry accounts and the extracts from the final accounts, follow as Exhibit 28.3.

Exhibit 28.3

Year to 31 December	Debtors at end of year (after bad debts written off)	Bad debts written off during year	Debts thought at end of year to be impossible to collect: 2% of debtors
	£	£	£
2009	6,000	423	120 (2% of £6,000)
2010	7,000	510	140 (2% of £7,000)
2011	7,750	604	155 (2% of £7,750)
2012	6,500	610	130 (2% of £6,500)

Dr		Provision for Doubtful Debts Account			Cr
2009		£	2009		£
Dec 31	Balance c/d	120	Dec 31 Profit and loss a/c		120
2010			2010		
Dec 31	Balance c/d	140	Jan 1 Balance b/d		120
			Dec 31 Profit and loss a/c		20
		140			140
2011			2011		
Dec 31	Balance c/d	155	Jan 1 Balance b/d		140
			Dec 31 Profit and loss a/c		15
		155			155
2012			2012		
Dec 31	Profit and loss a/c	25	Jan 1 Balance b/d		155
Dec 31	Balance c/d	130			
		155			
					155
			2013		
			Jan 1 Balance b/d		130

Dr		Bad Debts Account			Cr
2009		£	2009		£
Dec 31	Debtors	423	Dec 31 Profit and loss a/c		423
2010			2010		
Dec 31	Debtors	510	Dec 31 Profit and loss a/c		510
2011			2011		
Dec 31	Debtors	604	Dec 31 Profit and loss a/c		604
2012			2012		
Dec 31	Debtors	610	Dec 31 Profit and loss a/c		610

Profit and Loss Account(s) (extracts) for the year ended

		£	£
Gross profit for 2009, 2010, 2011			xxx
2009	*Less* Expenses:		
	Bad debts	423	
	Provision for doubtful debts (increase)	120	543
2010	*Less* Expenses:		
	Bad debts	510	
	Provision for doubtful debts (increase)	20	530
2011	*Less* Expenses:		
	Bad debts	604	
	Provision for doubtful debts (increase)	15	619
2012	Gross profit for 2012		xxx
	Add Reduction in provision for doubtful debts		25
			xxx
	Less Bad debts		610
			xxx

University Centre Library
The Hub at Blackburn College

Customer ID: ******97

Title: Book-keeping and accounts (7th ed.)
ID: BB32202
Due: Fri, 13 Apr 2018

Balance Sheet (extracts) as at 31 December

		£	£
2009	Debtors	6,000	
	Less Provision for doubtful debts	120	5,880
2010	Debtors	7,000	
	Less Provision for doubtful debts	140	6,860
2011	Debtors	7,750	
	Less Provision for doubtful debts	155	7,595
2012	Debtors	6,500	
	Less Provision for doubtful debts	130	6,370

28.8 Bad debts recovered

It is not uncommon for a *debt written off* in previous years to be *recovered* is occurs, the book-keeping procedures are that you should king the following entries:

int

ecovered account.

ating the debt in the ledger account of the debtor is to have a ccount as a guide for granting credit in the future. By the time bad, it will be recorded in the debtors' ledger account. Thus, covered, it must also be shown in the debtors' ledger account. eque is later received from the debtor in settlement of the f, other book-keeping entries are necessary:

ith the amount received ount with the amount received.

inancial year, the credit balance on the bad debts recovered ferred to either the bad debts account or direct to the credit loss account. The net effect of either of these entries is the ebts account will be transferred to the profit and loss account at the end of the financial year. In other words, the net profit will be the same no matter which method is used.

Note: A step-by-step guide to dealing with bad debts and provision for and debts in final accounts is shown in Section 29.14.

Chapter summary

- If a debt is unlikely to be paid then it is known as a bad debt.
- When the debt has been outstanding for a length of time the business usually decides to write if off. The debt is debited to the bad debts account and the customer's account is credited. The bad debt account is later credited and the profit and loss account debited where it is charged as an expense.

- A provision for doubtful debts is created in case some of the outstanding debts are not paid. The provision is charged to the profit and loss account and then deducted from the debtors in the balance sheet, thereby showing a realistic figure of the debts owed and what payment the business expects to receive.
- The provision for doubtful debts is calculated after any bad debts have been written off and deducted from the outstanding debtors.
- The provision for doubtful debts can be adjusted if the debtors at the end of the financial year either increase or decrease.
- To increase the provision debit the profit and loss account and credit the provision for doubtful debts account with the amount of the increase.
- To reduce the provision debit the provision for doubtful debts account and credit the profit and loss account with the amount of the reduction.
- A debt that has previously been written off but is subsequently paid by the debtors is known as a bad debt recovered.

EXERCISES

28.1 Data Computer Services commences in business on 1 January 2009, and during its first year of trading the following debts are found to be bad and the business decided to write them off as bad:

2009		
April 30	H Gordon	£1,110
August 31	D Bellamy Ltd	£640
October 31	J Alderton	£120

On 31 December 2009, the schedule of remaining debtors, amounting in total to £68,500, is examined, and it is decided to make a provision for bad debts of £2,200.

You are required to show:

(*a*) the bad debts account and the provision for doubtful debts account
(*b*) the charge to the profit and loss account
(*c*) the relevant extracts from the balance sheet as at 31 December 2009.

28.2 A business started on 1 January 2009, and its financial year end is 31 December.

Date: 31 Dec	Total debtors	Profit and loss	Dr/Cr	Final figure for Balance Sheet
2009	7,000			
2010	8,000			
2011	6,000			
2012	7,000			

The table shows the figure for debtors appearing in a trader's books on 31 December of each year from 2009 to 2012. The provision for doubtful debts is to be 1% of debtors from 31 December 2009. Complete the table indicating the amount to be debited or credited to the profit and loss accounts for the year ended on each 31 December, and the amount for the final figure of debtors to appear in the balance sheet on each date.

28.3X A business started on 1 January 2009 and its financial year end is 31 December annually. The table shows the debtors, the bad debts written off and the estimated doubtful debts at the end of year.

Year to 31 December	Debtors at end of year (after bad debts written off)	Bad debts written off during the year	Debts thought at end of year to be unlikely to collect
2009	12,000	298	100
2010	15,000	386	130
2011	14,000	344	115
2012	18,000	477	150

Show the Bad Debts Account and Provision for Doubtful Debts Account, as well as the extracts from the profit and loss account for each year and the balance sheet extracts.

28.4 Emford & Co was advised to create a provision for doubtful debts at the end of the business's accounting year, 31 December 2009. It was decided to use a rate of 5% based on trade debtors which totalled £18,600 at that date.

A year later, on 31 December 2010, when trade debtors totalled £19,240, the provision for doubtful debts was maintained at the same rate.

During 2011 the business experienced far fewer bad debts than had been expected and so on 31 December 2012 the rate was reduced to 2.5%. Trade debtors at this date totalled £20,400.

Task:
Complete the following table.

Date	Amount of provision for doubtful debts £	Amount of adjustment to existing provision £	Write either 'increase' or 'decrease' to indicate the effect on the *profit* for the year
31 December 2009			
31 December 2010			
31 December 2011			

Southern Examining Group AQA

Please note that this question is NOT from the live examinations for the current specification.

28.5X From the details below, write up the accounts shown in the ledger of C Bedford Ltd, a wholesaler, for the year ended 31 December 2008. You should show clearly the amounts transferred to the profit and loss account. Information of relevance is as follows:

● At 1 January 2008, T Strange owed C Bedford Ltd £2,000. On 30 November 2008, C Bedford Ltd is notified that T Strange has been declared bankrupt and Bedford receives a cheque for 25p for each £1 owed. The balance owing by T Strange is written off as a bad debt.

● C Bedford Ltd also maintains a provision for doubtful debts equivalent to 1% of outstanding debts at the end of the year. On 1 January 2008 the balance on this account is £500. At 31 December 2008 C Bedford is owed £52,000 by debtors.

NEAB (GCSE)

28.6X (*a*) On 1 January 2009, there was a balance of £2,500 in the provision for bad debts account and it was decided to maintain the provision at 5% of the debtors at the end of each year. The debtors on 31 December each year were as follows:

	£
2009	60,000
2010	40,000
2011	40,000

You are required to show the accounting entries for the three years ended 31 December 2009, 2010 and 2011 as follows:
(i) the provision for doubtful debts account
(ii) the profit and loss account
(iii) the balance sheet extract.
(*b*) Explain the difference between bad debts and a provision for doubtful debts.
(*c*) As more and more businesses are experiencing difficulty collecting debts they find it important to create a provision for doubtful debts to provide for such a contingency. What is the purpose of creating such a provision, and which accounting concept covers this area.

CHAPTER 29

Accruals, prepayments and other adjustments for financial statements

Learning objectives

After you have studied this chapter you should be able to:

- understand why it is necessary to adjust expense accounts for amounts owing or paid in advance
- adjust expense accounts for amounts owing (accruals) and paid in advance (prepayments)
- adjust revenue accounts for amounts owing at the end of a period
- show accruals, prepayments and revenue debtors in the balance sheet
- ascertain the amounts of expenses and revenue that should be shown in the profit and loss account after making adjustments for accruals and prepayments
- enter up the necessary account for goods taken for own use
- prepare financial statements for service sector organisations
- understand what is meant by goodwill and distinguish between various kinds of capital
- enter discounts allowed and received in the financial statements
- prepare financial statements, incorporating the above mentioned adjustments, for a sole trader using the fully worked example and step-by-step guide.

29.1 Introduction

The trading and profit and loss accounts that have been prepared in the previous chapters have included sales for a specific period and shown *all* the expenses deducted appertaining to the period, resulting in either a net profit or net loss. So far, it has been assumed that the expenses incurred have belonged exactly to the specific period of the trading and profit and loss account.

While this generally applies to most expenses incurred by a business there are occasions when some items of expenditure are paid in arrear and/or in advance. For example, a company had some repair work carried out on its premises totalling £2,000. At the end of the financial year ending 31 December 2010 the company had not received an invoice from the builder even though the work had been carried out in November 2010. In order to show a correct figure of profit for the period the amount of the repair bill £2,000 should be accrued and charged against the profit for the period. Similarly, if an expense is paid in advance at the end of the period an adjustment needs to be made to ensure that the profit for the period is correct.

This is discussed more fully in the following sections.

29.2 Adjustments needed for expenses owing or paid in advance

Not all businesses pay their rent exactly on time and, indeed, some businesses prefer to pay for their rent in advance. The following examples will illustrate the adjustments necessary if expenses are either owing, or paid in advance, at the end of a financial period.

Two businesses rent their premises for £1,200 per year.

1 Business A pays £1,000 during the year and owes £200 rent at the end of the year:

Rent expense used up during the year = £1,200
Rent actually paid in the year = £1,000.

2 Business B pays £1,300 during the year, including £100 in advance for the following year:

Rent expense used up during the year = £1,200
Rent actually paid for in the year = £1,300.

A profit and loss account for the 12 months needs 12 months' rent as an expense, i.e. £1,200. This means that in the above two examples the double entry accounts will have to be adjusted.

In all the examples following in this chapter, the trading and profit and loss accounts are for the period ended 31 December 2009.

29.3 Accrued expenses (i.e. expenses owing)

Assume that rent of £1,000 per year is payable at the end of every three months but that the rent is not always paid on time. Details are given in the table below.

Amount	Rent due	Rent paid
£250	31 March 2009	31 March 2009
£250	30 June 2009	2 July 2009
£250	30 September 2009	4 October 2009
£250	31 December 2009	5 January 2010

The rent account appears thus:

Dr		Rent Account		Cr
2009		£		
Mar 31	Cash	250		
Jul 2	"	250		
Oct 4	"	250		

The rent paid on 5 January 2010 will appear in the books for the year 2010 as part of the double entry.

The expense for 2009 is obviously £1,000 as that is the year's rent, and this is the amount needed to be transferred to the profit and loss account. But if £1,000 was put on the credit side of the rent account (the debit being in the profit and loss account), the account would not balance. We would have £1,000 on the credit side of the account and only £750 on the debit side.

To make the account balance, the £250 rent owing for 2009 but paid in 2010 must be carried down to 2010 as a credit balance because it is a liability on 31 December 2009. Instead of rent owing, it could be called rent accrued (or just simply an **accrual**). The completed account can now be shown, thus:

Dr		Rent Account			Cr
2009		£	**2009**		£
Mar 31	Cash	250	Dec 31 Profit and loss		1,000
Jul 2	"	250			
Oct 4	"	250			
Dec 31	Accrued c/d	250			
		1,000			1,000
			2010		
			Jan 1 Accrued b/d		250

The balance c/d has been described as 'accrued c/d', rather than as a balance. This is to explain what the balance is for; it is for an **accrued expense**.

29.4 Prepaid expenses

Insurance for a business is at the rate of £840 a year, starting from 1 January 2009. The business has agreed to pay this at the rate of £210 every three months. However, payments were not made at the correct times. Details were:

Amount	Insurance due	Insurance paid
£210	31 March 2009	£210 28 February 2009
£210 £210	30 June 2009 30 September 2009	£420 31 August 2009
£210	31 December 2009	£420 18 November 2009

The insurance account for the year ended 31 December 2009 will be shown in the books as:

Dr	Insurance Account		Cr
2009	£		
Feb 28 Bank	210		
Aug 31 "	420		
Nov 18 "	420		

The last payment shown of £420 is not just for 2009; it can be split as £210 for the three months to 31 December 2009 and £210 for the three months ended 31 March 2010. For a period of 12 months the cost of insurance is £840 and this is, therefore, the figure needing to be transferred to the profit and loss account.

If this figure of £840 is entered, then the amount needed to balance the account will be £210 and at 31 December 2009 there is a benefit of a further £210 paid for but not used up – an asset that needs carrying forward as such to 2010, i.e. as a debit balance. It is a **prepaid expense**. The account can now be completed as follows:

Dr	Insurance Account		Cr
2009	£	2009	£
Feb 28 Bank	210	Dec 31 Profit and loss	840
Aug 31 "	420		
Nov 18 "	420	Dec 31 Prepaid c/d	210
	1,050		1,050
2010			
Jan 1 Prepaid b/d	210		

Prepayment happens when items other than purchases are bought for use in the business and they are not fully used up in the period. For instance, packing materials and stationery items are normally not entirely used up over the period in which they are bought, there being a stock in hand at the end of the accounting period. This stock is, therefore, a form of prepayment and needs carrying down to the following period in which it will be used. This can be seen in the following example:

Year ended 31 December 2009:
Packing materials bought in the year £2,200
Stock of packing materials in hand as at 31 December 2009 £400.

Looking at the example, it can be seen that in 2009 the packing materials used up will have been (£2,200 – £400) = £1,800. We will still have a stock of £400 packing materials at 31 December 2009, to be carried forward to 2010 as an asset balance (debit balance). Thus:

Dr		Packing Materials Account		Cr
2009	£	2009		£
Dec 31 Bank	2,200	Dec 31 Profit and loss		1,800
		Dec 31 Stock c/d		400
	2,200			2,200
2010				
Jan 1 Stock b/d	400			

The stock of packing materials is not added to the stock of unsold goods in hand in the balance sheet, but it is added to the other prepayments of expenses.

29.5 Revenue owing at the end of period

The revenue owing for sales is already shown in the books. These are the debit balances on our customers' accounts, i.e. debtors. There may be other kinds of revenue, all of which have not been received by the end of the period (e.g. rent receivable). An example now follows.

Example: A business's warehouse is larger than is needed. The business rents part of it to another business for £800 per annum. Details for the year ended 31 December are as shown in the table below.

Amount	Rent due	Rent received
£200	31 March 2009	4 April 2009
£200	30 June 2009	6 July 2009
£200	30 September 2009	9 October 2009
£200	31 December 2009	7 January 2010

The account for 2009 will appear as follows:

Dr	Rent Receivable Account	Cr
	2009	£
	Apr 4 Bank	200
	Jul 6 Bank	200
	Oct 9 Bank	200

The rent received of £200 on 7 January 2010 will be entered in the books in 2010 (not shown).

Any rent paid by the business would be charged as a debit to the profit and loss account. Any rent received, being the opposite, is transferred to the credit of the profit and loss account, since it is revenue/income.

The amount to be transferred for 2009 is that earned for the 12 months, i.e. £800. The rent received account is completed by carrying down the balance owing as a debit balance to 2010. The £200 owing is an asset on 31 December 2009.

The rent receivable account can now be completed:

Dr		Rent Receivable Account		Cr
2009	£	2009		£
Dec 31 Profit and loss	800	Apr 4 Bank		200
		Jul 6 Bank		200
		Oct 9 Bank		200
		Dec 31 Accrued c/d		200
	800			800
2010				
Jan 1 Accrued b/d	200			

29.6 Expenses and revenue account balances and the balance sheet

In all the cases listed dealing with adjustments in the final accounts, there will still be a balance on each account after the preparation of the trading and profit and loss accounts. All such balances remaining should appear in the balance sheet. The only question left is where and how they should be shown.

The amounts owing for expenses are usually added together and shown as one figure. These could be called 'expense creditors', 'expenses owing' or 'accrued expenses'. The items would appear under current liabilities as they are expenses that have to be discharged in the near future.

The items prepaid are also added together and are called 'prepayments', 'prepaid expenses' or 'payments in advance'. They are shown under the debtors. Amounts owing for rents receivable or other revenue owing are usually added to debtors.

The balance sheet in respect of the accounts so far seen in this chapter would appear thus:

Balance Sheet as at 31 December 2009

	£	£	£
Current assets			
Stock		xxx	
Debtors		200	
Prepayments (210 + 400)		610	
Bank		xxx	
Cash		xxx	
		x,xxx	
Less Current liabilities			
Trade creditors	xxx		
Accrued expenses	250	xxx	
Net current assets			xxx

29.7 Expenses and revenue accounts covering more than one period

Students are often asked to draw up an expense or revenue account for a full year where there are amounts owing or prepaid at both the beginning and end of a year. We can now see how this is done.

Example 1: The following details are available:

(A) On 31 December 2008, three months' rent of £3,000 is owing.
(B) The rent chargeable per year is £12,000.
(C) The following payments are made in the year 2009: 6 January £3,000; 4 April £3,000; 7 July £3,000; 18 October £3,000.
(D) The final three months' rent for 2009 is still owing.

Now we can look at the completed rent account. The letters (A) to (D) give reference to the details above.

Dr			Rent Account				Cr
2009			£	2009			£
Jan 6	Bank	(C)	3,000	Jan 1	Owing b/d	(A)	3,000
Apr 4	Bank	(C)	3,000	Dec 31	Profit and loss	(B)	12,000
Jul 7	Bank	(C)	3,000				
Oct 18	Bank	(C)	3,000				
Dec 31	Accrued c/d	(D)	3,000				
			15,000				15,000
				2010			
				Jan 1	Accrued b/d		3,000

Example 2: The following details are available:

(A) On 31 December 2008, packing materials in hand amount in value to £1,850.
(B) During the year to 31 December 2009, £27,480 is paid for packing materials.
(C) There are no stocks of packing materials on 31 December 2009.
(D) On 31 December 2009, we still owed £2,750 for packing materials already received and used.

The packing materials account will appear thus:

Dr			Packing Materials Account		Cr
2009			£	2009	£
Jan 1	Stocks b/d	(A)	1,850	Dec 31 Profit and loss	32,080
Dec 31	Bank	(B)	27,480		
Dec 31	Owing c/d	(D)	2,750		
			32,080		32,080
				2010	
				Jan 1 Owing b/d	2,750

The figure of £32,080 is the difference on the account, and is transferred to the profit and loss account. We can prove it is correct through the following:

	£	£
Stock at start of year		1,850
Add Bought and used:		
Paid for	27,480	
Still owed for	2,750	30,230
Cost of packing materials used in the year		32,080

Example 3: Where different expenses are put together in one account, it can get even more confusing. Let us look at where rent and rates are joined together. Here are the details for the year ended 31 December 2009:

(A)   Rent is payable of £6,000 per annum.
(B)   Rates of £4,000 per annum are payable by instalments.
(C)   At 1 January 2009, rent £1,000 has been prepaid in 2008.
(D)   On 1 January 2009 rates are owed of £400.
(E)   During 2009, rent of £4,500 is paid.
(F)   During 2009, rates of £5,000 were paid.
(G)   On 31 December 2009, rent £500 is owing.
(H)   On 31 December 2009, rates of £600 have been prepaid.

A combined rent and rates account is to be drawn up for the year 2009 showing the transfer to the profit and loss account, and balances are to be carried down to 2010. Thus:

Dr				Rent and Rates Account			Cr
2009			£	2009			£
Jan 1 Rent prepaid b/d	(C)		1,000	Jan 1 Rates owing b/d	(D)		400
Dec 31 Bank: rent	(E)		4,500	Dec 31 Profit & loss a/c	(A)+(B)		10,000
Dec 31 Bank: rates	(F)		5,000				
Dec 31 Rent owing c/d	(G)		500	Dec 31 Rates prepaid c/d	(H)		600
			11,000				11,000
2010				2010			
Jan 1 Rates prepaid b/d	(H)		600	Jan 1 Rent owing b/d	(G)		500

29.8   Goods for own use

Traders will often take items out of their business stocks for their own use, without paying for them. There is nothing wrong about this, but an entry should be made to record the event. This is done as follows:

● **Credit** the purchases account, to reduce cost of goods available for sale
● **Debit** the drawings account, to show that the proprietor has taken the goods for private use.

In the United Kingdom, an adjustment may be needed for value added tax. If goods supplied to a trader's customers have VAT added to their price, then any such goods taken for own use will need such an adjustment. This is because the VAT regulations state that VAT should be added to the cost of goods taken. The double entry for the VAT content would be:

- **Debit** the drawings account
- **Credit** VAT account.

Adjustments may also be needed for other private items. For instance, if a trader's private insurance had been incorrectly charged to the insurance account, then the correction would be:

- **Credit** the insurance account
- **Debit** the drawings account.

29.9 Goodwill

Definition of goodwill

Goodwill is the value of a business over and above the total value of its net assets. For example a business may have the following assets:

	£
Buildings	450,000
Equipment	150,000
Debtors	60,000
Stock	80,000
	740,000

The owner decides to sell the business as a going concern to Ms Lee for £800,000. Ms Lee has, therefore, paid £60,000 more than the total of all the assets. This extra payment of £60,000 is for what is known as 'goodwill'.

Ms Lee has paid this extra amount because she wanted to take over the business as a going concern. Thus,

Purchased goodwill = Total price *less* the value of identifiable assets.

Goodwill is an intangible asset, that is, an asset that cannot be physically seen or touched. It represents the excess amount that has to be paid to acquire a part or whole of a business as a going concern over and above the value of the net assets owned by the business.

Reasons for payment of goodwill

When a business has been established for some time it has many possible advantages that are important to a prospective purchaser of the business, such as:

- good reputation
- large customer base
- experienced, efficient and reliable employees

● the business is situated in a good location
● good contact with suppliers
● possible good brand names that are known and recognised within the industry.

Few of the above advantages are available to a completely new business. For this reason, many people will decide to buy an existing business and pay an extra amount for goodwill.

29.10 Distinctions between various kinds of capital

The capital account represents the claim of the proprietor against the assets of a business at a point in time. The word 'capital' is, however, often used in a specific sense. The main uses are listed below.

Capital invested

This means the actual amount of money, or money's worth, brought into a business by the proprietor from outside interests. The amount of **capital invested** is not affected by the amounts of profits made by the business or any losses incurred.

Capital employed

The term **capital employed** has many meanings but basically it means the amount of money that is being used (or 'employed') in the business. If, therefore, all the assets were added up in value and the liabilities of the business deducted, the difference is the amount of money employed in the business (i.e. the net assets).

Another way of looking at the calculation of capital employed is to take the balance of the capital account and add this to any long-term loan. The result will be the same as the net assets, i.e. the capital employed.

Working capital (net current assets)

The difference between the current assets and current liabilities is often referred to as **working capital** or 'net current assets'. This amount represents the money that is available to pay the running expenses of the business and, ideally, the current assets should exceed the current liabilities twice over, i.e. in the ratio 2:1. In simple terms it means that, for every £1 owed, the business should be able to raise £2.

29.11 Financial statements in the services sector

All the accounts considered so far have been accounts for businesses that trade in some sort of goods. To enable the business to ascertain the amount of gross profit made on selling the goods, a trading account has been drawn up. There are, however, many organisations that do not deal in goods but instead supply customers with a 'service'. These will include professional firms such as accountants, solicitors, doctors, estate agents, management consultants and advertising agencies. Also businesses that provide such services as window cleaning, gardening, hairdressing, repairs and maintenance to washing machines, computer repairs, leisure and health clubs and so on. Since they do not deal in 'goods' there is no need for trading accounts to be drawn up; a profit and loss account, together with a balance sheet, is prepared instead.

The first item in the profit and loss account will be the revenue which might be called 'fees', 'charges', 'accounts rendered', 'takings', etc., depending on the nature of the organisation. Any other item of income will also be added (e.g. rent receivable). Following this, the expenses incurred in running the business will be deducted to arrive at the net profit or loss.

An example of the profit and loss account of a solicitor is illustrated in Exhibit 29.1.

Exhibit 29.1

E B Brown, Solicitor
Profit and Loss Account for the year ended 31 December 2010

	£	£
Revenue:		
Fees charged		87,500
Insurance commissions		1,300
		88,800
Less Expenses:		
Wages and salaries	29,470	
Rent and rates	11,290	
Office expenses	3,140	
Motor expenses	2,115	
General expenses	1,975	
Depreciation	2,720	50,710
Net profit		38,090

29.12 Treatment of discounts allowed and discounts received in final accounts

In Chapter 21 we dealt with recording cash discounts in the cash book and ledgers and you will recall that such a discount could be either 'discounts allowed', which represents a reduction given to our customers for prompt payment of their account or 'discounts received' when the reduction is given by a supplier to us when we pay their account within a specified period.

Using the example below of D Marston (Exhibit 29.2) let us assume that the discount allowed amounted to £310 and the discount received totalled £510. These items would appear in the trading and profit and loss account as follows:

Exhibit 29.2

Trading and Profit and Loss Account of D Marston
for the year ended 31 December 2010

	£	£
Gross profit		30,500
Less Expenses		
Discounts allowed	310	
Other expenses	10,000	10,310
		20,190
Add Income		
Discounts received		510
Net profit		20,700

29.13 Worked example of the financial statements for a sole trader

We have now covered all the adjustments that may be necessary before preparing the financial statements for a business. The adjustments covered are depreciation, from Chapter 27, writing off bad debts and the provision for doubtful debts from Chapter 28, and in this chapter we have dealt with accruals, prepayments, discounts allowed and received. You may also recall that Chapter 12 dealt with closing stock and sales returns and purchases returns and carriage inwards and outwards.

Shown in Exhibit 29.3 is a fully worked example that includes all the items mentioned above and in Section 29.14 you will find another step-by-step guide that deals with these rather tricky adjustments; remember there is also a step-by-step guide to preparing financial statements, preliminary level, in Section 12.9.

Exhibit 29.3

G Lea, a sole trader, extracted the following trial balance from his books for the year ended 31 March 2010.

G Lea

Trial Balance as at 31 March 2010

	Dr	Cr
	£	£
Purchases and sales	224,000	419,700
Stock 1 April 2009	51,600	
Capital 1 April 2009		72,000
Bank overdraft		43,500
Cash	900	
Carriage inwards	4,600	
Discounts	14,400	9,300
Sales returns	8,100	
Purchases returns		5,700
Carriage outwards	21,600	
Rent and insurance	17,400	
Provision for doubtful debts		6,600
Office equipment	20,000	
Delivery vans	27,000	
Debtors and creditors	119,100	61,200
Drawings	28,800	
Bad debts written off	400	
Wages and salaries	89,000	
General office expenses	4,500	
Provision for depreciation		
Office equipment		8,000
Delivery vans		5,400
	631,400	631,400

Notes:

(1) Stock 31 March 2010 was valued at £42,900
(2) Wages and salaries accrued £2,100 and office expenses owing £200 at 31 March 2010
(3) Rent prepaid 31 March 2010 was £1,800
(4) Increase the provision for doubtful debts to £8,100
(5) Provide for depreciation on the office equipment at 20% per annum using the straight line method.
(6) Provide for depreciation on the delivery vans at 20% per annum using the reducing balance method.

You are required to prepare the trading and profit and loss account for the year ended 31 March 2010 together with a balance sheet as at that date.

G Lea

Trading and Profit and Loss Account for the year ended 31 March 2010

	£	£	£
Sales			419,700
Less Sales returns			8,100
			411,600
Less Cost of goods sold			
Opening stock		51,600	
Add Purchases	224,000		
Add Carriage inwards	4,600		
	228,600		
Less Purchases returns	5,700	222,900	
		274,500	
Less Closing stock		42,900	231,600
Gross Profit			180,000
Add Discounts received	(G)		9,300
			189,300
Less Expenses			
Wages and salaries (89,000 + 2,100)	(C)	91,100	
Discounts allowed	(F)	14,400	
Carriage outwards		21,600	
Rent and insurance (17,400 − 1,800)	(A)	15,600	
Bad debts written off	(N)	400	
General office expenses (4,500 + 200)	(D)	4,700	
Increase in provision for doubtful debts (8,100 − 6,600)	(L)	1,500	
Depreciation:			
Office equipment	(H)	4,000	
Delivery vans	(J)	4,320	157,620
Net Profit			31,680

G Lea
Balance Sheet as at 31 March 2010

Fixed Assets			Cost	Total Depreciation	Net Book Value
		£	£	£	£
Office equipment	(I)		20,000	12,000	8,000
Delivery vans	(K)		27,000	9,720	17,280
			47,000	21,720	25,280
Current Assets					
Stock			42,900		
Debtors		119,100			
Less Provision for doubtful debts	(M)	8,100	111,000		
Prepaid expenses	(B)		1,800		
Cash in hand			900	156,600	
Less Current Liabilities					
Creditors			61,200		
Bank overdraft			43,500		
Expenses owing (2,100 + 200)	(E)		2,300	107,000	
Net Current Assets					49,600
					74,880
Financed by:					
Capital					72,000
Add Net Profit					31,680
					103,680
Less Drawings					28,800
					74,880

29.14 Step-by-step guide dealing with further adjustments to financial statements

Note: The letters (A) to (N) shown after each adjustment can be cross referenced to the Trading and Profit and Loss Account and Balance Sheet of G Lea.

1 Prepayments (amounts paid in advance)
In the financial statements

(*a*) If a trial balance is provided in a question then ensure that you *deduct* the amount of the prepayment from the appropriate expense account and put the resultant figure in the profit and loss account. Ensure that only the expenses incurred for that particular period are charged against the profits for that period. Refer to the worked example, note (3) rent prepaid £1,800. This amount should be deducted from the rent in the trial balance, i.e. £17,400 − £1,800 = £15,600, this figure should be entered as an expense in the profit and loss account (A).

(*b*) In the balance sheet show the amount of the *prepayment* in the current assets section directly under the debtors, i.e. prepaid expenses £1,800 (B).

2 Accruals (amount owing)
In the financial statements
(a) If a trial balance is provided in a question then *add* the amount of the accrual to the appropriate expense account and put this figure in the profit and loss account. Refer to the worked example, note (2) wages and salaries accrued £2,100 and office expenses owing £200. These figures should be added as follows:

$$\text{Wages and salaries} \quad £89,000 + £2,100 = £91,100$$
$$\text{General office expenses} \quad £4,500 + £200 \ = \ £4,700$$

The amounts to be charged as expenses to the profit and loss account are thus, wages and salaries £91,100 (C) and general office expenses £4,700 (D).

(b) In the balance sheet show the amount of the *accrual* under the heading current liabilities section directly under the creditors, i.e. expenses owing £2,100 + £200 = £2,300 (E).

3 Discounts allowed and received
Discount allowed
Charge as an expense in the profit and loss account. Refer to the worked example where the discount allowed £14,400 has been charged as an expense (F).
Discount received
Add as income in the profit and loss account directly underneath the gross profit figure. Again, refer to the worked example where there is discount received of £9,300 that has been added as income (G).

4 Depreciation
Straight line method (Refer to the worked example, note 5)
(a) Find the cost price of the office equipment £20,000
(b) Using percentage given 20%
calculate 20% of £20,000 = £4,000
then
(c) Charge £4,000 as an expense in the profit and loss account (H).
(d) In the balance sheet, deduct *total* depreciation £4,000 from this year plus depreciation deducted in previous years £8,000* = £12,000 from the cost price of the asset to give you the net book value of the asset £20,000 − £12,000 = £8,000. Enter each of these figures in the appropriate columns in the balance sheet (I). (*See trial balance credit side.)

Reducing balance method (Refer to the worked example, note 6)
(a) Find the cost price of the delivery vans £27,000
(b) Find the total amount of depreciation to date
(refer to trial balance credit side) £5,400
(c) Find the difference (£27,000 − £5,400) £21,600
(d) Using percentage given 20%
calculate 20% of £21,600 = £4,320
then
(e) Charge £4,320 as an expense in the profit and loss account (J).
(f) In the balance sheet, deduct *total* depreciation £4,320 from this year plus depreciation deducted in previous years £5,400* = £9,720 from the cost price of the asset to give you the net book value of the asset £27,000 − £9,720 =

£17,280. Enter these figures in the appropriate columns in the balance sheet (K). (*See trial balance credit side.)

5 Provision for doubtful debts

Creating a provision

(a) If a provision is to be created for the first time look in the question for details of the amount to be set aside. Let us assume in our worked example that a provision had been created in 2009 amounting to £6,600.

(b) The *provision for doubtful debts £6,600* would have been charged to the profit and loss account as an expense in 2009.

(c) In the balance sheet, the *provision for doubtful debts £6,600* would have been deducted from the debtors. The debtors are to be found under the heading of current assets.

Increasing the provision

(a) Refer to your question and ascertain the new provision, in our example the new provision is £8,100 for this year (see note 4).

(b) Find last year's provision, using our example the figure is £6,600 (this figure can be found in the trial balance, credit side).

(c) Charge the difference between the new and old provision, £8,100 − £6,600 = £1,500 to the profit and loss account (L).

(d) In the balance sheet, deduct the *new provision £8,100* from the debtors (M).

Reducing the provision

(a) Refer to your question and ascertain the new provision. Using our worked example we will assume that in 2011 it was decided to reduce the provision to £5,000.

(b) Find the old provision, again using our example this would be £8,100.

(c) Take the difference between the old and the new provision, £8,100 − £5,000 = £3,100 then add this amount as income in the profit and loss account.

(d) Deduct the *new provision for doubtful debts £5,000* from the debtors in the balance sheet.

6 Bad debts

Simply write them off as an expense in the profit and loss account. In our example you will see that bad debts written off are £400, this is shown as an expense in the profit and loss account (N).

Note: A model layout of the financial statements of a sole trader is shown in Appendix B.

Chapter summary

- It is important to ensure that expenses incurred in a particular period are charged against the profit for that period whether or not they have been paid. In the same way revenue earned in a period should be included as income for that period irrespective of whether the money has been received or is still owed.
- Items owing are called 'accruals', items paid in advance are called 'prepayments'.
- Adjustments need to be made in the expense and revenue accounts to ensure that expenses incurred or revenue due for the period are included in that year's financial statements.

- Expenses owing (accruals) are shown in the balance sheet under the heading of current liabilities while expenses prepaid (prepayments) are shown under current assets. Amounts owing for rents receivable or other revenue due is usually added to the debtors.
- If the owner of a business takes goods for his or her own use without paying for them then an adjustment is made by crediting the purchases account and debiting the drawings account, plus an adjustment for VAT if appropriate.
- Goodwill is the extra amount paid for an existing business above the value of its other assets.
- There are various forms of 'capital' used in a business; capital invested, capital employed and working capital.
- A fully worked example of the financial statements for a sole trader, including all adjustments, is illustrated using the step-by-step guide.

EXERCISES

29.1 The first financial year's trading of C Homer ended on 31 December 2009. You are required to present ledger accounts showing the amount transferred to the profit and loss account in respect of the following items:

(a) Rent: paid in 2009 amounted to £1,600; owing at 31 December 2009, £400.

(b) Insurance: paid in 2009 amounted to £900. Of the amount paid £265 was in respect of insurance for 2010.

(c) Motor expenses: paid in 2009, £7,215; owing at 31 December 2009, £166.

(d) Rates: paid six months' rates on 1 January 2009, £750; on 1 July 2009 paid nine months' rates for the period 31 March 2010, £1,125.

(e) K Whalley rented part of the buildings from C Homer for £400 per month from 1 January 2009. On 15 April 2009 he paid C Homer £2,000 and on 15 December 2009 he paid £4,400. Show these transactions in C Homer's accounts.

29.2 The following accounts are from T Norton's books during his first year of trading to 31 December 2009.

(a) General expenses: paid in 2009, £615; still owing at 31 December 2009, £56.

(b) Telephone: paid in 2009, £980; owing at 31 December 2009, £117.

(c) Norton received commission from the sale of goods. In 2009 he received £3,056 and was owed a further £175 on 31 December 2009.

(d) Carriage outwards: paid in 2009, £666; still owing at 31 December 2009, £122.

(e) Insurance: paid 1 January 2009 for nine months' insurance, £1,080; paid 1 October 2009 the sum of £1,080 for insurance to 30 June 2010.

Show the ledger accounts balanced off at the end of the year, showing balances carried down and the amounts transferred to the final accounts for the year 2009.

29.3X T Dale's financial year ended on 30 June 2009. Write up the ledger accounts, showing the transfer to the final accounts.

(a) Stationery: paid for the year to 30 June 2009, £855; stocks of stationery at 30 June 2008, £290; at 30 June 2009, £345.

(b) General expenses: paid for the year to 30 June 2009, £590; owing at 30 June 2008, £64; owing at 30 June 2009, £90.

(c) Rent and rates (combined account): paid in the year to 30 June 2009, £3,890; rent owing at 30 June 2008, £160; rent paid in advance at 30 June 2009, £250; rates owing at 30 June 2008, £205; rates owing at 30 June 2009, £360.

(d) Motor expenses: paid in the year to 30 June 2009, £4,750; owing as at 30 June 2008, £180; owing as at 30 June 2009, £375.

(e) Dale earned commission from the sales of goods. Received for the year to 30 June 2009, £850; owing at 30 June 2008, £80; owing at 30 June 2009, £145.

29.4 The following balances were part of the trial balance of C Cainen on 31 December 2009:

	Dr	Cr
	£	£
Stock at 1 January 2009	2,050	
Sales		18,590
Purchases	11,170	
Rent	640	
Wages and salaries	2,140	
Insurance	590	
Bad debts	270	
Telephone	300	
General expenses	180	

On 31 December 2009 you ascertain that:

(a) the rent for four months of 2010, £160, has been paid in 2009
(b) £290 is owing for wages and salaries
(c) insurance has been prepaid £190
(d) a telephone bill of £110 is owed
(e) stock is valued at £3,910.

Draw up Cainen's trading and profit and loss account for the year ended 31 December 2009.

29.5X The following were part of the trial balance of K Tyler on 31 December 2009:

	Dr	Cr
	£	£
Stock at 1 January 2009	8,620	
Sales		54,190
Purchases	30,560	
Sales returns	200	
Wages and salaries	4,960	
Motor expenses	2,120	
Rent and rates	1,200	
Discounts allowed	290	
Lighting expenses	580	
Computer running expenses	1,210	
General expenses	360	

Given the information that follows, you are to draw up a trading and profit and loss account for the year ended 31 December 2009.

    (*a*) stock on 31 December 2009 is £12,120

    (*b*) items prepaid: rates £160; computer running expenses £140

    (*c*) items owing: wages £510; lighting expenses £170

    (*d*) £700 is to be charged as depreciation of motor vehicles.

29.6   From the following trial balance of J Sears, a store owner, prepare a trading and profit and loss account for the year ended 31 December 2009 and a balance sheet as at that date, taking into consideration the adjustments shown below:

Trial Balance as at 31 December 2009

	Dr £	Cr £
Sales		80,000
Purchases	70,000	
Sales returns	1,000	
Purchases returns		1,240
Stock at 1 January 2009	20,000	
Provision for doubtful debts		160
Wages and salaries	7,200	
Telephone	200	
Store fittings	8,000	
Motor van	6,000	
Debtors and creditors*	1,960	1,400
Bad debts	40	
Capital		35,800
Bank balance	600	
Drawings	3,600	
	118,600	118,600

Adjustments:

    (*a*) closing stock at 31 December 2009 is £24,000

    (*b*) accrued wages £450

    (*c*) telephone prepaid £20

    (*d*) provision for bad debts to be increased to 10% of debtors

    (*e*) depreciation on store fittings £800, and motor van £1,200.

*Note: Sometimes, in examinations, two items will be shown on the same line. The examiner is testing to see whether the student knows which of the figures relate to the account titles. In Exercises 29.6 and 29.7X the item 'Debtors and creditors' is shown on the same line.

29.7X The following trial balance was extracted from the records of L Robinson, a trader, as at 31 December 2009:

	Dr	Cr
	£	£
Discounts allowed	410	
Discounts received		506
Carriage inwards	309	
Carriage outwards	218	
Sales returns	1,384	
Purchases returns		810
Sales		120,320
Purchases	84,290	
Stock at 31 December 2008	30,816	
Motor expenses	4,917	
Repairs to premises	1,383	
Salaries and wages	16,184	
Sundry expenses	807	
Rates and insurance	2,896	
Premises at cost	40,000	
Motor vehicles at cost	11,160	
Provision for depreciation – motors		3,860
Debtors and creditors*	31,640	24,320
Cash at bank	4,956	
Cash in hand	48	
Drawings	8,736	
Capital		50,994
Loan from P Hall (repayable 2012)		40,000
Bad debts	1,314	
Provision for doubtful debts		658
	241,468	241,468

Note: See footnote to exercise 29.6 for an explanation of why two figures are on one line.

The following matters are to be taken into account at 31 December 2009:

(a) stock £36,420
(b) expenses owing: sundry expenses £62; motor expenses £33
(c) prepayment: rates £166
(d) provision for doubtful debts to be reduced to £580
(e) depreciation for motor vehicles to be £2,100 for the year
(f) part of the premises were let to a tenant, who owed £250 at 31 December 2009
(g) loan interest owing to P Hall £4,000.

Draw up a trading and profit and loss account for the year ended 31 December 2009 and a balance sheet as at that date.

29.8 Freddy Tuilagi is a baker. His trial balance as at 30 September is as follows:

	Dr	Cr
	£	£
Motor van (at cost)	7,000	
Discount received		230
Bank		50
Opening stock	850	
General expenses	610	
Provision for depreciation: Equipment		2,000
Drawings	1,400	
Sales		30,490
Cash	30	
Creditors		845
Purchases	13,725	
Wages	3,880	
Advertising	420	
Telephone	160	
Equipment (at cost)	17,000	
Capital		11,460
	45,075	45,075

The following additional information is available at 30 September:

(1) Stock at cost amounted to £960.
(2) Over the year Freddy Tuilagi took purchases for his own use, at cost £320.
(3) The advertising was prepaid by £46.
(4) Depreciation is to be provided for as follows:
  - Equipment 30% reducing (diminishing) balance method
  - Motor van 15% straight line (on cost) method.
(5) Discounts received of £80 have not yet been entered in the books.

Required:
(*a*) Prepare Freddie Tuigali's trading, profit and loss account for the year ended 30 September.
(*b*) Prepare Freddie Tuigali's balance sheet as at 30 September.

City & Guilds Pitman qualifications

29.9X   Ben Axtell owns a sports shop. His business's financial year ended on 31 March 2009. The trading account for the year ended on that date has been prepared. The following information was gathered from the business's accounting records in order that the other year end financial statements could be prepared.

	£
Gross profit	56,738
Rent of shop premises	9,340
Business rates	4,070
Wages of shop assistants	19,360
Discounts received	133
Trade creditors	4,839
Stock in trade, 31 March 2009	32,980
Maintenance and servicing charges	740
Cash at bank	3,354
Advertising	1,450
Light and heat	1,740
Capital on 1 April 2008	32,056
Insurance	580
Drawings	17,240
Loan from Kay French	8,000
Loan interest	1,212
Shop furniture, fittings and equipment	
at cost	14,000
provision for depreciation, 1 April 2008	4,300

Additional information:

● Business rates, £320, were outstanding on 31 March 2009.
● Advertising costs, £414, were paid by cheque on 30 March 2009. This transaction was omitted from the accounting records.
● Insurance premiums, £65, were prepaid at 31 March 2009.
● The shop furniture, fittings and equipment should be depreciated by 15% per annum using the straight line method.
● The loan from Kay French is due to be repaid in 2013.

Tasks:
(a) Prepare the profit and loss account for the year ended 31 March 2009.
(b) Prepare a balance sheet as at 31 March 2009. The balance sheet should show clearly the subtotal for working capital.
(c) Show how the following accounts should appear in the ledger:
    (i) business rates;
    (ii) insurance.

Note: the accounts should show the figures given in the list above, and any entries arising from the additional information including the transfer of the correct amount to the profit and loss account.

Balance the accounts and bring down the balances.

Southern Examining Group

Please note that this question is NOT from the live examinations for the current specification.

Extended trial balance

Learning objectives

After you have studied this chapter you should be able to:

● enter balances from the general ledger and other records on the extended trial balance

● deal with adjustments, including accruals and prepayments, and enter them correctly on the extended trial balance

● enter the closing stock valuation on the extended trial balance

● deal with other adjustments such as depreciation and provision for doubtful debts and enter them on the extended trial balance

● deal with any errors and discrepancies and enter them on the extended trial balance

● extend the extended trial balance entries into appropriate columns of adjustments, profit and loss account and balance sheet and total them correctly.

30.1 Introduction

As previously mentioned in Chapter 8, a **trial balance** is a list of all balances on the double entry (the ledgers) accounts and the cash book at a particular point in time. The main purpose of the trial balance is to ensure that the books 'balance' and, if any errors are identified, to make the necessary corrections. Another important function of the trial balance is to provide the balances to be used in preparation of the financial statements of the business, the trading and profit and loss account and the balance sheet.

30.2 The extended trial balance

The extended trial balance is often referred to as a 'worksheet' which provides a useful aid where a large number of adjustments are needed prior to the preparation of the financial statements. The extended trial balance is drawn up on specially preprinted stationery on which suitable columns are printed. Exhibit 30.1 shows an example of an extended trial balance. You may wish to photocopy this format and use it when carrying out some of the student activities at the end of the chapter.

Exhibit 30.1 Format for an extended trial balance

Description	Ledger Balances		Adjustments		Profit and Loss		Balance Sheet	
	Dr £	Cr £	Dr £	Cr £	Dr £	Cr £	Dr £	Cr £

It should be noted, however, that some examining bodies may require a slightly different format which needs more columns. It is advisable to find out in which format the examining body, whose syllabus you are studying, require the extended trial balance to be shown.

30.3 Preparing the extended trial balance

Once the trial balance has been drawn up and balanced off correctly, the next task is to implement the following adjustments:

- accruals and prepayments
- include the closing stock valuation
- make provision for depreciation and provision for doubtful debts
- correct any errors.

30.4 A worked example

In Exhibit 30.2 you will find the trial balance which was extracted from the books of D Simpson, a retailer, at 31 December 2009.

Exhibit 30.2

Trial Balance of D Simpson as at 31 December 2009

	£	£
Purchases	138,872	
Sales		202,460
Carriage inwards	490	
Carriage outwards	1,406	
Sales and purchases returns	424	2,280
Stock 1 January 2009	9,820	
Wages and salaries	29,950	
Rent	11,000	
Rates and insurance	3,900	
Heating and lighting	1,254	
Motor vehicle	9,000	
Motor expenses	2,500	
Capital 1 January 2009		37,896
Bank overdraft		5,638
Fixtures and fittings	6,400	
Drawings	27,900	
Debtors	23,200	
Creditors		17,842
	266,116	266,116

Notes:
(a) Rent owing amounted to £1,000 as at 31 December 2009.
(b) Rates paid in advance amounted to £500.
(c) Closing stock was valued at £12,042 as at 31 December 2009.
(d) Depreciate the motor vehicle at 20% using the straight line method.
    [*Note:* Fixtures and fittings are not to be depreciated in this example.]
(e) Provide for the creation of a provision for doubtful debts amounting to 2% of the debtors.

You are required to:

1 Prepare an extended trial balance at 31 December 2009.
2 Prepare a trading and profit and loss account for the year ended 31 December 2009 and a balance sheet as at that date.

Since many students have difficulty in preparing extended trial balances the above example will be carried out using the 'step-by-step guide' shown below.

Step-by-step guide

Step 1

First of all draw up a trial balance in the usual way (refer to Section 8.3). Remember:

> Debit Balances are Assets or Expenses
> *and*
> Credit Balances are Liabilities, Capital or Income

If there have been no errors then the two sides should agree. Refer to Exhibit 30.3 and note that the balances have now been entered on the **extended trial balance** (**ETB**) under the heading 'ledger balances'.

Step 2

Deal with the adjustments at the bottom of the trial balance.
Note: Each item must be dealt with twice to comply with the double entry rules.
  Adjustments fall into four categories:

1 **Accruals**
2 **Prepayments**
3 **Closing stock valuation**
4 **Other adjustments:**
  depreciation provision
  provision for doubtful debts
  correction of errors

When dealing with adjustments think double entry, i.e.

> which account should be debited
> *and*
> which account should be credited

  When entering the adjustment on the extended trial balance first of all look to see if there is already an 'Account' for the transaction and, if so, use it. If not, then open an account at the foot of the extended trial balance. (This is illustrated in the following examples.)

Step 3

Deal with accruals and prepayments.

1 Accruals (amounts owing)

For example, referring to Exhibit 30.2(a) rent owing amounts to £1,000, which is entered as follows:

> Debit   Rent Account £1,000
> Credit   Accruals – Rent £1,000 (as this item is a liability).

This transaction is now shown in Exhibit 30.3 below as '(a)' under the 'adjustments' column – see the debit entry of £1,000 next to the 'Rent Account' and the credit entry of £1,000 entered below the totals of the trial balance under the heading 'Accruals – Rent'.

2 Prepayments (amounts paid in advance)

Exhibit 30.2(b) shows a rates prepayment of £500, which is entered as follows:

> Debit   Prepayments – rates £500
> Credit   Rates account £500.

This again is shown in Exhibit 30.3(b) under the adjustments column – see the debit entry of £500 entered below the totals of the trial balance under the heading 'Prepayment – rates £500' and the corresponding credit entry shown next to the 'rates account'.

3 Dealing with the closing stock valuation

At the end of the financial year a business usually undertakes a valuation of the stock. Exhibit 30.2(c) shows a closing stock of £12,042, which is entered as follows:

> Debit   Stock account (to be shown in the balance sheet as an asset)
> Credit   Stock account (shown in the profit and loss account as a deduction from the cost of goods sold calculation).

This is shown in Exhibit 30.3(c) under the trial balance totals is the adjustments column.

4 Dealing with other adjustments

Depreciation provision   Exhibit 30.2(d) requires provision for depreciation of 20% on motor vehicles using the straight line method. Motor vehicles cost £9,000, therefore, 20% of cost equals £1,800 depreciation to be charged against the profit and loss account. This transaction is entered on the extended trial balance under the adjustments column, see note (d) as follows:

> Debit   Depreciation of motor vehicle £1,800 (amount to be charged to profit and loss account)
> Credit   Depreciation provision of motor vehicle £1,800 (amount to be shown as a deduction from the value of the asset in the balance sheet).

Provision for doubtful debts   Exhibit 30.2(e) requires the creation of a provision for doubtful debts amounting to 2% of the debtors figure of £23,200 which amounts to £464. The entry in the extended trial balance will appear in the adjustments column – note (e) as follows:

> Debit   Creation of provision for doubtful debts £464 (this amount to be charged in the profit and loss account)
> Credit   Provision for doubtful debts £464 (this amount to be shown as deduction from the debtors in the balance sheet).

Correction of errors To keep the worked example as straightforward as possible, no errors require correcting in Exhibit 30.2. This topic will be covered later in this chapter.

Step 4

The next step is to add up both parts of the adjustments column. Providing the adjustments have been carried out correctly, the two columns should agree – in other words, the adjustments column acts rather like a mini trial balance.

Step 5

It is now necessary to add/subtract the figures *across* the extended trial balance and enter the *total* in either the profit and loss account or balance sheet column. This step requires a certain amount of skill from the students since they must be fully conversant with the position of each balance figure in the financial statements. A useful hint is to carry out this identification *before* starting the analysis by entering either of the following immediately before the description column (*see* Exhibit 30.3), namely:

PL   Profit and loss account
BS   Balance sheet

to indicate which analysis column to use.

It is important to note when carrying out the analysis that if the balance is shown as a debit balance in the ledger balance column then it will appear as a debit balance in either the profit and loss account column or the balance sheet column. The same thing applies to the credit balances, which will appear in either the profit and loss account column or balance sheet column as a credit balance. While carrying out the analysis, any figures appearing in the adjustments column must be taken into consideration; for example, referring to Exhibit 30.3(a), the balance of rent will be analysed as:

Rent £11,000 plus £1,000 (owing) = £12,000

This will be analysed into the profit and loss account column as a debit balance of £12,000.

Note: Refer to Exhibit 30.3 where this task has been carried out.

A further example can also be seen in Exhibit 30.3(b) where the prepayment of rates £500 will be analysed as follows:

Rates and Insurance	£3,900
Less amount paid in advance	500
	£3,400

The amount to be shown in the profit and loss account column will be £3,400 debit balance.

Exhibit 30.3 D Simpson – extended trial balance at 31 December 2009

	Description	Ledger Balances Dr £	Ledger Balances Cr £	Adjustments Dr £	Adjustments Cr £	Profit and Loss Dr £	Profit and Loss Cr £	Balance Sheet Dr £	Balance Sheet Cr £
PL	Purchases	138,872				138,872			
PL	Sales		202,460				202,460		
PL	Carriage inwards	490				490			
PL	Carriage outwards	1,406				1,406			
PL	Sales and purchases returns	424	2,280			424	2,280		
PL	Stock 1 January 2009	9,820				9,820			
PL	Wages and salaries	29,950				29,950			
PL	Rent	11,000		(a) 1,000		12,000			
PL	Rates and insurance	3,900			(b) 500	3,400			
PL	Heating and lighting	1,254				1,254			
BS	Motor vehicle	9,000						9,000	
PL	Motor expenses	2,500				2,500			
BS	Capital 1 January 2009		37,896						37,896
BS	Bank overdraft		5,638						5,638
BS	Fixtures and fittings	6,400						6,400	
BS	Drawings	27,900						27,900	
BS	Debtors	23,200						23,200	
BS	Creditors		17,842						17,842
		266,116	266,116						
BS	Accrual – Rent				(a) 1,000				1,000
BS	Prepayment – Rates			(b) 500				500	
BS	Stock 31 December 2009			(c) 12,042				12,042	
PL	Stock 31 December 2009				(c) 12,042		12,042		
PL	Depreciation – Motor vehicle			(d) 1,800		1,800			
BS	Depreciation – Provision for motor vehicle				(d) 1,800				1,800
PL	Provision for doubtful debts				(e) 464	464			
BS	Provision for doubtful debts			(e) 464					464
				15,806	15,806				
				(Step 4)					
	Net profit (Step 6)					14,402			14,402
						216,782	216,782	79,042	79,042
								(Step 7)	

Step 6

Add up the profit and loss account columns. The difference between the two figures will represent a profit or loss for the period. In our example of D Simpson the difference between these two columns is £14,402, representing a net profit. This figure will now be entered on the extended trial balance as net profit £14,402, a *debit entry* in the profit and loss account column.

The corresponding *credit entry* will appear as under the balance sheet columns.

Step 7

The only remaining task to carry out is to add up the balance sheet column totals and, provided all transactions have been carried out correctly, the totals should agree.

Note: Refer to Exhibit 30.3 where you can see that the extended trial balance balances with a total of £79,042.

The trading and profit and loss account and balance sheet of D Simpson for the year ended 31 December 2009 is shown in Exhibit 30.4.

Exhibit 30.4

D Simpson
Trading and Profit and Loss Account
for the year ended 31 December 2009

	£	£	£
Sales		202,460	
Less Sales returns		424	202,036
Less Cost of goods sold:			
Opening stock		9,820	
Purchases		138,872	
Carriage inwards		490	
		149,182	
Less Purchase returns	2,280		
Closing stock	12,042	14,322	134,860
Gross profit			67,176
Less Expenses:			
Carriage outwards		1,406	
Wages and salaries		29,950	
Rent (11,000 + 1,000)		12,000	
Rates and insurance (3,900 − 500)		3,400	
Heating and lighting		1,254	
Motor expenses		2,500	
Depreciation – Motor vehicle		1,800	
Creation of provision for doubtful debts		464	52,774
Net profit			14,402

D Simpson
Balance Sheet as at 31 December 2009

	£	Cost £	Total Dep'n £	Net Book Value £
Fixed assets:				
Fixtures and fittings		6,400	–	6,400
Motor vehicles		9,000	1,800	7,200
		15,400	1,800	13,600
Current assets:				
Stock		12,042		
Debtors	23,200			
Less Provision for doubtful debts	464	22,736		
Prepayments		500	35,278	
Less Current liabilities:				
Bank overdraft		5,638		
Creditors		17,842		
Accruals		1,000	24,480	
Net current assets				10,798
				24,398
Financed by:				
Capital: Balance 1 January 2009				37,896
Add Net profit for the year				14,402
				52,298
Less Drawings				27,900
				24,398

30.5 Other considerations

In the above example of D Simpson the transactions involving depreciation and provision for doubtful debts was kept as straightforward as possible to avoid complications. However, assuming it is the next accounting period of D Simpson, the following adjustments will now be shown:

1 Depreciate the motor vehicle by 20% using the straight line method (for the second year).
2 Increase the provision for doubtful debts to £550.
3 Write off a bad debt amounting to £100.

1 Depreciate the motor vehicle by 20% using the straight line method

First of all the amount of depreciation to be charged against the profit and loss account needs to be calculated. As the method of depreciation to be used is the straight line method, the amount of depreciation will be the same each year, namely, 20% of £9,000 = £1,800. This amount is then entered on the extended trial balance as follows:

D Simpson
Extended Trial Balance (extract) as at 31 December 2010

Description	Ledger balances		Adjustments		Profit and loss		Balance sheet	
	Dr £	Cr £	Dr £	Cr £	Dr £	Cr £	Dr £	Cr £
Motor vehicle	9,000						9,000	
Provision for depreciation motor vehicle*		1,800		1,800				3,600
Depreciation of motor vehicle			1,800		1,800			

The above example shows that the motor vehicle account remains a debit balance of £9,000 which appears in the balance sheet column as a debit (an asset). The provision for depreciation of motor vehicle* appears under the ledger balances column as £1,800, representing the amount of depreciation charged for the first year. To this figure another £1,800 is added representing the depreciation for this year showing a total of depreciation to date of £3,600. This is shown as a credit balance in the balance sheet column of the extended trial balance.

When the balance sheet is prepared it will appear as follows:

D Simpson
Balance Sheet (extract) as at 31 December 2010

	Cost	Total dep'n	Net book value
Fixed assets	£	£	£
Motor vehicle	9,000	3,600	5,400

The remaining debit balance of depreciation of motor vehicle £1,800 will be charged in the profit and loss account. This is shown in the extended trial balance under the profit and loss account column as a debit balance (see above in the extended trial balance extract).

2 Increase the provision for doubtful debts to £550

In the accounts for the year ended 31 December 2009, D Simpson created a provision for doubtful debts equal to 2% of the debtors which amounted to £464 (this is illustrated in the extract from extended trial balance below).

In the year to 31 December 2010 it was decided to increase the provision to £550, representing an increase of £86 (£550 *less* £464). To record this increase the following entries need to be made:

● Show the increase of provision for doubtful debts of £86 as a debit entry in the adjustments column to be charged in the profit and loss account.
● Increase the existing 'provision for doubtful debts account' by £86 to £550; this will be shown as a credit entry in the adjustments column of the extended trial balance. This figure is then extended to the balance sheet column as £550 (credit entry).

This can now be seen in the following extract from the extended trial balance.

D Simpson
Extended Trial Balance (extract) as at 31 December 2010

Description	Ledger balances		Adjustments		Profit and loss		Balance sheet	
	Dr £	Cr £	Dr £	Cr £	Dr £	Cr £	Dr £	Cr £
Provision for doubtful debts		464		86				550
Increase in provision for doubtful debts			86		86			

3 Write off a bad debt amounting to £100

After the preparation of the draft accounts one of the firm's debtors was reported to have been declared bankrupt. The balance on the debtor's account was £100 and it was decided to write the debt off as bad.

This would be entered on the extended trial balance as follows:

D Simpson
Extended Trial Balance (extract) as at 31 December 2010

Description	Ledger balances		Adjustments		Profit and loss		Balance sheet	
	Dr £	Cr £	Dr £	Cr £	Dr £	Cr £	Dr £	Cr £
Debtors (say)	26,000			100			25,900	
Bad debts			100		100			

The above entries show that the debtors, which we have assumed are £26,000 for this year ended 2010, have been reduced by £100 and will appear in the balance sheet as £25,900. The bad debt will also be charged to the profit and loss account. This is shown as a debit entry in both the adjustments column and the profit and loss account column.

30.6   A more complicated example

Exhibit 30.5 shows a worked example of a more complicated extended trial balance.

Exhibit 30.5

J Blake is a sole trader. He extracted the following list of balances from the books of his business on 31 March 2009:

	Dr £	Cr £
Sales		80,650
Purchases	45,380	
Sales returns	510	
Purchases returns		930
Discounts allowed	1,120	
Discounts received		390
Stock at 1 April 2008	12,460	
Motor van, at cost	12,500	
Office equipment	9,600	
Provision for depreciation of motor van 1 April 2008		3,800
Provision for depreciation of office equipment 1 April 2008		2,150
Salaries and wages	17,620	
Motor van running expenses	3,910	
Sundry expenses	1,140	
Rent and rates	3,200	
Bad debts	375	
Provision for doubtful debts 1 April 2008		320
Debtors	12,870	
Creditors		9,100
Bank	8,040	
Cash	60	
Drawings	7,000	
Capital		38,445
	135,785	135,785

This additional information is available at 31 March 2009:

(*a*) Stock was valued at £20,100.

(*b*) Salaries and wages of £490 are to be accrued.

(*c*) The following have been prepaid: rent and rates £790.

(*d*) An additional £270 is to be written off as bad debts, and the provision for doubtful debts is to be adjusted to 2% of debtors after writing off bad debts.

(*e*) Goods taken by Blake for his private use during the year amounted at cost to £370. No record of this has yet been made in the books.

(*f*) Depreciation is to be written off as follows: motor van £2,000; office equipment at 15% using the straight line method.

Exhibit 30.6 J Blake – extended trial balance at 31 March 2009

	Description	Ledger Balances Dr £	Ledger Balances Cr £	Adjustments Dr £	Adjustments Cr £	Profit and Loss Dr £	Profit and Loss Cr £	Balance Sheet Dr £	Balance Sheet Cr £
PL	Sales		80,650				80,650		
PL	Purchases	45,380			370	45,010			
PL	Sales returns/Purchase returns		930				930		
PL	Discounts	1,120				1,120			
PL	Stock at 1 April 2008	12,460				12,460			
BS	Motor van, at cost	12,500						12,500	
BS	Office equipment, at cost	9,600						9,600	
BS	Provision for dep'n – Motor van 1.4.2008		3,800		2,000				5,800
BS	Provision for dep'n – Office equip. 1.4.2008		2,150		1,440				3,590
PL	Salaries and wages	17,620		490		18,110			
PL	Motor van running expenses	3,910				3,910			
PL	Sundry expenses	1,140				1,140			
PL	Rent and rates	3,200			790	2,410			
PL	Bad debts	375		270		645			
BS	Provision for doubtful debts 1.4.2008		320	68					252
BS	Debtors	12,870			270			12,600	
BS	Creditors		9,100						9,100
BS	Bank	8,040						8,040	
BS	Cash	60						60	
BS	Drawings	7,000		370				7,370	
BS	Capital		38,445						38,445
		135,785	135,785						
BS	Accrual – Salaries and wages				490				490
BS	Prepayment – Rent and rates			790				790	
BS	Stock – 31 March 2009			20,100				20,100	
PL	Stock – 31 March 2009				20,100		20,100		
PL	Depreciation – Motor van			2,000		2,000			
PL	Depreciation – Office equipment			1,440		1,440			
PL	Reduction in provision for doubtful debts				68		68		
				25,528	25,528				
BS	Net profit (balancing figure)					13,383			13,383
						102,138	102,138	71,060	71,060

You are required to:

1 Prepare an extended trial balance as at 31 March 2009.
2 Prepare a trading and profit and loss account for the year ended 31 March 2009 and a balance sheet as at that date.

Remember to follow the 'Step-by-step guide' to assist you in following the workings of Exhibit 30.5 and note the order of dealing with the 'adjustments':

● accruals and prepayments
● deal with the closing stock valuation
● make provision for depreciation and provision for doubtful debts
● other adjustments
    – writing off the bad debt (refer back to Section 30.5(3) and Chaper 28)
    – goods taken for own use (see the worked example, Exhibit 30.6).

The extended trial balance of J Blake is now shown in Exhibit 30.6 and the trading and profit and loss account and balance sheet is shown in Exhibit 30.7 as follows:

Exhibit 30.7

J Blake
Trading and Profit and Loss Account for the year ended 31 March 2009

	£	£	£
Sales		80,650	
Less Sales returns		510	80,140
Less Cost of goods sold:			
Opening stock		12,460	
Add Purchases (45,380 – 370 own use)	45,010		
Less Purchase returns	930	44,080	
		56,540	
Less Closing stock		20,100	36,440
Gross profit			43,700
Add Income:			
Discount received		390	
Reduction in provision for doubtful debts			
(320 – 2% of (12,870 – 270))		68	458
			44,158
Less Expenses:			
Discounts allowed		1,120	
Salaries and wages (17,620 + 490)		18,110	
Motor van running expenses		3,910	
Rent and rates (3,200 – 790)		2,410	
Sundry expenses		1,140	
Bad debts (375 + 270)		645	
Depreciation: Motor van		2,000	
Office equipment		1,440	30,775
Net profit			13,383

J Blake
Balance Sheet as at 31 March 2009

		Cost	Total dep'n	Net book value
	£	£	£	£
Fixed assets:				
Office equipment		9,600	3,590	6,010
Motor van		12,500	5,800	6,700
		22,100	9,390	12,710
Current assets:				
Stock		20,100		
Debtors (12,870 – 270)	12,600			
Less Provision for doubtful debts	252	12,348		
Prepayments		790		
Cash at bank		8,040		
Cash in hand		60	41,338	
Less Current liabilities				
Creditors		9,100		
Accruals		490	9,590	
Net current assets				31,748
				44,458
Financed by:				
Capital				38,445
Add Net profit				13,383
				51,828
Less Drawings (7,000 + 370 goods for own use)				7,370
				44,458

Chapter summary

- The extended trial balance is often referred to as a 'worksheet' since it provides a useful aid where a large number of adjustments are needed prior to the preparation of the financial statements.
- Initially a trial balance is prepared in the usual way with debit balances consisting of assets or expenses and credit balances being liabilities, capital or income.
- At the end of the financial year there are often several adjustments to be made. These consist of accruals and prepayments, closing stock valuation and making provisions for depreciation and doubtful debts.
- It is important to remember that each adjustment must be recorded *twice* on the extended trial balance, one being a debit entry the other the credit entry.
- A careful systematic approach must be applied when entering items in the extended trial balance. Each category must be entered one step at a time, i.e. accruals, prepayments, dealing with the closing stock valuation and then other adjustments.
- It is important to ensure that the 'adjustment columns' add up correctly, rather like a mini-trial balance.

- The next step is to add/subtract the figures across the extended trial balance entering the total in either the profit and loss or balance sheet columns. The balancing figure in the profit and loss columns represents the *profit* or *loss* for the period which is also entered in the balance sheet columns. All columns are then added up with each section agreeing.
- Finally, the financial statements can be prepared, i.e. the trading and profit and loss accounts and the balance sheet.

EXERCISES

Note: A blank worksheet for preparing extended trial balance exercises is given in Appendix B.

30.1 Reconstruct the trial balance after making the necessary corrections.

S Dickinson
Trial Balance as at 30 September 2009

	Dr £	Cr £
Capital	59,868	
Motor vehicles	22,500	
Computer equipment	18,000	
Debtors	31,059	
Creditors		30,690
Purchases	245,259	
Sales		358,317
Wages and salaries		38,476
Motor expenses		3,428
Printing and stationery	3,600	
General expenses	8,235	
Cash at bank	5,850	
Stock 1 October 2008	23,004	
Rent and rates	31,500	
Heating and lighting		6,624
Interest received	6,417	
Insurance		10,332
Rent received	5,175	
Drawings		12,600
	460,467	460,467

30.2 From the following list of balances taken from the books of G Brammer you are required to draw up a trial balance as at 31 December 2009.

	£
Capital	100,000
Premises	66,250
Motor vehicle	17,000
Office equipment	2,438
Wages	19,637
Purchases	37,455
Sales	56,170
Commission received	1,050
Electricity	925
Telephone	1,125
Motor expenses	1,500
Printing, stationery and advertising	2,050
Creditors	8,500
Debtors	12,012
General expenses	2,371
Bank overdraft	3,505
Drawings	6,462

30.3X From the list of balances from the accounts of Fraser & Co, you are required to prepare a trial balance as at 31 December 2010.

Fraser & Co
List of Outstanding Balances as at 31 December 2010

	£
Purchases	334,500
Sales	511,050
Sales returns	10,050
Purchases returns	8,400
Stock 1 January 2010	33,000
Discount allowed	6,900
Discount received	8,250
Wages and salaries	55,750
Carriage inwards	2,100
Carriage outwards	3,300
Printing and stationery	4,200
Electricity	7,300
Motor expenses	18,250
Telephone	3,100
General expenses	2,900
Debtors	51,000
Creditors	32,400
Bad debts written off	1,650
Provision for doubtful debts at 31 December 2010	675
Cash in hand	1,200
Bank overdraft	35,100
Capital	57,825
Property	75,000
Plant and equipment	96,000
Provision for depreciation at 31 December 2010	
Property	15,000
Plant and equipment	37,500

30.4 The following is a list of balances extracted from the books of J Steadman, a sole trader, as at 31 January 2010.

J Steadman
List of Balances as at 31 January 2010

	£
Capital	58,260
Equipment	11,250
Furniture and fittings	6,000
Motor vehicles	17,370
Sales	96,030
Purchases	59,220
Cash at bank	750
General expenses	1,800
Wages	17,820
Rent, rates and insurance	7,650
Heating and lighting	2,100
Debtors	24,000
Creditors	10,800
Stock 1 February 2009	17,130

The following additional information is available as at 31 January 2010:

(*a*) Wages unpaid amounted to £351.
(*b*) Insurance paid in advance £600.
(*c*) Closing stock was valued at £14,730.

You are required to take the above adjustments into account and prepare the figures for the final accounts for J Steadman for the year ended 31 January 2010, using the extended trial balance.

Note: Remember to use the blank extended trial balance worksheet in Appendix B.

30.5X The following is a list of balances taken from the ledgers of Rigby & Co as at 31 July 2010, the end of the financial year.

Rigby & Co
List of Balances as at 31 July 2010

	£
Stock at 1 August 2009	29,150
Purchases	243,800
Sales	509,450
Sales returns	3,805
Purchases returns	2,655
Discounts allowed	6,620
Discounts received	5,750
Wages and salaries	76,500
Lighting and heating	9,250
Telephone, stationery and advertising	13,600
Motor expenses	10,500
General expenses	3,005
Rates and insurance	15,000
Motor vehicles:	
At cost	20,000
Accumulated depreciation	5,000
Fixtures and fittings:	
At cost	22,100
Accumulated depreciation	9,945
Creditors	21,900
Debtors	31,700
Drawings	22,325
Cash in hand	995
Cash at bank	10,985
Capital	114,635
Land and buildings	150,000

The following additional information is available as at 31 July 2010:

(a) Motor expenses owing £200.

(b) Insurance paid in advance £3,500.

(c) Closing stock was valued at £30,700.

(d) Depreciate motor vehicles at 25% and fixtures and fittings at 15% per annum using the straight line method.

You are required to take the above adjustments into account and prepare the figures for the final accounts of Rigby & Co for the year ended 31 July 2010, using the extended trial balance.

30.6 Amanda Carver is the proprietor of Automania, a business which supplies car parts to garages to use in servicing and repair work.

At the end of the financial year, on 30 April 2009, the balances were extracted from the general ledger and have been entered onto a trial balance, as shown below:

Automania
Trial Balance as at 30 April 2009

Description	Ledger balances	
	Dr £	Cr £
Capital		135,000
Drawings	42,150	
Rent	17,300	
Purchases	606,600	
Sales		857,300
Sales returns	2,400	
Purchases returns		1,260
Salaries and wages	136,970	
Motor vehicles (M.V.) at cost	60,800	
Provision for depreciation (M.V.)		16,740
Fixtures and fittings (F&F) at cost	40,380	
Provision for depreciation (F&F)		21,600
Bank		3,170
Cash	2,100	
Lighting and heating	4,700	
VAT		9,200
Stock at 1 May 2008	116,100	
Bad debts	1,410	
Provision for doubtful debts		1,050
Debtors control account	56,850	
Creditors control account		50,550
Sundry expenses	6,810	
Insurance	1,300	
Accruals		
Prepayments		
Depreciation		
Provision for doubtful debts – Adjustment		
Closing stock – Profit and loss		
Closing stock – Balance sheet		
	1,095,870	1,095,870

The following adjustments need to be taken into account as at 30 April 2009:

(*a*) Rent payable by the business is as follows:
- For the period to 31 July 2008 – £1,500 per month
- From 1 August 2008 – £1,600 per month

(*b*) The insurance balance includes £100 paid for the period 1 May 2009 to 31 May 2009.

(*c*) Depreciation is to be calculated as follows:
- Motor vehicles – 20% per annum straight line method
- Fixtures and fittings – 10% per annum reducing balance method

(*d*) The provision for doubtful debts is to be adjusted to a figure representing 2% of debtors.

(e) Stock has been valued at cost on 30 April 2009 at £119,360. However, this figure includes old stock, the details of which are as follows:
- Cost price of old stock   – £3,660
- Net realisable value of old stock – £2,060

Also included is a badly damaged car door which was to have been sold for £80 but will now have to be scrapped. The cost price of the door was £60.

(f) A credit note received from a supplier on 5 April 2009 for goods returned was filed away with no entries having been made. The credit note has now been discovered and is for £200 net plus £35 VAT.

Required:

(i) Make appropriate entries in the adjustments columns of the extended trial balance taking account of the above information. Show all workings.

(ii) Complete the extended trial balance showing clearly the profit or loss made by Automania for the year ended 30 April 2009.

Note: Use a photocopy of the blank extended trial balance form in Appendix B for your answer.

Association of Accounting Technicians (Amended)

30.7X Helen Grant is the owner of Road Runner, a business that buys and sells car tyres.

- The financial year end is 30 April 2009.
- You are employed to assist with the book-keeping.
- The business uses a manual system consisting of a general ledger, a sales ledger and a purchase ledger.
- Double entry takes place in the general ledger. Individual accounts of debtors and creditors are kept in memorandum accounts.
- You use a purchases day book and a sales day book. Totals from the day books are transferred into the general ledger.

At the end of the financial year on 30 April 2009, the following balances were taken from the general ledger.

	£
Sales	689,250
Purchases	414,875
Stock at 1 May 2008	69,376
Salaries and wages	115,654
General expenses	82,440
Shop fittings at cost	48,140
Provision for depreciation, shop fittings	17,890
Computer equipment at cost	12,900
Provision for depreciation, computer equipment	7,460
Debtors control account	58,200
Creditors control account	45,320
Bad debts	1,850
Provision for doubtful debts	2,010
Bank (debit balance)	4,658
Cash	550
VAT (credit balance)	13,500
Discount allowed	8,740
Discount received	3,658
Drawings	22,000
Bank deposit account	20,000
Capital	80,295

The following adjustments need to be made for the year ended 30 April 2009.

(*a*) Stock was valued at cost on 30 April 2009 at £58,450.

(*b*) Depreciation needs to be provided as follows:
- Shop fittings – 10% per annum straight line method
- Computer equipment – 25% per annum reducing balance method.

(*c*) General expenses include insurance of £2,400, which was paid for the year ended 31 October 2009.

(*d*) The provision for doubtful debts should be adjusted to 2.5% of the debtors.

(*e*) £2,000 is owed in wages on 30 April 2009.

(*f*) The bank deposit account was opened on 1 November 2008. Interest is paid at a fixed rate of 6% per annum.

Tasks:

1 Using the blank extended trial form in Appendix B enter the balances into the trial balance and total both columns, before taking into account the additional information.

2 Prepare journal entries to record the above adjustments; dates and narratives are not required.

3 Make appropriate entries in the adjustment columns of the extended trial balance taking account of all the journal entries.

4 Complete the extended trial balance showing clearly the profit or loss made by Helen Grant.

Association of Accounting Technicians (Amended)

CHAPTER 31

Stock valuation

Learning objectives

After you have studied this chapter you should be able to:

- understand that there can be more than one way of valuing stock
- calculate the value of stock using three different methods
- understand how the closing stock valuation affects the profit figures
- adjust stock valuations, where necessary, by a reduction to net realisable value
- adjust stock valuations in respect of goods on sale or return
- understand the importance of the final stock valuation figure that appears in the balance sheet and maintaining appropriate stock levels.

31.1 Different valuations of stock

Stock is the name given to goods purchased for re-sale; it can also include work in progress and raw materials, which you will learn about later in Chapter 38, Manufacturing accounts.

Most people would assume that there can only be one figure for the valuation of stock. This is, however, untrue. This chapter will examine how the valuation of stock can be calculated using different figures.

Assume that a business has just completed its first financial year and is about to value stock on hand at cost price. The business has only dealt with one type of goods. A record of the transactions is now shown in Exhibit 31.1.

Exhibit 31.1

Bought				Sold			
2009			£	2009			£
January	10	at £30 each	300	May	8	for £50 each	400
April	10	at £34 each	340	November	24	for £60 each	1,440
October	20	at £40 each	800				
	40		1,440		32		1,840

The balance of stock on hand at 31 December 2009 is 8 units. The total figure of purchases is £1,440 and that of sales is £1,840. The trading account for the first year of trading can now be completed if the closing stock is brought into the calculations.

But what value do we put on each of the 8 units left in stock at the end of the year? If all of the units bought during the year had cost £30 each, then the closing stock would be 8 × £30 = £240. However, we have bought goods at different prices. This means that the valuation depends on which goods are taken for this calculation: the units at £30, or those at £34, or yet others at £40.

Many businesses do not know exactly whether they have sold all the oldest units before they sell new units. For instance, a business selling spanners may not know whether the oldest spanners had been sold before the newest spanners.

The stock valuation will, therefore, be based on an accounting custom, and not on the facts of exactly which units were still in stock at the year end. The three main methods of doing this are now shown.

31.2 First in, first out method

This is usually known as **FIFO**, the first letters of each word. The method says that, as far as the accounts are concerned, the first goods to be received are the first to be issued. Using the figures in Exhibit 31.1, we can now calculate the closing figure of stock as follows:

2009	Received	Issued	Stock	£	£
Jan	10 × £30 each		10 × £30		300
April	10 × £34 each		10 × £30 10 × £34	300 340	640
May		8 × £30 each	2 × £30 10 × £34	60 340	400
Oct	20 × £40 each		2 × £30 10 × £34 20 × £40	60 340 800	1,200
Nov		2 × £30 each 10 × £34 each 12 × £40 each	8 × £40		320

The closing stock at 31 December 2009 is therefore valued at £320 using the FIFO method.

31.3 Last in, first out method

This is usually known as **LIFO**. As each issue of goods is made, the goods are said to be from the last batch received before that date. Where there is not enough left of the last batch, then the balance of goods needed is said to come from the previous batch still unsold.

From the information shown in Exhibit 31.1, the calculation under this basis can now be shown.

2009	Received	Issued	Stock	£	£
Jan	10 × £30 each		10 × £30		300
April	10 × £34 each		10 × £30 10 × £34	300 340	640
May		8 × £34 each	10 × £30 2 × £34	300 68	368
Oct	20 × £40 each		10 × £30 2 × £34 20 × £40	300 68 800	1,168
Nov		20 × £40 each 2 × £34 each 2 × £30 each	8 × £30		240

The closing stock at 31 December 2009 is therefore valued at £240 using the LIFO method.

31.4 Average cost method

Using what is known as the **AVCO** method, with each receipt of goods the average cost for each item of stock is recalculated. Further issues of goods are then at that figure, until another receipt of goods means that another recalculation is needed.

From the information in Exhibit 31.1, the calculation can be shown thus:

2009	Received	Issued	Average cost per unit of stock held	Number of units in stock	Total value of stock
			£		£
January	10 × £30		30	10	300
April	10 × £34		32*	20	640
May		8 × £32	32	12	384
October	20 × £40		37**	32	1,184
November		24 × £37	37	8	296

Notes: *In April, the average cost is calculated as follows:
stock 10 × £30 = £300 + stock received (10 × £34) £340 = total £640.
20 units in stock, so the average is £640 ÷ 20 = £32.

**In October, the average is calculated as follows:
stock 12 × £32 = £384 + stock received (20 × £40) £800 = £1,184.
32 units in stock, so the average is £1,184 ÷ 32 = £37.

The closing stock at 31 December 2009 is therefore valued at £296 using the AVCO method.

31.5 Stock valuation and the calculation of profits

Using the figures from Exhibit 31.1, with stock valuations shown by the three methods of FIFO, LIFO and AVCO, the trading accounts would appear as set out in the table.

Trading Account for the year ended 31 December 2009

	FIFO		LIFO		AVCO	
	£	£	£	£	£	£
Sales		1,840		1,840		1,840
Less Cost of sales						
Purchases	1,440		1,440		1,440	
Less Closing stock	320	1,120	240	1,200	296	1,144
Gross Profit		720		640		696

As can be seen from the table above, different methods of stock valuation will mean that different profits are shown.

31.6 Reduction to net realisable value

The **net realisable value** of stock is calculated as follows:

Net realisable value = Saleable value (what it can be sold for) *less* any expenses needed to complete the item or get it in a condition to be sold.

The concept of prudence is used when stock is valued. Stock should not be over-valued; otherwise, profits shown will be too high. Therefore, if the net realisable value of stock is less than the cost of the stock, prudence dictates that the figure to be taken for the final accounts is that of net realisable value.

Example 1: An item of stock was purchased at cost price £300. Unfortunately, the item was damaged in the warehouse and the cost of repair and repainting amounted to £50 after which it was estimated it could be sold for £200. The item would be valued as follows:

Saleable value £200 less cost of repair and repainting £50 = Net realisable value of £150.

31.7 Goods on sale or return

Goods received on sale or return

Sometimes we may receive goods from a supplier on a **sale or return** basis. This means that we do not have to pay for the goods until we sell them. If we do not sell them we have to return them to our supplier.

This means that the goods do not belong to us. If we have some goods on sale or return at the stocktaking date, they should not be included in our stock valuation.

Goods sent to our customers on sale or return

We may send goods on a sale or return basis to our customers. The stock will belong to us until it is sold. At our stocktaking date, any goods held by our customers on sale or return should be included in our stock valuation.

31.8 Stocktaking and the balance sheet date

Students often think that all the counting and valuing of stock is done on the last day of the accounting period. This might be true in a small business, but it is often impossible in larger businesses. There may be too many items of stock to do it so quickly.

This means that stocktaking may take place over a period of days. To get the figure of the stock valuation as on the last day of the accounting period, we will have to make adjustments. Exhibit 31.2 gives an example of such calculations.

Exhibit 31.2

Lee Ltd has a financial year that ends on 31 December 2009. The stocktaking is not in fact done until 8 January 2010. When the items in stock on that date are priced out, it is found that the stock value amounts to £28,850. The following information is available about transactions between 31 December 2009 and 8 January 2010.

(a) Purchases since 31 December 2009 amounted to £2,370 at cost.
(b) Sales returns since 31 December 2009 were £350 at selling price.
(c) Sales since 31 December 2009 amounted to £3,800 at selling price.
(d) The selling price is always cost price + 25%.

Lee Ltd
Computation of stock as on 31 December 2009

	£	£	£
			£
Stock (at cost) as at 8 January 2010			28,850
Add Items which were in stock on 31 December 2009 (at cost)			
		£	
Sales		3,800	
Less Profit content (20% of selling price)*		760	3,040
			31,890
Less Items which were not in stock on 31 December 2009 (at cost)			
	£	£	
Sales returns	350		
Less Profit content (20% of selling price)*	70	280	
Purchases (at cost)		2,370	2,650
Stock in hand as on 31 December 2009			29,240

Note: Stock is at cost (or net realisable value) and not at selling price. As this calculation has a sales figure in it, which includes profit, we must deduct the profit part to get to the cost price. This is true also for sales returns.

At one time it was very rare for auditors to attend at stocktaking time as observers. The professional accounting bodies now encourage auditors to be present if at all possible.

31.9 Stock levels

One of the most common faults found in the running of a business is that too high a level of stock is maintained. A considerable number of businesses that have problems with a shortage of finance will find that they can help matters by having a sensible look at the amounts of stock they hold. It would be a very rare business indeed which, had it not investigated the matter previously, could not reduce its stock level. The cash saved could be used more profitably and could also improve cash flow.

Chapter summary

- There are three methods of valuing stock namely: first in, first out (FIFO), last in, first out (LIFO) and the average cost method (AVCO).
- Each of the above methods gives a different closing stock valuation that subsequently affects the profit figure. The lower the closing stock figure the lower the profit while the higher the closing stock figure the higher the profit.
- Net realisable value is the sales value of goods less expenses before sale.
- When a business supplies goods to a customer on sale or return they belong to the supplier until such time as the customer decides they wish to purchase them and an order is placed.
- It may be necessary to make adjustments to the final stock figure which appears in the balance sheet depending upon when the physical stock take has taken place.
- It is important that businesses do not maintain a high level of stock since this means funds are tied up and could cause a cash flow problem.

EXERCISES

31.1   (*a*) From the following figures, calculate the closing stock in trade that would be shown using (i) FIFO, (ii) LIFO, (iii) AVCO methods.

2009	Bought	2009	Sold
January	24 at £10 each	June	30 at £16 each
April	16 at £12.50 each	November	34 at £18 each
October	30 at £13 each		

(*b*) Draw up trading accounts for 2009 using each of the three methods for stock valuation.

31.2X   (*a*) From the following figures, calculate the closing stock in trade that would be shown using (i) FIFO, (ii) LIFO, (iii) AVCO methods.

2009	Bought	2009	Sold
January	30 at £12 each	July	24 at £15.50 each
May	30 at £14 each	November	16 at £18 each

(*b*) Draw up trading accounts for 2009 using each of the three methods for stock valuation.

31.3 DC Ltd, whose financial year end was 31 December 2009, does not take a stock check until 8 January 2010, when it is shown to be £50,850 at cost. It is then established that:

(a) a calculation of 1,000 items at £1.60 was shown as £160
(b) during the period from the year end to 8 January 2010, no purchases were made but sales of £500 were made. The profit margin is 20%
(c) some goods costing £560 had a net realisable value of £425
(d) one stock sheet has been added up to be £2,499. The total should have been £4,299.

Calculate the correct figure of stock on 31 December 2009.

31.4X You are valuing stock at your business as it was at 31 December 2009. The actual date on which the stock was counted was 7 January 2010. The stock sheets show a total of £85,980 at cost as on that date. You are to adjust this figure to find out the stock as at 31 December 2009. The rate of gross profit is 25% on selling price.
On further scrutiny you find:

(a) goods received after 1 January and for which invoices bear the date of January amount to £3,987
(b) one of the stock sheets has been added up to give a total of £4,897 instead of £4,798
(c) goods selling at £480 have been sent to a customer on 'sale or return' during December – these had not been sold by the customer but they had been omitted from the stock figures
(d) an item of 360 units priced at £1.60 each has been extended on the stock sheets as £420
(e) goods amounting to £98 have been returned to suppliers during the first week of January.

31.5X (a) If the closing stock of a business had been mistakenly overvalued by £5,000 and the error has gone unnoticed, what would be the effect of the error on:
(i) this year's profit?
(ii) next year's profit?
(b) A company that sells videos and electrical goods values its closing stock at £72,050 (cost price) at 30 June 2009. However, it has found that this figure includes the following:
(i) Five videos that had cost £300 each have now been replaced by an improved model. In order to sell these obsolete models, it is thought that they will have to be sold at £250 each.
(ii) A hi-fi system that cost £500 has been damaged and it is estimated that repairs will cost £100 before it can be sold.

Calculate the value of the closing stock after taking into the account the above adjustments.

31.6 On 30 November 2009, the last day of its financial year, The Pine Warehouse made a cash sale of some pine tables and chairs. These had originally cost £1,000 and were sold for £1,500. Although the sale was immediately recorded in the accounts of the business and the cash had been paid at the time of the sale, the customer asked for delivery to take place on 22 December 2009. The tables and chairs were therefore still in stock at the financial year end. The proprietor of the business, Pat Hall, has suggested that the tables and chairs should be included in the valuation of the closing stock at the selling price of £1,500. Pat Hall comments to you: 'This seems to be in accordance with the prudence concept since profits can be recognised once they are realised.'
You are required to write a memo to Pat Hall stating whether or not you agree with the proposed accounting treatment for the tables and chairs. Clearly explain the reasons for your answer.

AAT

31.7X   (*a*) You are required to value the closing stock, after taking into account the necessary adjustments, in the following separate situations:

(i) Closing stock was valued at cost at £43,795. However, this figure includes two items, cost price £175 each, which have been damaged in storage. It has been estimated that if a total of £35 was spent on repairing them, they could be sold for £140 each.

(ii) The value of the closing stock had been valued at cost on 31 October 2009 at £107,300. However, this includes some discontinued kitchen cabinets the details of which are as follows:

Cost	£2,300
Normal selling price	£3,500
Net realisable value	£1,800

(*b*) Stock has always been valued by Electronics World Ltd on a FIFO basis and this includes the closing stock figure of £198,650 as at 31 May 2009. It has been suggested that the closing stock figure should now be recalculated on a LIFO basis.

(i) Assuming that the prices of electronic goods have been gradually rising throughout the year, would the change suggested increase profit for the year ended 31 May 2009, decrease profit or would profit remain the same?

(ii) Which accounting concept states that the company should not normally change its basis for valuing stock unless it has very good reasons for doing so?

AAT

CHAPTER 32

Errors not affecting trial balance agreement

Learning objectives

After you have studied this chapter you should be able to:

- appreciate that accounting transactions are entered twice; once on the debit side and once on the credit side on an account
- understand that there are two types of error, those that effect the agreement of the trial balance and those that do not
- appreciate that errors are usually identified after a period of time has elapsed
- distinguish between the different kinds of errors
- correct errors using the journal.

32.1 Introduction

In Part 1 of this book the system of double entry book-keeping was introduced whereby each transaction recorded in the books of account required two entries:

1 one entry must be on the debit side of an account, and
2 one entry must be on the credit side on an account.

At the end of an accounting period each account is balanced up and a trial balance drawn up to check the arithmetical accuracy of the book-keeping entries. Provided that every item has been entered correctly, the two sides of the trial balance should equal each other, i.e.

Total debit balances = Total credit balances

However, it is inevitable that errors will occur when data is entered into the books of account. There are two main classifications of errors:

1 those that affect the balancing of the trial balance
2 those that do not affect the balancing of the trial balance.

32.2 Errors affecting trial balance agreement

These errors result in the total of the debit columns in the trial balance *not* being the same as the total of the credit column. Suppose we correctly entered cash received of £103 from H Lee, our debtor, in the cash book as shown below:

Dr   **Cash Book (debit side only)**   Cr

	Cash	Bank	
	£	£	
2009	103		
May 1 H Lee			

However, when posting this item to H Lee's account we entered the amount received on the credit side as £13, see below:

Sales Ledger

Dr   H Lee Account   Cr

	2009	£
	May 1 Cash	13

When the trial balance is drawn up the totals will be different by (£103 − £13) = £90. This effect will arise in every case where a debit entry does not equal a credit entry for a transaction. Correction of these types of errors is covered in Chapter 33. In this present chapter errors that do not affect the trial balance agreement will be discussed.

32.3 Errors not affecting trial balance agreement

Although the trial balance totals agree, complete accuracy cannot be guaranteed. Certain errors can still be made which do not affect the balancing of the trial balance, i.e. the trial balance would still appear to balance even though certain errors have occurred. The errors that lead to this situation are listed below:

- **Errors of commission** - where a correct amount is entered, but in the wrong person's account, for example, a sale of goods to J. Black is entered in error, in J. Blake's account.
- **Errors of principle** - where an item is entered in the wrong type of account, for example, a fixed asset is entered in an expense account.
- **Error of original entry** - where an item is entered using an incorrect amount, for example, an invoice received showing goods purchased to the value of £925 is entered in both the purchases account and the supplier's account as £92.50.
- **Error of omission** - where a transaction is completely omitted from the books for example if a purchase invoice is accidentally thrown away and therefore never entered in the books of account.
- **Compensating errors** - where two errors of equal amounts but on opposite sides of the accounts cancel out each other.

● **Complete reversal of entries** – where the correct amounts are entered in the correct accounts but each item is shown on the wrong side of each account.

In Sections 32.5 to 32.10, to follow, each of the above errors are illustrated together with the journal entries required to correct the error.

32.4 Correction of errors

Most errors are discovered after a period of time has elapsed. Once identified they need to be corrected properly via the journal and not by crossing out items or tearing a page out of a ledger or even using correcting fluid. If the latter was permitted then there is more risk of fraudulent transactions taking place.

Corrections are recorded in the journal which, as already mentioned in Chapter 24, is a book of original entry. By entering them in the journal a permanent record is made for future reference.

Since many students have difficulty with journal entries you may remember from Chapter 24 that it is often useful to think 'double entry' before entering the details in the journal. In other words, think where the transaction has been entered in the double entry accounts and then where the entry should have been made; this then gives you the basis for preparing the journal entry. Work through the following sections with this in mind.

32.5 Errors of commission

An **error of commission** arises when a correct amount is entered in the books, but in the wrong person's account.

Example 1: D Long paid us £50 by cheque on 18 May 2009. The transaction is correctly entered in the cash book, but it was entered by mistake in the account for D Longman. This means that there had been both a debit of £50 and a credit of £50. It has appeared in the personal account as:

Dr	**D Longman Account**		Cr
	2009		£
	May 18 Bank		50

The error was found on 31 May 2009. This will now have to be corrected and requires two entries:

Accounting entries	Explanation
Debit D Longman's account	To cancel out the error on the credit side of that account
Credit D Long's account	To enter the amount in the correct account

The accounts will now appear thus:

Dr			D Longman Account			Cr
2009		£	2009			£
May 31 D Long:						
Error corrected		50	May 18 Bank			50

Dr			D Long Account			Cr
2009		£	2009			£
			May 31 Cash entered in error in			
May 1 Balance b/d		50	D Longman's account			50

The journal

The ways by which errors have been corrected should all be entered in the journal. The correction has already been shown above in double entry. In fact, the journal entries should be made before completing the double entry accounts for the transaction. For teaching purposes only in this chapter, the journal entries are shown last.

The journal entry will be thus:

The Journal		
	Dr	Cr
2009	£	£
May 31 D Longman	50	
D Long		50
Cheque received . . . entered in wrong		
personal account, now corrected.		

32.6 Errors of principle

An **error of principle** is where a transaction is entered in the wrong type of account. For instance, the purchase of a fixed asset should be debited to a fixed asset account. If in error it is debited to an expense account, then it has been entered in the wrong type of account.

Example 2: The purchase of a motor car for £5,500 by cheque on 14 May 2009 has been debited in error to a motor expenses account. In the cash book it is shown correctly. This means that there has been both a debit of £5,500 and a credit of £5,500.

It will have appeared in the expense account as:

Dr		Motor Expenses Account		Cr
2009	£			
May 14 Bank	5,500			

The error is detected on 31 May 2009 and is corrected. To do so, two entries are needed:

Accounting entry	Explanation
Debit Motor Car account **Credit** Motor Expenses account	To put the amount in the correct account To cancel the error previously made in the Motor Expenses account

The accounts then are corrected thus:

Dr	Motor Expenses Account		Cr
2009 May 14 Bank	£ 5,500	2009 May 31 Motor car error corrected	£ 5,500

Dr	Motor Car Account		Cr
2009 May 31 Bank: entered originally in Motor expenses	£ 5,500		

The journal

The journal entries to correct the error will be shown as:

The Journal			
		Dr	Cr
2009		£	£
May 31 Motor car		5,500	
Motor expenses			5,500
Correction of error whereby purchase			
of motor car was debited to motor			
expenses account.			

32.7 Errors of original entry

An **error of original entry** occurs where an original amount is incorrect and is then entered in double entry.

Example 3: Sales of £150 to T Higgins on 13 May 2009 have been entered as both a debit and a credit of £130. The accounts would appear thus:

Dr	T Higgins Account		Cr
2009 May 13 Sales	£ 130		

Dr	Sales Account		Cr
		2009 May 31 Sales day book (part of total)	£ 130

The error is found on 31 May 2009. The entries to correct it are now shown:

Dr		T Higgins Account		Cr
2009	£			
May 13 Sales	130			
May 31 Sales: error	20			

Dr	Sales Account		Cr
	2009	£	
	May 31 Sales day book	130	
	May 31 T Higgins:		
	error corrected	20	

The journal

To correct the error, the journal entries will be:

The Journal			
		Dr	Cr
2009		£	£
May 31 T Higgins		20	
Sales			20
Correction of error. Sales of £150			
had been incorrectly entered as £130.			

32.8 Errors of omission

Errors of omission are where transactions are not entered into the books at all.

Example 4: The purchase of goods from T Hope for £250 on 13 May 2009 had been completely omitted from the books. The error was found on 31 May 2009. The entries to correct it will be as follows:

Dr		Purchases Account		Cr
2009	£			
May 13 T Hope:				
error corrected	250			

Dr	T Hope Account		Cr
	2009	£	
	May 31 Purchases:		
	error corrected	250	

The journal

The journal entries to correct the error will be:

The Journal	Dr	Cr
	£	£
2009	250	
May 31 Purchases		
T Hope		250
Correction of error. Purchase omitted		
from books.		

32.9 Compensating errors

These errors are where they cancel each other out.

Example 5: Let us take a case where incorrect totals had purchases of £7,900 and sales of £9,900. The purchases day book adds up to be £100 too much. In the same period, the sales day book also adds up to be £100 too much.

If these were the only errors in our books, the trial balance totals would equal each other. Both totals would be wrong – they would both be £100 too much – but they would be equal. In this case, the accounts would have appeared as follows:

Dr	Purchases Account		Cr
2009	£		
May 13 Purchases	7,900		

Dr	Sales Account		Cr
		2009	£
		May 31 Sales	9,900

When corrected, the accounts will appear as:

Dr	Purchases Account		Cr
2009	£	2009	£
May 13 Purchases	7,900	May 31 The Journal:	
		error corrected	100

Dr	Sales Account		Cr
2009	£	2009	£
May 31 The Journal:		May 31 Sales	9,900
error corrected	100		

The journal

Journal entries to correct these two errors will be thus:

The Journal		Dr	Cr
		£	£
2009		100	
May 31 Sales			
Purchases			100
Correction of compensating errors.			
Totals of both purchases and sales day books			
incorrectly added up to £100 too much.			

32.10 Complete reversal of entries

This error is where the correct amounts are entered in the correct accounts, but each item is shown on the wrong side of each account.

Example 6: We pay a cheque for £200 on 28 May 2009 to D Charles. We enter it as follows in accounts with the letter (A). There has, therefore, been both a debit and a credit of £200.

Dr	Cash Book (A)				Cash	Bank	Cr
		Cash	Bank		Cash	Bank	
		£	£		£	£	
2009							
May 28 D Charles			200				

Dr	D Charles (A)		Cr
		2009	£
		May 28 Bank	200

This is incorrect. It should have been debit D Charles Account £200, credit Bank £200. Both items have been entered in the correct accounts, but each is on the wrong side of its account.

The way to correct this is more difficult to understand than with other errors. Let us look at how the items would have appeared if we had done it correctly in the first place. We will show the letter (B) behind the account names.

Dr	Cash Book (B)				Cash	Bank	Cr
		Cash	Bank		Cash	Bank	
		£	£	2009	£	£	
				May 28 D Charles		200	

Dr	D Charles (B)		Cr
2009		£	
May 28 Bank		200	

We found the error on May 31 and it was corrected as follows:

1 First we have to cancel the error. This would mean entering these amounts:

Dr:	D Charles	£200	
Cr:	Bank		£200

2 Then we have to enter up the transaction:

Dr:	D Charles	£200	
Cr:	Bank		£200

Altogether then, the entries to correct the error are twice the amounts first entered. When corrected, the accounts appear as follows, marked (C).

Dr			**Cash Book (C)**			*Cr*
	Cash £	Bank £		Cash £	Bank £	
2009			2009			
May 8 D Charles		200	May 31 D Charles: error corrected		400	

Dr		**D Charles Account (C)**		*Cr*
2009	£	2009	£	
May 28 Bank: error corrected	400	May 28 Bank	200	

You can see that accounts (C) give the same final answer as accounts (B).

			£	£
(B)	*Dr*:	D Charles	200	
	Cr:	Bank		200
(C)	*Dr*:	D Charles (£400 – £200)	200	
	Cr:	Bank (£400 – £200)		200

The journal

Journal entries. These would be shown as follows:

The Journal		
	Dr	Cr
2009	£	£
May 31 D Charles	400	
Bank		400
Payment of £200 on 28 May 2009 to		
D Charles incorrectly credited to his account,		
and debited to bank. Error now corrected.		

32.11 Casting

You will often notice the use of the expression **casting**, which means adding up. **Overcasting** means incorrectly adding up a column of figures to give an answer that is *greater* than it should be. **Undercasting** means incorrectly adding up a column of figures to give an answer that is *less* than it should be.

Chapter summary

- Periodically businesses balance their accounts and prepare a trial balance to check the arithmetical accuracy of the book-keeping entries. However, agreement in the trial balance does not necessarily mean that no errors have occurred.
- There are two types of errors: those that affect the balancing of the trial balance and those that do not.
- Errors that can occur and yet the trial balance still agree are errors of commission, principle, original entry, omission, compensating and complete reversal of entries.
- Once identified the errors are corrected by using the journal. However, it is sometimes easier for students to carry out the double entry first followed by the journal entry. In normal circumstances you would prepare the journal entry first followed by postings to the appropriate ledger accounts.
- The term 'casting' refers to figures that are added up. Overcasting means adding figures up to an amount greater than they should be, whereas, undercasting means adding a column of figures up to less than it should be.

EXERCISES

32.1 Show the journal entries necessary to correct the following errors:

(a) A sale of goods £678 to J Harkness had been entered in J Harker's account.
(b) The purchase of a machine on credit from L Pearson for £4,390 had been completely omitted from our books.
(c) The purchase of a motor vehicle for £10,800 had been entered in error in the motor expenses account.
(d) A sale of £221 to E Fletcher had been entered in the books – both debit and credit – as £212.
(e) Commission received £257 had been entered in error in the sales account.

32.2X Show the journal entries needed to correct the following errors:

(a) Purchases £699 on credit from K Webb had been entered in H Weld's account.
(b) A cheque of £189 paid for advertisements had been entered in the cash column of the cash book instead of in the bank column.
(c) Sale of goods £443 on credit to B Maxim had been entered in error in B Gunn's account.
(d) Purchase of goods on credit from K Innes £89 entered in two places in error as £99.
(e) Cash paid to H Mersey £89 has been entered on the debit side of the cash book and the credit side of H Mersey's account.

32.3 The following errors have been made in the accounting records of Berry Sports:

(*a*) £110 has been debited to the rent account instead of the rates account.

(*b*) Purchases returns valued at £300 have been debited to the purchases returns account and credited to the creditors control account.

(*c*) £2,000 has been debited to the insurance accounts and credited to the bank account instead of the correct amount of £200.

Record the journal entries in the main (general) ledger to correct the above.
Narratives are not required.

Association of Accounting Technicians

32.4 The following errors have been made in the main (general) ledger of Senator Safes:

(*a*) £300 has been debited to the miscellaneous expenses account instead of the rates account.

(*b*) Purchases returns have been entered in the accounting records as £706 instead of £607 (ignore VAT).

(*c*) A credit customer, Leeson and Company, has ceased trading. The amount outstanding on its account of £800 plus VAT has been written off as a bad debt in the subsidiary (sales) ledger only, but the net amount and VAT should also have been written off.

Record the journal entries necessary in the main (general) ledger to correct the errors shown above. Narratives are not required.

Association of Accounting Technicians

32.5X The following errors have been made in the main (general) ledger of McGee Autos:

(*a*) £25 has been credited to the discounts received account instead of to the interest received account.

(*b*) The total of the sales day book has been posted incorrectly as £51,010 instead of the correct amount of £50,101 (ignore VAT).

(*c*) A payment of £100 to settle a hotel bill has been incorrectly credited to the hotel expenses account and debited to the bank account.

Record the journal entries needed in the main (general) ledger to correct the errors shown above. Dates and narratives are not required.

Association of Accounting Technicians

32.6X John Granger is the owner of a business of a retail business trading in car accessories. John has been told that he ought to prepare a trial balance at regular intervals. However, he has doubts about the value of trial balances.

(*a*) Explain *two* benefits that can arise from the preparation of a trial balance.

(*b*) Point out the limitations of this accounting technique.

(*c*) Provide an example of a situation which illustrates the limitations of a trial balance.

Assessment and Qualifications Alliance (AQA)

32.7X D Singh, a retail trader, has a lot still to learn about accounting but has managed to draw up the following trial balance from his business records.

	£	£
Stock 1 April 2009		21,400
Stock 31 March 2010	15,600	
Discounts allowed		620
Discounts received	900	
Purchases	188,000	
Purchase returns	2,800	
Sales		264,200
Sales returns	2,200	
Buildings at cost	140,000	
Provision for depreciation of buildings	7,000	
Motor vehicles at cost	30,000	
Provision for depreciation of motor vehicles	9,000	
Capital: D Singh		169,200
Bank	14,200	
Debtors		22,600
Provision for doubtful debts	1,920	
Creditors	15,200	
General expenses	33,200	
Drawings	18,000	
	478,020	478,020

Required:

(*a*) Prepare a corrected trial balance as at 31 March 2010.

(*b*) After the preparation of the corrected trial balance, but before drawing up the final accounts, the following items were discovered:

(i)   A credit note for £148 had been received from FH Ltd. This was in respect of goods returned by Singh in December 2009. No entry was made in the books.

(ii) No entry has been made in the books in respect of £333 goods taken for own use.

(iii) A payment by a debtor, T Hall, of £168 has been credited in error to T Hallworth's account.

(iv) Free samples sent to a customer, L Shah, have been charged to him as though they were sales for £88.

(v)   A discount allowed to K Young of £64 was found to be incorrect. It should have been £94.

Show the journal entries needed for items (i) to (v) above.

CHAPTER 33

Suspense accounts and errors

Learning objectives

After you have studied this chapter you should be able to:

● understand the reason for using a suspense account
● create a suspense account in order to balance the trial balance
● correct errors using a suspense account
● recalculate profits after errors have been corrected
● appreciate the limitations of trial balances.

33.1 Introduction

In the previous chapter errors that did not affect the balancing of the trial balance were discussed. However, many errors may occur that do affect the balancing of the trial balance, for example:

● incorrect additions in any account
● making an entry on only one side of the accounts – for example, a debit but no credit, or a credit but no debit
● entering a different amount on the debit side from the amount on the credit side.

33.2 Suspense accounts

If a trial balance does not balance it is important that errors are located and corrected as soon as possible. When they cannot be found, then the trial balance totals should be made to agree with each other by inserting the amount of the difference between the two sides in a **suspense account**. This occurs in Exhibit 33.1 where there is a difference of £40.

Exhibit 33.1

Trial Balance as at 31 December 2009

	Dr	Cr
	£	£
Totals after all the accounts have been listed	100,000	99,960
Suspense account		40
	100,000	100,000

To make the two totals the same, a figure of £40 for the suspense account has been shown on the credit side. A suspense account is opened and the £40 difference is also shown there on the credit side.

Dr	Suspense Account		Cr
	2009		£
	Dec 31 Difference		
	per trial balance		40

33.3 Suspense account and the balance sheet

If the errors are not found before the financial statements are prepared, the suspense account balance will be included in the balance sheet. Where the balance is a credit balance, it should be included under current liabilities on the balance sheet. When the balance is a debit balance, it should be shown under current assets on the balance sheet. Large errors should always be found before the financial statements are drawn up.

33.4 Correction of errors

When errors are found, they must be corrected using double entry. Each correction must be described by an entry in the journal.

One error only

We will look at two examples:

Example 1: Assume that the error of £40 as shown in Exhibit 33.1 is found in the following year on 31 March 2010, the error being that the sales account was undercast by £40. The action taken to correct this is:

● Debit the suspense account to close it: £40.
● Credit the sales account to show item where it should have been: £40.

The accounts now appear as Exhibit 33.2.

Exhibit 33.2

Dr		Suspense Account		Cr
2010	£	2009		£
		Dec 31 Difference per		
Mar 31 Sales	40	trial balance		40

Dr		Sales Account		Cr
		2010		£
		Mar 31 Suspense		40

This can be shown in journal form as follows:

The Journal		
	Dr	Cr
2010	£	£
Mar 31 Suspense	40	
Sales		40
Correction of undercasting of sales by £40		
in last year's accounts.		

Example 2: The trial balance on 31 December 2009 shows a difference of £168. It was a shortage on the debit side. A suspense account is opened and the difference of £168 is entered on the debit side.

On 31 May 2010 the error is found. We had made a payment of £168 to D Miguel to close his account. It was correctly entered in the cash book, but it was not entered in Miguel's account.

To correct the error, the account of D Miguel is debited with £168, as it should have been in 2010, and the suspense account is credited with £168 so that the account can be closed. The accounts and journal entry now appear as in Exhibit 33.3.

Exhibit 33.3

Dr		D Miguel Account		Cr
2010	£	2010		£
May 31 Bank	168	Jan 1 Balance b/d		168

Dr		Suspense Account		Cr
2009	£	2010		£
Dec 31 Difference				
per trial balance	168	May 31 D Miguel		168

The Journal		Dr	Cr
		£	£
2010			
May 31 D Miguel		168	
Suspense			168
Correction of non-entry of payment last year			
in D Miguel's account.			

More than one error

We can now look at an example where the suspense account difference has been caused by more than one error.

Example 3: A trial balance at 31 December 2009 shows a difference of £77, being a shortage on the debit side. A suspense account is opened, and the difference of £77 is entered on the debit side of the account.

On 28 February 2010 all the errors from the previous year were found:

(*a*) A cheque of £150 paid to L Kent had been correctly entered in the cash book, but had not been entered in Kent's account.
(*b*) The purchases account has been undercast by £20.
(*c*) A cheque of £93 received from K Sand has been correctly entered in the cash book but has not been entered in Sand's account.

These three errors have resulted in a net error of £77, shown by a debit of £77 on the debit side of the suspense account.

These are corrected by:

● making correcting entries in the accounts for (*a*), (*b*) and (*c*)
● recording the double entry for these items in the suspense account.

Dr	L Kent Account		Cr
2010	£		
Feb 28 Suspense (*a*)	150		

Dr	Purchases Account		Cr
2010	£		
Feb 28 Suspense (*b*)	20		

Dr	K Sand Account		Cr
		2010	£
		Feb 28 Suspense (*c*)	93

Dr	Suspense Account		Cr
2010	£	2010	£
Jan 1 Balance b/d	77	Feb 28 L Kent (*a*)	150
Feb 28 K Sand (*c*)	93	Feb 28 Purchases (*b*)	20
	170		170

The Journal	Dr	Cr
2010	£	£
Feb 28 L Kent	150	
Suspense		150
Cheque paid omitted from Kent's account		
Feb 28 Purchases	20	
Suspense		20
Undercasting of purchases by £20 in		
last year's accounts		
Feb 28 Suspense	93	
K Sand		93
Cheque received omitted from Sand's		
account		

Only those errors that make the trial balance totals different from each other have to be corrected via the suspense account.

33.5   The effect of errors on profits

Some of the errors will have meant that the calculation of original profits will be wrong. Other errors will have no effect upon profits. We will use Exhibit 33.4 to illustrate the different kinds of errors. Exhibit 33.4 shows a set of accounts in which errors have been made.

Exhibit 33.4

S Brough
Trading and Profit and Loss Account for the year ended 31 December 2009

		£	£
Sales	(A)		165,000
Less Cost of goods sold			
Opening stock		10,000	
Purchases	(B)	122,000	
		132,000	
Less Closing stock		14,000	
			118,000
Gross profit			47,000
Less Expenses			
Rent	(C)	7,000	
Insurance	(D)	1,400	
Lighting		1,600	
Depreciation		5,000	
			15,000
Net profit			32,000

S Brough
Balance Sheet as at 31 December 2009

		£	£	£
		Cost	Depreciation	
Fixed assets				
Equipment		44,000	16,000	28,000
Current assets				
Stock		14,000		
Debtors	(E)	13,000		
Cash at bank		6,800		
Suspense	(G)	200	34,000	
Current liabilities				
Creditors	(F)	12,000	12,000	
Net current assets				22,000
Net assets				50,000
Financed by				
Capital Account				
Balance as at 1 January 2009				36,000
Add Net profit for the year				32,000
				68,000
Less Drawings				(18,000)
				50,000

Errors that *do not* affect profit calculations

If an error affects items only in the balance sheet, then the original calculated profit will not need altering. The example below shows this:

Example *4*: Assume that in Exhibit 33.4 the £200 debit balance on the suspense account shown in the balance sheet was because, on 1 November 2009, we paid £200 to a creditor T Monk and it was correctly entered in the cash book, but it was not entered anywhere else. The error was found on 1 June 2010.

We can see that when this error is corrected, only two items in the final accounts will have to be altered. These are (F) Creditors, which will have to be reduced by £200, and (G) Suspense account, which will now be cancelled and not shown in the balance sheet. Once the errors have been corrected by the journal entries, see below, the balance sheet will be correct. This means that neither the trading account nor the profit and loss account have been affected; the profit as shown for 2009 is correct.

The double entry records needed are as follows:

T Monk Account

2010	£	2010	£
June 1 Suspense (Correction)	200	Jan 1 Balance b/d	200

Suspense Account

2010	£	2010	£
Jan 1 Balance b/d (Difference		2010	
in last year's trial balance)	200	June 1 T Monk	200

The journal entries to correct it will be thus:

The Journal	Dr	Cr
	£	£
2010		
June 1 T Monk	200	
Suspense		200
Payment to T Monk on 1 November 2009		
not entered in his account.		
Correction now made.		

Errors that *do* affect profit calculations

If the error is in one of the numbers labelled (A), (B), (C) or (D) shown in the trading and profit and loss account, then the original profit will need altering. Example 5 shows this:

Example 5: Assume that in Exhibit 33.4 the £200 debit balance was because the rent account (C) was added up incorrectly: it should be shown as £7,200 instead of £7,000. The error was found on 1 June 2010. The journal entries to correct it are:

The Journal	Dr	Cr
	£	£
2010		
June 1 Rent	200	
Suspense		200
Correction of rent undercast last year.		

Rent last year should have been increased by £200. This would have reduced net profit by £200. A statement of corrected profit for the year is now shown.

S Brough
Statement of Corrected Net Profit for the year ended 31 December 2009

	£
Net profit per the accounts	32,000
Less Rent understated	200
Corrected net profit for the year	31,800

Where there have been several errors

Example 6: If in Exhibit 33.4 there had been four errors found in the ledger accounts of S Brough on 31 March 2010, their correction can now be seen. Assume that the net difference had also been £200, with the four errors as:

	£
(A) Sales overcast by	210
(B)* A credit purchase from C Hall of £59 was entered in the books, debit and credit entries, as	95
(D) Insurance undercast by	40
(E) Cash received from a debtor, L Young entered in the cash book only	50

Note: Error (B) is known as an **error of transposition**, the figures have been transposed.

Error (A) affected the profits: both gross and net profit were shown £210 too much because of this error. It also affected the Suspense account (G).

Error (B) showed purchases too high by (£95 − £59) = £36. This means that gross and net profits were shown £36 too little. The other item affected is (F) Creditors, which is shown as being £36 too much. This error does not affect (G) Suspense account.

Error (D) needs insurance increasing by £40. This will reduce the net profit by £40. It also affects the Suspense account (G).

Error (E) does not affect the profits at all. It affects only items in the balance sheet, namely (E) Debtors and (G) Suspense.

The entries in the ledger accounts are as follows:

General Ledger **Sales Account**

2010			£	
Mar 31 Suspense (Correction)	(A)		210	

General Ledger **Purchases Account**

			2010			£
			Mar 31 C Hall (Correction)	(B)		36

Purchases Ledger **C Hall Account**

2010			£	
Mar 31 Purchases (Correction)	(B)		36	

General Ledger **Insurance Account**

2010			£	
Mar 31 Suspense (Correction)	(D)		40	

Sales Ledger **L Young Account**

			2010			£
			Mar 31 Suspense (Correction) (E)			50

The entries in the suspense account and the journal entries will be as follows:

General Ledger **Suspense Account**

2010		£	2010		£
Jan 1 Balance b/d		200	Mar 31 Sales	(A)	210
Mar 31 L Young	(E)	50	" 31 Insurance	(D)	40
		250			250

The Journal		Dr	Cr
2010		£	£
(A) Mar 31 Sales		210	
Suspense			210
Sales overcast of £70 in 2009.			
(B) Mar 31 C Hall		36	
Purchases*			36
Credit purchase of £59 entered both as			
debit and credit as £95 in 2009.			
(D) Mar 31 Insurance		40	
Suspense			40
Insurance expense undercast by £40 in 2009.			
(E) Mar 31 Suspense		50	
L Young			50
Cash received omitted from L Young's account in 2009.			

Note: *In (B), the correction of the understatement of purchases does not pass through the Suspense account.

Now we can calculate the corrected net profit for the year 2009. Only items (A), (B) and (D) affect figures in the trading and profit and loss account. These are the only adjustments to be made to profit.

S Brough
Statement of corrected Net Profit for the year ended 31 December 2009

		£	£
Net profit per the accounts			32,000
Add Purchases overstated	(B)		36
			32,036
Less Sales overcast	(A)	210	
Insurance undercast	(D)	40	250
Corrected net profit for the year			31,786

33.6 Limitations of trial balances

In this and the previous chapter, you have seen various kinds of errors. Those in Chapter 32 were not revealed by trial balance totals being unequal. This shows a serious limitation in depending completely on the trial balance as an absolute check on the accuracy of the entries in the books of account. To refresh your memory, the kinds of *errors not disclosed by a trial balance* are:

● errors of commission
● errors of principle
● errors of original entry

- errors of omission
- compensating errors
- complete reversal of entries.

Even when the balances in a trial balance agree, there can be very large errors of various kinds, which may mean that profits have been wrongly calculated and that the balance sheet is incorrect. This current chapter has demonstrated these kinds of errors, where they have resulted in a difference being put into a suspense account until the error(s) have been found.

A very small amount in a suspense account could hide very large errors. For instance, a £50 credit in a suspense account could eventually be found to be either of the following:

- Sales overcast £10,000, debtors total overcast £10,050. If the errors are not found, then both the gross and net profits will be overstated by £10,000 and the figure of debtors in the balance sheet overstated by £10,050.
- Rent expense undercast by £2,000, total of creditors undercast by £1,950. In this case the net profit will be shown at £2,000 more than it should be, while creditors in the balance sheet will be understated by £1,950.

This shows that there is always a possibility of serious errors occurring without it being obvious at first sight.

Every attempt should be made to find errors. Opening a suspense account should be done only if all other efforts have failed.

33.7 Suspense accounts: examinations and business

Examinations

Unless it is part of a question, *do not* make your balance sheet totals agree by using a suspense account. The same applies to trial balances. Examiners are very likely to penalise you for including a suspense account when it should not be required.

Business

When preparing financial statements for a business every effort should be made to ensure that trial balance and balance sheet balance. However, if all else fails it may be necessary to open a suspense account and hopefully the error(s) may subsequently be located and posted to the suspense account, as shown in this chapter, and the balance eliminated.

Chapter summary

- If the totals in the trial balance do not agree it may be necessary to open a suspense account and enter the difference into the account until the error(s) can be located.
- In the unlikely event that the error(s) are not found when the balance sheet is prepared it may be necessary to include the suspense account. If the suspense

account shows a credit balance then it should be entered under the current liabilities whereas a debit balance would be shown under current assets.

● Any errors found should be corrected using a journal and subsequently posted to the appropriate double entry accounts. If the error affects the suspense account then the posting should be made to that account.

● Some errors may affect the gross profit and net profit calculations and adjustments have to be made to these profit figures.

● Other errors that do not affect the profit calculations may affect a figure in the balance sheet. If this is the case then the figure in the balance sheet will require amending.

● While the balancing of the trial balance is seen to ensure that the book-keeping entries have been carried out correctly the trial balance does have limitations in that certain errors occur which are not revealed by the trial balance agreement.

EXERCISES

33.1 On 31 March 2009 the following items are to be corrected via the journal. Show the corrections. Narratives are not required.

(*a*) T Thomas, a customer, had paid us a cheque for £900 to settle his debt. The cheque has now been returned to us marked 'Dishonoured'.

(*b*) We had allowed C Charles, a debtor, a cash discount of £35. Because of a dispute with her, we have now disallowed the cash discount.

(*c*) Office equipment bought for £6,000 has been debited to motor vehicles account.

(*d*) The copy sales invoice of sales to J Graham £715 was lost, and therefore was completely omitted from our books.

(*e*) Cash drawings of £210 have been correctly entered in the cash book, but have been credited to the wages account.

33.2 Jaspa West wishes to record the following in his books of account:

1 A cash receipt of £55 for rent has been recorded as a debit entry in the rent received account. The cash book entry had been correctly made. This matter should be corrected.

2 A debt of £150 owing by Mary Beagle will not be received and is to be written off as a bad debt.

3 The sales account has been overcast by £350. Therefore, this needs to be corrected.

4 A motor vehicle, costing £3,500, has been purchased on credit from C Williams.

5 A provision for bad debts of £225 is to be created.

Required:

(*a*) Write up the journal entries to record the above transactions.

(*b*) Give two examples of book-keeping errors which would not be revealed by the trial balance.

City & Guilds Pitman qualifications

33.3X John Laundau has just extracted a trial balance at 30 August, the end of his financial year. The debit side was greater than the credit side by £520 and a suspense account was opened for that amount. The auditors subsequently found the following errors:

1 £200 cash received from the sale of an old computer has been credited to the rent received account.

2 A payment of £100 for water entered in the cash book had not been entered in the water account.

3 The sales account had been undercast by £260.

4 A private purchase of a £1,000 computer had been included in the computer account.

5 Sale of goods to Lynne Beagle had been correctly entered in the sales account as £2,150 but had been entered in the personal account as £2,510.

6 No provision against doubtful debts had been created. This should have been 3% of the end of year total debtors of £7,000.

Required:

(*a*) Make appropriate journal entries, with narrative, to rectify the errors.

(*b*) Show how the suspense account would be cleared by the appropriate entries.

City & Guilds Pitman qualifications

33.4 H Logan extracted a trial balance as at 31 December 2009. He was unable to balance it, but as he urgently needed his accounts for tax purposes, he opened a suspense account and entered £705 debit balance in it.

The following year he found the errors now listed:

(*a*) The sales returns day book had been undercast by £100.

(*b*) Drawings of £80 had been debited to wages account.

(*c*) Carriage inwards £75 had been debited to carriage outwards.

(*d*) A payment of bank charges £270 had not been posted to the expense account.

(*e*) A sale of goods £385 to K Abbott on 30 December 2009 had not been entered at all.

(*f*) Discounts allowed of £218 had been credited to the discounts allowed account.

(*g*) A rent rebate of £200 had been entered in the cash book but not posted elsewhere.

(*h*) The purchases day book had carried forward a figure of £24,798 when it should have been £24,897.

Required:

1 Show the journal entries needed to correct the errors. Narratives are not required.

2 Show the suspense account balanced off.

3 If the original incorrect gross profit was shown as £129,487 and the original net profit was shown as £77,220 calculate the corrected figures for gross and net profits after the above items have been corrected.

33.5 The following trial balance was extracted by K Woodburn from her books as at 30 June 2009. She is unable to get the totals to agree.

Trial Balance as at 30 June 2009

	Dr £	Cr £
Sales		87,050
Purchases	62,400	
Discounts allowed and received	305	410
Salaries and wages	3,168	
General expenses	595	
Fixtures	10,000	
Stock 1 July 2008	12,490	
Debtors and creditors	8,120	5,045
Bank	6,790	
Drawings	4,520	
Capital		17,017
Suspense	1,134	
	109,522	109,522

The following errors are found:

(i) Sales day book overcast by £350.

(ii) Discounts allowed undercast by £100.

(iii) Fixtures, bought for £850, have been entered in the cash book but not in the fixtures account.

(iv) Credit purchases of £166 was entered in the purchases day book only, but not in the creditor's account.

(v) Cheque payment to a creditor of £490 had been debited to the drawings account in error.

You are required to:

(*a*) draw up the suspense account to record the corrections

(*b*) redraft the trial balance after all corrections have been made.

33.6X   T Sawyer extracted the following trial balance from his books. He could not get the totals to agree with each other.

Trial Balance as at 31 December 2009

	Dr £	Cr £
Capital		25,621
Drawings	13,690	
Sales		94,630
Purchases	60,375	
Sales and purchases returns	1,210	1,109
Wages and salaries	14,371	
Sundry expenses	598	
Stock 1.1.2009	8,792	
Debtors and creditors	11,370	4,290
Loan from J Chandler		5,000
Equipment	16,000	
Bank	5,790	
Suspense		1,546
	132,196	132,196

The following errors are discovered:

(i) Purchases day book was overcast by £258.

(ii) A repayment of loan £2,000 was debited in error to the wages account.

(iii) A cheque payment for equipment £1,500 has been entered in the equipment account but not in the cash book.

(iv) Purchases returns £168 have been entered in the purchases returns day book but not in the creditor's account.

(v) Sundry expenses £44 have been entered in the cash book but not in the sundry expenses account.

You are required to:

(*a*) draw up the suspense account, showing corrections

(*b*) redraft the trial balance after all corrections have been made.

33.7   The trial balance of Philip Hogan as at 31 December 2009 does not balance. The difference of £5,400 has been credited to a suspense account. The following errors were subsequently discovered:

(*a*) The sales day book is undercast by £3,000.

(*b*) Purchases received from Dawson & Co, amounting to £1,147, had been received on 31 December 2009, and included in the closing stock at that date. Unfortunately, the invoice had not been entered in the purchases day book.

(*c*) Motor repairs of £585 have been charged to the motor vehicles account.

(*d*) Credit sales of £675 made to J Greenway have been debited to the account of J Green.

(*e*) A payment of £425 in respect of electricity has been debited to the electricity account as £575.

(*f*) A cheque for £2,250 received from Teape Ltd, a debtor, has been correctly entered in the cash book but no entry has been made in Teape's account.

Required:
(i) Show the journal entries, including narratives, to correct the above errors, (ii) Write up the suspense account after correction of the above errors.

33.8X   A trial balance does not balance and a suspense account has been opened with a credit balance of £510. The following errors are then discovered.

(i)   Cash purchases of £450 were recorded in both the cash book and ledger as £540.

(ii) The total of the motor expenses account was undercast by £70.

(iii) Cash received from a debtor £150 is entered in the cash book only.

(iv) The sales account was undercast by £350.

(v) The insurance account was overcast by £80.

Required:
(*a*) Show the journal entries to correct the errors.

(*b*) Write up the suspense account showing correction of the errors.

(*c*) The net profit figure originally calculated for the year ended 31 December 2009 was £12,250. Calculate the corrected net profit figure.

NEAB (AQA) (GCSE)

PART 5

Financial statements of other organisations

This part is concerned with the accounting procedures that have to be followed with different forms of organisations. It also includes a chapter outlining the basic ratios that are used for analysis and interpretation of accounts.

CHAPTER 34

Single entry and incomplete records

Learning objectives

After you have studied this chapter you should be able to:

- appreciate why it is not always appropriate to use double entry for recording transactions
- understand the difference between mark-up and margin
- use accounting ratios to calculate missing figures in financial statements
- appreciate that many businesses use single entry for recording transactions
- ascertain the profit figure from incomplete records
- ascertain sales and purchases from incomplete records
- prepare financial statements from incomplete records.

34.1 Introduction

There are many types of businesses that are run by a person on their own such as the shopkeeper, market stall holder, window cleaner, and so on. In such cases it may be impractical for them to record their finances by the use of a full double entry system of book-keeping. In fact many of them would be unable to write up double entry records, it is more likely that they would enter details of a transaction once only thereby using a **single entry** system. Also many would fail to record every transaction resulting in **incomplete accounting records**.

Since accounting is carried out to assist management in the successful running of a business it is important to remember that the task should not be too onerous for the owner of the business. Many small businesses, like small retail shops, have all the information they require just by keeping a cash book and a record of their debtors and creditors, which in most cases is not recorded using double entry.

Where businesses use a single entry system of recording their financial transactions and indeed where not every transaction is recorded, resulting in incomplete accounting records, then the accountant may have to use ratios to help ascertain missing information.

The ratios, mark-up and margin, can be used to calculate missing figures from incomplete records and to show the relationship between profit and cost price and profit and selling price respectively.

34.2 Mark-up and margin

The purchase cost, gross profit and selling price of goods or services may be shown as:

> Cost price + Gross profit = Selling price

The gross profit when shown as a fraction or percentage of the **cost price** is known as the **mark-up**. The gross profit when shown as a fraction or percentage of the **selling price** is known as the **margin**.

The mark-up and margins can now be calculated using this example:

$$\text{Cost price} + \text{Gross profit} = \text{Selling price}$$
$$£4 \quad + \quad £1 \quad = \quad £5$$

Mark-up $= \dfrac{\text{Gross profit}}{\text{Cost price}}$ as a fraction, or if required as a percentage, multiply by 100:

$$£\frac{1}{4} = \frac{1}{4}, \text{ or } \frac{1}{4} \times 100 = 25\%$$

Margin $= \dfrac{\text{Gross profit}}{\text{Selling price}}$ as a fraction, or if required as a percentage, multiply by 100:

$$£\frac{1}{5} = \frac{1}{5}, \text{ or } \frac{1}{5} \times 100 = 20\%$$

Author's hint

Students often confuse the relationship between the selling price and profit (margin) and cost price and profit (mark-up). This can easily be remembered using the mnemonic 'Mrs Muc', as shown in Exhibit 34.1.

Exhibit 34.1

MaRgin   Sales   Mark-Up   Cost price

34.3 Calculating missing figures

We can use the ratios given in Section 34.2 to complete trading accounts where some of the figures are missing. For ease of illustrating this fact, all examples in this chapter:

- assume that all the goods in a business have the same rate of mark-up
- ignore wastages and theft of goods.

Example 1: The following figures apply for the year 2009:

	£
Stock 1.1.2009	400
Stock 31.12.2009	600
Purchases	5,200

A uniform rate of mark-up of 20% is applied.

Required: Find the gross profit and the sales figure.

Trading Account for the year ended 31 December 2009

	£	£
Sales		?
Less Cost of goods sold		
Stock 1.1.2009	400	
Add Purchases	5,200	
	5,600	
Less Stock 31.12.2009	600	
		5,000
Gross profit		?

Answer:

It is known that: Cost of goods sold + Gross profit = Sales

and you know that you can use
mark-up to find profit, because   Cost of goods sold + % mark-up = Sales

	£5,000	+	20%	= Sales

So sales =   £5,000   +   £1,000   = £6,000

The trading account can now be completed as shown below:

Trading Account for the year ended 31 December 2009

	£	£
Sales		6,000
Less Cost of goods sold		
Stock 1.1.2009	400	
Add Purchases	5,200	
	5,600	
Less Stock 31.12.2009	600	5,000
Gross profit		1,000

Example 2: Another business has the following figures for 2010:

	£
Stock 1.1.2010	500
Stock 31.12.2010	800
Sales	6,400

A uniform rate of margin of 25% is in use.

Required: Find the gross profit and the figure of purchases.

Trading Account for the year ended 31 December 2010

	£	£
Sales		6,400
Less Cost of goods sold		
Stock 1.1.2010	500	
Add Purchases	?	
	?	
Less Stock 31.12.2010	800	?
Gross profit		?

Answer:

Cost of goods sold + Gross profit   = Sales

Rearranging items:	Sales	– Gross profit = Cost of goods sold
	Sales	– 25% Margin = Cost of goods sold
	£6,400	– £1,600 (25% of £6,400) = £4,800

Now the following figures are known:

		£	£
Cost of goods sold:			
Stock 1.1.2010		500	
Add Purchases	(A)	?	
	(B)	?	
Less Stock 31.12.2010		800	
			4,800

The two missing figures are found by normal arithmetical deduction:

(B) *less* £800	= £4,800
Therefore (B)	= £5,600

So that:

£500 opening stock + (A)	= £5,600
Therefore (A)	= £5,100

The completed trading account can now be shown:

Trading Account for the year ended 31 December 2010

	£	£
Sales		6,400
Less Cost of goods sold		
Stock 1.1.2010	500	
Add Purchases	5,100	
	5,600	
Less Stock 31.12.2010	800	4,800
Gross profit		1,600

This technique is found very useful by retail stores when estimating the amount to be bought if a certain sales target is to be achieved. Alternatively, stock levels or sales figures can be estimated given information as to purchases and opening stock figures.

34.4 The relationship between mark-up and margin

As both of these figures refer to the same profit but are expressed as a fraction or a percentage of different figures, there is a relationship between them. If one is known as a fraction, the other can soon be found.

If the mark-up is known, in order to find the margin you need to take the same numerator to be the numerator of the margin. Then, for the denominator of the margin, take the total of the mark-up's denominator *plus* the numerator. An example can now be shown:

Mark-up	Margin
$\dfrac{1}{4}$	$\dfrac{1}{4+1} = \dfrac{1}{5}$
$\dfrac{2}{11}$	$\dfrac{2}{11+2} = \dfrac{2}{13}$

If the margin is known, to find the mark-up take the same numerator to be the numerator of the mark-up. Then, for the denominator of the mark-up, take the figure of the margin's denominator *less* the numerator:

Margin	Mark-up
$\dfrac{1}{6}$	$\dfrac{1}{6-1} = \dfrac{1}{5}$
$\dfrac{3}{13}$	$\dfrac{3}{13-3} = \dfrac{3}{10}$

34.5 Preparing final accounts from incomplete records

When a business has not kept full accounting records it is still necessary to prepare final accounts at the end of the business's financial year. The method used to prepare the accounts in these circumstances is to compare the capital at the beginning and end of the accounting period.

The only way that capital can be increased is by the owner putting in additional funds or by making profits. Consider a business where capital at the end of 2009 is

£20,000. During 2010 there had been no drawings or extra cash brought in by the owner. At the end of 2010 the capital was £30,000. The profits of the business for the year can be found as follows:

$$\text{Net profit} = \underset{\text{capital}}{\underset{\text{This year's}}{£30,000}} - \underset{\text{capital}}{\underset{\text{Last year's}}{£20,000}} = £10,000$$

If on the other hand the drawings had been £7,000, the profits must have been £17,000, calculated thus:

$$\text{Last year's capital} + \text{Profits} - \text{Drawings} = \text{This year's capital}$$
$$£20,000 \quad + \quad ? \quad - \quad £7,000 = \quad £30,000$$

We can see that £17,000 profits was the figure needed to complete the formula, filling in the missing figure by normal arithmetical deduction:

$$£20,000 + £17,000 - £7,000 = £30,000$$

Exhibit 34.2 shows the calculation of profit where insufficient information is available to draft a trading and profit and loss account, only information of assets and liabilities being known.

Exhibit 34.2

H Taylor has not kept proper book-keeping records, but he has kept notes in diary form of the transactions of his business. He is able to give you details of his assets and liabilities as at 31 December 2009 and at 31 December 2010 as follows:

			£
At 31 December 2009	*Assets:*	Motor van	10,000
		Fixtures	7,000
		Stock	8,500
		Debtors	9,500
		Bank	11,100
		Cash	100
	Liabilities:	Creditors	8,000
		Loan from J Ogden	6,000
At 31 December 2010	*Assets:*	Motor van (after depreciation)	8,000
		Fixtures (after depreciation)	6,300
		Stock	9,900
		Debtors	11,240
		Bank	11,700
		Cash	200
	Liabilities:	Creditors	8,700
		Loan from J Ogden	4,000
	Drawings were £9,000		

First of all a **statement of affairs** is drawn up as at 31 December 2009. This is the name given to what would have been called a balance sheet if it had been drawn up from a set of records. The capital is the difference between the assets and liabilities.

H Taylor
Statement of Affairs as at 31 December 2009

Fixed assets	£	£
Motor van		10,000
Fixtures		7,000
		17,000
Current assets		
Stock	8,500	
Debtors	9,500	
Bank	11,100	
Cash	100	
	29,200	
Less Current liabilities		
Creditors	8,000	
Net current assets		21,200
		38,200
Less Long-term liability		
Loan from J Ogden		6,000
		32,200
Financed by		
Capital (difference)		32,200

A statement of affairs is now drafted up as at the end of 2010. The formula of opening capital + profit – drawings = closing capital is then used to deduce the figure of profit.

H Taylor
Statement of Affairs as at 31 December 2010

Fixed assets	£	£
Motor van		8,000
Fixtures		6,300
		14,300
Current assets		
Stock	9,900	
Debtors	11,240	
Bank	11,700	
Cash	200	
	33,040	
Less Current liabilities		
Creditors	8,700	
Net current assets		24,340
		38,640
Less Long-term liability		
Loan from J Ogden		4,000
		34,640
Financed by		
Capital balance at 1.1.2010		32,200
Add Net profit	(C)	?
	(B)	?
Less Drawings		9,000
	(A)	?

Deduction of net profit   Opening capital + net profit − drawings = closing capital. Find the missing figures (A), (B) and (C) by deduction:

(A) is the figure needed to make the balance sheet totals equal, i.e. £34,640;
(B) is therefore £34,640 + £9,000 = £43,640;
(C) is therefore £43,640 − £32,200 = £11,440.

To check:

		£
Capital		32,200
Add Net profit	(C)	11,440
	(B)	43,640
Less Drawings		9,000
	(A)	34,640

Obviously, this method of calculating profit is very unsatisfactory as it is much more informative when a trading and profit and loss account can be drawn up. Therefore, whenever possible, the 'comparison of capital' method of ascertaining profit should be avoided and financial statements drawn up from the available records.

34.6 Step-by-step guide to incomplete records

In preparing final accounts from a single entry set of records a formal approach should be followed as shown below.

Note: You may find it useful to use this guide when studying the example shown below in the accounts of M Cole.

Step 1

Prepare a statement of affairs on the closing day of the *last* accounting period to ascertain the initial *opening capital*. Remember to include the cash and bank balances. (In our example the opening capital is £43,000.)

Step 2

Either draw up and balance a cash and bank summary or, if a cash and bank summary is shown, it may only be necessary to balance off the account. Remember to include the *final cash and bank balances in the final balance sheet*. (In our example the balances at 31 December 2009 are cash £100 and bank £30,500.)

Step 3

Calculate the figures for purchases and sales to be shown in the trading account. Remember that there are *two ways* that this may be achieved: either as a calculation or by using double entry 'T' accounts. (In our example the purchases are £74,500 and the sales £102,200.)

Step 4

Calculate the figures for expenses. If there are no accruals or prepayments either at the beginning or end of the accounting period, the expenses paid will equal the expenses used up during the period. If, however, there *are* accruals and prepayments, then it will be necessary to make adjustments, again, this may be carried out as a calculation or by using 'T' accounts. (In our example there is an 'accrual for rent', therefore it is necessary to calculate the rent for the year using either of the aforementioned methods, and the figure for the year is £3,000.) Remember that 'accounting for prepaid expenses' has been shown in Section 29.4.

Step 5 Depreciation

Check to see if you need to take account of any depreciation before preparing the final accounts. The amount of depreciation may be given or, alternatively, you may have to compare the value of each asset at the beginning of the period with that at the end of the period – the difference being **depreciation**. (In our example under (*f*) below we are told the value of the fixed asset of 'fixtures' is £8,000 and they are to be depreciated at 10% per annum. Thus 10% of £8,000 = £800 depreciation which has been charged to the profit and loss account and shown as a deduction from the fixtures in the balance sheet.)

Remember to check to see if there are any additions to assets and, if so, ensure that you include them on the balance sheet and depreciate them as indicated above.

Finally, prepare the financial statements:

- trading and profit and loss account, and
- balance sheet.

The above guide is now used in the following example to demonstrate the various stages. M Cole requires his final accounts to be drawn up for the year ended 31 December 2009 but has not kept full accounting records. He has, however, been able to provide the following information.

(*a*) The sales are mostly on a credit basis. No record of sales has been made, but £100,000 has been received, £95,000 by cheque and £5,000 by cash, from persons to whom goods have been sold.
(*b*) Amount paid by cheque to suppliers during the year = £72,000.
(*c*) Expenses paid during the year: by cheque, rent £2,000, general expenses £1,800; by cash, rent £500.
(*d*) M Cole took £100 cash per week (for 52 weeks) as drawings.
(*e*) Other information is available:

	At 31.12.2008 £	At 31.12.2009 £
Debtors	11,000	13,200
Creditors for goods	4,000	6,500
Rent owing	–	500
Bank balance	11,300	30,500
Cash balance	800	100
Stock	15,900	17,000

(*f*) The only fixed asset consists of fixtures that were valued at 31 December 2008 at
£8,000. These are to be depreciated at 10% per annum.

A step by step guide, shown below, is now used to demonstrate the various stages.

Step-by-step guide

Step 1

First, draw up a statement of affairs, taking into account all the opening figures, on
the closing day of the last accounting period. This is shown below:

M Cole
Statement of Affairs as at 31 December 2008

	£	£
Fixed Assets		
Fixtures		8,000
Current Assets		
Stock	15,900	
Debtors	11,000	
Bank	11,300	
Cash	800	
	39,000	
Less Current Liabilities		
Creditors	4,000	
Net current assets		35,000
		43,000
Financed by		
Capital (difference)		43,000
		43,000

Step 2

Next, a cash and bank summary, showing the totals of each separate item plus opening
and closing balances, is drawn up. Thus:

Dr	Cash	Bank		Cash	Bank Cr
	£	£		£	£
Balances 31.12.2008	800	11,300	Suppliers		72,000
Receipts from debtors	5,000	95,000	Rent	500	2,000
			General Expenses		1,800
			Drawings	5,200	
			Balances 31.12.2009	100	30,500
	5,800	106,300		5,800	106,300

Step 3

Calculate the figures for purchases and sales to be shown in the trading account.
Remember that the figures needed are the same as those which would have been
found if double entry records had been kept.

Purchases

In double entry, purchases means the goods that have been bought in the period, irrespective of whether or not they have been paid for during the period. The figure of payments to suppliers must therefore be adjusted to find the figure for purchases. In our example we have:

	£
Paid during the year	72,000
Less Payments made, but which were for goods which were purchased	
in a previous year (creditors 31.12.2008)	4,000
	68,000
Add Purchases made in this year, but for which payment has not yet	
been made (creditors 31.12.2009)	6,500
Goods bought in this year, i.e. purchases	74,500

The same answer could have been obtained if the information had been shown in the form of a total creditors account, the figure for purchases being the amount required to make the account totals agree:

Dr		Total Creditors' Account		Cr
	£		£
Cash paid to suppliers	72,000	Balances b/f	4,000
Balances c/d	6,500	Purchases (missing figure)	74,500
	78,500		78,500

Sales

The sales figure will only equal receipts where all the sales are for cash. Therefore, the receipts figures need adjusting to find sales. This can only be done by constructing a total debtors' account, the sales figure being the one needed to make the totals agree.

Dr		Total Debtors' Account		Cr
	£		£
Balances b/f	11,000	Receipts: Cash	5,000
		Cheque	95,000
Sales (missing figure)	102,200	Balances c/d	13,200
	113,200		113,200

Step 4   Expenses

Where there are no accruals or prepayments either at the beginning or end of the accounting period, then expenses paid will equal the expenses used up during the period. These figures will be charged to the trading and profit and loss account.

In contrast, where such prepayments or accruals exist, then an expense account should be drawn up for that particular item. When all known items have been entered, the missing figure will be the expenses to be charged for the accounting period.

In our example, only the rent account needs to be drawn up:

Dr		Rent Account		Cr
	£			£
Cheques	2,000	Rent (missing figure)		3,000
Cash	500			
Accrued c/d	500			
	3,000			3,000

Alternatively, the rent for the year can be found using the following calculation:

Accrual – Rent

		£
Paid:	Bank	2,000
	Cash	500
		2,500
Add: Owing 31.12.09		500
Rent for the year		3,000

Step 5

Check to see if any depreciation needs to be charged to the profit and loss account. In our example, Section 34.3 (*f*), it states that the fixtures are valued at £8,000 and should be depreciated at 10% per annum. Therefore, depreciation charge for the year is 10% of £8,000 = £800; this amount should be charged to the profit and loss account. In the balance sheet remember to deduct the depreciation from the fixtures, i.e. £8,000 – £800 = £7,200 to give you the net book value of the asset.

Now prepare the financial statements using all the information given in the details and the figures you have calculated.

M Cole
Trading and Profit and Loss Account for the year ended 31 December 2009

	£	£
Sales (Step 3)		102,200
Less Cost of goods sold		
Stock at 1.1.2009	15,900	
Add Purchases (Step 3)	74,500	
	90,400	
Less Stock at 31.12.2009	17,000	73,400
Gross profit		28,800
Less Expenses		
Rent (Step 4)	3,000	
General expenses	1,800	
Depreciation: Fixtures	800	5,600
Net profit		23,200

Balance Sheet as at 31 December 2009

Fixed Assets	£	£	£
Fixtures at 1.1.2009		8,000	
Less Depreciation (Step 5)		800	7,200
Current Assets			
Stock		17,000	
Debtors		13,200	
Bank (Step 2)		30,500	
Cash (Step 2)		100	
		60,800	
Less Current Liabilities			
Creditors	6,500		
Rent owing	500	7,000	
Net current assets			53,800
			61,000
Financed by			
Capital (Step 1)			
Balance 1.1.2009 (per opening statement of affairs)			43,000
Add Net profit			23,200
			66,200
Less Drawings			5,200
			61,000

34.7 Incomplete records and missing figures

In practice, part of the information relating to cash receipts or payments is often missing. If the missing information is in respect of one type of payment, then it is normal to assume that the missing figure is the amount required to make both totals agree in the cash column of the cash and bank summary. This does not happen with bank items since another copy of the bank statement can always be obtained from the bank.

Exhibit 34.3 shows an example when the drawings figure is unknown.

Exhibit 34.3

The following information on cash and bank receipts and payments is available:

	Cash	Bank
	£	£
Cash paid into the bank during the year	5,500	
Receipts from debtors	7,250	800
Paid to suppliers	320	4,930
Drawings during the year	?	–
Expenses paid	150	900
Balances at 1.1.2009	35	1,200
Balances at 31.12.2009	50	1,670

Dr		Cash	Bank			Cash	Bank Cr
		£	£			£	£
Balances 1.1.2009		35	1,200	Bankings	C	5,500	
Received from debtors		7,250	800	Suppliers		320	4,930
Bankings	C		5,500	Expenses		150	900
				Drawings		?	
				Balances 31.12.2009		50	1,670
		7,285	7,500			7,285	7,500

The amount needed to make the two sides of the cash columns agree is £1,265. Therefore, this is taken as the figure of drawings.

Exhibit 34.4 is an example of where the receipts from debtors have not been recorded.

Exhibit 34.4
Information of cash and bank transactions is available as follows:

	Cash	Bank
	£	£
Receipts from debtors	?	6,080
Cash withdrawn from the bank for business use (this is the amount which is used besides cash receipts from debtors to pay drawings and expenses)		920
Paid to suppliers		5,800
Expenses paid	640	230
Drawings	1,180	315
Balances at 1.1.2010	40	1,560
Balances at 31.12.2010	70	375

Dr	Cash	Bank		Cash	Bank Cr
	£	£		£	£
Balances 1.1.2010	40	1,560	Suppliers		5,800
Received from debtors	?	6,080	Expenses	640	230
Withdrawn from Bank C	920		Withdrawn from Bank C		920
			Drawings	1,180	315
			Balances 31.12.2010	70	375
	1,890	7,640		1,890	7,640

Receipts from debtors is, therefore, the amount needed to make each side of the cash column agree, namely £930.

It must be emphasised that balancing figures are acceptable only when all the other figures have been verified. Should, for instance, a cash expense be omitted when cash received from debtors is being calculated, then this would result in an understatement not only of expenses but also ultimately of sales.

34.8 Where there are two missing pieces of information

If both cash drawings and cash receipts from debtors were not known, it would not be possible to deduce both of these figures. The only course available would be to estimate whichever figure was more capable of being accurately assessed, use this as a known figure, and deduce the other figure. However, this is a most unsatisfactory position as both of the figures are no more than pure estimates, the accuracy of one relying entirely upon the accuracy of the other.

34.9 Cash sales and purchases for cash

Where there are cash sales as well as sales on credit terms, then the cash sales must be added to sales on credit to give the total sales for the year. This total figure of sales will be the one shown in the trading account.

Similarly, purchases for cash will need adding to credit purchases to give the figure of total purchases for the trading account.

Chapter summary

- Both margin and mark-up are based upon the formula, Cost price + Gross profit = Sales. When gross profit is shown as a percentage of the cost price this gives the mark-up. If the gross profit is shown as a percentage of the selling price this gives the margin. Remember *Mrs MUC*!
- Mark-up and margin can be used to ascertain missing figures in incomplete records.
- In many small businesses it may not be practical to use a full double entry accounting system; instead single entry is used.
- Where no proper accounts are kept, possibly the only way to ascertain the amount of profit is to compare the capital account at the beginning and end of an accounting period. Provided no additional funds have been invested in the business or drawings taken out then the difference must be either profit or loss.
- A statement of affairs is often prepared to ascertain the capital of the proprietor. This statement shows the value of the assets and liabilities at a specific date and by using the accounting equation the capital can be found.
- Using the step-by-step method the financial statements can be prepared from records not kept by the double entry system of book-keeping (see Section 34.6).
- Where there are missing figures it is possible to deduce the figure by careful analysis of data available and process of elimination.
- The disadvantage of single entry is that insufficient financial information is available to the owner(s) of the business.

EXERCISES

34.1 (a) If an item costs £20 and is sold for £25, what are the mark-up and margin, expressed as percentages?

(b) If the mark-up on a unit is $33\frac{1}{3}$%, what is the margin?

(c) If the margin is $16\frac{2}{3}$%, what is the mark-up?

34.2X (a) If an item costs £60 and is sold for £90, what are the mark-up and margin, expressed as percentages?

(b) If the margin on a unit is 50%, what is the mark-up?

(c) If the mark-up is 50%, what is the margin?

34.3 T Ashby is a trader who marks up the selling price of his goods to 25% above cost. His books give the following information at 31 July 2009:

	£
Stock as at 1 August 2008	19,744
Stock as at 31 July 2009	25,240
Sales for the year	120,000

You are required to create a trading account for Ashby showing:

(a) the cost of goods sold

(b) the value of purchases during the year

(c) the profit that Ashby made.

34.4 T Rigby produced from his trial balance as at 31 August 2009 the following information:

	£
Stock as at 1 September 2008	20,000
Purchases for the year	180,000

Rigby has a 'mark-up' of 50% on 'cost of sales'.
His average stock during the year was valued at £40,000.

You are required to:

(a) calculate the closing stock for Rigby as at 31 August 2009

(b) prepare his trading account for the year ended 31 August 2009

(c) ascertain the total amount of expenses that Rigby *must not exceed* if he is to maintain a net profit on sales of 10%.

34.5 The following figures have been extracted from the records of K Rogers, who does not keep a full record of his transactions on the double entry system:

			£
1 November	2009	Debtors	2,760
1 November	2009	Creditors	1,080
1 November	2009	Stock	2,010
31 October	2010	Debtors	3,090
31 October	2010	Creditors	1,320
31 October	2010	Stock	2,160

All goods were sold on credit and all purchases were made on credit. During the year ended 31 October 2010, cash received from debtors amounted to £14,610, whereas cash paid to creditors amounted to £9,390.

Required:

(*a*) Calculate the amount of sales and purchases for the year ended 31 October 2010.

(*b*) Draw up the trading account for the year ended 31 October 2010.

34.6X The following figures for a business are available:

			£
1 June	2008	Stock	11,590
1 June	2008	Creditors	3,410
1 June	2008	Debtors	5,670
31 May	2009	Stock	13,425
31 May	2009	Creditors	4,126
31 May	2009	Debtors	6,108
Year to 31 May 2009:			
Received from debtors			45,112
Paid to creditors			29,375

All goods were bought or sold on credit.

Required:

Draw up the trading account for the year 31 May 2009, deducing any figures that might be needed.

34.7 On 1 July 2009, D Lewinski commenced business with £60,000 in his bank account. After trading for a full year, he ascertained that his position on 30 June 2010 was as follows:

	£		£
Plant	36,000	Fixtures	3,600
Creditors	7,200	Bank balance	6,000
Debtors	9,300	Stock-in-trade	13,500
Cash in hand	1,350	Drawings	16,000

You are required to:

(*a*) calculate D Lewinski's capital at 30 June 2010

(*b*) prepare D Lewinski's balance sheet at 30 June 2010 (assuming a profit of £18,550), set out in such a manner as to show clearly the totals normally shown in a balance sheet.

34.8 J Marcano is a dealer who has not kept proper books of account. At 31 August 2009 her state of affairs was as follows.

	£
Cash	115
Bank balance	2,209
Fixtures	3,500
Stock	16,740
Debtors	11,890
Creditors	9,952
Motor van (at valuation)	3,500

During the year to 31 August 2010, her drawings amounted to £7,560. Winnings from the national lottery of £12,800 were put into the business. Extra fixtures were bought for £2,000. At 31 August 2010 Marcano's assets and liabilities were: cash £84; bank overdraft, £165; stock, £24,891; creditors for goods £6,002; creditors for expenses £236; fixtures to be depreciated by £300; motor van to be valued at £2,800; debtors, £15,821; prepaid expenses, £72.

You are required to draw up a statement showing the profit or loss made by Marcano for the year ended 31 August 2010.

34.9X   A Hanson is a sole trader who, although keeping very good records, does not operate a full double entry system. The following figures have been taken from his records:

	31 March 2008	31 March 2009
	£	£
Cash at bank	1,460	1,740
Office furniture	600	500
Stock	2,320	2,620
Cash in hand	60	80

Debtors on 31 March 2008 amounted to £2,980 and sales for the year ended 31 March 2009 to £11,520. During the year ended 31 March 2009, cash received from debtors amounted to £10,820.

Creditors on 31 March 2008 amounted to £1,880 and purchases for the year ended 31 March 2009 to £8,120. During the year ended 31 March 2009, cash paid to creditors amounted to £7,780.

During the year to 31 March 2009 no bad debts were incurred. Also during the same period, there was neither discounts allowed nor discounts received.

Required (with all calculations shown):
(*a*) Calculate debtors and creditors as at 31 March 2009.
(*b*) Calculate Hanson's capital as at 31 March 2008 and 31 March 2009.
(*c*) Calculate his net profit for the year ended 31 March 2009, allowing for the fact that during the year Hanson's drawings amounted to £2,540.

34.10   Leigh Osawa had not kept full accounting records. On 31 March 2009 he attempted to prepare his final accounts for his business but was unable to calculate the figure for total sales, rent and business rates for the year ended on that date.

The following information is available:

	Balance 1 April 2008	Balance 31 March 2009
	£	£
Trade debtors	23,460	28,270
Rent due	1,040	730
Business rates prepaid	390	440

The bank statements for the year ended 31 March 2009 reveal:

	£
Receipts from trade debtors	226,820
Payment for	
Rent	12,290
Business rates	4,680

It should be noted that trade debtors were allowed discounts of £280 during the year under review.

Set out detailed calculations of the amounts to be included in the final accounts for the year ended 31 March 2009 for:

(*a*) sales
(*b*) rent
(*c*) business rates.

Southern Examining Group AQA

Please note that this question is NOT from the live examinations for the current specification.

34.11X An accountant has prepared quarterly accounts for Linda Goodheart, who runs a small newsagent's shop. After he had prepared the accounts for the third quarter of the year to 31 July 2009, the trial balance was as follows:

	£	£
Fixtures and fittings, at cost	7,800	
Provision for depreciation of fixtures and fittings		1,600
Balance at bank	1,572	
Prepayment for shop expenses	250	
Trade creditors		11,980
Sundry debtors	11,156	
Capital account		20,632
Stock	13,434	
	34,212	34,212

Due to illness of her accountant, she has asked you to prepare the accounts for the final quarter of her financial year. Looking through the bank statements you have elicited this information:

	Quarter to 31/10/09
Paid into bank:	
Cash sales	16,216
Receipts from debtors	22,860
Bank interest	47
Cheque from creditor, who had been overpaid	381
Amounts withdrawn –	
Purchases	34,886
Shop expenses	5,401
For personal use	3,000
Wages	440

You have also discovered that:
(i)   all receipts and payments for the business go through the bank account
(ii) the business is owed £11,340 by customers at 31 October 2009
(iii) shop expenses are paid for at the time of purchase
(iv) sales produce a gross profit of 35%
(v)   fixtures and fittings are depreciated at the rate of 10% p.a. on cost
(vi) the stock at 31 October 2009 is valued at £16,111.

You are required (showing all workings) to:
(*a*) produce a summary bank account for the quarter to 31 October 2009
(*b*) prepare the business profit and loss account for the period from 1 August to 31 October 2009
(*c*) prepare the balance sheet as at 31 October 2009.

OCR (Accounting Stage II)

34.12X Ruth Eridge has not kept proper accounting records for her business which opened on 1 April 2008. On that date she opened a business bank account with £30,000 of her private funds.

A summary of her bank account for the year ended 31 March 2009 is shown below:

	£		£
Capital introduced	30,000	Drawings	14,500
Cash sales	64,200	Purchase of fixed assets	25,000
		Payments to suppliers of stock	27,800
		Business expenses	18,100
		Balance at bank 31 March 2009	8,800
	94,200		94,200

On 31 March 2009:

- unsold stock was valued at £7,700
- there were business expenses of £200 prepaid
- fixed assets were to be depreciated by £4,000
- the amount owing to trade creditors was £3,200.

Tasks:

(*a*) Prepare the business's trading and profit and loss account for the year ended 31 March 2009.

(*b*) Ruth Eridge would like to expand her business but will need £25,000 to finance the expansion. Advise Ruth of *two* ways in which she could finance the expansion of the business. In each case explain the financial implications of your suggestion.

Southern Examining Group AQA

Please note that this question is NOT from the live examinations for the current specification.

Club accounts

Learning objectives

After you have studied this chapter you should be able to:

- appreciate that non-profit-making organisations such as clubs, charities, associations and societies prepare different financial statements from profit-making organisations
- prepare a receipts and payments account
- prepare income and expenditure accounts and balance sheet for non-profit-making organisations
- calculate profits and losses from special activities and incorporate them into the financial statements
- appreciate that various forms of income may need special treatment
- be aware of treasurer's responsibilities.

35.1 Non-profit-making organisations

The organisations we have covered so far have all been profit-making businesses. However, there are other organisations whose objective is not to make a profit but instead provide facilities for their members to pursue a hobby, sporting activity or provide voluntary services. These clubs and associations do not have to prepare a trading and profit and loss account since they are not formed to carry on trading and make profits. Instead the financial statements prepared by them are either 'receipts and payments accounts' or 'income and expenditure accounts'.

35.2 Receipts and payments account

Receipts and payments accounts are usually prepared by the treasurer of the club or association. This account is a summary of the cash book for the period and if the organisation has no assets (other than cash) and no liabilities, a summary of the cash book tells the members all they need to know about the financial activities during a period. Exhibit 35.1 is an example of a receipts and payments account.

Exhibit 35.1

The Homers Running Club
Receipts and Payments Account for the year ended 31 December 2009

Receipts	£	Payments	£
Bank balance 1.1.2009	2,360	Groundsman's wages	10,000
Subscriptions received for 2009	11,640	Sports ground expenses	1,760
Rent received	1,000	Committee expenses	280
		Printing and stationery	110
		Bank balance 31.12.2009	2,850
	15,000		15,000

35.3 Income and expenditure accounts

When assets are owned, and/or there are liabilities, the receipts and payments account is not a good way of drawing up financial statements. Other than the cash received and paid out, it shows only the cash balances; the other assets and liabilities are not shown at all.

What is required is:

● a balance sheet, and
● an account showing whether the association's capital has increased.

The second of these two requirements is provided via an **income and expenditure account**. Such an account follows the same rules as trading and profit and loss accounts, the only differences being the terms used.

A comparison of terms used now follows:

Profit-making organisation	Non-profit organisation
1 Trading and profit and loss account	1 Income and expenditure account
2 Net profit	2 Surplus of income over expenditure
3 Net loss	3 Excess of expenditure over income

35.4 Profit or loss for a special purpose

Sometimes there are reasons why a **non-profit-making organisation** would want a profit and loss account. This is where something is done to make a profit. The profit is not to be kept, but used to pay for the main purpose of the organisation.

For instance, a football club may have discos or dances that people pay to attend. Any profit from these events helps to pay football expenses. For these discos and dances a trading and profit and loss account would be drawn up. Any profit (or loss) would be transferred to the income and expenditure account.

35.5 Accumulated fund

A sole trader or a partnership would have capital accounts. A non-profit-making organisation would instead have an **accumulated fund**. It is in effect the same as a capital account, for it is the difference between assets and liabilities.

For a sole trader or partnership:

> Capital = Assets – Liabilities

In a non-profit-making organisation:

> Accumulated Fund = Assets – Liabilities

35.6 Drawing up income and expenditure accounts

We can now look at the preparation of an income and expenditure account and a balance sheet of a club. This is drawn up on the basis of a trial balance.

Long Lane Football Club Trial Balance as at 31 December 2009		
	Dr £	Cr £
Sports equipment	8,500	
Club premises	29,600	
Subscriptions received		6,490
Staff wages	4,750	
Furniture and fittings	5,260	
Rates and insurance	1,910	
General expenses	605	
Accumulated fund 1 January 2009		42,016
Donations received		360
Telephone and postage	448	
Bank	2,040	
Bar purchases	9,572	
Creditors for bar supplies		1,040
Bar sales		14,825
Bar stocks 1 January 2009	2,046	
	64,731	64,731

The following information is also available:

(i) Bar stocks at 31 December 2009 amount in value to £2,362.

(ii) There is a need to provide for depreciation: sports equipment £1,700; furniture and fittings £1,315.

The club's trading account for its bar is as follows:

Long Lane Football Club Bar
Trading Account for the year ended 31 December 2009

	£	£
Sales		14,825
Less Cost of goods sold		
Opening stock	2,046	
Purchases	9,572	
	11,618	
Closing stock	2,362	
		9,256
Gross profit		5,569

The result of the club bar operation is calculated separately. The gross profit/loss will then be incorporated into the club's income and expenditure account for calculation of the overall result, as shown below:

Income and Expenditure Account
for the year ended 31 December 2009

	£	£
Income		
Gross profit from bar		5,569
Subscriptions		6,490
Donations received		360
		12,419
Less Expenditure		
Staff wages	4,750	
Rates and insurance	1,910	
Telephone and postage	448	
General expenses	605	
Depreciation: Furniture	1,315	
Sports equipment	1,700	
		10,728
Surplus of income over expenditure		1,691

Balance Sheet at 31 December 2009

	£	£	£
	Cost	*Depreciation*	*Net book value*
Fixed assets			
Club premises	29,600	–	29,600
Furniture and fittings	5,260	1,315	3,945
Sports equipment	8,500	1,700	6,800
	43,360	3,015	40,345
Current assets			
Bar stocks		2,362	
Cash at bank		2,040	
		4,402	

	£	£	£
Current liabilities			
Creditors for bar supplies		1,040	
Net current assets			3,362
Net assets			43,707
Accumulated fund			
Balance at 1 January 2009			42,016
Add Surplus of income over expenditure			1,691
			43,707

35.7 Subscriptions

No subscriptions owing

Where there are no **subscriptions** owing, or paid in advance, at the beginning and the end of a financial year, then the amount shown on the credit side of the subscriptions account can be transferred to the credit side of the income and expenditure account, as follows:

Dr		Subscriptions		Cr
2009	£	2009		£
Dec 31 Income & expenditure a/c	3,598	Dec 31 Bank (total received)		3,598

Income and Expenditure Account
for the year ended 31 December 2009 (extract)

Income:	£
Subscriptions	3,598

Subscriptions owing

On the other hand, there may be subscriptions owing at both the start and the end of the financial year. In a case where £325 was owing at the start of the year, a total of £5,668 was received during the year, and £554 was owing at the end of the year, then this would appear as follows:

Dr		Subscriptions		Cr
2009	£	2009		£
Jan 1 Owing b/d	325	Dec 31 Bank (total received)		5,668
Dec 31 Income & expenditure a/c		Dec 31 Balance c/d		554
(difference)	5,897			
	6,222			6,222

Income and Expenditure Account
for the year ended 31 December 2009 (extract)

Income:	£
Subscriptions	5,897

In the balance sheet, the subscription owing at the end of December 2009 would be shown under the heading of 'Current assets' as a debtor, as shown below:

Balance Sheet as at 31 December 2009 (extract)

Current assets	£
Stock	x,xxx
Debtors (xxx + 554)	xxx

Subscriptions owing and paid in advance

In the third case, at the start of the year there are both subscriptions owing from the previous year and also subscriptions paid in advance. In addition, there are also subscriptions paid in the current year for the next year (in advance) and subscriptions unpaid (owing) at the end of the current year. The example below concerns an amateur theatre organisation.

An amateur theatre organisation charges its members an annual subscription of £20 per member. It accrues for subscriptions owing at the end of each year and also adjusts for subscriptions received in advance. The following applies:

(A) On 1 January 2002, 18 members owed £360 for the year 2001.
(B) In December 2001, 4 members paid £80 for the year 2002.
(C) During the year 2002, the organisation received cash subscriptions of £7,420.

For 2001	£360
For 2002	£6,920
For 2003	£140
	£7,420

(D) At the close of 31 December 2002, 11 members had not paid their 2002 subscriptions.

Note: Dates have been deliberately set as 2001, etc., for easier understanding of this topic.

These facts are translated into the accounts as set out below:

Dr			Subscriptions			Cr
2002		£	2002			£
Jan 1 Owing b/d	(A)	360	Jan 1 Prepaid b/d	(B)		80
Dec 31 Income and expenditure a/c		*7,220	Dec 31 Bank	(C)		7,420
Dec 31 Prepaid c/d	(C)	140	Dec 31 Owing c/d	(D)		220
		7,720				7,720
2003			2003			
Jan 1 Owing b/d	(D)	220	Jan 1 Prepaid b/d	(C)		140

*The difference between the two sides of the account.

Income and Expenditure Account
for the year ended 31 December 2002 (extract)

Income:	£
Subscriptions	7,220

In this last case in the balance sheet as at 31 December 2002, the amounts owing for subscriptions (D), £220, will be shown under current assets as a debtor. The subscriptions (C) paid in advance for 2003 will appear as an item under current liabilities as subscriptions received in advance, £140, as shown below:

Balance Sheet as at 31 December 2002 (extract)

Current Assets	
Stock	xxx
Debtors (xxx + 220)	xx
Current Liabilities	
Subscriptions in advance	140

Note: Treasurers of clubs and societies are very much aware that if subscriptions are outstanding for a long time it is unlikely that they will ever be paid, the member may have lost interest or moved on to another organisation. Consequently, many clubs and indeed charities do not include unpaid subscriptions as an asset in the balance sheet.

35.8 Donations

Any **donations** received are shown as income in the year that they are received.

35.9 Entrance fees

New members often have to pay an entrance fee in the year that they join, in addition to the membership fee for that year. Entrance fees are normally included as income in the year that they are received.

35.10 Life membership

In some clubs and societies members can pay a one-off amount for **life membership**. This membership will last for their lifetime. In this case, all of the money received from life membership should not be credited to the income and expenditure account of the year in which it is received.

In a club where members joined at age 20 and would probably be members for 40 years, then one-fortieth ($2\frac{1}{2}\%$) of the life membership fee should be credited in the income and expenditure account each year. The balance not transferred to the income and expenditure account would appear in the balance sheet as a long-term liability. This is because it is the liability of the club to allow the members to use the club for the rest of their lives without paying any more for membership.

On the other hand, a club especially for people over the age of 60 would transfer a much bigger share of the life membership fee paid to the income and expenditure account. This is because the number of years of future use of the club will be far less because people are already old when they join. It may be, in those circumstances, that 10% of the life membership fee per year would be transferred to the credit of the income and expenditure account.

35.11　Treasurers' responsibilities

Treasurers of clubs or societies have a responsibility for maintaining proper accounting records in the same way as an accountant has when looking after the financial affairs of a business. It is important to ensure that any monies paid out by the treasurer have been properly authorised, especially when purchasing an item of capital expenditure (such as new sound equipment for a dramatic society). In such cases, the authorisation for purchase will more than likely have been approved at a committee meeting and noted in the minutes of the meeting. For smaller items of expenditure such as postages, telephone calls, etc., the club or society's rules will provide the treasurer with the authority to make payments against receipted bills.

It is also important for the treasurer to keep all invoices, receipted accounts and any other documents as evidence against payments. Treasurers should also provide receipts for any monies received. All documents should be filed and available at the year end for the club's auditor to carry out an audit and for preparation of the club's year-end financial statements.

Chapter summary

- The main objective of non-profit-making organisations is to provide members with facilities to pursue a leisure activity and not to trade and make profits.
- The financial statements prepared for non-profit-making organisations may either be a 'receipts and payments account' or 'income and expenditure account'.
- A 'receipts and payments account' is very much like a cash book summary.
- An 'income and expenditure account' is very similar to a trading and profit and loss account except that the terminology used is different. A profit/surplus in the Income and Expenditure Account is expressed as 'surplus of income over expenditure'. A loss would be referred to as 'excess of expenditure over income'.
- The 'accumulated fund' is basically the same as a capital account.
- Although clubs and societies are non-profit-making sometimes activities are held to generate profits for the benefit of the organisation and its members.
- The treatment of members' subscriptions may involve subscriptions owing and/or paid in advance.
- Donations should be treated as income in the year in which they are received.
- Entrance fees are usually treated as income in the year in which the member joins the organisation.
- Life membership subscriptions should be spread over the anticipated length of membership which is usually decided by the club's committee or may be set out in the rules and regulations.
- Club treasurers carry an important role and, as such, are responsible for maintaining the organisation's accounting records and looking after their financial affairs.

EXERCISES

35.1 You are given the following details of the Horton Hockey Club for its year to 30 June 2009:

Payments:	£
Teams' travel expenses	1,598
Groundsman's wages	3,891
Postage and stationery	392
Rent of pitches and clubhouse	4,800
General expenses	419
Cost of prizes for raffles	624
Receipts:	
Subscriptions	8,570
Donations	1,500
Receipts from raffles	3,816

Cash and bank balances:	£
1 July 2008	2,715
30 June 2009	4,877

You also find out that members owe £160 subscriptions on 30 June 2009. On that date, the club owed £400 for rent and £75 for wages.

You are required to draw up:
(*a*) a receipts and payments account for the year ended 30 June 2009.
(*b*) an income and expenditure account for the year ended 30 June 2009.

35.2X These are the financial details of the Superball Football Club for the year to 31 May 2009:

Payments:	£
Hire of transport	3,710
Ground maintenance costs	1,156
Groundsman's wages	5,214
Committee expenses	906
Costs of disco	1,112
Rent of ground	2,450
General expenses	814
Receipts:	
Members' subscriptions	8,124
Prize money for winning cup	1,000
Receipts from disco	3,149
Collections at matches	5,090

Cash and bank balances:	£
1 June 2008	905
31 May 2009	2,906

Members' subscriptions owing on 31 May 2008 amount to £160 and on 31 May 2009 to £94. On 31 May 2009 the rent had been prepaid £200, and owing were transport hire £90 and committee expenses £170.

You are required to draw up:
(*a*) a receipts and payments account for the year ended 31 May 2009.
(*b*) an income and expenditure account for the year ended 31 May 2009.

35.3 The following receipts and payments account for the year ending 31 May 2008 was prepared by the treasurer of the Down Town Sports and Social Club.

Receipts	£	Payments	£
Balance at bank 1 June 2007	286	Purchases of new equipment	166
Subscriptions	135	Bar stocks purchased	397
Net proceeds of jumble sale	91	Hire of rooms	64
Net proceeds of dance	122	Wages of part-time staff	198
Sale of equipment	80	Balance at bank 31 May 2008	352
Bar takings	463		
	1,177		1,177

Notes:

(i)   On 1 June 2007, the club's equipment was valued at £340. Included in this total, valued at £92, was the equipment sold during the year for £80.

(ii)   Bar stocks were valued as follows: 31 May 2007, £88; 31 May 2008, £101. There were no creditors for bar supplies on either of these dates.

(iii)   Allow £30 for depreciation of equipment during the year ending 31 May 2008. This is additional to the loss on equipment sold during the year.

(iv)   No subscriptions were outstanding at 31 May 2007, but on 31 May 2008 subscriptions due but unpaid amounted to £14.

Required (with calculations shown):

(*a*)   Calculate the accumulated fund of the club as at 1 June 2007.

(*b*)   Draw up the income and expenditure account of the club for the year ending 31 May 2008.

35.4X   The following trial balance was extracted from the books of the Upper Harbour Sports Club at the close of business on 31 March 2009:

	Dr £	Cr £
Club premises	13,500	
Sports equipment	5,100	
Bar purchases and sales	9,540	15,270
Bar stocks 1 April 2008	2,190	
Balance at bank	2,790	
Subscriptions received		8,640
Accumulated fund 1 April 2008		22,290
Salary of secretary	3,600	
Wages of staff	5,280	
Postage and telephone	870	
Office furniture	1,200	
Rates and insurance	1,230	
Cash in hand	60	
Sundry expenses	840	
	46,200	46,200

Notes:

(i)   All bar purchases and sales are on a cash basis. Bar stocks at 31 March 2009 were £2,460.

(ii)   No subscriptions have been paid in advance but subscriptions in arrears at 31 March 2009 amounted to £90.

(iii)   Rates pre-paid at 31 March 2009: £60.

(iv)   Provision for depreciation as follows: sports equipment £600; office furniture £120.

Required:

Prepare the bar trading account and the income and expenditure account of the club for the year ended 31 March 2009, together with a balance sheet as on that date. For this purpose, the wages of staff £5,280 should be shown in the income and expenditure account and not the bar trading account.

35.5 Amit Mall is the treasurer of the local tennis club. He needs to prepare some financial statements and has asked you to help.

The following information is available for the year ended 30 November 2009.

● The bank summary shows:

	£		£
Opening balance	850	Bar purchases	6,400
Subscriptions	33,000	Wages	25,500
Bar sales	8,700	General expenses	4,850
Bank loan	5,400	Purchase of land	12,000
Closing balance	800		
	48,750		48,750

● The year end balances are:

	30 November 2008 £	30 November 2009 £
Stock of bar purchases	680	890
Creditors for bar purchases	1,000	540
Subscriptions in arrear	1,000	4,000
Accrual for general expenses	150	250

● 20% of wages relate to the bar, 80% to other activities
● 30% of expenses relate to the bar, 70% to other activities
● the loan was taken out on 1 January 2008 at a rate of interest of 8% per annum
● the subscription is £100 per member per year.

Tasks:

1 Calculate the purchases made for the bar for the year ended 30 November 2009.
2 Calculate the net profit or loss made from the bar for the year ended 30 November 2009.
3 Calculate the total number of members who should have paid a subscription to the tennis club for the year ended 30 November 2009.
4 Calculate the surplus or deficit made by the tennis club for the year ended 30 November 2009.
5 List the assets and liabilities held by the tennis club on 30 November 2009.
6 The tennis club does not provide for depreciation of land. Briefly explain why.

Association of Accounting Technicians

35.6 The treasurer of a local amateur dramatic society is trying to ascertain the amount of subscriptions to transfer to the society's income and expenditure account for the year ended 31 December 2002 and asks for your help.

The following information is made available to you:

	2001 £	2002 £
Subscriptions in arrears	235	185
Subscriptions in advance	220	140

In addition, you are told that the amount received from members during the year 2002 amounted to £2,600, all of which was banked immediately.

Note: Dates have deliberately set as 2001 to make it easier for students answering this question.

You are required to draw up the society's subscriptions account for the year ended 31 December 2002, showing clearly the amount of subscriptions to be transferred to the income and expenditure account.

35.7X Pat Hall is the treasurer of a local tennis club that has 420 members. The subscription details for the club are as follows:

Subscriptions for year to 31 December 2007 – £220 per member
Subscriptions for year to 31 December 2008 – £240 per member
Subscriptions for year to 31 December 2009 – £250 per member

On 31 December 2007, six members had prepaid their subscriptions for 2008. By 31 December 2008, eight members will have prepaid their subscriptions for 2009. All other members have paid, and will continue to pay their subscriptions during the relevant year.

You are required (showing all your workings) to:
(*a*) calculate the subscriptions figure to be entered in the income and expenditure account for the year ended 31 December 2008
(*b*) calculate the total amount of money received for subscriptions during the year ended 31 December 2008.

Association of Accounting Technicians

35.8X Harry Green is the treasurer of his golf club.

● During the year ended 30 November 2009, the club received £110,000 in cash and cheques from members for annual subscriptions.
● The annual subscription is £50 per member.
● On 30 November 2008, four members were in arrears and two had paid in advance.
● On 30 November 2009, three members were in arrears and five had paid in advance.

Tasks:
(*a*) Prepare the subscription account, clearly showing the amount of subscriptions to be entered in the income and expenditure account for the year ended 30 November 2009.
(*b*) How many members does the golf club have?

Association of Accounting Technicians

35.9X The following items represented the assets and liabilities of the Torrevieja Club at 1 January 2009:

	£
Rent paid in advance	400
Cash at bank	800
Subscriptions in advance	1,200
Equipment	40,000
Lawn mower	600
Subscriptions in arrears	200
Insurance in arrears	100
Heating in advance	200

The Receipts and Payments Account for the year to 31 December 2009 reveals the following:

	£		£
Subscriptions	26,000	Purchase of lawn mower	1,100
Dinner and dance ticket sales	4,650	Soft drink purchases	3,600
Sale of existing lawn mower	700	Insurance	1,050
Soft drink sales	7,200	Rent	4,420
		Heating	1,450
		Dinner dance expenses	3,200

The following additional information is also available:

(i) The club depreciates its lawn mowers by 15% on those in existence at 31 December 2009.

(ii) Subscriptions in arrears at 31 December 2009 amounted to £750, while those in advance amounted to £590.

(iii) Unsold soft drinks at 31 December 2009 amounted to £1,400.

(iv) Dinner dance expenses in arrears at 31 December amounted to £160.

(v) Insurance paid in advance at 31 December 2009 amounted to £180.

You are required to:

(a) calculate the club's accumulated fund at 1 January 2009

(b) prepare the club's income and expenditure account for the year ended 31 December 2009

(c) prepare the club's balance sheet as at 31 December 2009.

City & Guilds Pitman qualifications

CHAPTER 36

Partnership accounts

Learning objectives

After you have studied this chapter you should be able to:

- understand exactly what a partnership is and the rules relating to the number of partners
- distinguish between limited and unlimited partners
- describe the main features of a partnership agreement
- understand the position if no partnership agreement exists
- draw up the capital and current accounts for the partnership
- prepare the financial statements of a partnership.

36.1 The need for partnerships

So far, we have considered mainly businesses owned by only one person. Businesses that set up to make a profit can often have more than one owner and there are various reasons for multiple ownership. There are two types of multiple ownership: **partnerships** and limited companies. This chapter deals only with partnerships. Limited companies will be the subject of later chapters.

Advantages of partnerships

Partnerships are easier to set up than limited companies and have much lower set-up costs. The advantages of partnerships include:

- More capital can be raised, i.e. with additional partners.
- Additional partners bring in a variety of skills and expertise that benefit the partnership.
- The experience or ability required to manage the business cannot always be provided by one person working alone.
- The responsibility of management could be shared by additional partners.
- A partnership of family members can bring a stronger desire to succeed within a dependable environment.

- Partnerships are ideal organisations for professional practices such as medicine, law and accounting.
- Profits from partnership are taxed as the personal income of the partnership.

Disadvantages of partnerships

The disadvantages include:

- The partners have unlimited liability (except a **limited partner**, see Section 36.3) and may be responsible for the debts of other partners.
- A partnership is dissolved on the death of a partner.
- It is difficult to liquidate or transfer partnerships.
- A partnership may have difficulty in raising sufficient capital for large-scale operations. Increased unlimited liability could also be a deterrent to expanding the business.

36.2 Nature of a partnership

A partnership has the following characteristics:

1 It is formed to make profits.
2 It must obey the law as given in the Partnership Act 1890. If there is a limited partner, as described in Section 36.3, the Limited Partnerships Act of 1907 must also be complied with.
3 Normally, there can be a minimum of 2 and a maximum of 20 partners. Exceptions are banks, where there cannot be more than 10 partners; also, there is no maximum limit for firms of accountants, solicitors, stock exchange members or other professional bodies receiving the approval of the relevant government body for this purpose.
4 Each partner (except for limited partners, described below) must pay his or her share of any debts that the partnership is unable to pay; they are personally liable. If necessary, partners could be forced to sell their private possessions to pay their share of any debts. This can be said to be 'unlimited' liability.

36.3 Limited partners

A partnership may be unlimited as previously discussed or limited. In a **limited partnership** there must be at least one partner who is not limited. All limited partnerships must be registered with the Registrar of Companies. Limited partners are not liable for the debts as in Section 36.2 (4) above. The following characteristics are found in limited partnerships:

1 Their liability for the debts of the partnership is limited to the capital they have invested in the partnership. They can lose that capital, but they cannot be asked for any more money to pay the debts unless they break the regulations relating to the involvement in the partnership (2 and 3 below).
2 The partners are not allowed to take out or receive back any part of their contribution to the partnership during its lifetime.

3 They are not allowed to take part in the management of the partnership business.
4 All the partners cannot be limited partners as mentioned above; there must be at least one partner with unlimited liability.

36.4 Partnership agreements

Agreements in writing are not necessary for partnerships. It is advisable, however, that a written **partnership agreement** is drawn up by a lawyer or accountant. This will ensure that there will be fewer problems between partners.

36.5 Content of partnership agreements

The written agreement can contain as much, or as little, as the partners want. The law does not say what it must contain. The usual accounting contents are:

1 The capital to be contributed by each partner.
2 The ratio in which profits (or losses) are to be shared.
3 The rate of interest, if any, to be paid on capital before the profits are shared.
4 The rate of interest, if any, to be charged on partners' drawings.
5 Salaries to be paid to partners.
6 Performance-related payments to partners.
7 Arrangement for the admission of a new partner.
8 Procedures to be carried out when a partner retires or dies.

Points 1 to 6 in the list above are now examined. Points 7 and 8 are outside the scope of this book but are covered in *Business Accounting 1* by Frank Wood and Alan Sangster.

1 Capital contributions

Partners need not contribute equal amounts of capital. What matters is how much capital each partner *agrees* to contribute.

2 Profit (or loss) sharing ratios

Although partners can in fact agree to share profits/losses in any ratio that they desire, it is often thought by students that profits should be shared in the same ratio as that in which capital is contributed. For example, suppose the capitals were Allen £20,000 and Beet £10,000; many people would share the profits in the ratio of two-thirds to one-third, even though the work to be done by each partner is similar. A look at the division of the first few years' profits on such a basis would be:

Years	1	2	3	4	5	Total
	£	£	£	£	£	£
Net profits	18,000	24,000	30,000	30,000	36,000	
Shared:						
Allen $^2/_3$	12,000	16,000	20,000	20,000	24,000	92,000
Beet $^1/_3$	6,000	8,000	10,000	10,000	12,000	46,000

It can be seen from the above table that Allen would receive £92,000, or £46,000 more than Beet. To treat each partner fairly, the difference between the two shares of profit when the duties of the partners are the same should be adequate to compensate Allen for putting extra capital into the business. Some might feel that £46,000 extra profits is far more than adequate for this purpose.

Consider, too, the position of capital-ratio sharing of profits when one partner has put in £99,000 and the other £1,000 as capital. In this case, one partner would get 99/100ths of the profits, while the other would get only 1/100th!

To overcome the difficulty of compensating for the investment of extra capital, the concept of interest on capital was devised.

3 Interest on capital

If the work to be done by each partner is of equal value but the capital contributed is unequal, it is reasonable to grant **interest on the partners' capital**. This interest is treated as a deduction prior to the calculation of profits and its distribution according to the profit-sharing ratio. The rate of interest is a matter of agreement between the partners, but it should equal the return that they would have received if they had invested the capital elsewhere.

Taking Allen and Beet's business again, but sharing the profits equally after charging 5% per annum interest on capital, the division of profits would become:

Years	1	2	3	4	5	Total
	£	£	£	£	£	£
Net profits	18,000	24,000	30,000	30,000	36,000	
Interest on capital						
Allen	1,000	1,000	1,000	1,000	1,000	
Beet	500	500	500	500	500	
Remainder shared:						
Allen $1/2$	8,250	11,250	14,250	14,250	17,250	65,250
Beet $1/2$	8,250	11,250	14,250	14,250	17,250	65,250

Summary	Allen	Beet
	£	£
Interest on capital	5,000	2,500
Balance of profits	65,250	65,250
	70,250	67,750

Here Allen has received £2,500 more than Beet which the partners consider appropriate for his having invested a larger amount over five years.

4 Interest on drawings

It is clearly in the best interests of the business that cash is withdrawn from the business by the partners in accordance with the two basic principles of: (*a*) as little as possible, and (*b*) as late as possible. The more cash that is left in the business, the more expansion can be financed, the greater the economies of having ample cash to take advantage of bargains and of not missing cash discounts.

To deter the partners from taking out cash unnecessarily, the concept can be used of charging the partners **interest on each withdrawal**, calculated from the date of withdrawal to the end of the financial year. The amount charged to them helps to swell the profits divisible between the partners. The rate of interest should be sufficient to achieve this without being too harsh.

Suppose that Allen and Beet have decided to charge interest on drawings at 5% per annum, and that their year end is 31 December. The following drawings are made:

Allen

Drawings		Interest		£
1 January	£1,000	5% of £1,000 for 1 year	=	50
1 March	£2,400	5% of £2,400 for 10 months	=	100
1 May	£1,200	5% of £1,200 for 8 months	=	40
1 July	£2,400	5% of £2,400 for 6 months	=	60
1 October	£ 800	5% of £800 for 3 months	=	10
		Interest charged to Allen	=	260

Beet

Drawings		Interest		£
1 January	£ 600	5% of £600 for 1 year	=	30
1 August	£4,800	5% of £4,800 for 5 months	=	100
1 December	£2,400	5% of £2,400 for 1 month	=	10
		Interest charged to Beet	=	140

The interest charged to each partner would vary depending on when and how much money was taken out as drawings.

5 Salaries to partners

One partner may have more responsibility or tasks than others. As a reward for this and rather than change the profit and loss sharing ratio, that partner may have a **partnership salary**, which is deducted before sharing the balance of profits.

6 Performance-related payments to partners

Partners may agree that commission or performance-related bonuses should be payable to some or all the partners in a way that is linked to their individual performance. As with salaries, these would be deducted before sharing the balance of profits.

36.6 An example of the distribution of profits

Taylor and Clarke have been in partnership for one year, sharing profits and losses in the ratio of Taylor three-fifths and Clarke two-fifths. They are entitled to 5% per annum interest on capital, Taylor having put in £20,000 and Clarke £60,000. Clarke is to have a salary of £20,000. They charge interest on drawings, Taylor being charged

£500 and Clarke £1,000. The net profit, before any distributions to the partners, amounts to £50,000 for the year ended 31 December 2009.

The results are shown in Exhibit 36.1.

Exhibit 36.1

	£	£	£
Net profit			50,000
Add Charged for interest on drawings:			
Taylor		500	
Clarke		1,000	
			1,500
			51,500
Less Salary: Clarke		20,000	
Interest on capital (@ 5%)			
Taylor	1,000		
Clarke	3,000		
		4,000	
			24,000
			27,500
Balance of profits shared:			
Taylor (three-fifths)		16,500	
Clarke (two-fifths)		11,000	27,500
			27,500

The £50,000 net profits have therefore been shared as follows:

	Taylor	Clarke
	£	£
Balance of profits	16,500	11,000
Interest on capital	1,000	3,000
Salary	–	20,000
	17,500	34,000
Less Interest on drawings	500	1,000
	17,000	33,000
	£50,000	

36.7 The financial statements

If the sales, stock and expenses of a partnership were exactly the same as that of a sole trader, then the trading and profit and loss account would be identical with that as prepared for the sole trader. However, a partnership would have an extra section shown under the profit and loss account. This section is called the profit and loss **appropriation account**, and it is in this account that the distribution of profits is shown. The heading to the trading and profit and loss account does not include the words 'appropriation account'. It is purely an accounting custom not to include it in the heading.

The trading and profit and loss account of Taylor and Clarke from the details given would appear as shown in Exhibit 36.2.

Exhibit 36.2

Taylor and Clarke
Trading and Profit and Loss Account
for the year ended 31 December 2009

(Trading Account – same as for sole trader)
(Profit and Loss Account – same as for sole trader)
Profit and loss appropriation account

	£	£	£
Net profit			50,000
Interest on drawings:			
Taylor		500	
Clarke		1,000	1,500
			51,500
Less:			
Interest on capital:			
Taylor	1,000		
Clarke	3,000	4,000	
Salary		20,000	24,000
			27,500
Balance of profits shared:			
Taylor (three-fifths)		16,500	
Clarke (two-fifths)		11,000	27,500
			27,500

36.8 Fixed and fluctuating capital accounts

There is a choice available in partnership accounts. Partnerships can operate either fixed capital accounts plus current accounts, or fluctuating capital accounts. Each option is described below, with a final comment on which is generally preferable.

Fixed capital accounts plus current accounts

With **fixed capital accounts**, the capital account for each partner remains year by year at the figure of capital put into the business by the partners. The profits, interest on capital, and the salaries to which the partner may be entitled are then credited to a separate current account for the partner, and the drawings and the interest on drawings are debited to it. The balance of the current account at the end of each financial year will then represent the amount of undrawn (or withdrawn) profits. A credit balance will be undrawn profits, while a debit balance will be drawings in excess of the profits to which the partner is entitled.

Using the financial information from Sections 36.6 and 36.7 for Taylor and Clarke their capital and current accounts, assuming drawings of £12,000 for Taylor and £20,000 for Clarke, would appear as follows:

Taylor

Dr		**Capital Account**		Cr
		2009		£
		Jan 1 Bank		20,000

Clarke

Dr		**Capital Account**		Cr
		2009		£
		Jan 1 Bank		60,000

Taylor

Dr		**Current Account**		Cr
2009	£	2009		£
Dec 31 Cash: Drawings	12,000	Dec 31 Profit and loss		
Dec 31 Profit and loss		appropriation account:		
appropriation account:		Interest on capital		1,000
Interest on drawings	500	Share of profits		16,500
Dec 31 Balance c/d	5,000			
	17,500			17,500
		2010		
		Jan 1 Balance b/d		5,000

Clarke

Dr		**Current Account**		Cr
2009	£	2009		£
Dec 31 Cash: Drawings	20,000	Dec 31 Profit and loss		
Dec 31 Profit and loss		appropriation account:		
appropriation account:		Interest on capital		3,000
Interest on drawings	1,000	Share of profits		11,000
Dec 31 Balance c/d	13,000	Salary		20,000
	34,000			34,000
		2010		
		Jan 1 Balance b/d		13,000

Notice that the salary of Clarke was not paid to him but was merely credited to his account. If in fact it was paid in addition to his drawings, the £20,000 cash paid would have been debited to the current account, changing the £13,000 credit balance into a £7,000 debit balance.

Examiners often ask for the capital accounts and current accounts to be shown in columnar form. For the previous accounts of Taylor and Clarke, these would appear as follows:

Capital Accounts

	Taylor	Clarke			Taylor	Clarke
	£	£	2009		£	£
			Jan 1 Bank		20,000	60,000

Current Accounts

	Taylor	Clarke		Taylor	Clarke
2009	£	£	**2009**	£	£
Dec 31 Cash: Drawings	12,000	20,000	Dec 31 Interest on capital	1,000	3,000
Dec 31 Interest on			Dec 31 Share of profits	16,500	11,000
drawings	500	1,000	Dec 31 Salary	–	20,000
Dec 31 Balances c/d	5,000	13,000			
	17,500	34,000		17,500	34,000
			2010		
			Jan 1 Balances b/d	5,000	13,000

Fluctuating capital accounts

In this arrangement of **fluctuating capital accounts** the distribution of profits would be credited to the capital account, and the drawings and interest on drawings is debited. Therefore, the balance on the capital account will change each year, i.e. it will fluctuate.

If fluctuating capital accounts had been kept for Taylor and Clarke, they would have appeared:

Taylor
Capital Account

Dr				Cr
2009	£	**2009**		£
Dec 31 Cash: Drawings	12,000	Jan 1 Bank		20,000
Dec 31 Profit and loss		Dec 31 Profit and loss		
appropriation account:		appropriation account:		
Interest on drawings	500	Interest on capital		1,000
Dec 31 Balance c/d	25,000	Share of profits		16,500
	37,500			37,500
		2010		
		Jan 1 Balance b/d		25,000

Clarke
Capital Account

Dr				Cr
2009	£	**2009**		£
Dec 31 Cash: Drawings	20,000	Jan 1 Bank		60,000
Dec 31 Profit and loss		Dec 31 Profit and loss		
appropriation account:		appropriation account:		
Interest on drawings	1,000	Interest on capital		3,000
Dec 31 Balance c/d	73,000	Salary		20,000
		Share of profits		11,000
	94,000			94,000
		2010		
		Jan 1 Balance b/d		73,000

Fixed capital accounts preferred

The keeping of fixed capital accounts plus current accounts is considered preferable to operating fluctuating capital accounts. When partners are taking out greater amounts than the share of the profits that they are entitled to, it is shown up by a debit balance on the current account and so acts as a warning.

36.9 Where no partnership agreement exists

Where no formal partnership agreement exists – either express or implied – Section 24 of the Partnership Act 1890 governs the situation. The accounting content of this section states:

● Profits and losses are to be shared equally.
● There is to be no interest allowed on capital.
● No interest is to be charged on drawings.
● Salaries are not allowed.
● If a partner puts a sum of money into a business in excess of the capital he or she has agreed to subscribe, that partner is entitled to interest at the rate of 5% per annum on such an advance.

This section applies where there is no agreement. There may be an agreement not by a partnership deed but in a letter, or it may be implied by conduct – for instance, when a partner signs a balance sheet that shows profits shared in some ratio other than equally. Where a dispute arises as to whether agreement exists or not, and this cannot be resolved by the partners, only the courts will be competent to decide.

36.10 The balance sheet

The capital side of the balance sheet will appear as follows for our example. Note that figures in brackets, e.g. '(20,000)', is an accounting convention indicating a negative amount.

Balance Sheet as at 31 December 2009

	£ Taylor	£ Clarke	£ Total
Capital accounts			
Balance	20,000	60,000	80,000
Current accounts			
Interest on capital	1,000	3,000	
Share of profits	16,500	11,000	
Salary	–	20,000	
	17,500	34,000	
Less Drawings	(12,000)	(20,000)	
Interest on drawings	(500)	(1,000)	
	5,000	13,000	18,000

If one of the current accounts had finished in debit – for instance, if the current account of Taylor had finished up as £5,000 debit – the figure of £5,000 would appear in brackets and the balances would appear net in the totals column:

	Taylor	Clarke	
	£	£	£
Closing balance	(5,000)	13,000	8,000

If the net figure, for example, the £8,000 just shown, turned out to be a debit figure, then this would be deducted from the total of the fixed capital accounts.

36.11 A fully worked exercise

We can now look at a fully worked exercise covering nearly all the main points shown in this chapter.

Kidd and Mellor are in partnership. They share profits in the ratio: Kidd three-fifths to Mellor two-fifths. The following trial balance was extracted as at 31 March 2009:

Trial balance as at 31 March 2009

	Dr £	Cr £
Equipment at cost	26,000	
Motor vehicles at cost	36,800	
Provision for depreciation at 31.3.2008:		
Equipment		7,800
Motor vehicles		14,720
Stock at 31 March 2008	99,880	
Debtors and creditors	83,840	65,100
Cash at bank	2,460	
Cash in hand	560	
Sales		361,480
Purchases	256,520	
Salaries	45,668	
Office expenses	1,480	
Motor expenses	2,252	
Heating and lighting	2,000	
Current accounts at 31.3.2008:		
Kidd		5,516
Mellor		4,844
Capital accounts:		
Kidd		86,000
Mellor		50,000
Drawings:		
Kidd	16,000	
Mellor	22,000	
	595,460	595,460

A set of final accounts for the year ended 31 March 2009 for the partnership are to be drawn up. The following notes are applicable at 31 March 2009:

(i)   Stock at 31 March 2009 was valued at £109,360.
(ii)   Office expenses owing £440.
(iii) Provision for depreciation: motor vehicles 20% of cost, equipment 10% of cost.
(iv)   Charge interest on capital at 6%.
(v)   Charge interest on drawings: Kidd £628, Mellor £892.
(vi)   Charge £15,000 for salary for Mellor.

The financial statements are now shown in Exhibit 36.3.

Exhibit 36.3

Kidd and Mellor
Trading and Profit and Loss Account for the year ended 31 March 2009

	£	£	£
Sales			361,480
Less Cost of sales:			
Opening stock		99,880	
Add Purchases		256,520	
		356,400	
Less Closing stock		109,360	247,040
Gross profit			114,440
Less Expenses:			
Salaries*		45,668	
Heating and lighting		2,000	
Office expenses (1,480 + 440)		1,920	
Motor expenses		2,252	
Depreciation: Motor vehicles	7,360		
Equipment	2,600	9,960	61,800
Net profit			52,640
Add Interest on drawings: Kidd		628	
Mellor		892	1,520
			54,160
Less Interest on capital: Kidd		5,160	
Mellor		3,000	8,160
			46,000
Less Salary: Mellor			15,000
			31,000
Balance of profits shared: Kidd (³/₅ths)		18,600	
Mellor (²/₅ths)		12,400	31,000
			31,000

*Does not include partner's salary.

Kidd and Mellor
Balance Sheet as at 31 March 2009

	Cost £	Depreciation £	NBV £
Fixed assets			
Equipment	26,000	10,400	15,600
Motor vehicles	36,800	22,080	14,720
	62,800	32,480	30,320
Current assets			
Stock	109,360		
Debtors	83,840		
Bank	2,460		
Cash	560	196,220	
Less Current liabilities			
Creditors	65,100		
Expenses owing	440	65,540	
Net Current assets			130,680
			161,000

	Kidd	Mellor	Total
Capital accounts			
Balance	86,000	50,000	136,000
Current accounts			
Balances as at 1.4.2008	5,516	4,844	
Add Interest on capital	5,160	3,000	
Add Salary	–	15,000	
Add Share of profits	18,600	12,400	
	29,276	35,244	
Less Drawings	(16,000)	(22,000)	
Less Interest on drawings	(628)	(892)	
Balances as at 31.3.2009	12,648	12,352	25,000
			161,000

Chapter summary

- Partnerships are formed with two or more partners carrying on in business with a view to making a profit.
- There are two types of partnership, an unlimited and a limited partnership.
- Where there is a limited partnership there must be at least one unlimited partner within the partnership. Limited partnerships should be registered with the Registrar of Companies and the Limited Partnership Act 1907 must be complied with.
- Limited partners cannot withdraw any of the capital they invested in the partnership nor may they take part in the management of the partnership.
- It is advisable for all partnerships to draw up a Partnership Agreement detailing the accounting requirements of the partnership (Section 36.5).
- If there is no partnership agreement then the provisions of the Partnership Act 1890 will apply (Section 36.9).
- The partners may use either fixed or fluctuating capital accounts.

● The financial statements of a partnership are: trading and profit and loss account that has an additional section called the 'appropriation account' and balance sheet. The balance sheet will show the capital and current accounts of all the partners.

EXERCISES

36.1 Stead and Jackson are partners in a retail business in which they share profits and losses equally. The balance on the partners' capital and current accounts at the year end 31 December 2009 were as follows:

	Capital Account £	Current Account £
Stead	24,000	2,300 Cr
Jackson	16,000	3,500 Cr

During the year, Stead had drawings amounting to £15,000 and Jackson £19,000. Jackson was to receive a partnership salary of £5,000 for extra duties undertaken. The net profit of the partnership, before taking any of the above into account, was £45,000.

You are required to:

(a) draw up the appropriation account for the partnership for the year ended 31 December 2009.

(b) show the partners' capital and current accounts.

36.2X Wain, Brown and Cairns own a garage, and the partners share profits and losses in the ratio of Wain 50%, Brown 30% and Cairns 20%. Their financial year end is 31 March 2009 and the following details were extracted from their books on that date:

	Wain £	Brown £	Cairns £
Capital account balances	30,000	50,000	70,000
Current account balances	2,400 Cr	3,100 Cr	5,700 Cr
Partnership salaries	10,000	8,000	–
Drawings	12,000	15,050	14,980

The net profit for the year ended 31 March 2009 amounted to £60,000 before taking any of the above into account.

You are required to:

(a) prepare an appropriation account for the year ended 31 March 2009.

(b) draw up the partners' capital and current accounts in columnar form for the year ended 31 March 2009.

36.3X The following balances were extracted from the books of Bradford and Taylor as at 31 December 2009:

		£
Capital accounts		
	Bradford	40,000
	Taylor	30,000
Current accounts		
	Bradford	3,450 Cr
	Taylor	2,680 Dr
Drawings		
	Bradford	8,000
	Taylor	12,000
	Net profit for the year	44,775

The following information is also available from their partnership agreement:
(i)   The partners are entitled to receive 5% interest on capital.
(ii) Taylor is to receive a partnership salary of £6,000.
(iii) Interest is to be charged on drawings as follows: Bradford £200; Taylor £125.
(iv) Bradford and Taylor are to share profits and losses in the ratio 3:2.

Required:
(*a*) Show the profit and loss appropriation account for the year ended 31 December 2009.
(*b*) Show the partners' capital and current accounts for the year ended 31 December 2009.
(*c*) Show how the profits and losses would be distributed and how much each partner would receive if there was no partnership agreement.

36.4 Simpson and Young are in partnership, sharing profits and losses in the ratio 3:2. At the close of business on 30 June 2009 the following trial balance was extracted from their books:

	Dr	Cr
	£	£
Buildings	28,000	
Motor vans (cost £16,000)	11,000	
Office equipment (cost £8,400)	5,600	
Stock 1 July 2009	18,000	
Purchases	184,980	
Sales		254,520
Wages and salaries	32,700	
Rent, rates and insurance	3,550	
Electricity	980	
Stationery and printing	420	
Motor expenses	3,480	
General office expenses	1,700	
Debtors and creditors	28,000	15,200
Capital accounts: Simpson		50,000
Young		20,000
Drawings: Simpson	10,000	
Young	5,000	
Current accounts: Simpson		640
Young		300
Cash at bank	7,250	
	340,660	340,660

Notes:

(i) Interest is to be allowed on capital accounts at the rate of 10% per annum, and no interest is to be charged on drawings.

(ii) Rates prepaid at 30 June 2009 amount to £250.

(iii) Wages due at 30 June 2009 are £500.

(iv) Provision for depreciation is as follows: motor van at 20% per annum on cost; office equipment at 10% using the reducing balance method.

(v) Stock 30 June 2009 was valued at £19,000.

Required:

Prepare the trading and profit and loss appropriation account for the year ended 30 June 2009, and a balance sheet as at that date.

36.5X Kirkham and Keeling are in partnership, sharing profits and losses in the ratio of 3:2. Their partnership agreement also provides for interest on capital to be given to the partners at 10% per annum, but no interest may be charged on drawings. The following trial balance was drawn up at the end of the financial year:

Trial Balance of Kirkham and Keeling as at 30 June 2009

	£	£
Premises	59,200	
Motor vehicles (cost £30,000)	24,000	
Computer equipment (cost £12,000 at 1.7.2007)	8,000	
Cash at bank	12,500	
Debtors	56,000	
Creditors		30,400
Sales		509,040
Purchases	369,960	
Stock 1 July 2008	36,000	
Salaries	65,400	
Electricity	1,960	
Telephone	840	
Motor expenses	3,960	
Printing, stationery and advertising	3,000	
Rates and insurance	7,100	
General expenses	3,400	
Capital accounts: Kirkham		100,000
Keeling		40,000
Current accounts: Kirkham		1,280
Keeling		600
Drawings: Kirkham	20,000	
Keeling	10,000	
	681,320	681,320

Notes:

(i) The closing stock has been valued at £38,000.

(ii) Insurance paid in advance at 30 June 2009 amounted to £1,000.

(iii) Motor expenses owing at 30 June 2009 amounted to £400.

(iv) You are to provide for depreciation on the motor vehicles at 20% on cost. The computer equipment is expected to last three years from the date of purchase.

You are required to prepare the trading and profit and loss appropriation account for the year ended 30 June 2009 and a balance sheet as at that date.

36.6 Bhayani and Donnell are in partnership, sharing profits and losses in the ratio 2:1. The following trial balance was extracted after the preparation of their trading account for the year ended 31 December:

	Dr	Cr
	£	£
Provision for depreciation: Vehicles		3,000
Provision for depreciation: Fittings		2,000
Bank balance		950
Drawings: Bhayani	2,000	
Donnell	600	
Vehicles (at cost)	35,000	
Fittings (at cost)	12,000	
Premises (at cost)	20,000	
Rent received		500
Debtors and creditors	25,700	15,600
Current accounts: Bhayani	600	
Donnell	nil	nil
Provision for doubtful debts		950
Gross profit		32,000
Heating and lighting	1,400	
Wages and salaries	4,100	
Cash	600	
Capital accounts: Bhayani		35,000
Donnell		12,000
	102,000	102,000

At 31 December the following information needs to be taken into consideration:
(i) The provision for doubtful debts is to be maintained at 3% of debtors.
(ii) Rent received of £100 has been paid in advance.
(iii) A heating invoice of £100 has yet to be paid.
(iv) £200 of wages have been prepaid.
(v) Depreciation needs to be provided for on the following basis:
  ● vehicles at 10% straight line method
  ● fittings at 15% reducing (diminishing) balance method.
(vi) The partnership agreement provides for the following:
  ● interest on drawings is charged at 6% per annum
  ● interest on capital is allowed at 8% per annum
  ● Donnell is to receive a salary of £3,263.

You are required to:
(a) prepare the partnership profit and loss account for the year ended 31 December
(b) prepare the partnership appropriation account for the year ended 31 December
(c) prepare each partner's current account at 31 December
(d) prepare the partnership balance sheet as at 31 December.

City & Guilds Pitman qualifications

36.7X Jane Hanford and Kevin Pearson are partners in a travel agency. They share profits and losses equally. On 31 March 2009 the business's final accounts were prepared. The following balances remained in the accounts.

	£
Cash at bank	3,460
Expenses due	240
Expenses prepaid	160
Furniture and equipment at net book value	45,000
Net profit for the year ended 31 March 2009	31,280
Trade creditors	6,300
Trade debtors	7,500
Capital accounts	
Jane Hanford	25,000
Kevin Pearson	20,000
Drawings for the year	
Jane Hanford	17,000
Kevin Pearson	13,000
Current account balances at 1 April 2008	
Jane Hanford	2,100
Kevin Pearson	1,200

From this information the partners' current accounts were prepared.

Current Accounts

	Jane Hanford £	Kevin Pearson £		Jane Hanford £	Kevin Pearson £
Drawings	17,000	13,000	Opening Balances	2,100	1,200
Balances c/f	740	3,840	Net Profit	15,640	15,640
	17,740	16,840		17,740	16,840

(*a*) Prepare the business's balance sheet as at 31 March 2009.

(*b*) Jane and Kevin want to expand the business but they disagree how this should be financed. Jane thinks that they ought to get a loan from the bank. Kevin thinks they ought to take on a new partner who could provide additional finance. What method of finance do you think they should choose? Give reasons for your choice.

AQA

CHAPTER 37

Limited company accounts

Learning objectives

After you have studied this chapter you should be able to:

- appreciate the reasons for forming a limited company
- understand the features of a limited company
- distinguish between a public limited company, private limited company and a company limited by guarantee
- appreciate the legal status of a limited company
- distinguish between the different types of share capital
- distinguish between ordinary and preference shares and debentures
- understand and prepare the financial statements of limited companies
- appreciate the concept of reserves and distinguish between revenue and capital reserves.

37.1 Introduction

In the previous chapter we considered partnerships which were owned and run by more than one person. Another type of business organisation is a **limited company**. If a business wishes to expand it will inevitably require additional capital; forming a limited company makes it possible to raise the required funds and also provides additional features that are attractive to the owner(s).

37.2 Features of a limited company

Many people consider it more beneficial to form a limited company rather than operate as either a sole trader or partnership for several reasons:

- **Limited liability** – the capital of a limited company is divided into **shares**. Shares can be of any nominal amount, for example, 10p, 25p, £1, £5, £10 per share. To become a member of a limited company, or a **shareholder**, a person must buy one or more of the shares.

If a shareholder has paid in full for the shares, their liability is limited to the amount they have paid for the shares. If the company loses all its assets, the most a shareholder can lose is the amount they paid for their shares. They are not liable to pay anything more out of their private money in respect of the company's losses. If, however, a shareholder has only partly paid for their shares they are required to pay the balance owing on the shares but nothing else.

This is known as **limited liability** and the company is known as a **limited company**. This simply means that shareholders may lose the amount invested in the company but their personal assets are safe, so encouraging investment but limiting the financial risk. At the same time limited companies are able to attract investments from a large number of people and organisations and raise large amounts of capital.

- **Separate legal entity** – one of the most important features of a limited company is its status in law as a **separate legal entity**. This means that the company is treated separately from the shareholders who own the company. Thus, a company may sue someone in its own name and likewise be sued in the company name.
- **Raising capital** – one of the main reasons for forming a limited company is to raise large amounts of capital to finance the business. The way in which companies raise capital is by issuing shares to prospective investors. In smaller private companies shares are issued to family and business colleagues who then become shareholders (i.e. members) of the company. Large public limited companies issue their shares to the general public, hence the name 'public' limited companies.

37.3 Public and private companies and companies limited by guarantee

There are two classes of company, the **public limited company** (abbreviated PLC) and the **private limited company** (abbreviated Ltd). In the UK, private limited companies far outnumber public limited companies. A public company must have a minimum of two **directors**.

A private limited company is usually, but not always, a smaller business, and may be formed by one or more people and have at least one director who may be the only shareholder. It is defined by the 2006 Companies Act as a company that is not a public company. The main differences between a private company and a public company are that a private company:

- can have an authorised share capital of less than £50,000, and from October 2009 need have no authorised share capital at all
- cannot offer its shares for subscription to the public at large, whereas public companies can.

Public limited companies are required to have a Company Secretary but this is no longer the case for private limited companies since the implementation of the Companies Act 2006. However, a private limited company may decide to have a company secretary, and in this case it is up to the company to specify the Company Secretary's duties and responsibilities.

Companies limited by guarantee do not have a share capital. Instead they rely on the guarantee of the members to contribute to the assets in the event of insolvency. Such companies would include charities and educational organisations.

37.4 Legal status of limited companies

Limited companies are governed by the various Companies Acts 1985, 1989 and more recently the Companies Act 2006. The 2006 Act will eventually replace the 1985 and 1989 Acts when all its sections are finally implemented in October 2009.

As mentioned above one of the main advantages of forming a limited company is that the company has its own separate legal identity from those of the shareholders and directors.

Under the Companies Act 2006 there are significant changes to be implemented in October 2009 concerning the formation of companies. Companies formed from that date will be required to state in their Memorandum of Association the following:

- that the subscribers would like to form a company under the Act
- that all subscribers wish to become members of the company and have at least one share each.

A company is also required to have Articles of Association which must be registered. The Articles contain the company's regulations and as such are often referred to as the *internal rule book*.

37.5 Share capital

The **share capital** is the capital of a company which is divided into shares which are then bought and owned by the shareholders. There are two main types of share capital namely, **authorised share capital** and **issued share capital**, it is important to distinguish between the two:

1 **Authorised share capital** – the total of the share capital that the company would be allowed to issue also called the 'nominal capital'.

   Note: In the new Companies Act 2006 a company will no longer be required to have authorised share capital and only the issued/allotted share capital will be included in the financial statements. However, since many of the examining bodies may still be using existing syllabuses when setting examination papers it was felt necessary to include the definition of authorised share capital.

2 **Issued share capital** – the amount of share capital actually issued and allotted to shareholders.

   If all of the authorised share capital has been issued then items (1) and (2) above are the same. The authorised share capital is included in the Balance Sheet as *a note to the accounts* for information only, whereas the issued capital is included in the *Financed by* section. If all the share capital has not been issued then the amount of the authorised share capital will be greater than the issued capital. The difference between the two being the *unissued capital* (see below).

There are also other meanings relating to share capital:

- **Called-up capital** – where only part of the amounts payable on each share has been asked for, the total amount requested on all the shares is known as the 'called-up capital'.
- **Uncalled capital** – the amount that is to be received in future, but which has not yet been requested.
- **Calls in arrear** – the amount for which payment has been requested (i.e. called for), but has not yet been paid by shareholders.
- **Paid-up capital** – the total of the amount of share capital that has been paid for by shareholders.

Exhibit 37.1 illustrates these different meanings.

Exhibit 37.1 **Better Enterprises Ltd**

Better Enterprises Ltd was formed with the legal right to be able to issue 100,000 shares of £1 each. The company has actually issued 75,000 shares. None of the shares has yet been fully paid-up; so far the company has made calls of 80p (£0.80) per share. All of the calls have been paid by shareholders, except for £200 owing from one particular shareholder. On this basis, therefore:

(a) *Authorised (or nominal) share capital is £100,000.
(b) Issued share capital is £75,000.
(c) Called-up capital is (75,000 × £0.80) = £60,000.
(d) Calls in arrear amounted to £200.
(e) Paid-up capital is £60,000 less (d) £200 = £59,800.

*See note above re authorised share capital.

37.6 Shares and dividends

Two main types of shares are issued by companies:

1 **Ordinary shares** – these are by far the most popular way that companies use to raise capital. Ordinary shareholders will receive a variable share of the profits in the form of a **dividend** based on the number of shares that each shareholder owns. If a company makes a loss no dividend would likely to be paid.

As owners of an ordinary share, shareholders can attend the **annual general meeting** and other company meetings and vote on agenda items. As stated earlier if a company fails, shareholders could lose all their investment since other creditors have first call on any assets left in the company.

2 **Preference shares** – shareholders buy these shares knowing that they will get an agreed percentage rate of dividend. They will be paid this agreed amount before dividends are paid to ordinary shareholders. Preference shareholders can attend company meetings but have no voting rights.

Dividends payable – a successful company is very likely to pay a dividend based on its net profit. It is, however, unlikely that all this profit will be available for distribution since the company may decide to retain a proportion in the form of **revenue reserves**.

Exhibit 37.2 shows how dividends are distributed between ordinary and preference shareholders.

Exhibit 37.2

Dee Dee Transport has issued 30,000 5% preference shares of £1 each and 300,000 ordinary shares of £1 each, which have all been taken up. The profit available for dividends over the past four years has been:

Year 1 – £12,000
Year 2 – £19,500
Year 3 – £24,000
Year 4 – £34,500

The profit would have been distributed as follows:

Year	1	2	3	4
	£	£	£	£
Profits available for dividends	12,000	19,500	24,000	34,500
Preference shares	1,500	1,500	1,500	1,500
Balance for Ordinary shares	(3.5%) 10,500	(6%) 18,000	(7.5%) 22,500	(11%) 33,000

In the above example, the preference share dividend remains constant at 5% whereas the ordinary share dividend depends upon the success or otherwise of the company's performance. In the above case the company has achieved a yearly growth in profits.

37.7 Debentures

A **debenture** is a loan which is taken out by a limited company. A company may borrow money from a bank or from other sources and when this happens a debenture certificate is issued by the lender. The features of a debenture include:

- A fixed rate of interest is paid by the company to the investor annually (the **debenture interest**).
- The interest must be paid irrespective of whether the company makes a profit.
- Debentures are often secured on the fixed assets of the business, thereby making it a safer investment for the investor.
- If the company gets into financial difficulties the debenture holders are one of the first claimants to be paid.

37.8 The financial statements of a limited company

Trading and profit and loss accounts

The trading and profit and loss account for limited companies are prepared in the same way as they would be for sole traders and partnerships. While there is no difference to the trading account the profit and loss account does contain *two* additional types of expense:

1 **Directors' remuneration** – **directors** are appointed by the shareholders and are employees of the company. As such they are entitled to receive what is termed **directors' remuneration**, in other words pay in return for their services to the company. Such remuneration is charged to the profit and loss account.
2 **Debenture interest** – this is interest that has to be paid each year to the debenture holder for lending the company money. As mentioned in Section 37.7 the interest is usually at a fixed rate and has to be paid even if the company makes a loss.

The layout of a trading and profit and loss account of a limited company showing where the above new items would appear is as follows:

Name of Company . . . Limited
Trading and Profit and Loss Account for the year ended . . .

	£	£
Sales		xxx
Less Cost of goods sold		
Opening stock	xxx	
Add: Purchases	xxx	
	xxx	
Less Closing stock	xxx	
Cost of sales		xxx
Gross profit		**xxx**
Less Expenses:		
Directors' remuneration	**xx**	
Debenture interest	**xx**	
Other overhead expenses	xx	
		xxx
Net profit		**xxx**

Appropriation account* (see page 473)

This section of the accounts shows how the net profits are to be apportioned, i.e. how the profits are to be taxed and the balance distributed. *Note that taxation is outside the scope of this book.* Items for distribution include:.

● dividends declared
● transfer to and from reserves
● amounts of goodwill written off
● amounts of **preliminary expenses** written off. (*Note:* these are all the costs incurred when a company is formed.)

Exhibit 37.3 shows the distribution of the company's profit for the first three years of trading as a new business.

Exhibit 37.3

Delta Ltd has a share capital of 200,000 ordinary shares of £1 each and 100,000 – 5% preference share of £1 each.

- The net profits for the first three year of business ending on 31 December are as follows:
    - 2009 = £35,936
    - 2010 = £40,728
    - 2011 = £47,500
- Transfers to reserves are made as follows:
    - 2009 = Nil
    - 2010 = General reserve £20,000
    - 2011 = Fixed asset replacement reserve £25,000
- Dividends were declared for each year on the preference shares and on the ordinary shares at:
    - 2009 = 6%
    - 2010 = 8%
    - 2011 = 10%

The appropriation section of the trading and profit and loss account for Delta Ltd for the three years would be as follows:

Delta Ltd
Profit and Loss Appropriation Accounts (1) For the year ended 31 December 2009

	£	£
Net profit for the year		35,936
Less Appropriations:		
Dividends:		
Preference dividend 5% (5% × £100,000)	5,000	
Ordinary dividend 6% (6% × £200,000)	12,000	(17,000)
Retained profits carried forward to next year		18,936

(2) For the year ended 31 December 2010

	£	£
Net profit for the year		40,728
Add Retained profits brought forward from last year		18,936
		59,664
Less Appropriations:		
Transfer to general reserve	20,000	
Dividends:		
Preference dividend 5% (5% × £100,000)	5,000	
Ordinary dividend 8% (8% × £200,000)	16,000	(41,000)
Retained profits carried forward to next year		18,664

(3) For the year ended 31 December 2011

	£	£
Net profit for the year		47,500
Add Retained profits brought forward from last year		18,664
		66,164
Less Appropriations:		
Transfer to fixed assets replacement reserve	25,000	
Dividends:		
Preference dividend 5% (5% × £100,000)	5,000	
Ordinary dividend 10% (10% × £200,000)	20,000	50,000
Retained profits carried forward to next year		16,164

Balance sheet

Exhibit 37.4 shows a balance sheet for a limited company (for internal use) together with explanations.

Exhibit 37.4

Balance Sheet as at 31 December 2009
Letters in brackets (A) to (F) refer to the notes following the balance sheet

		£	£	£
Fixed assets				
Intangible assets	(A)			
Goodwill				80,000
Tangible assets	(B)			
Buildings			72,000	
Machinery			44,800	
Motor vehicles			19,200	136,000
				216,000
Current assets				
Stock		48,000		
Debtors		24,000		
Bank		32,000	104,000	
Creditors: Amounts falling due within one year	(C)			
Dividends payable		8,000		
Creditors		40,000	48,000	
Net current assets	(D)			56,000
Total assets less current liabilities				272,000
Creditors: amounts falling due after more than one year	(E)			
Debenture loans				64,000
				208,000
Capital and reserves				
Called-up share capital	(F)			160,000
Revenue reserves				
General reserve				40,000
Profit and loss account				8,000
				208,000

Notes:
(A) Intangible assets are those not having a 'physical' existence; for instance, you can see and touch tangible assets under (B), i.e. buildings, machinery, etc., but you cannot see and touch goodwill, or intellectual property rights, etc.
(B) Tangible fixed assets are shown under a separate heading. Notice that figures are shown net of depreciation. In a note accompanying the accounts, the cost and depreciation on these assets would be given.
(C) Only items payable within one year go under this heading.
(D) The term 'net current assets' replaces the more familiar term of 'working capital'.
(E) These particular debentures are repayable several years hence. If they had been payable within one year, they would have been shown under (C).
(F) An analysis of share capital will be given in supplementary notes to the balance sheet.

Note: The latest examining boards syllabuses for units containing limited company accounts are still including an Appropriation Account. Therefore, appropriation accounts have been included both above in Section 37.8 and worked examples in Section 37.13. However, in recent accounting standards the distribution of a company's profit is shown as a note to the accounts. The note is similar to the appropriation account.

37.9 Reserves in the balance sheet

You will notice in the above balance sheet under the *Capital and reserves* section the heading **Revenue reserves**. Reserves are profits of the company which are transferred to a **reserve account** for use in future years. There are two types of reserves in a company – these are revenue reserves and capital reserves.

Revenue reserves are reserves that are transferred from the trading activities of the company, i.e. the net profit, and set aside for future use by the company. They often appear under the heading of *General reserve*. Another revenue reserve is retained profit, i.e. the balance of profit remaining after distribution of dividends and transfers to reserve accounts. This figure is shown at the bottom of the appropriation account as **Retained profit** *carried forward to next year* and is subsequently included in the balance sheet where it is shown as *Profit and loss account*.

Capital reserves, unlike revenue reserves, cannot be used for payment of dividends. The two most common capital reserves are the *share premium account* and the *revaluation reserve account*.

The **share premium** account arises when shares are issued at a premium, i.e. above their par or nominal value. For example a company may wish to expand its business and require additional funds. The nominal value of its ordinary shares is £1 but the valuation of each share is calculated to be £3. The extra funds acquired in this case, £2 per share, will be put into the share premium account while the remainder will be part of the ordinary share capital.

The revaluation reserve account arises when an asset of the company is revalued, for example, premises and buildings may have been purchased when the company was first established many years ago and since then have increased in value. The asset is thus revalued and the new valuation figure is shown in the assets section in the balance sheet. The difference between the original value, i.e. the cost price and the revaluation figure, is shown in the balance sheet under the heading reserves and described as 'revaluation reserve account'.

Note: It is thought by many that reserves represent money available whenever the company needs extra funding but this is not the case. Both revenue and capital reserves are not cash funds, they are reserves which are represented by the net assets owned by the company. The assets belong to the company which is owned by the shareholders.

37.10 Investments

Where a company buys shares in another company as an investment, the investment is shown as an asset in the balance sheet. It is shown as a separate item in the accounts between the fixed assets and the current assets. The market value of such investments is shown in the balance sheet as a note in brackets, for example:

Balance Sheet (Extracts)

	£
Investments at cost (market value £100,000)	75,000

In the above case, the market value is above cost. If the market value falls below cost, then the difference is written off to the profit and loss account, so that the balance sheet will then show the investment at the written-down figure.

37.11 Loan capital

The term **loan capital** includes money owing on debentures, and loans from banks and other sources not repayable in the near future.

37.12 Shareholders' funds

This is the amount of share capital and reserves 'owned' by the shareholders. In Exhibit 37.5 the **shareholders' funds** of Ashford Ltd would be:

	£
Called-up capital	150,000
General reserve	10,000
Profit and loss account	56,021
Shareholder' funds	216,021

37.13 A fully worked example of the financial statements

Two examples of a limited company's financial statements are now shown as Exhibits 37.5 and 37.6. In the first exhibit new items applicable to limited company accounts are shown while Exhibit 37.6 contains a more complicated example including preference shares and debentures.

Exhibit 37.5

The following trial balance is extracted from the books of an imaginary company called Ashford Ltd as at 31 December 2009. Note that the new items specific to limited companies have been highlighted in bold.

Ashford Ltd
Trial Balance as at 31 December 2009

	Dr £	Cr £
Ordinary share capital		**150,000**
Premises at cost	97,500	
Equipment at cost	82,500	
Provision for depreciation on equipment		23,700
Purchases	302,547	
Sales		475,215
Wages and salaries	61,310	
Directors' remuneration	**20,000**	
General expenses	48,252	
Rates and insurance	6,450	
Electricity	2,324	
Bad debts	1,122	
Provision for doubtful debts		1,291
Debtors	32,676	
Creditors		26,240
Stock as at 1 January 2009	38,534	
Bank	34,651	
Profit and loss account brought forward at 1 January 2009		**51,420**
	727,866	727,866

The following adjustments are needed:

(i)   The issued share capital is divided into 150,000 shares of £1 each and a dividend of 10% has been declared on these shares for 2009.
(ii)   Stock in trade at 31 December 2009 is valued at £43,713.
(iii)   Wages and salaries due at 31 December 2009 amount to £872.
(iv)   Rates and insurance paid in advance at 31 December 2009 amount to £450.
(v)   The provision for doubtful debts is to be increased to £1,407.
(vi)   A depreciation charge is to be made on equipment at the rate of 10% per annum on cost.
(vii) A transfer of £10,000 to a general reserve account is required.

Ashford Ltd
Trading and Profit and Loss Account for the year ended 31 December 2009

	£	£
Sales		475,215
Less Cost of goods sold:		
Opening stock	38,534	
Add Purchases	302,547	
	341,081	
Less Closing stock	43,713	297,368
Gross profit		177,847

		£	£
Less Expenses:			
Salaries and wages (61,310 + 872)		62,182	
Directors' remuneration	(A)	**20,000**	
General expenses		48,252	
Rates and insurance (6,450 – 450)		6,000	
Electricity		2,324	
Bad debts		1,122	
Increase in provision for doubtful debts (1,407 – 1,291)		116	
Depreciation: Equipment		8,250	148,246
Net profit			29,601
Add **Retained profits brought forward from last year**			51,420
			81,021
Less Appropriations:			
Transfer to general reserve		**10,000**	
Ordinary share dividends (10% of 150,000)	(B)	**15,000**	25,000
Retained profits carried forward to next year			56,021

Notes:
(A) Directors' remuneration is shown as an expense in the profit and loss account.
(B) The dividend of 10% is based on the issued ordinary share capital.

Ashford Ltd
Balance Sheet as at 31 December 2009

Fixed assets		£	£	£
Tangible assets	(A)			
Premises			97,500	
Equipment			50,550	148,050
Current assets				
Stock		43,713		
Debtors (32,676 + 450 – 1,407)		31,719		
Bank		34,651	110,083	
Creditors: Amounts falling due within one year				
Creditors (26,240 + 872)		27,112		
Dividend payable		15,000	42,112	
Net current assets				67,971
Total assets less current liabilities				216,021
Capital and reserves	(B)			
Called-up share capital				150,000
Revenue reserves				
General reserve			10,000	
Profit and loss account			56,021	66,021
				216,021

Notes:
(A) Notes to be given in an appendix as to cost, acquisitions and sales in the year and depreciation.
(B) 'Reserves' consist either of those undistributed profits remaining in the appropriation account, or those profits transferred to a reserve account appropriately titled (e.g. general reserve, fixed assets replacement reserve).

Exhibit 37.6

This worked example includes preference shares, debentures and share premium account.

The following trial balance was extracted from the books of an imaginary company called Dobson Ltd as at 31 December 2009:

Dobson Ltd
Trial Balance as at 31 December 2009

	Dr £	Cr £
8% Preference share capital		35,000
Ordinary share capital		125,000
10% Debentures (repayable 2015)		20,000
Share premium		21,000
Profit and loss account b/forward at		
1 January 2009		13,874
Equipment at cost	122,500	
Motor vehicles at cost	99,750	
Provision for depreciation: Equipment		29,400
Provision for depreciation: Motor vehicles		36,225
Stock 1 January 2009	136,132	
Sales		418,250
Purchases	232,225	
Sales returns	4,025	
General expenses	1,240	
Salaries and wages	46,260	
Directors' remuneration	18,750	
Rent, rates and insurance	18,095	
Motor expenses	4,361	
Debenture interest	1,000	
Bank	12,751	
Cash	630	
Debtors	94,115	
Creditors		93,085
	791,834	791,834

The following adjustments are needed:

(i)   Stock at 31.12.09 was £122,000.
(ii) Accrue rent £2,000.
(iii) Accrue debenture interest £1,000.
(iv) Depreciate the equipment at 10% on cost and motor vehicles at 20% on cost.
(v)   Transfer to general reserve £5,000.
(vi) It is proposed to pay the 8% preference dividend and a 10% dividend on the ordinary shares.
(vii) Authorised share capital is £35,000 in preference shares and £200,000 in £1 ordinary shares.

Dobson Ltd
Trading and Profit and Loss for the year ended 31 December 2009

		£	£
Sales			418,250
Less Sales returns			4,025
			414,225
Less Cost of goods sold:			
Opening stock		136,132	
Add Purchases		232,225	
		368,357	
Less Closing stock		122,000	246,357
Gross profit			167,868
Less Expenses:			
Salaries and wages		46,260	
Rent, rates and insurance (18,095 + 2,000)		20,095	
Motor expenses		4,361	
General expenses		1,240	
Directors' remuneration	(A)	18,750	
Debenture interest (1,000 + 1,000)	(B)	2,000	
Depreciation:			
Equipment (10% × 122,500)		12,250	
Motor vehicles (20% × 99,750)		19,950	124,906
Net profit			42,962
Add Retained profits brought forward from last year			13,874
			56,836
Less Appropriations			
Transfer to general reserve		5,000	
Preference share dividend (8% × 35,000)		2,800	
Ordinary share dividend (10% × 125,000)	(C)	12,500	20,300
Retained profits carried forward to next year			36,536

Notes:

(A) Directors' remuneration is shown as an expense in the profit and loss account.

(B) Debenture interest is an expense to be shown in the profit and loss account.

(C) The final dividend of 10% is based on the issued ordinary share capital and *not* on the authorised ordinary share capital.

Dobson Ltd
Balance Sheet as at 31 December 2009

	£	£	£
Fixed assets			
Tangible assets (A)			
Equipment*		80,850	
Motor vehicles*		43,575	124,425
Current assets			
Stock	122,000		
Debtors	94,115		
Bank	12,751		
Cash	630	229,496	
Creditors: Amounts falling due within one year			
Creditors (93,085 + 2,000)	95,085		
Dividends payable: Preference shares	2,800		
: Ordinary shares	12,500		
Debenture interest due	1,000	111,385	
Net current assets			118,111
			242,536
Creditors: Amounts falling due after more than one year			
10% Debentures			20,000
			222,536
Capital and reserves			
Called-up share capital			160,000
Capital reserve			
Share premium (B)			21,000
Revenue reserves			
General reserve			5,000
Profit and loss account			36,536
			222,536

Notes:
(A) Notes to be given in an appendix as to cost, acquisitions and sales in the year and depreciation.
(B) The share premium account is a capital reserve refer to Section 37.9.
(C) 'Reserves' consist either of those undistributed profits remaining in the appropriation account, or those transferred to a reserve account appropriately titled (e.g. general reserve, fixed assets replacement reserve) refer to Section 37.9.

Workings:
Equipment cost £122,500 less depreciation to date £41,650 (£29,400 + £12,250) gives a net book value of £80,850. Motor vehicles cost £99,750 less depreciation to date £56,175 (£36,225 + £19,950) gives a net book value of £43,375.

Chapter summary

- Limited companies are owned by shareholders who appoint directors to manage the company on their behalf.
- There are many features which make forming a limited company attractive to investors including limited liability whereby a shareholder may lose the amount invested in the company but their personal assets are safe.
- Limited companies are a separate legal entity to the shareholders and as such it can sue and be sued in its own name.
- A public company is one that can issue its shares publicly and there is no maximun number of shareholders. It must also have an issued share capital of at least £50,000. A private company must issue its shares privately.
- Authorised share capital is the maximum amount of share capital or number of shares the company would be allowed to issue. Note that in the Companies Act 2006, from October 2009, there will no longer be a requirement to have an authorised share capital.
- Issued share capital is the amount of share capital actually issued to shareholders, i.e. the called-up capital.
- There are two main types of shares: (1) preference shares – here the shareholders get an agreed percentage rate of dividend before the ordinary shareholders receive anything; (2) ordinary shares – the shareholders are entitled to a dividend after the preference shareholders have been paid their dividends. The amount they receive fluctuates depending on the profits available.
- A debenture is a loan to the company upon which a fixed rate of interest is paid annually. The interest must be paid even if the company makes a loss. Debentures are often secured on the assets of the business.
- The financial statements for a limited company consist of a trading and profit and loss account, which includes an appropriation section (see the note in Section 37.8), and a balance sheet.
- Both debenture interest and directors' remuneration must be charged to the profit and loss account.
- Any undistributed profits are carried forward to the next accounting period and must also be shown in the balance sheet. (Note: these can sometimes be referred to as 'retained profits' and 'profit and loss account balance'.)
- Reserve accounts contain appropriated profits that have been transferred for use in future years such as a general reserve or fixed asset reserve account. They are classed as revenue reserves and may be used to distribute as a dividend to shareholders.
- Share premium is another class of reserve that arises when shares are issued above the face or nominal value. The extra amount received above the nominal value is credited to the share premium account. This account is classed as a capital reserve which means it cannot be used to distribute as a dividend to shareholders.

EXERCISES

37.1 Draw up a balance sheet for LMT Ltd from the following as at 31 December 2009 for internal use.

	£
Buildings at cost	45,000
Machinery at cost	24,000
Fixtures at cost	12,000
Stock	18,000
Bank	6,000
Debtors	9,000
Depreciation to date:	
Buildings	18,000
Machinery	7,200
Fixtures	4,800
Authorised share capital: Ordinary shares £1	60,000
Issued share capital: Fully paid	36,000
Debentures: 10%	18,000
Proposed dividend owing	3,000
Creditors	9,000
General reserve	15,000
Profit and loss account (balancing figure, for you to ascertain)	?

37.2X C Blake Ltd has an authorised share capital of 90,000 ordinary shares of £1 each and 10,000 10% preference shares of £1 each. The company's trial balance, extracted after one year of trading, was as follows on 31 December 2009:

	£
Net profit for the year to 31 December 2009	11,340
Debentures	30,000
Issued ordinary share capital, fully paid	60,000
Issued preference share capital, fully paid	10,000
Creditors	3,550
Debtors	4,120
Cash	2,160
Stock	8,800
Provision for doubtful debts	350
Provision for depreciation: Equipment	4,500
Equipment at cost	45,000
Buildings at cost	50,000
Bank (use the balancing figure)	?

The directors decide to transfer £1,500 to the general reserve and to recommend a dividend of 12½% on the ordinary shares. The preference dividend was not paid until after January 2010.

You are required to:
(a) draw up the appropriation account for the year ended 31 December 2009
(b) draft a balance sheet as at 31 December 2009.

37.3 CA Company Ltd, manufacturing agricultural implements, made a net profit of £210,000 for the year to 31 December 2010. Retained profits at 31 December 2009 amounted to £17,000. At the directors' meeting, the following appropriations were agreed:

	£
To be transferred to general reserve	30,000
To be transferred to foreign exchange reserve	16,000

It had also been agreed that a dividend of 10% be proposed on the ordinary share capital. This amounted to 500,000 shares of £2 each. Preference share dividends of 10% have been paid during the year on 250,000 preference shares of £1 each.

You are required to draw up the company's profit and loss appropriation account for the year ended 31 December 2010.

37.4 The trial balance extracted from the books of Chang Ltd at 31 December 2009 was as follows:

	£	£
Share capital		100,000
Unappropriated profits brought forward from last year		34,280
Freehold premises at cost	65,000	
Machinery at cost	55,000	
Provision for depreciation on machinery account		
as at 31 December 2008		15,800
Purchases	201,698	
Sales		316,810
General expenses	32,168	
Wages and salaries	54,207	
Rent	4,300	
Lighting expenses	1,549	
Bad debts	748	
Provision for doubtful debts as at 31 December 2008		861
Debtors	21,784	
Creditors		17,493
Stock in trade as at 31 December 2008	25,689	
Bank balance	23,101	
	485,244	485,244

You are given the following additional information:

(i)   The authorised and issued share capital is divided into 100,000 shares of £1 each.
(ii) Stock in trade as at 31 December 2009 was £29,142.
(iii) Wages and salaries due at 31 December 2009 amounted to £581.
(iv) Rent paid in advance at 31 December 2009 amounted to £300.
(v)   A dividend of £10,000 is proposed for 2009.
(vi) The provision for doubtful debts is to be increased to £938.
(vii) A depreciation charge is to be made on machinery at the rate of 10% per annum at cost.

Required:
Draw up a trading and profit and loss account for the year ended 31 December 2009 and a balance sheet as at 31 December 2009.

37.5X On 30 September 2009, Reynolds Ltd had an authorised capital of £250,000, divided into 200,000 ordinary shares of £1 each and 50,000 7% preference shares of £1 each. All the preference shares were issued and fully paid, while 150,000 of the ordinary shares were issued and fully paid. The company also had a balance on the general reserve account of £45,000 and a balance brought forward on the profit and loss account of £30,000.

During the year ended 30 September 2010, the company made a net profit of £70,000, out of which a transfer of £8,000 was made to the general reserve account. The directors had paid an interim dividend of 6p per share on the ordinary share capital and now propose to pay the preference dividend and a final dividend of 14p per share on the ordinary share capital.

From the information given above you are required to prepare for Reynolds Ltd:

(*a*) a profit and loss appropriation account for the year ended 30 September 2010
(*b*) the capital and reserves section of the balance sheet as at 30 September 2010.

37.6   Jaspa West Ltd has an authorised share capital of £300,000, divided into 200,000 ordinary shares of £1 each and 100,000 8% preference shares of £1 each. The following balances remained in the accounts of the company after the preparation of the trading and profit and loss account for the year ended 31 December 2010:

	Dr	Cr
	£	£
Premises at cost	270,600	
Bank balance		21,400
Heating and lighting prepaid	3,800	
Provision for depreciation on machinery		18,400
Machinery at cost	72,600	
Preference share capital: fully paid		80,000
Ordinary share capital: fully paid		150,000
Profit and loss account b/f: 1 January 2010		92,000
Debtors and creditors	80,000	37,000
Stock	56,000	
Wages and salaries accrued		4,200
Net profit (for the year ended 31 December 2010)		80,000
	483,000	483,000

The directors have recommended:

- the creation of a general reserve, amounting to 40% of the year's net profit
- an ordinary dividend of 4%
- payment of the year's preference dividend.

You are required to:
(*a*) prepare the profit and loss appropriation account for the year ended 31 December 2010
(*b*) prepare the balance sheet as at 31 December 2010.

City & Guilds Pitman qualifications

37.7X   Cityjag plc has an authorised capital of 500,000 £1 ordinary shares and 250,000 £1 (9%) preference shares. The following balances remained in the books after the profit and loss account has been prepared for the year ended 31 December 2010:

	Dr	Cr
	£	£
140,000 £1 ordinary shares		140,000
90,000 £1 (9%) Preference shares		90,000
Profit and loss account balance 1 January 2010		10,000
Premises at cost	180,000	
Motor vehicles at cost	90,200	
Fixtures and fittings at cost	45,000	
Provision for depreciation on motor vehicles		30,200
Provision for depreciation on fixtures and fittings		25,000
Trade debtors and trade creditors	7,700	9,000
Bank	8,500	
Expenses prepaid and accrued	2,000	1,000
Stock at 31 December 2010	21,800	
General reserve		10,000
Net trading profit for the year ended 31 December 2010		40,000
	355,200	355,200

The directors of Cityjag plc have decided to transfer £20,000 to the general reserve; to recommend payment of the preference share dividend; and to recommend a dividend of 11% on ordinary shares.

From the information given, you are required to prepare for Cityjag plc

(*a*) a profit and loss appropriation account for the year ended 31 December 2010
(*b*) a balance sheet as at 31 December 2010.

NEAB (GCSE)

37.8X   Vivex plc's financial year ended on 31 March 2009. On this date the following balances remained in the company's books after the preparation of the profit and loss account.

	£000
Fixed assets at net book value	9,600
Rent receivable	60
Issued capital, £1 ordinary shares fully paid	7,000
Provision for doubtful debts	35
Trade debtors	695
Debenture interest due	40
Debentures (10%)	800
Expenses prepaid	30
Share premium	1,200
Profit and loss account balance, 1 April 2008	386
Trade creditors	374
General reserve, 1 April 2008	500
Bank overdraft	76
Stock	823
Net profit for year	797

On 31 March 2009 the directors agreed that there should be a transfer of £300,000 to the general reserve. They proposed that shareholders should receive a dividend of 7.5p per share.

Tasks:

(*a*) Prepare the company's profit and loss appropriation account for the year ended 31 March 2009.
(*b*) List the company's current liabilities at 31 March 2009.
(*c*) Prepare an extract from the company's balance sheet as at 31 March 2009 showing issued capital, reserves and the total of the shareholders' funds.

The directors of the company are concerned because the return on capital employed has been declining during recent years.

(*d*) Advise the directors of *two* ways in which the return on capital employed could be improved.

Southern Examining Group AQA

Please note that this question is NOT from the live examinations for the current specification.

CHAPTER 38

Manufacturing accounts

Learning objectives

After you have studied this chapter you should be able to:

- understand that a company manufacturing its own goods records the cost of manufacture in a Manufacturing Account
- calculate the prime cost and production cost of goods manufactured
- distinguish between direct costs and indirect costs
- prepare a manufacturing account
- calculate the production cost per unit.

38.1 Introduction to manufacturing accounts

Previous chapters have dealt with businesses involved in the buying and selling of goods or services, essentially trading operations. As such the trading and profit and loss accounts have been prepared to record the trading activities and ascertain the gross profit and net profit.

In the case of a company involved in producing goods a **manufacturing account** is drawn up to determine the actual cost of manufacture normally shown in the account as the **production cost**.

The actual cost is calculated by starting with direct materials, direct labour and direct expenses. The total of these costs is known as the **prime cost**. Other costs which are essential to the manufacture of the goods, but cannot be allocated to them specifically are known as **indirect manufacturing costs**.

The manufacturing account is prepared to provide the production costs which is necessary before the trading account and profit and loss account can be drawn up. The manufacturing account is an essential document for a company since it provides vital information to the owners in managing costs. It is normally only an internal document and Exhibit 38.1 shows how the cost of production is determined.

A manufacturing company builds up its cost in stages to determine the **total cost** as shown in Exhibit 38.1.

Exhibit 38.1 Total cost calculation

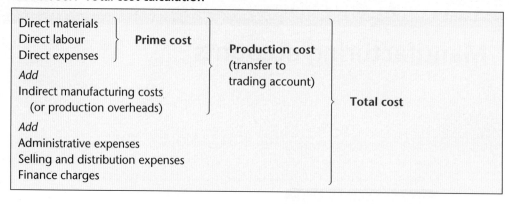

The prime cost and production cost appear in the manufacturing account. The production cost is transferred to the trading account. Administrative expenses, selling and distribution expenses and finance expenses appear in the profit and loss account.

38.2 Direct and indirect costs

Direct costs are those that can be directly identified with specific products or jobs. For example, referring to Exhibit 38.1, the direct costs identified are:

- Direct materials – raw materials required for the manufacture of a product.
- Direct labour – wages of the machine operator who makes the product.
- Direct expenses – expenses that can be identified to each unit of production, for example, the hire of a special machine, or the payment of a royalty for the use of a patent or copyright.

The total of all the **direct costs** is known as the **prime cost** (see Exhibit 38.1).

Indirect costs are those that occur in the factory or other places where production is being carried out but cannot be easily traced to the items being manufactured. Examples include:

- rent of premises and business rates
- insurance of premises
- depreciation of equipment
- factory heating and lighting
- wages of supervisors.

Indirect costs are also referred to as indirect manufacturing costs, production overheads or **factory overhead costs** (see Exhibit 38.1).

38.3 Administration expenses

Administration expenses consist of such items as managers' salaries, legal and accountancy charges, the depreciation of office equipment, and secretarial salaries.

38.4 Selling and distribution expenses

Selling and distribution expenses are items such as sales staff salaries and commission, carriage outwards, depreciation of delivery vehicles, advertising and display expenses.

38.5 Finance charges

Finance charges are those expenses incurred in providing finance facilities such as interest charged on a loan, bank charges and discounts allowed.

38.6 Format of financial statement

As previously mentioned if a company manufactures its own products then it would prepare a manufacturing account prior to the trading and profit and loss accounts thus:

- Manufacturing Account
- Trading Account
- Profit and Loss Account
- Balance Sheet.

Manufacturing account section

This is charged with the production cost of goods completed during the accounting period. It consists of:

- *Direct material* – this is found as follows:
    - (i) opening stock of raw materials
    - (ii) *add* the cost of purchases of raw materials plus carriage inwards charges
    - (iii) *less* closing stock of raw materials
    - (iv) this gives *the cost of raw material consumed.*
    To this figure *add* the following:
- *Direct labour*
- *Direct expenses*
- This now gives the figure of *prime cost.*

Now add:

- *Indirect manufacturing costs* such as wages of supervisor, factory rent, depreciation of equipment, etc.
- *Add* opening work in progress and *deduct* closing work in progress
- This now gives *production cost of goods completed.*

When completed the manufacturing account shows the total production costs relating to the goods manufactured and available for sale during the accounting period. This figure is then transferred to the trading account section of the trading and profit and loss accounts.

Note: Many students are so used to deducting expenses such as wages, rent, depreciation, etc. in profit and loss accounts that they can easily fall into the trap of *deducting* these instead of *adding* them in the manufacturing account. Remember we are building up the cost of manufacture so all costs are added.

Trading account section

This account includes:

- production cost brought down from the manufacturing account
- opening and closing stocks of finished goods
- sales.

When completed, this account will disclose the gross profit. This figure will then be carried down to the profit and loss account section of the final accounts.

The Manufacturing Account and the Trading Account can be shown in the form of a diagram.

Manufacturing Account

	£
Production costs for the period:	
Direct materials	xxx
Direct labour	xxx
Direct expenses	xxx
Prime cost	xxx
Indirect manufacturing costs (or production overheads)	xxx
*Production cost of goods completed c/d to trading account	xxx

Trading Account

		£	£
Sales			xxx
Less Production cost of goods sold:			
Opening stock of finished goods	(A)	xxx	
Add ***Production costs of goods completed b/d**		xxx	
Less Closing stock of finished goods	(B)	xxx	xxx
Gross profit			xxx

(A) is production costs of goods unsold in previous period.
(B) is production costs of goods unsold at end of the period.

Profit and loss account section

This section includes:

- gross profit brought down from the trading account
- all administration expenses
- all selling and distribution expenses
- all finance charges.

Since some of the charges usually found in the profit and loss account will have already been included in the manufacturing account only the remainder need charging to the profit and loss account.

When complete the profit and loss account will show the net profit.

Balance sheet

The balance sheet of a manufacturing company is virtually the same as balance sheets prepared for other organisations with one exception. In the *Current assets* section all three closing stocks must be included, i.e.:

- stock of raw materials
- stock of work-in-progress
- stock of finished goods.

38.7 A worked example of a manufacturing account

Exhibit 38.2 shows the necessary details for a manufacturing account. It has been assumed that there were no partly completed units (known as **work in progress**) either at the beginning or end of the period.

Exhibit 38.2

Details of production cost for the year ended 31 December 2009:

	£
1 January 2009, stock of raw materials	3,000
31 December 2009, stock of raw materials	4,200
Raw materials purchased	48,000
Manufacturing (direct) wages	126,000
Royalties	900
Indirect wages	54,000
Rent of factory – excluding administration and selling and distribution blocks	2,640
Depreciation of plant and machinery in factory	2,400
General indirect expenses	1,860

Manufacturing Account for the year ended 31 December 2009

	£	£
Stock of raw materials 1.1.2009		3,000
Add Purchases		48,000
		51,000
Less Stock of raw materials 31.12.2009		4,200
Cost of raw materials consumed		46,800
Manufacturing wages		126,000
Royalties		900
Prime cost		173,700
Indirect Manufacturing Costs		
Rent	2,640	
Indirect wages	54,000	
General expenses	1,860	
Depreciation of plant and machinery	2,400	60,900
Production cost of goods completed c/d		234,600

Sometimes, if a company has produced less than its customers have demanded, the company may well have bought an outside supply of finished goods. In this case, the trading account will have both a figure for purchases and for the production cost of goods completed.

38.8 Work in progress

The production cost to be carried down to the trading account is that of production cost of goods completed during the period. If items have not been completed, they cannot be sold. Therefore, they should not appear in the trading account.

For instance, if we have the following information, we can calculate the transfer to the trading account:

	£
Total production costs expended during the year	60,000
Production costs last year on goods not completed last year, but completed in this year (work in progress)	3,600
Production costs this year on goods which were not completed by the year end (work in progress)	5,280

The calculation is:	
Total production costs expended this year	60,000
Add Costs from last year, in respect of goods completed in this year (work in progress)	3,600
	63,600
Less Costs in this year, for goods to be completed next year (work in progress)	5,280
Production costs expended on goods completed this year	58,320

38.9 A worked example for a manufacturing account

Consider the case whose details are given in Exhibit 38.3.

Exhibit 38.3

	£
1 January 2009, Stock of raw materials	7,200
31 December 2009, Stock of raw materials	9,450
1 January 2009, Work in progress	3,150
31 December 2009, Work in progress	3,780
Year to 31 December 2009	
Wages: Direct	35,640
Indirect	22,950
Purchase of raw materials	78,300
Fuel and power	8,910
Direct expenses	1,260
Lubricants	2,700
Carriage inwards on raw materials	1,800
Rent of factory	6,480
Depreciation of factory plant and machinery	3,780
Internal transport expenses	11,620
Insurance of factory buildings and plant	11,350
General factory expenses	2,970

Manufacturing Account for the year ended 31 December 2009

	£	£
Stock of raw materials 1.1.2009		7,200
Add Purchases		78,300
Carriage inwards		1,800
		87,300
Less Stock of raw materials 31.12.2009		9,450
Cost of raw materials consumed		77,850
Direct wages		35,640
Direct expenses		1,260
Prime cost		114,750
Add Indirect Manufacturing Cost		
Fuel and power	8,910	
Indirect wages	22,950	
Lubricants	2,700	
Rent	6,480	
Depreciation of plant	3,780	
Internal transport expenses	11,620	
Insurance	11,350	
General factory expenses	2,970	70,760
		185,510
Add Work in progress 1.1.2009		3,150
		188,660
Less Work in progress 31.12.2009		3,780
Production cost of goods completed c/d		184,880

The trading account is concerned with finished goods. If in Exhibit 38.3 there had been £31,500 stock of finished goods at 1 January 2009 and £39,600 at 31 December 2009, and the sales of finished goods amounted to £275,000, then the trading account would appear thus:

Trading Account for the year 31 December 2009

	£	£
Sales		275,000
Less Cost of goods sold		
Stock of finished goods 1.1.2009	31,500	
Add Production cost of goods completed b/d	184,880	
	216,380	
Less Stock of finished goods 31.12.2009	39,600	176,780
Gross profit c/d		98,220

The profit and loss account is then constructed in the normal way.

38.10　Apportionment of expenses

Quite often, expenses will have to be divided between:

- Indirect manufacturing costs:　to be charged in the manufacturing account section

- Administration expenses:
- Selling and distribution expenses: } to be charged in the profit and loss account section
- Financial charges:

An instance of this could be the rent expense. If the rent is paid separately for each part of the organisation, then it is easy to charge the rent to each sort of expense. However, only one figure of rent might be paid, without any indication as to how much is for the factory part, how much is for the selling and distribution part and that for the administration buildings.

How the rent expense will be apportioned in the latter case will depend on circumstances, but will use the most equitable way of doing it. A range of methods may be used, including ones based upon:

- floor area
- property valuations of each part of the buildings and land.

38.11　Full set of final accounts: worked example

A complete worked example is now given. Note that in the profit and loss account the expenses have been separated to show whether they are administration expenses, selling and distribution expenses, or financial charges.

The trial balance in Exhibit 38.4 has been extracted from the books of J Jarvis, Toy Manufacturer, as on 31 December 2009.

Exhibit 38.4

J Jarvis
Trial Balance as at 31 December 2009

	Dr	Cr
	£	£
Stock of raw materials 1.1.2009	2,100	
Stock of finished goods 1.1.2009	3,890	
Work in progress 1.1.2009	1,350	
Wages (direct £18,000; factory indirect £14,500)	32,500	
Royalties	700	
Carriage inwards (on raw materials)	350	
Purchases of raw materials	37,000	
Productive machinery (cost £28,000)	23,000	
Computer equipment (cost £2,000)	1,200	
General factory expenses	3,100	
Lighting	750	
Factory power	1,370	
Administrative salaries	4,400	
Salesmen's salaries	3,000	
Commission on sales	1,150	
Rent	1,200	
Insurance	420	
General administration expenses	1,340	
Bank charges	230	
Discounts allowed	480	
Carriage outwards	590	
Sales		100,000
Debtors and creditors	14,230	12,500
Bank	5,680	
Cash	150	
Drawings	2,000	
Capital as at 1.1.2009		29,680
	142,180	142,180

Notes at 31.12.2009:

(i)   Stock of raw materials £2,400; stock of finished goods £4,000; work in progress £1,500.

(ii) Lighting, rent and insurance are to be apportioned: factory five-sixths, administration one-sixth.

(iii) Depreciation on productive machinery and computer equipment is at 10% per annum on cost.

J Jarvis
Manufacturing, Trading and Profit and Loss Account
for the year ended 31 December 2009

	£	£	£
Stock of raw materials 1.1.2009			2,100
Add Purchases			37,000
Carriage inwards			350
			39,450
Less Stock raw materials 31.12.2009			2,400
Cost of raw materials consumed			37,050
Direct labour			18,000
Royalties			700
Prime cost			55,750
Indirect Manufacturing Cost			
General factory expenses		3,100	
Lighting ⅝ths		625	
Power		1,370	
Rent ⅝ths		1,000	
Insurance ⅝ths		350	
Depreciation of plant		2,800	
Indirect labour		14,500	23,745
			79,495
Add Work in progress 1.1.2009			1,350
			80,845
Less Work in progress 31.12.2009			1,500
Production cost of goods completed c/d			79,345
Sales			100,000
Less Cost of goods sold			
Stock of finished goods 1.1.2009		3,890	
Add Production cost of goods completed		79,345	
		83,235	
Less Stock of finished goods 31.12.2009		4,000	79,235
Gross profit			20,765
Administration Expenses			
Administrative salaries	4,400		
Rent ⅙th	200		
Insurance ⅙th	70		
General expenses	1,340		
Lighting ⅛th	125		
Depreciation of computer equipment	200	6,335	
Selling and Distribution Expenses			
Sales representatives' salaries	3,000		
Commission on sales	1,150		
Carriage outwards	590	4,740	
Financial Charges			
Bank charges	230		
Discounts allowed	480	710	11,785
Net profit			8,980

J Jarvis
Balance Sheet as at 31 December 2009

	Cost	Total Depreciation	Net Book Value
	£	£	£
Fixed Assets			
Productive machinery	28,000	7,800	20,200
Computer equipment	2,000	1,000	1,000
	30,000	8,800	21,200
Current Assets			
Stock:			
Raw materials	2,400		
Finished goods	4,000		
Work in progress	1,500		
Debtors	14,230		
Bank	5,680		
Cash	150	27,960	
Less Current Liabilities			
Creditors	12,500	12,500	
Net current assets			15,460
			36,660
Financed by			
Capital			
Balance as at 1.1.2009			29,680
Add Net profit			8,980
			38,660
Less Drawings			2,000
			36,660

Unit cost of production

Once the total cost of production is calculated the production cost per unit can easily be ascertained. In the above example let us assume that 2,267 units were produced at the cost of £79,345 (see the Manufacturing Account). The cost per unit is as follows:

$$\frac{\text{Cost of production}}{\text{No. of units produced}} = \text{Cost per unit}$$

$$= \frac{£79,345}{2,267 \text{ units}} = £35.00 \text{ per unit}$$

38.12 Other terms used in manufacturing accounts

Fixed costs are costs that, in the short term, remain the same irrespective of the level of business activity. Examples of a fixed cost would be rent, business rates, insurance, etc., and such costs would have to be paid if the company produced 100 units or 1,000 units.

Variable costs vary depending on the level of production. For example, raw materials used in manufacture would vary depending upon the level of goods produced; the more goods produced the greater the cost of raw materials. If fewer goods were produced the costs of raw materials would be reduced.

Note: Students often find the preparation of manufacturing accounts difficult to grasp and may find it useful to remember the following areas in which they could easily make a mistake:

1 Remember to add any item appearing under the heading of 'Indirect Manufacturing Costs', i.e. rent, wages, depreciation, power and lighting, etc.
2 In the trading account 'Cost of Goods Sold' section ensure you use the **Production cost** of goods completed, i.e. £79,345, and *not* the **purchases** figure.
3 In the balance sheet, under current assets, be sure to include all *three closing stocks* if applicable to your question, i.e.
   (i)   stock of raw materials
   (ii) stock of work in progress
   (iii) stock of finished goods.

Chapter summary

- When a company manufactures its own products, rather than purchasing them, the cost of production can be found by preparing a manufacturing account.
- Direct costs are those costs that can be traced to the specific item being manufactured.
- Indirect costs, also known as 'indirect manufacturing costs', are those costs relating to the manufacture of an item that cannot be easily traced, for example, a supervisor's wages.
- The cost of producing an item is made up of direct materials, direct labour and direct expenses to arrive at the prime cost. To this figure is added any indirect manufacturing costs, plus the opening stock of work in progress less closing stock of work in progress to find the production cost of goods completed.
- Where a business manufactures its own goods the financial statements consist of: a manufacturing account, which gives the production cost of goods completed; the trading and the profit and loss account, which shows the gross and net profits respectively; and the balance sheet.
- It is important to adjust the manufacturing account for any work in progress at the start and end of the accounting period.
- Fixed costs remain the same whatever the level of productive activity whereas variable costs, such as raw materials, varies according to the number of units produced.
- The areas likely to cause errors when preparing financial statements for manufacturing organisations are:
  1 Manufacturing account – under the heading 'Indirect expenses' remember to *add* the expenses, i.e. rent, power and lighting, depreciation, etc.
  2 Trading account – when calculating the 'Cost of goods sold' ensure you use the 'Production cost of goods manufactured' not purchases!
  3 Balance sheet – include all *three* closing stock under the heading of 'Current assets', i.e. raw materials, work in progress and finished goods.

EXERCISES

38.1 From the following information, prepare the manufacturing and trading account of E Smith for the year ended 31 March 2009.

	£
Stocks at 1 April 2008:	
Finished goods	6,724
Raw materials	2,400
Work in progress	955
Carriage on purchases (raw materials)	321
Sales	69,830
Purchases of raw materials	21,340
Manufacturing wages	13,280
Factory power	6,220
Other manufacturing expenses	1,430
Factory rent and rates	2,300
Stocks at 31 March 2009	
Raw materials	2,620
Work in progress	870
Finished goods	7,230

38.2X From the following details, you are to draw up a manufacturing, trading and profit and loss account of P Lucas for the year ended 30 September 2009.

	30.9.2008	30.9.2009
	£	£
Stocks of raw materials, at cost	8,460	10,970
Work in progress	3,070	2,460
Finished goods stock	12,380	14,570

	£
For the year:	
Raw materials purchased	38,720
Manufacturing wages	20,970
Factory expenses	12,650
Depreciation:	
Plant and machinery	7,560
Delivery vans	3,040
Office equipment	807
Factory power	6,120
Advertising	5,080
Office and administration expenses	25,910
Sales representatives' salaries and expenses	26,420
Delivery van expenses	5,890
Sales	174,610
Carriage inwards	2,720

38.3   The Oldport Manufacturing Co's financial year ended on 30 April 2009. The following list includes some of the balances in the business's book at that date.

		£
Stocks 1 May 2008		
	Finished goods	27,900
	Raw materials	31,550
Wages		
	Direct manufacturing	67,525
	Indirect manufacturing	24,390
	Office	38,440
Purchases of raw materials		98,560
Factory rent and rates		22,400
Stocks 30 April 2008		
	Finished goods	31,280
	Raw materials	34,585

Tasks:

(a) Set out a detailed calculation of the company's prime cost. Select appropriate items from the information provided.

(b) Explain what is meant by the term 'variable costs'. Illustrate your answer with *one* example of a variable cost.

Southern Examining Group AQA

Please note that this question is NOT from the live examinations for the current specification.

38.4   Ace Crafts Ltd makes ornaments, which it sells in wooden cases. The following information is made available to you in respect of the year ended 31 December 2009:

	1 Jan 2009	31 Dec 2009
	£	£
Raw materials	36,000	46,400
Wooden cases	18,000	15,360
Work-in-progress	10,000	15,200

The activities for the year ended 31 December 2009 were:

	£
Raw materials purchased	70,400
Purchases of wooden cases	18,000
Carriage outwards	1,680
Carriage inwards on raw materials	1,120
Wages	170,000
Salary of factory manager	33,200
Factory power	14,560
Factory rates	2,280
Lighting	1,800
Administration expenses	19,200
Salesmen's salaries	47,600

The company completely finished the manufacture of 1,000 ornaments. All ornaments were sold immediately on completion for £80 each. In addition:

- Factory plant was valued at £100,000 on 1 January 2009. It depreciates by 20% for 2009.
- 80% of the wages are for productive workers, and 20% for factory overheads.
- 50% of the lighting is for the factory.

Required:

(*a*) Draw up a manufacturing account to disclose:

    (i)   cost of raw materials used

    (ii) cost of wooden cases used

    (iii) prime cost

    (iv) factory overheads

    (v) cost of production.

(*b*) Draft the trading and profit and loss account for the year ended 31 December 2009.

(*c*) Ascertain the production cost of each boxed ornament.

(*d*) Calculate the gross profit on each boxed ornament sold.

38.5X The following balances have been extracted from the books of Tan Guat Hoon as at 31 August 2009.

	£
Stock at 1 September 2008	
Raw materials	16,300
Work in progress	21,200
Finished goods	43,100
Provision for doubtful debts at 1 September 2008	1,460
Purchases of raw materials	71,200
Returns of raw materials	700
Sales	187,300
Discounts allowed	640
Discounts received	700
Production wages	21,300
Office salaries	11,300
Production equipment (cost £60,000)	29,400
Office equipment (at cost)	5,400
Carriage on raw materials	930
Rent and rates	8,000
Heat and light	1,100
Insurance	500

The following information is also relevant at 31 August 2009:

(i)   Closing stocks are:

    • Raw materials   £15,800

    • Work in progress £20,100

    • Finished goods   £36,400.

(ii)   The following amounts remain outstanding:

    • Rent and rates   £500

    • Heat and light   £220

    • Production wages £2,600.

(iii) £100 insurance has been prepaid.

(iv) Three-quarters of insurance relates to the factory and the remainder to the office.

(v)   Two-thirds of heat and light relates to the factory and the remainder to the office.

(vi) 80% of rent and rates relates to the factory and the remainder to the office.

(vii) The provision for doubtful debts is to be reduced to £1,010.

(viii) Depreciation is to be provided:

    – on production equipment at 30% reducing (diminishing) balance basis

    – on office equipment at 40% on cost.

You are required to:

(a) prepare a Manufacturing Account for the year ended 31 August 2009

(b) prepare a Trading, Profit and Loss Account for the year ended 31 August 2009.

City & Guilds Pitman qualifications

38.6X Toybox Products Ltd manufactures wooden toys for younger children. The following information is available about the company's financial year ended 30 April 2009.

	£
Direct wages	226,450
Indirect factory power	37,720
Sales of finished goods	545,800
Factory insurance	13,240
Purchases of raw materials	104,850
Returns inwards (finished goods)	3,620
Depreciation of factory plant and machinery	33,800
Indirect factory wages and salaries	24,390
Stocks at 1 May 2008	
Raw materials	11,250
Finished goods	21,480
Stocks at 30 April 2009	
Raw materials	14,740
Finished goods	26,260

Tasks:

(a) Prepare the company's manufacturing account for the year ended 30 April 2009. The account should show subtotals for:
 - raw materials consumed
 - prime cost
 - total factory overheads.

(b) Prepare a trading account for the year ended 30 April 2009.

The company's directors had been hoping to expand the company. However, during recent months sales have decreased because of increasing competition.

Tasks:

(c) Explain *three* ways in which it might be possible to overcome competition and increase sales.

(d) Recommend *two* ways in which the company could finance an expansion programme. In each case explain the effect of the recommendation on the company's cash resources.

Southern Examining Group AQA

Please note that this question is NOT from the live examinations for the current specification.

CHAPTER 39

Analysis and interpretation of accounts

Learning objectives

After you have studied this chapter you should be able to:

- appreciate the importance of analysing financial statements for the benefit of interested parties
- distinguish between profitability and liquidity
- calculate and analyse ratios
- understand the term 'capital employed'
- calculate and understand the importance of working capital.

39.1 Interpretation of accounts

The whole purpose of recording and classifying financial information about a business, and communicating this to the owners and managers in the form of the financial statements, is to assess the performance of the business. The information contained in the financial statements can be used to evaluate various aspects of the company by the use of accounting ratios.

For the ratios to be a reliable guide to performance, two criteria need to be applied:

1 The financial statements used for calculating the current ratios must be *up to date.*
2 Each ratio must be *compared* with the same ratio from the previous year's accounts or with those from a competitor's accounts.

The concept of comparison is crucial, since this identifies trends in the business and allows action to be taken.

The analysis of a business using accounting ratios is widely practised by both internal and external parties and the main ones are listed in Exhibit 39.1.

Exhibit 39.1

39.2 Profitability and liquidity

There are two basic but essential factors in the operation of a business, the first is to maintain, and if possible, increase profit. The ability to make profit is known as **profitability**.

The second essential factor is for the business to have sufficient funds at all times so that it can pay its debts as they become due. The level of funds available to pay creditors is known as **liquidity**.

The importance of both these factors cannot be too highly stressed. A business which operates with a good profits record and sound liquidity will become well regarded by both customers and suppliers.

If a business is consistently unable to generate profits it will fail. Even when a business makes a profit but has weak liquidity it would demonstrate a failure to control its cash flow. Late or slow payments to creditors could lead to suppliers not wishing to deal with the company. Once a business gains a poor financial reputation it could affect its trading performance which would further weaken it and cause it to fail.

39.3 Profitability ratios

The **profitability ratios** measure the success or otherwise of a business's trading activities in respect of profit during an accounting period. The main ratios used to examine profitability are:

- **gross profit margin/sales**
- **gross profit mark-up/cost of sales**
- **net profit margin/sales**

- **expenses (or overheads)/sales**
- **return on capital employed (ROCE)**
- **stock turnover ratio.**

1 Gross profit as percentage of sales

The basic formula is:

$$\frac{\text{Gross profit}}{\text{Sales}} \times 100 = \text{Gross profit as percentage of sales (Gross profit margin)}$$

This is the amount of gross profit for every £100 of sales and is known as the gross profit margin (refer to Chapter 34 for margin and mark-up). If the answer turns out to be 15% this would mean that for every £100 of sales £15 gross profit is made before any expenses are paid.

This ratio is used as a test of the profitability of the sales. Even if sales are increased it may not mean that the gross profit will increase. The trading accounts in Exhibit 39.2 illustrate this.

Exhibit 39.2

D. Clive

Trading Accounts for the years ended 31 December 2009 and 2010

	2009		2010	
	£	£	£	£
Sales		70,000		80,000
Less Cost of goods sold				
Opening stock	5,000		9,000	
Add Purchases	60,000		72,000	
	65,000		81,000	
Less Closing stock	9,000	56,000	11,000	70,000
Gross profit		14,000		10,000

In the year 2009 the gross profit as a percentage of sales was:

$$\frac{14,000}{70,000} \times 100 = 20\%$$

In the year 2010 it became:

$$\frac{10,000}{80,000} \times 100 = 12^{1}/2\%$$

Sales had increased, but as the gross profit percentage had fallen by a relatively greater amount, the gross profit had fallen. There can be many reasons for such a fall in the gross profit percentage.

- Perhaps the goods being sold have cost more, but the selling price of the goods has not risen to the same extent.
- Perhaps, in order to increase sales, reductions have been made in the selling price of goods.

- There could be a difference in how much has been sold of each sort of goods, called the sales mix, between this year and last, with different kinds of goods carrying different rates of gross profit per £100 of sales.
- There may have been a greater wastage or theft of goods.

These are only some of the possible reasons for the decrease. The point of calculating the ratio is to find out why and how such a change has taken place.

2 Gross profit to cost of sales

The basic formula is:

$$\frac{\text{Gross profit}}{\text{Cost of sales}} \times 100 = \begin{array}{c}\text{Gross profit as a percentage of cost of sales} \\ \text{(Gross profit mark-up)}\end{array}$$

This ratio shows the percentage of profit to the cost of sales, in other words the amount the trader has marked up its products. For example, if a trader buys a product for £1 and decides to mark it up by 20% (20% of £1 = 20p) then the selling price becomes £1.20.

Using the figures in Exhibit 39.2, the gross profit as a percentage of cost of sales would be as follows:

In the year 2009 the gross profit as a percentage of cost of sales:

$$\frac{14,000}{56,000} \times 100 = 25\%$$

In the year 2010 it became:

$$\frac{10,000}{70,000} \times 100 = 14.29\%$$

3 Net profit margin to sales

Here the formula is:

$$\frac{\text{Net profit}}{\text{Sales}} \times 100 = \text{Net profit as percentage of sales}$$

This calculation will show how much net profit has been made for every £100 of sales. It brings the expenses (or overheads) into the calculation, as opposed to the gross profit percentage, which ignores expenses. Changes in the ratio will be due either to:

- the gross profit ratio changing, and/or
- the expenses per £100 of sales changing.

When changes are due to expenses, they will be examined to see if anything can be done in future to minimise the expenses and ensure that a reasonable net profit is made.

4 Expenses to sales ratio

This ratio is calculated as follows:

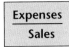

$$\frac{\text{Expenses}}{\text{Sales}}$$

Normally, this is referred to as a percentage and is calculated as follows:

$$\text{Expenses as a percentage of sales} = \frac{\text{Expenses}}{\text{Sales}} \times 100 = x\%$$

It is useful to compare the expenses/sales percentage with the previous results. If an increase was evident this would indicate an increase in the expenses of the business and would require further investigation by management. If the result remained stable or in fact had reduced this would indicate that expenses incurred in running the business had been carefully monitored.

5 Return on capital employed ratio (ROCE)

This ratio is calculated as follows:

$$\frac{\text{Net profit}}{\text{Capital employed}}$$

Normally, this is referred to as a percentage and is calculated as follows:

$$\text{Return of capital employed} = \frac{\text{Net profit}}{\text{Capital employed}} \times 100 = x\%$$

It shows (as a percentage) the net profit made for each £100 of capital employed. The higher the ratio, the more profitable the business. This is the most important ratio of all.

There has never been an agreed definition of the term 'capital employed'. Very often it has been taken to mean the average capital. For this, the opening capital for the period is added to the closing capital and then the total is divided by two. In an examination, use the method stated by the examiner. If you are given only the closing capital, use the closing capital figure.

In the following example, two businesses of sole traders (A) and (B) have made the same profits, but the capital employed in each case is different. From the balance sheets that follow, the return on capital employed is calculated using the average of the capital account as capital employed.

Balance Sheets	(A)	(B)
	£	£
Fixed Assets + Current Assets – Current Liabilities	100,000	160,000
Capital Accounts:		
Opening balance	80,000	140,000
Add Net profits	36,000	36,000
	116,000	176,000
Less Drawings	16,000	16,000
	100,000	160,000

Return on capital employed is calculated thus for the two businesses:

$$(A) \quad \frac{£36,000}{(£80,000 + £100,000) \div 2} \times 100\% = 40\%$$

$$(B) \quad \frac{£36,000}{(£140,000 + £160,000) \div 2} \times 100\% = 24\%$$

The ratio illustrates that what is important is not simply how much profit has been made but how well the capital has been employed. Business (A) has made far better use of its capital, achieving a return of £40 net profit for every £100 invested, whereas (B) has received a net profit of only £24 per £100.

In this case, only the accounts of sole traders have been dealt with, so that a straightforward example could be used. In Section 39.6 other meanings of 'capital employed' will be considered, when dealing with:

● sole traders who have received loans to help finance their businesses
● partnerships
● limited companies.

6 Stock turnover ratio

Every business should operate both to keep its stock to as low a figure as possible without losing profitability, and to sell its goods as quickly as possible. The stock turnover ratio measures how well the business is managing to do these things. Any increase in stocks or slowdown in sales will show a lower ratio.

The ratio is calculated as follows:

$$\frac{\text{Cost of goods sold}}{\text{Average stock}} = \text{Stock turnover ratio}$$

If only the opening and closing stocks are known the average stock is found by adding these two figures and dividing them by two (i.e. averaging them). The higher this ratio, the more profitable the business. For example, if £5 gross profit was made on a particular product and the stock turnover is 6 times a year then the business would make a gross profit of £5 × 6 = £30. If, however, the stock turnover ratio increased to 9, then gross profit would be £5 × 9 = £45.

39.4 Liquidity ratios

A business that has satisfactory liquidity (see Section 39.2) will have sufficient funds, normally referred to as 'working capital', to pay creditors at the required time. The ability to pay creditors on time is vital to ensure that good business relationships are maintained.

The ratios used to examine liquidity, i.e. the **liquidity ratios**, are:

1 **Current ratio (working capital ratio)**
2 **Acid test ratio (quick ratio)**

3 **Debtors : sales ratio (debtors' collection period)**
4 **Creditors : purchases ratio (creditors' payment period).**

Each of the liquidity ratios stated can be compared period by period to see whether that particular aspect of liquidity is getting better or worse. In the case of the current ratio, it was often thought in the past that the ideal ratio should be around 2:1 and that, ideally, the acid test ratio should be in the region of 1:1 to 1.5:1. However, in recent years it has become recognised that such a fixed figure cannot possibly apply to every business, as the types and circumstances of businesses vary so widely.

1 Current ratio (or working capital ratio)

The current ratio measures current assets against current liabilities. It will compare assets that will be turned into cash within the next 12 months with any liabilities that will have to be paid within the same period. The current ratio is thus stated as:

$$\frac{\text{Current assets}}{\text{Current liabilities}}$$

If, therefore, the current assets are £125,000 and the current liabilities are £50,000, the current ratio will be:

$$\frac{£125,000}{£50,000} = 2.5\text{:}1, \text{ or } 2.5 \text{ times}$$

If the ratio increases by a large amount, the business may have more current assets than it needs. If the ratio falls by a large amount, then perhaps too little is being kept as current assets.

2 Acid test ratio (or quick ratio)

To determine a further aspect of liquidity, the **acid test ratio** takes into account only those current assets that are cash or can be changed very quickly into cash. This will normally mean Cash + Bank + Debtors. You can see that this means exactly the same as current assets less stock. The acid test ratio may, therefore, be stated as:

$$\frac{\text{Current assets less stock}}{\text{Current liabilities}}$$

For instance, if the total of current assets is £40,000 and stock is £10,000, and the total of current liabilities is £20,000, then the ratio will be:

$$\frac{£40,000 - £10,000}{£20,000} = 1.5\text{:}1, \text{ or } 1.5 \text{ times}$$

This ratio shows whether there are enough liquid assets to be able to pay current liabilities quickly. It is dangerous if this ratio is allowed to fall to a very low figure. If suppliers and others cannot be paid on time, supplies to the business may be reduced or even stopped completely. Eventually, the business may not have enough stock to be able to sell properly. In that case, it may have to cease business.

3 Debtors to sales ratio (debtors' collection period)

This ratio assesses how long it takes for debtors to pay what they owe. The calculation is made as follows:

$$\frac{\text{Debtors}}{\text{Sales for the year}} \times 12 = \text{Number of months that debtors (on average) take to pay up}$$

For example:

	(C)	(D)
Sales for the year	£240,000	£180,000
Debtors as per balance sheet	£60,000	£30,000

In business (C), debtors therefore take three months on average to pay their accounts, calculated from:

$$\frac{£60,000}{£240,000} \times 12 = 3 \text{ months}$$

In business (D), debtors therefore take two months on average to pay their accounts, given from:

$$\frac{£30,000}{£180,000} \times 12 = 2 \text{ months}$$

If the ratio is required to be shown in days instead of months, the formula should be multiplied by 365 instead of 12. The higher the ratio, the worse a business is at getting its debtors to pay on time. The lower the ratio, the better it is at managing its debtors.

Businesses should make certain that debtors pay their accounts on time. There are two main reasons for this. First, the longer a debt is owed, the more likely it will become a bad debt. Second, any payment of money can be used in the business as soon as it is received, and so this increases profitability; it can help reduce expenses. For example, it would reduce a bank overdraft and therefore reduce the bank overdraft interest.

4 Creditors to purchases ratio (creditors' payment period)

This ratio shows how long it takes a business (on average) to pay its suppliers. The calculation is made as follows:

$$\frac{\text{Creditors}}{\text{Purchases for the year}} \times 12 = \text{Number of months it takes (on average) to pay up suppliers}$$

For example:

	(E)	(F)
Purchases for the year	£120,000	£90,000
Creditors as per balance sheet	£40,000	£22,500

Business (E) therefore takes four months' credit on average from its suppliers, i.e.

$$\frac{£40,000}{£120,000} \times 12 = 4 \text{ months}$$

Business (F) takes on average three months to pay its suppliers, i.e.

$$\frac{£22,500}{£90,000} \times 12 = 3 \text{ months}$$

Taking longer to pay suppliers could be a good thing or a bad thing, depending upon circumstances. If so long is taken to pay that possible discounts are lost, or that suppliers refuse to supply again, then it would be undesirable. On the other hand, paying before it is necessary simply takes money out of the business early without gaining any benefit.

39.5 Other ratios

There are many more ratios that may be used in analysing financial information, too many to mention in this book. There may be the need, say, to ascertain the amount of sales per employee or production ratios in a manufacturing company. However, another ratio that is useful to business organisations is the **fixed assets to sales ratio**.

Fixed assets to sales ratio

This ratio measures the level of efficiency of the fixed assets in generating sales. It is calculated as follows:

$$\frac{\text{Sales}}{\text{Fixed assets}} = \text{Fixed asset to sales ratio}$$

The greater the ratio the higher the level of efficiency, whereas a lower ratio indicates that the company is not operating as effectively. This may be caused by a decrease in sales or an increase in the fixed assets.

39.6 Definition of capital employed in various circumstances

In Section 39.3 (5), it was pointed out that there is not one single agreed definition of the term 'capital employed'. In answering an exam question in this area, you must follow the examiner's instructions, if any are given; otherwise, state what basis you have used.

Sole proprietorships

'Capital employed' could mean any of the following:

- closing balance on capital account at the end of a financial period
- average of opening and closing balances on the capital account for the accounting period
- capital balances plus any long-term loans.

Partnerships

'Capital employed' could mean any of the following:

- closing balance on the fluctuating capital accounts at the end of a financial period
- average of opening and closing balances on the fluctuating capital accounts for an accounting period
- total of fixed capital accounts plus total of partners' current accounts at the end of a financial period
- average of opening and closing balances on the partners' capital and current accounts for an accounting period
- any of the above, plus long-term loans to the partnership.

Limited companies

Given the following details, different figures for capital employed may be used.

	£
(a) Ordinary share capital	100,000
(b) Preference share capital	40,000
(c) Total of different types of reserves including balance in profit and loss account	35,000
(d) Debentures	60,000

- To calculate return on ordinary shareholders' funds, it would be (a) £100,000 + (c) £35,000 = £135,000.
- To calculate return on total shareholders' fund, it would be (a) £100,000 + (b) £40,000 + (c) £35,000 = £175,000.
- To calculate return on total capital employed, i.e. including borrowed funds, it would be (a) £100,000 + (b) £40,000 + (c) £35,000 + (d) £60,000 = £235,000.

Any question involving return of capital employed for limited companies should be read very carefully indeed. Use the method suggested by the examiner. If no indication is given, use that of (a) + (c) above, but you must state what method you have used.

39.7 Definition of working capital

Working capital is the amount by which current assets exceed current liabilities. It is also known as 'net current assets' (see Chapter 11).

It is vital for businesses to have sufficient working capital to enable them to have funds available to pay everyday running expenses. Working capital tends to circulate through a business, as shown in the diagram in Exhibit 39.3. As it flows, profits are made as stock is sold to debtors; the quicker it is sold, the quicker the business makes profits.

Exhibit 39.3

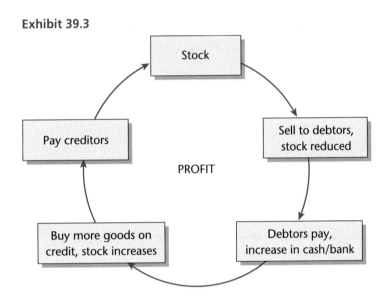

39.8 A fully worked example of calculating ratios

A fully worked example of calculating ratios and interpreting accounts is shown in Exhibit 39.4. Check all the calculations yourself and see whether your conclusions about the changes in the ratios agree with the author's.

Exhibit 39.4

The following are the final accounts for two similar types of retail stores:

Trading and Profit and Loss Accounts

	J		K	
	£	£	£	£
Sales		80,000		120,000
Less Cost of goods sold:				
Opening stock	25,000		22,500	
Add Purchases	50,000		91,000	
	75,000		113,500	
Less Closing stock	15,000	60,000	17,500	96,000
Gross profit		20,000		24,000
Less Depreciation	1,000		3,000	
Other expenses	9,000	10,000	6,000	9,000
Net profit		10,000		15,000

Balance Sheets

	J		K	
Fixed Assets	£	£	£	£
Equipment at cost	10,000		20,000	
Less Depreciation to date	8,000	2,000	6,000	14,000
Current Assets				
Stock	15,000		17,500	
Debtors	25,000		20,000	
Bank	5,000		2,500	
	45,000		40,000	
Less Current Liabilities				
Creditors	5,000		10,000	
Net current assets		40,000		30,000
		42,000		44,000
Financed by:				
Capital				
Balance at start of year		38,000		36,000
Add Net profit		10,000		15,000
		48,000		51,000
Less Drawings		6,000		7,000
		42,000		44,000

We will now calculate the following ratios (with all calculations shown correct to one decimal place):

(a) Gross profit as a percentage of sales
(b) Net profit as a per entage of sales
(c) Expenses as a percentage of sales
(d) Stock turnover ratio
(e) Rate of return of net profit on capital employed (use the average of the capital account for this purpose)
(f) Current ratio
(g) Acid test ratio (quick ratio)
(h) Debtors : Sales ratio
(i) Creditors : Purchases ratio

	J	K
(a) Gross profit as a % of sales	$\dfrac{£20,000}{£80,000} \times 100\% = 25\%$	$\dfrac{£24,000}{£120,000} \times 100\% = 20\%$
(b) Net profit as a % of sales	$\dfrac{£10,000}{£80,000} \times 100\% = 12.5\%$	$\dfrac{£15,000}{£120,000} \times 100\% = 12.5\%$
(c) Expenses as a % of sales	$\dfrac{£10,000}{£80,000} \times 100\% = 12.5\%$	$\dfrac{£9,000}{£120,000} \times 100\% = 7.5\%$
(d) Stockturn	$\dfrac{£60,000}{(£25,000 + £15,000) \div 2} = 3 \text{ times}$	$\dfrac{£96,000}{(£22,500 + £17,500) \div 2} = 4.8 \text{ times}$
(e) Rate of return on capital employed	$\dfrac{£10,000}{(£38,000 + £42,000) \div 2} \times 100\% = 25\%$	$\dfrac{£15,000}{(£36,000 + £44,000) \div 2} \times 100\% = 37.5\%$
(f) Current ratio	$\dfrac{£45,000}{£5,000} = 9{:}1$	$\dfrac{£40,000}{£10,000} = 4{:}1$
(g) Acid test ratio	$\dfrac{£45,000 - £15,000}{£5,000} = 6{:}1$	$\dfrac{£40,000 - £17,500}{£10,000} = 2.25{:}1$
(h) Debtors : Sales ratio	$\dfrac{£25,000}{£80,000} \times 12 = 3.75 \text{ months}$	$\dfrac{£20,000}{£120,000} \times 12 = 2 \text{ months}$
(i) Creditors : Purchases ratio	$\dfrac{£5,000}{£50,000} \times 12 = 1.2 \text{ months}$	$\dfrac{£10,000}{£91,000} \times 12 = 1.3 \text{ months}$

Having calculated the ratios, we will now attempt briefly to see what we have learned from studying the accounts and the ratios. At this stage in your studies, we would not expect a very long analysis. Instead, you should know what your examiner would expect of you in the examination.

You should not just say that the ratios differ. You should try to see why the ratios are different. Show the examiner that you are looking at the ratios as though they belong to a business for which the ratios mean something. He will not give you any marks for this part of the question if you talk only about the arithmetic of the ratios.

Business K is more profitable, both in terms of actual net profits (£15,000 compared with £10,000), but also in terms of capital employed. K has managed to achieve a return of £37.50 for every £100 invested, i.e. 37.5%. J has managed a lower return of 25%.

The conclusions are only possible reasons because you must know more about the business before you can give a definite answer.

- Possibly K managed to sell far more merchandise because of lower prices, i.e. it took only 20% margin as compared with J's 25% margin.
- Maybe K made more efficient use of mechanised means in the business. Note that it has more equipment, and perhaps as a consequence it kept other expenses down to £6,000 as compared with J's £9,000.

- K did not have as much stock lying idle. K turned over stock 4.8 times in the year, as compared with 3 times for J.
- J's current ratio of 9:1 was far greater than normally needed. K kept it down to 4:1. J therefore had too much money lying idle.
- The acid test ratio for J was higher than necessary and followed a similar trend to that shown by the current ratio.
- One reason for the better current and acid test ratios for K was that debts were collected on a 2 months' average.
- J also paid creditors more quickly than K – but only slightly faster.

When all these factors are considered, it is clear that business K is being run much more efficiently and, consequently, more profitably.

39.9 Summary of the formulae

For easy reference the various ratios, percentages and formulae used in this chapter are summarised in Exhibit 39.5.

Exhibit 39.5

Gross profit margin as a percentage of sales	$= \dfrac{\text{Gross profit}}{\text{Sales}} \times 100 = \text{x\%}$
Gross profit mark-up as a percentage of sales	$= \dfrac{\text{Gross profit}}{\text{Cost of sales}} \times 100 = \text{x\%}$
Net profit margin as a percentage of sales	$= \dfrac{\text{Net profit}}{\text{Sales}} \times 100 = \text{x\%}$
Expenses as a percentage of sales	$= \dfrac{\text{Expenses}}{\text{Sales}} \times 100 = \text{x\%}$
Return on capital employed (ROCE)	$= \dfrac{\text{Net profit}}{\text{Capital employed}} \times 100 = \text{x\%}$
Stock turnover	$= \dfrac{\text{Cost of goods sold}}{\text{Average stock}} = \text{x times a year}$
where average stock	$= \dfrac{\text{Opening stock} + \text{Closing stock}}{2}$
Current ratio (working capital ratio)	$= \dfrac{\text{Current assets}}{\text{Current liabilities}} = \text{x:1}$
Acid test ratio (quick ratio)	$= \dfrac{\text{Current assets} - \text{Stock}}{\text{Current liabilities}} = \text{x:1}$
Debtors : Sales ratio (debtors' collection period)	= Number of months debtors (on average) take to pay
	$= \dfrac{\text{Debtors}}{\text{Sales for the year}} \times 12 = \text{x months}$

(If days instead of months are required, the formula should be multiplied by 365 instead of 12.)

Creditors : Purchases ratio (creditors' payment period)

= Number of months it takes (on average) to pay suppliers

$$= \frac{\text{Creditors}}{\text{Purchases for the year}} \times 12 = \text{x months}$$

(If days instead of months are required, the formula should be multiplied by 365 instead of 12.)

Fixed Asset : Sales ratio

$$= \frac{\text{Sales}}{\text{Fixed assets}} = \text{x:1}$$

39.10 Multiple-choice questions

Now attempt Set No 3 of the multiple-choice questions in Appendix C, which contains 27 questions.

Chapter summary

- Financial statements are analysed and interpreted for internal and external parties. It is important to remember that a ratio on its own is of no use at all. It must be compared with previous years' results or the results of a competitor to be meaningful.
- Profitability and liquidity are equally important factors when running a business.
- The use of the profitability ratios ensure owners of a business keep a careful check on figures such as cost of goods, sales, expenses, gross and net profits.
- Liquidity ratios measure the ability of a business to pay its debts as they fall due and ensure smooth cash flow.
- Working capital is found by deducting the total current assets from the total current liabilities.
- There are various methods of calculating capital employed depending upon the type of business, i.e. sole trader, partnership or limited company.
- Working capital is found by deducting current liabilities from the current assets. It is vital for businesses to have sufficient working capital to ensure they can pay their debts as they fall due.

Note: In Appendix B you will find a worksheet that you can photocopy and use to answer questions on ratio analysis.

EXERCISES

39.1 The following accounts are of two companies that each sell sports goods:

Trading and Profit and Loss Accounts

	M Ltd		N Ltd	
	£	£	£	£
Sales		360,000		250,000
Less Cost of goods sold:				
Opening stock	120,000		60,000	
Add Purchases	268,000		191,500	
	388,000		251,500	
Less Closing stock	100,000	288,000	64,000	187,500
Gross profit		72,000		62,500
Less Expenses:				
Wages	8,000		11,300	
Directors' remuneration	12,000		13,000	
Other expenses	8,800	28,800	3,200	27,500
Net profit		43,200		35,000
Add Retained profits from last year		16,800		2,000
		60,000		37,000
Less Appropriations:				
General reserve	8,000		2,000	
Dividends	40,000	48,000	30,000	32,000
Retained profits carried to next year		12,000		5,000

Balance Sheets

	M Ltd		N Ltd	
	£	£	£	£
Fixed Assets:				
Fixtures at cost	200,000		180,000	
Less Depreciation to date	50,000	150,000	70,000	110,000
Motor vans at cost	80,000		120,000	
Less Depreciation to date	30,000	50,000	40,000	80,000
		200,000		190,000
Current Assets:				
Stock	100,000		64,000	
Debtors	60,000		62,500	
Bank	40,000		3,500	
	200,000		130,000	
Less Current Liabilities				
Creditors	50,000		65,000	
Net current assets		150,000		65,000
		350,000		255,000
Financed by:				
Issued share capital		300,000		200,000
General reserve		38,000		50,000
Profit and loss		12,000		5,000
		350,000		255,000

Required:

(*a*) Calculate the following ratios to one decimal place:

    (i)   current ratio

    (ii)   acid test ratio

    (iii) stockturn

    (iv) debtors : sales ratio

    (v)   creditors : purchases ratio

    (vi) gross profit as a percentage of sales

    (vii) net profit as a percentage of sales

    (viii) rate of return on shareholders' funds.

(*b*) Compare the results of the two companies, giving possible reasons for the different results.

39.2X   The owners of Hailstone company and Taylor company are having a friendly argument over the relative performance of their two similar businesses. The following information is available:

	Hailstone company	Taylor company
	£	£
Cash	4,000	100
Sales	200,000	200,000
Operating expenses	8,000	80,000
Closing stock	8,000	30,000
Debtors	3,000	33,000
Bank overdraft	nil	5,000
Opening stock	10,000	40,000
Capital employed	320,000	320,000
Creditors	7,500	50,000
Purchases	140,000	60,000

Required:

(*a*) For each company, calculate to one decimal place:

    (i)   gross profit margin

    (ii) stock turnover (use cost of goods sold divided by average stock)

    (iii) net profit margin

    (iv) return on capital employed

    (v) debtors collection period

    (vi) current ratio.

(*b*) Comment on the performance of each of the companies, using the ratios you have calculated.

City & Guilds Pitman qualifications

39.3X   The following figures are extracted from the final accounts of a company for the year ended 31 December 2009:

	£
Opening stock	5,000
Purchases	32,000
Closing stock	7,000
Sales	60,000
Debtors	7,500

For the year ended 31 December 2009, calculate:

(*a*) cost of goods sold

(*b*) average stock

(c) rate of stock turnover

(d) debtors' collection period.

For the year ended 31 December 2008, the following had been calculated.

- Rate of stock turnover (stockturn)　　=　6 times p.a.
- Debtors' collection period　　　　　　=　31 days (1 month)

(e) With that additional information in mind, state which you think was the better year out of 2008 and 2009. Give *two* reasons to support your answer.

NEAB (GCSE)

PART 6

Associated accounting topics

This part is concerned with the use of conputerised accounting systems. Also covered is a chapter on how ethics affects you personally in the workplace.

Computers and accounting systems

Learning objectives

After you have studied this chapter you should be able to:

- appreciate the uses of computer technology in recording financial information
- appreciate the different types of financial accounting packages available for all types of organisations
- understand the functions and benefits of computer accounting software
- appreciate the benefits of having online facilities within a computer system to provide for internet usage
- realise the importance of backing up data when using a computerised accounting package
- understand the importance of security when using an accounting package and the benefits of using a password
- describe the advantages and disadvantages of using a computerised accounting system.

40.1 Introduction

Today there is widespread use of computers to operate accounting systems. Sophisticated technology is now available at a reasonable cost. Large- to medium-sized concerns have used specially written packages for a number of years but smaller enterprises were initially discouraged from setting up their own systems by the cost of such packages. However, small businesses can now afford to use a computerised system using off-the-shelf packages such as Sage or QuickBooks. These packages carry out the same double entry functions of data processing and recording financial information as manual systems and also offer other features such as management information.

The rapid development of the internet means that accounting information and transactions can be carried out online. Consequently businesses that do not have computer facilities could easily get left behind and miss out on the opportunities that internet access provides.

40.2 Functions of computerised accounting packages

A **computerised accounting package** offers all the functions that a manual system provides but in addition it provides useful reports and management information. Since the system is integrated, basic data is entered, processed and automatically posted to supplier and customer accounts and the general (nominal) ledger updated. At the same time stock records are updated and, in some instances, automatic re-ordering systems are in place. The main functions of a computerised accounting package are listed below.

Sales

Preparation and printing of sales invoices, credit notes and month end statements. Data from the above documents is entered, processed and recorded:

- in the customer accounts in the sales ledger
- by automatic update of the stock records.

Purchases

Data from the purchase invoice and credit notes is entered, processed and recorded:

- in the supplier accounts in the purchase ledger
- by automatic update of the stock records
- via a print out of remittance advices.

Bank account

- Recording data such as customer receipts, supplier payments, other payments and receipts.
- Many banks offer online banking facilities which have the added advantage of the organisation's bank account being completely up to date.
- All receipts and payments are linked to the personal accounts of the debtors and creditors and the system provides for such transactions to automatically update these accounts.

General (nominal) ledger

Automatic updating of the general (nominal) ledger.

Wages/salaries

Organisations have the option of using a combined computerised accounting and wages/salary package; alternatively, they may use a separate 'payroll package'. Such packages perform all the necessary payroll functions.

Stock control

As mentioned above under sales and purchases these functions are linked to the stock records. This means that stock records are automatically updated after each sales invoice and purchases invoice is entered into the system so providing an accurate figure of stock held at any particular point in time.

At the end of the financial year when an organisation undertakes stocktaking the use of a computerised system enables up-to-date stock lists to be made available. These lists are used in the physical stocktake and enable variances to be identified and amended.

The functions are summarised in Exhibit 40.1.

Exhibit 40.1 Integrated computerised accounting system

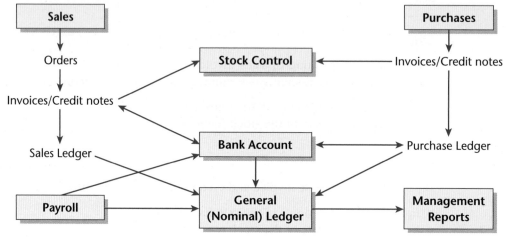

Exhibit 40.1 can be compared to Exhibit 2.1 (see page 10). The source documents and their entry in the books of prime entry are clearly shown.

Management reports

One of the main features of a computerised accounting system is the facility to provide the owners of the business and/or management with useful financial data and reports. At the end of each month or specific accounting period certain 'month end/year end' functions are carried out to provide the following information:

- day books for customers and suppliers
- general (nominal) ledger and bank account transactions
- activity reports on all ledger transactions
- an audit trail
- analysis reports for aged debtors and creditors
- financial statements including the trial balance, trading and profit and loss accounts and balance sheet
- ratio analysis.

Other useful functions

Spreadsheets   The use of spreadsheets is another facility that a computer has to offer. Spreadsheets can be used to provide financial budgets or cash-flow budgets, a fixed asset register, calculation of loan interest payments plus many other uses.

Internet access   As mentioned above internet access can provide such things as online banking, payment of suppliers and other payments such as wages/salaries. An organisation having its own website can advertise its products and services and offer online ordering systems. In addition the internet is a useful source of information and data that an organisation may from time to time need to access.

40.3   Data back-up

It is important that data held on the computer is regularly saved. The regularity has to be determined by the business relative to the type of operation and could mean every few minutes, after a specified computer task or after a longer time scale, say, every hour.

It is also vital to back up data held on the system. Back-up can be achieved by copying data onto a floppy disc, a CD or by transferring it to another computer, either on the premises or at a remote location. A recent development for storing information is USB pen drives, or memory sticks, which are small but robust solid state devices and are easily carried in a pocket or briefcase.

Some large organisations may deem it essential to keep their CDs, floppy discs, etc. containing stored information off-site in a secure location. This is particularly the case where the loss of such data could have catastrophic implications for the business.

40.4   Security

All organisations regard their financial information as sensitive and as such it should remain confidential except where legislation demands certain information be made available to external bodies.

Staff working on computerised accounting systems will be allocated passwords which will restrict access to their area of work. Passwords should be changed regularly to help prevent the possibility of non-authorised persons accessing the system.

When a system uses internet connections there is the constant threat of fraudulent access and corruption. Most computer systems have packages to resist viruses and attack by hacking. These have to be constantly reviewed and updated.

40.5   Computerised accounting systems

The following advantages and disadvantages of using accounting packages are detailed below.

Advantages

- Data is inputted and processed very rapidly, far faster than in a manual system.
- Greater accuracy since data is only input once and transactions carried out automatically whereas with a manual system data may have to be entered twice or more.

- Documents such as invoices, credit notes, statements, remittance advices can be produced automatically.
- Constant updating of the accounting records gives the accurate state of customers' accounts enabling remedial action to be taken as necessary.
- Management information can quickly be made available in report form, i.e. aged debtors and creditors analysis reports.
- A system connected to the internet can make financial transactions electronically.
- More efficient use of resources, for example, less accounting staff.

Disadvantages

- The cost of installation can be considerable together with the ongoing costs of maintenance and updating.
- The introduction of the system will affect most other areas of the business leading to considerable disruption. Staff may also be resentful of any new system.
- Staff will need to be trained to use the system and training costs have to be considered.
- System downtime can be very disruptive.
- Data back-up is essential at regular intervals.
- Fraudulent access can seriously affect the business operation and its profitability.
- Security measures are vital, for example, passwords for staff and protection against viruses and hacking.
- Health risks associated with the operation of computer keyboards and screens, which include eyestrain, back problems due to poor posture, and muscular fatigue in the arm and wrist from keyboard use. Regular rest intervals away from work stations are essential.

Chapter summary

- Computers are widely used in organisations for operating accounting systems.
- Most computerised accounting packages are integrated systems linking together the sales ledger, purchase ledger, general (nominal) ledger and the bank account.
- The computerised accounting package also produces various documents such as invoices, credit notes, statements and remittance advices.
- Other features include providing financial information for the owners of the business and/or management and the use of the internet for online facilities and spreadsheets for such things as preparing budgets, etc.
- It is essential that users of computerised accounting packages regularly back up data using one of the various methods available.
- Security within any system is paramount for any organisation and every effort must be made to ensure that data is safe and secure.
- Organisations must consider the benefits of operating a computer accounting package such as the speed at which data is entered, accuracy, cost effectiveness and the information output, such as management reports.
- The disadvantages include the cost of installing equipment, buying software and providing training together with security concerns. There may also be some resentment from staff and lack of motivation.

EXERCISES

40.1 A flag manufacturer's business has recently received a large increase in orders from overseas to meet the requirements of major sporting events. This demand for flags has had a considerable effect on the present manual accounting system. The Finance Director has decided that he would like to introduce a fully integrated computer accounting system. He intends to put his case forward at the next Directors' Meeting and asks you to prepare some notes on his behalf.

Required:
Prepare notes for the Finance Director to present at the meeting including the main advantages to be gained by making the change. You must also anticipate the arguments that may be used by a board member objecting to the proposed change.

40.2 The security of data is a very important consideration when using a computerised accounting package. Explain the measures that a medium-sized company could initiate to provide protection for the company against the security of its financial data and records.

40.3X You work in the accounts department of an advertising agency where a new member of staff has recently joined the accounts team. You have been asked to help her settle in the department and provide training on the computerised accounting system. One of the areas that you feel is very important is security and backing up data.

Required:
Draft a memo to the trainee outlining the importance of security of financial data and the agency's procedures for backing up data.

40.4X (a) Outline the benefits that are available to a small business when it has internet facilities.
(b) If the firm decided to obtain the services of a web designer to develop a website what benefits would this provide to the business?
(c) If the website was developed what do you think are the disadvantages to offering such a service?

40.5X A local garage, which carries out servicing and repairs mainly to cars and small commercial vehicles, is run by the owner with two other employees. The book-keeping and accounting is carried out on a part-time basis by an employee who works one day per week. She uses a manual accounting system to deal with customer invoices and payments, paying suppliers for goods received, banking monies received, petty cash and paying wages.

The owner is considering a computerised accounting system but is unsure as to the benefits to be gained from a large initial investment.

Required:
Put forward the benefits that might be gained but also consider the adverse aspects of such an investment.

CHAPTER 41

Ethics: getting it right as a professional

Learning objectives

After you have studied this chapter you should be able to:

- appreciate how ethics affects you personally at home, with friends and in the workplace
- reflect on the factors on which your ethical behaviour is based
- be aware that codes of ethical behaviour have been introduced by most accountancy bodies
- appreciate that conflict may occur in dealing with an ethical dilemma or problem and the steps to take to resolve this.

41.1 This chapter is for you personally

You may wonder why ethics appears in a book whose aim is to develop your accountancy skills. Since you have reached the final chapter in the book it is assumed that you intend to make a career in finance and accounting.

You will already have been influenced by ethics but may not have been fully aware of how it has affected you. Your upbringing at home, your progress through school and college will have shaped and developed your behaviour. This revolves round the 'right thing to do' and the 'wrong thing to do'. The object of this chapter is to introduce you to the topic and encourage you to reflect on your own values and beliefs and how they affect your personal behaviour.

Accountancy is a profession and being a member of such a profession means more than 'just a job of work'. Being technically competent and nothing else is not sufficient. The way you act and make decisions in the workplace is crucial to the role of being a professional.

41.2 What are you taking to the party?

This question is asking what you have gained from your upbringing and life experiences in developing your personal behaviour. You might describe this as your own 'code of conduct' which will probably have been influenced by family/cultural/ religious/ educational aspects.

It is expected that you will have gained:

- values – what you have decided will guide you through life
- attitudes – developed through experience and can change through new positive/ negative experiences
- beliefs – a conviction that something is true
- awareness – *self:* a developing understanding of a certain subject or situation; *others:* an ability of how to interact with family, friends and colleagues
- discipline – in terms of personal behaviour the ability to maintain self-control.

At this point consider the first three aspects discussed above and then add your own perceptions. Try to think of at least three elements for each aspect below.

An example is done for you.

Values   *Honesty* ....

Attitudes   ....

Beliefs   ....

41.3 Ethics

On a personal level **ethics** may be sufficiently described as the morals governing human behaviour. Professional ethics, however, are more clearly defined and are generally referred to as 'a code of behaviour considered correct for a particular group, association or profession'.

41.4 What you need to be successful in your workplace

The level and range of ethical requirements for each employee in the workplace will change relative to their duties and status. For example, an employee with no contact with clients or customers will have different requirements to employees such as sales staff.

Mechanical
Any aspiring professional should:

- Be skilled up to a technical level appropriate to their job requirements.
- Behave responsibly in carrying out their duties.
- Be prepared to undertake training to enhance their skills in terms of job, technological, environmental and legal requirements. Most professional bodies require members to undertake Continual Professional Development (CPD) to ensure that they are up-to-date and competent in all areas of their work.
- Know the need to keep confidential the work of the business except in permitted circumstances, for example, compliance with legal requirements.

Inter-personal

Any aspiring professional should:

- Work honestly and diligently with colleagues.
- Behave responsibly and fairly in a straightforward and honest manner to all people whether they be colleagues, clients, customers, contractors, etc.
- Conduct oneself courteously at all times.
- Not undermine colleagues to gain a personal advantage.

41.5 Ethical codes

Over the past few years the issue of ethical behaviour in the finance industry has been highly topical. In the USA, during this time, there have been some high-profile corporate failures, which led to the ethical culture and behaviour within these companies being questioned.

As a result the International Federation of Accountants (IFAC), through its ethics committee, issued its Code of Ethics for Professional Accountants, the latest issue being in June 2005. The aim of the code is 'to strengthen the worldwide accountancy profession' and is mandatory for those accountancy bodies that are members of IFAC. Therefore most accountancy bodies in the UK have now adopted the IFAC code with some additions and extra guidance.

As a student or full member of an accountancy institution you will be required to comply with that institution's code. To ensure that members are familiar with the requirements of the codes, seminars and training programmes have been initiated by the professional bodies as part of their CPD programmes. You should be also aware that many institutions have incorporated such codes into the assessment process for student members.

Larger accountancy firms have their own ethical codes. As an employee you would be expected to comply with that code from the commencement of your employment. It is likely to be covered in your training at the induction stage or by participating in internal sessions.

41.6 Conflict

Until IFAC produced its first Code of Ethics in 2001, most codes of ethics in the accountancy profession consisted of sets of detailed rules that had to be followed to the letter. That was the problem in most of the famous corporate failures; it was the letter rather than the spirit that was being observed. Most regulators were producing ever-increasingly lengthy and unwieldy lists of rules to combat ever-increasing breaches of the regulations. It was then that IFAC decided to produce a code, which was a framework of principles:

A professional accountant is expected to comply with the following fundamental principles:

(a) Integrity – A professional accountant should be straightforward and honest in all professional and business relationships.

> *(b) Objectivity – A professional accountant should not allow bias, conflict of interest or undue influence to override professional or business judgements.*
>
> *(c) Professional Competence and Due Care – A professional accountant has a continuing duty to maintain professional knowledge and skill at the level required to ensure that a client or employer receives competent professional service based on current developments in practice, legislation and techniques. A professional accountant should act diligently and in accordance with applicable technical and professional standards when providing professional services.*
>
> *(d) Confidentiality – A professional accountant should respect the confidentiality of information acquired as a result of professional and business relationships and should not disclose any such information to third parties without proper and specific authority unless there is a legal or professional right or duty to disclose. Confidential information acquired as a result of professional and business relationships should not be used for the personal advantage of the professional accountant or third parties.*
>
> *(e) Professional behaviour – A professional accountant should comply with relevant laws and regulations and should avoid any action that discredits the profession.*

Professional accountants, including students, have to abide by these fundamental principles. Although there are detailed examples for guidance, the principles override any illustrations. Therefore, when making professional judgements the professional accountant has to consider these principles sufficiently for any such decisions to be able to withstand professional scrutiny if necessary at later date.

Problems can arise when we take account of the influences on us when deciding what course of action to follow, whether professional or personal. The influences can include:

- Personal – the need to behave within one's own integrity.
- Company – working in the best interests of your employer.
- Professional body – upholding the aims and standards of your institution or association.
- Public interest – *'a distinguishing mark of a profession is acceptance of its responsibility to the public. Therefore, a professional accountant's responsibility is not exclusively to satisfy the needs of an individual client or employer'* (IFAC Code of Ethics, Introduction). In the first edition (2001) of its Code, it was stated: *'The accountancy profession's public consist of clients, credit grantors, governments, employers, employees, investors, the business and financial community and others who rely on the objectivity and integrity of professional accountants. . . .'*

You can see that all these considerations can lead to uncertainty in arriving at the correct decision. However, remember that management are responsible for implementing and maintaining ethical standards. An ethical dilemma or problem is not the sole responsibility of the person affected but should be dealt with as stated in the code. This may be as a team in a particular department, as a company-wide issue or at a professional or regulatory disciplinary hearing.

41.7   Your next step

Assuming you are involved in accountancy you need to evaluate your present situation relative to your work, academic studies and your status, even as a student member of an accountancy body. As a junior member in the workplace, professional ethics may have little effect due to your level of work. If you are in the initial stages of your accountancy studies you will need to be familiar with the assessment requirements of your particular accountancy body.

It is worth remembering that professional ethics have an impact on companies, institutions, associations, etc. irrespective of the activity being carried out. You will need to be involved whatever your role.

Chapter summary

- This chapter introduces the concept of your personal behaviour, which can be referred to as your own code of conduct.
- Ethical behaviour is now an important aspect of working as a professional accountant and is referred to under both inter-personal and mechanical aspects.
- Codes of behaviour have been introduced in the UK by most of the professional firms, institutions, associations, etc. Within an organisation, it is management's role to implement and maintain the relevant ethical code. Nevertheless every professional accountant has his or her own responsibilities and has to be accountable for his or her actions.
- Ethical dilemmas and problems are not the sole responsibility of the person affected but should be resolved based on teamwork appropriate to the scale of the problem.

Appendices

The Appendices provide ancillary information to aid understanding of the main narrative of the book. Test questions are also included.

Glossary of accounting terms

The chapter where the term first appears is shown at the end of each definition.

Account	The place in a ledger where all the transactions relating to a particular asset, liability or capital, expenses or revenue item are recorded. Accounts are part of the double entry book-keeping system. They are sometimes referred to as 'T accounts' or ledger accounts. (**4**)
Accounting	A skill or practice of maintaining accounts and preparing reports to aid the financial control and management of a business. (**1**)
Accounting concepts	The rules which lay down the way in which the activities of a business are recorded. (**13**)
Accounting equation	If a business starts trading it will require resources, expressed as: resources supplied by the owner = resources in the business or capital = assets − liabilities. (**3**)
Accounting system	The period in which a business operates its financial year. It involves recording all trading activities from source documents to the preparation of final accounts. (**2**)
Accrual	An accrued expense. An amount owing. (**29**)
Accrual concept	Where net profit is the difference between revenues and expenses. (**13**)
Accrued expense	An expense that has been incurred and the benefit received but that has not been paid for at the end of the accounting period. Also referred to as an accrual. (**29**)
Accumulated fund	A form of capital account for a non-profit-making organisation. (**35**)
Acid test ratio	A ratio comparing current assets less stock with current liabilities. Also known as the 'quick ratio'. (**39**)
Advice note	A note sent to a customer by the supplier prior to goods being despatched, advising of the goods to be despatched and the estimated date of delivery. (**14**)
Ageing debtors schedule	A list of amounts owing by debtors and how long the debt has been outstanding. (**28**)
Amortisation	A term used instead of depreciation when assets are used up simply because of the time factor. (**26**)
Analytical day books	Book of original entry in which sales and/or purchase invoices are entered. The book has various analysis columns, which are totalled

at the end of the month and posted to the general ledger and control accounts. (19)

Annual General Meeting (AGM)
A meeting held every year to which all shareholders in a company are invited to attend. At the meeting, the latest set of final accounts is considered, together with the appointment or removal of directors and/or auditors. (37)

Appreciation
The increase in value over the cost of an asset, usually land and buildings. (26)

Appropriation account
An addition to the Profit and Loss Account of partnerships. The appropriation account shows how profit earned is divided. In accordance with the partnership deed or agreement. (36)

Assets
Resources owned by the business. (3)

Authorised share capital
The total amount of share capital or number of shares which a company can have in issue at any given time. (37)

Automated Direct Debit Instruction Service (AUDDIS)
A fast method for businesses to make repayments. (20)

AVCO
A method by which the goods used are priced out at average cost. (31)

Bad debt
A debt owing to a business which is unlikely to be paid. (28)

Bad debt recovered
A debt, previously written off, that is subsequently paid by the debtor. (28)

Balance sheet
A statement showing the assets, capital and liabilities of a business. (2)

Balancing the account
Finding and entering the difference between the two sides of an account. (7)

Bank cash book
The cash book for other than petty cash. (22)

Bank draft
This is raised by the bank from funds held by a business and is passed to the supplies for whom it is a secure and guaranteed method of payment. (20)

Bank giro credit (BGC)
Method used by businesses to pay creditors, wages and/or salaries. A bank giro credit list and slips containing information about each person or organisation to be paid and the amount payable are sent to the bank, together with one cheque to cover all the payments. The bank then automatically transfers the funds from the business's account to the account of each of the respective people or organisations. (23)

Bank guarantee/debit card
Used by customers when paying by cheque and this tells the seller that a bank or card company guarantees that payment will be made. (20)

Bank overdraft
What results when we have paid more out of our bank account than we have paid into it. (21)

Bank reconciliation statement
A calculation comparing the cash book balance with the bank statement balance. (17)

Bank statement
Copy of our current account given to us by our bank. (20)

Bankers' Automated Clearing Service (BACS)
Computerised payment transfer system that is a very popular way of paying creditors, wages and salaries. (2)

Book-keeping	The recording of accounting data. (**1**)
Books of original entry	Books where the first entry of a transaction is made. (**15**)
Budgets	The usual term for financial plans. (**1**)
Business entity concept	Concerning only transactions that affect the business, and ignoring the owner's private transactions. (**13**)
Called-up capital	Where only part of the amounts payable on each share have been asked for. The total amount requested on all the shares is known as the 'called-up capital'. (**37**)
Calls in arrear	The amount for which payment has been requested (i.e. called for), but has not yet been paid by shareholders. (**37**)
Capital	The total of resources supplied to a business by its owner. (**3**)
Capital employed	This term has many meanings, but basically it means the amount of money that is being used up (or 'employed') in the business. It is the balance of the capital account plus any long-term loan or, alternatively, the total net assets of the business. (**29**)
Capital expenditure	When a business spends money to buy or add value to a fixed asset. (**9**)
Capital invested	The amount of money, or money's worth, brought into a business by its proprietor from outside. (**29**)
Capital reserve	Reserves which cannot be used for the payment of dividends. The two most common types of capital reserve are the Share Premium Account and Revaluation Reserve Account. (Capital reserves are outside the scope of this book.) (**37**)
Carriage inwards	Cost of transport of goods into a business. (**12**)
Carriage outwards	Cost of transport of goods to the customers of a business. (**12**)
Carriage paid	The cost of transport that has been included in the cost of the goods. (**14**)
Cash book	Book of original entry for cash and bank receipts and payments. (**2**)
Cash discount	An allowance given for quick payment of an account owing. (**21**)
Cash float	The sum held as petty cash. (**22**)
Casting	Adding up figures. (**32**)
Cheque	A cash free method of transferring money using a form of standard format. It is used to instruct one's own bank to transfer money from one's own account to another person or business. (**20**)
Cheque counterfoil	On which to record details of the cheque issued. (**2**)
CHAPS	Clearing House Automated Payment System. A computerised system that has developed to facilitate the same day transfer of large amounts of money. (**20**)
Club accounts	Accounts prepared for non-profit-making organisations such as the local tennis club. (**35**)
COD	Literally 'Cash on delivery'. (**14**)
Coding of invoices	A process used, particularly in computerised accounting, to code the invoice to the supplier or purchaser, and also to the relevant account in the general ledger. (**16**)

Company limited by guarantee	These do not have share capital but rely on members' guarantees in the event of insolvency. (**37**)
Compensating error	Where two errors of equal amounts but on opposite sides of the accounts, cancel out each other. (**32**)
Complete reversal of entries	Where the correct amounts are entered in the correct accounts but each item is shown on the wrong side of each account. (**32**)
Computerised accounting packages	A software accounting package which involves the inputting of financial data. The data is recorded in both the individual account and ledgers in one transaction. The package also provides additional financial management reports and information. (**40**)
Conservatism	An older term for 'prudence'. (**13**)
Consistency concept	To keep the same method, except in special cases. (**13**)
Contra	A contra is where both the debit and credit entries are shown in the cash book. (**21**)
Control account	An account which checks the arithmetical accuracy of a ledger. (**25**)
Cost of conversion	Consists of specific, attributable production costs and overheads. (**13**)
Cost of goods sold	This is calculated as follows: Opening stock plus purchases during the period less the value of the stock at the end of the period (closing stock). (**10**)
Cost of purchase	The purchase price less trade discounts, etc. (**13**)
Cost price	The basic price before any mark ups, etc. (**27**)
Credit	The right-hand side of the accounts in double entry. (**4**)
Credit card	Issued by organisations such as Visa, Mastercard and involve electronic transfer of money to the seller by the credit card company who will bill the buyer for repayment. (**20**)
Credit control	The measures and procedures a business undertakes to ensure that its customers pay their accounts when they fall due. This includes evaluating the credit worthness of customers before allowing them credit. (**15**)
Credit note	A document sent to a customer showing allowance given by supplier in respect of unsatisfactory goods. (**2**)
Credit transfer	An amount paid by someone direct into our bank account. (**20**)
Creditor	A person to whom money is owed for goods or services. (**2**)
Creditors : purchases ratio	A ratio assessing how long it takes a business to pay its creditors. Also known as 'creditors' payment period'. (**39**)
Current assets	Assets consisting of cash, goods for resale, or items having a shorter life. (**3**)
Current liabilities	Liabilities to be paid for in the near future. (**3**)
Current ratio	A ratio comparing current assets with current liabilities. Also known as the 'working capital' ratio. (**39**)
Debenture	Loan to a company. (**37**)
Debenture interest	An agreed percentage of interest paid to a debenture holder for lending a company money. (**37**)

Debit	The left-hand side of the accounts in double entry. (4)
Debit note	A document sent to a supplier showing allowance given for unsatisfactory goods. (2)
Debtor	A person who owes money to the business for goods or services supplied. (2)
Debtors : Sales ratio	A ratio assessing how long it takes debtors to pay a business. Also known as 'debtors' collection period'. (39)
Delivery note	A note which accompanies goods being despatched, enabling the customer to check what goods have been received. The carrier often retains a copy and asks the customer to sign this to verify that the customer has received the goods. (14)
Depletion	The wasting away of an asset as it is used up. (26)
Depreciation	The part of the cost of the fixed asset consumed during its period of use by a business. (26)
Direct costs	Costs which can be traced to the item being manufactured. (38)
Direct debit	Payment made out of payer's bank, direct to payee's bank, on *payee's* instructions. (20)
Directors	Officials appointed by shareholders to manage the company for them. (37)
Directors' remuneration	Directors are legally employees of the company and any pay they receive is called directors' remuneration. (37)
Discounts allowed	A reduction given to customers who pay their accounts within the time allowed. (21)
Discounts received	A reduction given to us by a supplier when we pay their account before the time allowed has elapsed. (21)
Dishonoured cheque	A cheque that is found to be worth nothing. (23)
Dividends	The amount given to shareholders as their share of the profits of the company. (37)
Donation	A monetary gift donated to the club or society, monies received should be shown as income in the year that they are received. (35)
Double entry book-keeping	A system where each transaction is entered twice, once on the debit side and once on the credit side. (2)
Doubtful debt	A debt which may not be paid in the time requested. (28)
Drawee	The bank on which a cheque is drawn. (20)
Drawer	The person making out a cheque and using it for payment. (20)
Drawings	Cash or goods taken out of a business by the owner for private use. (6)
Dual aspect concept	Dealing with both aspects of a transaction. (13)
E&OE	Appears on some invoices and other documents. Abbreviation stands for 'errors and omissions excepted'. Basically it is a warning that errors or omissions may exist on documents. (14)
EFTPOS	Electronic Funds Transfer at Point of Sale. A system used by most large retail businesses which involves the use of electronic cash

registers. This automatically transfers payments from the purchaser's account to the seller's bank account. (**20**)

Equity	Another name for the capital of the owner. Also described as 'net worth'. (**3**)
Error of commission	Where a correct amount is entered, but in the wrong person's account. (**32**)
Errors, complete reversal of entries	See 'complete reversal of entries'. (**32**)
Error of omission	Where a transaction is completely omitted from the books. (**32**)
Error of original entry	Where an item is entered, but both debit and credit entries are of the same incorrect amount. (**32**)
Error of principle	Where an item is entered in the wrong type of account, for example, a fixed asset entered in an expense account. (**32**)
Error of transposition	Where figures are transposed incorrectly. (**33**)
Ethics	The moral principles governing human conduct generally referred to as 'a code of behaviour considered correct for a particular group, association, profession'. (**41**)
Ex works	An indication that the price of certain goods does not include delivery costs. (**14**)
Exempted businesses	Businesses that do not have to add VAT to the price of goods and services supplied by them, and that cannot obtain a refund of VAT paid on goods and services purchased by them. (**18**)
Exempt supplies	Supplies which are outside the scope of VAT and, therefore, VAT cannot be charged. (**18**)
Expenses	Costs of operating the business. (**6**)
Expenses : Sales ratio	A ratio which indicates whether costs are rising against sales or whether sales are falling against expenses. (**39**)
Extended trial balance (ETB)	A trial balance with additional columns added to enable adjustments to be made prior to the preparation of the financial statements. The extended trial balance is often referred to as a 'worksheet'. (**30**)
Factoring	A system used by a business to improve its cash flow. This involves 'selling' its debtors to a factoring company, which is then responsible for collecting debts as they become due and which keeps a percentage of the money collected, usually around 10%. (**15**)
Factory overhead costs	Refer to: Indirect manufacturing costs. (**38**)
FIFO	A method by which the first goods to be received are said to be the first to be sold. (**31**)
Final accounts	At the end of the accounting period or year a business usually prepares its final accounts, which includes the trading and profit and loss account and balance sheet. (**12**)
Financial statements	Formal documents produced by an organisation to show the financial status of the business at a particular time. These include the trading and profit and loss account and the balance sheet. (**1**)

Fixed assets	Assets bought which have a long life and are to be used in the business. (**3**)
Fixed assets to sales ratio	A measurement of the efficiency of fixed assets in generating sales. (**39**)
Fixed capital accounts	Capital accounts which consist only of the original capital invested in the business. (**36**)
Fixed costs	Costs that remain the same (in the short term) irrespective of levels of production or business activity. (**38**)
Flat rate scheme	A special VAT scheme for small businesses. (**18**)
Fluctuating capital accounts	Capital accounts whose balances change from one period to the next. (**36**)
Folio columns	Columns used for entering reference numbers. (**21**)
General ledger	All accounts other than those for customers and suppliers. (**2**)
Going concern concept	Where a business is assumed to continue for a long time. (**13**)
Goodwill	The extra amount paid for an existing business above the value of its other assets. (**29**)
Goods received note	A note that details exactly what goods have been received. (**14**)
Gross loss	When the 'cost of goods sold' exceeds 'sales', then the business has incurred a gross loss. (**10**)
Gross profit	Found by deducting cost of goods sold from sales. (**9**)
Gross profit as a percentage of sales (Gross profit margin)	A ratio which states gross profit as a percentage of sales; can indicate how effectively a business has controlled their cost of goods. (**39**)
Gross profit to cost of sales (Gross profit mark-up)	The percentage of gross profit to the cost of sales. (**39**)
Historical cost concept	The normal means of valuing the assets of a business based on their cost price. (**13**)
Impersonal accounts	All accounts other than debtors' and creditors' accounts. (**2**)
Imprest system	A system used for controlling expenditure of small cash items which are recorded in the petty cash book. A cash 'float' of a fixed amount is provided initially to the person responsible for operating the petty cash system. Any cash paid out during a particular period, i.e. a week, is reimbursed to the petty cashier so restoring the 'float' to its original sum. (**22**)
Inadequacy	When an asset is no longer used because of changes within an organisation due to growth, competition or product range changes. (**26**)
Income and expenditure account	An account for a non-profit-making organisation to find the surplus or loss made during a period. (**35**)
Incomplete records	Where only some transactions are recorded in the books of account, the missing information has to be obtained by other means. (**34**)
Indirect manufacturing costs	Costs which occur in a factory or other production facility but cannot be easily traced to the items being manufactured. (**38**)

Input VAT	The VAT charged to a business on its purchases and expenses (inputs). (**18**)
Inputs	The value of goods and services purchased by a business. (**18**)
Intangible fixed asset	A fixed asset that cannot be physically seen or touched. (**37**)
Interest on capital	An amount, at an agreed rate of interest, that is credited to a partner based on the amount of capital contributed by him/her. (**36**)
Interest on drawings	An amount, at an agreed rate of interest, that is based on the drawings taken out and is debited to the partners. (**36**)
Invoice	A document prepared by the seller and sent to the purchaser whenever a business buys goods or services on credit. It gives details of the supplier and the customer, the goods purchased and their price. (**2**)
Issued share capital	The amount of the authorised share capital of a company that has been issued to shareholders. (**37**)
Journal	A book of account used to record rare or exceptional transactions that should not appear in the other books of original entry in use. (**2**)
Lease	An agreement to rent property for a period of time. (**26**)
Liabilities	Total of money owed for assets supplied to the business. (**3**)
Life membership	Where members pay one amount for membership to last them their lifetime. (**35**)
LIFO	A method by which the goods sold are said to have come from the last lot of goods to be received. (**31**)
Limited company	An organisation owned by its shareholders, whose liability is limited to their share capital. (**1**)
Limited liability	The liability of shareholders, in a company, is limited to any amount they have agreed to invest. (**37**)
Limited partner	A partner whose liability is limited to the capital invested in the firm. (**36**)
Limited partnership	A form of partnership in which limited partners' liabilities are limited to their investment and in which general partners with unlimited liability operate the business. (**36**)
Liquidity	The ability of a business to pay its debts as they fall due and to meet unexpected expenses within a reasonable settlement period. (**39**)
Liquidity ratios	Ratios that attempt to indicate the ability of a business to meet its debts as they become due and include current ratio and acid test ratio. (**39**)
Loan capital	Money owing by a company for debentures and for loans from banks and other sources that are not repayable in the near future. (**37**)
Loan interest	The extra amount levied by the lender of funds to recompense them for making the loan. (**9**)
Long-term liabilities	Liabilities not having to be paid for in the near future. (**11**)
Loss	Result of selling goods for less than they have cost the business. (**6**)

Manufacturing account	An account in which production cost is calculated. (**38**)
Margin	Profit shown as a percentage or fraction of the selling price. (**34**)
Mark-up	Profit shown as a percentage or fraction of the cost price. (**34**)
Matching concept	Another term for the accrual concept. (**13**)
Materiality concept	To record something in a special way only if the amount is not a small one. (**13**)
Memorandum account	An account which is not part of the double-entry system. These may be the personal accounts of debtors or creditors where the control account is part of the double entry and the personal accounts are classified as 'memorandum accounts'. Alternatively, the sales and purchases ledgers may be part of the double entry and the control accounts classified as 'memorandum accounts'. (**25**)
Money measurement concept	Accounting is only concerned with the money measurement of things and where most people will agree to the monetary value of a transaction. (**13**)
Narrative	A description and explanation of the transaction recorded in the journal. (**24**)
Net book value	The cost of a fixed asset with depreciation deducted, also known as 'book value'. (**26**)
Net current assets	The value of current assets less that of current liabilities. Also known as 'working capital'. (**11**)
Net loss	This occurs when total expenses exceed the gross profit. (**12**)
Net monthly	Appears at the foot of an invoice and means the full amount of the invoice is due for payment within one month of the invoice date. (**14**)
Net profit	Gross profit less expenses. (**9**)
Net profit as a percentage of sales	A ratio that states net profit as a percentage of sales and brings expenses into the calculation. (**39**)
Net realisable value	The value of goods calculated as the selling price less expenses before sale. (**13**)
Net worth	See 'equity'. (**3**)
Nominal accounts	Accounts in which expenses, revenue and capital are recorded. (**2**)
Nominal ledger	Ledger for impersonal accounts (also called general ledger). (**2**)
Non-profit-making organisations	Clubs, associations and societies operated to provide a service or activity for members since their main purpose is not trading or profit making. (**35**)
Non-trading organisations	These include clubs, associations and other non-profit-making organisations that are normally run for the benefit of their members to engage in a particular activity. (**1**)
Objectivity	Using a method that everyone can agree to. (**13**)
Obsolescence	Becoming out of date. (**26**)
Opening entry	An entry needed to open a new set of books of account. (**24**)

Ordinary shares	Shares entitled to dividends after the preference shareholders have been paid their dividends. (**37**)
Output VAT	The VAT charged by a business on its supplies (outputs). (**18**)
Outputs	The value of goods and services sold to a business. (**18**)
Overcasting	Incorrectly adding up a column of figures to give an answer which exceeds the correct total. (**32**)
Paid-up capital	The total of the amount of share capital that has been paid for by shareholders. (**37**)
Partly exempt businesses	These will sell some goods that are exempt from VAT and some goods that are either standard-rated or zero-rated. They may reclaim part of the input VAT paid by them. (**18**)
Partnership	A group of a minimum of two people and a maximum of twenty, who together are carrying on a particular business with a view to making profit. (**1**)
Partnership agreement	The contractual relationship, either written or verbal, between partners, which usually covers details such as how profits or losses should be shared and the relevant responsibilities of the partners. (**36**)
Partnership salaries	Agreed amounts payable to partners in respect of duties undertaken by them. (**36**)
Payee	The person to whom a cheque is paid. (**20**)
Payer	The person who pays a cheque. (**20**)
Paying-in slip	Form used for paying money into a bank account. (**2**)
Personal accounts	Accounts for both creditors and debtors. (**2**)
Petty cash book	A cash book used for making small (petty) payments. Payments are usually analysed and the totals of each column later posted to the various accounts in the general ledger. The source document used for entry into the petty cash book is a petty cash voucher. (**2**)
Petty cash voucher	The form used by anyone requesting payment for a small item of expenditure incurred on behalf of the business. The form gives details of the expense and should be signed and duly authorised. (**2**)
Posting	The act of using one book as a means of entering the transactions to another account. (**2**)
Preference shares	Shares that are entitled to an agreed rate of dividend before the ordinary shareholders receive anything. (**37**)
Preliminary expenses	All the costs that are incurred when a company is formed. (**37**)
Prepaid expense	An expense – usually a service – that has been paid for in one accounting period, the benefit of which will not be received until a subsequent period. It is a payment for an expense that has been paid for in advance. (**29**)
Prepayment	Also referred to as 'prepaid expense'. (**29**) (See above)
Prime cost	Direct materials plus labour plus direct expenses. (**38**)
Prime documents	Another term for source documents. (**2**)
Private ledger	Ledger for capital and drawings accounts. (**2**)

Private limited company	A legal entity with at least two shareholders, where the liability of the shareholders is limited to the amount of their investment. The public cannot subscribe for its shares. (**1**)
Production cost	Prime cost plus indirect manufacturing costs. (**38**)
Profit	The result when goods are sold for more than they cost. (If they are sold for less than they cost, then a *loss* is incurred.) (**6**)
Profit and loss account	Account in which net profit is calculated. (**10**)
Profitability	The effective operation of a business to make ongoing profits to ensure its long-term viability. (**39**)
Profitability ratios	Ratios that attempt to indicate the trend in a business's ability to make profit. These include gross profit and net profit to sales and return on capital employed. (**39**)
Pro-forma invoice	A type of invoice that is occasionally raised when the seller wishes to secure payment prior to the goods or services being supplied. (**14**)
Provision for doubtful debts	An account showing the expected amounts of debtors, who at the balance sheet date, may not be able to pay their outstanding accounts. (**28**)
Provision for depreciation account	The account where depreciation is accumulated for balance sheet purposes. In the balance sheet the cost price of the asset is shown, less the depreciation to date, to give the net book value. (**27**)
Prudence concept	To ensure that profit is not shown as being too high, or assets shown at too high a value. (**13**)
Public limited company	A legal entity with many shareholders since the public can subscribe for its shares. Shareholder liability is limited to the amount of their investment. (**1**)
Purchase invoice	A document received by purchaser showing details of goods bought and their prices. (**2**)
Purchase order	This is a document prepared by the purchaser and it contains details of the goods or services required by the purchaser. (**14**)
Purchases	Goods bought by the business for the purpose of selling them again. (**5**)
Purchases day book	Book of original entry for credit purchases. (**2**)
Purchases journal	Another name for the purchases day book. (**2**)
Purchases ledger	A ledger for suppliers' personal accounts. (**2**)
Purchase ledger control account	An account containing the total of the various individual personal ledger account balances. By comparing the balance on the control account with the outstanding balances in a subsidiary ledger the arithmetical accuracy can be checked and errors rectified. (**25**)
Purchases returns	Goods returned by the business to its suppliers. See also returns outwards. (**5**)
Purchases returns day book	Book of original entry for goods returned to suppliers. (**2**)
Quick ratio	Same as the acid test ratio. (**39**)
Quotation	A formal document prepared by a supplier which is an offer to supply goods or services. (**14**)

Real accounts	Accounts in which property of all kinds is recorded. (**2**)
Realisation concept	The point at which profit is treated as being earned. (**13**)
Receipt	A form acknowledging receipt of money for goods or services rendered. (**2**)
Receipts and payments account	A summary of the cash book of a non-profit-making organisation. (**35**)
Reducing balance method	Depreciation calculation which is at a lesser amount every following period. (**26**)
Remittance advice	A document which accompanies payments by cheque or via BACS and gives details of the payment. (**14**)
Reserve accounts	The transfer of apportioned profits to accounts for use in future years. (**37**)
Retained profits	Profits earned in a year but not paid out in dividends. (**37**)
Return on capital employed (ROCE)	A ratio that shows the net profit made for each £100 of capital employed. (**39**)
Returns inwards	Goods returned to the business by its customers. (**2**)
Returns inwards day book	Book of original entry for goods returned by customers. (**2**)
Returns note	Document identifying sales returns. (**14**)
Returns outwards	Goods returned by the business to its suppliers. (**2**)
Returns outwards day book	Book of original entry for goods returned to suppliers. (**2**)
Revenue expenditure	Expenses needed for the day-to-day running of the business. (**9**)
Revenue reserve	Reserves of a company which are available for distribution as a dividend. (**37**)
Revenues	Monetary value of goods and services supplied to the customers. (**6**)
Sale or return	Goods that do not belong to the person holding them. (**31**)
Sales	Goods sold by the business. (**5**)
Sales day book	Book of original entry for credit sales. (**2**)
Sales invoice	A document showing the details of goods sold and the prices of those goods. (**15**)
Sales journal	Another name for sales day book. (**2**)
Sales ledger	A ledger for customers' personal accounts. (**2**)
Sales ledger control account	See 'purchases ledger control account'. (**25**)
Sales returns	Goods returned to the business by its customers. (**5**)
Sales returns day book	Book of original entry for goods returned by customers. (**2**)
Selling price	The price a good/service is sold at. (**34**)
Separate legal entity	A feature of a limited company. (**37**)
Shareholder	An owner of shares in a company. (**37**)
Shares	The division of the capital of a limited company into parts. (**37**)
Share capital	The capital of a company divided into shares owned by its shareholders. (**37**)
Shareholders' funds	The amount of share capital and reserves 'owned' by the shareholders. (**37**)

Share premium	The excess in price of an issued share over its nominal value. (**37**)
Single entry	Where transactions are only recorded once in the books of account. (**34**)
Slip system	This involves putting information, such as lists of invoices, in slip form which can then be entered directly into the ledger accounts, eliminating the need to enter them in the day books. Also used by banks whereby a customer makes out a paying-in slip to pay money into their account, the slip is used to enter details of the transaction. The slip is used as documentary evidence. (**15**)
Sole trader	A business owned by one person only. (**1**)
Source documents	Where original information is found (e.g. sales and purchases invoices and credit notes). (**2**)
Spreadsheets	A computer program which consists of rows and columns. The program carries out calculations and is a useful facility when preparing financial budgets such as cash flow forecasts. (**40**)
Standard-rated businesses	These will have to add VAT to the value of the sales invoice, but they can also claim back VAT paid on purchases. (**18**)
Standing order	Payment made out of payer's bank, direct to payee's bank, on the *payer's* instructions. (**20**)
Statement of account	This is normally sent to purchasers at the end of each month and it states the amount owing to the supplier at the end of that particular month. (**14**)
Statement of affairs	A statement from which the capital of the owner is deduced by estimating assets and liabilities. Then Capital = Assets *less* Liabilities. (**34**)
Stock	Unsold goods. (**3**)
Stock turnover (or stockturn) ratio	A ratio comparing the cost of goods sold to the average stock. It shows the number of times stock is sold in an accounting period. (**39**)
Straight line method	Depreciation calculation which remains at an equal amount each year. (**26**)
Subjectivity	Using a method which other people may not agree to. (**13**)
Subscriptions	Amounts paid by members of a club or society, usually on an annual basis, to enable them to participate in the activities of the organisation. (**35**)
Suspense account	Account showing balance equal to difference in trial balance. (**33**)
T accounts	Accounts presented in the shape of a T. (**4**)
Total cost	Production cost plus administration, selling and distribution expenses. (**38**)
Trade discount	A reduction given to a customer when calculating the selling prices of goods. (**15**)
Trading account	Account in which gross profit is calculated. (**10**)
Trading and profit and loss account	Combined account in which both gross and net profits are calculated. (**2**)

Transaction	Events which change two items in the balance sheet. (**4**)
Trial balance	A list of all the balances in the books at a particular point in time. The balances are shown in debit and credit columns. These columns should balance provided no errors have occurred. (**2**)
Uncalled capital	The amount that is to be received in future, but which has not yet been requested. (**37**)
Undercasting	Incorrectly adding up a column of figures to give an answer which is less than the correct total. (**32**)
Unpresented cheque	A cheque which has been sent but has not yet gone through the bank account of the receiver of it. (**23**)
Value Added Tax (VAT)	A tax charged on the supply of most goods and services. The tax is borne by the final consumer of the goods or services, not by the business selling them to the consumer. VAT is administered by HMRC. (**18**)
Variable cost	Costs that vary depending on levels of production or business activity. (**38**)
Work in progress	Items not completed at the end of a period. (**38**)
Working capital	The amount by which the current assets exceed the current liabilities. Also known as 'net current assets'. (**11**)
Working capital ratio	Same as the current ratio. (**29**)
Zero-rated businesses	Businesses that do not have to add VAT to goods and services supplied to others by them, but they can receive a refund of VAT paid on goods and services purchased by them. (**18**)
Zero-rated supplies	Goods or services where VAT is charged at the rate of 0%. (**18**)

Model layouts for financial statements and worksheets

Many students have difficulty remembering the layout of the financial statements of various businesses. In this appendix you will find suggested model layouts of the financial statements, which include the trading and profit and loss account and balance sheet for the following organisations:

- sole trader
- partnership – including the appropriation account
- limited company
- a manufacturing account.

Also included are suggested working sheets for answering questions on petty cash, ratio analysis and the extended trial balance. You may find it useful to photocopy the above documents and put them in your file for reference and to use when answering questions on these topics.

In this appendix you will find the following suggested model layouts of financial statements and worksheets; these are shown with column lines for ease of working:

- **Financial statements:**
  1. Sole trader
  2. Partnership
  3. Limited company
     Trading and profit and loss account
     Balance sheet
  4. Manufacturing account

- **Worksheets:**
  5. Petty cash book
  6. Worksheet for accounting ratios
  7. Worksheet for extended trial balance

1 Sole trader financial statements

Trading and Profit and Loss Account – Sole trader

Trading and Profit and Loss Account of . . . for the year ended . . .		
	£	£
Sales		xxx
Less Sales returns		xx
		xxx (a)
Less Cost of goods sold		
Opening stock	x	
Add Purchases	x	
Add Carriage inwards	x	
	xx	
Less Purchases returns	x	
	xx	
Less Closing stock	x	xxx (b)
Gross profit (a) – (b)		xxx (c)
Less Expenses		
Bad debts (written off)	x	
Wages and salaries	x	
Rates	x	
Insurance	x	
Rent	x	
General expenses	x	
Postages	x	
Stationery	x	
Carriage outwards	x	
Discounts allowed	x	
Heating	x	
Electricity	x	
Depreciation	x	
Increase in provision for doubtful debts	x	xxx (d)
(c) – (d)		xxx (e)
Add income*		
Discounts + interest received	x	
Reductions in provision for doubtful debts	x	xx (f)
Net profit (e) + (f)		£xxx (g)

The left margin labels read: **Trading Account** (upper section) and **Profit and Loss Account** (lower section).

Note: Alternatively, the Income can be added to Gross Profit before deducting expenses.

Balance Sheet – Sole trader

Balance Sheet of . . . as at . . .			
	Cost (a)	Total depreciation (b)	Net book value (a) – (b)
Fixed assets	£	£	£
Premises	x	x	x
Motor vehicle	x	x	x
Office furniture	x	x	x
Office equipment	x	x	x
Machinery	x	x	x
	xx	xx	x (c)
Current assets			
Stock (closing)	x		
Debtors (*Less* Provision for doubtful debts)	x		
Prepayments	x		
Cash at bank	x		
Cash in hand	x	xx (d)	
Less Current liabilities			
Creditors	x		
Expenses owing	x		
Bank overdraft	x	xx (e)	
Net current assets (d) – (e)			xx (f)
(c) + (f)			xxx (g)
Less Long-term liabilities			
Long-term loan			x (h)
Net assets (g) – (h)			£x,xxx (i)
			£x,xxx
Financed by			
Capital			xxx
Add Profit			x
			xxx
Less Drawings			x
			£x,xxx (i)

2 Partnership financial statements

Alan and Graham
Trading and Profit and Loss Account for the year ended . . .

	£	£	£
Trading Account – Same as sole trader *Profit and Loss Account – Same as sole trader* *Profit and Loss Appropriation Account**			
Net Profit			xxx (a)
Add Interest charged on drawings			
Alan		x	
Graham		x	xx (b)
(a) + (b)			xxx (c)
Less Interest on capital			
Alan	x		
Graham	x	xx	
Salary			
Graham	x	x	xx (d)
(c) – (d)			xxx (e)
Share of Profits:			
Alan		xx	
Graham		xx	
			xxx (e)

*Note: The Appropriation Account is usually shown under the general heading of Trading and Profit and Loss Account.

Alan and Graham
Balance Sheet as at . . .

	£ *Alan*	£ *Graham*	£ *Total*
Asset section of the balance sheet – Same as sole trader *Extract showing Financed by section only*			
Financed by:			
Capital Accounts			
Balance	xx	xx	xxx (a)
Current Accounts			
Balance b/d	xx	xx	
Add Share of profit	x	x	
Salary – Graham	–	x	
Interest on capital	x	x	
	xx	xx	
Less Drawings	(x)	(x)	
Interest on drawings	(x)	(x)	
	xx	xx	
			xxx (b)
(a) + (b) =			£x,xxx (c)

3 Limited company financial statements

Name of Company . . . Limited
Trading and Profit and Loss Account for the year ended . . .

	£	£	
Sales		xxx	
Less Sales returns		x	
		xxx	(a)
Less Cost of goods sold			
Opening stock	xxx		
Add Purchases	xxx		
Add Carriage inwards	xxx		
	xxx		
Less Purchase returns	xxx		
	xxx		
Less Closing stock	xx	xxx	(b)
Gross Profit (a) – (b)		xxx	(c)
Less Expenses:			
Salaries and wages	xx		
Directors' remuneration	xx		
General expenses	xx		
Rates and insurance	xx		
Motor expenses	xx		
Debenture interest	xx		
Bad debts written off	xx		
Depreciation – Motors	xx		
– Equipment	xx	xxx	(d)
Net Profit (c) – (d)		xxx	(e)
Add Retained profits from last year		xx	(f)
(e) + (f)		xxx	(g)
Less Appropriations:			
Transfers to general reserve	xx		
Interim dividends paid:			
Preference shares	xx		
Ordinary shares	xx		
Final dividends paid:			
Preference shares	xx		
Ordinary shares	xx	xxx	(h)
Retained profits carried forward		£x,xxx	(i)
to next year (g) – (h)			

Name of Company . . . Limited
Balance Sheet as at . . .

	£	£	£
Fixed assets			
Intangible assets			
Goodwill			xx (a)
Tangible assets (A)			
Premises		xxx	
Equipment		xxx	
Motors		xxx	xxx (b)
(a) + (b)			xxx (c)
Current assets			
Stock	xx		
Debtors	xx		
Bank	xx		
Cash	xx	xxx (d)	
Creditors: amounts falling due within one year			
Creditors	xx		
Bank overdraft	xx		
Dividends payable	xx		
Debenture interest due	xx	xxx (e)	
Net Current assets (d) – (e)			xxx (f)
Total assets less current liabilities (c) + (f)			xxx (g)
Creditors: amounts falling due after more than one year			
Debentures			xxx (h)
(g) – (h)			x,xxx (i)
Capital and reserves (B)			
Called-up share capital			x,xxx (j)
Capital-reserve			
Share premium		xxx	
Revenue reserves			
General reserve		xxx	
Profit and loss account		xxx	xxx (k)
(j) + (k)			£x,xxx (i)

Notes: Based on UK legislation
(A) Notes to be given in appendix as to cost, acquisitions and sales in the year and depreciation.
(B) 'Reserves' consist either of those unused profits remaining in the appropriation account, or those transferred to a reserve account appropriately titled (e.g. general reserve, fixed asset replacement reserve, etc.).

4 Manufacturing Account

Name of firm
Manufacturing Account for the year ended . . .

	£	£	
Stock of raw materials (opening)		xxx	
Add Purchases		xxx	
Add Carriage inwards		xxx	
		xxx	(a)
Less Stock of raw materials (closing)		xxx	(b)
Cost of raw materials consumed (a) – (b)		xxx	(c)
Direct labour		xxx	(d)
Direct expenses			
Royalties		xx	(e)
Prime cost (c) + (d) + (e)		xxx	(f)
Add Indirect manufacturing cost			
General factory overheads	xx		
Lighting	xx		
Power	xx		
Rent	xx		
Insurance	xx		
Indirect labour	xx		
Depreciation of plant	xx	xxx	(g)
(f) + (g)		xxx	(h)
Add Work in progress (opening)		xx	(i)
(h) + (i)		xxx	(j)
Less Work in progress (closing)		xx	(k)
Production cost of goods completed c/d (j) – (k)		xxx	

Note: The 'Production cost of goods completed' will be entered in the trading account, refer to Chapter 38. The rest of the trading account and profit and loss account is the same as for sole traders and partnerships.

Balance Sheet Extract as at . . .

	£	£	£
Current assets			
Stock – raw materials	xx		
– work in progress	xx		
– finished goods	xx		

Note: All three closing stocks of raw materials, work in progress and finished goods are included in the Balance Sheet.

5 Petty Cash Book

Receipts £	Date	Details	Voucher Number	Total £	VAT £	£	£	£	£	£

6 Accounting ratios – Calculation sheet

Profitability Ratios – Section 39.3

Ratio	Formula	Year 1	Year 2
1 Gross profit margin as a % of sales	$\dfrac{GP}{Sales} \times 100 = x\%$		
2 Gross profit mark-up as a % of sales	$\dfrac{GP}{Cost\ of\ Sales} \times 100 = x\%$		
3 Net profit margin as a % of sales	$\dfrac{NP}{Sales} \times 100 = x\%$		
4 Expenses as a % of sales	$\dfrac{Expenses}{Sales} \times 100 = x\%$		
5 Return on capital employed (ROCE)	$\dfrac{NP}{Capital\ Employed} \times 100 = x\%$		
6 Stock turnover, e.g. 5 times	$\dfrac{Cost\ of\ Goods\ Sold}{Average\ Stock} = x\ Times\ a\ year$		

Liquidity Ratios – Section 39.4

1 Current (or working capital ratio)	$\dfrac{Current\ Assets}{Current\ Liabilities} = x{:}1$		
2 Acid test (or quick ratio)	$\dfrac{Current\ Assets - Stock}{Current\ Liabilities} = x{:}1$		
3 Debtors to sales ratio (for months) (debtors' collection period)	$\dfrac{Debtors}{Sales\ for\ year} \times 12 = x\ Months$		
or Debtors to sales ratio (for days)	$\dfrac{Debtors}{Sales\ for\ year} \times 365 = x\ Days$		
4 Creditors to purchases (for months) (creditors' payment period)	$\dfrac{Creditors}{Purchases\ for\ year} \times 12 = x\ Months$		
or Creditors to purchases (for days)	$\dfrac{Creditors}{Purchases\ for\ year} \times 365 = x\ Days$		

Asset Utilisation – Section 39.5

Fixed assets to sales ratio	$\dfrac{Sales}{Fixed\ Assets} = x{:}1$		

7 Format for an extended worksheet

Description	Ledger Balances		Adjustments		Profit and Loss		Balance Sheet	
	Dr	Cr	Dr	Cr	Dr	Cr	Dr	Cr
	£	£	£	£	£	£	£	£

Multiple-choice questions

Each multiple-choice question has four suggested answers, either letter (A), (B), (C) or (D). You should read each question and then decide which choice is best, either (A) or (B) or (C) or (D). Write down your answers on a separate piece of paper. You will then be able to repeat the set of questions later without the distraction of previously written attempts.

When you have completed a set of questions, check your answers against those given in Appendix D.

Set No 1: Questions MC1–MC20

MC1 Which of the following statements is *in*correct?
   (A)   Assets – Liabilities = Capital
   (B)   Capital – Liabilities = Assets
   (C)   Assets = Capital + Liabilities
   (D)   Assets – Capital = Liabilities.

MC2 Which of the following is not an asset?
   (A)   Debtor
   (B)   Motor Vehicle
   (C)   Creditor
   (D)   Stock of Goods.

MC3 Which of the following is a liability?
   (A)   Cash balance
   (B)   Loan from J Owens
   (C)   Debtor
   (D)   Buildings.

MC4 Which of the following is *in*correct?

	Assets £	Liabilities £	Capital £
(A)	9,460	2,680	6,780
(B)	7,390	1,140	6,250
(C)	6,120	2,490	4,630
(D)	8,970	3,580	5,390

MC5   Which of the following statements is *in*correct?

		Effect upon	
		Assets	*Liabilities*
(A)	Paid creditor by cheque	− Bank	+ Creditors
(B)	Bought goods on credit	+ Stock	+ Creditors
(C)	Received cash from debtor	+ Cash	
		− Debtor	
(D)	Sold goods for cash	+ Cash	
		− Stock	

MC6   Which of the following are correct?

	Accounts	*To record*	*Entry in the account*
(i)	Assets	a decrease	Debit
		an increase	Credit
(ii)	Capital	a decrease	Debit
		an increase	Credit
(iii)	Liabilities	a decrease	Debit
		an increase	Credit

(A)   (i) and (ii)
(B)   (i) and (iii)
(C)   (ii) and (iii)
(D)   None of them.

MC7   Which of the following are correct?

		Account to be debited	*Account to be credited*
(i)	Bought motor van by cheque	Motor van	Bank
(ii)	Paid a creditor, T Allen, by cheque	Cash	T Allen
(iii)	Loan repaid to C Kirk by cheque	Loan from Kirk	Bank
(iv)	Sold goods for cash	Sales	Cash

(A)   (i) and (ii) only
(B)   (ii) and (iii) only
(C)   (iii) and (iv) only
(D)   (i) and (iii) only.

MC8   Which of the following are *in*correct?

		Account to be debited	*Account to be credited*
(i)	Sold goods on credit to P Moore	P Moore	Sales
(ii)	Bought fixtures on credit from Furnishers Ltd	Fixtures	Furnishers Ltd
(iii)	Introduce more capital in cash	Capital	Cash
(iv)	A debtor, L Sellars, pays by cheque	Cash	L Sellars

(A)   (iii) and (iv) only
(B)   (ii) and (iii) only
(C)   (i) and (iv) only
(D)   (i) and (iii) only.

MC9 Which of the following should not be called 'sales'?
- (A) Goods sold, to be paid for in one month's time
- (B) Goods sold, cash being received immediately
- (C) Item previously included in purchases, now sold on credit
- (D) Sale of a motor lorry not now required.

MC10 Which of the following should not be called 'purchases'?
- (A) Items bought for the prime purpose of resale
- (B) Goods bought on credit
- (C) Office stationery purchased
- (D) Goods bought for cash.

MC11 Which of the following are *in*correct?

		Account to be debited	Account to be credited
(i)	B Ash returns goods to us	Sales returns	B Ash
(ii)	Goods bought on credit from L Thomas	L Thomas	Purchases
(iii)	Motor van bought on credit from X L Garages	Purchases	X L Garages
(iv)	Goods sold for cash	Cash	Sales

- (A) (i) and (ii) only
- (B) (i) and (iii) only
- (C) (ii) and (iii) only
- (D) (iii) and (iv) only.

MC12 Of the following, which are correct?

		Account to be debited	Account to be credited
(i)	Surplus office furniture sold for cash	Cash	Sales
(ii)	We returned goods to F Ward	F Ward	Sales returns
(iii)	Goods bought for cash	Purchases	Cash
(iv)	Goods sold on credit to F Clarke	F Clarke	Sales

- (A) (i) and (ii) only
- (B) (iii) and (iv) only
- (C) (ii) and (iii) only
- (D) (ii) only.

MC13 What is the amount of capital, given the following information? Buildings £30,000, Stock £5,600, Bank £750, Creditors £2,200, Loan from K Noone £7,000:
- (A) £29,150
- (B) £36,350
- (C) £41,150
- (D) None of the above.

MC14 Which of these statements is *in*correct?
- (A) Profit is another word for capital
- (B) A loss decreases capital
- (C) Profit increases capital
- (D) Drawings decreases capital.

MC15 Which of the following are *in*correct?

		Account to be debited	Account to be credited
(i)	Paid insurance by cheque	Insurance	Bank
(ii)	Paid telephone bill by cash	Telephone	Cash
(iii)	Received refund of part of motor expenses by cheque	Cash	Motor Expenses
(iv)	Took cash out of business for personal use	Drawings	Capital

(A) (i) and (iii) only
(B) (ii) and (iv) only
(C) (iii) and (iv) only
(D) (iv) only.

MC16 Of the following, which are correct?

		Account to be debited	Account to be credited
(i)	Paid rent by cheque	Rent	Cash
(ii)	Received commission in cash	Commissions	Cash
(iii)	Introduced extra capital in cash	Cash	Capital
(iv)	Sold surplus stationery for cash	Cash	Stationery

(A) None of them
(B) (i) and (iv) only
(C) (ii) and (iii) only
(D) (iii) and (iv) only.

MC17 What is the balance on the following account on 30 June 2009?

Dr		N Garth		Cr
2009	£	2009		£
June 18 Bank	400	June 1 Purchases		870
June 22 Returns	44	June 15 Purchases		245
		June 29 Purchases		178

(A) A debit balance of £849
(B) A credit balance of £829
(C) A credit balance of £849
(D) There is a nil balance on the account.

MC18 What was the balance on the account of N Garth, in MC17, on 20 June?
(A) A credit balance of £671
(B) A debit balance of £715
(C) A credit balance of £715
(D) A debit balance of £671.

MC19 Of the following, which *best* describes a trial balance?
(A) Is the final account in the books
(B) Shows all the asset balances
(C) Is a list of balances on the books
(D) Discloses the financial position of a business.

MC20   When should the trial balance totals differ?
    (A)   Only when it is drawn up by the accountant
    (B)   When drawn up before the profit and loss account is prepared
    (C)   If drawn up half-way through the financial year
    (D)   Never.

Set No 2: Questions MC21–MC55

MC21   Gross profit is:
    (A)   Excess of cost of goods sold over sales
    (B)   Purchases + Sales
    (C)   Net profit less expenses
    (D)   Excess of sales over cost of goods sold.

MC22   Net profit is calculated in the:
    (A)   Trial balance
    (B)   Trading account
    (C)   Profit and loss account
    (D)   Balance sheet.

MC23   The credit entry for net profit is shown in the:
    (A)   Capital account
    (B)   Profit and loss account
    (C)   Balance sheet
    (D)   Trading account.

MC24   The value of closing stock is found by:
    (A)   Adding opening stock to purchases
    (B)   Deducting purchases from sales
    (C)   Looking in the stock account
    (D)   Doing a stock-taking.

MC25   Which of the following are *not* part of the double entry system?
    (i)   Trading account
    (ii)   Balance sheet
    (iii)   Trial balance
    (iv)   Profit and loss account.

    (A)   (i) and (ii)
    (B)   (i) and (iii)
    (C)   (ii) and (iii)
    (D)   (ii) and (iv).

MC26   Which is the *best* definition of a balance sheet?
    (A)   A list of balances after calculating net profit
    (B)   A statement of all liabilities
    (C)   A trial balance at a different date
    (D)   A list of balances before calculating net profit.

MC27 The descending order in which current assets should be shown in the balance sheet are:
- (A) Debtors, Bank, Stock, Cash
- (B) Stock, Debtors, Bank, Cash
- (C) Stock, Debtors, Cash, Bank
- (D) Cash, Bank, Debtors, Stock.

MC28 Carriage inwards is charged to the trading account because:
- (A) It is not a balance sheet item
- (B) It is not part of motor expenses
- (C) Sales returns also goes in the trading account
- (D) It is basically part of the cost of buying goods.

MC29 Given figures showing Sales £28,500, Opening stock £4,690, Closing stock £7,240, Carriage inwards £570 and Purchases £21,360, the cost of goods sold figure is:
- (A) £19,830
- (B) £19,380
- (C) £18,810
- (D) Another figure.

MC30 If someone owns a grocery store, which of the following are *not* capital expenditure?
- (i) Rent
- (ii) Motor van
- (iii) Fixtures
- (iv) Fire insurance.

- (A) (ii) and (iii)
- (B) (i) and (ii)
- (C) (i) and (iii)
- (D) (i) and (iv).

MC31 The purchases day book is *best* described as:
- (A) A list of purchases bought on credit
- (B) Containing suppliers' accounts
- (C) A list of purchases bought for cash
- (D) Part of the double entry system.

MC32 Customers' personal accounts are found in:
- (A) The private ledger
- (B) General ledger
- (C) Purchases ledger
- (D) Sales ledger.

MC33 Which of the following are *not* personal accounts?
- (i) Debtors
- (ii) Drawings
- (iii) Rent
- (iv) Creditors.

(A)   (iii) only
(B)   (i) and (ii) only
(C)   (i) and (iv) only
(D)   (ii) and (iii) only.

MC34   A debit balance of £500 in the cash columns of the cash book would mean:
(A)   The book-keeper has made a mistake
(B)   We have £500 cash in hand
(C)   We have spent £500 cash more than we have received
(D)   Someone has stolen £500 cash.

MC35   A sum of £200 withdrawn from the bank and placed in the cash till is entered:
(A)   Debit bank column £200: Credit bank column £200
(B)   Debit cash column £200: Credit bank column £200
(C)   Debit bank column £200: Credit cash column £200
(D)   Debit cash column £400: Credit cash column £400.

MC36   A contra item is where:
(A)   Cash is banked before it has been paid out
(B)   Where double entry is completed within the cash book
(C)   Where the proprietor has repaid his capital in cash
(D)   Where sales have been paid by cash.

MC37   An invoice shows a total of £3,200 less a $2\frac{1}{2}$% cash discount. If this was paid in time, the amount of the cheque paid would be for:
(A)   £2,960
(B)   £3,040
(C)   £3,120
(D)   £2,800.

MC38   The total of the discounts received column in the cash book is posted to:
(A)   The credit of the discounts received account
(B)   The credit of the discounts allowed account
(C)   The debit of the discounts allowed account
(D)   The debit of the discounts received account.

MC39   A bank overdraft is *best* described as:
(A)   A business wasting its money
(B)   Having more receipts than payments
(C)   A business having bought too many goods
(D)   A business having paid more out of its bank account than it has put in it.

MC40   A cash discount is *best* described as a reduction in the sum to be paid:
(A)   If goods are bought on credit and not for cash
(B)   If either cheque or cash payment is made within an agreed period
(C)   If cash is paid instead of cheques
(D)   If trade discount is also deducted.

MC41 If a sales invoice shows 12 items of £250 each, less trade discount of 20% and cash discount of 5%, then the amount to be paid, if the payment is made within the credit period, will be for:
- (A) £2,440
- (B) £2,360
- (C) £2,280
- (D) £2,500.

MC42 The total of the sales day book is entered on:
- (A) The debit side of the sales day book
- (B) The credit side of the sales account in the general ledger
- (C) The debit side of the sales account in the general ledger
- (D) The debit side of the sales day book.

MC43 A trade discount is *best* described as:
- (A) A discount given if the invoice is paid
- (B) A discount given for cash payment
- (C) A discount given to suppliers
- (D) A discount given to traders.

MC44 The sales day book does *not* contain:
- (A) Credit sales made without deduction of trade discount
- (B) Credit sales made to overseas customers
- (C) Cash sales
- (D) Credit sales which eventually turn out to be bad debts.

MC45 The purchases day book consists of:
- (A) Cash purchases
- (B) Suppliers' ledger accounts
- (C) A list of purchases invoices
- (D) Payments for goods.

MC46 The total of the purchases day book is transferred to the:
- (A) Debit side of the purchases account
- (B) Credit side of the purchases day book
- (C) Debit side of the purchases day book
- (D) Debit side of the purchases ledger.

MC47 The balances in the purchases ledger are usually:
- (A) Credit balances
- (B) Contras
- (C) Nominal account balances
- (D) Debit balances.

MC48 Debit notes are entered in the:
- (A) Purchases returns day book
- (B) Sales returns day book
- (C) Purchases account
- (D) Purchases returns account.

MC49 A statement of account:
    (A)   Is used instead of an invoice
    (B)   Means that customers need not keep accounts
    (C)   Saves sending out invoices
    (D)   Acts as a reminder to the purchaser of the amount owed.

MC50 Originally we bought 80 items at £60 each, less trade discount of 25%. We now return 5 items, so we will issue a debit note amounting to:
    (A)   £270
    (B)   £240
    (C)   £225
    (D)   £220.

MC51 A cheque given to you by a customer and banked by you, but for which he has proved not to have enough funds to meet it, is known as:
    (A)   A dishonoured cheque
    (B)   A debit transfer
    (C)   A standing order
    (D)   A bank error.

MC52 Which of the following are not true? A bank reconciliation statement is:
    (i)   Drawn up by the bank monthly
    (ii)   Not part of the double entry system
    (iii) Part of the double entry system
    (iv) Drawn up by our cashier.

    (A)   (i) and (ii)
    (B)   (i) and (iii)
    (C)   (ii) and (iv)
    (D)   (iii) and (iv).

MC53 The journal is:
    (A)   Part of the double entry system
    (B)   A form of sales day book
    (C)   A form of diary
    (D)   A supplement to the balance sheet.

MC54 Given a desired cash float of £700, if £541 is spent in the period and the opening cash float has been £700, how much will be reimbursed at the end of the period?
    (A)   £541
    (B)   £700
    (C)   £159
    (D)   None of the above.

MC55 A petty cash book:
    (A)   Is used only in limited companies
    (B)   Is used when there is a bank overdraft
    (C)   Is used for small cheque payments
    (D)   Will keep down the number of entries in the general ledger.

Set No 3: Questions MC56–MC82

MC56 The straight line method of depreciation consists of:
(A) Unequal amounts of depreciation each year
(B) Increasing amounts of depreciation each year
(C) Reducing amounts of depreciation each year
(D) Equal amounts of depreciation each year.

MC57 Depreciation is:
(A) The cost of a current asset wearing away
(B) The cost of a replacement for a fixed asset
(C) The salvage value of a fixed asset plus its original cost
(D) The part of the cost of the fixed asset consumed during its period of use by the business.

MC58 A business bought a machine for £50,000. It is expected to be used for 6 years, then sold for £5,000. What is the annual amount of depreciation if the straight line method is used?
(A) £7,000
(B) £8,000
(C) £7,500
(D) £6,750.

MC59 When a separate provision for depreciation account is in use, then book-keeping entries for the year's depreciation are:
(A) Debit profit and loss: Credit the balance sheet
(B) Debit profit and loss: Credit asset account
(C) Debit asset account: Credit provision for depreciation account
(D) Debit profit and loss: Credit provision for depreciation account.

MC60 In a trial balance, the balance on the provision for depreciation account is:
(A) Shown as a credit item
(B) Not shown, as it is part of depreciation
(C) Shown as a debit item
(D) Sometimes shown as a credit, sometimes as a debit.

MC61 If a provision for depreciation account is not in use, then the entries for the year's depreciation would be:
(A) Debit asset account, credit profit and loss account
(B) Credit asset account, debit provision for depreciation account
(C) Credit profit and loss account, debit provision for depreciation account
(D) None of the above.

MC62 A provision for doubtful debts is created:
(A) When debtors become bankrupt
(B) When debtors cease to be in business
(C) To provide for possible bad debts
(D) To write off bad debts.

MC63 When final accounts are prepared, the bad debts account is closed by a transfer to the:
(A) Balance sheet
(B) Profit and loss account
(C) Trading account
(D) Provision for doubtful debts account.

MC64 These questions relate to the following assets and liabilities:

	£		£
Stock	1,000	Machinery	750
Cash at bank	750	Debtors	750
Cash in hand	50	Fixtures	250
Creditors	500	Motor vehicle	750
Capital	3,800		

(i) The balance sheet totals are (use the vertical presentation):
(A) £4,800.   (B) £3,800.   (C) £4,000.   (D) £4,500.

(ii) Current liabilities are:
(A) £1,750.   (B) £500.   (C) £3,800.   (D) £2,550.

(iii) Working capital is:
(A) £3,050.   (B) £2,050.   (C) £500.   (D) £800.

Pitman Qualifications

MC65 If we take goods for own use, we should:
(A) Debit drawings account: Credit purchases account
(B) Debit purchases account: Credit drawings account
(C) Debit drawings account: Credit stock account
(D) Debit sales account: Credit stock account.

MC66 A debit balance brought down on a packing materials account means:
(A) We owe for packing materials
(B) We have no stock of packing materials
(C) We have lost money on packing materials
(D) We have a stock of packing materials unused.

MC67 A credit balance brought down on a rent account means:
(A) We owe that rent at that date
(B) We have paid that rent in advance at that date
(C) We have paid too much rent
(D) We have paid too little in rent.

MC68 Working capital is a term meaning:
(A) The amount of capital invested by the proprietor
(B) The excess of the current assets over the current liabilities
(C) The capital less drawings
(D) The total of fixed assets + current assets.

MC69 In the trading account, the sales returns should be:
- (A) Added to cost of goods sold
- (B) Deducted from purchases
- (C) Deducted from sales
- (D) Added to sales.

MC70 If £750 was added to rent instead of being added to a fixed asset:
- (A) Gross profit would not be affected
- (B) Gross profit would be affected
- (C) Both gross and net profits would be affected
- (D) Just the balance sheet items would be affected.

MC71 Of the following, which should *not* be entered in the journal?
- (i) Cash payments for wages
- (ii) Bad debts written off
- (iii) Credit purchases of goods
- (iv) Sale of fixed assets.

- (A) (i) and (ii)
- (B) (i) and (iii)
- (C) (ii) and (iii)
- (D) (iii) and (iv).

MC72 Which of the following do *not* affect trial balance agreement?
- (i) Purchases £585 from C Owens completely omitted from the books
- (ii) Sales £99 to R Morgan entered in his account as £90
- (iii) Rent account added up to be £100 too much
- (iv) Error on sales invoice of £14 being entered in the books.

- (A) (i) and (iv)
- (B) (i) and (ii)
- (C) (i) and (iii)
- (D) (iii) and (iv).

MC73 Which of the following *are* errors of principle?
- (i) Rent entered in buildings account
- (ii) Purchases £150 completely omitted from books
- (iii) Sale of machinery £500 entered in sales account
- (iv) Cheque payment to R Kago entered only in cash book.

- (A) (ii) and (iii)
- (B) (iii) and (iv)
- (C) (i) and (ii)
- (D) (i) and (iii).

MC74 When trial balance totals do not agree, the difference is entered in:
- (A) The balance account
- (B) A suspense account
- (C) An errors account
- (D) The profit and loss account.

MC75 Which of these errors would be disclosed by the trial balance?
- (A) Error on a purchase invoice
- (B) Purchases from T Morgan entered in C Morgan's account
- (C) Carriage outwards debited to sales account
- (D) Overcast of total on sales account.

MC76 All these questions refer to the following trading and profit and loss account.

Trading Account and Profit and Loss Account			
		£	£
Sales			24,770
Less Sales returns			270
			24,500
Less Cost of goods sold:			
Opening stock		700	
Add Purchases	18,615		
Less Purchases returns	280		
	18,335		
Add Carriage Inwards	320	18,655	
		19,355	
Less Closing Stock		980	18,375
Gross Profit			6,125
Less Expenses:			
Wages		1,420	
Rent (360 + 90)		450	
General expenses		220	
Carriage outwards		360	?
Net Profit			?

(i) The missing net profit figure should be:
   (A) £1,675.   (B) £21,675.   (C) £3,675.   (D) £4,675.

(ii) Total expenses were:
   (A) £210.   (B) £2,450.   (C) £810.   (D) £2,575.

(iii) The cost of goods sold totalled:
   (A) £18,375.   (B) £19,500.   (C) £24,500.   (D) £24,770.

(iv) The expense item of Rent totalled:
   (A) £360.   (B) £270.   (C) £90.   (D) £450.

(v) The turnover is:
   (A) £24,770.   (B) £24,500.   (C) £19,355.   (D) £18,375.

(vi) The net cost of purchases is:
   (A) £18,615.   (B) £18,335.   (C) £18,655.   (D) £18,375.

(vii) Purchases returned totalled:
   (A) £360.   (B) £320.   (C) £280.   (D) £270.

(viii) Gross profit as a percentage on net sales is:
   (A) 20%.   (B) 30%.   (C) 25%.   (D) $33^1/_3$%.

(ix) Net profit as a percentage on net sales is:
   (A) 10%.   (B) 20%.   (C) 25%.   (D) 15%.

(x) The value of unsold goods was:

(A) £980.　　　(B) £24,500.　　　(C) £6,125.　　　(D) £19,355.

Pitman Qualifications

MC77 Answer the following questions using the following trial balance and the information given below:

Trial Balance as at 31 December

	£	£
Capital		5,600
Furniture and fittings	5,880	
Stock January 1	700	
Drawings	1,200	
Bank overdraft		1,260
Salaries	3,560	
General expenses	190	
Purchases/sales	4,020	9,840
Discount all'd/rec'd	150	130
Rent and rates	820	
Returns in/out	90	80
Trade debtors/creditors	1,500	1,070
Provision for doubtful debts		130
	£18,110	£18,110

Notes:

(*a*) Salaries owing at 31 December – £140
(*b*) Rent and rates paid in advance – £220
(*c*) Depreciate furniture and fittings by 10% p.a.
(*d*) Closing stock valuation – £800
(*e*) Increase the provision for doubtful debts to bring it up to 10% of debtors' balances.

(i) What will be the yearly depreciation charge?
　　(A) £5,292.　　　(B) £6,468.　　　(C) £588.　　　(D) £5,886.

(ii) What will be the salaries figure shown on the profit and loss account?
　　(A) £140.　　　(B) £3,700.　　　(C) £3,420.　　　(D) £3,560.

(iii) The rent and rates figure shown on the profit and loss account will be:
　　(A) £600.　　　(B) £820.　　　(C) £220.　　　(D) £1,040.

(iv) The new provision for doubtful debts will be:
　　(A) £1,650.　　　(B) £1,450.　　　(C) £150.　　　(D) £110.

(v) What will be the gross profit on the trading account?
　　(A) £5,910.　　　(B) £5,830.　　　(C) £4,630.　　　(D) £4,430.

(vi) The net profit on the profit and loss account will be:
　　(A) £1,420.　　　(B) £792.　　　(C) £1,400.　　　(D) £812.

(vii) The book value of furniture and fittings on the balance sheet will be:
　　(A) £5,292.　　　(B) £6,000.　　　(C) £6,368.　　　(D) £5,880.

(viii) What will be the turnover for the year?
　　(A) £9,840.　　　(B) £3,840.　　　(C) £9,750.　　　(D) £4,640.

(ix) Using the adjusted sales figure, the stock turnover for the year will be:
　　(A) 10.　　　(B) 11.　　　(C) 12.　　　(D) None of these.

(x) What will be the capital figure at end of year?
　　(A) £4,100.　　　(B) £5,600.　　　(C) £5,192.　　　(D) £6,392.

Pitman Qualifications

MC78 Given last year's capital as £57,500, this year's capital as £64,300, and drawings as £11,800, then profit must have been:
(A) £18,600
(B) £18,100
(C) £16,600
(D) £19,600.

MC79 Given last year's capital as £74,500, closing capital as £46,200, and drawings of £13,400, then:
(A) Profit for the year was £14,900
(B) Loss for the year was £14,900
(C) Loss for the year was £15,900
(D) Profit for the year was £16,800.

MC80 Given this year's closing capital as £29,360, the year's net profit as £8,460 and drawings as £5,320, what was the capital at the beginning of the year?
(A) £29,360
(B) £26,220
(C) £34,680
(D) None of the above.

MC81 In a commercial business, an 'accumulated fund' would be known as:
(A) Fixed assets
(B) Total assets
(C) Net current assets
(D) Capital.

MC82 A receipts and payments account does not show:
(A) Cheques paid out during the year
(B) The accumulated fund
(C) Receipts from sales of assets
(D) Bank balances.

Answers to multiple-choice questions

Set 1

1	B	2	C	3	B	4	C	5	A
6	C	7	D	8	A	9	D	10	C
11	C	12	B	13	D	14	A	15	C
16	D	17	C	18	C	19	C	20	D

Set 2

21	D	22	C	23	A	24	D	25	C
26	A	27	B	28	D	29	B	30	D
31	A	32	D	33	D	34	B	35	B
36	B	37	C	38	A	39	D	40	B
41	C	42	B	43	D	44	C	45	C
46	A	47	A	48	A	49	D	50	C
51	A	52	B	53	C	54	A	55	D

Set 3

56	D	57	D	58	C	59	D	60	A
61	D	62	C	63	B	64	(i) B (ii) B (iii) B	65	A
66	D	67	A	68	B	69	C	70	A
71	B	72	A	73	D	74	B	75	D

76 (i) C (ii) B (iii) A (iv) D (v) B (vi) B (vii) C (viii) C (ix) D (x) A

77 (i) C (ii) B (iii) A (iv) C (v) A (vi) B (vii) A (viii) C (ix) D (x) D

78	A	79	B	80	B	81	D	82	B

Answers to exercises

*Set out in this Appendix are the answers to the Exercises at the end of each chapter, **excluding** those with suffix 'X' in the Exercise number.*

Chapter 1 Introduction to accounting principles

1.1 Refer to text Section 1.4.
1.2 Refer to text Section 1.5 and Exhibit 1.4.
1.3 Refer to text Section 1.7.

Chapter 2 The accounting system

2.1 Refer to text Section 2.3.
2.2 Refer to text Section 2.3.
2.4 Refer to text Section 2.6.

Chapter 3 The balance sheet and the accounting equation

3.1
(a) £26,373
(b) £62,486
(c) £77,100
(d) £986,763
(e) £10,265
(f) £404,903

3.3
(a) Asset
(b) Asset
(c) Liability
(d) Asset
(e) Liability
(f) Asset

3.5 Wrong: Assets – Creditors, Loan from C Shaw
Liabilities – Debtors, Stock of Goods

3.7

	£
Assets	
Shop premises	50,000
Motor vehicle	10,000
Stock of goods	5,000
Cash at bank	7,000
Cash in hand	100
	72,100
Less Liabilities	
Loan from Uncle	30,000
Owed for stock	2,100
	32,100
CAPITAL INTRODUCED	40,000

3.9

Balance Sheet of T Lymer as at 31 December 2010

	£	£	£
Fixed assets:			
Office furniture			8,640
Delivery van			12,000
			20,640
Current assets:			
Stock		4,220	
Debtors		10,892	
Cash at Bank		11,722	26,834
Less Current liabilities:			
Creditors		12,651	12,651
Net current assets			14,183
			£34,823
Financed by:			
Capital			34,823
			£34,823

3.11

	Assets £	Capital £	Liabilities £
(a)	+400		+400
(b)	+500		+500
(c)	−50		−50
(d)	−330		−330
(e)	+5,000	+5,000	
(f)	+880		
	−880		
(g)	+45		
	−45		
(h)	+77		
	−77		

Chapter 4 The double entry system for assets, liabilities and capital

4.1

Account to be debited	Account to be credited
(a) Motor van	Cash
(b) Office machinery	J Grant & Son
(c) Cash	Capital
(d) Bank	J Beach
(e) A Barrett	Cash

4.3

Bank

(1) Capital	25,000	(2) Office Furniture	1,500
		(5) Motor Van	6,000
		(15) Planers Ltd	7,500
		(31) Machinery	2,800

Capital

| | | (1) Bank | 25,000 |

Office Furniture

| (2) Bank | 1,500 | (8) J. Walker & Sons | 600 |

Machinery

| (3) Planers Ltd | 7,500 | | |
| (31) Bank | 2,800 | | |

Planers Ltd

| (15) Bank | 7,500 | (3) Machinery | 7,500 |

Motor Van

| (5) Bank | 6,000 | | |

J. Walker & Sons

| (8) Office Furniture | 600 | (23) Cash | 600 |

Cash

| | | (23) J. Walker & Sons | 600 |

4.5

A Burton

Capital Account

| | | (1) Bank | 15,000 |

Bank Account

(1) Capital	15,000	(3) Motor vehicles	6,500
		(9) Furniture	1,150
		(17) Cash	200
		(25) Computex Ltd	1,000
		(27) Motor vehicles	2,450
		(31) Computex Ltd	1,400

Motor Vehicles Account

| (3) Bank | 6,500 | | |
| (27) Bank | 2,450 | | |

Furniture Account

(9) Bank	1,150		
(19) Cash	42		
(29) Cash	100		

Computer Equipment Account

| (12) Computex Ltd | 2,400 | | |

Computex Ltd Account

| (25) Bank | 1,000 | (12) Computer equipment | 2,400 |
| (31) Bank | 1,400 | | |

Cash Account

| (17) Bank | 200 | (19) Furniture | 42 |
| | | (29) Furniture | 100 |

Chapter 5 The double entry system for the asset of stock

5.1

Account to be debited	Account to be credited
(a) Purchases	P Hart
(b) Cash	Sales
(c) Motor vehicles	Morgan Motors
(d) Purchases	Cohens Ltd
(e) P Hart	Purchases returns
(f) H Perkins	Sales
(g) Bank	Sales
(h) Cash	Office furniture
(i) Sales returns	H Perkins
(j) Purchases	P Griffith

5.3

Paul Garner

Capital

			(1) Cash	4,000

Purchases

(2) Flynn Bros	1,230			
(4) Cash	345			
(20) Flynn Bros	450			

Sales

		(7) Cash	120
		(16) D Knott	600
		(23) Bateson's Ltd	570

Computer Equipment

(14) Bank	1,000		

Bateson's Ltd

(23) Sales	570	(30) Sales returns	109

Sales Returns

(30) Bateson's Ltd	109		

Cash

(1) Capital	4,000	(4) Purchases	345
(7) Sales	120	(10) Bank	3,500

Flynn Bros

(25) Purchases returns	75	(2) Purchases	1,230
(27) Bank	1,605	(20) Purchases	450

Bank

(10) Cash	3,500	(14) Computer Equip	1,000
		(27) Flynn Bros	1,605

D Knott

(16) Sales	600		

Purchases Returns

		(25) Flynn Bros	75

5.4

Grace Andrews

Capital

		(1) Bank	10,000
		(1) Cash	100

Cash

(1) Capital	100	(10) Office furniture	65
(30) Sales	280		

Shop Fittings

(3) Duffy & Son	1,900		

Barrett's Fashions

(15) Purchases returns	180	(5) Purchases	2,378
		(28) Purchases	1,434

Office Furniture

(10) Cash	65		

Purchases Returns

		(15) Barrett's Fashions	180

Bank

(1) Capital	10,000	(9) Computer	1,020
(12) Sales	800	(22) Duffy & Son	1,900
(25) Sales	600	(30) Motor vehicles	4,750

Duffy & Son

(22) Bank	1,900	(3) Shop fittings	1,900

Purchases

(5) Barrett's Fashions	2,378		
(28) Barrett's Fashions	1,434		

Computer

(9) Bank	1,020		

Sales

		(12) Bank	800
		(25) Bank	600
		(30) Cash	280

Motor Vehicles

(30) Bank	4,750		

Chapter 6 The double entry system for expenses and revenue

6.1

	Account to be debited	Account to be credited
(a)	Rent	Cash
(b)	Purchases	Cash
(c)	Bank	Rates
(d)	General exps	Bank
(e)	Cash	Commissions recd
(f)	T Jones	Purchases returns
(g)	Cash	Sales
(h)	Office fixtures	Bank
(i)	Wages	Cash
(j)	Drawings	Cash

6.3

Bank

Jan 1	Capital	20,000	Jan 3 Rent	1,000
Jan 25	Sales	800	Jan 4 Motor van	5,000
			Jan 19 Insurance	220
			Jan 31 Electricity	78

Capital

	Jan 1 Bank	20,000

Rent

Jan 3 Bank	1,000

Motor Van

Jan 4 Bank	5,000

Cash

Jan 5 Sales	1,005	Jan 10 Motor expenses	75
		Jan 12 Wages	120
		Jan 31 Wages	135

Motor Expenses

Jan 10 Cash	75

Wages

Jan 12 Cash	120
Jan 31 Cash	135

Insurance

Jan 19 Bank	220

Electricity

Jan 31 Bank	78

Purchases

Jan 4 M Parkin	580
Jan 4 J Kane	2,400
Jan 17 M Parkin	670

Sales

	Jan 5 Cash	1,005
	Jan 25 Bank	800

M Parkin

	Jan 4 Purchases	580
	Jan 17 Purchases	670

J Kane

	Jan 4 Purchases	2,400

6.5

Bank

Jul 1 Capital	8,000	Jul 2 Rent	375
		Jul 3 Shop Fittings	800
		Jul 6 Insurance	130
		Jul 13 Printing & Stationery	120
		Jul 30 High Lane Motors	5,000

Capital

	Jul 1 Bank	8,000

Rent

Jul 2 Bank	375

Shop Fittings

Jul 3 Bank	800

Insurance

Jul 6 Bank	130

Chapter 7 Balancing off accounts

6.5 (cont'd)

Motor Van

Jul 7 High Lane Motors	5,000		

Cash

Jul 11 Sales	1,500	Jul 15 Wages	200
Jul 21 Sales	780	Jul 25 Motor expenses	89
		Jul 31 Wages	300
		Jul 31 Stationery	45

Printing and Stationery

Jul 13 Bank	120
Jul 31 Cash	45

Wages

Jul 15 Cash	200
Jul 31 Cash	300

Motor Expenses

Jul 25 Cash	89

Purchases

Jul 5 A Jackson	450
Jul 5 D Hill	675
Jul 5 E Frudd	1,490
Jul 18 A Jackson	890

Sales

		Jul 11 Cash	1,500
		Jul 21 Cash	780

A Jackson

		Jul 5 Purchases	450
		Jul 18 Purchases	890

D Hill

		Jul 5 Purchases	675

E Frudd

		Jul 5 Purchases	1,490

High Lane Motors

Jul 30 Bank	5,000	Jul 7 Motor van	5,000

7.1

D Binns

(1) Sales	1,035	(9) Sales returns	60
		(25) Cash	450
		(31) Balance c/d	525
	1,035		1,035
(1) Balance b/d	525		

M Lowe

(3) Sales	99	(31) Balance c/d	99
(1) Balance b/d	99		

C Cade

(1) Sales	450	(12) Bank	450

H Teate

(1) Sales	630	(9) Sales returns	30
		(16) Bank	600
	630		630

J Watts

(3) Sales	627	(31) Balance c/d	762
(31) Sales	135		
	762		762
(1) Balance b/d	762		

7.2

G Birks

(11) Purchases returns	87	(2) Purchases	687
(27) Cash	300	(17) Purchases	120
(31) Balance c/d	420		
	807		807
		(1) Balance b/d	420

B Dixon

(21) Bank	1,320	(5) Purchases	1,320

A Weale

(31) Purchases returns	42	(2) Purchases	180
(31) Balance c/d	138		
	180		180
		(1) Balance b/d	138

T Potts

(11) Purchases returns	33	(2) Purchases	1,012
(31) Balance c/d	979		
	1,012		1,012
		(1) Balance b/d	979

K Lee

(31) Balance c/d	150	(5) Purchases	150
		(1) Balance b/d	150

7.3

D Binns

	Dr £	Cr £	Balance £	
(1) Sales	1,035		1,035	Dr
(9) Sales returns		60	975	Dr
(25) Cash		450	525	Dr

C Cade

	Dr £	Cr £	Balance £	
(1) Sales	450		450	Dr
(12) Bank		450	0	Dr

H Teate

	Dr £	Cr £	Balance £	
(1) Sales	630		630	Dr
(9) Sales returns		30	600	Dr
(16) Bank		600	0	Dr

J Watts

	Dr £	Cr £	Balance £	
(3) Sales	627		627	Dr
(31) Sales	135		762	Dr

M Lowe

	Dr £	Cr £	Balance £	
(3) Sales	99		99	Dr

7.5

T Tickle

(1) Sales	690	(14) Sales returns	46
(31) Balance c/d	30	(25) Bank	674
	720		720

D Stott

(19) Purchases returns	19	(3) Purchases	116
(23) Bank	97		
	116		116

J Rhodes

(31) Balance c/d	98	(3) Purchases	98

J Abmed

(29) Cash	367	(11) Purchases	367

S Ames

(1) Sales	330	(14) Sales returns	45
(9) Sales	645	(30) Bank	500
		(31) Balance c/d	430
	975		975

D Owen

(19) Purchases returns	36	(3) Purchases	347
(31) Balance c/d	446	(11) Purchases	135
	482		482

T Johnson

(9) Sales	376	(31) Bank	376

Debtors   S Ames

Creditors   T Tickle
D Owen
J Rhodes

Chapter 8 The trial balance

8.1

Capital

	May 1 Bank	2,500

Bank

May 1 Capital	2,500	May 12 K Gibson	76
May 9 C Bailey	250	May 12 D Ellis	370
May 10 H Spencer	150	May 31 C Mendez	87
		May 31 Balance c/d	2,367
	2,900		2,900
Jun 1 Balance b/d	2,367		

8.1 (cont'd)

Cash

	£		£
May 6 Sales	500	May 8 Rent	120
		May 15 Stationery	60
		May 19 Rent	120
		May 31 Balance c/d	200
	500		500
Jun 1 Balance b/d	200		

Rent

	£		£
May 8 Cash	120	May 31 Balance c/d	240
" 19 Cash	120		
	240		240
Jun 1 Balance b/d	240		

Stationery

	£		
May 15 Cash	60		

Purchases

	£		£
May 2 D Ellis	540	May 31 Balance c/d	1,082
May 2 C Mendez	87		
May 2 K Gibson	76		
May 18 D Ellis	145		
May 18 C Mendez	234		
	1,082		1,082
Jun 1 Balance b/d	1,082		

Sales

	£		£
May 31 Balance c/d	1,496	May 4 C Bailey	430
		May 4 B Hughes	62
		May 4 H Spencer	176
		May 6 Cash	500
		May 25 C Bailey	90
		May 25 B Hughes	110
		May 25 H Spencer	128
	1,496		1,496
		Jun 1 Balance b/d	1,496

H Spencer

	£		£
May 4 Sales	176	May 10 Bank	150
May 25 Sales	128	May 31 Balance c/d	154
	304		304
Jun 1 Balance b/d	154		

D Ellis

	£		£
May 12 Bank	370	May 2 Purchases	540
May 31 Balance c/d	315	May 18 Purchases	145
	685		685
		Jun 1 Balance b/d	315

C Mendez

	£		£
May 31 Bank	87	May 2 Purchases	87
May 31 Balance c/d	234	May 18 C Mendez	234
	321		321
		Jun 1 Balance b/d	234

K Gibson

	£		£
May 12 Bank	76	May 2 Purchases	76

C Bailey

	£		£
May 4 Sales	430	May 9 Bank	250
May 25 Sales	90	May 31 Balance c/d	270
	520		520
Jun 1 Balance b/d	270		

B Hughes

	£		£
May 4 Sales	62	May 31 Balance c/d	172
May 25 Sales	110		
	172		172
Jun 1 Balance b/d	172		

Trial Balance as at 31 May 2009

	Dr £	Cr £
Capital		2,500
Bank	2,367	
Cash	200	
Rent	240	
Stationery	60	
Purchases	1,082	
Sales		1,496
H Spencer	154	
D Ellis		315
C Mendez		234
C Bailey	270	
B Hughes	172	
	4,545	4,545

8.2

Bank

Mar 1	Capital	8,000	Mar 17	M Hyatt		84
Mar 24	J Carlton	95	Mar 21	Betta Ltd		500
			Mar 31	Motor van		4,000
			Mar 31	Balance c/d		3,511
		8,095				8,095
Apr 1	Balance b/d	3,511				

Cash

Mar 5	Sales	870	Mar 6	Wages	140
Mar 30	J King (Loan)	600	Mar 9	Purchases	46
			Mar 12	Wages	140
			Mar 31	Balance c/d	1,144
		1,470			1,470
Apr 1	Balance b/d	1,144			

Capital

	Mar 1	Bank	8,000

Motor Van

Mar 31	Bank	4,000

Purchases Returns

Mar 31	Balance c/d	44	Mar 18	T Braham	20
			Mar 27	K Henriques	24
		44			44
			Apr 1	Balance b/d	44

Wages

Mar 6	Cash	140	Mar 31	Balance c/d	280
Mar 12	Cash	140			
		280			280
Apr 1	Balance b/d	280			

Purchases

Mar 2	K Henriques	76	Mar 31	Balance c/d	864
Mar 2	M Hyatt	27			
Mar 2	T Braham	560			
Mar 9	Cash	46			
Mar 10	M Hyatt	57			
Mar 10	T Braham	98			
		864			864
Apr 1	Balance b/d	864			

Sales

Mar 31	Balance c/d	1,074	Mar 5	Cash	870
			Mar 7	H Elliott	35
			Mar 7	L Lane	42
			Mar 7	J Carlton	72
			Mar 13	L Lane	32
			Mar 13	J Carlton	23
		1,074			1,074
			Apr 1	Balance b/d	1,074

Shop Fixtures

	Mar 15	Betta Ltd	500

J King (Loan)

	Mar 30	Cash	600

H Elliott

	Mar 7	Sales	35

L Lane

Mar 7	Sales	42	Mar 31	Balance c/d	74
Mar 13	Sales	32			
		74			74
Apr 1	Balance b/d	74			

J Carlton

Mar 7	Sales	72	Mar 24	Bank	95
Mar 13	Sales	23			
		95			95

8.5 Trial Balance of P Brown as at 31 May 2009

	Dr £	Cr £
Capital		20,000
Drawings	7,000	
General expenses	500	
Sales		38,500
Purchases	29,000	
Debtors	6,800	
Creditors		9,000
Bank	15,100	
Cash	200	
Plant and equipment	5,000	
Heating and lighting	1,500	
Rent	2,400	
	67,500	67,500

8.6 Trial Balance of S Higton as at 30 June 2009

	Dr £	Cr £
Capital		19,956
Sales		119,439
Stationery	1,200	
General expenses	2,745	
Motor expenses	4,476	
Cash at bank	1,950	
Stock 1 July 2008	7,668	
Wages and salaries	9,492	
Rent and rates	10,500	
Office equipment	6,000	
Purchases	81,753	
Heating and lighting	2,208	
Rent received		2,139
Debtors	10,353	
Drawings	4,200	
Creditors		10,230
Motor vehicle	7,500	
Interest received		1,725
Insurance	3,444	
	153,489	153,489

8.2 (cont'd)

K Henriques

Mar 27 Purchases returns	24		Mar 2 Purchases	76
Mar 31 Balance c/d	52			
	76			76
			Apr 1 Balance b/d	52

M Hyatt

Mar 17 Bank	84		Mar 2 Purchases	27
			Mar 10 Purchases	57
	84			84

T Brabam

Mar 18 Purchases returns	20		Mar 2 Purchases	560
Mar 31 Balance c/d	638		Mar 10 Purchases	98
	658			658
			Apr 1 Balance b/d	638

Betta Ltd

Mar 21 Bank	500		Mar 15 Shop Fixtures	500

Trial Balance as at 31 March 2009

	Dr £	Cr £
Bank	3,511	
Cash	1,144	
Capital		8,000
Motor van	4,000	
Purchases returns		44
Wages	280	
Purchases	864	
Sales		1,074
Shop fixtures	500	
J King (Loan)		600
H Elliott	35	
L Lane	74	
K Henriques		52
J Braham		638
	10,408	10,408

Chapter 9 Capital and revenue expenditures

9.1

Newton Data Systems

Type of expenditure	Reason
(a) Revenue	Use up in the short term
(b) Capital	Adds to value of computer equipment
(c) Revenue	Used up in the short term
(d) Revenue	Used up in the short term
(e) Capital	Adds to the value of the computer
(f) Question is not clear	
(1) If spent on improving building Construction = Capital	Add to value of fixed assets
(2) If spent on extra wages for Security guards = Revenue	Used up in the short term

9.2

Cairns Engineering Co

	Capital	Revenue
	£	£
(a) New stationery and brochures	–	411
(b) New pickup truck	18,000	–
(c) New lathe	5,200	–
(d) Delivery costs – lathe	200	–
(e) Electricity – wiring	1,800	
– electricity costs		2,100
(f) Wages – Re: improvements	20,000	
– Other		45,000
	45,200	47,511

Brief description of capital and revenue expenditure – see text.

9.4

T Taylor
Revised Profits Year to 31 December 2009

	£
Gross profit before corrections	95,620
Add (a) Purchases overstated	311
	95,931
Less (c) Sale of building	10,000
Revised gross profit	85,931
Net profit before corrections	28,910
Less Gross profit overstated (10,000 – 311)	9,689
	19,221
Add (d) Loan interest overstated	500
Revised net profit	19,721

Error (b) does not affect gross profit or net profit calculations.

Chapter 10 Trading and profit and loss account: an introduction

10.1

L Simpson
Trading and Profit and Loss Account
for the year ended 31 December 2009

	£	£
Sales		38,220
Less Cost of goods sold:		
Purchases	24,190	
Less Closing stock	4,310	
		19,880
Gross profit		18,340
Less Expenses:		
Rent	4,170	
Wages and salaries	5,390	
Postage and stationery	840	
Electricity expenses	710	
General expenses	370	
		11,480
Net profit		6,860

10.3

G Singh
Trading and Profit and Loss Account
for the year ended 31 December 2009

	£	£
Sales		73,848
Less Cost of goods sold:		
Purchases	58,516	
Less Closing stock	10,192	
		48,324
Gross profit		25,524
Less Expenses:		
Wages	8,600	
Motor expenses	2,080	
Rates	2,680	
Insurance	444	
General expenses	420	
		14,224
Net profit		11,300

Chapter 11 The balance sheet

10.5

Mrs P Stewart
Trial Balance as at 31 March 2010

	Dr £	Cr £
Sales		24,765
Purchases	13,545	
Staff wages	2,100	
Drawings	5,500	
Rent and rates	1,580	
Electricity	565	
Motor expenses	845	
Insurance	345	
General expenses	245	
Cash in hand	135	
Cash at bank	2,675	
Creditors		3,285
Vehicle	5,875	
Fixtures and fittings	1,495	
Capital		6,855
	34,905	34,905

Closing stock £2,345

Mrs P Stewart
Trading and Profit and Loss Account
for the year ended 31 March 2010

	£	£
Sales		24,765
Less Cost of goods sold		
Purchases	13,545	
Less Closing stock	2,345	
	11,200	
		13,565
Gross profit		13,565
Less Expenses		
Staff wages	2,100	
Rent and rates	1,580	
Electricity	565	
Motor expenses	845	
Insurance	345	
General expenses	245	
		5,680
Net profit		7,885

11.1

G Singh
Balance Sheet as at 31 December 2009

	£	£	£
Fixed Assets			
Premises			20,000
Motor vehicle			12,000
			32,000
Current Assets			
Stock	10,192		
Debtors	7,800		
Cash at bank	6,616		
Cash in hand	160		
		24,768	
Less Current Liabilities			
Creditors	6,418		
		6,418	
Net current assets			18,350
			50,350
Financed by			
Cash introduced			48,000
Add Net profit for the year			11,300
			59,300
Less Drawings			8,950
			50,350

11.3

Mrs P Stewart
Balance Sheet as at 31 March 2009

	£	£	£
Fixed Assets			
Fixtures and fittings			1,495
Motor car			5,875
			7,370
Current Assets			
Stock	2,345		
Debtors	–		
Bank	2,675		
Cash	135		
		5,155	
Less Current Liabilities			
Creditors	3,285		
		3,285	
Net current assets			1,870
Total net assets			9,240
Financed by			
Capital			6,855
Add Net profit			7,885
			14,740
Less Drawings			5,500
			9,240

11.4

Miss V Holland
Balance Sheet as at 30 June 2009

	£	£	£
Fixed Assets			
Equipment			2,885
Van			3,400
			6,285
Current Assets			
Stock in hand	1,465		
Trade debtors	2,375		
Cash in hand	150		
		3,990	
Current Liabilities			
Trade creditors	4,565		
Bank overdraft	1,785		
		6,350	
Net current liabilities			(2,360)
			3,925
Long-term Liabilities			
Loan from mother			2,000
Net assets			1,925
Financed by			
Capital account			
Cash introduced			2,000
Net profit			2,525
			4,525
Drawings			2,600
			1,925

12.3

T Mann
Trading and Profit and Loss Account
for the year ended 31 December 2009

	£	£	£
Sales			52,790
Less Sales returns			490
			52,300
Less Cost of goods sold			
Opening stock		5,690	
Add Purchases	31,000		
Carriage inwards	1,700		
	32,700		
Less Purchases returns	560		
		32,140	
		37,830	
Less Closing stock		4,230	
			33,600
Gross profit			18,700
Less Expenses:			
Rent		1,460	
Salaries and wages		5,010	
Motor expenses		3,120	
Carriage outwards		790	
General expenses		420	
			10,800
Net profit			7,900

12.5

Suzanne Curtis
Trading and Profit and Loss Account
for the year ended 30 June 2009

	£	£	£
Sales			111,600
Less Sales returns			1,230
			110,370
Less Cost of sales			
Opening stock		14,208	
Add Purchases		71,244	
Add Carriage inwards		1,860	
		87,312	
Less Purchases returns		1,932	
		85,380	
Less Closing stock		17,700	
			67,680
Gross profit			42,690
Less Expenses:			
Salaries and wages		23,172	
Rent and rates		1,824	
Insurance		468	
Motor expenses		2,656	
Telephone internet charges		2,624	
Carriage outwards		1,200	
Electricity		996	
General expenses		1,884	
			34,824
Net profit			7,866

Chapter 12 Financial statements: further considerations

12.1

T Clarke
Trading Account for the year ended 31 December 2009

	£	£
Sales		38,742
Less cost of goods sold		
Opening stock	6,924	
Add Purchases	26,409	
Add Carriage inwards	670	
	34,003	
Less Closing stock	7,489	
		26,514
Gross profit		12,228

12.5 (cont'd)

Suzanne Curtis
Balance Sheet as at 30 June 2009

	£	£	£
Fixed Assets			
Buildings			50,000
Fixtures and fittings			2,100
Motor vehicles			10,800
			62,900
Current Assets			
Stock	17,700		
Debtors	23,376		
Cash at bank	2,892		
		43,968	
Less Current Liabilities			
Creditors		20,386	
Net current assets			23,582
			86,482
Financed by:			
Capital – Balance at 1.7.2008			85,816
Add Net profit			7,866
			93,682
Less Drawings			7,200
			86,482

12.8

J Smailes
Trading and Profit and Loss Account
for the year ended 31 March 2009

	£	£	£
Sales			92,340
Less Cost of sales			
Opening stock		18,160	
Add Purchases	69,185		
Add Carriage inwards	420		
	69,605		
Less Purchases returns	640		
		68,965	
		87,125	
Less Closing stock		22,390	
			64,735
Gross profit			27,605
Less Expenses			
Wages and salaries		10,240	
Carriage outwards		1,570	
Rent and rates		3,015	
Communication expenses		624	
Commissions payable		216	
Insurance		405	
Sundry expenses		318	
			16,388
Net profit			11,217

J Smailes
Balance Sheet as at 31 March 2009

	£	£	£	£
Fixed Assets				
Buildings				20,000
Fixtures				2,850
				22,850
Current Assets				
Stock		22,390		
Debtors		14,320		
Bank		2,970		
Cash		115		
			39,795	
Less Current Liabilities				
Creditors		8,160	8,160	
Net current assets				31,635
				54,485
Less Long-term liabilities				
Loan				10,000
				44,485
Capital				
Balance at 1.4.2008				40,888
Add Net profit				11,217
				52,105
Less Drawings				7,620
				44,485

Chapter 13 Accounting concepts, standards and policies

13.1
(a) Materiality
(b) Business entity
(c) Prudence
(d) Historical cost
(e) Money measurement
(f) Accruals
(g) Realisation
(h) Going concern
(i) Consistency
(j) Materiality.

13.4 The *historical cost concept* is an accounting concept whereby the assets of a business are recorded in the accounts at cost price. Refer to text, Section 13.4.
Advantages of using the cost method of valuation are that the assets can easily be verified since there will be an invoice available for checking the purchase price; and, also, no valuations need be carried out on assets whose value may be subjective. Refer to text, Section 13.4.

13.5 The accounting concept the accounts clerk should follow in these circumstances would be that of prudence. Since it appears that the Priory Paper Co has disappeared it is unlikely that the debt of £187.00 will be recovered. In the circumstances the business will have no option but to write the debt off.

13.7 'FRS 18 Accounting policies' recommends the following four objectives to be considered when selecting an accounting policy: relevance, reliability, comparability, understandability.

13.8

MEMO

To   James
From   Payroll Manager   Today's date

Further to our conversation I would advise you not to divulge any confidential information to one of your colleagues. As you are no doubt aware any information that you observe in your position within the Payroll Department is confidential and should not be discussed with anyone other than myself as Payroll Manager.

Your colleague should be advised accordingly.

Chapter 14 Business documentation

14.1 (a) Remittance advice – see Section 14.11.
(b) Goods received note (GRN) – see Section 14.12.
(c) Credit note – see Section 14.9.
(d) Invoice – see Section 14.6.

14.3 (a) Purchase order.
(b) Advice note.
(c) Invoice.
(d) Remittance advice.

Chapter 15 Division of the ledger: sales day book and sales ledger

15.1 (a) Sales day book/sales ledger/personal account
(b) Cash book/general ledger/nominal account
(c) Purchases day book/purchases ledger/personal account
(d) Cash book/general ledger/nominal account
(e) Sales day book/sales ledger/personal account
(f) Sales returns day book/sales ledger/personal account
(g) Purchases returns day book/purchases ledger/personal account
(h) General journal/general ledger/real account

15.3

Sales Day Book

(1)	J Gordon	187
(3)	G Abrahams	166
(6)	V White	12
(10)	J Gordon	55
(17)	F Williams	289
(19)	C Richards	66
(27)	V Wood	28
(31)	L Simes	78
		881

Sales Ledger

J Gordon

(1)	Sales	187
(10)	Sales	55

G Abrahams

(3)	Sales	166

V White

(6)	Sales	12

F Williams

(17)	Sales	289

C Richards

(19)	Sales	66

V Wood

(27)	Sales	28

L Simes

(31)	Sales	78

General Ledger

Sales Account

(31) Sales day book	881

15.5 Dabell's Stationery Supplies Ltd.

Sales Day Book — page 26

Date		Name	Invoice No	Total £
April	1	Fisher & Co	6265	1,459
April	3	Elder (Office Supplies)	6266	73
April	5	Haigh (Mfr) Ltd	6267	56
April	11	Ardern & Co (Solicitors)	6268	1,598
April	15	I Rafiq	6269	540
April	20	Royle's Business Systems	6270	2,456
April	22	Fisher & Co	6271	23
April	22	Ardern & Co (Solicitors)	6272	345
April	25	Elder (Office Supplies)	6273	71
April	27	Haigh (Mfr) Ltd	6274	176
				6,797

Sales Ledger

Ardern & Co Account SL 1

(1) Balance b/d	472	(30) Balance c/d	2,415
(11) Sales	1,598		
(22) Sales	345		
	2,415		2,415
(1) Balance b/d	2,415		

Elder (Office Supplies) Account SL 2

(1) Balance b/d	75	(30) Balance c/d	219
(3) Sales	73		
(25) Sales	71		
	219		219
(1) Balance b/d	219		

Fisher & Co Account SL 3

(1) Balance b/d	231	(30) Bank	231
(1) Sales	1,459	(30) Balance c/d	1,482
(22) Sales	23		
	1,713		1,713
(1) Balance b/d	1,482		

Haigh (Mfr) Ltd Account SL 4

(1) Balance b/d	1,267	(30) Bank	1,000
(5) Sales	56	(30) Balance c/d	499
(27) Sales	176		
	1,499		1,499
(1) Balance b/d	499		

I Rafiq Account SL 5

(1) Balance b/d	330	(30) Bank	330
(15) Sales	540	(30) Balance c/d	540
	870		870
(1) Balance b/d	540		

Royle's Business Systems Ltd Account SL 6

(1) Balance b/d	750	(30) Balance c/d	3,206
(20) Sales	2,456		
	3,206		3,206
(1) Balance b/d	3,206		

List of outstanding debtors as at 30 April 2009

	Amount (£)
Ardern & Co	2,415
Elder (Office Supplies)	219
Fisher & Co	1,482
Haigh (Mfr) Ltd	499
I Rafiq	540
Royle's Business Systems	3,206
	8,361

15.7 See text, Section 15.15.

15.8 See text, Section 15.16.

Chapter 16 The purchases day book and purchases ledger

16.1 *Workings of purchases invoices*

(1) K King	4 radios × 30 =	120	
	3 music centres × 160 =	480	
		600	
	Less trade discount 25%	150	
			450
(3) A Bell	2 washing machines × 200 =	400	
	5 vacuum cleaners × 60 =	300	
	2 dish dryers × 150 =	300	
		1,000	
	Less trade discount 20%	200	
			800
(15) J Kelly	1 music centre × 300 =	300	
	2 washing machines × 250 =	500	
		800	
	Less trade discount 25%	200	
			600
(20) B Powell	6 radios × 70 =	420	
	Less trade discount $33\frac{1}{3}\%$	140	
			280
(30) B Lewis	4 dish dryers × 200 =	800	
	Less trade discount 20%	160	
			640

(a)

Purchases Day Book

(1)	K King	450
(3)	A Bell	800
(15)	J Kelly	600
(20)	B Powell	280
(30)	B Lewis	640
		2,770

(b)

Purchases Ledger

K King

(1) Purchases	450

A Bell

(3) Purchases	800

J Kelly

(15) Purchases	600

B Powell

(20) Purchases	280

B Lewis

(30) Purchases	640

(c)

General Ledger

Purchases Account

(31) Purchases day book	2,770

Purchase Ledger

Barton Food's Ltd Account — PL 10

July 1	Purchases	PB 1	78.50
July 8	Purchases	PB 1	101.30

Henmore Eggs Account — PL 11

July 3	Purchases	PB 1	56.26
July 12	Purchases	PB 1	48.20
July 31	Purchases	PB 1	62.60

Fernley & Co Account — PL 12

July 10	Purchases	PB 1	98.00
July 23	Purchases	PB 1	43.20

Bridge Catering Co Account — PL 13

July 14	Purchases	PB 1	142.00

Ruffoni Creams Account — PL 14

July 19	Purchases	PB 1	132.82

Ace Packaging Co Account — PL 15

July 25	Purchases	PB 1	217.75

General Ledger

Purchases Account — GL 28

July 31	Credit Purchases for the month	PB 1	980.63

16.3

Surprise Desserts

Purchase Day Book *page 1*

Date		Invoice No	Folio	Amount £
July 1	Barton Foods Ltd	201	PL 10	78.50
July 3	Henmore Eggs	202	PL 11	56.26
July 8	Barton Foods Ltd	203	PL 10	101.30
July 10	Fernley & Co	204	PL 12	98.00
July 12	Henmore Eggs	205	PL 11	48.20
July 14	Bridge Catering Co	206	PL 13	142.00
July 19	Ruffoni Creams	207	PL 14	132.82
July 23	Fernley & Co	208	PL 12	43.20
July 25	Ace Packaging Co	209	PL 15	217.75
July 31	Henmore Eggs	210	PL 11	62.60
			GL 28	980.63

Chapter 17 Sales returns day book and purchases returns day book

17.1

Purchases Day Book

(1)	H Lloyd	119
(4)	D Scott	98
(4)	A Simpson	114
(4)	A Williams	25
(4)	S Wood	56
(10)	A Simpson	59
(18)	M White	89
(18)	J Wong	67
(18)	H Miller	196
(18)	H Lewis	119
(31)	A Williams	56
(31)	C Cooper	98
		1,096

Purchases Returns Day Book

(7)	H Lloyd	16
(7)	D Scott	14
(25)	J Wong	5
(25)	A Simpson	11
		46

General Ledger
Purchases Account

(31)	Purchases day book	1,096

Purchases Returns Account

		(31) Purchases returns day book	46

Purchases Ledger
H Lloyd

(7)	Returns	16	(1) Purchases	119

D Scott

(7)	Returns	14	(4) Purchases	98

A Simpson

(7)	Returns	11	(4) Purchases	114
(25)	Returns		(10) Purchases	59

A Williams

	(4) Purchases	25
	(31) Purchases	56

S Wood

	(4) Purchases	56

M White

	(18) Purchases	89

J Wong

(25)	Returns	5	(18) Purchases	67

H Miller

	(18) Purchases	196

H Lewis

	(18) Purchases	119

C Cooper

	(31) Purchases	98

Framework Ltd

17.3

Sales Ledger
J Forbes (Fancy Gifts) Account

(1)	Balance b/d	745	(31) Bank	745
(23)	Sales	1,234	(31) Balance c/d	1,234
		1,979		1,979
(1)	Balance b/d	1,234		

Goodwin & Co Account

(1)	Balance b/d	276	(31) Balance c/d	604
(11)	Sales	328		
		604		604
(1)	Balance b/d	604		

L & P Moss Account

(1)	Balance b/d	390	(31) Bank	200
(27)	Sales	2,500	(31) Balance c/d	2,690
		2,890		2,890
(1)	Balance b/d	2,690		

Purchases Ledger

M & P Fitzsimmons Account

(28)	Purchases returns	200	(1) Balance b/d	800
(31)	Bank	500	(22) Purchases	756
(31)	Balance c/d	856		
		1,556		1,556
			(1) Balance b/d	856

L Horne Account

(12)	Purchases returns	42	(1) Balance b/d	450
(31)	Balance c/d	1,058	(2) Purchases	650
		1,100		1,100
			(1) Balance b/d	1,058

M Ward & Sons Account

(31)	Bank	245	(1) Balance b/d	245
(31)	Balance c/d	334	(31) Purchases	334
		579		579
			(1) Balance b/d	334

(b)

D Wilson Ltd Ledger

G Christie & Sons

2009		
May 1	Sales	752

G Christie & Son Ledger

D Wilson Ltd

2009		
May 1	Purchases	752

18.2

Sales Day Book

		Total	VAT	Net
2009				
Aug 1	M Sinclair & Co	188	28	160
Aug 8	M Brown & Associates	282	42	240
Aug 19	A Axton Ltd	94	14	80
Aug 31	T Christie	47	7	40
		611	91	520

Sales Ledger

M Sinclair & Co

(1) Sales	188

M Brown & Associates

(8) Sales	282

A Axton Ltd

(19) Sales	94

T Christie

(31) Sales	47

General Ledger

Sales

(31) Credit sales for the month	520

Value Added Tax

(31) Sales book: VAT content	91

Chapter 18 Value added tax (VAT)

18.1 (a) Style of invoice will vary. Invoice number to be 10586

Calculations:

	£
3 sets of Boy Michael golf clubs × £240	720
150 Watson golf balls at £8 per 10 balls	120
4 Faldo golf bags at £30	120
	960
Less trade discount 33 1/3%	320
	640
Add VAT 17 1/2%	112
	752

18.3

Sales Day Book – R Colman Ltd

	Total	VAT	Net
(1) B Davies & Co	188	28	160
(4) C Grant Ltd	235	35	200
(16) C Grant Ltd	141	21	120
(31) B Karloff	94	14	80
	658	98	560

Purchases Day Book – R Colman Ltd

	Total	VAT	Net
(10) G Cooper & Son	470	70	400
(10) J Wayne Ltd	282	42	240
(14) B Lugosi	47	7	40
(23) S Hayward	47	7	40
	846	126	720

Sales Ledger

B Davies & Co

(1) Sales	188

C Grant Ltd

(4) Sales	235
(16) Sales	141

B Karloff

(31) Sales	94

Purchases Ledger

G Cooper & Son

	(10) Purchases	470

J Wayne Ltd

	(10) Purchases	282

B Lugosi

	(14) Purchases	47

S Hayward

	(23) Purchases	47

General Ledger

Sales

	(31) Sales day book	560

Purchases

(31) Purchases day book	720	

Value Added Tax

(31) VAT content in purchases book	126	(31) VAT content in sales book	98
		(31) Balance c/d	28
	126		126

18.5

(a) Ivy & Co

VAT Account

Dr					Cr
2009			2009		
April 30	Purchases Day Book	8,750	April 30	Sales Day Book	9,205
May 31	Purchases Day Book	7,350	May 31	Sales Day Book	8,400
June 30	Purchases Day Book	9,625	June 30	Sales Day Book	10,500
June 30	Balances c/d	2,380			
		28,105			28,105
			July 1	Balance b/d	2,380

(b) The outstanding balance of £2,380 is the amount of VAT due to HMRC for the quarter ending 30 June 2009.

When Ivy & Co pays this amount to HMRC this will clear the amount in the VAT account.

18.7

Lawton Photography

	Calculation	Amount of invoice
	£	£
Total amount of equipment delivered	2,320.00	
Less Trade discount of $12\frac{1}{2}\%$, $£2,320 \times \frac{12.50}{100}$	290.00	
	2,030.00	2,030.00
Less Cash discount of $2\frac{1}{2}\%$, $£2,030 \times \frac{2.50}{100}$	50.75	
	1,979.25	
Add VAT @ $17\frac{1}{2}\%$, $£1,979.25 \times \frac{17.5}{100}$	346.37	346.37
		2,376.37

Note: VAT is calculated when $2\frac{1}{2}\%$ discount has been deducted but the invoice amount ignores this discount since the customer may not pay within the 7 days. If the customer fails to pay within 7 days no adjustment to the VAT needs to be made.

Chapter 19 VAT entries from sales and purchases day books

19.1
(a)

Curtain Design Company
Sales Day Book

Date	Details	Folio	Total £	VAT £	Ready-made £	Custom-made £
2009						
Nov 1	Jarvis Arms Hotel	SL 1	2,702.50	402.50		2,300.00
Nov 8	Springs Nursing Home	SL 2	1,175.00	175.00	1,000.00	
Nov 15	J P Morten	SL 3	258.50	38.50	220.00	
Nov 17	Queen's Hotel	SL 4	1,762.50	262.50		1,500.00
Nov 30	W Blackshaw	SL 5	105.75	15.75	90.00	
			6,004.25	894.25	1,310.00	3,800.00
				GL 3	GL 1	GL 2

(b)
Sales Ledger
Jarvis Arms Hotel Account — SL 1

Nov 1	Sales	2,702.50	

Spring's Nursing Home Account — SL 2

Nov 8	Sales	1,175.00	

J P Morten Account — SL 3

Nov 15	Sales	258.50	

Queen's Hotel Account — SL 4

Nov 17	Sales	1,762.50	

W Blackshaw Account — SL 5

Nov 30	Sales	105.75	

(c)
General Ledger
Sales – Ready-Made Account — GL 1

			Nov 30	Day book	1,310.00

Sales – Custom-Made Account — GL 2

			Nov 30	Day book	3,800.00

Value Added Tax Account — GL 3

			Nov 30	VAT on sales	894.25

19.2
(a)

Hall Engineering Co
Purchases Day Book

Date	Details	Folio	Total £	VAT £	Engineering parts £	Printing and stationery £	Motor expenses £
2009							
May 1	Black's Engineering Co	PL 1	611.00	91.00	520.00		
May 3	Ace Printing Co	PL 2	170.37	25.37		145.00	
May 24	Morgan's Garage	PL 3	141.00	21.00			120.00
May 26	Martin's Foundry	PL 4	822.50	122.50	700.00		
May 28	Office Supplies	PL 5	148.05	22.05		126.00	
May 29	Black's Engineering Co	PL 1	258.50	38.50	220.00		
			2,151.42	320.42	1,440.00	271.00	120.00
				GL 4	GL 1	GL 2	GL 3

(b)
Purchases Ledger
Black's Engineering — PL 1

			May 1	Purchases	611.00
			May 29	Purchases	258.50

Ace Printing Co — PL 2

			May 3	Purchases	170.37

Morgan's Garage — PL 3

			May 24	Purchases	141.00

Martin's Foundry — PL 4

			May 26	Purchases	822.50

Office Supplies — PL 5

			May 28	Purchases	148.05

(c)
General Ledger
Purchases – Engineering Parts — GL 1

May 31	Day book	1,440.00	

Printing and Stationery — GL 2

May 31	Day book	271.00	

Motor Expenses — GL 3

May 31	Day book	120.00	

VAT — GL 4

May 31	VAT on Purchases	320.42	

19.3 Sales Day Book – Smart Campers

Date 2009	Name of Customer	Invoice Total	VAT	Horsforth	Moortown	Otley
May 2	Outdoor Centre	326.04	29.64		296.40	
May 8	Premier Leisure	980.55	89.14	891.41		
May 16	Airedale Sport	223.17	20.29			202.88
May 28	Empire Products	1,075.43	97.76		977.67	
		2,605.19	236.83	891.41	1,274.07	202.88

Smart Campers: Workings:

Outdoor Centre/Moortown   £
2 May 12 Flair cool boxes at £15.90 each   190.80
       6 Camping stoves at £29.95 each   179.70
                                                    370.50
       Less Trade discount 20%   74.10
                                                    296.40
       Add VAT at 10%   29.64
                                                    326.04

Premier Leisure/Horsforth   £
8 May 10 Explorer rucksacks at £34.99 each   349.90
       Less Trade discount 20%   69.98
                                                    279.92
       12 Trekker ridge tents at £59.95 each   719.40
       Less Trade discount 15%   107.91
                                                    611.49
                                                    891.41
       Add VAT at 10%   89.14
                                                    980.55

Airedale Sport/Otley   £
16 May 8 Palma cool bags at £7.85 each   62.80
        12 Flair cool boxes at £15.90 each   190.80
                                                    253.60
        Less Trade discount 20%   50.72
                                                    202.88
        Add VAT at 10%   20.29
                                                    223.17

Empire Products/Moortown   £
28 May 14 Dome tents at £47.90 each   670.60
        8 Trekker ridge tents at £59.95 each   479.60
                                                  1,150.20
        Less Trade discount 15%   172.53
                                                    977.67
        Add VAT at 10%   97.76
                                                  1,075.43

Chapter 20 Business banking

20.1, 20.2, 20.3 and 20.4
The answer to each question can be found in the chapter text.

20.7 (a) Howard Photographics
(b) Central Bank
(c) Ben Brown Limited.

Chapter 21 Cash books

21.1

Cash Book

	Cash	Bank			Cash	Bank
(1) Capital		4,000		(2) Fixtures		660
(4) Sales	225			(4) Rent	140	
(6) T Thomas		188		(12) Wages	275	
(8) Sales		308		(15) Cash		200
(10) J King	300			(20) Stationery	60	
(14) J Walters (Loan)		500		(22) J French		166
(15) Bank	200			(28) Drawings	100	
(30) J Scott		277		(31) Balances c/d	216	4,247
(31) Sales	66					
	791	5,273			791	5,273
(1) Balances b/d	216	4,247				

21.2

Cash Book

	Cash	Bank			Cash	Bank
2009				2009		
May 1 Balance b/d	14.72			May 1 Balance b/d		820.54
3 P Wrench		432.36		2 Stationery	10.00	37.50
3 R Whitworth		634.34		6 SW Rail		450.80
3 Summers		341.00		9 Fabulous Fabrics Ltd		348.32
12 Sales	76.00			11 Mellors Mfg. Co		221.30
17 Trentham Traders		32.81		14 HMRC		250.00
24 Sales	350.00			20 Foreign Currency		3.20
26 Cash C		300.00		26 Bank C	300.00	
31 J Summers		1,231.00		27 Salaries		5,720.00
31 Bradnop Mfg. Co		725.00		31 Balance c/d	130.72	
31 Taylors		2,330.50				
31 Balance c/d		1,824.65				
	440.72	7,851.66			440.72	7,851.66
June 1 Balance b/d	130.72			June 1 Balance b/d		1,824.65

21.4

Cash Book

	Disc	Cash	Bank			Disc	Cash	Bank
(1) Capital			6,000	(1) Fixtures				950
(3) Sales		407		(2) Purchases				1,240
(5) N Morgan	10		210	(4) Rent			200	
(9) S Cooper	20		380	(7) S Thompson & Co	4			76
(14) L Curtis			115	(12) Rates				410
(20) P Exeter	2		78	(16) M Monroe	6		114	
(31) Sales			88	(31) Balances c/d			93	4,195
	32	407	6,871		10		407	6,871

General Ledger

Discounts Allowed

(31) Cash Book	32

Discounts Received

(31) Cash Book	10

21.5

Cash Book

	Disc	Cash	Bank			Disc	Cash	Bank
(1) Balances b/d		211	3,984	(2) T Adams	4			76
(4) C Potts			98	(2) C Bibby	13			247
(6) Sales			49	(2) D Clarke	22			418
(9) R Smiley	4		156	(7) Stationery			65	
(9) J Turner	16		624	(12) Motor expenses			100	
(9) R Pimlott	13		507	(21) Insurance				120
(18) Sales		98		(23) Expenses			60	
(28) R Godfrey (Loan)			500	(31) Stationery			84	27
				(31) Balances c/d				5,030
	33	309	5,918		39		309	5,918

General Ledger

Discounts Allowed

(31) Cash Book	33

Discounts Received

(31) Cash Book	39

Chapter 22 Petty cash and the imprest system

22.1

Petty Cash Book

Receipts £ p	Date	Details	Voucher Number	Total £ p	VAT £ p	Postage £ p	Cleaning £ p	Motor Expenses £ p	Stationery £ p	Sundry Expenses £ p
2009										
18.52	June 1	Balance b/d								
131.48	June 1	Cash								
	June 1	Window cleaner	32	10.00			10.00			
	June 3	Postage stamps	33	7.60		7.60				
	June 4	Petrol	34	37.60	5.60			32.00		
	June 6	Stationery	35	9.75	1.45				8.30	
2.00	June 10	Jean Ford stamps	8							
	June 14	Office cleaner	36	20.00			20.00			
	June 16	Parcel postage	37	1.35		1.35				
	June 19	Magazine	38	3.00						3.00
	June 21	Computer disks	39	7.95	1.05				6.90	
	June 23	Petrol	40	14.10	2.10			12.00		
	June 27	Refreshments	41	4.20						4.20
	June 29	Office cleaner	42	20.00			20.00			
				135.55	10.20	8.95	50.00	44.00	15.20	7.20
	June 30	Balance c/d		16.45						
152.00				152.00						
16.45	July 1	Balance b/d								
133.55	July 1	Cash								

Amount required to restore imprest = Float required   £ 150.00
Less Cash in hand   16.45
Amount required   133.55

22.4

(a)

Petty Cash Book – S Dickinson (Estate Agents)

Receipts £	Date 2009	Details	Voucher no	Total payment £	VAT £	Travelling £	Postage £	Stationery £	Office expenses £	Ledger postings £
120.00	Mar 1	Cash	CB 1							
	2	Postage Stamps	1	6.50			6.50			
	3	Rail Fare	2	23.00		23.00				
	7	Parcel	3	4.00			4.00			
	9	Window Cleaning	4	8.00					8.00	
	12	Envelopes	5	3.10	0.46			2.64		
	14	Office Tea, etc.	6	6.40					6.40	
	16	Petrol	7	10.00	1.49	8.51				
	19	Disks – Computer	8	13.00	1.94				11.06	
	20	Dusters and Polish	9	1.73	0.26				1.47	
	23	Postage Stamps	10	2.40			2.40			
	27	Ledger a/c J Cheetham	11	7.30						7.30
	31	Magazine	12	6.40					6.40	
				91.83	4.15	31.51	12.90	2.64	33.33	7.30
		Balance c/d		28.17	GL 5	GL 1	GL 2	GL 3	GL 4	C 44
120.00				120.00						
28.17	Apr 1	Balance b/d								
91.83	Apr 1	Cash	CB 1							

(b)

General Ledger

Travelling Expenses Account — GL 1

2009			
Mar 31	Petty Cash	PCB 1	31.51

Postage Account — GL 2

2009			
Mar 31	Petty Cash	PCB 1	12.90

Stationery Account — GL 3

2009			
Mar 31	Petty Cash	PCB 1	2.64

Office Expenses Account — GL 4

2009			
Mar 31	Petty Cash	PCB 1	33.33

VAT Account — GL 5

2009			
Mar 31	Petty Cash	PCB 1	4.15

Cash Book (Bank Column Only) — CB 1

2009			
Mar 31	Petty Cash	PCB 1	91.83

Purchase Ledger

J Cheetham Account — C 44

2009					2009		
Mar 31	Petty Cash	PCB 1	7.30		Feb 1	Balance b/d	7.30

(c)

MEMORANDUM

To	Ms S Dickinson	Ref
From	Student's Name	Date 31 March 2009
Subject	Petty Cash Imprest System	

Advantages of Imprest System:

1. *Control:* The petty cash can be checked easily at any time because cash in hand plus vouchers paid out for the period should always equal the amount of the 'float'.
2. *Responsibility:* It is an ideal opportunity to appoint junior staff and give them some responsibility and test their honesty.
3. *Efficiency:* It relieves the accountant by dealing with numerous small cash payments and reduces the posting to the general ledger.

Chapter 23 Bank reconciliation statements

Note: Both in theory and in practice you can start with the cash book balance working to the bank statement balance, or you can reverse this method. Many teachers and lecturers have their preferences, but this is a personal matter only. Examiners sometimes ask for them using one way, sometimes the other. Students should therefore be able to tackle them both ways.

23.1 (a)

Cash Book

2009 (Totals so far)		2009 (Totals so far)	
Dec 31 J. Walters	2,328	Dec 31 Bank charges	497
	54	Dec 31 Balance c/d	22
			1,863
	2,382		2,382

(b) **Bank Reconciliation Statement as at 31 December 2009**

Balance per cash book	1,863
Add Unpresented cheque	115
	1,978
Less Bankings not yet on bank statement (249 + 178)	427
Balance per bank statement	1,551

OR

Bank Reconciliation Statement as at 31 December 2009

Balance per bank statement	1,551
Add Bankings not yet on bank statement (249 + 178)	427
	1,978
Less Unpresented cheque	115
Balance per cash book	1,863

23.3 (a)

Cash Book – James Baxter

2009	£	2009	£
Mar 31 BGC	929	Mar 31 Balance b/d	2,804
– A May	2,003	Mar 31 Standing order	
		– Oak plc	100
		Mar 31 Bank charges	28
	2,932		2,932

(b)

James Baxter
Bank Reconciliation Statement as at 31 March 2009

	£
Bank overdraft per cash book	2,003
Add Banking not entered on bank statement	160
	2,163
Less Unpresented cheque	490
Bank overdraft per bank statement	1,673

OR

James Baxter
Bank Reconciliation Statement as at 31 March 2009

	£
Balance per bank statement	1,673 O/D
Less Banking not entered on bank statement	160
	1,513 O/D
Add Unpresented cheque	490
Balance per cash book	2,003 O/D

23.5 (a)

Cash Book – K Talbot

	£		£
Balance b/d	4,500	RB Insurance	600
Bank interest received	720	Bank charges	90
KB Ltd	780	Dishonoured cheque: C Hill	210
Bank deposit account	4,200	Balance c/d	9,300
	10,200		10,200

(b)

K Talbot
Bank Reconciliation Statement as at 31 December 2009

	£
Balance per cash book	9,300
Add Unpresented cheques (750 + 870)	1,620
	10,920
Less Banking not recorded	2,070
Balance per bank statement	8,850

OR

K Talbot
Bank Reconciliation Statement as at 31 December 2009

	£
Balance per bank statement	8,850
Add Cash not yet credited	2,070
	10,920
Less Unpresented cheques (750 + 870)	1,620
Balance per cash book	9,300

Chapter 24 The journal

24.1

The Journal

Date	Details	Dr	Cr
		£	£
2009			
Jan 1	Computer	4,000	
	Data Systems Ltd		4,000
Jan 5	Drawings	120	
	Purchases		120
Jan 8	Bad debts	220	
	J Oddy		220
Jan 15	Motor vehicle	15,500	
	Bank		15,500
Jan 29	Office furniture and fittings	250	
	J Street		250

24.3 (a)

The Journal as at 1 May 2009

	Dr	Cr
Bank	2,910	
Cash	160	
Equipment	5,900	
Premises	25,000	
Debtor: J Carnegie	540	
Creditors: R Smith		890
T Thomas		610
Loan: J Higgins		4,000
Capital		29,010
	34,510	34,510

(b)

Cash Book

	Cash	Bank		Cash	Bank
(1) Balances b/d	160	2,910	(5) R Smith		500
(31) Sales	8,560	8,000	(12) J Higgins		1,000
(31) Cash C		8,000	(31) Bank C	8,000	
			(31) Loan interest		200
			(31) Balance c/d	720	9,210
	8,720	10,910		8,720	10,910

Ledger accounts

Equipment

(1) Balance b/d	5,900		

Premises

(1) Balance b/d	25,000		

R Smith

(5) Bank	500	(1) Balance b/d	890

J Carnegie

(1) Balance b/d	540	(31) Sales returns	400
(24) Sales	2,220		

T Thomas

		(1) Balance b/d	610
		(2) Purchases	2,100

J Higgins (Loan)

(12) Bank	1,000	(1) Balance b/d	4,000

Loan Interest

(31) Bank	200		

Capital

		(1) Capital	29,010

Sales Returns

(31) J Carnegie	400		

Sales

		(24) J Carnegie	2,220
		(31) Cash	8,560

Purchases

(2) T Thomas	2,100		

24.3 *(cont'd)*

J Green
Trial Balance as at 31 May 2009

	Dr £	Cr £
Cash	720	
Bank	9,210	
Equipment	5,900	
Premises	25,000	
R Smith		390
J Carnegie	2,360	
T Thomas		2,710
J Higgins		3,000
Loan interest	200	
Capital		29,010
Sales		10,780
Purchases	2,100	
Sales returns	400	
	45,890	45,890

Chapter 25 Control accounts

25.1

Sales Ledger Control Account

(1)	Balance b/d	4,560	(31) Sales returns	460
(31)	Sales day book	10,870	(31) Cheques and cash	9,615
			(31) Discounts allowed	305
			(31) Balances c/d	5,050
		15,430		15,430

25.2

Sales Ledger Control Account

(1)	Balances b/d	6,708	(31) Discounts	300
(31)	Sales day book	11,500	(31) Cash and cheques	8,970
			(31) Bad debts	115
			(31) Sales returns	210
			(31) Balances c/d	8,613
		18,208		18,208

25.6 *(a)*

Sales Ledger – Shery Tatupu

L Barker

2009			2009		
Mar 31	Credit sales	18,642	Jan 1	Balance b/d	62
			Mar 31	Bank	15,023
			Mar 31	Discount	142
			Mar 31	Balance c/d	3,415
		18,642			18,642

D Blackhurst

2009			2009		
Jan 1	Balance b/d	1,466	Mar 31	Sales returns	88
Mar 31	Credit sales	16,428	Mar 31	Bank	16,009
			Mar 31	Balance c/d	1,797
		17,894			17,894

H Brackenbridge

2009			2009		
Mar 31	Credit sales	19,886	Jan 1	Balance b/d	58
			Mar 31	Bank	17,332
			Mar 31	Discount	227
			Mar 31	Balance c/d	2,269
		19,886			19,886

(b)

Sales Ledger Control Account

2009			2009		
Jan 1	Balance b/d	1,346	Mar 31	Sales returns	88
Mar 31	Credit sales	54,956	Mar 31	Bank	48,364
			Mar 31	Discounts	369
			Mar 31	Balance c/d	7,481
		56,302			56,302

(c) **Sales Ledger Outstanding Balances at 31 March 2009**

	£
L Barker	3,415
D Blackhurst	1,797
H Brackenbridge	2,269
	7,481
Balance per Sales Ledger Control Account	7,481

Pitman Qualifications

Chapter 26 Depreciation of fixed assets

26.1

K Richardson

Straight Line	
Cost	40,000
Year 1 Depreciation	7,000
	33,000
Year 2 Depreciation	7,000
	26,000
Year 3 Depreciation	7,000
	19,000
Year 4 Depreciation	7,000
	12,000
Year 5 Depreciation	7,000
	5,000

40,000 – 5,000 = 35,000 ÷ 5 = 7,000

Reducing Balance	
Cost	40,000
Year 1 Depreciation 40% of 40,000	16,000
	24,000
Year 2 Depreciation 40% of 24,000	9,600
	14,400
Year 3 Depreciation 40% of 14,400	5,760
	8,640
Year 4 Depreciation 40% of 8,640	3,456
	5,184
Year 5 Depreciation 40% of 5,184	2,074
	3,110

26.2

(a) Straight Line	
Cost	37,500
Year 1 Depreciation	5,535
	31,965
Year 2 Depreciation	5,535
	26,430
Year 3 Depreciation	5,535
	20,895
Year 4 Depreciation	5,535
	15,360

37,500 – 15,360 = 22,140 ÷ 4 = 5,535

(b) Reducing Balance	
Cost	37,500
Year 1 Depreciation 20% of 37,500	7,500
	30,000
Year 2 Depreciation 20% of 30,000	6,000
	24,000
Year 3 Depreciation 20% of 24,000	4,800
	19,200
Year 4 Depreciation 20% of 19,200	3,840
	15,360

26.6

(a) Reducing Balance	
Dumper cost	6,000
Year 1 Depreciation 20%	1,200
	4,800
Year 2 Depreciation 20% of 4,800	960
	3,840
Year 3 Depreciation 20% of 3,840	768
	3,072

(b) Straight Line	
Dumper cost	6,000
Year 1 Depreciation	976*
	5,024
Year 2 Depreciation	976
	4,048
Year 3 Depreciation	976
	3,072

* Calculation: $\dfrac{6,000 - 3,072}{3} = \dfrac{2,928}{3} = 976$

Chapter 27 Double entry records for depreciation and the disposal of assets

27.1

(a)

Motor Cars

2009		
Jan 1	Bank	12,500

(b)

Provision for Depreciation: Motor Cars

			2009		
			Dec 31	Profit and loss	2,500
2010			2010		
Dec 31	Balance c/d	4,500	Dec 31	Profit and loss	2,000
		4,500			4,500
2011			2011		
Dec 31	Balance c/d	6,100	Jan 1	Balance b/d	4,500
			Dec 31	Profit and loss	1,600
		6,100			6,100

(c)

Profit and Loss Account (extracts) – A White

(2009)	Provision for depreciation: Motors	2,500
(2010)	Provision for depreciation	2,000
(2011)	Provision for depreciation	1,600

(d)

Balance Sheets (extracts) – A White

	2009	2010	2011
Motor car at cost	12,500	12,500	12,500
Less Depreciation to date	2,500	4,500	6,100
Net book value	10,000	8,000	6,400

27.3

(a)

Computer

2009			2009		
Jan 1	Balance b/d	9,500	Jan 1	Computer disposals	9,500

27.3 (cont'd)

(b) Provision for Depreciation: Computer

2009	£	2009	£
Dec 31 Balance c/d	1,900	Dec 31 Profit and loss	1,900
2010		**2010**	
Dec 31 Balance c/d	3,800	Jan 1 Balance b/d	1,900
		Dec 31 Profit and loss	1,900
	3,800		3,800
2011		**2011**	
Dec 31 Balance c/d	5,700	Jan 1 Balance b/d	3,800
		Dec 31 Profit and loss	1,900
	5,700		5,700
2012		**2012**	
Jan 1 Computer disposals	5,700	Jan 1 Balance b/d	5,700

(c) Computer Disposals

2012		2012	
Jan 1 Computer	9,500	Jan 1 Depreciation	5,700
Dec 31 Profit and loss	450	" 1 Bank	4,250
	9,950		9,950

(d) Profit and Loss Account (extracts)

(2009) Provision for depreciation	1,900		
(2010) Provision for depreciation	1,900		
(2011) Provision for depreciation	1,900	(2009) Profit on sale of computer	450

(e) Balance Sheets (extracts)

	2009	2010	2011
Computer at cost	9,500	9,500	9,500
Less Depreciation to date	1,900	3,800	5,700
Net book value	7,600	5,700	3,800

27.4

(a) Motor Van Disposals

Motor van	12,000	Provision for depreciation	9,700
		Bank	1,850
		Profit and loss: loss on sale	450
	12,000		12,000

(b) Machinery Disposals

Machinery	27,900	Provision for depreciation	19,400
Profit and loss: profit on sale	2,770	Bank	11,270
	30,670		30,670

(c) Fixtures Disposals

Fixtures	8,420	Provision for depreciation	7,135
		Bank	50
		Profit and loss: loss on sale	1,235
	8,420		8,420

(d) Buildings Disposals

Buildings	200,000	Provision for depreciation	110,000
Profit and loss: profit on sale	59,000	Bank	149,000
	259,000		259,000

Chapter 28 Bad debts and provisions for doubtful debts

28.1

Data Computer Services

(a) Bad Debts Account

2009	£	2009	£
Apr 30 H Gordon	1,110	Dec 31 Profit and loss	1,870
Aug 31 D Bellamy	640		
Oct 31 J Alderton	120		
	1,870		1,870

Provision for Doubtful Debts Account

	£	2009	£
		Dec 31 Profit and loss	2,200

(b) Profit and Loss Account
for the year ended 31 December 2009 (extracts)

Gross profit		xxx
Less Expenses:		
Bad debts written off	1,870	
Provision for doubtful debts	2,200	

(c) Balance Sheet as at 31 December 2009 (extract)

Debtors	68,500
Less Provision for doubtful debts	2,200
	66,300

28.2

Date 31 Dec	Total debtors	Profit and loss	Dr/Cr	Final figure for balance sheet
2009	7,000	70	Dr	6,930 (net)
2010	8,000	10	Dr	7,920 (net)
2011	6,000	20	Cr	5,940 (net)
2012	7,000	10	Dr	6,930 (net)

28.4

Emford & Co

Date	Amount of provision for doubtful debts £	Amount of adjustment to existing provision £	Write either 'increase' or 'decrease' to indicate the effect on the *profit* for the year
31 December 2009	930	930	Decrease
31 December 2010	962	32	Decrease
31 December 2011	510	452	Increase

(c)

Motor Expenses Account

2009			2009		
Dec 31	Bank	7,215	Dec 31	Profit and loss	7,381
Dec 31	Owing c/d	166			7,381
		7,381			
			2010		
			Jan 1	Owing b/d	166

(d)

Rates Account

2009			2009		
Jan 1	Bank	750	Dec 31	Profit and loss	1,500
Jul 1	Bank	1,125	Dec 31	Prepaid c/d	375
		1,875			1,875
2010					
Jan 1	Prepaid b/d	375			

(e)

Rents Receivable Account

2009			2009		
Dec 31	Profit and loss	4,800	Apr 15	Bank	2,000
Dec 31	In advance c/d	1,600	Dec 15	Bank	4,400
		6,400			6,400
			2010		
			Jan 1	In advance b/d	1,600

29.2

T Norton

(a)

General Expenses Account

2009			2009		
Dec 31	Bank	615	Dec 31	Profit and loss	671
Dec 31	Owing c/d	56			671
		671			
			2010		
			Jan 1	Owing b/d	56

(b)

Telephone Account

2009			2009		
Dec 31	Bank	980	Dec 31	Profit and loss	1,097
Dec 31	Owing c/d	117			1,097
		1,097			
			2010		
			Jan 1	Owing b/d	117

Chapter 29 Accruals, prepayments and other adjustments for financial statements

29.1

C Homer

(a)

Rent Account

2009			2009		
Dec 31	Bank	1,600	Dec 31	Profit and loss	2,000
Dec 31	Owing c/d	400			2,000
		2,000			
			2010		
			Jan 1	Owing b/d	400

(b)

Insurance Account

2009			2009		
Dec 31	Bank	900	Dec 31	Profit and loss	635
		900	Dec 31	Prepaid c/d	265
2010					900
Jan 1	Prepaid b/d	265			

29.3 (cont'd)

(c) Commission Received Account

2009			2009	
Dec 31	Profit and loss	3,231	Dec 31 Bank	3,056
			Dec 31 Owing c/d	175
		3,231		3,231
2010				
			Jan 1 Owing b/d	175

(d) Carriage Outwards Account

2009			2009	
Dec 31	Bank	666	Dec 31 Profit and loss	788
Dec 31	Owing c/d	122		
		788		788
			2010	
			Jan 1 Owing b/d	122

(e) Insurance Account

2009			2009	
Jan 1	Bank	1,080	Dec 31 Profit and loss	1,440
Oct 1	Bank	1,080	Dec 31 Prepaid c/d	720
		2,160		2,160
2010				
Jan 1	Prepaid b/d	720		

29.4

C Cainen
Trading and Profit and Loss Account
for the year ended 31 December 2009

Sales		18,590
Less Cost of goods sold:		
Opening stock	2,050	
Add Purchases	11,170	
	13,220	
Less Closing stock	3,910	
		9,310
Gross profit		9,280
Less Expenses:		
Rent (640 – 160)	480	
Wages and salaries (2,140 + 290)	2,430	
Insurance (590 – 190)	400	
Bad debts	270	
Telephone (300 + 110)	410	
General expenses	180	
		4,170
Net profit		5,110

29.6

J Sears
Trading and Profit and Loss Account
for the year ended 31 December 2009

Sales		80,000
Less Sales returns		1,000
		79,000
Less Cost of goods sold:		
Opening stock	20,000	
Add Purchases	70,000	
	90,000	
Less Purchase returns	1,240	
	88,760	
Less Closing stock	24,000	
		64,760
Gross profit		14,240
Less Expenses:		
Wages and salaries (7,200 + 450)	7,650	
Telephone (200 – 20)	180	
Bad debts	40	
Provision for doubtful debts (1,960 × 10% – 160)	36	
Depreciation:		
Store fittings	800	
Motor van	1,200	
		9,906
Net profit		4,334

J Sears
Balance Sheet as at 31 December 2009

	Cost	Depreciation	Net Book Value
Fixed Assets			
Store fittings	8,000	800	7,200
Motor van	6,000	1,200	4,800
	14,000	2,000	12,000
Current Assets			
Stock		24,000	
Debtors	1,960		
Less Provision for doubtful debts	196		
		1,764	
Prepaid expenses		20	
Bank		600	
		26,384	
Less Current Liabilities			
Creditors	1,400		
Expenses owing	450		
		1,850	
Net current assets			24,534
			36,534
Financed by:			
Capital			
Balance 1.1.2009			35,800
Add Net profit			4,334
			40,134
Less Drawings			3,600
			36,534

29.8

Freddy Tuilagi
Trading and Profit and Loss Account
for the year ended 30 September

Sales			30,490
Less Cost of goods sold:			
Opening stock		850	
Add Purchases (13,725 – 320)		13,405	
		14,255	
Less Closing stock		960	
			13,295
Gross profit			17,195
Add Discounts received (230 + 80)			310
			17,505
Less Expenses:			
General expenses		610	
Wages		3,880	
Advertising (420 – 46)		374	
Telephone		160	
Depreciation – Equipment		4,500	
– Motor van		1,050	
			10,574
			6,931

Freddy Tuilagi
Balance Sheet as at 30 September

	Cost £	Depreciation £	Net Book Value £
Fixed Assets			
Equipment	17,000	6,500	10,500
Motor van	7,000	1,050	5,950
	24,000	7,550	16,450
Current Assets			
Stock		960	
Prepayments		46	
Cass in hand		30	
		1,036	
Less Current Liabilities			
Bank overdraft		50	
Creditors (845 – 80)		765	
		815	
Net current assets			221
			16,671
Financed by:			
Capital		11,460	
Add Net profit		6,931	
		18,391	
Less Drawings (1400 + 320)		1,720	
			16,671

Chapter 30 Extended trial balance

30.1

S Dickinson
Trial Balance as at 30 September 2009

	Dr £	Cr £
Capital		59,868
Motor vehicles	22,500	
Computer equipment	18,000	
Debtors	31,059	
Creditors		30,690
Purchases	245,259	
Sales		358,317
Wages and salaries	38,476	
Motor expenses	3,428	
Printing and stationery	3,600	
General expenses	8,235	
Cash at bank	5,850	
Stock 1 October 2008	23,004	
Rent and rates	31,500	
Heating and lighting	6,624	
Interest received		6,417
Insurance	10,332	
Rent received		5,175
Drawings	12,600	
	460,467	460,467

30.2

G Brammer
Trial Balance as at 31 December 2009

	Dr £	Cr £
Capital		100,000
Premises	66,250	
Motor vehicle	17,000	
Office equipment	2,438	
Wages	19,637	
Purchases	37,455	
Sales		56,170
Commission received		1,050
Electricity	925	
Telephone	1,125	
Motor expenses	1,500	
Printing, stationery and advertising	2,050	
Creditors		8,500
Debtors	12,012	
General expenses	2,371	
Bank overdraft		3,505
Drawings	6,462	
	169,225	169,225

30.4

J Steadman – Extended trial balance as at 31 January 2010

	Description	Ledger Balances Dr £	Ledger Balances Cr £	Adjustments Dr £	Adjustments Cr £	Profit and Loss Dr £	Profit and Loss Cr £	Balance Sheet Dr £	Balance Sheet Cr £
BS	Capital		58,260						58,260
BS	Equipment	11,250						11,250	
BS	Furniture and fittings	6,000						6,000	
BS	Motor vehicles	17,370						17,370	
PL	Sales		96,030				96,030		
PL	Purchases	59,220				59,220			
BS	Cash at bank	750						750	
PL	General expenses	1,800				1,800			
PL	Wages	17,820		(a) 351		18,171			
PL	Rent, rates and insurance	7,650			(b) 600	7,050			
PL	Heating and lighting	2,100				2,100			
BS	Debtors	24,000						24,000	
BS	Creditors		10,800						10,800
PL	Stock 1 February 2009	17,130				17,130			
		165,090	165,090						
BS	Accrual – Wages				(a) 351				351
BS	Prepayment – Insurance			(b) 600				600	
BS	Stock – 31 January 2010			(c) 14,730				14,730	
PL	Stock – 31 January 2010				(c) 14,730		14,730		
				15,681	15,681				
	Net profit					5,289			5,289
						110,760	110,760	74,700	74,700

50.6 (ii)

Automania – Extended trial balance as at 30 April 2009

Type	Description	Ledger Balances Dr £	Ledger Balances Cr £	Adjustments Dr £	Adjustments Cr £	Profit and Loss Dr £	Profit and Loss Cr £	Balance Sheet Dr £	Balance Sheet Cr £
BS	Capital		135,000						135,000
BS	Drawings	42,150						42,150	
PL	Rent	17,300		1,600		18,900			
PL	Purchases	606,600				606,600			
PL	Sales		857,300				857,300		
PL	Sales returns	2,400				2,400			
PL	Purchases returns		1,260		200		1,460		
PL	Salaries and wages	136,970				136,970			
BS	Motor vehicles (MV) at cost	60,800						60,800	
BS	Provision for depreciation (MV)		16,740		12,160				28,900
BS	Fixtures and fittings (F & F) at cost	40,380						40,380	
BS	Provision for depreciation (F & F)		21,600		1,878				23,478
BS	Bank		3,170						3,170
BS	Cash	2,100						2,100	
PL	Lighting and heating	4,700				4,700			
BS	VAT		9,200		35				9,235
PL	Stock 1 May 2008	116,100				116,100			
PL	Bad debts	1,410				1,410			
PL/BS	Provision for doubtful debts		1,050		87				1,137
BS	Debtors control account	56,850						56,850	
BS	Creditors control account		50,550	*235					50,315
PL	Sundry expenses	6,810				6,810			
PL	Insurance	1,300			100	1,200			
		1,095,870	1,095,870						
BS	Accruals				1,600				1,600
BS	Prepayments			100				100	
PL	Depreciation – Motor vehicles			12,160		12,160			
PL	Depreciation – Fixtures & fittings			1,878		1,878			
PL	Provision for doubtful debts – Adjustment			87		87			
PL	Closing stock – Profit and loss				117,700		117,700		
BS	Closing stock – Balance sheet			117,700				117,700	
				133,760	133,760				
	Net profit					67,245			67,245
						976,460	976,460	320,080	320,080

*Note: Made up of £200 purchases returns plus VAT £35 = £235

30.6 (cont'd)

(i) Workings

(a) Rent:

1.5.2008 to 31.7.2008 = 3 months × 1,500 =	4,500
1.8.2008 to 30.8.2009 = 9 months × 1,600 =	14,400
	18,900
Rent paid during year	17,300
Rent owing at 30.4.2009	1,600

(b) Insurance paid in advance - 100

(c) Depreciation:

Motor vehicles = 20% SLM = 20% of £60,800 =	12,160
Fixtures and fittings = 10% RBM = F & F cost	40,380
Less Depreciation to date	21,600
Net book value	18,780
Therefore 10% of £18,780 =	1,878

(d) Increase in provision for doubtful debts to 2% of debtors

= 2% of £56,850 (new provision) =	1,137
Less Old provision =	1,050
Therefore increase =	87

(e)

Stock valuation 30.4.2009		£119,360
Less Reduction in value of old stock		
3,660 – 2,060 =	1,600	
Less Badly damaged car door =	60	1,660
New stock valuation 30.4.2009		£117,700

(f) Debit – Creditors control £235

Credit – Purchases returns £200

Credit – VAT £35

Chapter 31 Stock valuation

31.1 (a) (i) FIFO 6 × £13 = £78 stock valuation at 31 December 2009.

(ii) LIFO

2009	Received	Issued	Stock	£	£
Jan	24 × £10		24 × £10	240	
April	16 × £12.50		24 × £10 16 × £12.50	240 200	440
June		14 × £10 16 × £12.50	10 × £10		100
Oct	30 × £13		10 × £10 30 × £13	100 390	490
Nov		4 × £10 30 × £13	6 × £10		60

Closing stock would be valued at £60 on a LIFO basis.

(iii) AVCO

2009	Received	Issued	Average cost per unit	No. of units in stock	Total value of stock
Jan	24 × £10		£10.00	24	£240
April	16 × £12.50		£11.00	40	£440
June		30	£11.00	10	£110
Oct	30 × £13		£12.50	40	£500
Nov		34	£12.50	6	£75

Closing stock would be valued at £75 on an average cost basis.

(b) **Trading Accounts for the year ended 31 December 2009**

	FIFO		LIFO		AVCO	
Sales		1,092		1,092		1,092
Less Cost of goods sold						
Purchases	830		830		830	
Less Closing stock	78		60		75	
		752		770		755
Gross Profit		340		322		337

31.3

DC Ltd
Stock Valuation as at 31 December 2009

	£	£
Value at 8 January 2010		50,850
Add (*a*) Error in calculation (1,600 − 160)	1,440	
(*b*) Sales at cost (500 − 100)	400	
(*d*) Casting error (4,299 − 2,499)	1,800	
		3,640
		54,490
Less (*c*) Reduce to NRV (560 − 425)		135
Corrected value of stock at 31 December 2009		54,355

31.6 The Pine Warehouse

The tables and chairs sold to the customer on 30 November 2009 should not be included in the closing stock figure at the end of the financial year since they are no longer the property of The Pine Warehouse; they belong to the customer who has already paid for them and is the legal owner. Stock should be valued at the lower of 'cost' or 'net realisable value' and certainly not at selling price. In any case, the profit of £500 has already been entered in the books for the year to 30 November 2009, as it was included in cash sales.

Chapter 32 Errors not affecting trial balance agreement

(To economise on space, all narratives for journal entries in these answers are omitted.)

32.1							
(*a*)	J Harkness	Dr	678	J Harker	Cr	678	
(*b*)	Machinery	Dr	4,390	L Pearson	Cr	4,390	
(*c*)	Motor van	Dr	10,800	Motor expenses	Cr	10,800	
(*d*)	E Fletcher	Dr	9	Sales	Cr	9	
(*e*)				Sales	Dr	257	Commissions received	Cr	257

32.3

Berry Sports
Journal

		Dr £	Cr £
Dec 1	Rates	100	
Dec 1	Rent		100
Dec 1	Creditors Control*	600	
Dec 1	Purchases Return		600
Dec 1	Bank	1,800	
Dec 1	Insurance		1,800

*Note: First the error has to be cancelled:

Dr Creditors Control	300	
Cr Purchases Return		300

Then the transaction requires entering:

Dr Creditors Control	300	
Cr Purchases Return		300

Thus the amounts are double the original amount, i.e. £600

32.4

Senator Safes
Journal

	Dr £	Cr £
Rates	300	
Miscellaneous Expenses		300
Purchases Returns	99	
Creditors Control		99
(*Note:* 706 − 607 = 99)		
Bad Debts	800	
VAT	140	
Debtors Control*		940

Note: The question stated the sales ledger is a subsidiary ledger, i.e. the accounts are classed as memorandum accounts, therefore, the bad debt will need to be credited to the debtors control account.

Chapter 33 Suspense accounts and errors

33.1

The Journal

		Dr £	Cr £
(a)	T. Thomas	900	
	Bank		900
(b)	C. Charles	35	
	Discounts allowed		35
(c)	Office equipment	6,000	
	Motor vehicles		6,000
(d)	J. Graham	715	
	Sales		715
(e)	Wages	210	
	Drawings	210	
	Suspense		420

33.2

Jaspa West

		Dr	Cr
(a)	(1) Suspense	110	
	Rent Received		110
	Correction of error rent received £55		
	debited in error to Rent Received		
	(2) Bad Debts	150	
	Mary Beagle		150
	Debt owed by Mary Beagle written		
	off as bad		
	(3) Sales	350	
	Suspense		350
	Sales overcast by £350		
	(4) Motor Vehicle	3,500	
	C Williams		3,500
	Purchase of motor vehicle on credit		
	(5) Profit and Loss	225	
	Provision for doubtful debts		225
	Creation of provision for doubtful debts		

(b) Two examples of errors which would not be revealed by the trial balance would be: Two from, errors of omission, commission, principle, original entry, compensating and complete reversal of entries.

33.3 1

The Journal

		Dr	Cr
(a)	Sales returns	100	
	Suspense		100
(b)	Drawings	80	
	Wages		80
(c)	Carriage inwards	75	
	Carriage outwards		75
(d)	Bank charges	270	
	Suspense		270
(e)	Sales ledger control (K Abbott)	385	
	Sales		385
(f)	Discounts allowed (2 × 218)	436	
	Suspense		436
(g)	Suspense	200	
	Rent		200
(b)	Purchases (24,897 − 24,798)	99	
	Suspense		99

2

Suspense Account

	£			£
Balance b/f	705	(a)	Sales returns	100
(g) Rent	200	(d)	Bank charges	270
		(f)	Discounts received	436
		(b)	Purchases	99
	905			905

3

Original incorrect gross profit				129,487
Add (e)	Sales omitted			385
				129,872
Less (a)	Sales returns omitted		100	
(c)	Carriage in understated		75	
(b)	Purchases understated		99	274
				129,598
Original net profit				77,220
Add Increase in gross profit, i.e. it also increases net profit (129,598 − 129,487)				111
				77,331
Add (b)	Wages overstated		80	
(c)	Carriage outwards overstated		75	
(g)	Rent rebate omitted		200	355
				77,686
Less (d)	Bank charges omitted		270	
(f)	Discounts allowed understated		436	706
Corrected figure of net profit				76,980

33.5

(a)

Suspense

	£			£
Balance as per T.B.	1,134	(i)	Sales over-cast	350
(iv) Creditor	166	(ii)	Discounts under-cast	100
		(iii)	Fixtures omitted	850
	1,300			1,300

(b)

K Woodburn

Trial Balance as at 30 June 2009

	Dr	Cr
Sales (87,050 − 350)		86,700
Purchases	62,400	
Discounts allowed and received	405	410
Salaries and wages	3,168	
General expenses	595	
Fixtures (10,000 + 850)	10,850	
Stock 1 July 2008	12,490	
Debtors and creditors	8,120	4,721
Bank	6,790	
Drawings (4,520 − 490)	4,030	
Capital		17,017
	108,848	108,848

Note: Discounts allowed 305 + (ii) 100 = 405
Creditors 5,045 + (iv) 166 − (v) 490 = 4,721

33.7

The Journal

		Dr	Cr
(a)	Suspense	3,000	
	Sales		3,000
	Correction of error sales day book undercast by £3,000		
(b)	Purchases	1,147	
	Dawson & Co		1,147
	Goods purchased on credit from Dawson & Co		
(c)	Motor repairs	585	
	Motor vehicles		585
	Motor repairs posted in error to motor vehicles account		
(d)	J Greenway	675	
	J Green		675
	Goods sold on credit to J Greenway posted in error to J Green's account		
(e)	Suspense	150	
	Electricity		150
	Payment of electricity account incorrectly debited £150 too much		
(f)	Suspense	2,250	
	Teape Ltd		2,250
	Payment of £2,250 received from Teape Ltd not credited to their account		

Philip Hogan
Suspense Account

	£		£
Sales (a)	3,000	Balance b/d	5,400
Electricity (e)	150		
Teape Ltd (f)	2,250		
	5,400		5,400

Note that items (b), (c) and (d) do not pass through the suspense account, as they do not affect the balancing of the books.

Chapter 34 Single entry and incomplete records

34.1 (a) (i) Mark-up = 25%
      (ii) Margin = 20%
    (b) Margin = 25%
    (c) Mark-up = 20%

34.3 First, draw up a trading account and insert the figures given in the question. The gross profit can now be calculated. Since mark-up is 25%, then margin is 20%. Consequently, gross profit is 20% of £120,000 = £24,000.
Cost of goods sold = Sales − Gross Profit = £120,000 − £24,000 = £96,000. Purchases can now be found arithmetically.

T Ashby
Trading Account for the year ended 31 July 2009

	£	£
Sales		120,000
Less Cost of goods sold (a)		
Opening stock	19,744	
Add Purchases	101,496	
	121,240	
Less Closing stock (b)	25,240	96,000
Gross profit (c)		24,000

34.4 (a) Average stock value = £40,000

Therefore $\dfrac{£20,000 + (a)}{2} = £40,000$ and (a) is found to be £60,000.

Cost of goods sold is then calculated as £140,000. Mark-up is 50%, so sales = £140,000 + (£140,000 × 50%) = £210,000.

(b)
T Rigby
Trading Account for the year ended 31 August 2009

	£	£
Sales		210,000
Less Cost of sales:		
Opening stock	20,000	
Add Purchases	180,000	
	200,000	
Less Closing stock (a)	60,000	140,000
Gross profit		70,000

(c) If net profit on sales is not to be less than 10% of sales (=£21,000), this means that Rigby can afford up to £49,000 in expenses, i.e. Gross profit £70,000 − £49,000 expenses = £21,000 net profit.

34.5 (a)

Total Debtors

Balances b/d	2,760	Cash	14,610
Sales (difference)	14,940	Balances c/d	3,090
	17,700		17,700

Total Creditors

Cash	9,390	Balances b/d	1,080
Balances c/d	1,320	Purchases (difference)	9,630
	10,710		10,710

(b)
K Rogers
Trading Account for the year ended 31 October 2010

	£	£
Sales		14,940
Less Cost of Goods Sold		
Opening Stock	2,010	
Add Purchases	9,630	
	11,640	
Less Closing Stock	2,160	9,480
Gross Profit		5,460

34.7 (a) Capital is £6,000.
(b)
D Lewinski
Balance Sheet as at 30 June 2010

	£	£
Fixed assets		
Plant		36,000
Fixtures		3,600
		39,600
Current assets		
Stock	13,500	
Debtors	9,300	
Bank	6,000	
Cash	1,350	
	30,150	
Less Current liabilities		
Creditors	7,200	
Net current assets		22,950
		62,550
Financed by:		
Capital		
Cash introduced		60,000
Add Net profit		18,550
		78,550
Less Drawings		16,000
		62,550

34.8

J Marcano
Statement of Affairs as at 31 August 2009

	£	£
Fixed assets		
Fixtures		3,500
Motor van		3,500
		7,000
Current assets		
Stock	16,740	
Debtors	11,890	
Bank	2,209	
Cash	115	
	30,954	
Less Current liabilities		
Creditors	9,952	
		21,002
		28,002

Statement of Affairs as at 31 August 2010

	£	£	£
Fixed assets			
Fixtures		5,500	
Less Depreciation		300	
			5,200
Motor van		3,500	
Less Depreciation		700	
			2,800
			8,000
Current assets			
Stock		24,891	
Debtors		15,821	
Prepaid expenses		72	
Cash		84	
		40,868	
Less Current liabilities			
Trade creditors	6,002		
Expenses owing	236		
Bank overdraft	165		
		6,403	
Net current assets			34,465
			42,465
Capital			
Balance as at 31.8.2009			28,002
Add Cash introduced			12,800
Add Net profit	(C)		9,223
			50,025
Less Drawings	(B)		7,560
	(A)		42,465

(A) Found as the figure to make balance sheet totals agree 42,465.
(B) Less 7,560 = (A) 42,465, therefore (B) is 50,025.
(C) Missing figure to total 50,025 = 9,223.

Leigh Osawa

34.10
(a) Sales

Trade Debtors Account

	£		£
2008		2009	
Apr 1 Balance b/f	23,460	Mar 31 Receipts	226,820
2009		Mar 31 Discounts	280
Mar 31 Sales (missing figure)	231,910	Mar 31 Balance c/d	28,270
	255,370		255,370
Apr 1 Balance b/d	28,270		

(b) Rent

Rent Account

	£		£
2009		2008	
		Apr 1 Balance (rent owing) b/d	1,040
Mar 31 Bank: rent	12,290	2009	
		Mar 31 Profit & Loss	11,980
Mar 31 Balance (rent owing) c/d	730		
	13,020		13,020
		Apr 1 Balance (rent owing) b/d	730

(c) Business Rates

Business Rates Account

	£		£
2008		2009	
Apr 1 Balance (prepaid) b/d	390	Mar 31 Profit & Loss	4,630
2009			
Mar 31 Bank: business rates	4,680	Mar 31 Balance (prepaid) c/d	440
	5,070		5,070
Apr 1 Balance (prepaid) b/d	440		

Chapter 35 Club accounts

35.1 (a)

Horton Hockey Club
Receipts and Payments Account
for the year ended 30 June 2009

Receipts		Payments	
Bank balance b/f	2,715	Teams' travel expenses	1,598
Subscriptions	8,570	Groundsman's wages	3,891
Donations	1,500	Postage and stationery	392
Receipts from raffles	3,816	Rent of pitches and club house	4,800
		General expenses	419
		Prizes for raffles	624
		Bank balance c/f	4,877
	16,601		16,601

(b)

Horton Hockey Club
Income and Expenditure Account
for the year ended 30 June 2009

Income:		
Subscriptions (8,570 + 160)		8,730
Donations		1,500
Profit on raffles (3,816 − 624)		3,192
		13,422
Less Expenditure:		
Teams' travel expenses	1,598	
Groundsman's wages (3,891 + 75)	3,966	
Postage and stationery	392	
Rent of pitches and club house (4,800 + 400)	5,200	
General expenses	419	
		11,575
Surplus of income over expenditure		1,847

35.3 (a) Accumulated fund as at 1 June 2007:

Bar stocks	88
Equipment	340
Bank	286
	714

(b)

Down Town Sports and Social Club
Income and Expenditure Account
for the year ended 31 May 2008

Income	£	£	£
Subscriptions			149
Net proceeds of jumble sale			91
Net proceeds of dance			122
Contribution from Bar:			
Bar takings		463	
Less Cost of supplies:			
Opening Stock	88		
Add Purchases	397		
	485		
Less Closing stock	101	384	
Total income			79
			441
Less Expenditure			
Wages		198	
Hire of rooms		64	
Loss on equipment		12	
Depreciation		30	304
Surplus of income over expenditure			137

35.5

1 Bar Purchases

	£
Payments via Bank	6,400
Less Opening Creditors	1,000
	5,400
Add Closing Creditors	540
Bar Purchases	5,940

2 Bar
Trading and Profit and Loss Account
for the year ended 30 November 2009

	£	£
Sales		8,700
Less Cost of bar sales		
Opening stock	680	
Add Bar purchases (see Task 1)	5,940	
	6,620	
Less Closing stock	890	
		5,730
Gross Profit		2,970
Less Expenses		
Wages (20% × 25,500)	5,100	
General expenses ((4,850 + 250 − 150) × 30%)	1,485	
		6,585
Net Loss		3,615

3

Subscription Account

	£		£
Balance (owing) b/d	1,000	Bank	33,000
Income and Expenditure Account (difference)	36,000	Balance (owing) c/d	4,000
	37,000		37,000

Total number of members = $\frac{36,000}{100}$ = 360 Members

4

Income and Expenditure Account
for the year ended 30 November 2009

		£
Income		
Subscriptions (See Task 3)		36,000
Expenditure		
Loss on bar (See Task 2)	3,615	
Wages (80% × 25,500)	20,400	
General expenses ((4,850 + 250 – 150) × 70%)	3,465	
Interest on bank loan (8% × 5,400 × 11/12)	396	
		27,876
Surplus of income over expenditure		8,124

5

	£
Assets	
Land	12,000
Stock	890
Subscriptions owing	4,000
	16,890
Liabilities	
Bank	800
Creditors	540
Accrual (General expenses)	250
Loan	5,400
Interest	396
	7,386

6 Land is usually classified as a non-wasting fixed asset. It does not tend to go down in value and therefore is not normally depreciated.

35.6

Amateur Dramatic Society
Subscriptions Account

In arrears b/d	235	In advance b/d	220
In advance c/d	140	Bank	2,600
Income and expenditure	2,630	In arrears c/d	185
	3,005		3,005
In arrears b/d	185	In advance b/d	140

Chapter 36 Partnership accounts

36.1 (a)

Stead and Jackson
Appropriation Account
for the year ended 31 December 2009

	£
Net profit	45,000
Less Salary: Jackson	5,000
	40,000
Balance of profits shared:	
Stead ½	20,000
Jackson ½	20,000
	40,000

(b)

Capital Accounts

	Stead	Jackson			Stead	Jackson
				2009		
				Dec 31 Balance b/d	24,000	16,000

Current Accounts

		Stead	Jackson			Stead	Jackson
2009				2009			
Dec 31	Drawings	15,000	19,000	Dec 31	Balance b/d	2,300	3,500
Dec 31	Balances c/d	7,300	9,500	Dec 31	Salary		5,000
				Dec 31	Share of profits	20,000	20,000
		22,300	28,500			22,300	28,500
				2010			
				Jan 1	Balance b/d	7,300	9,500

36.4

Simpson and Young
Trading and Profit and Loss Appropriation Account for the year ended 30 June 2009

	£	£
Sales		254,520
Less Cost of sales:		
Opening stock	18,000	
Add Purchases	184,980	
	202,980	
Less Closing stock	19,000	183,980
Gross profit		70,540
Less Expenses:		
Wages and salaries (32,700 + 500)	33,200	
Rent, rates and insurance (3,550 – 250)	3,300	
Electricity	980	
Stationery and printing	420	
Motor expenses	3,480	
General office expenses	1,700	
Depreciation: Motor van (20% of 16,000)	3,200	
Office equipment (10% of 5,600)	560	46,840
Net profit		23,700
Less Interest on capital:		
Simpson (10% of 50,000)	5,000	
Young (10% of 20,000)	2,000	7,000
		16,700
Share of profits:		
Simpson ³/₅ths	10,020	
Young ²/₅ths	6,680	16,700

Simpson and Young
Balance Sheet as at 30 June 2009

	Cost £	Accumulated Depreciation £	Net Book Value £
Fixed assets			
Buildings	28,000	–	28,000
Office equipment	8,400	3,360 (W1)	5,040
Motor vans	16,000	8,200 (W2)	7,800
	52,400	11,560	40,840
Current assets			
Stock	19,000		
Debtors	28,000		
Prepayments	250		
Cash at bank	7,250	54,500	
Less Current liabilities			
Creditors	15,200		
Accruals	500	15,700	
Net current assets			38,800
			79,640

	Simpson	Young	Total
Financed by:			
Capital accounts	50,000	20,000	70,000
Balance b/f			
Current accounts			
Balance b/f	640	300	
Add Share of profit	10,020	6,680	
Add Interest on capital	5,000	2,000	
	15,660	8,980	
Less Drawings	10,000	5,000	
	5,660	3,980	9,640
			79,640

(W1) Provision for depreciation on office equipment:
8,400 – 5,600 + 560 = 3,360
(W2) Provision for depreciation on motor vans:
16,000 – 11,000 + 3,200 = 8,200

36.6 (a)

Bhayani and Donnell
Profit and Loss Account for the year ended 31 December

	£	£
Gross profit		32,000
Add Reduction in provision for doubtful debts		179
Add Rent received (500 – 100)		400
		32,579
Less Expenses:		
Heating and lighting (1,400 + 100)	1,500	
Wages and salaries (4,100 – 200)	3,900	
Depreciation: Vehicles (10% of 35,000)	3,500	
Fittings 15% of (12,000 – 2,000)	1,500	10,400
Net profit		22,179

(b)

Bhayani and Donnell
Appropriation Account for the year ended 31 December

	£	£
Net profit b/fwd		22,179
Add Interest charged on drawings:		
Bhayani (6% of 2,000)	120	
Donnell (6% of 600)	36	156
		22,335
Less Salary: Donnell		3,263
Interest on capital:		
Bhayani (8% of 35,000)	2,800	
Donnell (8% of 12,000)	960	7,023
		15,312
Balance of profits shared:		
Bhayani 2/3	10,208	
Donnell 1/3	5,104	15,312

(c)

Bhayani – Current Account

	£		£
Jan 1 Balance b/d	600	Dec 31 Profit and loss appropriation account:	
Dec 31 Drawings	2,000	Interest on capital	2,800
Dec 31 Profit and loss appropriation account:		Share of profit	10,208
Interest on drawings	120		
Dec 31 Balance c/d	10,288		
	13,008		13,008
		Jan 1 Balance b/d	10,288

Donnell – Current Account

	£		£
Dec 31 Drawings	600	Dec 31 Profit and loss appropriation account:	
Dec 31 Profit and loss appropriation account:		Interest on capital	960
Interest on drawings	36	Share of profit	5,104
Dec 31 Balance c/d	8,691	Salary	3,263
	9,327		9,327
		Jan 1 Balance b/d	8,691

(d)

Bhayani and Donnell
Balance Sheet as at 31 December

Fixed assets	Cost £	Total Depreciation £	Net Book Value £
Premises	20,000	–	20,000
Fittings	12,000	3,500	8,500
Vehicles	35,000	6,500	28,500
	67,000	10,000	57,000

Current assets	£	£	£
Debtors	25,700		
Less Provision for doubtful debts	771	24,929	
Prepayments (wages)		200	
Cash		600	
		25,729	
Less Current liabilities			
Creditors		15,600	
Bank overdraft		950	
Accruals (heating)		100	
Rent received in advance		100	16,750
Net current assets			8,979
			65,979

Financed by:	Bhayani £	Donnell £	£
Capital accounts			
Balance	35,000	12,000	
			47,000
Current accounts			
Balance 1 January	(600)	nil	
Add Interest on capital	2,800	960	
Salary		3,263	
Share of profits	10,208	5,104	
	12,408	9,327	
Less Drawings	(2,000)	(600)	
Interest on drawings	(120)	(36)	
	10,288	8,691	
			18,979
			65,979

Chapter 37 Limited company accounts

37.1

LMT Ltd
Balance Sheet as at 31 December 2009

	Cost	Accumulated depreciation	Net book value
Fixed Assets			
Buildings	45,000	18,000	27,000
Machinery	24,000	7,200	16,800
Fixtures	12,000	4,800	7,200
	81,000	30,000	51,000
Current Assets			
Stock		18,000	
Debtors		9,000	
Bank		6,000	
		33,000	
Less Creditors falling due within one year			
Creditors	9,000		
Proposed dividend	3,000	12,000	
Net current assets			21,000
			72,000
Less Long-term Liabilities			
10% Debentures			18,000
			54,000
Financed by:			
Capital and reserves			
Called-up share capital			36,000
Revenue reserves			
General reserve		15,000	
Retained profits as per profit and loss account		(C)?	(B)?
			(A)?

Note: The Authorised Share Capital is 60,000 £1 ordinary shares.

(A) is the figure needed to make balance sheet total agree, i.e. 54,000.
(B) is the figure needed to add up to 54,000; therefore B = 54,000 − 36,000 = 18,000
(C) + 15,000 = B. (C) must be the missing figure of 3,000.

Note that depreciation has been shown in this answer in order to assist students.

37.3

CA Company Ltd
Profit and Loss Appropriation Account for the year ended 31 December 2010

Net profit b/d		210,000
Add Retained profits from last year		17,000
		227,000
Less Transfer to general reserve	30,000	
Transfer to foreign exchange reserve	16,000	
Preference dividend paid (250,000 × £1 × 10%)	25,000	
Proposed ordinary dividend 10% (500,000 × £2 × 10%)	100,000	171,000
Retained profits carried forward to next year		56,000

37.4

Chang Ltd
Trading and Profit and Loss Account
for the year ended 31 December 2009

Sales			316,810
Less Cost of goods sold:			
Opening stock		25,689	
Add Purchases		201,698	
		227,387	
Less Closing stock		29,142	198,245
Gross profit			118,565
Less Expenses:			
Wages and salaries (54,207 + 581)		54,788	
Rent (4,300 − 300)		4,000	
Lighting expenses		1,549	
Bad debts		748	
Provision for doubtful debts (938 − 861)		77	
General expenses		32,168	
Depreciation: Machinery (55,000 × 10%)		5,500	98,830
Net profit			19,735
Add Retained profits b/f from last year			34,280
			54,015
Less Proposed dividend			10,000
Retained profits c/f to next year			44,015

Chang Ltd
Balance Sheet as at 31 December 2009

	£	£
Fixed Assets		
Premises		65,000
Machinery	55,000	
Less Aggregate depreciation (15,800 + 5,500)	21,300	33,700
		98,700
Current Assets		
Stock		29,142
Debtors	21,784	
Less Provision for doubtful debts	938	20,846
Prepayments		300
Bank		23,101
		73,389
Less Creditors falling due within one year		
Dividend payable	10,000	
Creditors	17,493	
Expenses owing	581	28,074
Net current assets		45,315
		144,015
Financed by:		
Capital and reserves		
Called-up share capital		100,000
Revenue reserves		
Profit and loss account		44,015
		144,015

37.6 (a)

Jaspa West Ltd
Profit and Loss Appropriation Account for the year ended 31 December 2010

	£	£
Net profit		80,000
Add Retained profits b/f from last year		92,000
		172,000
Less Appropriations:		
General reserve (40% × 80,000)		32,000
Dividends payable		
Preference shares (8% × 80,000)	6,400	
Ordinary shares (4% × 150,000)	6,000	44,400
Retained profits c/f to next year		127,600

(b)

Jaspa West Ltd
Balance Sheet as at 31 December 2010

	Cost £	Depreciation to date* £	Net Book Value £
Fixed assets			
Premises	270,600	–	270,600
Machinery	72,600	18,400	54,200
	343,200	18,400	324,800
Current assets			
Stock	56,000		
Debtors (80,000 + 3,800)	83,800	139,800	
Creditors: Amounts falling due within one year			
Creditors (37,000 + 4,200)	41,200		
Bank	21,400		
Dividends payable (6,400 + 6,000)	12,400	75,000	
Net current assets			64,800
			389,600
Financed by:			
Capital and reserves			
Called-up capital			
Preference shares			80,000
Ordinary shares			150,000
			230,000
Revenue reserves			
General reserve		32,000	
Profit and loss account		127,600	159,600
			389,600

Note: The Authorised Share Capital is 200,000 £1 ordinary shares and 100,000 8% preference shares.

*Depreciation has been shown in this answer to comply with the examining body requirements.

Pitman Qualifications

617

Chapter 38 Manufacturing accounts

38.1

E Smith
Manufacturing and Trading Account for the year ended 31 March 2009

	£	£
Stock of raw material 1.4.2008		2,400
Add Purchases		21,340
Carriage inwards		321
		24,061
Less Stock of raw materials 31.3.2009		2,620
Cost of raw materials consumed		21,441
Manufacturing wages		13,280
Prime cost		34,721
Add Factory overhead expenses:		
Rent and rates	2,300	
Power	6,220	
Other expenses	1,430	9,950
		44,671
Add Work in progress 1.4.2008		955
		45,626
Less Work in progress 31.3.2009		870
Production cost of goods completed c/d		44,756
Sales		69,830
Less Cost of goods sold		
Stock finished goods 1.4.2008	6,724	
Add Production cost of goods completed b/d	44,756	
	51,480	
Less Stock finished goods 31.3.2009	7,230	44,250
Gross profit		25,580

38.3

The Oldport Manufacturing Co

(a) Calculation of prime cost

	£
Stock raw materials 1 May 2008	31,550
Add Purchases raw materials	98,560
	130,110
Less Stock raw materials 30 April 2009	34,585
	95,525
Direct Labour – Wages manufacturing	67,525
Prime cost	163,050

(b) Variable costs are those costs that change according to the number of units produced.
Examples one from: direct material or direct labour, that may be used, for example, in the manufacture of a wheelbarrow.

38.4 (a)

Ace Crafts Ltd
Manufacturing Account for the year ended 31 December 2009

	£	£	£
Stock of raw materials 1.1.2009			36,000
Add Purchases		70,400	
Add Carriage inwards		1,120	
			71,520
			107,520
Less Stock of raw materials 31.12.2009 (i)			46,400
Cost of raw materials used			61,120
Stock of cases 1.1.2009		18,000	
Add Purchases		18,000	
		36,000	
Less Stock of cases 31.12.2009 (ii)		15,360	
Cost of wooden cases used			20,640
Wages (170,000 × 4/5)			136,000
Prime cost			217,760
Add Factory overhead expenses:			
Indirect wages (170,000 × 1/5) (iii)	34,000		
Manager's salary (iv)	33,200		
Power	14,560		
Rates	2,280		
Lighting (1,800 × 1/2)	900		
Depreciation	20,000		104,940
			322,700
Add Work-in-progress 1.1.2009			10,000
			332,700
Less Work-in-progress 31.12.2009			15,200
Production cost of goods completed c/d (v)			317,500

(b)

Ace Crafts Ltd
Trading and Profit and Loss Account for the year ended 31 December 2009

	£	£
Sales (80 × 6,250)		500,000
Less Production cost of goods sold b/d		317,500
Gross profit		182,500
Less Expenses:		
Administration expenses	19,200	
Salesmen's salaries	47,600	
Lighting (1,800 × 1/2)	900	
Carriage outwards	1,680	69,380
Net profit		113,120

(c) Production cost = £317,500 ÷ 6,250 = £50.80 per unit.
(d) Gross profit = £182,500 ÷ 6,250 = £29.20 per unit.

Chapter 39 Analysis and interpretation of accounts

39.1 (a)

	M Ltd	N Ltd

(i) *Current ratio*

$$\frac{£200,000}{£50,000} = 4 : 1 \qquad \frac{£130,000}{£65,000} = 2 : 1$$

(ii) *Acid test ratio*

$$\frac{200,000 - 100,000}{£50,000} = 2 : 1 \qquad \frac{130,000 - 64,000}{£65,000} = 1 : 1$$

(iii) *Stockturn*

$$\frac{£288,000}{£120,000 + £100,000 \div 2} = 2.6 \text{ times} \qquad \frac{£187,500}{£60,000 + £64,000 \div 2} = 3.0 \text{ times}$$

(iv) *Debtors : Sales ratio*

$$\frac{£60,000}{£360,000} \times 12 \text{ months} = 2 \text{ months} \qquad \frac{£62,500}{£250,000} \times 12 \text{ months} = 3 \text{ months}$$

(v) *Creditors : Purchases ratio*

$$\frac{£50,000}{£268,000} \times 12 \text{ months} = 2.2 \text{ months} \qquad \frac{£65,000}{£191,500} \times 12 \text{ months} = 4 \text{ months}$$

(vi) *Gross profit %*

$$\frac{£72,000}{£360,000} \times 100\% = 20\% \qquad \frac{£62,500}{£250,000} \times 100\% = 25\%$$

(vii) *Net profit %*

$$\frac{£43,200}{£360,000} \times 100\% = 12\% \qquad \frac{£35,000}{£250,000} \times 100\% = 14\%$$

(viii) *Rate of return on shareholders' funds*

$$\frac{£43,200}{£350,000} \times 100\% = 12.3\% \qquad \frac{£35,000}{£255,000} \times 100\% = 13.7\%$$

(b) Briefly N Ltd gives a better return to shareholders because of (viii) above.

Reasons include:

● M Ltd's current ratio is higher. This indicates that M Ltd is in a better liquidity position.
● N Ltd's stock turnover is higher than that of M Ltd. This shows that N Ltd manages its sales performance more effectively.
● The gross profit percentage of N Ltd is 5% higher than that of M Ltd. This is due to better purchasing and selling prices. Net profit margins differ by a smaller margin of 2%, suggesting, that M Ltd has tighter control of its overhead expenses when compared with its sales volume (8% compared with 11%).

Chapter 40 Computers and accounting systems

40.1

To: Director of Finance
From: Administrative Assistant
Date: June 2010
Re: Proposed Integrated Computerised Accounting System

Points in favour of the new system:

● Faster data input and automatic processing.
● Greater accuracy especially via automatic posting.
● Documentation such as invoices, credit notes, statements, remittance advices produced automatically.
● Up-to-date information on customers' accounts, etc. is readily available.
● Provides management information.
● The system may be linked to the internet to allow for transactions such as ordering goods to be carried out electronically.
● Provides access to the organisation's bank account via the internet.
● More efficient and makes better use of resources.

Arguments against the new system:

● The cost of the installation plus ongoing costs of maintenance and updating software.
● Training costs of staff.
● Staff resentment of new system.
● System downtime may be disruptive.
● Fraudulent access can seriously affect business operation and profitability.
● Security measures that are necessary.
● Health and safety issues associated with using computers.

40.2 Measures a medium-sized company may adopt to safeguard the security of its financial data and records would include:

● All company's financial information should be regarded as confidential except where legislation states otherwise. Staff should be made aware of this requirement in the company's code of conduct.
● Staff should be allocated passwords to monitor accessibility to specific areas of work.
● Passwords need to be changed frequently.
● Installation of anti-virus computer packages to prevent the threat of fraud.
● Ensure data is saved and backed up regularly.
● Store back-up data in an off-site location if deemed necessary.

Index